TRANSMATH®

Understanding Algebraic Expressions

John Woodward
Mary Stroh

ISBN 13: 978-1-60697-042-3
ISBN: 1-60697-042-9

181972

Printed in the United States of America
Published and distributed by

17855 Dallas Parkway • Suite 400 • Dallas, Texas 75287 • 1-800-547-6747
www.voyagerlearning.com

Table of Contents

UNIT 2 *(continued)*

UNIT 3

UNIT 4

UNIT 5

Table of Contents

UNIT 8

UNIT 9

Table of Contents

Unit 1 Fractions and Decimal Numbers

Problem Solving: Statistics

I only have 0.341 seconds to hit this ball. Who made up this crazy game anyway???

Can you top this data?

Softball Statistics

Softball pitcher **Monica Abbott** has a record **.848** "career win" percentage.
She's won more than 80% of the games she has played!

Ty Cobb holds baseball's highest career batting average of **.366**.
Sara Graziano, who played softball for Coastal Carolina, has a career batting average of **.625**.
She hit more than half of the balls pitched to her!

OBJECTIVES

Building Number Concepts

- Use models to show the relationship between fractions and decimal numbers
- Use a variety of methods to add, subtract, multiply, and divide rational numbers
- Use rounding and estimation strategies with rational numbers

Problem Solving

- Find the mean, median, mode, and range of a set of data
- Read, create, and interpret box-and-whisker plots and scatter plots
- Identify direct and indirect relationships in data using a scatter plot

▶**Fair Shares and Operations on Fractions**

What are fair shares?

A fraction is the relationship between a part and a whole. Let's look at the fraction $\frac{4}{6}$. In a fraction, the part is called the numerator, and the whole is called the denominator.

$$\begin{array}{l} \text{part} \rightarrow \ 4 \ \leftarrow \text{numerator} \\ \text{whole} \rightarrow \ 6 \ \leftarrow \text{denominator} \end{array}$$

We can use shapes to show the part-to-whole relationship for $\frac{4}{6}$. In the models below, four parts are shaded out of a total, or whole, of six parts.

We can show the part-to-whole relationship for $\frac{4}{6}$ using shapes.

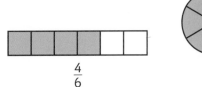
$\frac{4}{6}$

$\frac{4}{6}$

$\frac{4}{6}$

$\frac{4}{6}$

The parts of the fraction are equal in size or area within each shape. We call the equal parts within a shape "fair shares."

6 equal parts, or "fair shares"

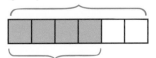

4 parts-to-whole

The next model shows examples of shapes that have been divided into fair shares and shapes that have not been divided into fair shares. In the shapes that are not divided into fair shares, some of the parts in the shape are bigger than others. This is how we know they are not divided into fair shares.

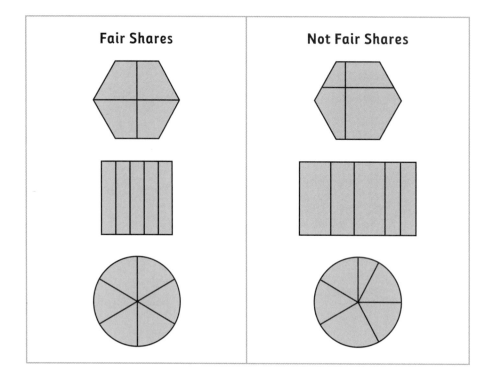

How do we add and subtract fractions with the same denominators?

Fair shares are essential to adding and subtracting fractions. They allow us to find exact sums or differences. The models below show how we add fractions that have the same fair shares. We start with $\frac{2}{4}$ and add $\frac{1}{4}$. We are adding fair shares of the same size or area. Example 1 shows that when we use fair shares to add or subtract fractions, we just add the numerators. The denominator stays the same.

Example 1

Add fractions using fair shares.

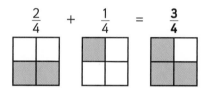

We subtract fractions in a similar way. We subtract, or take away, fair shares. We also demonstrate this with arrays. In Example 2, we subtract $\frac{3}{4} - \frac{1}{4}$. We begin with $\frac{3}{4}$ and then take away, or cross out, one of the parts.

Example 2

Subtract fractions using fair shares.

$$\frac{3}{4} - \frac{1}{4} = \frac{2}{4}$$

These operations apply to all kinds of fractions, even fractions that are greater than 1. The next two examples show addition and subtraction of fractions with a sum that is greater than 1. We use more than one square for each number because our fractions are greater than 1.

In the addition example, we add $\frac{5}{6}$ and $\frac{2}{6}$. The sum is represented by one array that is totally shaded and a second array with one part shaded.

Example 3

Add fractions where the sum is greater than 1.

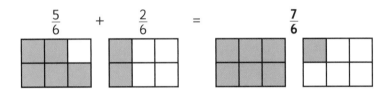

$$\frac{5}{6} \quad + \quad \frac{2}{6} \quad = \quad \frac{7}{6}$$

In the subtraction example, we start with two figures to show the problem. We subtract $\frac{2}{4}$ from $\frac{7}{4}$. We show this by shading one whole array and three of the four parts of the second array to represent $\frac{7}{4}$. Then we cross out two of the parts to get $\frac{5}{4}$. We still need two squares to demonstrate the answer. The answer $\frac{5}{4}$ is greater than 1.

Example 4

Subtract fractions greater than 1.

$$\frac{7}{4} \quad - \quad \frac{2}{4} \quad = \quad \frac{5}{4}$$

%÷ Apply Skills
≤x Turn to *Interactive Text*,
page 2.

mBook Reinforce Understanding
Use the *mBook Study Guide*
to review lesson concepts.

6 Unit 1 • Lesson 1

▶Problem Solving: **Organizing Data**

Vocabulary
minimum
maximum
range
mode
mean

How do we organize data in a way that is meaningful?

Carmen is a manager at a shoe store. She is in charge of buying shoes from shoe companies in New York and Los Angeles to sell in her store.

Carmen needs to figure out what kinds of shoes to buy based on what is popular. The most popular running shoe is QuikTrax. She has to be sure that she has enough pairs of QuikTrax to sell.

Here is Carmen's spreadsheet showing sales of QuikTrax shoes for the last nine weeks.

Week	Number of Pairs of Shoes Sold
May 1 to May 7	47
May 8 to May 14	39
May 15 to May 21	31
May 22 to May 28	39
May 29 to June 4	49
June 5 to June 11	57
June 12 to June 18	50
June 19 to June 25	48
June 26 to July 2	54
Total	**414**

Carmen wants to look at different parts of the data. She wants to find the lowest number of sales, the greatest number of sales, and the average sales for all nine weeks. This will help her determine how many pairs of running shoes to buy.

The data above are organized by date. It is not easy to find the data Carmen needs. We need to organize the data so that Carmen can make sense of the numbers.

Here are five words that we use to describe the important data Carmen is interested in.

Word	Definition
Minimum (Min)	Smallest value
Maximum (Max)	Largest value
Range	Difference between the min and the max
Mode	Number that appears the most
Mean	Average

The table below lists the number of pairs of shoes sold from smallest to largest. Now it is easy to see the **minimum** and the **maximum** .

Week	Number of Pairs of Shoes Sold	
May 15 to May 21	31 ←	minimum (min)
May 8 to May 14	39	
May 22 to May 28	39	the number that appears the most—the **mode**
May 1 to May 7	47	
June 19 to June 25	48	
May 29 to June 4	49	
June 12 to June 18	50	
June 26 to July 2	54	
June 5 to June 11	57 ←	maximum (max)
Total	**414**	

Now it is easy to see that the *minimum* sales occurred the week of May 15 to May 21, when the store only sold 31 pairs of shoes. The *maximum* sales occurred the week of June 5 to June 11, when the store sold 57 pairs of shoes.

From this, we determine the **range** . The *range* is how far the data stretch from lowest to highest. To find the range, we subtract the minimum from the maximum. In this set of data, the range is 57 − 31, or 26.

Ordering numbers this way is also helpful for seeing the **mode** . The *mode* is the number that appears the most in the set of data. In these data, it's 39. Every other number only appears once. The number 39 appears twice.

Another number that is helpful for Carmen is the average number of QuikTrax shoes sold. Another word for average is **mean** . We find the mean by dividing the total number of pairs of shoes sold during the nine weeks by the number of weeks.

Total Pairs of Shoes ÷ Number of Weeks = Mean

Example 1

Find the mean, or the average, number of pairs of QuikTrax shoes sold over nine weeks. Use the table on the previous page.

Total Pairs of Shoes ÷ Number of Weeks = Mean

414   ÷   9   =   46

The average, or mean, is 46 pairs of shoes per week.

Different ways of looking at data tell us different things. The minimum and the maximum tell us about what is happening at the extremes of the data set—the largest data and the smallest data. Sometimes data can be extreme, and the minimum and the maximum stand out from the rest of the data.

We look at the mean because it tells us about what is generally happening over time. The mean is the average number. It is our best prediction of what will happen next.

POWER CONCEPT

Mean, mode, and range tell us different things about a set of data.

Problem-Solving Activity
Turn to *Interactive Text*, page 3.

mBook Reinforce Understanding
Use the *mBook Study Guide* to review lesson concepts.

Homework

Activity 1

Add and subtract the fractions with like denominators.

1. $\frac{3}{5} + \frac{2}{5}$

2. $\frac{1}{3} + \frac{1}{3}$

3. $\frac{7}{9} - \frac{1}{9}$

4. $\frac{8}{10} - \frac{7}{10}$

5. $\frac{4}{6} + \frac{8}{6}$

6. $\frac{15}{3} - \frac{14}{3}$

Activity 2

Tell which of the following shapes are divided into fair shares. Write the letter on your paper.

(a)

(b)

(c)

(d)

(e)

(f)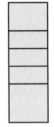

Activity 3

Tell the minimum, maximum, range, mode, and mean for the sets of data. Remember to put the data in order.

1. 6, 5, 2, 6, 3, 8, 1, 4, 6, 9

2. 1, 1, 9, 8, 2, 4, 3

3. 10, 30, 50, 70, 90, 50

Activity 4 • Distributed Practice

Solve.

1. 27 + 39

2. 23 − 19

3. 34 · 2

4. 270 ÷ 5

5. 409 − 118

6. 125 + 778

7. 123 · 4

8. 226 ÷ 2

▶Equivalent Fractions

Vocabulary
common denominator least common denominator (LCD)

Why do we need the same fair shares?

Let's look again at adding and subtracting fractions with the same denominators. We learned that fractions have a part-to-whole relationship. When we add, we combine the parts. The model shows how the whole, or denominator, stays the same. It is because the circles are divided into fair shares. What changes is the number of parts because we are adding them together.

Look what happens when we add fractions with the same denominator.

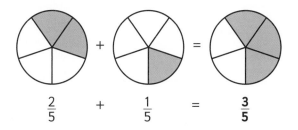

$$\frac{2}{5} \quad + \quad \frac{1}{5} \quad = \quad \frac{3}{5}$$

This process does not work as easily when the wholes, or denominators, are not the same. Let's look at the next model. We can combine the parts, but we cannot tell what the answer is. Should the answer be in halves or thirds or something else?

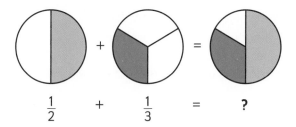

$$\frac{1}{2} \quad + \quad \frac{1}{3} \quad = \quad ?$$

We see what the answer looks like. We could probably give an approximate answer to the problem if we had to. But we cannot give an exact answer because of the way the fractions are set up.

To get an exact answer when we add and subtract fractions with uncommon denominators, we need to use the same fair share for each fraction. This is the **common denominator** .

Let's look at how we change fractions to make common denominators.

Example 1

Make common denominators using fraction bars.

$$\frac{1}{2}$$

$$+ \frac{1}{3}$$

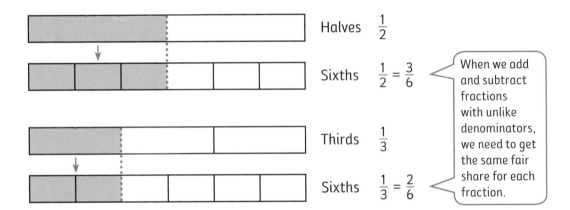

Halves $\frac{1}{2}$

Sixths $\frac{1}{2} = \frac{3}{6}$

Thirds $\frac{1}{3}$

Sixths $\frac{1}{3} = \frac{2}{6}$

> When we add and subtract fractions with unlike denominators, we need to get the same fair share for each fraction.

Both halves and thirds line up with sixths. We turn $\frac{1}{2}$ into $\frac{3}{6}$ and we turn $\frac{1}{3}$ into $\frac{2}{6}$. This way, the denominators will be the same, or common.

Once we have denominators where the whole, or total, is divided into the same fair shares, we can find an exact answer to the problem.

We use fraction bars to add our new fractions and get an exact answer.

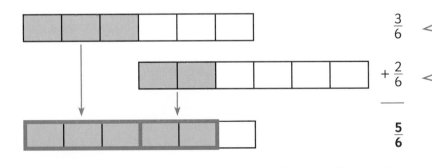

$$\frac{3}{6}$$

$$+ \frac{2}{6}$$

$$\frac{5}{6}$$

> When we make the denominators the same, we are finding equivalent fractions for each fraction in the original problem. We are not just changing the denominator. We are also changing the numerator.

Fraction bars help us make common denominators. We get the exact answer when we add or subtract fractions with common denominators. This process works with fractions that can be easily converted, like the conversion from $\frac{1}{2}$ to $\frac{3}{6}$.

But with most fractions, we need a method other than fraction bars to find common denominators.

POWER CONCEPT

When we make denominators the same, we also make equivalent fractions.

How do we make equivalent fractions?

Let's look at two ways to find a common denominator.

Example 1

Use a table of multiples to find the common denominator.

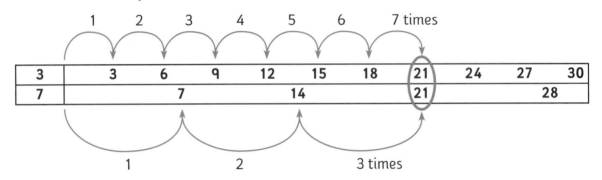

A common denominator for the denominators 3 and 7 is 21.

A table of multiples of two numbers helps us find the **least common denominator**, or **LCD**. The LCD is the first multiple that is the same for both 3 and 7. Each row shows how we count by the multiple of the number. We count by each number until we get to the first multiple that is the same for 3 and 7. In this case, the LCD is 21.

When we add or subtract fractions, we convert each fraction so that the denominators are the same. We can use fraction bars, or we can use tables of multiples. We can also simply multiply by a fraction equal to 1 to make an equivalent fraction. Let's see how to multiply a fraction by a fraction equal to 1 to make an equivalent fraction.

Remember, a fraction equal to 1 is any fraction with the same number in the numerator and in the denominator.

Example 2

Multiply by a fraction equal to 1 to find the common denominator, then solve the problem.

$$\frac{2}{3} - \frac{1}{7}$$

$$\frac{2}{3} \cdot \boxed{\frac{7}{7}} = \frac{14}{21}$$

$$\frac{1}{7} \cdot \boxed{\frac{3}{3}} = \frac{3}{21}$$

$$\frac{14}{21} - \frac{3}{21} = \frac{11}{21}$$

We can check our work using fraction bars. In this case, we see that the fraction bars for thirds and sevenths line up with the fraction bar for twenty-firsts. But it is sometimes hard to work with fraction bars because the fair shares can be very small.

Example 3

Use fraction bars to check the answer.

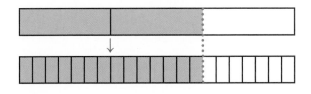

$$\frac{2}{3} = \frac{14}{21}$$

$$\frac{1}{7} = \frac{3}{21}$$

The answer is the same: $\frac{14}{21} - \frac{3}{21} = \frac{11}{21}$.

Another method for finding the common denominator involves multiplying the two denominators together. There are cases when this method is the best one to use. Other times multiplying denominators gives us a denominator that is far larger than what we need.

Example 4

Multiply two denominators to get a common denominator.

$$\frac{7}{10} - \frac{3}{20} \rightarrow \frac{}{10} \cdot \frac{}{20} = \frac{}{200}$$

A common denominator for these fractions is 200.

Now we want to find the equivalent numerators for each of the fractions. We multiply the original fractions by a fraction equal to 1 that will get us 200 for a denominator.

$$\frac{7}{10} \cdot \frac{20}{20} = \frac{140}{200} \qquad \frac{3}{20} \cdot \frac{10}{10} = \frac{30}{200}$$

$$\frac{140}{200} - \frac{30}{200} = \frac{110}{200}$$

A simpler approach is to find the LCD.

In this case, although 200 is a common denominator, it is not the *least common denominator*. Using 200 for the common denominator makes the numbers large and the computations more difficult.

What are some common situations that require addition and subtraction of fractions?

There are times when we have to add or subtract fractions with denominators that are not the same. Let's look at an example.

Problem:

Hector rides his bicycle to school every day. He rides $2\frac{1}{3}$ miles down Perry Street to Grove Street. From Grove Street he rides $\frac{1}{4}$ mile to the school. How far does Hector ride to school?

We need to add $2\frac{1}{3} + \frac{1}{4}$.

Steps for Adding Fractions With Unlike Denominators

STEP 1

Find the LCD.
The simplest method is to
count up by each number. The least common denominator is 12.

3	3	6	9	12	15	18
4	4	8	12	16	20	24

STEP 2

Find equivalent fractions by multiplying each fraction by a number equal to 1.

We start with $\frac{1}{3}$. Because 3 goes into 12 four times, we multiply our fraction by $\frac{4}{4}$.

$$\frac{1}{3} \cdot \frac{4}{4} = \frac{4}{12}$$

Next, we multiply $\frac{1}{4}$ by a fraction equal to 1. Because 4 goes into 12 three times, we use $\frac{3}{3}$.

$$\frac{1}{4} \cdot \frac{3}{3} = \frac{3}{12}$$

STEP 3

Add the new numbers together.
We can't forget the whole number that came before the fraction.

$$
\begin{array}{r}
2\frac{4}{12} \\
+ \ \frac{3}{12} \\
\hline
2\frac{7}{12}
\end{array}
$$

Hector rides his bike $2\frac{7}{12}$ miles to school.

 **Apply Skills**
Turn to *Interactive Text*, page 5.

 **Reinforce Understanding**
Use the *mBook Study Guide* to review lesson concepts.

Activity 1

Add and subtract.

1. $\frac{1}{5} + \frac{3}{5}$

2. $\frac{7}{8} - \frac{2}{8}$

3. $\frac{1}{2} + \frac{3}{4}$

4. $\frac{4}{8} - \frac{1}{4}$

5. $\frac{2}{3} + \frac{1}{5}$

6. $\frac{7}{9} - \frac{1}{6}$

Activity 2

Select the fraction that is equivalent.

1. $\frac{1}{2}$

   (a) $\frac{2}{5}$

   (b) $\frac{2}{4}$

   (c) $\frac{1}{4}$

2. $\frac{3}{4}$

   (a) $\frac{9}{12}$

   (b) $\frac{6}{10}$

   (c) $\frac{1}{3}$

3. $\frac{2}{5}$

   (a) $\frac{2}{9}$

   (b) $\frac{4}{10}$

   (c) $\frac{3}{7}$

4. $\frac{5}{7}$

   (a) $\frac{5}{9}$

   (b) $\frac{3}{7}$

   (c) $\frac{10}{14}$

Activity 3

Select the least common denominator (LCD) for each of the problems.

1. $\frac{1}{2} + \frac{2}{5}$

   (a) The LCD is 5.

   (b) The LCD is 10.

   (c) The LCD is 2.

2. $\frac{3}{8} - \frac{1}{4}$

   (a) The LCD is 8.

   (b) The LCD is 32.

   (c) The LCD is 4.

3. $\frac{4}{6} + \frac{2}{9}$

   (a) The LCD is 54.

   (b) The LCD is 18.

   (c) The LCD is 9.

Activity 4 • Distributed Practice

Solve.

1. Find the missing numbers in the lists of multiples. Write the answers on your paper.

3	3	(a)	9	12	(b)	(c)	21	
4	4	8	(d)	16	(e)	24	(f)	32

2. What is the LCD for the problem $\frac{2}{3} + \frac{5}{4}$?

3. Write the multiples for 5 starting at 5 and ending at 50.

4. Write the multiples for 10 starting at 10 and ending at 100.

5. What is the LCD for the problem $\frac{3}{5} - \frac{3}{10}$?

Lesson 3 ▸ Multiplying Fractions

Problem Solving:
▸ More Statistics

▸ Multiplying Fractions

Vocabulary
proper fraction

What happens when we multiply fractions?

Let's review two important points that help us stay organized when we add, subtract, or multiply fractions.

Look at the table. It shows what happens when we multiply two whole numbers. When we multiply two whole numbers, the product is never smaller than the other two whole numbers.

Multiplication of Whole Numbers	Product
$3 \cdot 4 =$	12
$6 \cdot 7 =$	42
$200 \cdot 5 =$	1,000
$18 \cdot 1 =$	18

When we multiply fractions, the result is usually the opposite. The product of two proper fractions is usually smaller than the fractions being multiplied. In a **proper fraction**, the numerator is less than the denominator.

Multiplication of Proper Fractions	Product
$\frac{1}{2} \cdot \frac{1}{4} =$	$\frac{1}{8}$
$\frac{3}{5} \cdot \frac{1}{2} =$	$\frac{3}{10}$
$\frac{1}{8} \cdot \frac{2}{3} =$	$\frac{2}{24}$
$\frac{4}{6} \cdot \frac{1}{5} =$	$\frac{4}{30}$

This model shows what happens when we multiply 3 · 4. Another way of saying this problem is, "We are multiplying 3 sets of 4."

3 · 4

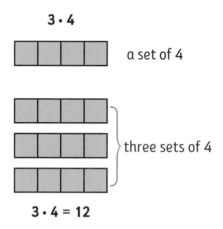

a set of 4

three sets of 4

3 · 4 = 12

POWER CONCEPT

When multiplying two whole numbers, the product is never smaller than either of the whole numbers being multiplied.

Now let's look at what happens when we multiply $\frac{1}{2} \cdot \frac{2}{3}$. Another way of saying this problem is, "What is $\frac{1}{2}$ of $\frac{2}{3}$?"

$$\frac{1}{2} \cdot \frac{2}{3}$$

We use the model to identify $\frac{2}{3}$

$\frac{2}{3}$

Then we find $\frac{1}{2}$ of the $\frac{2}{3}$

$\frac{1}{2}$ of $\frac{2}{3}$

POWER CONCEPT

When we multiply two fractions, we take a portion of a fraction.

The model shows the product $\frac{2}{6}$. The two colored and striped squares are the parts. The whole is all six parts.

$$\frac{1}{2} \cdot \frac{2}{3} = \frac{2}{6}$$

%÷
=×
Apply Skills
Turn to *Interactive Text*, page 7.

mBook **Reinforce Understanding**
Use the *mBook Study Guide* to review lesson concepts.

▶**Problem Solving: More Statistics**

Vocabulary
median

Why is the mean important?

In the first lesson of this unit, Carmen, the manager of a shoe store, used her spreadsheet to keep track of the mean number of QuikTrax shoes she sold over nine weeks. Here is the table of data.

Week	Number of Pairs of Shoes Sold
May 1 to May 7	47
May 8 to May 14	39
May 15 to May 21	31
May 22 to May 28	39
May 29 to June 4	49
June 5 to June 11	57
June 12 to June 18	50
June 19 to June 25	48
June 26 to July 2	54
Total	414

To find the mean, divide the total of the data by the number of data points.

Carmen calculated the mean by dividing the total number of pairs of shoes sold by the number of weeks.

$$\underbrace{414}_{\substack{\text{total} \\ \text{data}}} \div \underbrace{9}_{\substack{\text{number} \\ \text{of weeks}}} = \underbrace{46}_{\text{mean}}$$

The mean is $414 \div 9 = 46$.

The mean is useful because it helps us make a good guess or prediction. For example, if Carmen wanted to predict how many QuikTrax shoes would be sold next week, the best guess would be the mean. She would predict 46 pairs of shoes.

The mean is just one way of thinking about what is average or typical.

What is the median?

Another important idea is the **median** . The median is halfway between the minimum and the maximum of a set of numbers. That is, when we count from smallest to largest, it is the number in the middle. The illustration shows that a number like the median is easiest to see when we organize the data from smallest to largest.

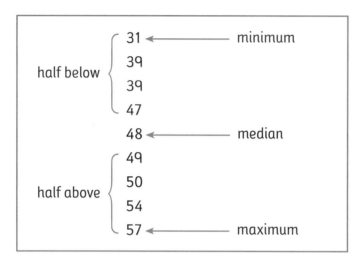

How do we find the median when we have an even set of numbers?

When we have an even set of numbers, the median is halfway between the two middle numbers.

How do we decide which number is the median if the two numbers in the middle are the same?

If the two numbers in the middle are the same, both numbers are the median.

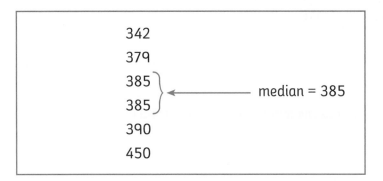

How do we present the data to find the mean and the median?

To find the mean and the median in a set of data, we present the data in two ways:

- an ordered list from low to high
- a simple tally chart

Example 1 shows an ordered list from low to high. Example 2 shows a simple tally chart. Both charts show how many students in one class are at a specific height. Some students are shorter than the rest of the class, and some are taller. But what is the average, or mean, height? Also, what is the middle point, or median, where half of the students are below and half are above?

Example 1

Find the mean and the median height of the students using the ordered list.

These are the heights of students from one classroom.

Ordered List (height measured in inches)
61
61
62
62
64
64
65
65
65
65
67
68
68
68
68
68
68
69
69
70
70
71
72

To find the mean, we divide the total number of inches by the total number of students.

The total number of inches is 1,530. The total number of students in the class is 23.

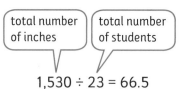

total number of inches   total number of students

1,530 ÷ 23 = 66.5

The mean is 66.5 inches.

To find the median, look for the middle point in the list.

The median is 68 inches.

When we have a long list of data, it is sometimes easier to organize the data in a tally chart. A tally chart uses marks to count the number of times each number appears in the list. In Example 2, we use Xs for the marks.

Example 2

Find the mean and the median height of the students using the tally chart.

Tally Chart (height measured in inches)	
61	x x
62	x x
63	
64	x x
65	x x x x
66	
67	x
68	x x x x x x — median
69	x x
70	x x
71	x
72	x

In the tally chart, we need to remember to count the marks by each number. There are 23 marks, so we divide the sum of the heights by 23 to find the mean.

1,530 ÷ 23 = 66.5

The mean is 66.5 inches.

To find the median, we locate the middle point in the count of students. We start at the first mark and the last mark in the tally chart. Then we move toward the middle number from each end, one mark at a time, until we reach the point in the middle. This point is 68.

The median is 68 inches.

Problem-Solving Activity
Turn to *Interactive Text*, page 8.

mBook **Reinforce Understanding**
Use the *mBook Study Guide* to review lesson concepts.

Homework

Activity 1

Add and subtract.

1. $\frac{1}{5} + \frac{2}{5}$

2. $\frac{7}{8} - \frac{5}{8}$

3. $\frac{1}{2} + \frac{1}{4}$

4. $\frac{7}{8} - \frac{1}{2}$

5. $\frac{2}{4} + \frac{1}{3}$

6. $\frac{5}{6} - \frac{1}{9}$

Activity 2

Select the problem that matches the area model.

1.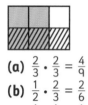

   (a) $\frac{2}{3} \cdot \frac{2}{3} = \frac{4}{9}$

   (b) $\frac{1}{2} \cdot \frac{2}{3} = \frac{2}{6}$

   (c) $\frac{1}{3} \cdot \frac{1}{2} = \frac{1}{6}$

2.

   (a) $\frac{3}{4} \cdot \frac{2}{3} = \frac{6}{12}$

   (b) $\frac{1}{4} \cdot \frac{3}{4} = \frac{3}{16}$

   (c) $\frac{1}{3} \cdot \frac{1}{4} = \frac{1}{12}$

3.

   (a) $\frac{2}{3} \cdot \frac{1}{3} = \frac{2}{9}$

   (b) $\frac{1}{3} \cdot \frac{3}{4} = \frac{3}{12}$

   (c) $\frac{1}{3} \cdot \frac{1}{2} = \frac{1}{6}$

Activity 3

For each of the data sets, tell the mean and the median.

1. 2, 3, 4, 3, 5, 3, 2, 4, 1

2. 20, 10, 30, 20

3. 300, 200, 100

4. 15, 13, 17, 12, 23, 18, 17, 13

Activity 4 • Distributed Practice

Solve.

1. Write the multiples of 6 starting at 6 and ending at 60.

2. Write the multiples of 8 starting at 8 and ending at 80.

3. What is the LCD for $\frac{1}{5}$ and $\frac{1}{6}$? Use the lists of multiples below to help you.

5	5	10	15	20	25	30	35	40	45	50
6	6	12	18	24	30	36	42	48	54	60

4. $500 \div 100$

5. $558 + 552$

6. $65 \cdot 3$

7. $712 - 383$

Lesson 4 | ▶Multiply and Simplify

Problem Solving:
▷Putting It All Together

▶Multiply and Simplify

Vocabulary
improper fraction

What is the traditional method for multiplying fractions?

Multiplying fractions is a relatively easy process. It is easy because we do not have to change denominators. We just multiply straight across.

$$\frac{3}{4} \cdot \frac{1}{2} = \frac{3}{8} \qquad \frac{7}{2} \cdot \frac{2}{7} = \frac{14}{14} \qquad \frac{6}{8} \cdot \frac{3}{7} = \frac{18}{56} \qquad \frac{6}{3} \cdot \frac{4}{2} = \frac{24}{6}$$

Remember:

When we add or subtract fractions, we are looking for an exact answer. That is why we must have the same denominators when we add or subtract:

$$\frac{1}{4} + \frac{2}{3}$$

- Is the answer written in fourths, or is it written in thirds? We have to have fair shares.
- We change $\frac{1}{4} + \frac{2}{3}$ into $\frac{3}{12} + \frac{8}{12}$ to get fair shares.
- Now we add so that the problem makes sense.

$$\frac{3}{12} + \frac{8}{12} = \frac{11}{12}$$

When we multiply fractions, we are taking a portion of one of the fractions. When we multiply $\frac{2}{3} \cdot \frac{1}{2}$, we are taking $\frac{2}{3}$ of $\frac{1}{2}$. Think of it as taking a "fraction of a fraction."

$$\frac{2}{3} \cdot \frac{1}{2} = \frac{2}{6} = \frac{1}{3}$$

How do we simplify the answer?

In most cases, we need to simplify the answers to problems. The larger fractions can be broken down into simpler fractions. We simplify by pulling out a fraction equal to one. The fraction we find contains the greatest common factor of the numerator and the denominator placed over itself. In a fraction, any number over itself is always equal to 1. Also, any number times 1 is the same number.

Example 1

Simplify the answer.

$$\frac{3}{4} \cdot \frac{2}{4} = \frac{6}{16}$$

$$\frac{6}{16} = \frac{3}{8} \cdot \boxed{\frac{2}{2}}$$

Because 2 is the greatest common factor of 6 and 16, we use $\frac{2}{2}$ as our fraction.

$$= \frac{3}{8} \cdot 1$$

$$= \frac{3}{8}$$

Sometimes the numerator is bigger than the denominator. These are called **improper fractions**. We usually change improper fractions to mixed numbers when we simplify the answer.

Example 2

Simplify the answer when it is an improper fraction.

$$\frac{3}{4} \cdot \frac{3}{2} = \frac{9}{8}$$

The answer, $\frac{9}{8}$, is an improper fraction.

We make a mixed number this way:

$$\frac{9}{8} = \frac{8}{8} + \frac{1}{8}$$

We need to find the whole number in the fraction.

$$= 1\frac{1}{8}$$

When do we simplify more than once?

There are times when we have to change our answer to a proper fraction or mixed number and still need to simplify the answer. In Example 1, we simplify the answer more than once.

Example 1

Write the answer in simplest form.

$$\frac{4}{5} \cdot \frac{3}{2} = \frac{12}{10}$$

First, we change the answer to a mixed number.

$$\frac{12}{10} = \frac{10}{10} + \frac{2}{10}$$

$$= 1\frac{2}{10} \quad \boxed{\text{Next, we simplify } \frac{2}{10}}$$

Next, we simplify $\frac{2}{10}$. We find the greatest common factor of the numerator and the denominator. It is 2.

$$\frac{2}{10} = \frac{1}{5} \cdot \frac{2}{2}$$

$$= \frac{1}{5} \cdot 1$$

$$= \frac{1}{5}$$

> Be sure to simplify all answers. The products of multiplication problems, as well as the answers to all operations with fractions, should be simplified.

So, $\frac{12}{10} = 1\frac{1}{5}$

The final answer after simplifying is $1\frac{1}{5}$.

When working with mixed numbers, we simplify all of our answers.

%÷ Apply Skills
<x Turn to *Interactive Text*, page 10.

mBook Reinforce Understanding
Use the *mBook Study Guide* to review lesson concepts.

▶**Problem Solving: Putting It All Together**

Vocabulary

outlier

How do we use statistics to make sense of data?

We have worked with the minimum, maximum, mean, mode, and median. The mean, or average, helps us predict the next number in the set of data.

But the mean alone can sometimes give us an incomplete picture of the data. We need to look at all the numbers (min, max, range, mean, and median) if we want to have a good understanding of a set of data.

The data set below shows the number of cars sold at Wilson's Autos. The data are written in order from low to high. This makes it easier to find the *min*, *max*, *mode*, and *median*. It also helps us compare the mean with the other data.

Example 1

Find the mean, median, mode, and range of the data in the table.

Week	Number of Cars Sold	
July 9 to July 15	21	← min
June 4 to June 10	29	
June 18 to June 24	29	← mode
July 16 to July 22	37	
July 23 to July 29	38	← median
July 2 to July 8	39	
July 30 to Aug. 5	40	
June 11 to June 17	44	
June 25 to July 1	47	← max
Total	324	

The table shows:

- the min = 21, the max = 47
- the range = 26 (47 − 21)
- the mode = 29 (the number that occurs most frequently in the list)
- the mean = 36 (the total, 324, divided by the number of data points, 9)

The median of 38 is close to the mean of 36. In a data set, when the mean and the median are close together, then either one is a good indication of what is "about average."

Let's look at what happens when we have some extreme numbers.

Let's say that Wilson's Autos wants to sell all the cars it has before new cars come in October. It decides to run a big sale. The sale was so successful that Wilson's Autos started to run out of cars by the week of September 17. That is why the number of auto sales per week drops off so much for the last two weeks of September.

Example 2

Find the mean, median, mode, and range of the data with extreme numbers.

Week	Number of Cars Sold	
Sept. 24 to Sept. 30	1	← minimum
Sept. 17 to Sept. 23	7	
Sept. 10 to Sept. 16	78	
Aug. 20 to Aug. 26	83	← median = 84
Aug. 13 to Aug. 19	85	mean = 68
Aug. 6 to Aug. 12	92	
Sept. 3 to Sept. 9	95	
Aug. 27 to Sept. 2	103	← maximum
Total	**544**	

The table shows:

- The min and the max are easy to see. The min is 1, and the max is 103.

- The range is 103 − 1, or 102.

- The median is the halfway point in the set of numbers. We have an even number of weeks. To determine the halfway point, we find the midway point between 83 and 85. The median is 84.

- Because there is no number that occurs most often, or more than once, there is no mode.

To get the mean, we add all the cars sold and divide by the total number of weeks:

544 ÷ 8 = 68

There are two weeks of very low sales, but most of the numbers in the data set are between 78 and 103.

Notice the gap between the mean, 68, and the median, 84.

Now let's look at what happens when we take out the two extreme numbers, 1 and 7. Numbers like this in a data set are called **outliers**. An outlier is any number that is significantly larger or smaller than the other numbers in the data set.

Example 3

Find the mean, median, mode, and range of the data after removing the outliers.

Week	Number of Cars Sold
Sept. 10 to Sept. 16	78
Aug. 20 to Aug. 26	83
Aug. 13 to Aug. 19	85
Aug. 6 to Aug. 12	92
Sept. 3 to Sept. 9	95
Aug. 27 to Sept. 2	103
Total	**536**

median = 88.5
mean = 89.3

Let's look at what happened when we removed the outliers:

- Now the minimum is 78 and the maximum is still 103.
- The range is 103 − 78, or 25. This is a much smaller range than before.
- The median did not change that much from before, from 84 to 88.5.
- The mean changed a great deal, from 68 to 89.3.

When we have extreme numbers, the mean is affected. In this case, it is less when the outliers 1 and 7 are included. This is why the median is a better overall indicator of week-by-week auto sales throughout the eight weeks.

Another way to understand the effect of extremes on the mean and the median is to change one of the numbers to an extremely large number. Suppose that instead of selling one car for the week of September 24–September 30, Wilson's Autos sold 1,000 cars. Now the max is the most extreme number.

The table in Example 4 shows the change in the data.

Example 4

Compare the median and mean when an outlier has been added to the data set.

Week	Number of Cars Sold
Sept. 17 to Sept. 23	7
Sept. 10 to Sept. 16	78
Aug. 20 to Aug. 26	83
Aug. 13 to Aug. 19	85
Aug. 6 to Aug. 12	92
Sept. 3 to Sept. 9	95
Aug. 27 to Sept. 2	103
Sept. 24 to Sept. 30	1,000
Total	**1,543**

median = 88.5
mean = 192.9

The table shows:

- The outlier 1,000 has a great effect on the mean, causing it to jump from 68 to 192.9.

- The change in the median is very small, moving from 84 to 88.5. This makes the median a much better description of this data than the mean.

When we think about data, we look at both the mean and the median. We also look at the min and max and see if they are extreme compared to the other numbers. When the mean and the median are close, then either number is a good description of the data. When they are far apart, the median tends to be a better description of the data. There is less of a change to the median based on outliers.

POWER CONCEPT

When the mean and the median are close, either number is a good description of the center of the data. When they are far apart, the median tends to be a better description of the center of the data.

Problem-Solving Activity
Turn to *Interactive Text*, page 11.

mBook Reinforce Understanding
Use the *mBook Study Guide* to review lesson concepts.

Activity 1

Add and subtract.

1. $\frac{1}{4} + \frac{1}{8}$
2. $\frac{5}{6} - \frac{2}{3}$
3. $\frac{1}{3} + \frac{1}{9}$
4. $\frac{5}{8} - \frac{1}{4}$
5. $\frac{2}{3} + \frac{3}{4}$
6. $\frac{4}{9} - \frac{1}{6}$

Activity 2

Multiply across and simplify the answer.

Model $\frac{1}{3} \cdot \frac{2}{4}$ Answer: $\frac{1 \cdot 2}{3 \cdot 4} = \frac{2}{12} = \frac{2}{2} \cdot \frac{1}{6} = \frac{1}{6}$

1. $\frac{1}{5} \cdot \frac{2}{10}$
2. $\frac{3}{4} \cdot \frac{2}{3}$
3. $\frac{4}{6} \cdot \frac{1}{4}$
4. $\frac{1}{2} \cdot \frac{3}{9}$

Activity 3

Select the true statement.

1. Data Set: 1, 2, 3, 4, 5
   (a) The mean is bigger than the median.
   (b) The mean is the same as the median.
   (c) The mean is smaller than the median.

2. Data Set: 4, 6, 9, 11, 14
   (a) The mode is 9.
   (b) The median is 9.
   (c) The range is 9.

Activity 4 • Distributed Practice

Solve.

1. What is the least common denominator for the problem $\frac{1}{6} + \frac{1}{9}$?

2. $45 + 22 + 37$
3. $267 - 199$
4. $48 \cdot 2$
5. $236 \div 4$
6. $629 + 481$
7. $222 \cdot 3$

▶**Dividing Fractions**

What happens when we divide fractions?

Before we talk about dividing fractions, it's important to remember what it means to divide whole numbers. Here's a very simple model using a number line. We see that the unit 4 breaks up 12 three times. The unit 4 is a single unit.

Example 1

Use a number line to show division of whole numbers.

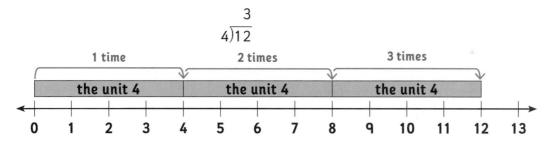

Now look at what happens when we divide a whole number by a fraction. The fraction $\frac{1}{2}$ is a single unit that breaks up 5. It breaks it up 10 times.

Example 2

Use a number line to show a whole number divided by a fraction.

$$5 \div \frac{1}{2} = 10 \quad \text{or} \quad \frac{1}{2}\overline{)5}^{\,10}$$

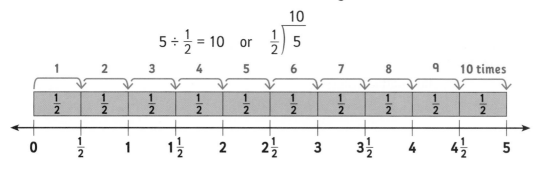

We use the number line to help us understand what is happening when we divide one fraction by another fraction. In each of the previous examples, we broke up a whole number by a unit. We call this unit the divisor. In Example 1, this divisor was a whole number, and in Example 2 it was a fraction. In the next example, we will break up a fraction by a unit that is also a fraction.

Example 3

Use a number line to show division of fractions.

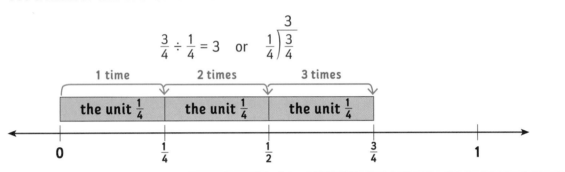

$$\frac{3}{4} \div \frac{1}{4} = 3 \quad \text{or} \quad \frac{1}{4}\overline{)\frac{3}{4}} = 3$$

Let's think about the difference between division of whole numbers and division of fractions. Look at the difference in the quotient in the two problems below. Generally, when we divide whole numbers, the quotient is smaller than the number being divided (the dividend). When we divide fractions, this is generally the opposite.

Whole Numbers	Fractions
$5\overline{)30}$ gives 6	$\frac{3}{4}\overline{)\frac{2}{3}}$ gives $\frac{8}{9}$

The quotient 6 is smaller than the number 30. The quotient $\frac{8}{9}$ is larger than the number $\frac{2}{3}$.

Remembering this difference between quotients and what we see when we use the number line helps us make sense of what is happening when we divide one fraction by another fraction.

POWER CONCEPT

When we divide one fraction by another, the quotient is often larger than the dividend.

What is the shortcut for dividing fractions?

The shortcut for dividing fractions is to flip over, or invert, the second fraction, then multiply. This is the *traditional method* for dividing fractions.

$$\frac{4}{8} \div \frac{1}{4}$$

Invert and multiply

$$\frac{4}{8} \div \frac{1}{4} = \frac{4}{8} \cdot \frac{4}{1}$$

$$\frac{4}{8} \cdot \frac{4}{1} = \frac{16}{8}$$

Simplify the answer

$$\frac{16}{8} = \frac{2}{1} \text{ or } 2$$

The number line helps us see why this shortcut works. We divide the divisor $\frac{1}{4}$ into the fraction. It breaks up the fraction $\frac{4}{8}$ exactly 2 times.

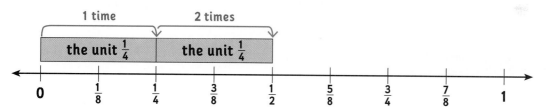

Let's practice the traditional method for dividing fractions in Example 1.

Example 1

Solve the problem using the traditional method for dividing fractions.

The shortcut for dividing fractions is to invert the second fraction, then multiply.

$$\frac{2}{4} \div \frac{6}{8} \quad = \quad \frac{2}{4} \cdot \frac{8}{6} = \frac{16}{24} \quad = \quad \frac{16}{24} = \frac{2}{3}$$

% ÷
≤ x Apply Skills
Turn to *Interactive Text*, page 13.

Monitoring Progress
Quiz 1

mBook Reinforce Understanding
Use the *mBook Study Guide* to review lesson concepts.

Activity 1

Multiply across and simplify the answer.

1. $\frac{1}{2} \cdot \frac{3}{4}$ 2. $\frac{4}{5} \cdot \frac{2}{3}$ 3. $\frac{4}{6} \cdot \frac{1}{2}$ 4. $\frac{2}{5} \cdot \frac{5}{10}$

Activity 2

Divide using invert and multiply. Simplify the answer.

1. $\frac{4}{5} \div \frac{1}{5}$ 2. $\frac{8}{9} \div \frac{1}{3}$ 3. $\frac{4}{1} \div \frac{1}{4}$

Activity 3

Answer the questions about the important statistics for the data set.

Data Set: 1, 2, 2, 3, 4, 4, 5, 6, 6, 6, 7, 8, 25

1. The number 25 is called a(n) _____ because it is so different from the other data.

2. The number 25 impacts the _____ more than the median.

3. The number 6 is called the _____.

4. The range is 24 because it represents the distance between the _____ and the _____.

Activity 4 • Distributed Practice

Solve.

1. List the first 6 multiples for 6 and 9. Find any common multiples.

2. List the factors of 36 and 48. What is the greatest common factor?

3. What is the least common denominator for $\frac{3}{5} - \frac{1}{9}$?

4. $\frac{3}{2} + \frac{5}{4}$ 5. $\frac{6}{7} - \frac{5}{7}$

6. $\frac{4}{6} - \frac{2}{9}$ 7. $420 \div 10$

▸**Mixed Practice With Fractions**

Vocabulary
reciprocal

When do we change the denominator and when don't we?

Working with fractions can be confusing. Sometimes we change the denominator, and sometimes we don't. This is why we have spent so much time thinking about key ideas or observations behind each operation. Here is a brief review.

When we add or subtract fractions, we need to have the same fair shares.

If we do not have the same fair shares, or the same denominators, then we get an answer that we cannot describe. Adding $\frac{1}{2}$ and $\frac{1}{3}$ does not give us halves or thirds. The answer does not make sense. By using the same fair shares, we get an answer that is exact. Take a look at the fraction bars below.

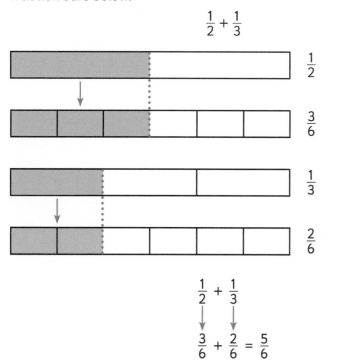

When we multiply fractions, we do not change the denominator.

When we multiply, we take a portion of the fraction. This is why the answer is usually smaller than the numbers we are multiplying.

$$\frac{3}{4} \cdot \frac{1}{2}$$

$$\frac{3}{4} \cdot \frac{1}{2} = \frac{3}{8}$$

When we divide fractions, we do not change the denominator.

We break up a fraction with another fraction. The answer to a division problem with two fractions is usually larger than the number we are dividing.

$$\frac{5}{8} \div \frac{1}{8}$$

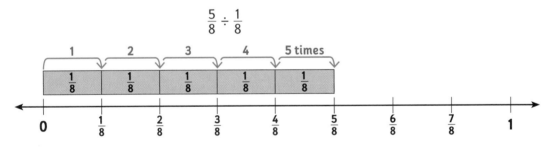

The traditional way to divide fractions is to invert, or flip over, the second fraction, then multiply.

$$\frac{5}{8} \cdot \frac{8}{1} = \frac{40}{8} = 5$$

What are reciprocals?

When we use the traditional method for dividing fractions, we invert one of the fractions. When we invert a fraction, we make a **reciprocal**. A reciprocal is the inverse of the fraction. Reciprocals are important. We use them a lot in algebra.

Fraction	Reciprocal
$\frac{1}{5}$	$\frac{5}{1}$
$\frac{7}{4}$	$\frac{4}{7}$
$\frac{25}{17}$	$\frac{17}{25}$
$\frac{2}{1}$	$\frac{1}{2}$

When we multiply a fraction and its reciprocal, we always get 1.

Multiplying by the Reciprocal
$\frac{1}{5} \cdot \frac{5}{1} = \frac{5}{5} = 1$
$\frac{7}{4} \cdot \frac{4}{7} = \frac{28}{28} = 1$
$\frac{25}{17} \cdot \frac{17}{25} = \frac{425}{425} = 1$
$\frac{2}{1} \cdot \frac{1}{2} = \frac{2}{2} = 1$

%÷
=× **Apply Skills**
Turn to *Interactive Text*, page 15.

mBook **Reinforce Understanding**
Use the *mBook Study Guide* to review lesson concepts.

▶**Problem Solving: Box-and-Whisker Plots**

Vocabulary

box-and-whisker plot

What are box-and-whisker plots?

We know that the median is a useful statistic when analyzing data. It is the halfway point in a set of data when the numbers are listed from low to high. Sometimes we want to find out how all the numbers in the data set relate to the median. **Box-and-whisker plots**, a kind of graph, help us understand how all the data are distributed from low to high.

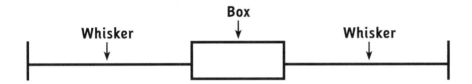

When we make box-and-whisker plots, we break the data into three parts. The first whisker contains the lowest $\frac{1}{4}$ of the data. The box in the middle contains the middle $\frac{1}{2}$ of the data, and the last whisker contains the highest $\frac{1}{4}$ of the data.

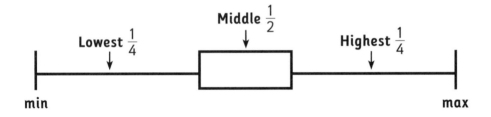

How do we make a box-and-whisker plot from a table of data?

Let's see how a box-and-whisker plot helps us organize data.

It is Sports Day at Union High School. There are many track-and-field events, and all students are encouraged to try them. Fifteen students try the long jump. Their longest jumps are recorded.

The data are in order from shortest to longest jumps. It is easier to find the median when we organize the data this way.

Student	Distance (in inches)
Amber	82
Oscar	87
Autumn	88
Brittany	90
Joshua	91
Marcus	92
Mikaela	93
Ryan	94 ← ———— median
Pablo	98
Seth	108
Tracey	110
Miguel	115
Paige	118
DeAnne	121
Lamar	123

Now we break the numbers into three different parts: (1) the lowest $\frac{1}{4}$, (2) the middle $\frac{1}{2}$, and (3) the highest $\frac{1}{4}$.

Long Jump Data (in inches)		
Lowest $\frac{1}{4}$	Middle $\frac{1}{2}$	Highest $\frac{1}{4}$
Amber: 82	Joshua: 91	Miguel: 115
Oscar: 87	Marcus: 92	Paige: 118
Autumn: 88	Mikaela: 93	DeAnne: 121
Brittany: 90	Ryan: 94	Lamar: 123
	Pablo: 98	
	Seth: 108	
	Tracey: 110	

min ↓ ↓ ↓ max

82 90 100 110 123

median = 94

We see where the median is inside the box. It is not in the middle of the box but toward the lower end.

Now we use the box-and-whisker plot to see how each student did compared to the median and to each other.

- The lowest $\frac{1}{4}$ of the jumpers jumped between 82 and 90 inches. Some of the students are not that far from the median of 94 inches.

- The middle $\frac{1}{2}$ of the students jumped between 90 and 110 inches. Some of the jumpers in this group, like Seth and Tracey, are in the middle $\frac{1}{2}$, but they are a good distance away from the median.

- Finally, the highest $\frac{1}{4}$ of the students jumped between 110 and 123 inches. They are the top $\frac{1}{4}$ of the jumpers in the group. DeAnne and Lamar are at the top, and they are a long way from the median.

What is the difference between the median and the halfway point between the min and the max?

When we compare the numbers below the median with those above the median in the box-and-whisker plot for the long jump data, we see right away that the range is smaller in the lower half. The box-and-whisker plots help us see how the numbers are distributed in a list of numbers, even if the list is ordered from low to high.

The range in the lower half is from the minimum of 82 to the median of 94. That is only 12 points. In the upper half, though, there is a range of 29 points from the median to the maximum.

This plot shows that even though the median is the halfway point in a set of data, it does not mean that it is exactly halfway between the minimum and the maximum.

Let's draw another box-and-whisker plot to illustrate this.

During Sports Day, some of the students take part in the discus throw. These are their results:

Discus Throw (in feet)		
Samuel	20	← min
Bud	21	
Aubrey	22	
Nate	23	
Jordan	25	← median
Jesus	40	
Tom	50	
Patrice	80	← max

- The median is the halfway point of the data. Because we have an even number of throwers, we find the point between Nate's and Jordan's scores, 24.

- The range is the difference between the largest and smallest scores, $80 - 20 = 60$. The halfway point from the min to the max is $20 + 30 = 50$. There is a difference of 26 between the median and the halfway point in the range. Most of the scores fall well below the halfway point.

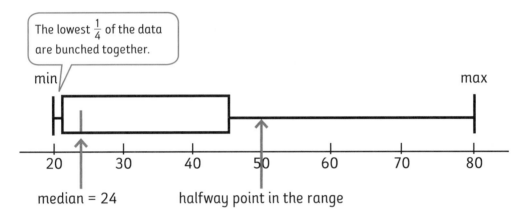

The lowest $\frac{1}{4}$ of the data are bunched together.

median = 24   halfway point in the range

A box-and-whisker plot clearly shows where the extreme scores are and how numbers in a set of data can be bunched together or spread out.

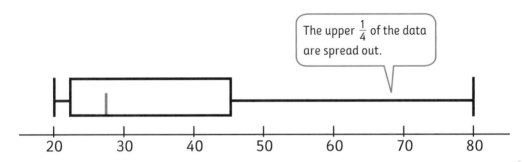

The upper $\frac{1}{4}$ of the data are spread out.

Box-and-whisker plots help us understand the data better and interpret it properly.

POWER CONCEPT

Box-and-whisker plots help us understand how data are distributed.

 Problem-Solving Activity
Turn to *Interactive Text*, page 16.

 mBook Reinforce Understanding
Use the *mBook Study Guide* to review lesson concepts.

Activity 1

Add, subtract, multiply, and divide the following fractions. Be careful to use the correct strategy. Simplify the answers if necessary.

1. $\frac{1}{2} + \frac{3}{4}$ 2. $\frac{4}{5} - \frac{2}{3}$ 3. $\frac{1}{6} \div \frac{1}{2}$

4. $\frac{2}{5} \cdot \frac{1}{3}$ 5. $\frac{2}{6} - \frac{1}{9}$ 6. $\frac{3}{5} \div \frac{1}{5}$

Activity 2

Give the reciprocal for each of the numbers.

Model 8   1. $\frac{1}{3}$ 2. $\frac{4}{5}$ 3. 9

Answer: $\frac{1}{8}$ 4. $\frac{6}{8}$ 5. 10   6. $\frac{2}{7}$

Activity 3

Give the missing part in the problems involving reciprocals.

Model $4 \cdot$ _____ $= 1$

Answer: $\frac{1}{4}$

1. _____ $\cdot \frac{4}{5} = 1$ 2. $\frac{3}{2} \cdot$ _____ $= 1$ 3. $5 \cdot \frac{1}{5} =$ _____

4. $\frac{7}{8} \cdot$ _____ $= 1$ 5. _____ $\cdot \frac{1}{8} = 1$ 6. $\frac{4}{3} \cdot \frac{3}{4} =$ _____

Activity 4 • Distributed Practice

Solve.

1. Find the first six multiples of 5 and 10. Give the common multiples.

2. What are the common factors of 8 and 12?

3. What is the least common denominator for the problem $\frac{1}{3} + \frac{1}{4}$?

4. What is the greatest common factor of 56 and 64?

5. $160 - 78$ 6. $32 \cdot 9$

7. $150 \div 4$ 8. $1,027 + 873$

9. $411 \cdot 3$ 10. $600 \div 30$

Decimal Numbers

Problem Solving:
Drawing Box-and-Whisker Plots

▶**Decimal Numbers**

Vocabulary
rational number

How are decimal numbers like fractions?

We have learned a lot about fractions in this unit. We will now focus on decimal numbers. Fractions and decimal numbers are both **rational numbers** . These are numbers that can be written as fractions. We can think about fractions and decimal numbers as different names for the same location on the number line.

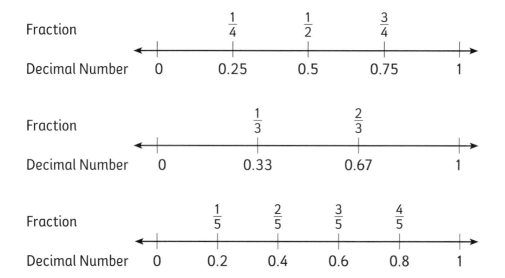

We use decimal numbers because they are easier to work with than fractions. Imagine if you had to add the following three fractions together.

$$\frac{3}{5} + \frac{4}{10} + \frac{14}{15}$$

The answer, $\frac{58}{30}$, is a large fraction that is difficult to understand. We know that it is bigger than 1 because $\frac{30}{30} = 1$. But how much bigger is it?

Understanding this problem is easier if we convert the fractions to decimal numbers and then add them.

How do we convert fractions to decimal numbers?

Example 1 shows how to convert fractions to decimal numbers and then round them to the hundredths place.

Example 1

Convert the fractions to decimal numbers and solve the problem.

$$\frac{3}{5} + \frac{4}{10} + \frac{14}{15}$$

To get the decimal numbers, we divide the fractions.

$$\begin{array}{ccc} 0.6 & 0.4 & 0.93 \\ 5\overline{)3} & 10\overline{)4} & 15\overline{)14} \end{array}$$

Fractions	$\frac{3}{5}$	+	$\frac{4}{10}$	+	$\frac{14}{15}$	=	$\frac{58}{30}$
Decimal numbers	**0.6**	+	**0.4**	+	**0.93**	=	**1.93**

When we convert fractions to decimal numbers, we change the fraction into the base-10 system. Each place value for a decimal number is a power of 10.

Thousandths ←
Hundredths ←
Tenths ←

$$\frac{3}{8} = 8\overline{)3} \quad 0.375$$

Finally, it is important to remember that when we convert fractions into decimal numbers, the numbers still have the same value or quantity. The fraction and the decimal number are equivalent.

Example 2

Use area models to show that $\frac{3}{4}$ and 0.75 are equivalent.

$$\frac{3}{4} = 4\overline{)3} = 0.75$$

$\frac{3}{4}$ 0.75

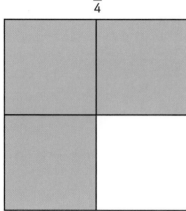   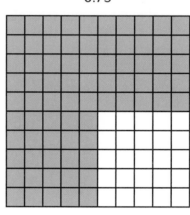

Part	3	75
Whole	4	100

Both fractions and decimal numbers are part-to-whole relationships.

The models show that $\frac{3}{4}$ and 0.75 have the same area.

% ÷ **Apply Skills**
< x Turn to *Interactive Text*,
page 18.

mBook **Reinforce Understanding**
Use the *mBook Study Guide*
to review lesson concepts.

▶**Problem Solving: Drawing Box-and-Whisker Plots**

How do we create box-and-whisker plots?

The method for creating box-and-whisker plots is simple. It involves medians. Let's look at another event at Sports Day—the high jump. Here is how everyone did.

Student	Height (in inches)	
Brittany	45	
Joshua	49	
Autumn	50	
Marcus	53	
Erica	54	
Oscar	54	
Ryan	55	
Pablo	56	◄——— median = 56
Amber	57	
Tracey	58	
Mikaela	60	
Lamar	62	
DeAnne	64	
Seth	64	
Paige	65	

We start with the median and divide the list into two groups. The first group is the group below, or lower than, the median. The second group is the group above, or higher than, the median. We find the median of each of these groups.

Group 1	
Student	Height (in inches)
Brittany	45 ←——— min
Joshua	49
Autumn	50
Marcus	53 ←——— median for group 1 (lower) = 53
Erica	54
Oscar	54
Ryan	55
Pablo	56 ←——— median for the whole group = 56

Group 2	
Student	Height (in inches)
Amber	57 ←——— min
Tracey	58
Mikaela	60
Lamar	62 ←——— median for group 2 (upper) = 62
DeAnne	64
Seth	64
Paige	65 ←——— max

Now we are ready to draw the box-and-whisker plot. Follow these four steps.

Steps for Drawing a Box-and-Whisker Plot

STEP 1
Draw vertical lines for the min and the max.

STEP 2
Use the lower and upper median numbers to make the sides of the box. Draw the rest of the box.

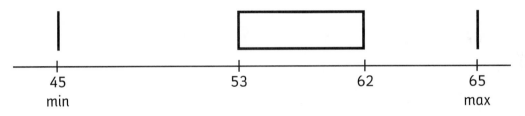

STEP 3
Draw horizontal lines that connect the min and the max to the box.

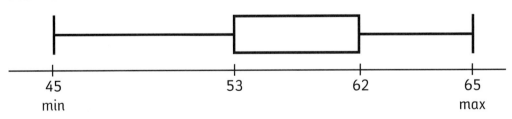

STEP 4
Put a mark for the median of the entire group of numbers in the box.

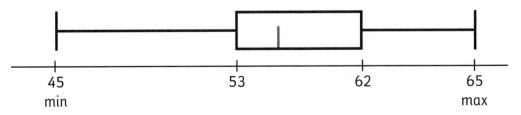

Remember, the whisker on the left of the box contains the lowest $\frac{1}{4}$ of the numbers. The box represents the middle $\frac{1}{2}$ of the numbers, and the whisker on the right contains the highest $\frac{1}{4}$ of numbers. In this example, the numbers stand for different heights that students jumped.

Once we have the box-and-whisker plot, we can make sense of all the high jumps.

- Erica jumped 54 inches. She is near the bottom of the middle half of numbers. She also isn't that far below the median of 56.

- Her friend DeAnne jumped much higher. She is near the top of the highest $\frac{1}{4}$ of heights. DeAnne is well above the median.

- Finally, Pablo jumped 56 inches. He is near the center of the middle group of numbers and right on the median.

Problem-Solving Activity
Turn to *Interactive Text*,
page 19.

mBook **Reinforce Understanding**
Use the *mBook Study Guide*
to review lesson concepts.

Activity 1

Convert the fractions to decimal numbers.

1. $\frac{1}{2}$

2. $\frac{4}{5}$

3. $\frac{3}{4}$

4. $\frac{1}{4}$

5. $\frac{2}{3}$

6. $\frac{3}{8}$

Activity 2

Select the best answer for each of the questions about decimal numbers.

1. The decimal number 0.35 has a 3 in the tenths place and a 5 in the _____ place.
   (a) thousands
   (b) hundredths
   (c) thousandths

2. We can check that $\frac{4}{5}$ = 0.8 by doing this computation on the calculator.
   (a) $4 \div 5$
   (b) $4 + 5$
   (c) $4 \cdot 5$

3. The decimal number 0.87 is the same as what fraction?
   (a) $\frac{8}{7}$
   (b) $\frac{87}{10}$
   (c) $\frac{87}{100}$

4. What are the fraction/decimal number equivalents for "three hundredths"?
   (a) $0.3 = \frac{3}{10}$
   (b) $0.03 = \frac{3}{100}$
   (c) $0.003 = \frac{3}{1,000}$

Activity 3

Look at the data. Imagine how it would look in a box-and-whisker plot. Answer the questions about the data and how it would be arranged in the plot.

Data Set: 45, 34, 55, 87, 62, 79, 39, 75, 95

1. What number represents the median of this data? Is this the same as or different than the actual midpoint of the data?

2. Write a number that falls in the lower $\frac{1}{4}$.

3. What is the min?

4. Write a number that falls in the upper $\frac{1}{4}$.

5. What is the max?

Activity 4 • Distributed Practice

Solve.

1. $120 \div 12$

2. $437 + 223$

3. $15 \cdot 8$

4. $601 - 379$

5. $\frac{3}{4} + \frac{1}{8}$

6. $\frac{7}{9} - \frac{1}{3}$

7. $\frac{5}{11} \cdot \frac{1}{2}$

8. $\frac{3}{4} \div \frac{1}{8}$

9. $\frac{4}{5} \div \frac{1}{5}$

10. $\frac{5}{9} - \frac{1}{6}$

▶Working With Decimal Numbers

Vocabulary
benchmark **repeating decimal** **irrational number**

How do we round decimal numbers?

In Lesson 7, we learned to change a fraction into a decimal number by dividing the denominator into the numerator. The result was often a decimal number with many digits to the right of the decimal point. Decimal numbers like this are difficult to read and understand. For example:

$$\frac{9}{14} = 14\overline{)9}^{0.64286}$$

Reading decimal numbers means knowing about place value.

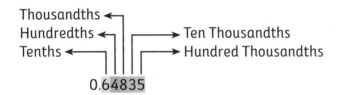

This number is difficult to read. It is read "64,835 hundred thousandths." If we understand place value, we will know the meanings of the numbers.

But for most of us, in our day-to-day life, we do not work with such precise numbers. Instead, we round the decimal number to a more manageable decimal place, such as tenths, hundredths, or thousandths.

The rules for rounding decimal numbers are the same as we used for whole numbers. In this case, we will round 0.64835 to the hundredths place.

Example 1

Round 0.64835 to the hundredths place.

0.6 4 8 3 5

> Remember: If the number is five or greater, we round up to the next digit.

We look at the number to the right of the hundredths place and circle it.

0.6 4 ⑧ 3 5

The 8 in the thousandths place is greater than 5, so we round up.

0.65

Now our decimal number is rounded to 0.65 or "65 hundredths."

Now let's change the decimal number slightly, to 0.64235, and round to the hundredths place. The number in the thousandths column is less than five. We do not round up because 2 is less than five.

Example 2

Round 0.64235 to the hundredths place.

0.6 4 ② 3 5

0.64

Because the number to the right of the hundredths place is less than five, we do not round up. We drop all the numbers to the right of the hundredths place and round to 0.64, or "64 hundredths."

How does rounding help us understand a number's meaning?

An important part of working with decimal numbers is knowing what a rational number is close to on the number line. There are some important rational numbers that we need to remember, called **benchmarks**. The number line below shows some of the most common benchmarks for fractions and decimal numbers. We remember these numbers because they help us understand how big a decimal number is.

Example 1

Find the approximate location of 0.64285 on the number line.

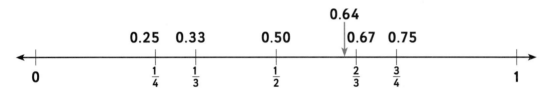

The decimal number 0.64 is close to 0.67, or $\frac{2}{3}$. That means 0.64285 is about $\frac{2}{3}$.

Benchmarks can be found between any whole numbers or they can be the whole numbers themselves. Let's look at what happens with a decimal number greater than 1.

Example 2

Find the approximate location of 2.83 on the number line.

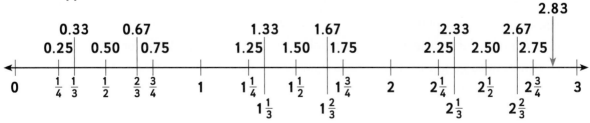

Look for the number 2 on the number line. Then find which benchmark 0.83 is closest to. The decimal part 0.83 is close to the benchmark 0.75.

So 2.83 is about 2.75, or $2\frac{3}{4}$.

How do we work with decimal numbers that never end?

Sometimes when we change a fraction into a decimal number, we get a pattern. The numbers keep repeating themselves. These are called **repeating decimals** .

Look at the repeating pattern we get when we convert $\frac{3}{11}$ and $\frac{4}{7}$ to decimal numbers. There is a special way to write this kind of number. We put a line over the top to show that the pattern repeats itself.

repeating pattern   written as

$$0.27272727272727$$
$$11\overline{)3}$$
           $0.\overline{27}$

repeating pattern   written as

$$0.571428571428$$
$$7\overline{)4}$$
           $0.\overline{571428}$

With repeating decimal numbers, we stop the decimal after the pattern is shown once. We put a line over the repeated part of the decimal.

There are also other kinds of decimal numbers that never end, but they do not have a pattern. These are called **irrational numbers** . One of the most famous irrational numbers is pi. We use pi to find the circumference and area of a circle. It is a comparison of the diameter and the circumference of a circle. The decimal number for pi is 3.14159265 . . . The three dots at the end mean that the decimal number goes on infinitely.

We can get close to pi by changing $\frac{22}{7}$ into a decimal number. There are even contests for people who can remember the most decimal places for pi. People have memorized pi to more than 1,000 decimal places. There is no pattern to irrational numbers like pi.

Apply Skills
Turn to *Interactive Text*,
page 21.

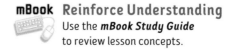

mBook **Reinforce Understanding**
Use the *mBook Study Guide*
to review lesson concepts.

▶Problem Solving: Interpreting Box-and-Whisker Plots

How do we interpret box-and-whisker plots?

Now let's put together all that we have learned about box-and-whisker plots. We use the concepts of minimum, maximum, range, mean, and especially median to understand a set of data. Let's look at some data from two different sporting events. All of the numbers have been rounded to the closest decimal number benchmarks. We will interpret the data by entering information from tables into box-and-whisker plots.

Example 1

Interpret the box-and-whisker plot for the hammer throw.

Hammer Throw	
Name	**Feet**
Marcus	22
Tracey	22.5
Oscar	23
Seth	24.25
Paige	24.25
Michael	24.5
Lamar	25.5
Amber	26
Ryan	26
Robert	26.5
Autumn	27.5
Brittany	29
DeAnne	29.25
Joshua	29.5
Total	**359.75**

Mean = 25.7

Median = 25.75

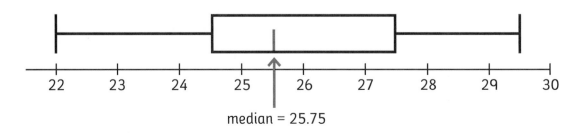

median = 25.75

What does the data tell us?

- The mean and the median are about the same. In fact, the median is close to the middle of the box, which means it is in the center of the middle $\frac{1}{2}$ of the scores.

- We see from the box-and-whisker plot that the lower and upper quarters, or whiskers, are about the same. That means people in the lower and upper quarters are spread out about the same distance.

- The range is only 7.5 points and the median is just about halfway between the minimum and the maximum. We have a pretty evenly distributed set of data, beginning with a minimum of 22 and reaching a maximum of 29.5.

Example 2

Interpret the box-and-whisker plot for the shot put.

Shot Put	
Name	**Feet**
Brittany	5
Seth	6
DeAnne	6.5
Amber	13
Paige	14.5
Lamar	14.75
Robert	15.5
Tracey	16.75
Autumn	17
Erica	17.25
Joshua	17.5
Ryan	18
Oscar	18.25
Michael	18.5
Marcus	19
Total	**217.5**

Mean = 14.5

Median = 16.75

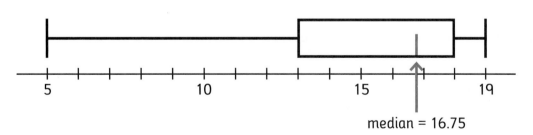

median = 16.75

What does the data tell us?

- The lower $\frac{1}{4}$ whisker is a lot longer than the upper $\frac{1}{4}$ whisker. That means there is a bigger spread of scores between the very lowest distance, or minimum of 5, and the bottom of the box, 13. It is a much bigger distance than the top of the box, 18, and the maximum of 19. So, some students could not throw the shot very far.

- The range in the lower $\frac{1}{4}$ was from 5 feet to 13 feet. That is quite a difference than the highest $\frac{1}{4}$ of the scores. These students were very close to each other. The top three students threw within 1 foot of each other.

- There is a bit of a difference between the mean and the median, but it isn't as clear as the differences between the lower and upper quarters of the scores.

In summary, the set of scores for the hammer throw show us that students are fairly evenly distributed from a minimum of 22 to a maximum of 29.5.

The shot put data tell us that there are some students in the lower $\frac{1}{4}$ who couldn't throw very far and the best students in the group were very close together in their throws.

The shape of the box-and-whisker plot helps us think about the data in the tables.

Problem-Solving Activity
Turn to *Interactive Text*,
page 22.

mBook **Reinforce Understanding**
Use the *mBook Study Guide*
to review lesson concepts.

Activity 1

Look at the calculator display for each of the fraction-to-decimal number conversions. Round the numbers to the nearest hundredths place.

Model $\frac{1}{9}$ | 0.111111111 | Answer: 0.11

1. $\frac{2}{3}$ | 0.66666666666666

2. $\frac{3}{8}$ | 0.375

3. $\frac{13}{7}$ | 1.85714285714285

4. $\frac{6}{11}$ | 0.54545454545454

5. $\frac{1}{3}$ | 0.33333333333333

6. $\frac{6}{7}$ | 0.85714285714285

Activity 2

Rewrite each of the repeating decimal numbers using the line over the top to represent the repeating part.

Model $\frac{3}{11} = 0.272727272727272 = 0.\overline{27}$

1. $\frac{2}{7} = 0.285714285714285714$

2. $\frac{4}{11} = 0.363636363636363636$

3. $\frac{5}{9} = 0.5555555555555555555$

4. $\frac{1}{6} = 0.1666666666666666666$

Activity 3

Select the best answer for the questions about decimal numbers.

1. When a decimal number does not seem to have an end and there is no pattern to it, we call this a(n) _____ number.
   (a) rational
   (b) whole
   (c) irrational

2. If you were asked to round 0.275 to the nearest hundredths place, the answer would be _____.
   (a) 0.28
   (b) 0.27
   (c) 0.3

3. Pi is an example of an irrational number because _____.
   (a) it repeats but doesn't end
   (b) it doesn't end and it doesn't repeat
   (c) it ends but doesn't repeat

4. If you were asked to round 0.119 to the nearest tenths place, the answer would be _____.
   (a) 0.1
   (b) 0.2
   (c) 0.12

Activity 4 • Distributed Practice

Solve.

1. $480 \div 12$

2. $999 + 1{,}011$

3. $47 \cdot 9$

4. $3{,}201 - 1{,}987$

5. $\frac{3}{5} + \frac{2}{4}$

6. $\frac{3}{5} - \frac{1}{3}$

7. $\frac{2}{3} \cdot \frac{4}{5}$

8. $\frac{3}{8} \div \frac{1}{4}$

9. $\frac{9}{5} - \frac{7}{5}$

10. $\frac{5}{12} + \frac{4}{6}$

▶Adding and Subtracting Decimal Numbers

Problem Solving:
▶Scatter Plots

▶**Adding and Subtracting Decimal Numbers**

How do we add or subtract decimal numbers?

Adding or subtracting decimal numbers is a lot like working with whole numbers. Both operations can involve regrouping. Example 1 shows how we regroup with decimal numbers. It doesn't matter whether we have to regroup whole numbers or decimal numbers, the process is still the same.

Example 1

Add or subtract the decimal numbers.

$$
\begin{array}{r}
{\scriptstyle 1\ 1}\\
48.32\\
+\ \ 7.81\\
\hline
56.13
\end{array}
\qquad
\begin{array}{r}
{\scriptstyle 7\ 13}\\
48.32\\
-\ \ 7.81\\
\hline
40.51
\end{array}
\qquad
\begin{array}{r}
{\scriptstyle 1}\\
48.32\\
+\ \ 9.12\\
\hline
57.44
\end{array}
\qquad
\begin{array}{r}
{\scriptstyle 3\ 18}\\
48.32\\
-\ \ 9.12\\
\hline
39.20
\end{array}
$$

Many of the errors we make when adding or subtracting decimal numbers arise when the numbers are uneven. Lining decimal numbers up by the decimal point is important. There are two ways we do this. One way is to write the numbers so that the decimal points are all in a straight line. We begin by placing the decimal points first in a column, then writing the numbers.

The second method is to make all of the decimal numbers have the same place value. All we do is add zeros to the end of each number. This way they are the same length.

Let's look at both methods:

Example 2

Add the decimal numbers.

Method 1	**Method 2**
Line up the decimal points.	Add zeros.

Method 1:
```
  4.031
  1.2
+ 3.55
-------
  8.781
```

Method 2:
```
  4.031
  1.200
+ 3.550
-------
  8.781
```

Remember that the portion of the decimal number to the right of the decimal point is always less than 1. If we use number sense, we can tell if we have incorrectly lined up the decimal numbers.

Improve Your Skills

A student solved the problem 34.8 − 2.5.

The student's answer
```
  34.8
−  2.5    ERROR
------
  14.3
```

The correct answer
```
  34.8
−  2.5    CORRECT
------
  32.3
```

Using good number sense, we can tell right away that the student's answer is wrong. If we round the numbers, subtracting 3 from 35 will give us a much larger answer than 14.3.

While this method is a good way to check our work quickly, there are errors that we may not see, especially if we are working with long decimal numbers. When we are not sure about our answer, working the problem again or checking it with a calculator is always a good strategy.

 **Apply Skills**
Turn to *Interactive Text*, page 24.

 **Reinforce Understanding**
Use the *mBook Study Guide* to review lesson concepts.

▶Problem Solving: Scatter Plots

What are scatter plots?

A lot of things in life have an effect on each other. A formal word for these things is variables. Think about driving a car. How dangerously somebody drives a car is one variable. How many accidents somebody has over a period of time is another variable. It's likely that the more dangerously a person drives, the more likely they are to have a car accident. There is a relationship between these two variables.

One way to show this relationship is to use a **scatter plot** . We start with a list of numbers that show the relationship between two activities or events. Let's say we rate how dangerous someone drives by using the numbers 1 through 10. A rating of 1 is a very safe driver and a 10 is a very dangerous driver. Here is the list.

Driver Rating	Number of Car Accidents
1	0
2	1
3	1
4	2
5	4
6	5
7	10
8	14
9	16
10	19

Next, we use a grid to plot these relationships. One axis will be the rating of the driver. The other axis will be the number of accidents.

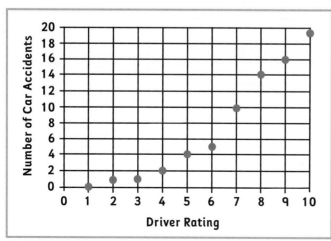

The scatter plot helps us see a clear pattern in these data.

- The person who has a low rating for dangerous driving has a low number of accidents.
- The person with a high rating has a high number of accidents.

This means that the more dangerously people drive, the more likely they are to have accidents.

The points move up in a gradual curve going from the lower left corner to the upper right corner. When there is this kind of pattern to the data on the scatter plot, we can make predictions. For example, we can predict that a person with a rating of 10 would probably have around 18 accidents.

Not all relationships have such a clear pattern. In some relationships it is more difficult to make predictions. The next scatter plot shows the relationship between the ability to play a piano and the ability to play basketball. Each ability is rated from 1 to 10. A rating of 1 means low ability and a 10 means very high ability.

Example 1

Plot the data on a scatter plot and analyze the information.

Ability to Play Piano	Ability to Play Basketball
7	1
2	2
8	3
5	4
9	6
6	7
3	8
7	9

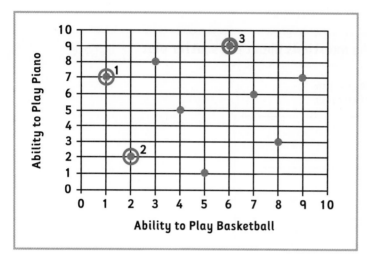

The data tell us:

- Person 1 has an above average piano-playing ability, but a low ability at basketball.

- Person 2 has low abilities at both piano and basketball.

- Person 3 has excellent ability at piano and good ability at basketball.

The lack of any pattern to the points makes sense when we look at the points that are circled.

Some scatter plots do not show a pattern. When there is no pattern, we cannot make a prediction. As we think about scatter plots, it is important to keep these two examples in mind. If the scatter plots show a certain direction, then we say there is a relationship between the two variables. If the points are all over the place with no clear direction, then it is safer to say that there is no relationship between the two variables.

Problem-Solving Activity
Turn to *Interactive Text*, page 25.

mBook Reinforce Understanding
Use the *mBook Study Guide* to review lesson concepts.

Activity 1

Select the best answer for each of the questions about the scatter plot.

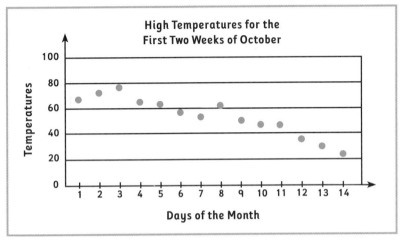

1. How would you describe the pattern in the scatter plot?
   (a) High temperatures are getting higher.
   (b) High temperatures are getting lower.
   (c) High temperatures stay about the same.

2. If you were to predict the high temperature on the 15th of October, what would you predict?
   (a) The high temperature will be between 60–80 degrees.
   (b) The high temperature will be between 40–60 degrees.
   (c) The high temperature will be between 20–40 degrees.

3. If you were to estimate the high temperature on the last day of September of the same year, what would you estimate?
   (a) The high temperature was between 60–80 degrees.
   (b) The high temperature was between 40–60 degrees.
   (c) The high temperature was between 20–40 degrees.

4. How would you describe the relationship between the two variables from looking at the scatter plot?
   (a) The two variables change in the same way.
   (b) The two variables change in opposite ways.
   (c) There is no relationship between the two variables.

Activity 2

Add and subtract the decimal numbers. Be sure to line up the numbers carefully on your paper. Check your answers by rounding to the nearest whole numbers.

1. $34.5 + 29.7$

2. $81.6 - 7.8$

3. $15.01 + 22.33 + 49.87$

4. $201.76 - 89.98$

5. $127.5 + 227.3 + 899.7$

6. $321.5 - 22.09$

Activity 3

Round to the nearest whole number and estimate the answer.

1. $3.1 + 2.4$

2. $9.1 - 4.07$

3. $27.9 + 44.8$

4. $98.01 - 29.8$

5. $129.458 + 634.229$

6. $878.005 - 499.87$

Activity 4 • Distributed Practice

Solve.

1. $300 + 900$

2. $420 - 198$

3. $55 \cdot 8$

4. $420 \div 7$

5. $\frac{3}{4} + \frac{2}{5}$

6. $\frac{5}{9} - \frac{1}{6}$

7. $\frac{1}{2} + \frac{4}{5}$

8. $\frac{13}{4} \div \frac{4}{1}$

9. $\frac{9}{10} - \frac{2}{5}$

10. $\frac{5}{8} \cdot \frac{3}{7}$

▶**Comparing Decimal Numbers**

How do we compare decimal numbers?

When we add or subtract decimal numbers, we have to make sense of our answer. It is easy to be confused by decimal numbers, so we need strategies for determining whether one decimal number is larger or smaller than another number.

A good example is racing. Runners are always comparing their times to what they have run before, their fastest time in an event, and how fast other runners are in the same event. Below are some times for Gail Johnson. Her main event is the 200-meter dash. At the end of the week she always compares how she did with her fastest time the week before.

Example 1

Compare decimal numbers.

Gail's fastest time the week before was 23.92 seconds.

Practice Runs	Best Times (in seconds)
Monday	24.5
Tuesday	24.2
Wednesday	23.83
Thursday	23.81
Friday	23.02

Compared to Gail's fastest time the week before, how much faster did Gail run . . .

- on Wednesday?
  23.92 − 23.83 = 0.09 seconds
- on Thursday?
  23.92 − 23.81 = 0.11 seconds
- on Friday?
  23.92 − 23.02 = 0.9 seconds

When we compare these numbers, they look different. But they are actually very close. Which one is a bigger decimal number: 0.09, 0.11, or 0.9? There are two strategies we use to understand the size of decimal numbers.

Remember the Connection Between Decimal Numbers and Fractions

The first way is to remember the connection between decimal numbers and fractions. Example 2 shows how we convert the decimal numbers so that they have the same place value. Then we compare the two numbers as fractions.

Example 2

Find out which is bigger: 0.09, 0.11, or 0.9.

We make the comparison this way:

0.09 is the same as $\frac{9}{100}$ (read the decimal number "9 hundredths").

0.11 is the same as $\frac{11}{100}$ (read the decimal number "11 hundredths").

0.90 is the same as $\frac{90}{100}$ (read the decimal number "90 hundredths").

The three decimal numbers are ordered from smallest to biggest this way: 0.09, 0.11, and 0.90.

Use a Decimal Ruler to Order Decimal Numbers

A second way to compare decimal numbers is to think about numbers on a decimal ruler. Once again, we see in Example 3 that we need to convert tenths to hundredths. We do that by adding a zero on the right. We convert 0.9 to 0.90. Then think about how we count on the number line.

Example 3

Use a decimal ruler to order the decimal numbers 0.09, 0.11, and, 0.9.

We begin by changing 0.9 to 0.90.

Where are 0.09, 0.11, and 0.90 on the decimal ruler?

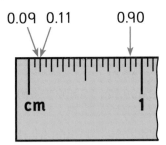

These two strategies help us make sense of decimal numbers and make comparisons.

 **Apply Skills**
Turn to *Interactive Text*, page 27.

 **Monitoring Progress**
Quiz 2

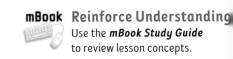 **mBook Reinforce Understanding**
Use the *mBook Study Guide* to review lesson concepts.

Homework

Activity 1

Add and subtract the decimal numbers. Round the answers to the nearest tenths place.

1. $56.02 + 89.09$

2. $99.63 - 89.87$

3. $129.74 + 229.01$

4. $506.06 - 317.12$

Activity 2

Put the decimal numbers in order from smallest to largest.

1. 0.1, 0.09, 0.19

2. 0.07, 0.005, 0.75

3. 1.23, 1.03, 0.031

4. 2.06, 2.6, 2.9

5. 0.09, 0.098, 0.089

6. 17.34, 17.04, 17.7

Activity 3

Answer the questions about data and statistics.

1. What type of graph would be the most helpful if you were interested in finding the top $\frac{1}{4}$ of the data?
   (a) pie graph
   (b) scatter plot
   (c) box-and-whisker plot

2. What type of graph would be the most helpful if you were examining the relationship between date and temperature?
   (a) pie graph
   (b) scatter plot
   (c) box-and-whisker plot

3. What is the mode of the data set?
   Data Set: 1, 2, 3, 4, 4, 4, 5, 6, 7, 8, 8, 9, 10, 11, 12
   (a) 4
   (b) 5
   (c) 6

4. What explains the large difference in the mean and median of the data set?
   Data Set: 10, 12, 14, 16, 21, 22, 66
   Median: 16   Mean: 23
   (a) Odd number of data in the set.
   (b) Extreme data in the set.
   (c) Not enough numbers in the set.

5. What is the range for the data set?
   Data Set: 1, 2, 2, 3, 4, 7, 8, 12, 12, 12, 12, 13, 17
   (a) 16
   (b) 17
   (c) 18

Activity 4 • Distributed Practice

Solve.

1. $527 + 298$

2. $306 - 167$

3. $43 \cdot 7$

4. $356 \div 8$

5. $\frac{5}{4} + \frac{1}{2}$

6. $\frac{5}{3} - \frac{8}{9}$

7. $\frac{1}{3} + \frac{4}{2}$

8. $\frac{3}{4} \div \frac{4}{5}$

9. $\frac{8}{12} - \frac{1}{6}$

10. $\frac{3}{9} + \frac{7}{6}$

▸**Multiplication of Decimal Numbers**

How do we multiply decimal numbers?

When we multiplied fractions, we found the product was usually smaller than the factors we were multiplying. The same is true for decimal numbers. Let's look at the problem 0.6 · 0.4. It was solved on a calculator. The answer, 0.24, is smaller than 0.6 or 0.4.

$$0.6 \cdot 0.4 = 0.24$$

The 100-square grid is a good way to see what happens when we multiply decimal numbers. First, we change the numbers 0.6 and 0.4 to their equivalents 0.60 and 0.40 because we are using a 100-square grid.

The first grid shows 0.60. The second grid shows 0.60 in color and 0.40 with diagonal lines.

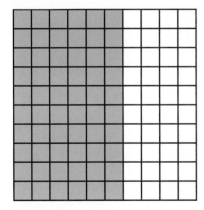
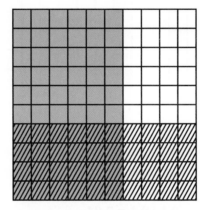

0.60 is shaded   0.40 is shaded with diagonals

The overlap is 0.24 or 24 out of the 100 squares.

That is the same answer we got when we worked the problem on a calculator.

$$0.6 \cdot 0.4 = 0.24$$

Here is one more example of multiplication of decimal numbers. This time we will use a problem with a very small answer. We begin by converting 0.1 to 0.10.

Example 1

Use a 100-square grid to multiply decimal numbers.

0.1 · 0.1

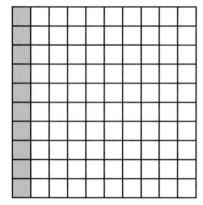

0.10 is shaded

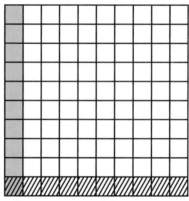

The second 0.10 is shaded with diagonals.

The overlap is 0.01 or 1 out of 100 squares. That is the same answer that we get when we solve the problem using a calculator.

0.1 · 0.1 = 0.01

When we look at multiplication with decimal numbers using an area model, it becomes clearer why the answer is smaller than the numbers we start with.

 **Apply Skills**
Turn to **Interactive Text**, page 29.

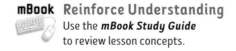 **mBook** **Reinforce Understanding**
Use the **mBook Study Guide** to review lesson concepts.

▶Problem Solving: **Direct Relationships**

What is a direct relationship on a scatter plot?

In the last lesson, we learned how to examine relationships between variables. For example, in the summer the hotter it gets, the more people go swimming. Another common relationship is that the more you eat, the more you weigh. We call these **direct relationships**. When one variable goes up or increases, the other variable increases as well.

Example 1 shows a scatter plot based on what happens when a person keeps going to school. The data start in the 12th grade, or the end of high school. The points show a consistent pattern—as education goes up, so does income.

Example 1

Use a scatter plot to show the relationship between years of education and income.

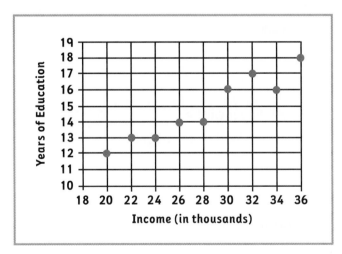

The scatter plot shows a consistent pattern: As the amount of education goes up, income also goes up.

In a direct relationship, both variables increase or decrease at the same time.

Not all direct relationships are easy to read. Let's look at Example 2. This plot shows data for high school basketball players. The players were rated from 1 (a very poor player) to 10 (an excellent player).

Example 2

Use a scatter plot to show the relationship between practicing basketball and the ability to play basketball.

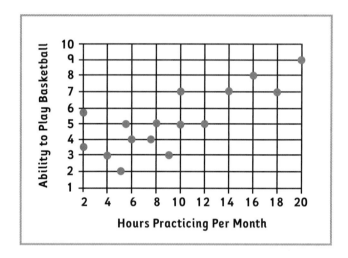

The data show:

- The more a player practices, the better that player will be.
- However, there are some players who practice a lot, but do not get that much better.
- There are other players who do not have to practice that much because they have natural talent.

This type of situation creates a more complicated pattern.

The more data we have, the easier it is to find a pattern. When there isn't a clear pattern, we might need to do more research to find more data.

 **Problem-Solving Activity**
Turn to *Interactive Text*,
page 30.

 **mBook Reinforce Understanding**
Use the *mBook Study Guide*
to review lesson concepts.

Homework

Activity 1

Select the 100-square grid that matches the problem.

1. $0.8 \cdot 0.9 = 0.72$

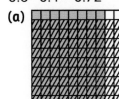

(a)   (b)   (c)

Activity 2

Select the problem that goes with each of the 100-square grids shown below.

1.

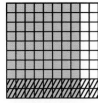

(a) $0.8 \cdot 0.2 = 0.16$
(b) $0.08 \cdot 0.2 = 0.016$
(c) $0.80 \cdot 0.02 = 0.016$

2.

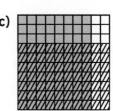

(a) $0.04 \cdot 0.2 = 0.008$
(b) $0.40 \cdot 0.20 = 0.08$
(c) $0.4 \cdot 0.2 = 0.08$

3.

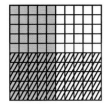

(a) $0.25 \cdot 0.2 = 0.050$
(b) $0.05 \cdot 0.05 = 0.0025$
(c) $0.5 \cdot 0.5 = 0.25$

4.

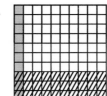

(a) $0.1 \cdot 0.3 = 0.03$
(b) $0.1 \cdot 0.03 = 0.003$
(c) $0.01 \cdot 0.03 = 0.0003$

Activity 3

Tell if the following scatter plots show a direct relationship. Explain your answer.

Model Is this a direct relationship?

Answer: No, it's not a direct relationship. The amount of snow that falls does not relate to the test scores.

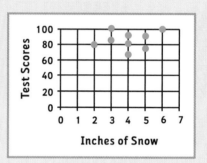

1. Is this a direct relationship?

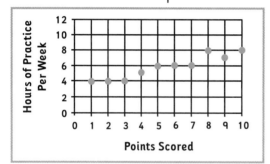

2. Is this a direct relationship?

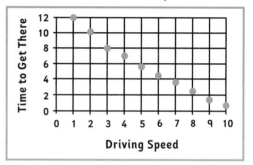

Activity 4 • Distributed Practice

Solve.

1. $\frac{1}{4} + \frac{1}{2}$

2. $\frac{2}{3} - \frac{1}{9}$

3. $\frac{1}{6} \cdot \frac{3}{2}$

4. $\frac{3}{4} \div \frac{4}{5}$

5. $\frac{1}{3} \cdot \frac{1}{6}$

6. $\frac{5}{9} \div \frac{1}{9}$

7. $1.23 + 2.47$

8. $10.01 - 8.9$

9. $3.7 + 8.02 + 2.99$

▶**Traditional Multiplication of Decimal Numbers and Number Sense**

What is the traditional method for multiplying decimal numbers?

The traditional method for multiplication is useful because it gives us a shortcut. It also lets us multiply numbers with a lot of digits. This is important because using square grids is difficult when the decimal numbers have a lot of digits. In many cases, it would not work.

The traditional method for multiplying decimal numbers is similar to that for multiplying whole numbers. Let's see how it works.

Steps for Multiplying Decimal Numbers

STEP 1	
Line up the numbers just as we would with whole numbers.	$\begin{array}{r} 7.7 \\ \times\,4.5 \\ \hline \end{array}$

STEP 2	
Multiply just as we would with whole numbers.	$\begin{array}{r} {\scriptstyle 2 \atop \scriptstyle 3} \\ 7.7 \\ \times\,4.5 \\ \hline 385 \\ +\,3080 \\ \hline 3465 \end{array}$

STEP 3	
To find out where to put the decimal point in the answer, we count the number of digits to the right of the decimal point in both numbers in the problem. Starting from the right of our answer, we count over that many digits and place a decimal point.	$\begin{array}{r} {\scriptstyle 2 \atop \scriptstyle 3} \\ 7.7 \quad {\scriptstyle 1} \\ \times\,4.5 \quad {\scriptstyle 1} \\ \hline 385 \\ +\,3080 \\ \hline 34.65 \quad {\scriptstyle 2} \end{array}$

Here is a good exercise for thinking about multiplying decimal numbers. In Example 1, there are three problems with the correct digits in each answer but no decimal point. Where do we put the decimal point?

Example 1

Place the decimal point in the answers.

$25.3 \cdot 10.6 = 26818$

$25.3 \cdot 0.106 = 26818$

$25.3 \cdot 1.06 = 26818$

In each case, we count the number of digits to the right of the decimal point in the problem. Then we count the same number of digits from the right in the answer and put the decimal point there.

two digits after the decimal points

$25.3 \cdot 10.6 = 268.18$

four digits after the decimal points

$25.3 \cdot 0.106 = 2.6818$

three digits after the decimal points

$25.3 \cdot 1.06 = 26.818$

How do we use number sense to check our answers?

There are two main number sense strategies that we use to check multiplication problems involving decimal numbers.

First, we round whenever possible. In the problem 25.3 · 10.6, the decimal number 25.3 rounds to 25 and 10.6 rounds to 11.
We find an approximate answer in our head: 25 · 11 = 275.
This means the exact answer must be near 275. The number 268 is close to 275, so it is probably the correct answer.

In the second strategy, we use rounding and convert decimal numbers to fractions. In the problem 25.3 · 0.106, the decimal number 25.3 rounds to 25 and 0.106 rounds to 0.11, or $\frac{11}{100}$. What is $\frac{11}{100}$ of 25.3? It is 2.5. The number 2.5 is close to the exact answer 2.6818.

It is useful to think about decimal numbers this way. Even though we can use a calculator or a computer to find exact answers, sometimes we enter the numbers incorrectly. That is why number sense strategies are a good way of determining if we have the correct answer.

Speaking of Math

We tell how we solved a multiplication problem with decimal numbers by explaining our thinking like this:

- *I line up the numbers to the right, not by the decimal point.*
- *I multiply the decimal numbers as if they were whole numbers.*
- *Once I get the answer, I count the digits to the right of the decimal points in my factors.*
- *Then I count the same number from the right digit in my answer and put a decimal point.*
- *I check my answer by rounding the numbers to whole numbers or fractions that are easy to use.*

 **Apply Skills**
Turn to *Interactive Text*, page 32.

 **mBook** **Reinforce Understanding**
Use the *mBook Study Guide* to review lesson concepts.

▶**Problem Solving: Indirect Relationships**

What do indirect relationships look like?

Indirect relationships are a different kind of relationship. With indirect relationships, every time one variable goes up, the other variable in a relationship goes down. The scatter plot in Example 1 shows such a pattern. The data in the scatter plot involve a number of people who all weighed 250 pounds at the beginning of an exercise program. All of them went on the same diet. The only thing that changed was the amount of exercise. Some of the people exercised a little bit each week and others exercised a lot.

Example 1

Look at the scatter plot to find what happens when people exercise.

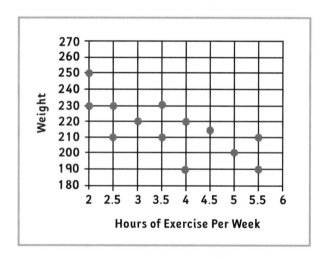

Notice the general direction of the points. They start out high and then decrease as they move across the graph. The weight is going down as the number of hours of exercise across the bottom is going up.

In an indirect relationship, the value of one variable increases when the other variable decreases.

Indirect relationships are all around us. The more police you have in a city, the less crime there is. The more time people spend working at jobs, the less time they have for hobbies or outside activities. These are just a few examples of where we find indirect relationships in the world around us.

 Problem-Solving Activity
Turn to *Interactive Text*,
page 33.

 mBook **Reinforce Understanding**
Use the *mBook Study Guide*
to review lesson concepts.

Activity 1

Select the correct answer for each of the multiplication problems.

1. $0.8 \cdot 0.9$
   (a) 0.72
   (b) 0.072
   (c) 7.2

2. $0.02 \cdot 0.25$
   (a) 0.50
   (b) 0.0050
   (c) 0.050

3. $0.75 \cdot 0.2$
   (a) 0.15
   (b) 0.015
   (c) 1.50

4. $0.5 \cdot 4.8$
   (a) 0.024
   (b) 0.24
   (c) 2.40

Activity 2

Multiply using the traditional method. Check your work using rounding.

1. $0.75 \cdot 0.8$

2. $0.029 \cdot 0.1$

3. $0.54 \cdot 0.7$

4. $0.25 \cdot 0.4$

5. $0.1 \cdot 0.08$

6. $2.5 \cdot 0.5$

Homework

Activity 3

Tell which of the graphs below represent indirect relationships. Explain your answer.

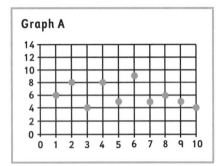

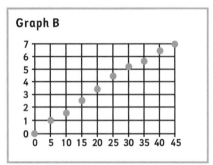

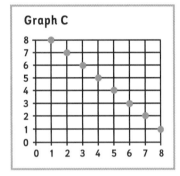

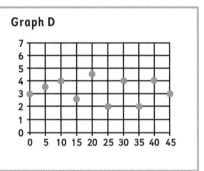

Activity 4 • Distributed Practice

Solve.

1. $\frac{2}{3} \cdot \frac{4}{5}$

2. $\frac{1}{2} \div \frac{2}{3}$

3. $\frac{4}{6} + \frac{3}{2}$

4. $\frac{7}{8} - \frac{1}{4}$

5. $\frac{3}{4} \div \frac{1}{4}$

6. $\frac{3}{9} \cdot \frac{3}{4}$

7. $14.01 - 7.6$

8. $4.78 + 2.95 + 8.7$

9. $107.2 - 95.09$

10. $127.85 + 495.76$

▶**Division of Decimal Numbers**

How do we divide decimal numbers?

When we talked about the division of fractions, we discussed that the quotient was often larger than the other two numbers in the problem. The same is true with the division of decimal numbers.

We use the same 100-square grid model that we used with multiplication to help understand the division of decimal numbers. Look at the problem:

$$0.6 \div 0.2$$

Because we use a 100-square grid, we convert 0.6 and 0.2 to their hundredths equivalents, 0.60 and 0.20. First, we shade the portion of the grid equivalent to 0.60.

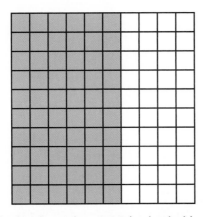

The decimal number 0.60 is shaded in color.

Then we show what 0.20 would look like. It divides, or breaks up, the number 0.60. The illustration shows that it breaks up 0.60 exactly three times.

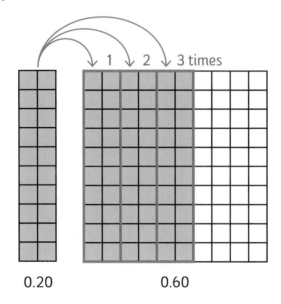

0.20   0.60

The decimal number 0.20 divides, or breaks up, 0.60 three times.

$$0.60 \div 0.20 = 3$$

Let's look at another example.

Example 1

Divide 0.05 into 0.20 using a 100-square grid.

We think of 0.05 as 5 out of 100 and 0.20 as 20 out of 100.

This grid shows 0.20.

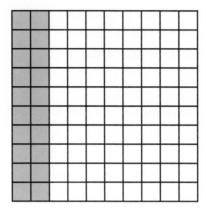

The decimal number 0.20 is shaded in color.

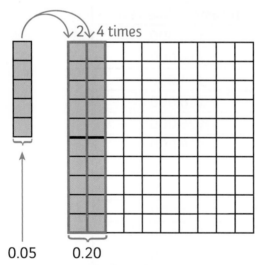

2 4 times

0.05   0.20

The decimal number 0.05 divides, or breaks up, 0.20 four times.

$$0.20 \div 0.05 = 4$$

POWER CONCEPT

When we divide by a decimal number less than 1, the quotient is usually larger than the dividend.

When we look at division of decimal numbers using an area model, it is clearer why the answer is larger than the numbers we started with.

Apply Skills
Turn to *Interactive Text*, page 35.

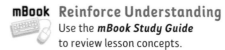

mBook Reinforce Understanding
Use the *mBook Study Guide* to review lesson concepts.

▶**Problem Solving: The Line of Best Fit**

Vocabulary

line of best fit

What is the line of best fit?

When we look at a scatter plot, sometimes it is hard to tell the direction of the points. We make it easier by putting a line through the points to show the direction. This line is called the **line of best fit** .

How do we draw a line of best fit? The answer involves medians. Here is an example using a direct relationship. Let's go back to the relationship that used the variables of education and income. This is a direct relationship because the more you have of one, the more you tend to have of the other.

The data here show how much money 15 people make. The people have between 7 and 21 years of education. This means the first point on the scatter plot shows how much the person with a seventh-grade education made in a year. It's $23,000. The last point is someone who went to college and graduate school and has 21 years of education. This person made $67,000 in one year.

Years of Education	Income in One Year
7	$23,000
8	$19,000
9	$34,000
10	$26,000
11	$36,000
12	$28,000
13	$37,000
14	$42,000
15	$41,000
16	$50,000
17	$63,000
18	$60,000
19	$54,000
20	$75,000
21	$67,000

Next, we see how to make the line of best fit.

Steps for Finding the Line of Best Fit

STEP 1

Create a scatter plot with the data.

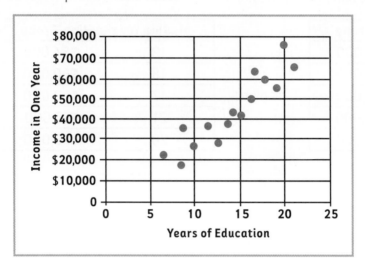

STEP 2

Divide the points into three groups.

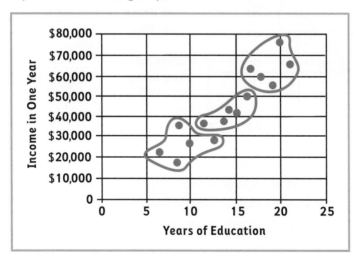

STEP 3

Find the medians for the low and the high groups of numbers.
We make a table of the data from these two groups and sort them
from low to high so that we can find the medians.

Median for the Low Group	
8	$19,000
7	$23,000
10	$26,000 ← median
9	$34,000
11	$36,000

Median for the High Group	
19	$54,000
18	$60,000
17	$63,000 ← median
21	$67,000
20	$75,000

STEP 4

Place the two medians on the scatter plot and connect them to make
the line of best fit.

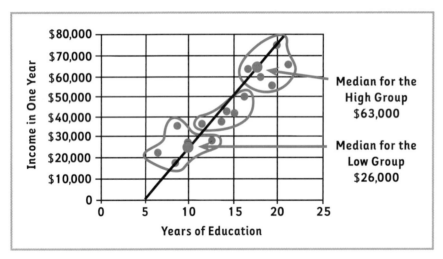

The line of best fit now shows us a clear direction in the data. It does not
have to go through all or any of the points plotted on the graph. The line
can help us predict other data that might appear on the graph.

Problem-Solving Activity
Turn to *Interactive Text*,
page 36.

mBook Reinforce Understanding
Use the *mBook Study Guide*
to review lesson concepts.

Homework

Activity 1

Select the problem that is represented by the 100-square grid.

1.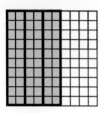

   (a) 0.6 ÷ 0.3 = 2
   (b) 0.6 ÷ 0.2 = 3
   (c) 0.6 ÷ 0.2 = 0.3

2.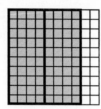

   (a) 0.8 ÷ 0.2 = 4
   (b) 0.8 ÷ 0.4 = 0.2
   (c) 0.8 ÷ 0.4 = 2

Activity 2

Select the correct 100-square grid for each of the problems. Then write the answer.

1. 0.75 ÷ 0.25

   (a)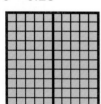

   (b)

   (c)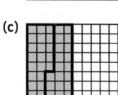

2. 0.8 ÷ 0.1

   (a)

   (b)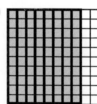

   (c)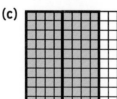

Activity 3

Answer the questions about the data sets.

1. Data Set: 23, 27, 28, 32, 45, 75, 100
   What is the median?
   (a) 23
   (b) 100
   (c) 32

2. Data Set: 1, 2, 3, 4, 5, 5, 6, 6, 6
   What is the mode?
   (a) 4
   (b) 5
   (c) 6

3. Data Set: 20, 40, 60, 80, 100
   What is the range?
   (a) 80
   (b) 60
   (c) 40

4. Data Set: 1, 2, 3, 3, 5, 7, 7, 9, 25
   Which number is called an outlier?
   (a) 1
   (b) 9
   (c) 25

Activity 4 • Distributed Practice

Solve.

1. $\frac{1}{3} \cdot \frac{1}{5}$

2. $\frac{1}{2} + \frac{2}{3}$

3. $\frac{4}{6} \cdot \frac{3}{2}$

4. $\frac{7}{8} \div \frac{1}{4}$

5. $\frac{3}{4} - \frac{1}{2}$

6. $\frac{3}{9} \div \frac{1}{3}$

7. $104.01 - 79.67$

8. $14.78 + 22.3 + 28.09$

9. $0.67 \cdot 0.8$

10. $0.12 \cdot 9$

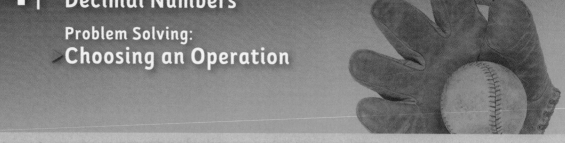

Lesson 14 | ▸The Traditional Method for Dividing Decimal Numbers

Problem Solving:
▸Choosing an Operation

▸The Traditional Method for Dividing Decimal Numbers

How do we use the traditional method for dividing decimal numbers?

The traditional method for dividing decimal numbers involves a shortcut that makes it easier to work with the numbers. There are three names for numbers in a division problem.

$$3 \longleftarrow \text{Quotient}$$
$$\text{Divisor} \longrightarrow 3.4\overline{)10.2} \longleftarrow \text{Dividend}$$

Example 1 shows how we change the divisor into a whole number in order to make it easier to divide. When we move the decimal point in one number, we need to do the same thing to the other number. So, if we change the divisor, we also need to change the dividend.

Example 1

Change the place value in the divisor and the dividend by moving the decimal points.

$3.4\overline{)10.2}$	$3.4\overline{)10.2}$	changes to	$34\overline{)102}$ with quotient 3
$0.25\overline{)15}$	$0.25\overline{)15}$	changes to	$25\overline{)1,500}$ with quotient 60
$0.02\overline{)0.104}$	$0.02\overline{)0.104}$	changes to	$2\overline{)10.4}$ with quotient 5.2
$1.2\overline{)0.156}$	$1.2\overline{)0.156}$	changes to	$12\overline{)1.56}$ with quotient 0.13

> Don't forget to change both numbers by the same amount.

How do we use good number sense when we divide decimal numbers?

Here is another exercise for thinking about decimal numbers when we divide. We did something similar when we multiplied decimal numbers in a previous lesson. Look at the problems in Example 1. There are two problems with the correct digits in the answers. Where do we put the decimal point?

Example 1

Use estimation to decide where the decimal point goes.

$210.05 \div 6.7 = 314$

- First, we round 210.05 to 210 and 6.7 to 7.
- We know that $210 \div 7 = 30$.
- Since the answer should be around 30, we put the decimal point in place to make our answer close to 30.

The answer is 31.4.

$210.05 \div 67 = 314$

- First, we round 210.05 to 210 and round 67 to 70.
- We know that $210 \div 70 = 3$.
- Since the answer is around 3, we put the decimal point in place to make our answer close to 3.

The answer is 3.14.

These skills are important even if we do most of our computations using a calculator. If we enter numbers incorrectly on a calculator, we need to be able to see that the answer does not make sense. So, number sense strategies help us determine if we have the correct answer.

 **Apply Skills**
Turn to *Interactive Text*, page 38.

 **Reinforce Understanding**
Use the *mBook Study Guide* to review lesson concepts.

▶**Problem Solving: Choosing an Operation**

Which operation do we use?

There are many times in life when we have to use math. We are not told what operation to use like in the problems that we solve in math class. We have to figure out what operation to use. When this happens, we need to think carefully about the problem.

Let's look at some situations where we need to choose an operation.

Problem:

An artist wants to make a frame for her new picture. She needs to know how much frame material to buy to go all the way around the picture. What operation should she use?

Since the artist wants to know the distance around the picture, she will have to measure each side of the picture and then add the lengths together.

The operation is addition.

Problem:

Your friend wants to give every student in his class three cookies. There are 25 students in the class. Which operation should he use?

Since we want every student to have three cookies, we could use either addition or multiplication to solve the problem. To add, we would need to add $3 + 3 + 3 + \ldots$ 25 times. This is a lot of work. It would be easier to write the multiplication problem $25 \cdot 3$ and solve it.

The operation is multiplication.

Problem-Solving Activity
Turn to *Interactive Text*, page 39.

mBook Reinforce Understanding
Use the *mBook Study Guide* to review lesson concepts.

Activity 1

Select the correct answer to each division problem.

1. $0.9 \div 0.3$
   (a) 0.27
   (b) 3
   (c) 0.03

2. $1.5 \div 0.75$
   (a) 0.2
   (b) 0.02
   (c) 2

3. $0.65 \div 0.5$
   (a) 0.13
   (b) 1.3
   (c) 0.013

4. $0.78 \div 0.02$
   (a) 39
   (b) 3.9
   (c) 0.39

Activity 2

Place the decimal point in the correct location in each of the problems to find the correct quotient.

Model $1.00 \div 0.5 = 020$
   The decimal point goes after the 2: 2.0.

1. $0.75 \div 0.25 = 0300$

2. $0.38 \div 0.2 = 0190$

3. $0.05 \div 0.5 = 0100$

4. $0.27 \div 0.9 = 0300$

5. $4.5 \div 0.05 = 0900$

Activity 3

Select the decimal operation you would use for each of the problems. Then set up the problem and solve.

Model   Tony needs to cut a board that is 0.68 inches long into 4 equal parts. How big is each part?

Answer: Division. $0.68 \div 4 = 0.17$ inches

1. Michael and McKay had lunch together. Michael's lunch cost $3.48. McKay's lunch cost $2.56. What was the total?

2. Ellen had a doctor's appointment and had to leave work 1.5 hours early today. Her boss deducted the time from her hours for the day, which were 7.5. How much time did she get paid for that day?

3. April gets paid $7.50 per hour. If she works 9.5 hours, what is her pay?

4. Albert is trying to figure out the tip for his meal. He wants to tip 15 percent, which is the same as 0.15. His meal cost $6.25. What is the tip?

5. Elizabeth has 3.5 yards of red fabric left over from last holiday season. She needs 0.25 yards of fabric to cover each jar lid she is decorating. How many lids can she cover with the leftover fabric?

Activity 4 • Distributed Practice

Solve.

1. $\frac{1}{2} + \frac{3}{5}$

2. $\frac{3}{4} - \frac{2}{3}$

3. $\frac{1}{6} \cdot \frac{1}{2}$

4. $\frac{1}{8} \div \frac{3}{4}$

5. $1.75 + 2.38$

6. $15.08 - 12.99$

7. $13.5 \cdot 0.8$

8. $6.8 \div 0.2$

9. $18.9 + 22.7 + 85.79$

10. $10.5 \div 0.5$

▸**Fractions and Decimal Numbers**

What are basic fraction and decimal number concepts?

Fractions and decimal numbers point to the same location on a number line. They are just different ways of describing the same number.

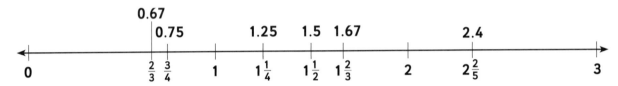

The concept of fractions is based on fair shares. That means we can take a shape and break it into equal parts. Fair shares are important when we add or subtract fractions because they allow us to add or subtract the same units.

When we change fractions into decimal numbers, we divide the denominator into the numerator. This changes the fraction into a base-10 number. Look at Review 1. We listen for the place value when we read the number.

Review 1

How are fractions and decimal numbers related?

Fraction	Decimal Number	We Say	Place Value
$\frac{4}{10}$	0.4	four tenths	Tenths
$\frac{1}{4}$	0.25	twenty-five hundredths	Hundredths
$\frac{3}{8}$	0.375	three hundred and seventy-five thousandths	Thousandths

There are different ways to show fractions and decimal numbers. Review 2 shows fraction bars and a 100-square grid. Each one helps us better understand these two kinds of rational numbers.

Review 2

How do we use models to show how fractions and decimal numbers are related?

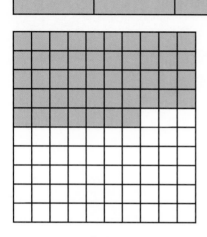

$\frac{3}{5}$

0.47

We use different models for fractions and decimal numbers. Fraction bars help us see fractions. We use a 100-square grid to show decimal numbers up to the hundredths place.

What do we need to remember when we work with fractions?

The rules for how to add, subtract, multiply, and divide fractions are different. It is important to be able to keep track of what we need to do. We begin by looking at the operation.

Review 1

What do we need to remember when we add or subtract fractions?

When adding and subtracting fractions, we need to have the same denominators. This is because we can only add or subtract the same fair shares. Without fair shares, the answer would not make sense.

$$\frac{2}{3} + \frac{1}{2} = ? \qquad \frac{4}{6} + \frac{3}{6} = \frac{7}{6}$$

Review 2

What do we need to remember when we multiply fractions?

When multiplying fractions, we use one fraction to take a portion of another fraction. If we work with fractions less than 1, the answer is usually smaller than the numbers we started with. We use a model to show what this looks like.

$$\frac{3}{4} \cdot \frac{1}{2} = \frac{3}{8}$$

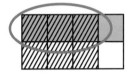

The overlap is 3 out of 8 sections, or $\frac{3}{8}$.

Review 3

What do we need to remember when we divide fractions?

Division is about breaking up one number with another number. We use one fraction as the unit to break up another fraction. In the problem $\frac{1}{2} \div \frac{1}{4}$, we break up $\frac{1}{2}$ by the unit $\frac{1}{4}$. Fraction bars help us see this.

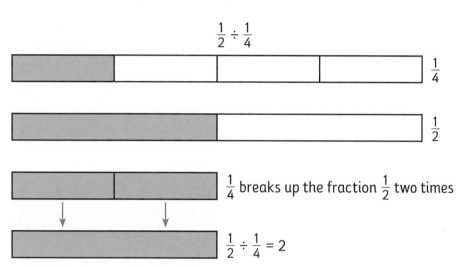

We saw the traditional methods for operating with fractions. We learned that the traditional methods are shortcuts for solving difficult problems.

What are the traditional methods for working with fractions?

Models help us see why addition, subtraction, multiplication, and division of fractions work. They help us build good number sense about these operations. They are not always the most efficient way to find an answer. It is faster to use the traditional methods for these operations. It's important for us to have good number sense and good computational skills.

Addition and Subtraction:

Use equivalent fractions to make the denominators the same.

$$\frac{2}{3} + \frac{1}{2}$$

$$\frac{2}{3} \cdot \frac{2}{2} = \frac{4}{6}$$

$$\frac{1}{2} \cdot \frac{3}{3} = \frac{3}{6}$$

$$\frac{2}{3} + \frac{1}{2} = \frac{4}{6} + \frac{3}{6} = \frac{7}{6}$$

Multiplication:

Multiply across. Do not change denominators.

$$\frac{1}{2} \cdot \frac{3}{4} = \frac{3}{8}$$

Division:

Invert the second fraction and multiply across. Do not change denominators.

$$\frac{1}{2} \div \frac{1}{4}$$

$$\frac{1}{2} \cdot \frac{4}{1} = \frac{4}{2}, \text{ or } 2$$

What do we need to remember when working with decimal numbers?

Operations on decimal numbers are less of a problem. We do not have to convert or simplify as we do with fractions. Here are some key ideas for working with decimal numbers.

Adding or subtracting decimal numbers:

We make sure to line up the decimal points. An easy way to do this is to add zeros to the end of the decimal number if the numbers are not the same length.

Original problem	Add a zero to make the same place values
3.242	3.242
− 1.15	− 1.150
	2.092

Multiplying decimal numbers using the traditional method:

We multiply the two numbers as if they were whole numbers. When we get the answer, we count the number of places to the right of the decimal point in our problem, then count over that many places in the answer and place the decimal point.

$$\begin{array}{r} 3.25 \\ \times\ \ 0.7 \\ \hline 2.275 \end{array}$$ three numbers to the right of the decimal point

Start all the way to the right and count over three places to the left and place the decimal point.

Dividing decimal numbers:

We start by making the divisor a whole number. If we move the decimal point in the divisor, we have to do the same thing with the dividend. We add a zero to the dividend if we need to.

divisor   dividend   40

$0.13\overline{)5.2}$ $13\overline{)520}$

How do we check our answers?

Number sense with fractions and decimal numbers is important. We use estimations to see if we have the right answer. This is especially true with decimal numbers. One of the easiest ideas to remember is that the decimal part of a number is always less than 1. If we want to find an approximate answer to a decimal number problem, we round to the nearest whole number. Let's look at an example with exact and estimated answers to different decimal number problems.

Review 1

How do we check our answers using estimation?

Exact Answer	Approximate Answer
$\begin{array}{r} 33.75 \\ 2.103 \\ +\ \ 4.7 \\ \hline 40.553 \end{array}$	$\begin{array}{r} 34 \\ 2 \\ +\ \ 5 \\ \hline 41 \end{array}$
$\begin{array}{r} 3.39 \\ \times\ \ \ 5.2 \\ \hline 17.628 \end{array}$	$\begin{array}{r} 3 \\ \times\ 5 \\ \hline 15 \end{array}$
$2.4\overline{)12.24}^{\ 5.1}$	$2\overline{)12}^{\ 6}$
$24\overline{)122.4}^{\ 5.1}$	$20\overline{)120}^{\ 6}$

The estimated answers are very close to the exact answers.

%÷
<x Apply Skills
Turn to *Interactive Text*,
page 41.

mBook **Reinforce Understanding**
Use the *mBook Study Guide*
to review lesson concepts.

▶**Problem Solving: Statistics**

What is important about the median?

There are many ways to think about a set of data. The first job to do with any set of data is to organize it from low to high or high to low. It makes it much easier to find important information when it is organized this way.

We also need to find the average, or mean. This number is the best way to predict any other number that might be added to the set of data. For example, let's say we are keeping track of average car sales for 11 months. We find out that on average 280 cars were sold each month. The best prediction for the 12th month would be that 280 cars would be sold.

Review 1 shows a set of data that has been organized from low to high. Now we can find the minimum, maximum, range, and median. We add the total data and divide by the number of scores to find the mean.

Review 1

What are the min, max, range, mean, and median in the set of data?

27, 35, 37, 41, 46, 52, 133

Mean = $7\overline{)371}$ with quotient 53

Min = 27

Max = 133

Range = 133 − 27 = 106

Median = 41

In Review 1 the mean is 53 and the median is 41. There is a noticeable difference between the two. This is because the max of 133 is extreme compared to the other numbers. Extreme values like this are called outliers. If we took out the 133, we would have just six scores. As Review 2 shows, we would have a mean of 39.67 and a median of 39. Now both numbers are good indicators of the data set.

Review 2

What are the min, max, range, mean, and median in the set of data?

$$27, 35, 37, 41, 46, 52$$

Mean = $6\overline{)238}$ ... 39.67

Min = 27

Max = 52

Range = 52 − 27 = 25

Median = 39

How do we represent data visually?

We can show data in a number of ways. Sometimes when we look at data on a graph or plot, it is easier to make sense of it. One way to show data is the box-and-whisker plot. We learn a lot about data by looking at the length of the three different parts of the plot. Let's look at two plots. Each plot tells a different story about the lower $\frac{1}{4}$, middle $\frac{1}{2}$, and upper $\frac{1}{4}$ of the data set.

Review 1

How do we analyze the data on the box-and-whisker plot?

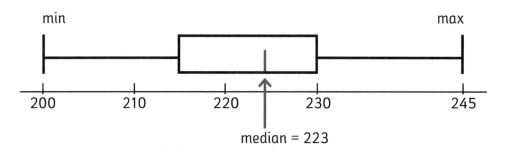

median = 223

Let's look at what this plot tells us:

- This plot shows an evenly distributed set of data between the minimum (200) and the maximum (245).

- The median is near the middle of the box, which means it is about halfway in the middle $\frac{1}{2}$ of the data.

- Also, the whiskers are about equal in length, which means there is about as much of a spread in the lower $\frac{1}{4}$ of the data as there is in the upper $\frac{1}{4}$ of the data.

Not every box-and-whisker plot will be as evenly distributed as the plot in Review 1. Sometimes the plot shows us that the data is not distributed evenly.

Review 2

How do we analyze the data on the box-and-whisker plot?

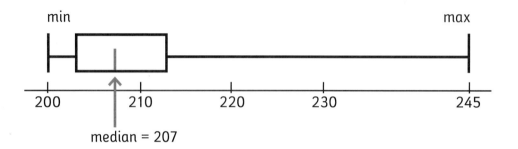

median = 207

This is a very different kind of plot. This is what the plot tells us:

- We see right away the two whiskers are not balanced.

- This means there is a big spread in the scores in the upper $\frac{1}{4}$ of the distribution compared to the lower $\frac{1}{4}$ where all the scores are packed together.

- Half of the scores are between 200 and 207, compared with the other half, which are between 207 and 245.

These data are unbalanced, and most scores are at the lower end of the range.

Now let's look at scatter plots.

What do we need to remember about scatter plots?

Scatter plots are another way to understand data. In scatter plots, we look for relationships between variables.

Review 1

What is a direct relationship?

In one type of relationship called a direct relationship, "the more we have of one, the more we have of the other." A good example of this is, "The more you push down on the gas pedal in a car, the faster the car goes." Points on a scatter plot tend to move from the lower left corner to the upper right corner.

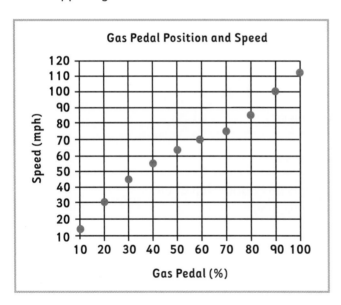

Review 2

What is an indirect relationship?

The opposite is an indirect relationship where "the more we have of one, the less we have of another." A good example of this is, "The more you practice, the less time it takes to run a lap." The points are high on the left and move lower as we go to the right on the scatter plot.

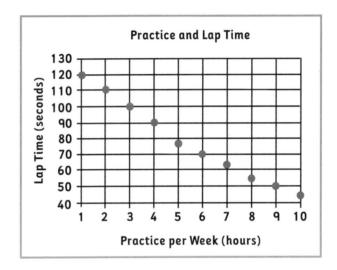

Of course, there are always times when there is no relationship at all. For example, eating more spinach does not make you smarter. Also, lifting more weights does not make you taller.

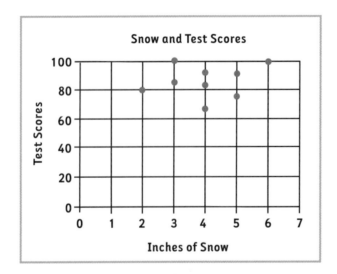

 Problem-Solving Activity
Turn to *Interactive Text*,
page 43.

 mBook Reinforce Understanding
Use the *mBook Study Guide*
to review lesson concepts.

Ridge Ending

Ridge

Bifurcation

Dot

Crossover

Lake

Every person's fingerprints are unique. Fingerprints do not change as people age.

Biometrics: On the Case

Biometrics is the examination of unique features or patterns, such as fingerprints, to identify people. Biometrics can be used to solve crimes or as a form of security.

Examples of biometrics include:

DNA testing: Checks a person's genetic code using a chemical analysis.

Retinal scans: Scans unique patterns of blood vessels in the eye. Not even twins have the same retinal patterns.

Hand geometry: Measures hand size and shape.

Face recognition: Measures people's facial features.

OBJECTIVES

Building Number Concepts

- Use variables to describe patterns
- Use variables to represent unknown values in formulas and equations
- Convert between equations and statements using words

Problem Solving

- Represent part-to-whole and part-to-part relationships using ratios
- Recognize and represent proportional relationships
- Use proportions to identify similar shapes

Lesson 1 | ▸Understanding Variables

Problem Solving:
▸**Strategies for Solving Problems**

▸Understanding Variables

What are variables?

Variables are used in math sentences to fill in for unknown values. In these problems, we use either a blank line or a variable to represent the unknown or missing number.

Using a blank line

_____ + 8 = 15   or

Using a variable

$x + 8 = 15$

In simple problems like this, it's easy to solve for the variable. We can do one of two things:

- We can think about what number is added to 8 to make 15.
- We can take 8 away from 15, and what is left is our answer.

Whether we use a blank line or a variable, the answer is still 7. No other number will work in this math sentence.

Another way variables are used in math sentences is to represent a general pattern. When a variable is used in this way, there are many numbers that can replace a variable to make a math sentence true. Properties of numbers demonstrate this use of variables.

Example 1

Identify the general pattern of these statements.

$5 + 0 = 5$

$10.7 + 0 = 10.7$

$150 + 0 = 150$

Any number plus 0 equals itself is a property of numbers.

We use a variable to demonstrate this property.

$m + 0 = m$

As we move from one statement to the next, we ask ourselves, "What is the same and what is changing?" We have to look at all three of the statements to answer this.

- The numbers 5, 10.7, and 150 are the parts that have changed from one statement to the next.
- Zero stays the same.
- The general pattern using a variable is: $m + 0 = m$.

We check our pattern by selecting any other number to try in the statement.

For instance, we try replacing the variable, m, with the value 100: $100 + 0 = 100$. Is this statement true? It is. In fact, we can substitute any value for m and the statement $m + 0 = m$ remains true.

Example 2 shows the same property we saw in Example 1 but in a slightly different way. We look at a subtraction statement describing a similar property of numbers. Any number minus itself equals 0.

Example 2

Identify the general pattern being shown by these three statements.

$$6 - 6 = 0$$
$$\frac{1}{2} - \frac{1}{2} = 0$$
$$1{,}253 - 1{,}253 = 0$$

What is the general pattern?

$n - n = 0$

Again, we ask ourselves, "What is the same and what is changing?" We have to look at all three of the statements to answer this.

- The numbers 6, $\frac{1}{2}$, and 1,253 are the parts that have changed from one statement to the next.
- Zero stays the same in each one of them.
- The general pattern using a variable is: $n - n = 0$.

We check the statement by selecting any other number to try in the general pattern. For instance, try replacing the variable, n, with the value 500: $500 - 500 = 0$. Is this statement true? It is. In fact, we can substitute any value for n and the statement $n - n = 0$ remains true.

Another important pattern involves multiplying by 1. Let's look at Example 3.

Example 3

Identify the pattern.

$3 \cdot 1 = 3$

$\frac{1}{2} \cdot 1 = \frac{1}{2}$

$1.35 \cdot 1 = 1.35$

What is the general pattern?

$n \cdot 1 = n$

The important thing to remember is that there are two ways we can use variables.

Two Ways We Use Variables

1. We use variables to represent a single number that is unknown in a math sentence.

$$x + 9 = 16 \qquad x = 7$$

In this case, only one number makes the statement true.

2. We use variables to represent a general pattern where the variable can have many values.

$$x + 0 = x \qquad x = \text{any number}$$

In this case, any number makes the statement true.

% ÷
=
< × **Apply Skills**
Turn to *Interactive Text*, page 46.

mBook **Reinforce Understanding**
Use the *mBook Study Guide* to review lesson concepts.

▶**Problem Solving: Strategies for Solving Problems**

How does the "Draw a Picture" strategy help us solve problems efficiently?

There are many problem-solving strategies for solving complex problems. For instance, good problem-solvers often draw a picture of the problem so that they can visualize it better.

Example 1 shows how a picture can help us solve a problem.

Example 1

Draw a picture to help solve the problem.

Problem:

If a rectangle has a base of 5 units and a perimeter of 16 units, what is the height of the rectangle?

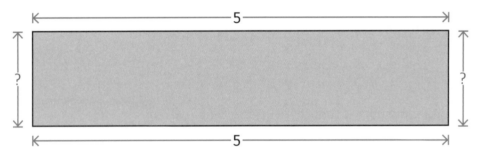

A picture helps us gain a better understanding of the problem.

- Each of the long sides is 5 units.
- We don't know what the height is.
- We use ? to show that we don't know what the measurements are.
- We add the two sides we know: 5 + 5 = 10.

We were told in the problem that the total perimeter is 16 units. We subtract 10 from 16 and get 6.

The perimeter is the sum of all the sides of the rectangle. So, the other two sides of the rectangle must be equal to 6 units and they must be the same number.

The height of the rectangle is 3 units.

How does the "Look for a Pattern" strategy help us solve problems efficiently?

There are several other problem-solving strategies. One of these strategies we will call "Look for a Pattern." This strategy helps save time when solving many different types of problems.

Look for a Pattern—Number Pattern

Example 1 shows how looking for a pattern can help us solve a problem.

Example 1

Look for a pattern to help solve the problem.

Problem:

How many times do we write the digit 9 when writing a list of whole numbers from 0 to 50?

We could write out all the numbers like this:

0, 1, 2, 3, 4, 5, 6, 7, 8, 9, 10, 11, 12, 13, 14, 15, etc.

It would take a long time to write all the numbers from 0 to 50. Instead, we could look for a pattern.

- Write out the numbers from 0–10. How many 9s are there? One.
- Next look at 11–20, then 21–30, and so on. For each set of 10, the digit 9 appears once.

Here is an organized list showing the pattern:

Range of Numbers	Number(s) With 9	Number of 9s
0–10	9	1
11–20	19	1
21–30	29	1
31–40	39	1
41–50	49	1
Total		5

There are 5 sets of numbers. There is one 9 in each set.

The digit 9 appears 5 times in the list of numbers from 0 to 50.

This is just one kind of problem that can be solved using a pattern. It involves a number pattern. Example 2 will use this strategy for solving a problem involving a geometric pattern.

Look for a Pattern—Geometric Pattern

Example 2

Look for a pattern to help solve the problem.

Problem:
Without counting every triangle, tell how many total triangles there are in the picture.

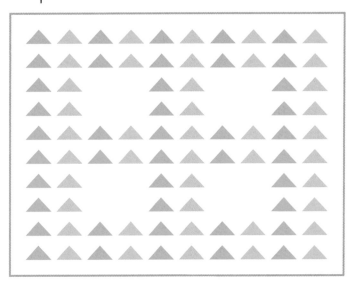

Finding the pattern in the picture helps us solve this problem.

- Notice that the geometric pattern is the same for every two rows.
- Count the number of orange and purple triangles in the first two rows and multiply that number by 3 because the pattern in these rows appears three times. We get 60 triangles.
- Then count the number of orange and purple triangles in the next two rows and multiply that number by 2 because the pattern in these rows appears two times. We get 24 triangles.
- Now add 60 and 24.

There are 84 triangles.

 **Problem-Solving Activity**
Turn to *Interactive Text*, page 47.

 **mBook Reinforce Understanding**
Use the *mBook Study Guide*
to review lesson concepts.

Activity 1

Tell the missing value for the variable.

1. $a + 7 = 13$ 2. $18 - b = 9$ 3. $c - 9 = 8$

4. $9 + d = 15$ 5. $e \cdot 7 = 21$ 6. $42 \div f = 6$

Activity 2

Select the statement that best describes the pattern.

Model $1 \cdot 8 = 8$
$1 \cdot 20 = 20$
$1 \cdot 500 = 500$

   (a) $x \cdot 1 = x$ **(b)** $1 \cdot x = x$ **(c)** $1 \cdot 1 = x$

   Answer: b, $1 \cdot x = x$

1. $0 \cdot 1 = 0$
$0 \cdot 50 = 0$
$0 \cdot 100 = 0$

   (a) $x \cdot 1 = x$ **(b)** $1 \cdot x = x$ **(c)** $0 \cdot x = 0$

2. $3 + 0 = 3$
$\frac{1}{2} + 0 = \frac{1}{2}$
$325 + 0 = 325$

   (a) $3 + x = 3$ **(b)** $x + 0 = x$ **(c)** $x + \frac{1}{2} = x$

3. $5 \cdot 1 = 5$
$66 \cdot 1 = 66$
$107.5 \cdot 1 = 107.5$

   (a) $x \cdot 1 = x$ **(b)** $1 \cdot 1 = x$ **(c)** $5 \cdot x = 5$

4. $44 - 44 = 0$
$375 - 375 = 0$
$1\frac{1}{2} - 1\frac{1}{2} = 0$

   (a) $44 - 44 = x$ **(b)** $x - 0 = x$ **(c)** $x - x = 0$

Activity 3

A value has been inserted for the variable in each of the following general statements. Is the statement true or false? Write T or F on your paper.

Model $x + 1 = x$

Replace x with 5.

$5 + 1 = 5$

Answer: False

1. $0 - y = y$
    Replace y with 10. $\rightarrow$ $0 - 10 = 10$
    Is the statement true or false?

2. $1 \cdot h = h$
    Replace h with 5. $\rightarrow$ $1 \cdot 5 = 5$
    Is the statement true or false?

3. $w - 0 = w$
    Replace w with 6. $\rightarrow$ $6 - 0 = 6$
    Is the statement true or false?

4. $a \cdot a = 1$
    Replace a with 2. $\rightarrow$ $2 \cdot 2 = 1$
    Is the statement true or false?

5. $0 \cdot b = 0$
    Replace b with 25. $\rightarrow$ $0 \cdot 25 = 0$
    Is the statement true or false?

Activity 4 • Distributed Practice

Solve.

1. $1.75 \cdot 0.1$

2. $\frac{12}{2} - \frac{10}{2}$

3. $567.05 - 49.97$

4. $\frac{3}{9} + \frac{1}{3}$

5. $42.7 \div 0.7$

6. $\frac{4}{5} \cdot \frac{5}{9}$

7. $\frac{3}{7} - \frac{1}{7}$

8. $22.75 + 33.75 + 5.25$

Lesson 2 ▶Patterns With More Than One Variable
Problem Solving: ▶More With Patterns

▶Patterns With More Than One Variable

Vocabulary
commutative property for addition

How do we use more than one variable to represent a pattern?

In the last lesson, we learned how to use a variable to write a general pattern about properties of numbers. Here are two very important properties:

> **Properties of Numbers:**
>
> $a + 0 = a$ (anything plus 0 equals itself)
>
> $b \cdot 1 = b$ (anything times 1 equals itself)

Sometimes we need more than one variable to represent a property. For instance, think about the **commutative property for addition** . This is the property that allows us to move numbers around when we add them.

Example 1 shows some number sentences that demonstrate the commutative property.

Example 1

Show the commutative property of addition.

If we are adding numbers, we can add them in any order.

$$5 + 6 = 6 + 5$$

$$\frac{1}{2} + \frac{1}{3} = \frac{1}{3} + \frac{1}{2}$$

$$2.2 + 3.3 = 3.3 + 2.2$$

Just like the properties we used in the last lesson, we can use a general statement with variables to describe the pattern in the commutative property. The only difference is that with this property we need more than one variable.

Example 2 shows the general statement using two variables to describe the commutative property. Notice that two numbers change in each of the statements. We need two different variables to represent this pattern.

Example 2

Write a general statement for the commutative property.

$5 + 6 = 6 + 5$

$\dfrac{1}{2} + \dfrac{1}{3} = \dfrac{1}{3} + \dfrac{1}{2}$

$2.2 + 3.3 = 3.3 + 2.2$

General Statement:

$a + b = b + a$

We can check our general statement by replacing the two variables with any two values.

Let's replace the variables in the general statement with the numbers 1 and 2.

Is this statement true?

$$\dfrac{a}{1} + \dfrac{b}{2} \quad = \quad \dfrac{b}{2} + \dfrac{a}{1}$$

$1 + 2 = 3$ $1 + 2 = 3$

Both sides equal 3.

The statement is true.

It's important to understand that the commutative property is true for any number of addends we have in our problem. For instance, $2 + 3 + 4 = 4 + 3 + 2$ shows the commutative property for three different addends. Both sides equal 9.

What do you think the impact will be on the general statement using variables? We will need a third variable.

Example 3 demonstrates writing a general statement about the commutative property when we have three addends, using the variables x, y, and z.

Example 3

Write a general statement about the commutative property for three addends.

We need to look carefully at the placement of each number to write the general statement correctly.

$4 + 2 + 1 = 2 + 4 + 1$
$3 + 7 + 8 = 7 + 3 + 8$
$5 + 6 + 9 = 6 + 5 + 9$

General Statement:

$$x + y + z = y + x + z$$

Notice that the first, middle, and last variable on the left side of the equal sign have been moved or "commuted" on the right-hand side so that they are in a new order: middle, first, last.

We can check the general statement by replacing the variables x, y, and z with any three numbers.

Let's look at 30, 50, and 20.
$30 + 50 + 20 = 50 + 30 + 20$

Is the statement true?
$30 + 50 + 20 = 100$
The left side equals 100.

$50 + 30 + 20 = 100$
The right side also equals 100.
The statement is true.

POWER CONCEPT

The commutative property for addition tells us that we can change the order of the numbers in any addition problem.

Since the commutative property states that we can add the numbers in any order, there are other general statements that would also work.

For instance, $x + y + z = z + y + x$ or $x + y + z = x + z + y$ would also work. We just make sure we are representing the pattern that is shown in the three statements when we write our general patterns.

Improve Your Skills

Your friend says that $3 - 2$ is the same as $2 - 3$ because of the commutative property. **ERROR**

We know that $3 - 2 = 1$ and that $2 - 3 = -1$.

The commutative property does not work for subtraction. Your friend would be correct to say that $3 + 2$ is the same as $2 + 3$. **CORRECT**

As we begin to analyze more and more complex patterns, we see how powerful variables can be. We have been looking at properties of numbers that work for many numbers. It would be impossible to look at all the possible patterns, so variables give us a general way to look at patterns in one simple statement.

%÷
≤× **Apply Skills**
Turn to *Interactive Text*,
page 49.

mBook **Reinforce Understanding**
Use the *mBook Study Guide*
to review lesson concepts.

▶Problem Solving: **More With Patterns**

How do patterns help determine what comes next in a sequence?

In the last lesson, we learned that the "Look for a Pattern" strategy helps us efficiently solve problems. We saw, for instance, that we didn't have to count all the triangles in the design. We could find the total by using a pattern. Sometimes, in complex problems involving sequences, the pattern itself is the answer to the problem, and we use it to determine the next item in the sequence.

Let's look at the pattern cards in Example 1. We will look for a pattern in the first three cards to determine what the fourth card should look like.

Example 1

Use the pattern to determine what the fourth card will look like.

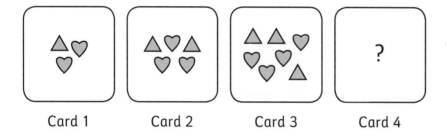

Card 1   Card 2   Card 3   Card 4

Examine the first three cards to find the pattern. It helps to organize the information in a table to keep it straight:

Card	Triangles	Hearts
1	1	2
2	2	3
3	3	4
4	?	?

What patterns do we see?

- The number of triangles is always the same as the card number.
- The number of hearts is always one more than the number of triangles.

We make a general statement about this pattern using variables.

Each card has x triangles and $x + 1$ hearts.

Notice that "one more" is written as $x + 1$. Once we know the general pattern, we can figure out what the fourth card will look like.

- The number of triangles is the same as the card number. There will be four triangles in the fourth card.
- The number of hearts is always one more than the number of triangles. There will be five hearts in the fourth card.

The fourth card should look like this:

Card 1   Card 2   Card 3   Card 4

This pattern involved addition. We always had one more heart, or + 1 hearts, than we had triangles. Not all patterns are addition patterns.

Example 2 shows a pattern with cards that involves multiplication.

Example 2

Use the pattern to determine what the fourth card will look like.

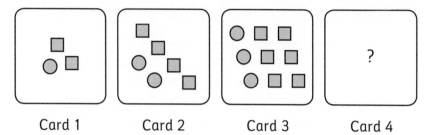

| Card 1 | Card 2 | Card 3 | Card 4 |

What patterns do we see?

- The number of circles is always the same as the card number.

Card	Circles	Squares
1	1	2
2	2	4
3	3	6
4	?	?

- There are always twice as many squares as circles.

We make this general statement about this pattern using variables:

Each card has m circles and $2 \cdot m$ squares.

"Twice as many" is written as $2 \cdot m$. Once we know the general pattern, we can figure out what the fourth card will look like.

- There will be four circles in the fourth card.
- There will be $2 \cdot 4$ or 8 squares in the fourth card.

The fourth card should look like this:

| Card 1 | Card 2 | Card 3 | Card 4 |

 Problem-Solving Activity
Turn to *Interactive Text*, page 50.

 mBook Reinforce Understanding
Use the *mBook Study Guide* to review lesson concepts.

Activity 1

Tell the missing value for the variable.

1. $m \div 8 = 6$
2. $4 \cdot 7 = n$
3. $5 + p = 14$

4. $r - 8 = 9$
5. $35 \div 5 = t$
6. $3 \cdot u = 18$

Activity 2

Tell if the general statement describes the pattern shown by the number sentences. Write Yes or No on your paper.

1. Does $x + y = y + x$ describe the pattern shown by these number sentences?

   $4 + 5 = 5 + 4$

   $3 + 2 = 2 + 3$

   $7 + 8 = 8 + 7$

2. Does $a \cdot b \cdot c = c \cdot b \cdot a$ describe the pattern shown by these number sentences?

   $3 \cdot \frac{1}{3} \cdot 1 = \frac{1}{3} \cdot 1 \cdot 3$

   $2 \cdot 4 \cdot 6 = 4 \cdot 6 \cdot 2$

   $8 \cdot 1.2 \cdot 3 = 1.2 \cdot 3 \cdot 8$

3. Does $a \cdot 0 = 0$ describe the pattern shown by these number sentences?

   $0 \cdot 0 = 0$

   $3 \cdot 3 = 9$

   $\frac{1}{4} \cdot \frac{1}{4} = \frac{1}{16}$

4. Does $0 + w = w$ describe the pattern shown by these number sentences?

   $0 + \frac{1}{3} = \frac{1}{3}$

   $0 + 0.25 = 0.25$

   $0 + 5 = 5$

5. Does $k + m + n = k + n + m$ describe the pattern shown by these number sentences?

   $5 + 6 + 7 = 5 + 7 + 6$

   $\frac{1}{2} + \frac{2}{2} + \frac{3}{2} = \frac{1}{2} + \frac{3}{2} + \frac{2}{2}$

   $1.2 + 3.7 + 2.9 = 1.2 + 2.9 + 3.7$

Activity 3

For each set of pattern cards, tell if it's an addition pattern (AP) or a multiplication pattern (MP). Write AP or MP on your paper. Then draw Card 4.

1.

Card 1 Card 2 Card 3

2.

Card 1 Card 2 Card 3

3.

Card 1 Card 2 Card 3

Activity 4 • Distributed Practice

Solve.

1. $\frac{3}{4} \cdot \frac{1}{5}$

2. $207.98 + 519.12$

3. $\frac{4}{5} - \frac{1}{10}$

4. $4.25 + 3.75 + 8.95$

5. $\frac{8}{12} \div \frac{1}{3}$

6. $1.11 \cdot 0.2$

7. $109.09 - 87.81$

8. $\frac{1}{3} + \frac{1}{6} + \frac{1}{9}$

▶**Substitution**

Vocabulary
substitution

What is substitution?

Substitution is an important concept to understand when working with variables. We use substitution when we replace a variable with a number value. We have already done this as a way to check our general statements in the last two lessons.

Example 1 shows substitution in a problem where only one value makes the statement true.

Example 1

Find the value of x.

$x \cdot 8 = 72$

In this problem, the variable x stands for just one number. The number is 9. We can substitute the value, 9, into the number sentence for the variable x.

$9 \cdot 8 = 72$

We can also use substitution to find specific cases of general patterns.

Example 2 shows substitution for a general pattern we looked at in Lesson 1, $m + 0 = m$.

Example 2

Substitute the given value for m.

Substitute 2 for m in m + 0 = m.

$$m + 0 = m$$
$$\downarrow \quad \downarrow \quad \downarrow$$
$$2 + 0 = 2$$

Substitute 0.03 for m in m + 0 = m.

$$m \quad + \quad 0 \quad = \quad m$$
$$\downarrow \qquad \downarrow \qquad \downarrow$$
$$0.03 \quad + \quad 0 \quad = \quad 0.03$$

Substitute $\frac{1}{4}$ for m in m + 0 = m.

$$m + 0 = m$$
$$\downarrow \quad \downarrow \quad \downarrow$$
$$\frac{1}{4} + 0 = \frac{1}{4}$$

We substituted different values for $m \left(2, 0.03, \text{ and } \frac{1}{4}\right)$ and showed that the statement remained true in each case.

Substitution helps us make sense of general patterns because it gives us a way to look at specific cases. We also use substitution to look at specific cases of patterns with more than one variable.

Example 3 shows how we substitute values for the two variables x and y to show specific cases of the general pattern.

Example 3

Substitute values for x and y in the general statement $x + y = y + x$.

Substitute $x = 2$ and $y = 4$.

$x + y = y + x$

$2 + 4 = 4 + 2$ Both sides equal 6.
The statement is true.

Substitute $x = \frac{1}{3}$ and $y = \frac{2}{3}$.

$x + y = y + x$

$\frac{1}{3} + \frac{2}{3} = \frac{2}{3} + \frac{1}{3}$ Both sides equal $\frac{3}{3}$, or 1.
The statement is true.

Substitute $x = 0.4$ and $y = 0.6$.

$x + y = y + x$

$0.4 + 0.6 = 0.6 + 0.4$ Both sides are equal to 1.0.
The statement is true.

Substitution is an important tool in algebra. It helps us understand the general pattern better when we see specific cases. It also helps us determine if statements are true or false.

% ÷
=
< × **Apply Skills**
Turn to *Interactive Text*,
page 52.

mBook Reinforce Understanding
Use the *mBook Study Guide*
to review lesson concepts.

▶Problem Solving: **Pattern Cards**

How do we analyze patterns?

We have now solved problems by analyzing pattern cards with addition and multiplication patterns. We will practice working with multiplication patterns again using pattern cards.

Example 1

Tell how many diamonds should be drawn on Card 3.

Card 1   Card 2   Card 3

Examine the first two cards to find the pattern. It helps to organize the information in a table to keep it straight.

The number of diamonds is always three times the number of hearts. Here is our general statement about this pattern:

Card	Hearts	Diamonds
1	1	3
2	3	9
3	2	?

Each card has x hearts and $3 \cdot x$ diamonds.

Once we know the general pattern, we can figure out what is missing in the third card. There are two hearts, so there must be $3 \cdot 2$ or 6 diamonds. The third card should look like this:

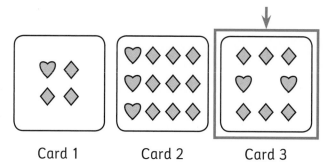

Card 1   Card 2   Card 3

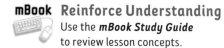

Problem-Solving Activity
Turn to *Interactive Text*, page 54.

mBook Reinforce Understanding
Use the *mBook Study Guide* to review lesson concepts.

Activity 1

Tell the one value that can be substituted for the variable in each problem.

1. What is the value of a in $a + 7 = 10$?

2. What is the value of b in $22 - b = 14$?

3. What is the value of x in $7 \cdot x = 63$?

4. What is the value of y in $y \div 8 = 4$?

Activity 2

For each of the general statements, substitute values for the variables and tell if the statement is true or false.

1. Substitute values for x and y in $x + y = y + x$ and tell if the general statement is true or false.

2. Substitute a value for z in $1 + z = z$ and tell if the general statement is true or false.

3. Substitute values for a, b, and c in $a + b + c = c + b + a$ and tell if the general statement is true or false.

4. Substitute a value for w in $1 \cdot w = w$ and tell if the general statement is true or false.

Activity 3

Tell what needs to go in Card 3 in each set of pattern cards.

1. How many circles should be added to Card 3?

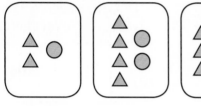

Card 1   Card 2   Card 3

2. How many squares should be added to Card 3?

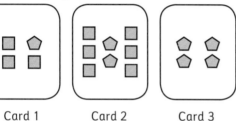

Card 1   Card 2   Card 3

3. How many hearts should be added to Card 3?

Card 1   Card 2   Card 3

Activity 4 • Distributed Practice

Solve.

1. $7.98 \cdot 0.1$

2. $\frac{3}{4} + \frac{5}{8}$

3. $90.02 - 79.98$

4. $\frac{2}{3} + \frac{1}{4} + \frac{1}{6}$

5. $27.3 \div 0.09$

6. $\frac{4}{5} \cdot \frac{5}{8}$

7. $\frac{4}{6} - \frac{1}{3}$

8. $99.87 + 101.35 + 115.75 + 98.75$

Problem Solving:
▶Word Problems With Ratios

▶**Ratios**

Vocabulary
ratio

What is a ratio?

In the past, we compared numbers in many different ways.

- We used fractions to compare the part to the whole. For example, the fraction $\frac{3}{4}$ compares the 3 parts to the whole 4.
- We used percents to compare a number to 100. For example, 90 percent is a comparison of 90 to 100.

A **ratio** also compares two numbers.

Here is a pattern that we analyzed in Lesson 3. We described the pattern using this statement:

Each card has x hearts and $3 \cdot x$ diamonds.

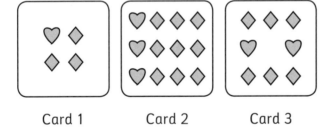

Card 1   Card 2   Card 3

Since this is true for every card, we use a ratio to describe the pattern. We can write the ratio of hearts to diamonds in three ways:

- 1 to 3
- 1 : 3
- $\frac{1}{3}$

We often use ratios in our everyday lives. Let's look at some situations in which people might use ratios.

In cooking—A cookie recipe calls for 1 cup of sugar and 2 cups of flour. The ratio of sugar to flour is 1 to 2.

$$\frac{\text{Sugar}}{\text{Flour}} = \frac{1C}{2C} \qquad \text{or} \qquad \text{sugar : flour is 1 : 2}$$

Knowing the ratio will help us double the recipe.

In painting—To paint a room a shade of light blue, we need to mix 3 cans of blue paint with 1 can of white paint. The ratio of blue paint to white paint is 3 to 1.

$$\frac{\text{Blue}}{\text{White}} = \frac{3 \text{ cans}}{1 \text{ can}} \qquad \text{or} \qquad \text{blue : white is 3 : 1}$$

Knowing the ratio will help us mix the correct shade if we run out of paint after the first mixture.

In the classroom—There are three eighth-grade math classes. One has very few boys compared to the number of girls. The boy-to-girl ratio in this class is 6 to 18.

$$\frac{\text{Boys}}{\text{Girls}} = \frac{6}{18} \qquad \text{or} \qquad \text{boys : girls is 6 : 18}$$

If the classes were changed to be more balanced by gender, the boy-to-girl ratio would change.

In maintenance—Many power tools, such as leaf blowers, chain saws, or lawn mowers, require a mixture of oil and gas to run correctly. The lawn mower calls for a mixture of 1 part oil to 16 parts gas. The ratio of oil to gas is 1 to 16.

$$\frac{\text{Oil}}{\text{Gas}} = \frac{1}{16} \qquad \text{or} \qquad \text{oil : gas is 1 : 16}$$

Knowing the ratio is important because the wrong mixture of oil to gas can result in the power tool breaking down or even starting a fire.

Why can't we just call them fractions?

In some cases, ratios and fractions represent the same thing. In fact, a fraction is a special type of ratio. However, fractions and ratios do not always mean the same thing. Let's look at some examples that help us understand the relationship between ratios and fractions.

Example 1

Read the problem and examine the relationship between the ratio and a fraction.

Problem:

   If there are 12 girls in a class of 26 students, what is the ratio of girls to total students in the class?

This is a part-to-whole relationship. We are comparing the number of girls in the class to the total number of students in the class. We can write this ratio of girls to total number of students as 12 to 26 or $\frac{12}{26}$. In this case, the ratio is like a fraction because it is a part-to-whole relationship.

In other cases, we use ratios to describe part-to-part relationships.

Example 2

Read the problem and examine the relationship between the ratio and a fraction.

Problem:

   If there are 12 girls in a class of 26 students, what is the ratio of girls to boys in the class?

This ratio represents a part-to-part relationship. If there are 26 students in the class and 12 are girls, there are 26 − 12, or 14, boys in the class. The girl-to-boy ratio is 12 to 14:

$$\frac{\text{Number of Girls}}{\text{Number of Boys}} = \frac{12}{14}$$

In this case, the ratio is not a fraction because it describes two parts of a whole.

This is how ratios differ from fractions.

- Fractions are always part-to-whole relationships.
- Ratios may be part-to-whole relationships or they can be part-to-part relationships.

This is also the reason we need to be careful and always label the parts of the ratio. Otherwise, people will assume we are talking about a fraction and a part-to-whole relationship. Notice the labels in the girl-to-boy ratio in Example 2.

We can describe all kinds of relationships between numbers using ratios. In Example 3, we demonstrate how many different kinds of comparisons we can make about a simple hand of cards.

Example 3

Make comparisons with ratios for the set of cards.

Ratio of cards with hearts to cards with diamonds:	2 to 1
Ratio of cards with diamonds to cards with clubs:	1 to 2
Ratio of cards with hearts to cards with clubs:	2 to 2
Ratio of cards with hearts to all cards:	2 to 5
Ratio of cards with spades to all cards:	0 to 5

These are just a few of the many ratios we could write. Ratios allow us the flexibility to compare any two things—suits of cards, numbers, colors—that we are interested in.

Ratios should always be labeled. The labels tell us what we need to know about the comparison being made by the ratio.

 **Apply Skills**
Turn to *Interactive Text*, page 56.

 **Reinforce Understanding**
Use the *mBook Study Guide* to review lesson concepts.

▶Problem Solving: **Word Problems With Ratios**

How do we use ratios to solve word problems?

Word problems involving ratios are easy to solve when we break them into manageable pieces. However, sometimes the numbers we need to solve the problems are not given. Let's look at an example.

Example 1

Solve the problem.

Problem:

In a recent survey of 100 homeowners, 25 had cats and 37 had dogs. The others had no pets. What is the ratio of pet owners to non-pet owners in the survey?

STEP 1
Label the ratio we are looking for.
The problem is asking for the ratio of pet owners to non-pet owners.

Our label looks like this: $\dfrac{\text{Pet Owners}}{\text{Non-Pet Owners}}$

STEP 2
Think about the numbers for our ratio.
We are not given either of these numbers in the problem, but we are given numbers that we can use to compute them.

Computing the number of pet owners:

Cat Owners + Dog Owners = 25 + 37 = 62

Pet Owners = 62

Computing the number of non-pet owners:

Total Homeowners Surveyed = 100

Total Homeowners − Pet Owners = 100 − 62 = 38

Non-Pet Owners = 38

STEP 3
We have the numbers we need. Now we are ready to set up our ratio:

$$\frac{\text{Pet Owners}}{\text{Non-Pet Owners}} \qquad \frac{62}{38}$$

The ratio of pet owners to non-pet owners is 62 to 38.

POWER CONCEPT

Breaking the problem into small steps makes it more manageable to solve.

 Problem-Solving Activity
Turn to *Interactive Text*, page 57.

 mBook Reinforce Understanding
Use the *mBook Study Guide* to review lesson concepts.

Activity 1

Substitute the value for the variable.

1. $a + 12 = 27$
2. $35 - b = 32$
3. $\frac{1}{5} + \frac{2}{5} = c$
4. $8 \cdot 6 = d$
5. $e \div 9 = 7$
6. $\frac{1}{10} \cdot \frac{3}{4} = f$

Activity 2

Select the ratio that represents the statement.

1. There are 25 students in the class and 15 are boys. What is the boy-to-girl ratio?
   (a) 25 to 15
   (b) 12 to 15
   (c) 15 to 10

2. In a survey of 100 students, 67 watch TV every night. What is the ratio of students who watch TV every night to total students?
   (a) 67 to 100
   (b) 33 to 100
   (c) 33 to 67

3. There are 302 students in the freshman class. Of the students, 150 are taking algebra and 152 are taking geometry. What is the ratio of students taking algebra to students taking geometry?
   (a) 150 to 152
   (b) 152 to 150
   (c) 150 to 302

4. There are 10 houses on your street. Of the owners, 5 have dogs, 2 have cats, and 3 have no pets. What is the ratio of people who do not have pets to the total number of houses?
   (a) 5 to 10
   (b) 2 to 10
   (c) 3 to 10

5. The radio station awarded prizes to 3 callers out of 30 callers during the morning show today. What is the ratio of non-prize winners to prize winners?
   (a) 3 to 30
   (b) 27 to 30
   (c) 27 to 3

Activity 3

Tell whether the statements are true or false.

1. The ratio of hearts to diamonds in a hand of cards is 3 to 2. This is a part-to-whole comparison.

2. Fractions always compare part-to-whole relationships.

3. Ratios always compare part-to-whole relationships.

4. If you have a power tool that requires an oil-to-gas ratio of 1 to 16, this means you need to put 1 part of oil for every 16 parts of gas.

Activity 4 • Distributed Practice

Solve.

1. $\frac{5}{8} \cdot \frac{3}{5}$

2. $192.37 + 246.85$

3. $\frac{8}{9} - \frac{1}{3}$

4. $125.07 + 229.37 + 889.11 + 507.07$

5. $\frac{5}{9} \div \frac{3}{5}$

6. $1.22 \cdot 0.02$

7. $101.01 - 99.99$

8. $\frac{5}{6} + \frac{1}{9} + \frac{1}{2}$

▶**Using Variables in Formulas**

Why are variables so important in formulas?

One of the most powerful uses of variables is in formulas. We worked with variables in formulas when we computed area and perimeter of geometric shapes.

Example 1 shows how variables are used in the area formula for a triangle. We use substitution to find the area of the triangle. Remember that area is measured in square units.

Example 1

Find the area of the triangle.

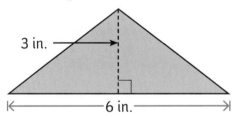

3 in.

6 in.

Area of a triangle = $\frac{1}{2}$ · base · height

We write this formula with variables like this:

$$A = \frac{1}{2} \cdot b \cdot h$$

Where A is the area, b is the base, and h is the height.

To find the area of the triangle, all we need to do is substitute the values for the variables b and h in the formula, and then compute A.

$$A = \frac{1}{2} \cdot b \cdot h$$

$$A = \frac{1}{2} \cdot 6 \cdot 3$$

$$A = 9 \text{ square inches}$$

Substituting values for variables is very common when using area formulas.

Example 2 shows us another well-known formula. It is the area formula for a square.

Example 2

Find the area of the square.

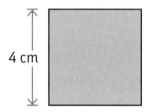

4 cm

Area of a square is $A = s^2$

We substitute the value for the side measurement of the square like this:

$$A = s^2$$

$$\downarrow$$

$$A = 4^2$$

$$A = 16 \text{ square cm}$$

Another type of measurement involving variables in formulas is perimeter.

Example 3 demonstrates the formula for the perimeter of a rectangle. Remember, when we find perimeter, we add up all the sides. Since a rectangle has four sides—two lengths and two widths—we double these measurements. Unlike area, perimeter is not measured in square units. There is only one dimension to perimeter because we are just measuring the distance around the outside of the shape.

Example 3

Find the perimeter of the rectangle.

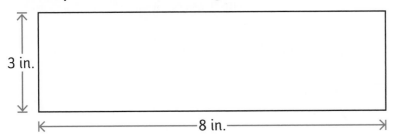

3 in.

8 in.

Perimeter of a rectangle is $P = 2 \cdot$ length $+ 2 \cdot$ width

We rewrite this formula using variables:

$$P = (2 \cdot l) + (2 \cdot w)$$

We include the parentheses because we want to double the length and the width before we add them together. Now we can substitute and solve.

$$P = (2 \cdot l) + (2 \cdot w)$$
$$P = (2 \cdot 8) + (2 \cdot 3)$$
$$P = 16 + 6$$
$$\mathbf{P = 22\ in}$$

One other common type of measurement using variables in formulas is the circumference of a circle.

Example 4 demonstrates how we use variables and substitution to calculate the circumference of a circle. When we measure the circumference of a circle, we are measuring around the outside.

Example 4

Find the circumference of the circle.

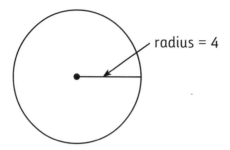

radius = 4

Circumference of a circle is C = 2 · π · radius

We rewrite this formula using variables:

$$C = 2 \cdot \pi \cdot r$$

Remember π (pi) is about 3.14. The radius of this circle is 4. We can substitute the value for π and the value for the variable, r, to calculate the circumference of the circle.

$$C = 2 \cdot \quad \pi \quad \cdot \quad r$$

$$\downarrow$$

$$C = 2 \cdot 3.14 \cdot 4$$
$$C = 25.12$$

All these formulas represent general patterns. We use them as a way to describe the measurements of shapes in general. For instance, the areas of all rectangles, regardless of their bases or heights, are computed by multiplying base by height. When we substitute values for the variables, we are looking at specific rectangles and their areas.

It helps us understand formulas better when we work with them flexibly. Suppose we know the area of a shape but not one of its dimensions. We use the formula to find the missing dimension. We substitute the values we know and compute the missing part.

How do we use formulas flexibly?

Example 1 demonstrates how to find the missing dimension if we know the area and one dimension of a rectangle.

Example 1

Find the missing dimension.

Problem:

Shaq is building a shed in his yard to store his outdoor tools. The area of each of the rectangular walls of the shed is going to be 36 sq. ft. with a base of 9 ft. Shaq wants to know what the height of the walls will be. Use the area formula to find the height of one of the walls.

Area of the wall = 36 sq. ft.	height = ?

base = 9 ft.

Area of a rectangle is $A = b \cdot h$

(where A = area, b = base, and h = height)

Put the values we know into the formula. This is where our problem-solving is a little different. Instead of substituting the dimensions and computing the area, we substitute the area and the base and compute the height.

$$A = b \cdot h$$
$$36 = 9 \cdot h$$

Now we find the value for the remaining variable. In this case, we find the value of h using what we know about basic facts.

$$36 = 9 \cdot h \rightarrow 36 = 9 \cdot 4$$

The answer is 4.

Each wall of the shed needs to be 4 feet tall.

 **Apply Skills** Turn to *Interactive Text*, page 59.

 **Monitoring Progress** Quiz 1

 **mBook Reinforce Understanding** Use the *mBook Study Guide* to review lesson concepts.

Activity 1

Find the value for the variable.

1. What is the value of x in $x + 129 = 237$?

2. What is the value of y in $9 \cdot y = 72$?

3. What is the value of a in $a - 146 = 229$?

4. What is the value of z in $56 \div z = 8$?

5. What is the value of b in $6 \cdot 5 = b$?

6. What is the value of w in $81 \div w = w$?

Activity 2

Compute the areas of each shape by substituting values for the variables in the formulas.

1. The area of a triangle is $A = \frac{1}{2} \cdot b \cdot h$

   What is the area of a triangle with a base that is 5 inches and a height that is 4 inches?

2. The area of a rectangle is $A = b \cdot h$
   What is the area of a rectangle with a base of 3 cm and a height of 9 cm?

3. The area of a square is $A = s^2$
   What is the area of a square with a side measurement of 10 cm?

4. The area of a parallelogram is $A = b \cdot h$
   What is the base of a parallelogram with an area of 48 square inches and a height of 8 inches?

Activity 3

Tell what should go in Card 3 by analyzing the patterns in the pattern cards.

1. How many hearts should be in Card 3?

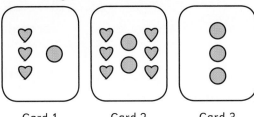

Card 1   Card 2   Card 3

2. How many squares should be in Card 3?

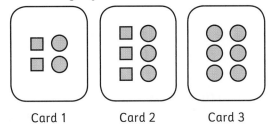

Card 1   Card 2   Card 3

3. How many triangles should be in Card 3?

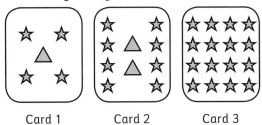

Card 1   Card 2   Card 3

Activity 4 • Distributed Practice

Solve.

1. $31.2 \cdot 0.2$

2. $\frac{4}{9} + \frac{1}{7}$

3. $560.05 - 388.97$

4. $\frac{1}{4} + \frac{1}{2} + \frac{1}{3}$

5. $36.6 \div 0.6$

6. $\frac{4}{9} \cdot \frac{1}{7}$

7. $\frac{10}{12} - \frac{1}{3}$

8. $129.05 + 334.99 + 827.49 + 600.11$

Problem Solving:
▸Solving Word Problems Using Proportions

▸Proportions

Vocabulary

proportion

What are proportions?

In Lesson 4, we looked at common ratios. One of these ratios was used in a recipe. If we want to make more than what the recipe is for, we can double or triple the amounts in the recipe. For example, the instructions at right are on the side of a box of pancake mix.

Following this recipe, there is only enough for two people. To have enough for two more people, more batter is needed. The recipe needs to be doubled. We use a **proportion** to determine the amount of milk and mix needed for the larger batch. A proportion is two ratios that are equal.

Pancakes
1 cup milk
2 cups mix

Serves 2.

Example 1 shows how we use a proportion to double this recipe.

Example 1

Determine the amount of each ingredient needed to double the recipe.

We start with the ratio for the recipe:

$$\frac{\text{Milk}}{\text{Mix}} \qquad \frac{1C}{2C}$$

Multiply the numerator by 2 and the denominator by 2. The ratios, $\frac{1}{2}$ and $\frac{2}{4}$, are equal because we are multiplying by a fraction equal to 1. It's easy to see that the amount of milk doubled and the amount of mix doubled.

$$\frac{\text{Milk}}{\text{Mix}} \qquad \frac{1C}{2C} \cdot \frac{2}{2} = \frac{2C}{4C}$$

The proportion is written with the two equal ratios connected by an equal sign.

$$\frac{1C}{2C} = \frac{2C}{4C}$$

Another good place to use proportions is with pattern cards. If the pattern is a multiplication pattern, it may be represented with a proportion.

Example 2

Write a proportion to demonstrate the multiplication pattern shown in the pattern cards.

How many diamonds should there be in Card 3?

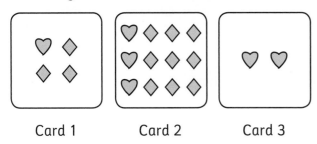

Card 1   Card 2   Card 3

We begin this problem by analyzing the first two cards to find the pattern. It helps to organize the information in a table to keep it straight.

Card	Hearts	Diamonds
1	1	3
2	3	9
3	2	?

We write the ratios for Card 1 and Card 2 this way.

Card 1 $\dfrac{\text{Hearts}}{\text{Diamonds}}$ $\dfrac{1}{3}$

Card 2 $\dfrac{\text{Hearts}}{\text{Diamonds}}$ $\dfrac{3}{9}$

The multiplication pattern is "times 3."

$$\dfrac{\text{Hearts}}{\text{Diamonds}} \qquad \dfrac{1}{3} \cdot \dfrac{3}{3} = \dfrac{3}{9}$$

The proportion is:

$$\dfrac{1}{3} = \dfrac{3}{9}$$

We can also use a proportion to find out how many diamonds need to go in Card 3.

$$\frac{\text{Hearts}}{\text{Diamonds}} \qquad \frac{1}{3} = \frac{2}{x}$$

hearts in Card 3

diamonds in Card 3

We use a variable to represent the unknown part. We now examine the proportion to see what we need to multiply by.

We ask ourselves, $1 \cdot ? = 2$?

The answer is 2. We multiply $\frac{1}{3}$ by $\frac{2}{2}$.

$$\frac{\text{Hearts}}{\text{Diamonds}} \qquad \frac{1}{3} \cdot \frac{2}{2} = \frac{2}{6}$$

We set the ratios equal to one another to write the proportion:

$$\frac{\text{Hearts}}{\text{Diamonds}} \qquad \frac{1}{3} = \frac{2}{6}$$

There should be 6 diamonds in Card 3.

Sometimes we are asked to find cards that have a proportional relationship in the pattern. Example 3 shows how to determine which cards are proportional.

Example 3

Determine which two cards represent a proportional relationship.

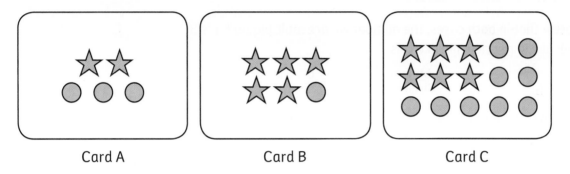

Card A   Card B   Card C

We analyze the numbers of stars and circles on the cards and organize the information in a table to keep it straight.

Card	Stars	Circles
A	2	3
B	5	1
C	6	9

We need to determine which cards are related to each other by multiplication. If we compare the stars in Cards A and B, we are comparing 2 and 5. Is there a multiplication relationship? No.

Card	Stars
A	2
B	5

This is not a multiplication relationship.

When we compare the stars in Cards A and C, we are comparing 2 and 6. Is there a multiplication relationship? Yes.

$2 \cdot 3 = 6$

Card	Stars
A	2
C	6

This is a multiplication relationship.

We know that the stars are proportional in Cards A and C. Let's see if the circles are proportional. Is there a multiplication relationship? Yes.

$3 \cdot 3 = 9$

Card	Circles
A	3
C	9

This is a multiplication relationship.

Notice that in both cases, the number we are multiplying by is 3. We look at the relationship like this:

$$\frac{\text{Stars}}{\text{Circles}} \qquad \frac{2}{3} \cdot \frac{3}{3} = \frac{6}{9}$$

We have found the proportional cards. The proportion looks like this:

$$\frac{\text{Stars}}{\text{Circles}} \qquad \frac{2}{3} = \frac{6}{9}$$

Card A is proportional to Card C.

Sometimes we are given proportions with just one missing part. The missing part is represented by a variable. We have to find the value of the variable. This is not difficult to do because we know that proportions are always multiplication relationships.

Example 4

Find the missing part in the proportion.

$$\frac{3}{8} = \frac{x}{16}$$

The missing part is represented by the variable x. We need to find the value of x. Identify the proportional parts that are known, 8 and 16. Ask, "What times 8 equals 16?" The answer is 2. Now multiply 3 and 2 to figure out x: $3 \cdot 2 = 6$

Substitute the value 6 for the variable x.

$$\frac{3}{8} = \frac{6}{16}$$

POWER CONCEPT

Proportions are relationships between ratios that are based on multiplication.

%÷ **Apply Skills**
<x Turn to *Interactive Text*,
page 62.

mBook **Reinforce Understanding**
Use the *mBook Study Guide*
to review lesson concepts.

▶**Problem Solving: Solving Word Problems Using Proportions**

How do we solve word problems using proportions?

Proportions are very helpful in solving some types of word problems. Remember that proportions work for multiplication relationships.

Example 1 shows how to use a proportion to help solve a word problem.

Example 1

Solve the word problem.

Problem:

A factory wants to paint one of its buildings dark green. The instructions for mixing the dark green paint call for 1 gallon of yellow paint and 5 gallons of blue paint. This is only enough for one side of the building. How much of each color paint will the factory need in order to mix enough paint for all four sides of the building?

What is the problem asking for?
It is asking, "How much paint is needed for all four sides of the building?"

What do we know?
We know the ratio of yellow paint to blue paint is 1 to 5. That is enough to paint one side of the building. We need four times that amount to paint all four sides.

$$\frac{\text{Yellow Paint}}{\text{Blue Paint}} \qquad \frac{1}{5} \cdot \frac{4}{4} = \frac{4}{20}$$

The proportion is:

$$\frac{\text{Yellow Paint}}{\text{Blue Paint}} \qquad \frac{1 \text{ gallon}}{5 \text{ gallons}} = \frac{4 \text{ gallons}}{20 \text{ gallons}}$$

The factory will need to buy 4 gallons of yellow paint and 20 gallons of blue paint.

In the next example, we are given a problem that can be solved by setting up a proportion with a variable. We need to find the missing part of the proportion. We find the value of the variable by examining the problem to see what we need to multiply by.

Example 2

Solve the word problem.

Problem:

Mrs. Horton needs to distribute 2 rubber bands and 3 paper clips to each student for the science experiment. She figures that she will need 60 paper clips. How many rubber bands will she need?

Begin by setting up a proportion that represents the problem. Use a variable for the missing part of the proportion.

$$\frac{\text{Rubber Bands}}{\text{Paper Clips}} \qquad \frac{2}{3} = \frac{x}{60}$$

Now we have the proportion set up. Analyze the numbers to find the multiplication pattern. What times 3 equals 60? The answer is 20.

We multiply by 20: $2 \cdot 20 = 40$.

Replace the x with 40.

$$\frac{\text{Rubber Bands}}{\text{Paper Clips}} \qquad \frac{2}{3} = \frac{40}{60}$$

$x = 40$

The number of rubber bands needed is 40.

Problem-Solving Activity
Turn to *Interactive Text*, page 63.

mBook Reinforce Understanding
Use the *mBook Study Guide* to review lesson concepts.

Homework

Activity 1

Tell the value of the variable.

1. $a + 80 = 170$
2. $270 \div b = 90$
3. $40 \cdot 5 = c$
4. $d - 120 = 150$
5. $e \cdot 70 = 560$
6. $f \div 8 = 90$

Activity 2

Tell the missing value in each of the proportions.

1. $\frac{3}{4} = \frac{x}{8}$
2. $\frac{4}{5} = \frac{12}{y}$
3. $\frac{1}{3} = \frac{w}{15}$
4. $\frac{5}{w} = \frac{15}{24}$

Activity 3

Tell which two pattern cards in each set represent a proportional relationship. Then tell the proportion.

1. Which two cards are proportional? What is the proportion?

   Card 1   Card 2   Card 3

2. Which two cards are proportional? What is the proportion?

 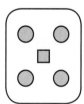

   Card 1   Card 2   Card 3

3. Which two cards are proportional? What is the proportion?

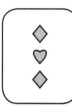 

   Card 1   Card 2   Card 3

Activity 4 • Distributed Practice

Solve.

1. $\frac{4}{8} \cdot \frac{1}{3}$
2. $290.04 + 109.67$
3. $\frac{3}{8} - \frac{1}{4}$
4. $1.23 + 2.37 + 4.09 + 3.11$

▶Translating Word Statements Into Number Statements

Problem Solving:
▶More Proportions With Variables

▷**Translating Word Statements Into Number Statements**

How do we translate word statements into addition and subtraction number statements?

When working with variables, we focused on numbers and substitution. Now we will use variables to translate word statements into number statements. Here is an example of how to use a variable to translate a word statement into a number statement.

Example 1

Translate the word statement into a number statement.

Word Statement:

Jenni is 5 years older than her brother Marshall.

STEP 1
Assign a variable to key words.
We will use the variable M to represent Marshall's age, and the variable J to represent Jenni's age.

M = Marshall's age

J = Jenni's age

STEP 2
Determine what operation is being used.
The word statement tells us that Jenni is 5 years older than Marshall. How can we write "5 years older" using numbers? It is "+ 5." We are using addition.

STEP 3
Write the number statement.
$J = M + 5$

We should stop and ask ourselves if the statement makes sense. Marshall's age plus 5 equals Jenni's age. Is that the same as "Jenni is 5 years older than her brother Marshall?" Yes, it is the same.

These steps show us how to set up a general number statement about their ages. What if we want to know how old Jenni is, and we are told that Marshall is 12 years old?

Example 2 shows how to substitute numbers into the number statement to get a specific instance of the pattern.

Example 2

Translate the word statement into a number statement to show a general pattern.

Word Statement:

How old is Jenni when Marshall is 12 years old?

Begin with the general number statement: $J = M + 5$

To find Jenni's age when Marshall is 12, substitute 12 for M.

$$J = M + 5$$

$$\downarrow$$

$$J = 12 + 5$$

Substituting the numbers in the equation, we see that Jenni is 17 years old when Marshall is 12 years old.

In this specific instance of the general pattern, Marshall is 12 and Jenni is 17. Let's think about how this information will change in a year. Each person will be one year older—Marshall will be 13 and Jenni will be 18. That is a different example of the general pattern. Does our general number statement still work? Let's try it.

$$J = M + 5$$

$$\downarrow$$

$$J = 13 + 5$$

Yes, Jenni will be 18 when Marshall is 13.

A person's age is something that changes. This is the type of situation where a general pattern can be described with a variable. We substitute a number each time we want to know the values for a specific example of the general pattern. In this instance, it was finding a person's age when we know the other person's age.

Let's look at another situation where something changes. Students are commonly required to attend school 180 days a year. The number of days until the end of the school year changes as the days go by. If x = the day number and y = the number of days left, then the general number statement looks like this: $180 - x = y$.

Example 3 shows how to use the general statement to find how many days are left in the school year.

Example 3

Translate the word problem into a number statement using a variable where something changes.

Problem:

How many days of school are left on Day 1? On Day 10? And on Day 100?

On Day 1: $180 - x = y$

$180 - 1 = 179$ There are 179 days left.

On Day 10: $180 - x = y$

$180 - 10 = 170$ There are 170 days left.

On Day 100: $180 - x = y$

$180 - 100 = 80$ There are 80 days left.

The two general number statements we have examined so far have represented addition and subtraction relationships. We used $M + 5$ to represent the relationship between Jenni's age and Marshall's age. We used $180 - x$ to determine how many school days are left on any given day of the school year. We can write number statements that involve multiplication and division relationships as well.

How do we translate a word statement into a multiplication number statement?

Example 1 shows a general number statement about a multiplication relationship.

Example 1

Translate the word problem into a multiplication number statement.

Problem:

Each student is required to have two lockers in the school building— one for books and one for athletic gear for gym class. Write a general number statement that describes the number of lockers that are being used in the building. If there are 900 students in the school, how many lockers are in use?

STEP 1
Assign a variable to key words.

- The number of students = the variable s.
- The number of lockers = the variable n.

STEP 2
Determine what operation is being used.
This is a multiplication relationship. For every student there are 2 times as many lockers. We can represent this as $2 \cdot s$.

STEP 3
Write the number statement.

number of lockers			number of students

$$n \quad = \quad 2 \quad \cdot \quad s$$

This statement tells us that there are always "two times as many lockers as there are students."

STEP 4

Substitute values for the variables and solve.

Now we substitute values for the variables. If there are 900 students in the building, we calculate the number of lockers in use like this:

$$n = 2 \cdot s$$

$$1{,}800 = 2 \cdot 900$$

There are 1,800 lockers in use at the school.

It's important that we read these problems carefully and understand what relationship we are representing. Let's see how we can avoid making one common mistake.

Improve Your Skills

A student translated the word statement below into a number statement.

Word Statement:

There are four times as many students on campus as there are teachers.

We will use these variables to represent the statement:

s = students t = teachers

The student wrote the number sentence $4 \cdot s = t$. **ERROR**

> This statement represents the exact opposite situation—there are four times as many teachers as students.

Here is the correct way to represent this statement: $4 \cdot t$. **CORRECT**

> This statement tells us that there are four times as many students as teachers.

Translating word statements accurately into number statements is a very important skill in everyday life and in higher-level math classes.

> A common mistake is to write the number sentence in the order of the words.

%÷ Apply Skills
=× Turn to *Interactive Text*, page 65.

mBook Reinforce Understanding
Use the *mBook Study Guide* to review lesson concepts.

▶Problem Solving: **More Proportions With Variables**

How do we show proportional relationships?

We have explored how to use variables to show proportional relationships. Let's review how to show proportional relationships using pattern cards.

Example 1

Draw pattern cards that show this proportional relationship:

$$\frac{\text{Stars}}{\text{Moons}} \qquad \frac{3}{1} = \frac{6}{y}$$

Begin by analyzing the multiplication relationship in the proportion. Compare 3 and 6. What are we multiplying by?

> Remember, proportions are relationships between numbers that are based on multiplication.

We are multiplying by 2: $3 \cdot 2 = 6$.

We multiply the number of moons by 2 as well: $1 \cdot 2 = 2$.

Substitute the value 2 for the variable y. The complete proportion looks like this:

$$\frac{\text{Stars}}{\text{Moons}} \qquad \frac{3}{1} = \frac{6}{2}$$

Now we can draw the pattern cards.

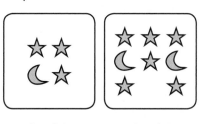

Card A   Card B

Problem-Solving Activity
Turn to *Interactive Text*, page 67.

mBook Reinforce Understanding
Use the *mBook Study Guide* to review lesson concepts.

Activity 1

Fill in the value for the variable.

1. $x \cdot 7 = 42$
2. $56 \div n = 8$
3. $12 - w = 9$
4. $8 + 7 = y$
5. $z - 5 = 7$
6. $b \div 8 = 6$
7. $c - 8 = 7$
8. $15 = 6 + d$

Activity 2

Select the number statement that matches the word statement.

1. Mack is 3 years older than Jake. If M is Mack's age and J is Jake's age, then
   (a) $M = 3 + J$
   (b) $J = 3 + M$
   (c) $J = 3 - M$

2. There are two times as many girls as boys in history class. If x is the number of girls and y is the number of boys, then
   (a) $2 \cdot x = y$
   (b) $2 \cdot y = x$
   (c) $y = x \cdot 2$

3. There is a 10 point difference between the lowest score and the highest score on the test. If a is the highest score and f is the lowest score, then
   (a) $f = a + 10$
   (b) $f - 10 = a$
   (c) $a - 10 = f$

4. Christy is 10 years younger than Jim. If C is Christy's age and J is Jim's age, which of the following demonstrates Jim's age?
   (a) $J = C + 10$
   (b) $C = J + 10$
   (c) $C - 10 = J$

Activity 3

For each set of pattern cards, tell how many hearts should be drawn on Card B.

1. $\dfrac{\text{Diamonds}}{\text{Hearts}}\ \dfrac{2}{1}=\dfrac{4}{x}$

   Card A   Card B

2. $\dfrac{\text{Squares}}{\text{Hearts}}\ \dfrac{1}{3}=\dfrac{3}{y}$

   Card A   Card B

3. $\dfrac{\text{Triangles}}{\text{Hearts}}\ \dfrac{4}{5}=\dfrac{12}{z}$

   Card A   Card B

4. $\dfrac{\text{Stars}}{\text{Hearts}}\ \dfrac{3}{2}=\dfrac{6}{m}$

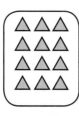

   Card A   Card B

Activity 4 • Distributed Practice

Solve.

1. $2.13 \cdot 0.11$

2. $\dfrac{4}{5}+\dfrac{3}{10}$

3. $\dfrac{11}{12}-\dfrac{2}{3}$

4. $\dfrac{1}{6}+\dfrac{2}{3}+\dfrac{1}{8}$

5. $72.8 \div 0.8$

6. $3.99 \cdot 0.01$

7. $\dfrac{4}{9}-\dfrac{1}{3}$

8. $\dfrac{1}{3} \div \dfrac{3}{5}$

▶**Translating Number Statements Into Word Statements**

How do we translate a number statement into a word statement?

In the previous lesson, we looked at translating a word statement into a number statement. Sometimes it helps us gain a deeper understanding of a concept if we look at the reverse—translating number statements into word statements.

Let's translate the following number statement.

$A = 5 \cdot B$

Steps for Translating Number Statements Into Word Statements

STEP 1

Examine the relationship that is being represented.

Do this by stating the numbers in a general word form:

Something is five times more than something else.

STEP 2

Think of a situation where this statement might apply.

There are many different situations that could be represented by this number statement. We will use pattern cards as an example.

STEP 3

Assign the variables to objects that can be counted.

A will represent the number of stars on Card A.

B will represent the number of stars on Card B.

STEP 4

Think of numbers that might work to replace the variables.

In this number statement, it is easier for us to choose a value for *B* first since it is the number being multiplied.

Let's say $B = 2$.

If this is true, then $A = 10$.

$A = 5 \cdot B$

$10 = 5 \cdot 2$

STEP 5

Use pictures to see if the numbers make sense.

Card A   Card B

STEP 6

Write the word statement that describes the picture.

There are five times as many stars on Card A as there are on Card B.

Our word statement now matches the number statement.

Translating number statements to word statements is all about understanding the relationships between numbers and variables. Remember that there are many different situations that could be represented by a single number statement. Let's look at another example with a different type of situation.

Example 1 demonstrates a word statement for the number statement $m = k + 3$.

Notice that the relationship is an addition relationship. This will require a little different thinking than the last example.

Example 1

Write two different word statements that can be described by the number statement $m = k + 3$.

Word Statement 1:

Suppose m is Enrico's age and k is Carmen's age.

When we make a word statement, we may have to change the order of the variables and numbers. We see this below.

Enrico is 3 years older than Carmen.

Does this statement make sense? Yes, $m = k + 3$.

Word Statement 2:

Let's say every time we take the school bus to another school for a game, there needs to be 3 adults. How many people are on the bus?

Let m = the number of people on the bus.

Let k = the number of players on the bus.

Would the statement $m = k + 3$ represent this situation? Let's write the statement as a word statement and analyze it.

The total number of people on the bus is the number of players plus 3 adults.

Is the total number of people (m) equal to the number of players (k) plus 3 adults? Yes.

This word statement is represented by the number statement $m = k + 3$.

Reversing a process helps us make sure we answer the statement correctly.

While it is less common to be asked to translate numbers to words in this way, it is still a good skill to practice. Mainly, it gives us flexibility in thinking about statements using variables.

Apply Skills
Turn to *Interactive Text*, page 69.

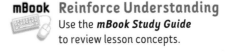
mBook Reinforce Understanding
Use the *mBook Study Guide* to review lesson concepts.

▶Problem Solving: **Identifying Proportions**

How do we identify proportions?

The most important idea to remember with proportions is that they represent multiplication relationships. Let's look at some pattern cards and identify which ones represent proportional relationships.

Example 1 demonstrates how to recognize proportions. There are five pattern cards but only two of them are proportional. Remember, we are looking for the multiplication relationships.

Example 1

Examine the pattern cards and identify which are proportional.

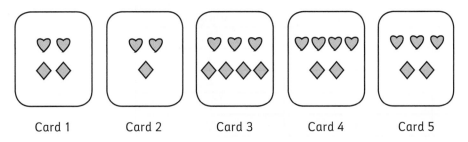

| Card 1 | Card 2 | Card 3 | Card 4 | Card 5 |

A good place to start is to look at the ratio of hearts to diamonds for each card. Then create a table or chart.

Card	Hearts	Diamonds
1	2	2
2	2	1
3	3	4
4	4	2
5	3	2

Next, we look for the proportional relationships. In other words, we look for multiplication relationships—hearts compared to hearts, diamonds compared to diamonds.

This is a complex comparison because there are so many cards. The best way to start is to look for numbers that may have a multiplication relationship. In this list, Cards 2 and 4 could represent multiplication relationships, but Cards 3 and 5 do not have a multiplication relationship with the other numbers (nothing times 2 equals 3, nothing times 3 equals 4).

We eliminate Cards 3 and 5. Cards 1, 2, and 4 remain.

Card	Hearts	Diamonds
1	2	2
2	2	1
3	3	4
4	4	2
5	3	2

Is there a proportional relationship between the remaining cards?

Compare Cards 1 and 2.

$$\frac{\text{Hearts}}{\text{Diamonds}} \qquad \frac{2}{2} \qquad \frac{2}{1}$$

Is this a proportional relationship? The hearts are but the diamonds are not: $2 \cdot 1 = 2$ but $2 \cdot 1$ does not equal 1. No, this is not a proportional relationship.

Compare Cards 1 and 4.

$$\frac{\text{Hearts}}{\text{Diamonds}} \qquad \frac{2}{2} \qquad \frac{4}{2}$$

Is this a proportional relationship? The hearts are but the diamonds are not: $2 \cdot 2 = 4$ but $2 \cdot 2$ does not equal 2.

Compare Cards 2 and 4.

$$\frac{\text{Hearts}}{\text{Diamonds}} \qquad \frac{2}{1} \qquad \frac{4}{2}$$

Is this a proportional relationship? The hearts are: $2 \cdot 2 = 4$. And the diamonds are: $1 \cdot 2 = 2$. We found the proportion.

Card 2 and Card 4 are proportional. The proportion is written like this:

$$\frac{\text{Hearts}}{\text{Diamonds}} \qquad \frac{2}{1} = \frac{4}{2}$$

This is a complex process. We must work slowly and carefully, comparing one pair of cards at a time. Remember to begin by eliminating any cards that obviously do not have a multiplication relationship. In Example 1 above, it was the cards with three hearts. This will change from one situation to the next. We have to analyze the cards we are working with carefully.

Problem-Solving Activity
Turn to *Interactive Text*, page 70.

mBook Reinforce Understanding
Use the *mBook Study Guide*
to review lesson concepts.

Activity 1

Tell the value of the variable that represents the missing part in each proportion.

1. $\frac{2}{3} = \frac{x}{12}$

2. $\frac{3}{4} = \frac{9}{y}$

3. $\frac{4}{w} = \frac{16}{20}$

4. $\frac{z}{5} = \frac{4}{10}$

5. $\frac{5}{b} = \frac{30}{36}$

6. $\frac{m}{10} = \frac{80}{100}$

Activity 2

Select the word statement that best matches the number statement.

1. $3 \cdot x = r$

   If x is the number of teachers and r is the number of students, then

   (a) There are 3 times as many teachers as students.

   (b) There are 3 more teachers than students.

   (c) There are 3 times as many students as teachers.

2. $a = b + 4$

   If a is Marius' age and b is Kyle's age, then

   (a) Marius is 4 years older than Kyle.

   (b) Kyle is 4 years older than Marius.

   (c) Marius is 4 times older than Kyle.

3. $m - 5 = n$

   If m is the number of points Zach scored and n is the number of points Larry scored, then

   (a) Zach scored 5 less points than Larry.

   (b) Larry scored 5 more points than Zach.

   (c) Zach scored 5 more points than Larry.

Activity 3

Tell which two cards represent a proportional relationship. Then write the proportion.

1. Which two cards are proportional? Write the proportion.

| Card 1 | Card 2 | Card 3 | Card 4 | Card 5 |

2. Which two cards are proportional? Write the proportion.

 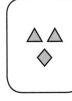

| Card 1 | Card 2 | Card 3 | Card 4 | Card 5 |

3. Which two cards are proportional? Write the proportion.

| Card 1 | Card 2 | Card 3 | Card 4 | Card 5 |

Activity 4 • Distributed Practice

Solve.

1. $\frac{5}{8} \cdot \frac{1}{3}$

2. $29.71 + 32.85$

3. $209.01 - 166.98$

4. $12.85 + 13.97 + 14.01 + 15.76$

5. $\frac{5}{9} \div \frac{1}{9}$

6. $12.1 \cdot 0.2$

7. $\frac{4}{3} - \frac{1}{2}$

8. $248.8 \div 0.02$

▶**Problem Solving: Using Proportions in Geometry**

What is similarity?

Proportions play a role in geometry. Look at the pattern in the figure below. Notice that each triangle is bigger than the triangle inside of it.

We may not see it right away, but the triangles are proportional. Each bigger triangle has sides that are bigger by a constant amount.

Look carefully at the numbers in the table. They show the lengths of the base and height of each triangle. There is a pattern.

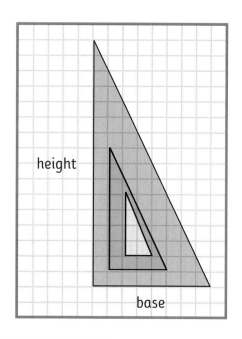

Triangle	Base	Height
Yellow	2 units	4 units
Red	4 units	8 units
Purple	8 units	16 units

It is easier to see the pattern if we write the numbers as the ratio of base to height and then compare the ratios.

Triangle	Yellow	Red	Purple
Base / Height	$\frac{2}{4}$	$\frac{4}{8}$	$\frac{8}{16}$

These ratios are all equal. They represent proportions.

Example 1 shows how we know they are proportional.

Example 1

Set up equivalent fractions to show that the triangles are proportional.

The dimensions of the yellow triangle are proportional to the dimensions of the red triangle. Each part is two times bigger.

Here are the equivalent fractions:

$$\frac{\text{Base}}{\text{Height}} \qquad \overset{\text{Yellow}}{\frac{2}{4}} \quad \cdot \quad \frac{2}{2} \quad = \quad \overset{\text{Red}}{\frac{4}{8}}$$

The dimensions of the red triangle are proportional to the dimensions of the purple triangle. Each part is two times bigger.

Here are the equivalent fractions:

$$\frac{\text{Base}}{\text{Height}} \qquad \overset{\text{Red}}{\frac{4}{8}} \quad \cdot \quad \frac{2}{2} \quad = \quad \overset{\text{Purple}}{\frac{8}{16}}$$

The dimensions of the yellow triangle are proportional to the dimensions of the purple triangle. Each part is four times bigger.

Here are the equivalent fractions:

$$\frac{\text{Base}}{\text{Height}} \qquad \overset{\text{Yellow}}{\frac{2}{4}} \quad \cdot \quad \frac{4}{4} \quad = \quad \overset{\text{Purple}}{\frac{8}{16}}$$

Proportion is an important idea in geometry. When an object is bigger in every way by the same proportional amount, the objects are similar. The yellow, red, and purple triangles are all similar triangles.

For example, in the triangles, each side in the red triangle is two times bigger than that side in the yellow triangle. The sides are proportional.

Because each side is two times bigger, we have a scaling factor of 2.

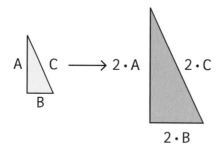

Comparing the yellow triangle to the purple triangle, we see that each side in the purple triangle is four times bigger than in the yellow triangle. The sides are proportional.

Because each side is four times bigger, we have a scaling factor of 4.

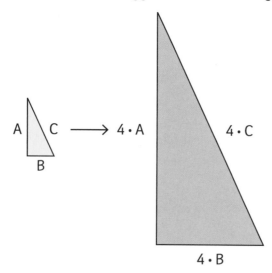

We call these three triangles similar triangles. Their sides are proportional.

How do we draw similar shapes?

When we draw similar shapes, we have to make sure that the dimensions are proportional. That means one shape should be drawn "a certain number of times" bigger or smaller than the other shape.

Example 1 demonstrates how to draw a similar shape that is larger than the original shape.

Example 1

Draw a shape that is similar to Shape M.

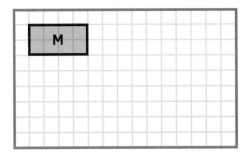

First, figure out the dimensions of Shape M.

    Shape M:

      Height = 2

      Base = 4

Once we know the dimensions of the shape, we can draw a shape that is similar. This new shape can be bigger or smaller.

In order to find a similar shape, we make a shape that is "x times bigger or smaller." Let's make a shape with sides that are two times bigger than Shape M.

To do this we multiply the base and the height of Shape M by 2.

The dimensions of Shape N will be:
Height = 2 · 2 = 4
Base = 4 · 2 = 8

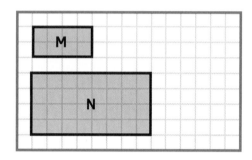

The dimensions are 4 by 8. We can write a proportion to show that the shapes are similar.

	Shape M		Shape N
Height	$\frac{2}{4}$	$=$	$\frac{4}{8}$
Base			

Shape M is similar to Shape N. The scaling factor is 2.

To make a similar shape that is larger, we multiplied the base and height by the same number.

We can also draw similar shapes that are smaller than the original shape.

Example 2

Draw a shape with sides that are three times smaller than Shape X. Identify the dimensions and the scaling factor.

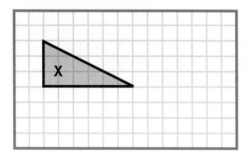

First, we figure out the dimensions of Shape X.

Shape X:

Height = 3

Base = 6

To make a shape with sides that are three times smaller, we have to think about the multiplication relationships.

$? \cdot 3 = 6$ and $? \cdot 3 = 3$

Then, we fill in the blanks. We will call this Shape Y.

$2 \cdot 3 = 6$ and $1 \cdot 3 = 3$

Shape Y:

Height = 1

Base = 2

We write a proportion to show that the shapes are similar.

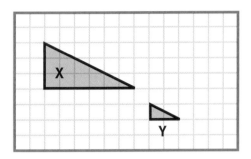

	Shape X		Shape Y
$\dfrac{\text{Height}}{\text{Base}}$	$\dfrac{3}{6}$	$=$	$\dfrac{1}{2}$

The scaling factor is the number we use to multiply or divide the numbers in the original ratio.

The scaling factor is 3.

Speaking of Math

Here is how you can explain your thinking when you are comparing proportional shapes:

- *First, I use the dimensions of each shape to write a ratio for the shapes.*
- *Next, I check the ratios to see if there is a multiplication relationship between the ratios.*
- *If there is a multiplication relationship, then I can find the scaling factor between the similar shapes.*

Problem-Solving Activity
Turn to *Interactive Text*, page 72.

mBook Reinforce Understanding
Use the *mBook Study Guide* to review lesson concepts.

Activity 1

Write the missing number in each proportion.

1. $\frac{3}{6} = \frac{1}{x}$

2. $\frac{4}{8} = \frac{8}{y}$

3. $\frac{w}{5} = \frac{9}{15}$

4. $\frac{1}{4} = \frac{z}{12}$

5. $\frac{6}{9} = \frac{2}{a}$

6. $\frac{2}{c} = \frac{4}{20}$

Activity 2

Tell the dimensions of the similar shapes described in each problem.

Model   A triangle has a base of 3 units and a height of 5 units. What are the dimensions of a similar triangle with sides that are twice the size?

Answer: The base is 3 · 2, or 6 units, and the height is 5 · 2, or 10 units.

1. A square is 3 centimeters by 3 centimeters. What are the dimensions of a similar square with sides that are three times that size?

2. A rectangle is 4 inches by 8 inches. What are the dimensions of a similar rectangle with sides that are twice the size?

3. A triangle has a base of 2 centimeters and a height of 4 centimeters. What are the dimensions of a similar triangle with sides that are four times that size?

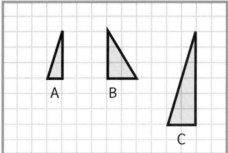

Activity 3

Tell which two shapes are similar and write the proportion. What is the scaling factor?

Activity 4 • Distributed Practice

Solve.

1. $\frac{3}{2} \cdot \frac{5}{4}$

2. $1.99 + 30.7$

3. $10.44 - 8.57$

4. $12.6 \div 0.2$

5. $\frac{8}{4} \div \frac{2}{1}$

6. $1.2 \cdot 8.4$

7. $\frac{3}{4} - \frac{1}{2}$

8. $1.25 + 3.75 + 2.9$

▶**Problem Solving: Figuring Out the Formula**

How do we find the formula from a set of data?

We have looked at formulas for computing the area, perimeter, or circumference of geometric shapes. There are many different kinds of formulas that we use every day. There are interest formulas, discounts, tips, tax, and many others.

Example 1 demonstrates how to use a formula for finding a discount amount.

Example 1

Calculate the discount on a $60 pair of jeans that are 25 percent off.

The formula is $D = 0.25 \cdot R$.

R = regular price

D = discount

We are given the regular price in the problem, $R = 60$.

We substitute 60 for R in the problem:

$D = 0.25 \cdot R$

$\downarrow$

$D = 0.25 \cdot 60$

$D = 15$

The discount on the jeans is $15.

When we know the cost of the item and the percent of discount, it's easy to compute the discount using this formula. This is one way we use algebra in our everyday lives. But, in some situations, we do not know the formula and need to figure it out by analyzing patterns in the data we are given.

One example of this is a cell phone bill. If we get the bill and look it over, all we see are descriptions of services, subtotals, and totals. We are not given the formulas for computing the charges. We just know the bottom line of how much we owe for each service and the total cost.

Let's take a look at how Jack Reed, Ace Detective, came up with a formula to understand one of these charges.

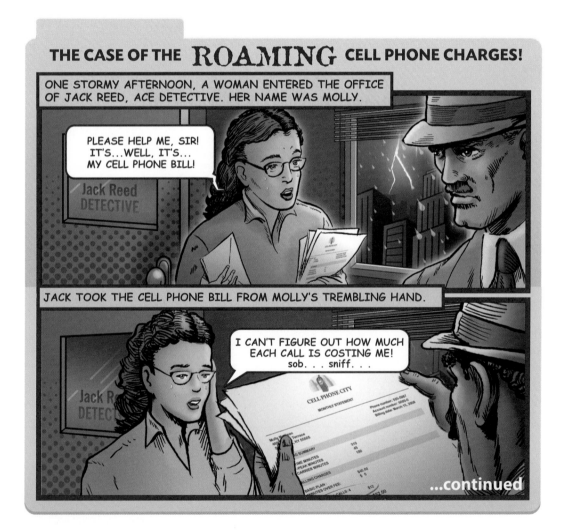

It's not always easy to see the pattern in a formula. Sometimes we need to look for things that have been added, subtracted, multiplied or divided. Jack Reed, Ace Detective, needed to multiply to write the formula and figure out roaming charges. Sometimes we might have to use more than one operation to create the formula.

Let's look at another situation that involves writing a formula that uses more than one operation.

Mrs. Bradshaw, Intergalactic Soccer Mom, was in charge of the fundraising effort for her daughter's soccer team. Her job was to count the money earned from the latest fundraiser— $5 raffle tickets.

Scanning the record sheet, she was surprised by the amounts recorded by each girl.

Player's Name	Number of Tickets	Amount Collected
Rebecca	5	$20
Brianna	10	$45
Stacy	7	$30
Tamara	5	$20
Lauren	15	$70
Rochelle	12	$55
Louisa	20	$95
Tyra	25	$120

Marcia, Marcia! The amount collected by each girl doesn't add up!

The tickets were $5 each. The amount collected by each girl should have been 5x, where x is the number of tickets sold. But this was not the case.

These examples show us just how powerful variables are in math sentences. There is much more flexibility in working problems this way. This is important as we learn about using algebra in real-life situations because we are not always given the same information in every problem we solve. Sometimes we just substitute numbers into a formula. Other times we look at the data for a pattern and generalize it in order to come up with the formula.

 **Problem-Solving Activity**
Turn to *Interactive Text*, page 76.

 Monitoring Progress
Quiz 2

 **mBook** **Reinforce Understanding**
Use the *mBook Study Guide* to review lesson concepts.

Activity 1

Select the best translation for each statement.

1. Matthew's roaming charges are $3 for every call made out of the area. If x is the total amount due for roaming charges and c is the number of calls made out of the area, then
   (a) $3 = x \cdot c$
   (b) $x = 3 \cdot c$
   (c) $3 \cdot x = c$

2. Members of the gym pay $\frac{1}{2}$ the amount of what nonmembers pay for using the gym. If y is the cost for members and z is the cost for nonmembers, then
   (a) $y = z + \frac{1}{2}$
   (b) $y - \frac{1}{2} = z$
   (c) $z \cdot \frac{1}{2} = y$

3. $A = 3 \cdot B$
   If A and B are similar shapes, then
   (a) A is 3 times bigger than B.
   (b) B is 3 more than A.
   (c) A is 3 less than B.

Activity 2

Give dimensions for a similar shape in each problem.

1. Shape A is a 2×4 rectangle. Shape B is a similar shape with dimensions $? \times ?$ if the scaling factor is 2.

2. Shape C is a 3×3 square. Shape D is a similar shape with dimensions $? \times ?$ if the scaling factor is 3.

3. Shape W is a 1×2 rectangle. Shape X is a similar shape with dimensions $? \times ?$ if the scaling factor is 10.

Activity 3

Select the correct formula for each problem. Inputs are represented by x and outputs are represented by y.

1. Manuel sold candy bars in his neighborhood for a school fundraiser. The table shows how many bars he sold and how much he collected. If x is the number of bars sold and y is the money collected, which formula represents the data?

Candy Bars Sold	Money Collected
5	$10
6	$12
7	$14
2	$4

   (a) $x = 2 \cdot y$ (b) $y = 2 \cdot x$ (c) $x \cdot y = 2$

2. Franco helps his grandfather pick up apples under the tree in the fall. His grandfather pays him to help. The table shows how many bushels of apples Franco collected and how much money he earned. If x is the number of bushels collected and y is the money Franco earned, which formula represents the data?

Bushels of Apples	Money Earned
8	$4
6	$3
10	$5
2	$1

   (a) $y = x - 4$ (b) $x = y \cdot 2$ (c) $y + 4 = x$

Activity 4 • Distributed Practice

Solve.

1. $\frac{2}{3} \cdot \frac{4}{5}$

2. $19.29 + 3.07$

3. $44.01 - 19.78$

4. $567.85 + 689.97 + 598.01 + 499.76$

5. $\frac{2}{8} \div \frac{1}{4}$

6. $1.11 \cdot 0.9$

7. $\frac{5}{8} - \frac{1}{6}$

8. $0.333 \div 0.3$

▶**Problem Solving: Proportions and Map Reading**

How do we use proportions to find actual distances on a map?

Any time we try to figure out actual distances from a map, we are using proportions. Look at the map of Colorado. Let's figure out how many miles it is to fly directly from one city to another. Flying makes calculations a little easier because we can use straight lines for the distance between two cities.

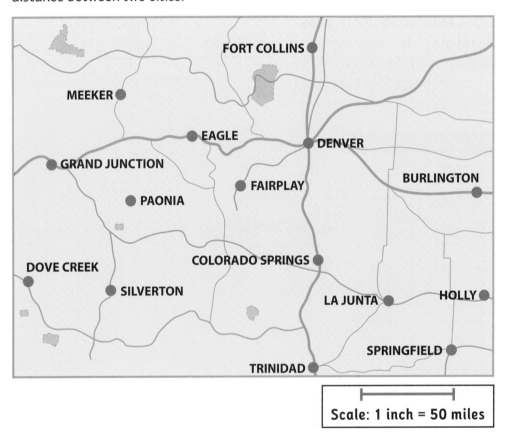

Scale: 1 inch = 50 miles

We have to read the scale carefully when we read a map. Notice that for this map, 1 inch represents 50 miles. This key shows the ratio of inches on the map to actual miles. We use a ruler to measure distances between cities on the map, and calculate the actual distance based on this scale.

Let's figure out how far it is from Denver to Grand Junction.

Example 1 shows how to make a proportion problem out of measurements from the map to calculate this distance.

Example 1

Calculate the distance in miles from Denver to Grand Junction.

When we measure the distance from Denver to Grand Junction on the map, we see it is about 3 inches.

Here are the proportions:

$$\frac{\text{Inches}}{\text{Miles}} \quad \frac{1}{50} = \frac{3}{x}$$

> The miles from Denver to Grand Junction.

The x in the proportion shows that we don't know how many miles it is from Denver to Grand Junction. The distance is the unknown. We solve this problem and calculate the actual distance by finding the value for the variable. We need to multiply by 3.

$$\frac{\text{Inches}}{\text{Miles}} \quad \frac{1}{50} = \frac{3}{x}$$

> Replace x with 50 · 3, or 150.

$x = 150$ miles

The distance from Denver to Grand Junction is 150 miles.

When we use scales on maps, we are actually using proportions. On this map, the scale gives the ratio of inches on the map to actual miles. To figure out an actual distance, use this ratio as part of a proportional problem.

The ratio of inches to miles for this proportion problem is $\frac{1}{50}$.

Example 2 shows how we compute the distance in miles from Grand Junction to Springfield.

Example 2

Compute how far it is in miles from Grand Junction to Springfield.

$$\frac{\text{Inches}}{\text{Miles}} \quad \frac{1}{50} = \frac{5}{x}$$

X = the miles from Grand Junction to Springfield.

Find the value for the variable.

$$\frac{\text{Inches}}{\text{Miles}} \quad \frac{1}{50} = \frac{5}{x}$$

Replace x with $50 \cdot 5$, or 250.

$x = 250$ miles

The distance from Grand Junction to Springfield is 250 miles.

What is a good rule of thumb?

"It's a good rule of thumb" is a common expression. Figuratively, it means that something is good to use as a general guide. But we can actually use our thumbs as an approximate ruler too. From the tip of our thumbs to the first joint is about 1 inch. This isn't an exact measurement because the distance varies from person to person. But the top segment of our thumb is a good tool to use for some purposes— it's a measure that equals about one inch that we always have with us. It can be especially helpful if we are trying to measure actual distances on a road map where there are a lot of twists and turns.

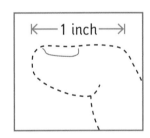

Example 1 shows the distance if we want to hike from Canyon View to Devil's Kitchen. We move our thumbs along the twists and turns of the trail from Canyon View to Devil's Kitchen. The

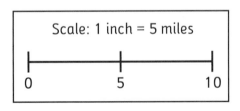

distance is about 3 thumb units, or about 3 inches. Look at the map to find the scale. For this map, 1 inch equals 5 miles. Let's do a proportion.

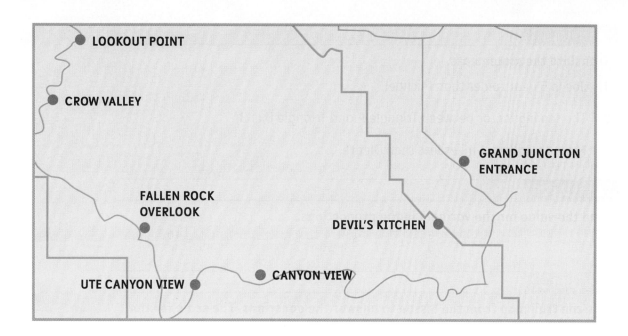

- LOOKOUT POINT
- CROW VALLEY
- GRAND JUNCTION ENTRANCE
- FALLEN ROCK OVERLOOK
- DEVIL'S KITCHEN
- UTE CANYON VIEW
- CANYON VIEW

Example 1

Estimate the actual distance from Canyon View to Devil's Kitchen.

The proportion is:

$$\frac{\text{Inches}}{\text{Miles}} \qquad \frac{1}{5} = \frac{3}{x}$$

> X = the miles from Canyon View to Devil's Kitchen.

Find the value for the variable.

$$\frac{\text{Inches}}{\text{Miles}} \qquad \frac{1}{5} = \frac{3}{x}$$

> Replace x with $5 \cdot 3$ or 15.

$x = 15$ miles

The distance from Canyon View to Devil's Kitchen is about 15 miles.

Maps are a very good place to use proportions. Maps are based on scaling. Scaling is about multiplication relationships.

Proportions are a powerful tool for representing multiplication relationships.

 **Problem-Solving Activity**
Turn to *Interactive Text*, page 79.

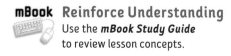 **mBook** **Reinforce Understanding**
Use the *mBook Study Guide*
to review lesson concepts.

Activity 1

Translate the statements.

1. Joe is 5 years older than Michael.

2. The scaling factor between Triangle A and Triangle B is 3.

3. Melinda walked 4 miles less than Diedre.

Activity 2

Find the value for the variable in the proportions.

1. $\frac{1}{50} = \frac{4}{x}$ 2. $\frac{1}{5} = \frac{6}{y}$ 3. $\frac{1}{50} = \frac{8}{z}$ 4. $\frac{1}{5} = \frac{10}{w}$

Activity 3

Use the trail map from the lesson to answer the questions. The scale for the map is 1 inch = 10 miles. Use proportions and equivalent fractions to set up your answer. Be sure to state what the answer is at the end.

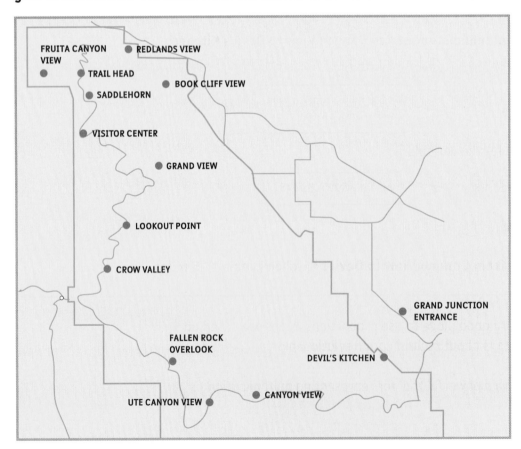

1. Use your thumb to measure the approximate distance between the Visitor Center and Lookout Point. Measure from point to point in a straight line. Round to the nearest inch. What is this distance in miles?

2. Use your thumb to measure the approximate distance between the Visitor Center and Crow Valley. Measure from point to point in a straight line. Round to the nearest inch. What is this distance in miles?

3. Use your thumb to measure the approximate distance between the Trail Head and Fallen Rock Overlook. Measure from point to point in a straight line. Round to the nearest inch. What is this distance in miles?

4. Use your thumb to measure the approximate distance between the Trail Head and Devil's Kitchen. Measure from point to point in a straight line. Round to the nearest inch. What is this distance in miles?

Activity 4 • Distributed Practice

Solve.

1. $\frac{1}{2} \cdot \frac{2}{3}$

2. $\frac{4}{6} \div \frac{1}{3}$

3. $\frac{8}{9} - \frac{1}{2}$

4. $\frac{32}{64} + \frac{10}{8}$

5. $1.17 - 0.89$

6. $2.5 \cdot 3$

7. $92.01 - 89.98$

8. $14.7 \div 0.07$

▸**Problem Solving: Translating Percent Problems**

How do we write percent problems using variables?

In everyday life, we often find problems that require us to work with percents. Variables can help us solve percent problems. A common type of problem with percents is the discount problem.

Before we even know the problem, we can set up a general statement for discount problems.

First, we choose variables.

d = the amount of the discount

c = the original cost of the item

p = percent of the discount

A discount amount is computed by multiplying the original cost by the percent of the discount.

$d = c \cdot p$

Let's look at a problem.

Problem:

James went shopping for a television. The original cost was $400, but it was on sale for 25% off. What is the amount of the discount on the television?

We substitute the variables with the price and percent to determine the discount.

$$d = \quad c \quad \cdot \quad p$$

$$\downarrow \qquad \downarrow$$

$$d = 400 \cdot 25\%$$

In order to work with the percent, we have to change it into a decimal number. So our problem is:

$d = 400 \cdot 0.25$

$d = 100$

The amount of the discount on the television is $100.

We can use the general statement $d = c \cdot p$ as a formula for discounts. But we do need to be careful to adjust the formula for the problem we are trying to solve. For instance, the discount may be a different percent. In addition, the cost changes from problem to problem. We need to make sure we understand what the problem is asking.

Example 1

Compute the discount on a $50 sweater that is 10% off.

First, we remember our discount formula.

$d = c \cdot p$

Next, we substitute the variables with the cost of the item and percent of discount. Remember, we change 10% to 0.10 to make the computation easier.

$d = c \cdot p$

$d = 50 \cdot 0.10$

$d = 5$

The discount amount is $5.

Discount problems are just one type of percent problem. Another common percent problem that is used in everyday life involves figuring out the tip for a meal at a restaurant. A common tip is 15%, or 0.15, of the total bill for the meal. Since the percent is the same for most tips, this is a good use of a formula. We only need to adjust the cost of the meal each time.

Example 2 shows how to figure a 15% tip on a meal that costs $49.99.

Example 2

Compute a 15% tip for a $49.99 meal.

First, we choose variables.

t = amount of tip

c = cost of the meal

p = percent of the meal that we want to tip

We multiply the cost of the meal by the percent that we want to tip to find the amount of our tip.

$t = c \cdot p$

Then, we substitute the values we know for the variables. Remember, we convert the 15% to 0.15 to make the computation easier.

$$t = \quad c \quad \cdot \quad p$$

$$t = 49.99 \cdot 0.15$$

When calculating a tip, we do not need to find an exact amount. The computation is easier if we use rounding. We round $49.99 to $50.

$t = 50 \cdot 0.15$

$t = \$7.50$

The tip should be about $7.50.

Another type of percent problem is the interest problem. This is very much like the discount problem. We have different amounts of money that we are computing interest for, as well as different percents of interest.

Example 3 shows a simple interest of 5% earned on $1,000 in the bank.

Example 3

Compute the interest earned on $1,000 when the interest rate is 5%.

First, we choose variables.

i = amount of interest

r = interest rate

a = account balance

Then we set up the general statement or formula.

$i = r \cdot a$

We convert 5% to 0.05 and substitute our values for the variables.

$i = \quad r \quad \cdot \quad a$

$\qquad \downarrow \qquad \downarrow$

$i = 0.05 \cdot \$1,000$

$i = \$50$

The interest earned on $1,000 at a rate of 5% is $50.

The final type of percent problem we will look at in this lesson is the computation of sales tax. We know that there is tax on items we buy at the store. Sales tax varies from state to state, usually somewhere between 5% and 8%.

Example 4 shows the amount of tax charged on a $150 purchase if we are shopping in a state with a 6% sales tax.

Example 4

Compute the sales tax on $150 when the sales tax is 6%.

First, we choose variables.

t = tax

p = percent charged for tax

c = cost of the purchase

Then we set up the general statement or formula.

$t = p \cdot c$

Now we substitute the values in the formula.

$t = p \cdot c$

$t = 0.06 \cdot 150$

$t = \$9$

The tax is $9 on the $150 purchase.

Writing a formula using variables to represent the "unknowns" in the problem helps us organize our thinking.

Problem-Solving Activity
Turn to *Interactive Text*, page 82.

mBook Reinforce Understanding
Use the *mBook Study Guide* to review lesson concepts.

Activity 1

Convert the following percents to decimal numbers.

1. 35%   2. 15%   3. 5%   4. 20%   5. 10%

Activity 2

Select the correct answer for each of the percent problems.

1. What is the discount on a $200 item that is 15% off?
   (a) $3
   (b) $30
   (c) $170

2. What is the tax on a $500 item at a 6% tax rate?
   (a) $3
   (b) $30
   (c) $470

3. What tip would you pay on a $60 meal at a 15% tip rate?
   (a) $9
   (b) $90
   (c) $69

4. How much interest will you earn at 2% on $1,000?
   (a) $20
   (b) $200
   (c) $800

Activity 3

Solve the word problems involving percents.

1. What is the discount on a $100 item that is 10% off?

2. What is the discount on a $200 item that is 10% off?

3. How much would a 15% tip be on a $150 meal?

4. How much interest will you earn on $500 at 1%?

5. How much interest will you earn on $1,000 at 2%?

6. What is the tax on a $375 item at a 5% tax rate?

Activity 4 • Distributed Practice

Solve.

1. $\frac{1}{3} \cdot \frac{4}{8}$

2. $1.29 + 15.09$

3. $332.11 - 219.34$

4. $7.8 - 3.9$

5. $\frac{2}{3} \div \frac{1}{2}$

6. $2.1 \cdot 7$

7. $\frac{5}{2} - \frac{1}{3}$

8. $0.44 \div 0.4$

Problem Solving:
▸Complex Pattern Cards

▸**Simplifying Ratios**

Why do we simplify ratios?

When we worked with fractions, we discovered that our answers were not complete until we simplified the fraction. We simplified fractions, or reduced fractions to lowest terms, by pulling out a fraction equal to 1 that represented the greatest common factor of the numerator and the denominator.

Example 1 shows how to simplify the fraction $\frac{12}{16}$.

Example 1

Simplify the fraction $\frac{12}{16}$.

We begin by thinking of the factors of 12 and 16.

12	1	2	3	④	6	12
16	1	2	④	8	16	

The common factors are 1, 2, and 4. The largest of these is 4. We pull out the factor 4 from both the numerator and the denominator.

$$\frac{12}{16} = \frac{4}{4} \cdot \frac{3}{4}$$

The simplified fraction is $\frac{3}{4}$.

We don't always have to simplify ratios when we write an answer, but sometimes we need to simplify them to find a proportional amount. We use the same procedure we used for simplifying fractions.

Example 2 shows a situation where we need to simplify a ratio in order to solve the problem. The procedure is the same as the one used for simplifying fractions.

Example 2

Solve the problem by simplifying the ratio.

Problem:

Eastern High School runs a summer sports camp for students. Last summer, there were 20 adults working at the camp and there were 60 students. This summer they will have 75 students, and they want to keep the adults-to-students ratio the same as last year. How many adults will they need?

We begin by looking at the adults-to-students ratio in the first summer.

$$\frac{\text{Adults}}{\text{Students}} \qquad \frac{20}{60}$$

We want to complete this proportion:

$$\frac{\text{Adults}}{\text{Students}} \qquad \frac{20}{60} = \frac{x}{75}$$

There is not a multiplication relationship that we know of for $60 \cdot ? = 75$. We have to first reduce the ratio in order to find a proportional ratio.

We reduce ratios the same way we reduce fractions. We find the greatest common factor and pull it out of each number. In this ratio, we are looking for the greatest common factor of 20 and 60.

20 ① ② ④ ⑤ ⑩ ⑳
60 ① ② 3 ④ ⑤ 6 ⑩ 12 15 ⑳ 30 60

The common factors are 1, 2, 4, 5, 10, and 20. The largest of these is 20. We pull out a factor of 20 from both numbers.

$$\frac{\text{Adults}}{\text{Students}} \qquad \frac{20}{60} = \frac{1}{3}$$

Now that we have a simplified ratio, we use it to figure out the multiplication relationship for the proportion.

$$\frac{\text{Adults}}{\text{Students}} \qquad \frac{1}{3} = \frac{x}{75}$$

We see that the scaling factor is 25: $3 \cdot 25 = 75$. We multiply both numbers by 25. The proportion is:

$$\frac{\text{Adults}}{\text{Students}} \qquad \frac{1}{3} = \frac{25}{75}$$

The answer is 25 adults are needed for the second summer.

We have to read each problem carefully to see if the ratio can be reduced. Sometimes we do not see a multiplication relationship at first. Example 3 shows another situation where we must reduce the ratio in order to complete the proportion.

Example 3

Determine if the two rectangles are similar.

One rectangle has dimensions of 4×6 and the other has dimensions of 6×9. Are they similar?

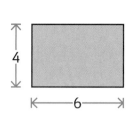 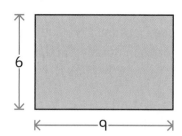

When we set up the proportion using these dimensions, it is not easy to see a multiplication relationship.

$$\frac{\text{Height}}{\text{Base}} \qquad \frac{4}{6} \cdot \frac{?}{?} = \frac{6}{9}$$

There is no whole-number multiplication relationship involved in the statements $4 \cdot ? = 6$ or $6 \cdot ? = 9$. We might think that they are not proportional.

We need to check to see if the ratios can be reduced.

We start by looking at the dimensions of the first rectangle: 4×6.
Can we reduce this ratio? Yes. The numbers 4 and 6 have common factors.

4	①	②	4	
6	①	②	3	6

The greatest common factor is 2. We pull out the common factor 2.

$$\frac{\text{Height}}{\text{Base}} \qquad \frac{4}{6} = \frac{2}{3}$$

Look at this reduced ratio and the ratio that represents the dimension of the second rectangle, 6×9.

$$\frac{\text{Height}}{\text{Base}} \qquad \frac{2}{3} = \frac{6}{9}$$

This proportion is true. If we multiply both numbers in the first ratio by $\frac{2}{3} \cdot \frac{3}{3} = \frac{6}{9}$ we end up with $\frac{6}{9}$, the second ratio in the proportion.

The answer is yes. These rectangles are similar. They have proportional sides.

The ratio of the height to the base is 2 : 3 for each of the rectangles.

%÷
=×
<× **Apply Skills**
Turn to *Interactive Text*, page 85.

mBook **Reinforce Understanding**
Use the *mBook Study Guide* to review lesson concepts.

▶Problem Solving: **Complex Pattern Cards**

How do we decide if complex cards are proportional?

We have looked at finding proportional pattern cards in the past few lessons. We did this by looking specifically for multiplication relationships. We were able to find multiplication patterns in each of the sets of cards we examined.

When we have ratios in the sets of cards that can be reduced, the process is much more complex. We may not always see the multiplication pattern at first glance. When this is the case, we begin by reducing the ratio and then continue with our search for the card or cards that are proportional.

Example 1

Determine which of the cards are proportional.

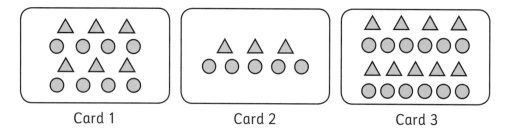

Card 1   Card 2   Card 3

We begin by organizing the information from the cards in a table.

Card	Triangles	Circles
1	6	8
2	3	5
3	9	12

Next we analyze the numbers and look for multiplication patterns.

- Comparing Cards 1 and 2, we see a possibility with 3 and 6 but not 5 and 8.

- Comparing Cards 2 and 3, we see a possibility with 3 and 9 but not 5 and 12.

We have to reduce the ratios to find the proportional relationships. We ask ourselves, "Which of the cards have ratios that can be reduced?" Set up the ratios for the three cards and examine them.

Card 1 $\dfrac{\text{Triangles}}{\text{Circles}}$ $\dfrac{6}{8}$

Card 2 $\dfrac{\text{Triangles}}{\text{Circles}}$ $\boxed{\dfrac{3}{5}}$ $\Bigg\}$ cannot be reduced

Card 3 $\dfrac{\text{Triangles}}{\text{Circles}}$ $\dfrac{9}{12}$

The ratio in Card 2 cannot be reduced, but the ratios in Cards 1 and 3 can. Let's start by reducing the ratio in Card 1. What are common factors for 6 and 8?

6	①	②	3	6
8	①	②	4	8

The greatest common factor is 2. We pull out the factor 2 from both numbers.

$$\dfrac{\text{Triangles}}{\text{Circles}} \qquad \dfrac{6}{8} = \dfrac{3}{4}$$

Now let's see if this is proportional to Card 3 in the set of pattern cards.

$$\dfrac{\text{Triangles}}{\text{Circles}} \qquad \dfrac{3}{4} = \dfrac{9}{12}$$

Cards 1 and 3 are proportional. If we multiply $\dfrac{3}{4}$ by $\dfrac{3}{3}$, we get $\dfrac{9}{12}$.

Let's look at these two cards again and separate them into groupings that show the ratio of triangles to circles—3 triangles for every 4 circles.

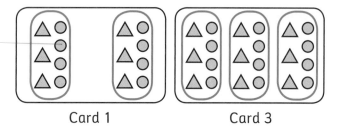

Card 1   Card 3

There are equal groupings of the ratio of triangles to circles in each of the cards. This means when we group them in this ratio, there are no circles or triangles left over. That is how we know they are proportional.

Problem-Solving Activity
Turn to *Interactive Text*, page 87.

mBook **Reinforce Understanding**
Use the *mBook Study Guide* to review lesson concepts.

Activity 1

Find the missing number in each of the proportions.

1. $\frac{x}{3} = \frac{4}{12}$

2. $\frac{3}{6} = \frac{15}{y}$

3. $\frac{2}{w} = \frac{8}{12}$

4. $\frac{4}{5} = \frac{z}{20}$

Activity 2

Reduce each of the ratios.

1. The ratio of girls to boys is 12 to 14.

2. The ratio of oil to gas is 2 to 8.

3. The ratio of pancake mix to milk is 3 to 6.

4. The ratio of stars to diamonds is 18 to 24.

5. The ratio of hearts to circles is 20 to 30.

Activity 3

Tell which two pattern cards in each group are proportional. You will need to reduce the ratios to find them.

1. Which two cards are proportional?

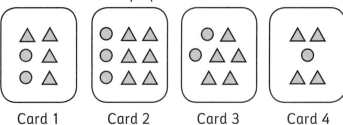

Card 1   Card 2   Card 3   Card 4

2. Which two cards are proportional?

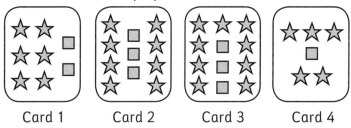

Card 1   Card 2   Card 3   Card 4

3. Which two cards are proportional?

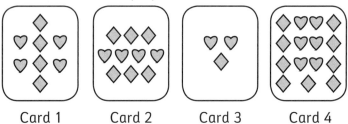

Card 1   Card 2   Card 3   Card 4

Activity 4 • Distributed Practice

Solve.

1. $\frac{3}{9} + \frac{4}{16}$

2. $\frac{11}{12} - \frac{2}{4}$

3. $\frac{7}{8} \cdot \frac{1}{3}$

4. $27.1 - 18.9$

5. $3.4 \cdot 5$

6. $\frac{3}{4} \div 4$

7. $16.8 \div 4$

8. $439.89 + 226.23$

▸**Making Sense of Proportional Reasoning**

What are some common mistakes with ratios and proportions?

In the last lesson, we learned that sometimes proportions are tricky when one or more of the ratios needs to be simplified. We think they are not proportional when they really are. We don't see the multiplication pattern until we simplify the ratios. We need to watch out for this common mistake.

Sometimes we are deceived by pictures as well when we are comparing two numbers or measurements. Look at the two pairs of intersecting lines. The picture can be deceiving in terms of comparing the sizes of the angles.

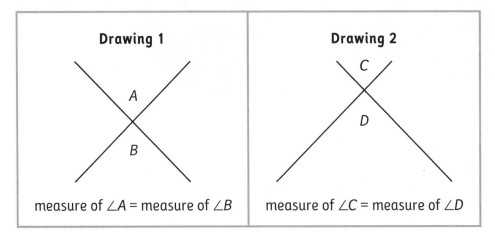

Angles *A* and *B* are measured where the lines intersect in Drawing 1. It's easy to see that the measure of angle *A* equals the measure of angle *B*. They look like the same size in the picture.

Now let's look at Drawing 2. Does the measure of angle *C* equal the measure of angle *D*? They are equal, but it doesn't look that way. *D* looks like a larger angle than *C* even though the measures are equal.

The same kind of misunderstandings can happen with ratios and proportions. That is why we need to check our thinking with the numbers we are comparing, using ratios and the numbers that represent a proportional relationship.

Look at the problem in Example 1. The two drawings show spinners. Is there an equal chance of landing on red in each of the pictures? We answer this question by thinking about proportions.

Example 1

Determine if the chances of landing on red are the same in each drawing.

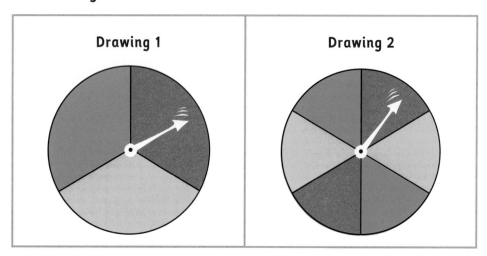

| Drawing 1 | Drawing 2 |

- In Drawing 1, there is a 1 out of 3, or $\frac{1}{3}$, chance of the spinner landing on red.
- In Drawing 2, there is a 2 out of 6, or $\frac{2}{6}$, chance of the spinner landing on red.

The chances of landing on red are the same because the ratios are equal.

Chances of landing on red: $\frac{1}{3} = \frac{2}{6}$.

Example 2 shows another picture of spinners. In this case, the chances of landing on red are not the same. Once again, proportions help us figure that out.

Example 2

Determine if the chances of landing on red are the same in each drawing.

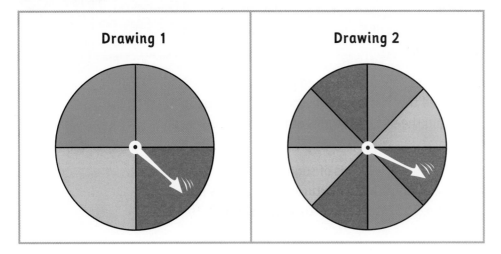

- In Drawing 1, there is a 1 out of 4, or $\frac{1}{4}$, chance of the spinner landing on red.
- In Drawing 2, there is a 3 out of 8, or $\frac{3}{8}$, chance of the spinner landing on red.

The chances of landing on red are not the same because the ratios are not equal.

Chances of landing on red: $\frac{1}{4} \neq \frac{3}{8}$.

Where do we use proportional thinking?

One place we use proportional thinking is in the area of probability.

- The probability of flipping heads on a coin is 1 out of 2.
- The chance of rolling a 4 using one die is 1 out of 6.

When we compare two ratios, we set up a proportion. We also use this type of thinking with cards.

- The chance of drawing a queen out of a card deck is 4 out of 52. It is not 1 out of 52 because there are 4 queens in a card deck.

4 : 52

Another context for thinking about ratios and proportions is mixtures. We discussed this in previous lessons, but it is a good context for remembering the different types of relationships we can compare with ratios.

- We mix 2 cups of flour with 3 cups of sugar to make a 5-cup mixture. The ratio of flour to the mixture is 2 to 5. This is a part-to-whole ratio. The ratio of flour to sugar is 2 to 3. This is a part-to-part ratio.

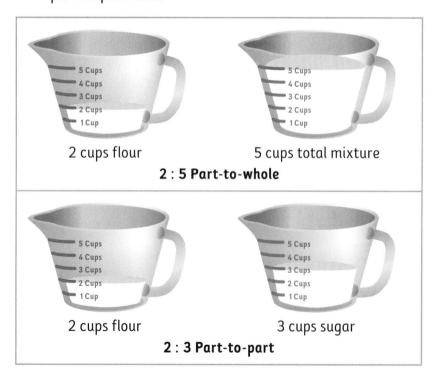

2 cups flour　　5 cups total mixture

2 : 5 Part-to-whole

2 cups flour　　3 cups sugar

2 : 3 Part-to-part

Apply Skills
Turn to *Interactive Text*,
page 89.

Reinforce Understanding
Use the *mBook Study Guide*
to review lesson concepts.

Homework

Activity 1

Reduce the ratios.

1. $\dfrac{\text{Eggs}}{\text{Milk}}$ $\dfrac{2\,\text{C}}{4\,\text{C}}$

2. $\dfrac{\text{Oil}}{\text{Gas}}$ $\dfrac{2\ \text{parts}}{8\ \text{parts}}$

3. $\dfrac{\text{Boys}}{\text{Girls}}$ $\dfrac{12}{14}$

4. $\dfrac{\text{Stars}}{\text{Diamonds}}$ $\dfrac{10}{30}$

Activity 2

Look at the spinners and tell if there is an equal chance of landing on red in each of the drawings. Answer Yes or No.

1. Is there an equal chance of landing on red?

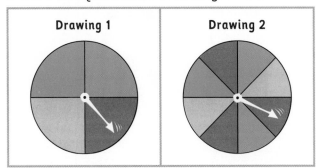

2. Is there an equal chance of landing on red?

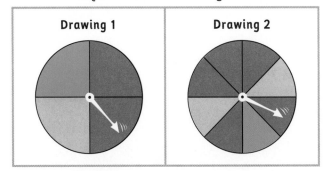

3. Is there an equal chance of landing on red?

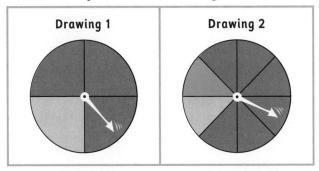

Activity 3

Select the jar that would give you the better chance of pulling out a red marble. Answer Jar 1 or Jar 2, or the same if both jars have the same chance.

1.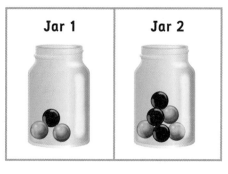

2.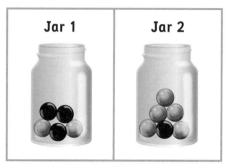

3.

4.

Activity 4 • Distributed Practice

Solve.

1. $12.7 - 11.9$

2. $\frac{3}{5} \div \frac{2}{4}$

3. $107.01 - 89.84$

4. $\frac{5}{8} + \frac{3}{4}$

5. $32.9 \cdot 2$

6. $14.7 \div 7$

7. $\frac{4}{5} \cdot \frac{2}{3}$

8. $\frac{5}{6} - \frac{3}{9}$

▶**Variables**

Why are variables important?

Variables help us describe patterns that occur in the world around us. Variables are used as part of mathematical statements, and we can substitute a wide range of numbers for the variable. One of the easiest ways to understand the use of a variable is through a formula.

We have learned about the areas of rectangles, triangles, and circles. Each of these areas can be written with formulas using variables. Notice that the variable *A* always stands for *area*. For each of the variables, we can substitute a wide range of numbers.

Review 1

How are variables used in formulas?

A = area

$A = b \cdot h$
b = base
h = height

$A = \frac{1}{2} \cdot b \cdot h$
b = base
h = height

$A = \pi \cdot r^2$
r = radius

Variables can also represent a missing value in relationships like proportions. In these cases, we use variables to help us set up a proportion and identify the value that we want to find.

Review 2 shows how variables are used in proportions.

Review 2

How are variables used in proportions?

Problem:

The school lunchroom sells 2 oranges for every 3 apples. How many oranges did they sell if they sold 9 apples?

$$\frac{\text{Oranges}}{\text{Apples}} \qquad \frac{2}{3} \qquad \frac{x}{9}$$

We use a variable to represent the unknown number of oranges. To find the value of x, we think, 3 times what equals 9? The answer is 3.

$$\frac{\text{Oranges}}{\text{Apples}} \qquad \frac{2 \cdot 3}{3 \cdot 3} \begin{array}{l} = 6 \\ = 9 \end{array}$$

They sold 6 oranges.

Variables also help us make general statements. Review 3 shows how we use a variable to figure out the weight of different quantities of rails used on railroad tracks. The simple statement allows us to figure out the weight for any number of rails.

Review 3

How are variables used to make a general statement?

Problem:

Railroads are a way to transport things across the country. Tracks need to be replaced when they get old. A six-foot rail weighs about 280 pounds. What is a way we can figure out the weight of different quantities of rails?

b = the number of rails

k = the total weight of the rails

Our general statement is:

$$k = 280 \cdot b$$

We can check this by substituting different numbers of rails.

How much do 10 rails weigh?

$$k = 280 \cdot b$$

$$k = 280 \cdot 10$$
$$k = 2{,}800$$

Answer: 2,800 pounds

How much would 30 rails weigh?

$$k = 280 \cdot b$$

$$k = 280 \cdot 30$$
$$k = 8{,}400$$

Answer: 8,400 pounds

We can work in the other direction based on a general statement such as the one shown in Review 4. We need to think about a situation where we could use the same statement again and again using different values for the variable.

Review 4

How do we write a word statement that describes a math statement with a variable?

$y = h + 3$

y = the time in New York

h = the time in Los Angeles

Word statement:

The time in New York is 3 hours ahead of the time in Los Angeles.

Sometimes word problems involve percents. We use variables to help make sense of these kinds of percent problems. Review 5 shows some common percent problems.

Review 5

How do variables help us think about percent problems?

Calculating Percent Discount

In a discount problem, we find the amount of the discount. We can use a simple discount formula to do this.

$d = c \cdot p$

d = the amount of the discount

c = the original cost of the item

p = percent of the discount

Calculating a Tip

To find the amount of a tip, we can use another formula:

$$t = c \cdot p$$

t = amount of tip

c = cost of the meal

p = percent of the meal that we want to tip

We multiply the cost of the meal by the percent that we want to tip to find the amount of our tip.

Calculating Interest

We can use variables to find the amount of interest we earn or pay at a specific interest rate. This involves another simple formula:

$$i = r \cdot a$$

i = amount of interest

r = interest rate

a = account balance

Calculating Sales Tax

Another way we use percents is in calculating sales tax. Variables help us write a formula for this.

$$t = p \cdot c$$

t = tax

p = percent charged for tax

c = cost of the purchase

> It is important to remember that we are multiplying by a percent, not by a whole number.

Apply Skills
Turn to *Interactive Text*, page 92.

Reinforce Understanding
Use the *mBook Study Guide* to review lesson concepts.

▶Problem Solving: **Ratios and Proportions**

What do we need to know about ratios and proportions?

Ratios are a special kind of relationship between numbers. They can be *part-to-whole relationships* just like fractions. But they can also be *part-to-part relationships*. We can make both of these relationships out of almost any kind of situation. Review 1 shows an example.

Review 1

What are different ways to write ratios?

Problem:

There are 3 people in the class who are left-handed. The other 22 people in the class are right-handed.

Part-to-whole relationship:

3 left-handed + 22 right-handed = 25 people

The total or whole = 25

$$\frac{\text{Left-handed}}{\text{Total}} \qquad \frac{3}{25} \qquad \frac{\text{Right-handed}}{\text{Total}} \qquad \frac{22}{25}$$

Part-to-part relationship:

$$\frac{\text{Left-handed}}{\text{Right-handed}} \qquad \frac{3}{22}$$

Proportions are equal ratios, and we make proportions by using multiplication. In fact, multiplication is the key idea in understanding proportions. We have used cards as a way of showing what a proportion looks like. We can see this in Review 2.

How do we decide if a relationship is proportional?

A proportion is two ratios that are equal. When a multiplication relationship exists between two ratios, we say that two things are proportional.

Let's look at these two cards. Is the relationship proportional?

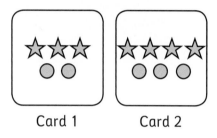

Card 1   Card 2

The relationship between these two cards is *not* proportional. We are just adding one star and one circle to the second card.

Is the relationship proportional in the next set of cards?

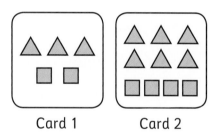

Card 1   Card 2

The relationship between the two cards *is* proportional. There are two times as many triangles and squares in Card 2 as there are in Card 1. The proportion is shown below.

$$\frac{\text{Triangles}}{\text{Squares}} \qquad \frac{3}{2} \cdot \frac{2}{2} = \frac{6}{4}$$

There are times when relationships do not look proportional. These situations remind us that we need to think carefully about the problem and determine if we can use multiplication to show that two ratios are equivalent.

We use proportions to help us decide if two shapes are similar. Review 3 shows us how this works.

Review 3

How do we use proportions to decide if two shapes are similar?

Similar shapes are proportional. Using what we know about proportions, we can compare parts of shapes to see if they are proportional.

Let's see how this works with triangles.

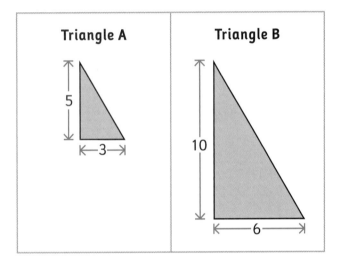

Let's look at the ratios of base to height for both triangles.

$$\frac{\text{Base}}{\text{Height}} \qquad \begin{array}{c} \text{Triangle A} \\ \frac{3}{5} \end{array} \qquad \begin{array}{c} \text{Triangle B} \\ \frac{6}{10} \end{array}$$

There is a multiplication relationship between the ratios. We multiply the base and height in Triangle A by 2 to find the base and height of Triangle B. The dimensions of these triangles are proportional, so the shapes are similar.

Triangle A is similar to Triangle B.

 **Problem-Solving Activity**
Turn to *Interactive Text*, page 94.

 **mBook Reinforce Understanding**
Use the *mBook Study Guide*
to review lesson concepts.

I'm exhausted! My wings are tired. How much farther?

Ten minutes less than the last time you asked, Dad!

MIGRATION FACT

Snow geese summer in the Arctic tundra and winter in the American South, Southwest, and East Coast regions. These geese live only in North America. Their yearly round-trip migration is more than 5,000 miles and they will travel at speeds of 50 mph or more.

OBJECTIVES

Building Number Concepts

- Represent inequalities using symbols and number lines
- Represent written statements using inequalities
- Create written statements from inequalities

Problem Solving

- Solve rate problems using proportions
- Find unit rates using proportions
- Compare two rates using proportions

▶**Inequalities**

Vocabulary
inequality ray

What are inequalities?

In the last unit, we substituted variables for numbers, or values. We also learned how to show them on a number line.

Example 1 shows the kind of problem that we worked.

Example 1

Show the value of x on a number line.

> To represent a specific number on a number line, use a circle or a dot.

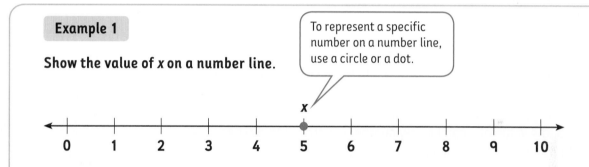

- The number line shows that $x = 5$.
- The dot is on the 5 and is filled in.

The number line shows that $x = 5$. When this is not the case, we can also use a symbol other than the equal sign. This kind of statement is called an **inequality**. For example:

$$x > 5$$

> This inequality reads "x is *greater than* 5."

greater than

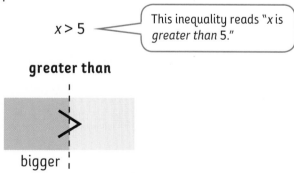

bigger

- We read the statement from left to right.
- The wider part of the symbol is on the same side as the bigger side of the inequality.

Let's see how we show an inequality on a number line. We use a **ray**, or a line that extends in only one direction, to graph the inequality.

> On a number line, the ray drawn to the right of an open circle shows that x is more than that number but not equal to it.

Example 2

Show x > 5 on a number line.

- Notice the open circle on 5 and the ray pointing to the right.
- An open circle on a number line shows that the variable does not equal that number.

In this case, the open circle shows that x is not equal to 5.

The ray shows that the value for x is any number greater than 5.

In $x > 5$, the value of x can be *any* number greater than 5. There are an infinite number of values that can make $x > 5$ true.

In this statement, x could be 5.01, 6, 7, 8, 9.25, $9\frac{1}{2}$, 10.33, and so on. All of these numbers are greater than 5.

Now let's look at another inequality that uses a different symbol.

POWER CONCEPT

In an inequality, the value for the variable is a *range of numbers*.

We use a different symbol when we want to show less than.
For example:

$$x < 23$$

This inequality reads "x is *less than* 23."

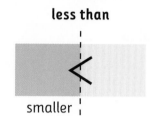

less than

smaller

- We read the statement from left to right.
- The small part of the symbol is on the same side as the smaller side of the inequality.

Example 3

Show x < 23 on a number line.

> A ray drawn to the left of an open circle shows that x is less than that number but not equal to it.

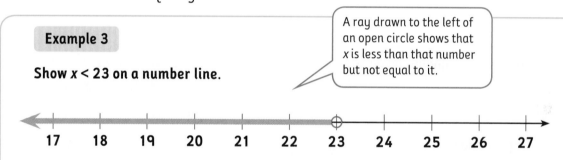

- There is an open circle that shows x does not equal 23.
- The ray is drawn to the left of the open circle.
- In x < 23, the value of x can be any number less than 23.

Examples of what the value of x could be include 22.99, 21, $20\frac{1}{2}$, $19\frac{3}{4}$, 18.01, 0, −1, −2.5, −25, and so on. There are an infinite number of values that can make x < 23 true.

Inequalities are important. They show that we can substitute a range of numbers for a variable. A variable does not stand for just one value. Many different numbers can work in an inequality.

What do the symbols ≥ and ≤ mean?

The symbols ≥ and ≤ are also used in inequalities. For example:

$$x \geq 5$$

This inequality reads "x is *greater than or equal to* 5."

greater than or equal to

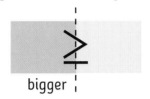

bigger

- Again, read from left to right.
- Remember that the wider part of the symbol is on the same side as the bigger side of the inequality.

Example 1 shows an inequality using ≥.

Example 1

Show $x \geq 5$ on a number line.

- Again, the inequality stands for a range of numbers, but this time the possible numbers *include the number 5.*
- Notice that the circle or dot on the 5 is filled in. One possible value for *x* is 5.

We also use the symbol ≤ in inequalities. For example:

$$x \leq 15$$

This inequality reads "x is *less than or equal to* 15."

less than or equal to

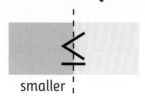

smaller

- Again, read from left to right.
- Remember that the small part of the symbol is on the same side as the smaller side of the inequality.

Example 2 shows an inequality using ≤.

Example 2

Show $x \leq 23$ on a number line.

This inequality reads "x is *less than or equal to* 23." Here is what the inequality $x \leq 23$ looks like on a number line.

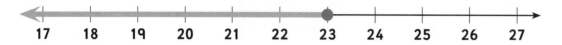

17 18 19 20 21 22 23 24 25 26 27

- Again, there is a range of numbers that we can substitute for x.
- The filled-in circle shows that one of the possible numbers is 23.

The table shows the symbols of inequality.

Symbol	Meaning
>	Greater than
≥	Greater than or equal to
<	Less than
≤	Less than or equal to

%÷ Apply Skills
≤× Turn to *Interactive Text*, page 97.

mBook Reinforce Understanding
Use the *mBook Study Guide* to review lesson concepts.

▶Problem Solving: **Rate**

What is rate?

Rate is a comparison of numbers that are measured in different units. We can use proportions to solve rate problems.

In geometry, we use proportions to create similar shapes of different sizes. We can expand the size of a shape by the same amount so the dimensions are proportional.

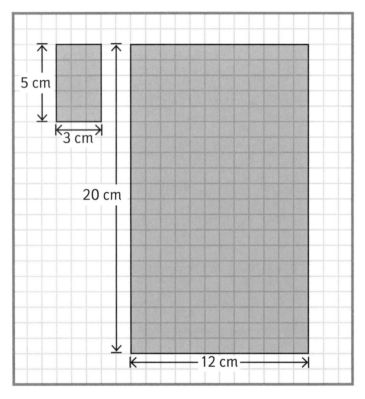

$$\frac{\text{Base}}{\text{Height}} \qquad \frac{3\text{ cm}}{5\text{ cm}} = \frac{12\text{ cm}}{20\text{ cm}}$$

If we are walking in the city, we may be able to walk 3 blocks in 5 minutes. How long would it take us to walk 12 blocks? We could use proportions to solve this problem.

$$\frac{\text{City Blocks}}{\text{Minutes}} \qquad \frac{3}{5} = \frac{12}{20}$$

> This is a special kind of proportion called a rate because it compares two units that are different.

In the rectangle example, we are comparing units that are the same— base (centimeters) and height (centimeters). A rate problem compares two different units. In the city block example, we are comparing city blocks (distance) with minutes (time).

Lesson 1

One type of rate problem involves how long it takes to do something. We might hear someone say, "At this rate, we should be there in about two hours." Example 1 shows us how to solve this type of rate problem.

Example 1

Solve a rate problem involving time and distance.

Problem:

We are on the freeway driving at a speed of 60 miles per hour. The freeway sign says that it is 120 miles until we get to our destination. At this rate, how long will it take us to get there?

- Multiply 60 miles by a number to get 120.
- Then multiply the hours by the same number to determine the time.

Miles $60 \cdot 2 = 120$
Hours $1 \cdot 2 = 2$

It will take us two hours to get to our destination.

Another use of rate involves charges. We might hear the person at the movie rental store say, "The charge on overdue movies is $2 per day."

Example 2

Solve a rate problem involving cost and time.

Problem:

We rented *Revenge of the Newts* and it was due on Monday. We forgot to return it, and are 5 days late returning the movie. With an overdue charge of $2 per day, how much do we owe?

- Multiply the charge and the days by the same amount. Since the movie is 5 days late, we multiply by 5.

$$\frac{\text{Charge}}{\text{Day}} \quad \frac{\$2 \cdot 5}{1 \cdot 5} = \frac{\$10}{5}$$

We owe $10 in overdue charges.

> If we are two weeks late in returning a movie, it will still cost us $2 per day. That is one way of saying that the rate remains the same.

Let's try this again with one more example.

Some items, like trees, are sold by a unit rate. You may hear a salesperson say, "This tree is $5 per foot, so it's going to cost $20 for a four-foot tree."

Example 3

Solve a rate problem involving height and cost.

Problem:

Bill's Nursery sells trees. The taller the tree, the more it costs. If a tree is $5 per foot, how much would it cost to buy a tree that is 8-feet tall?

What is the comparison?   Height of tree to the cost

What is the rate? $\dfrac{\text{Cost}}{\text{Height}}$ $\dfrac{\$5}{1} = \dfrac{\$40}{8}$

An 8-foot tall tree costs $40.

Once again, we are comparing two different quantities. We also assume that as one thing changes, the other changes in the same way.

No matter how tall the tree is, it will still cost us $5 per foot. It's important to know what the **unit rate** is. Unit rate is how much it costs for one unit.

The unit rate tells us what one of something is worth.

In real-world rate problems, the most difficult part is determining what information is important. Often we are given additional information that does not really help solve the problem.

Now let's see how to analyze a problem and identify the important information.

Example 4

Find the important information in this problem.

Problem:

Lotus Speedway is having a race for first-time drivers. These drivers are new to racing, so they don't drive as fast as the professionals we see on TV. The race starts at 2:00 PM, and there are 18 drivers. About halfway through the race, the fastest car is driving 4 laps in 6 minutes. His racing crew wants to figure out how long it will take to finish the last 20 laps of the race.

What is the comparison?   Laps *to* minutes

What is the rate? $\dfrac{\text{Laps}}{\text{Minutes}} \quad \dfrac{4}{6} = \dfrac{20}{x}$

> The variable *x* stands for what we need to know.

- First, what are we multiplying by? We ask ourselves, "$4 \cdot ? = 20$?" The answer is 5.
- Then we multiply 6 by 5 and get 30.

The completed proportion looks like this:

$$\dfrac{\text{Laps}}{\text{Minutes}} \quad \dfrac{4}{6} = \dfrac{20}{30}$$

The answer is 30. It will take 30 minutes for the fastest car to finish the last 20 laps of the race.

Problem-Solving Activity
Turn to *Interactive Text*, page 99.

mBook **Reinforce Understanding**
Use the *mBook Study Guide*
to review lesson concepts.

Activity 1

Describe each of the inequalities in words.

Model The inequality $x > 5$ means _____ .

Answer: x is greater than 5

1. The inequality $y < 6$ means _____ .

2. The inequality $5 \leq x$ means _____ .

3. The inequality $z > 9$ means _____ .

4. The inequality $m \geq 10$ means _____ .

5. The inequality $17 > n$ means _____ .

Activity 2

Tell whether each of the statements is true or false. On your paper, write T for true or F for false for each problem.

Model If $x > 20$, a possible value of x is 19.

Answer: F

1. If $y \leq 22$, a possible value of y is 22.

2. If $60 > z$, a possible value of z is 59.

3. If $w \geq 34$, a possible value of w is 46.

4. If $x < 22$, a possible value of x is 22.

Copy the number line onto a sheet of paper for each of the problems. Then draw each inequality on a number line.

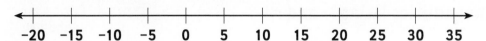

1. $m \leq 15$

2. $n \geq 0$

3. $x < 35$

4. $y > -5$

Solve.

1. $14.7 + 29.8 = a$

2. $437.6 - 250.8 = b$

3. $5.8 \cdot 10 = c$

4. $40.9 \div 10 = d$

5. $428 + e = 795$

6. $9 \cdot f = 72$

7. $g - 58 = 46$

8. $84 \div h = 12$

▶**Translating Inequalities Using > and <**

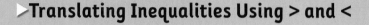

Vocabulary
word statement

How do we translate statements with > and < symbols?

In the last lesson, we learned the four symbols of inequality:

Meaning	Symbol
Greater than something	>
Greater than or equal to something	≥
Less than something	<
Less than or equal to something	≤

Let's use the symbols > and < to translate **word statements** into inequalities. A word statement uses words to describe a relationship.

Maxine's brother Simon is older than Maxine. She is 12.

How would we use an inequality to represent Simon's age?

- The information we have doesn't tell us how old Simon is, so we don't know what number his age is *equal to*.

- We just know what number it's *greater than*.

Use the variable B to represent the brother's age in an inequality. Simon's age is greater than 12.

$$B > 12$$

Does this inequality represent the information given? Yes. All we know is that Simon is older than Maxine and that Maxine is 12. Let's see how this inequality is represented on a number line.

> Notice that the circle is not filled in. This shows that Simon's age does not equal 12. It's greater than 12.

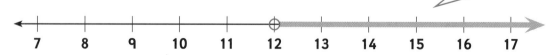

Now let's look at a situation where a word statement is translated into an inequality involving the symbol <.

Example 1

Translate a word statement into an inequality.

Word Statement:

Isaiah is shorter than Miguel. Miguel is 6 feet tall. How tall is Isaiah?

- We don't know what Isaiah's height is *equal to*. We just know Isaiah's height is shorter than or *less than* Miguel's.
- We know that Isaiah's height is less than 6 feet.

> This description of Miguel's height and Isaiah's height is a "less than" statement.

Look at the inequality that describes Isaiah's height. Use the variable I to represent Isaiah's height.

$$I < 6$$

Now look at how this inequality is represented on a number line.

Notice the open circle at 6 shows that Isaiah's height does not equal 6 feet. It is less than 6 feet. We are not told anything else about his height. All we know is that he is shorter than 6 feet.

The symbols > and < can be used to represent statements that use the words *higher than, bigger than, smaller than,* or *taller than.* All of these statements are represented mathematically using inequalities.

Apply Skills
Turn to *Interactive Text*, page 101.

mBook Reinforce Understanding
Use the *mBook Study Guide* to review lesson concepts.

▶**Problem Solving: Decreasing and Increasing Rates**

What happens when we go the other way?

The rate problems we worked on earlier involved making rates bigger.
Example 1 shows how we set up a proportion to show an increase.

Example 1

Set up the proportion with a variable.

Problem:

A runner can run 2 miles in 12 minutes. How long will it take him to
run 4 miles at this rate?

$$\frac{\text{Miles}}{\text{Minutes}} \qquad \frac{2}{12} = \frac{4}{x}$$

> x is the minutes it takes to run 4 miles at this rate.

Complete the proportion by finding the value of the variable.

$$\frac{\text{Miles}}{\text{Minutes}} \qquad \frac{2}{12} = \frac{4}{24}$$

At this rate, the runner will run 4 miles in 24 minutes.

We also use proportions to figure out what would happen in less time.

Example 2

Use a proportion to solve this problem.

Problem:

Let's say it took a runner 48 seconds to run 400 yards. How long will
it take her to run 100 yards at this rate?

$$\frac{\text{Yards}}{\text{Seconds}} \qquad \frac{400}{48} = \frac{100}{x}$$

> x is the seconds it takes to run 100 yards at this rate.

$$\frac{\text{Yards}}{\text{Seconds}} \qquad \frac{400}{48} = \frac{100}{12}$$

At this rate, it would take her 12 seconds to run 100 yards.

Here is another problem involving a proportion that represents rates that decrease.

Example 3

Use a proportion to solve the problem.

Problem:

It takes workers in a factory 45 minutes to make 30 computers. How many computers can they make in 15 minutes?

- First we set up the proportion. The two variables are minutes and computers.

We know it takes 45 minutes to make 30 computers. We want to know how many the workers can make in 15 minutes. The proportion looks like this:

$$\frac{\text{Minutes}}{\text{Computers}} \qquad \frac{45}{30} = \frac{15}{x}$$

> In this proportion, the variable x represents the number of computers that can be produced in 15 minutes.

- Next, we ask ourselves, "15 · ? = 45?" The answer is 3.
- Finally, we ask ourselves, "? · 3 = 30?" The answer is 10.

We write the completed proportion like this:

$$\frac{\text{Minutes}}{\text{Computers}} \qquad \frac{45}{30} = \frac{15}{10}$$

> At this rate, the workers can make 10 computers in 15 minutes.

The workers can make 10 computers in 15 minutes.

📝 **Problem-Solving Activity**
Turn to *Interactive Text*, page 103.

mBook **Reinforce Understanding**
Use the *mBook Study Guide* to review lesson concepts.

Activity 1

Select the inequality that best represents the word statement.

1. Betty is 13. She is older than Jim. Use the variable j in an inequality that represents Jim's age.

   (a) $j > 13$ **(b)** $j < 13$ **(c)** $13 < j$

2. Trent scored more points than Heath. Heath scored 12 points. Use the variable t in an inequality that represents the number of points Trent scored.

   (a) $12 > t$ **(b)** $12 < t$ **(c)** $t < 12$

3. The manager earns more money than the clerks at the store. The manager makes $600 a week. Use the variable c in an inequality that represents the clerk's pay.

   (a) $c > 600$ **(b)** $c < 600$ **(c)** $c \geq 600$

4. Everyone in the class scored lower on the test than Micah. Micah scored 95. Use the variable x in an inequality that represents the score of any other person in the class.

   (a) $x \leq 95$ **(b)** $x > 95$ **(c)** $x < 95$

Activity 2

Select the word statement that best fits the inequality.

1. $b > 57$, where b is Mr. Beardsley's age.
   (a) Mr. Beardsley is 57 years old.
   (b) Mr. Beardsley is younger than 57.
   (c) Mr. Beardsley is older than 57.

2. $m < 85$, where m is Marty's score on the quiz.
   (a) Marty's score is 85.
   (b) Marty's score is lower than 85.
   (c) Marty's score is higher than 85.

3. $t > 10$, where t is how many minutes it takes Tim to run a mile.
   (a) It takes Tim more than 10 minutes to run a mile.
   (b) Tim runs a mile in 10 minutes or less.
   (c) Tim can run the mile in less than 10 minutes.

Activity 3

Solve the rate problems by completing the proportions.

1. It took Mariah 3 hours to read 240 pages. How many pages can she read in 1 hour at the same rate?

    $\dfrac{\text{Hours}}{\text{Pages}}$ $\quad \dfrac{3}{240} = \dfrac{1}{x}$

2. It takes Flo's florists 12 hours to make 6 arrangements of flowers. At that rate, how long does it take them to make just one arrangement of flowers?

    $\dfrac{\text{Arrangements of Flowers}}{\text{Hours}}$ $\quad \dfrac{6}{12} = \dfrac{1}{y}$

3. It takes Michael 6 hours to drive 300 miles. At that rate, how far has he driven after 3 hours?

    $\dfrac{\text{Miles}}{\text{Hours}}$ $\quad \dfrac{300}{6} = \dfrac{z}{3}$

Activity 4 • Distributed Practice

Solve.

1. $\dfrac{4}{5} \cdot \dfrac{1}{2} = a$

2. $8 + b = 29$

3. $17.2 + 13.8 = c$

4. $72 \div d = 9$

5. $\dfrac{3}{8} + \dfrac{4}{6} = e$

6. $21 - 19 = f$

7. $42.7 \div 7 = g$

8. $47 \cdot h = 94$

9. $38.5 - 16.7 = j$

▶**Using ≥ and ≤**

How do we translate statements with ≥ and ≤ symbols?

Let's review the four symbols for inequalities we have used so far.

Meaning	Symbol
Greater than something	>
Greater than or equal to something	≥
Less than something	<
Less than or equal to something	≤

In the previous lesson, we used < and > symbols to translate word statements into inequalities. Now let's translate statements using the ≤ and ≥ symbols.

Let's say that the outside temperature today is *at least* 75 degrees.

> That means the temperature could be 75 degrees or it could be higher.

How would we use an inequality to represent the temperature?

> Use the variable x to represent the outside temperature.

$$x ≥ 75$$

> This inequality reads "the temperature is *greater than or equal to* 75 degrees."

We usually don't hear it stated that way in everyday language. We are more likely to hear someone say, "The temperature is *at least* 75 degrees."

Notice the phrase "at least" includes 75 in the range of values.

This is how we show this statement on a number line.

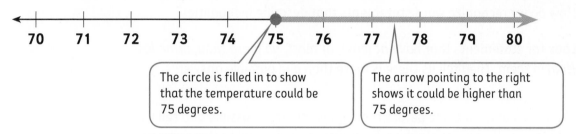

The circle is filled in to show that the temperature could be 75 degrees.

The arrow pointing to the right shows it could be higher than 75 degrees.

Now let's use the symbol ≤ to translate a statement that describes something as *less than or equal to*.

Manny is looking for a birthday card for his younger cousin. He knows that his cousin is *not older than* 12 years old.

How would we show this inequality?

Use the variable x to represent the age of Manny's cousin.

$x \leq 12$

This inequality means that his cousin could be 12 or he could be younger.

This is how the inequality looks on a number line.

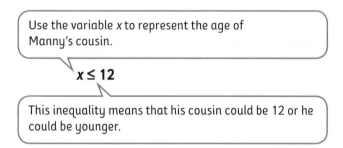

Again, the circle is filled in.

This inequality states that Manny's cousin is *less than or equal to* 12 years old. However, we would usually say, "The oldest he could be is 12," or, "He is 12 or younger."

It's important to learn how to translate phrases into inequalities.

What are other phrases that mean inequality?

How do we recognize word statements that describe inequalities?

Look for statements that have *at least, at most, no more than,* or *no less than* in them. They tell us there is more than one possible answer.

The words *at most* come before the highest number possible and tell us that the number we are looking for is less than or equal to this number. The words *at least* come before the lowest number possible and tell us that the number could be greater than or equal to this number.

All of these statements require the $\geq$ symbol for *greater than or equal to* and the $\leq$ symbol for *less than or equal to*. Let's look at some of these key phrases in word statements.

Example 1

Translate the word statements into inequalities.

In Seattle the daytime high temperature for October 9 is *at most* 75 degrees.

Use the variable t to represent temperature. $t \leq 75$

The bus can hold *no more than* 25 students.

Use the variable s to represent the number of
students the bus can carry. $s \leq 25$

There were *at least* 500 teenagers at the concert.

Use the variable t to represent the number of
teenagers at the concert. $t \geq 500$

Yasu earned *no less than* a 75 percent on any of his math quizzes or tests.

Use the variable y to represent Yasu's scores. $y \geq 75$

% ÷
≡ ×
< x   **Apply Skills**
Turn to *Interactive Text*,
page 105.

mBook   **Reinforce Understanding**
Use the *mBook Study Guide*
to review lesson concepts.

Activity 1

Tell whether each of the statements is true or false. For each problem, write T for true or F for false on your paper.

Model If $x > 20$, a possible value of x is 21.

　　　　Answer: T

1. If $y \leq 99$, a possible value of y is 99.

2. If $z < 99$, a possible value of z is 99.

3. If $w \geq 111$, a possible value of w is 111.

4. If $111 < t$, a possible value of t is 99.

Activity 2

Look at each of the number lines. Tell whether the number line shows the inequality that is given. Answer Yes or No.

Model　$x > 43$　Answer: No

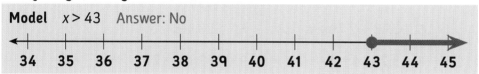

1. $m \geq 95$

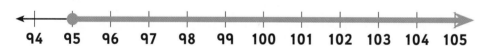

2. $n < 40$

3. $15 > y$

4. $43 \leq z$

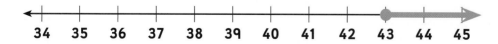

Activity 3

Write an inequality for each of the word problems. State what the variable represents.

Model The high temperature for the day was 75 degrees.

Answer: $t \leq 75$, where t stands for high temperature for the day.

1. It's at least 25 miles farther to the resort.

2. Martin has an older sister. Martin is 12.

3. Elijah is the tallest boy in the class. He is 6 feet tall.

4. The predicted high temperature for today is at most 55 degrees.

Activity 4 • Distributed Practice

Solve.

1. $\frac{1}{4} + \frac{2}{3} = x$

2. $74 - y = 68$

3. $\frac{3}{9} \div \frac{1}{9} = z$

4. $25 \cdot w = 100$

5. $3.98 + 2.79 = c$

6. $420 \div 6 = b$

7. $c + 537 = 814$

8. $3.25 \cdot 4 = d$

9. $143 - v = 22$

▶ **Problem Solving: Solving Word Problems Using Unit Rates**

How much for just one?

Often we may want to know the value of just one of something. The value of one of something is called the *unit rate*.

We use this concept often without actually thinking about unit rate. For instance, in the grocery store, it is easier if we compare the cost of just one unit, such as an ounce or a pound.

If we see a sign advertising four boxes of cereal for $10, we might ask ourselves how much it costs for just one box.

Let's look at a problem involving unit rate.

Example 1

Find the unit rate.

Problem:

It costs $6 to buy 3 cartons of milk. What is the cost of 1 carton?

Set up a proportion with a variable.

$$\frac{\text{Cost}}{\text{Carton}} \qquad \frac{\$6}{3} = \frac{x}{1}$$

> x is the cost for 1 carton.

Complete the proportion by finding the value of x.

$$\frac{\text{Cost}}{\text{Carton}} \qquad \frac{\$6}{3} = \frac{\$2}{1}$$

One carton of milk costs $2. The unit rate is $2 per carton.

Another way we talk about unit rate is when we use the term *miles per hour*. This term means the number of miles we travel in one hour. Miles per hour is a unit rate. It's the value of just one of something every one hour. Example 2 shows this situation.

Example 2

Find the unit rate.

Problem:

Quentin's dad drove him to a soccer tournament. They drove 240 miles in 4 hours. About how far did they drive in just 1 hour? What was the rate in miles per hour?

Set up a proportion with a variable.

$$\frac{\text{Miles}}{\text{Hour}} \qquad \frac{240}{4} = \frac{m}{1}$$

> *m* is the miles traveled in 1 hour.

Complete the proportion by finding a value for *m*.

$$\frac{\text{Miles}}{\text{Hour}} \qquad \frac{240}{4} = \frac{60}{1}$$

We see now that *m* = 60. This means Quentin and his dad drove 60 miles in 1 hour. Another way of saying this is "60 miles per hour."

The unit rate is 60 miles per hour.

Notice that each proportion starts with the units written in words.

Writing the words out is a good habit to practice with this type of problem. We want to remind ourselves what the numbers stand for. That way, when we solve for a variable, we know exactly what that variable represents. In the example about Quentin and his dad, the variable *m* stands for miles. In the previous example, the variable *x* stands for the cost in dollars.

Example 3 shows another problem involving unit rate.

Example 3

Find the unit rate.

Problem:

We are at the state fair. We use tickets to pay for the rides. Each ride requires the same number of tickets. We can take 4 rides on 20 tickets. How many tickets does it take for 1 ride?

Set up a proportion with a variable.

$$\frac{\text{Tickets}}{\text{Ride}} \qquad \frac{20}{4} = \frac{t}{1}$$

t stands for the number of tickets.

Complete the proportion by finding the value for *t*.

$$\frac{\text{Tickets}}{\text{Ride}} \qquad \frac{20}{4} = \frac{5}{1}$$

We can see that $t = 5$.

We need 5 tickets to take 1 ride.

How do we solve word problems using unit rates?

Sometimes we have to compute the unit rate for something to find the better deal. We usually expect that items marked "3 for $_____"
or "5 for $_____" are better deals than buying just one item.
However, this is not always the case.

To compare these different pricing methods, we find the unit rate.
Example 1 shows how we analyze this type of situation to determine the better deal.

Example 1

Find the unit rate.

Problem:

Monica needs soup. The store has a special—5 cans for $10. If she buys just 1 can of soup, the cost is $2.20. Which is the better deal?

We compare the cost of 1 can of soup for $2.20 to the special deal of 5 cans for $10. We set up a proportion to find the unit rate.

$$\frac{\text{Cost}}{\text{Number of Cans}} \qquad \frac{\$10}{5} = \frac{x}{1}$$

- First we ask ourselves, "1 • ? = 5?" The answer is 5.
- Then we need to find the value for x in the statement, "$x \cdot 5 = \$10$."

It's $2. We complete the proportion by filling in the value for x.

$$\frac{\text{Cost}}{\text{Number of Cans}} \qquad \frac{\$10}{5} = \frac{\$2}{1}$$

The unit price is $2.

We now compare the unit rate of $2 to the cost for 1 can—$2.20.
Buying soup at 5 for $10 is the better deal because it's $2 per can, not $2.20 per can.

Grocery stores often use this pricing method. We expect items marked "3 for $_____" to be the best deals. However, that is not always the case.

Example 2 shows a different situation. Sometimes the special pricing methods are not the best deal.

Find the unit rate.

Problem:

Marcus needs to wear ties for his new job. At the department store, ties are $19 each or 3 for $60.

We need to compare the cost of just 1 tie to the special deal by finding the unit rate. We set up the proportion like this:

$$\frac{\text{Cost}}{\text{Number of Ties}} \qquad \frac{\$60}{3} = \frac{x}{1}$$

- First we ask ourselves, "$1 \cdot ? = 3$?" The answer is 3.
- Then we need to find the value for x in this statement, "$x \cdot 3 = \$60$."

The cost is $20. We complete the proportion by filling in the value for x.

$$\frac{\text{Cost}}{\text{Number of Ties}} \qquad \frac{\$60}{3} = \frac{\$20}{1}$$

When we compare the two pricing methods, we see that the "special deal" is not the better deal.

The unit rate is $20 per tie.

If we buy the ties individually, they are $19 per tie.

📝 **Problem-Solving Activity**
Turn to *Interactive Text*, page 108.

⌨ **mBook Reinforce Understanding**
Use the *mBook Study Guide* to review lesson concepts.

Homework

Activity 1

Simplify the ratios.

Model $\frac{6}{12}$ Answer: $\frac{6}{12} = \frac{1}{2}$

1. $\frac{7}{14}$

2. $\frac{3}{12}$

3. $\frac{4}{20}$

4. $\frac{5}{15}$

5. $\frac{8}{48}$

Activity 2

Set up the unit rate problems as proportions. Tell what the variable represents. Show the units in words. Find the unit rate.

Model   It costs \$8 for 4 sandwiches. How much does it cost for just 1 sandwich?

Answer: $\frac{\text{Cost}}{\text{Sandwich}}$ $\frac{\$8}{4} = \frac{x}{1}$ X stands for the cost of 1 sandwich.

$\frac{\text{Cost}}{\text{Sandwich}}$ $\frac{\$8}{4} = \frac{\$2}{1}$ The cost of one sandwich is \$2.

1. Nguyen paid \$40 for 4 CDs. If all 4 cost the same amount, what was the cost of just 1 CD?

2. Sheldon paid \$180 for 6 pairs of contact lenses. What was the cost of just 1 pair of lenses?

3. Britt can do 45 sit-ups in 3 minutes. How many sit-ups can she do in just 1 minute?

Activity 3

Tell the better deal in each case by finding the unit rate.

1. What's the better deal, 1 apple for \$.50, or 3 for \$1?

2. What's the better deal, 1 pair of jeans for \$60 or 3 for \$200?

3. What's the better deal, 1 T-shirt for \$19 or 2 for \$40?

4. What's the better deal, 1 CD for \$15 or 2 for \$25?

5. What's the better deal, 3 juices for \$1 or \$.75 for 1 juice in the vending machine?

Activity 4 • Distributed Practice

Solve.

1. $\frac{4}{5} + \frac{2}{5} = x$

2. $35 - w = 19$

3. $4.75 + 2.98 = z$

4. $a + 385 = 410$

5. $\frac{1}{2} \cdot \frac{3}{5} = b$

6. $139.7 - 48.19 = c$

7. $\frac{4}{5} \div \frac{1}{5} = d$

8. $e \div 7 = 50$

▶**Logic and Number Lines**

How do we use logic to think about number lines?

We use logic in mathematics to help us think about different situations.

Let's think about a game of chance. We have a spinner that is divided into three equal parts, and the parts are colored red, yellow, and green. Each part is $\frac{1}{3}$ of the circle. What are the chances of the spinner landing on red or yellow? The chances are $\frac{2}{3}$.

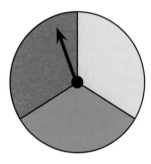

Now, what are the chances of landing on red *and* yellow?

When we think about this logically, it is impossible for the spinner to land on both of these colors. It can only land on one of them. The chances are 0 that the spinner will land on red *and* yellow.

Let's make the game more challenging using a coin. If we flip 2 heads in a row, we win. There are only 4 possible outcomes for 2 tosses of a coin. We see in the table that only one of them is a head *and* a head. That means there is only a 1 out of 4 or $\frac{1}{4}$ chance of flipping a head and a head.

First Toss	Second Toss
Head	Head
Head	Tail
Tail	Head
Tail	Tail

These examples are about events where there is only one value for each event. In the last example, we could only have:

- a head for the first event (the first toss).
- a head for the second event (the second toss).

What if we have one event with a single value and one with a range of values? What about situations where both events have a range of values?

We use different number lines to help us think about sentences that use *and*. Number lines help us see a range of variables that could make a statement true. Example 1 shows events with a range of values.

Example 1

Use number lines to show a range of values.

Problem:

To vote in this state, someone must have lived here for at least 6 months *and* be 18 years of age or older. How can we use number lines to understand the requirements for voting?

Let *x* be the number of months someone has lived in the state. They could have lived here for 6 months, 30 months, or 200 months. It doesn't matter. This means $x \geq 6$.

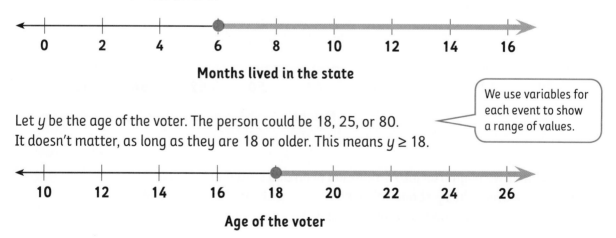

Months lived in the state

Let *y* be the age of the voter. The person could be 18, 25, or 80. It doesn't matter, as long as they are 18 or older. This means $y \geq 18$.

> We use variables for each event to show a range of values.

Age of the voter

We use two number lines because we are talking about two different events, or conditions.

Number lines are a good way to think about what happens in *and* statements.

We must use two different number lines because we have two different things measured in two different units. In Example 2, pay close attention to the units of measurement on each of the two number lines.

> It's very important to understand why we use two different number lines.

Example 2

Use number lines to show different units.

Problem:

To go on the bumper cars ride, one must be 8 years old or older *and* be taller than 48 inches. How can we use number lines to understand the requirements for the bumper cars ride?

Let *x* be the age. A person can be 8, 9, or 15 years old, or older. This means $x \geq 8$.

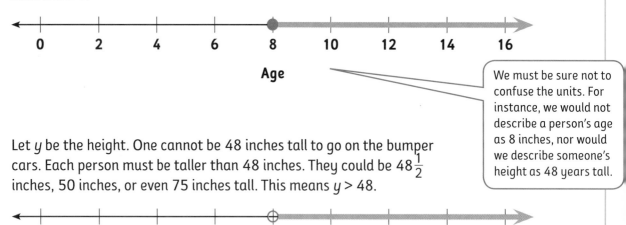

Age

> We must be sure not to confuse the units. For instance, we would not describe a person's age as 8 inches, nor would we describe someone's height as 48 years tall.

Let *y* be the height. One cannot be 48 inches tall to go on the bumper cars. Each person must be taller than 48 inches. They could be $48\frac{1}{2}$ inches, 50 inches, or even 75 inches tall. This means $y > 48$.

Height

Sometimes we might run into a situation in an *and* statement where one of the events has just one value, and the other event has a range of values. Example 3 shows how we represent this situation using number lines.

Example 3

Use number lines to show different units, where one event has a single value and the other has a range of values.

Problem:

We are trying to win a prize for shooting baskets. All the shots are the same distance from the basket. To win we must make 10 baskets *and* make them in less than 60 seconds.

Let x be the number of baskets. We cannot make fewer than 10 baskets, and we stop when we make 10 baskets. This means $x = 10$.

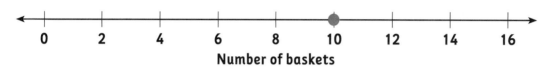

Number of baskets

Let y be the time. We have less than 60 seconds to make the baskets. We could do it in 25 seconds, 32 seconds, or 59 seconds. This means $y < 60$.

Time

Logic statements like these help us think about the range of variables in different situations. They also help us compare different things with different units of measure.

When we use *and* statements, we use number lines to help us logically see the range of values for each of the conditions in the statement. We need two different number lines because we are analyzing two different conditions.

%÷
≷× **Apply Skills**
Turn to *Interactive Text*, page 111.

Monitoring Progress
Quiz 1

mBook **Reinforce Understanding**
Use the *mBook Study Guide* to review lesson concepts.

Activity 1

Select the number lines that represent the logic of the *and* statements.

1. You must be at least 12 years old and no less than 48 inches tall to ride the rollercoaster.

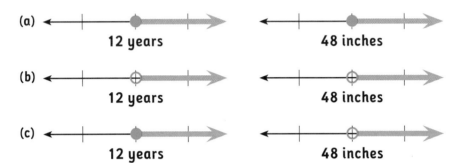

2. You must be 18 years old or older and have no speeding tickets on your driving record to deliver pizzas.

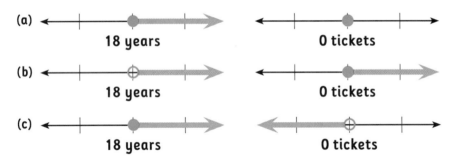

3. You must be no more than 8 years of age and weigh 60 pounds or less to play on the jungle gym at Kiddie Playland.

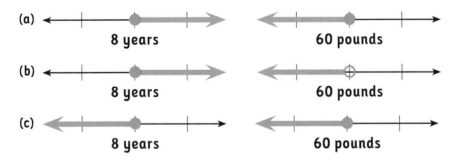

Activity 2

Select the word statement that best matches the inequality.

1. $m > 15$

   If m is Monty's age, then
   (a) Monty is older than 15.
   (b) Monty is younger than 15.
   (c) Monty is no more than 15 years old.

2. $x \leq 25$

   If x is the cost of a DVD player, then
   (a) the DVD player costs more than $25.
   (b) the DVD player costs less than $25.
   (c) the cost of the DVD player is $25 or less.

3. $y < 5$

   If y represents the number of people allowed on a ride at a time, then
   (a) there can be no more than 5 people.
   (b) there can be no less than 5 people.
   (c) there must be less than 5 people.

Activity 3

Complete the proportion to find the unit rate for each.

1. $\dfrac{\text{Miles}}{\text{Hours}} \quad \dfrac{360}{6} = \dfrac{x}{1}$

2. $\dfrac{\text{Apples}}{\text{Cost}} \quad \dfrac{1}{w} = \dfrac{12}{\$1.20}$

3. $\dfrac{\text{Pages}}{\text{Hours}} \quad \dfrac{480}{4} = \dfrac{z}{1}$

Activity 4 • Distributed Practice

Solve.

1. $a \cdot 30 = 270$

2. $\frac{4}{8} + \frac{1}{2} = b$

3. $6.2 \cdot 3 = c$

4. $5 \cdot d = 150$

5. $4.8 \div 4 = e$

6. $542 + f = 611$

7. $\frac{3}{4} - \frac{1}{2} = g$

8. $h - 198 = 227$

Lesson 6 | Problem Solving: ▸Simplifying Rates

▸**Problem Solving: Simplifying Rates**

When do we need to simplify rates?

We have been working with rates throughout this unit. Example 1 shows a rate problem similar to those we have been solving so far.

Example 1

Solve the simple rate problem.

Problem:

At the grocery store, 4 large bags of potato chips cost $6. How much will it cost to buy 12 bags of chips?

We begin by setting up the proportion with the variable:

$$\frac{\text{Cost}}{\text{Bag of Chips}} \qquad \frac{\$6}{4} = \frac{x}{12}$$

- We ask ourselves, "4 • ? = 12?" We find that it is 3.
- Then we multiply $6 • 3 = x, and x = 18.

The completed proportion looks like this:

$$\frac{\text{Cost}}{\text{Bag of Chips}} \qquad \frac{\$6}{4} = \frac{\$18}{12}$$

The 12 bags of chips will cost $18.

The rate problems we have worked so far have been relatively easy because we can see the multiplication relationship right away.

In Example 1, the problem is: 4 · ? = 12. We know 4 is a factor of 12, so it is not too difficult to solve.

Some rate problems are not as easy to solve because we cannot see the multiplication relationship right away. In these problems, we need to simplify the rate to find the multiplication relationship.

Example 2 shows how we simplify the rate before we can complete the proportion.

Example 2

Simplify the rate problem.

Problem:

We can buy 4 large bags of potato chips for $6. How much will it cost to buy 10 bags of chips?

Again, we begin by setting up the proportion with the variable:

$$\frac{\text{Cost}}{\text{Bag of Chips}} \qquad \frac{\$6}{4} = \frac{w}{10}$$

- First we ask, "4 · ? = 10?" We find this is not an easy multiplication problem.
- So we must ask, "Can the rate be simplified?" In this case, yes. We can simplify $\frac{6}{4}$.

We use the same method that we used for simplifying fractions:

Factors of 6 → 1, 2, 3, 6
Factors of 4 → 1, 2, 4

The greatest common factor is 2. We pull 2 out of 6 and 4.

$$\frac{6}{4} = \frac{3}{2}$$

The simplified rate is $\frac{3}{2}$. Now we substitute that for $\frac{6}{4}$ in our proportion:

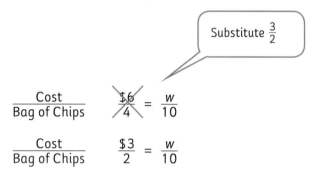

Substitute $\frac{3}{2}$

$$\frac{\text{Cost}}{\text{Bag of Chips}} \qquad \frac{\$6}{4} = \frac{w}{10}$$

$$\frac{\text{Cost}}{\text{Bag of Chips}} \qquad \frac{\$3}{2} = \frac{w}{10}$$

Now we can complete the proportion easily.

- We ask ourselves, "2 • ? = 10?" We see that it is 5.
- Then we multiply $3 • 5 to get $15.

The completed proportion looks like this:

$$\frac{\text{Cost}}{\text{Bag of Chips}} \qquad \frac{\$3}{2} = \frac{\$15}{10}$$

It will cost $15 for 10 bags of chips.

After a while, we will be able to see right away when something must be simplified.

Example 3 demonstrates another situation where the rate needs to be simplified.

Example 3

Simplify the rate problem.

Problem:

We want to buy soft drinks for a party. We can buy 6 two-liter bottles of cola for $15. We think we'll need 14 bottles for the party. How much will they cost?

We begin by setting up the proportion with the variable:

$$\frac{\text{Cost}}{\text{Soft Drinks}} \qquad \frac{\$15}{6 \text{ bottles}} = \frac{y}{14 \text{ bottles}}$$

- We ask ourselves, "6 · ? = 14?" We find this is not an easy multiplication problem.
- Then we ask ourselves, "Can we simplify?" The answer is yes.

The numbers 6 and 15 have a greatest common factor of 3. If we pull out 3 from both, we are left with $\frac{5}{2}$. Now we substitute $\frac{5}{2}$ for $\frac{15}{6}$ in the proportion and try again.

Again, we begin by setting up the proportion with a variable:

$$\frac{\text{Cost}}{\text{Soft Drinks}} \qquad \frac{\$5}{2 \text{ bottles}} = \frac{y}{14 \text{ bottles}}$$

- We ask ourselves, "2 · ? = 14?" We know that it's 7.
- Now we can complete the proportion: $\$5 \cdot 7 = y$ and $y = \$35$.

The completed proportion looks like this:

$$\frac{\text{Cost}}{\text{Soft Drinks}} \qquad \frac{\$5}{2 \text{ bottles}} = \frac{\$35}{14 \text{ bottles}}$$

The cost of 14 bottles of cola for the party will be $35.

Let's look at one final example of simplifying rates.

In this example, the simplified fraction is also the unit rate. Sometimes the best way to solve a complex rate problem is to find the unit rate. Example 4 shows a rate problem that is solved in this way.

> Unit rate is easy to work with because it is easy to multiply by the number 1.

Example 4

Solve a rate problem by finding the unit rate.

Problem:

We can buy 5 candles for $15. How much does it cost to buy 7 candles?

As always, we begin by setting up the proportion with a variable.

$$\frac{\text{Cost}}{\text{Candles}} \qquad \frac{\$15}{5} = \frac{z}{7}$$

- We ask, "$5 \cdot ? = 7$?" This is not an easy multiplication problem.
- So we ask ourselves, "Can we simplify the rate?" Yes, 5 and 15 have a greatest common factor of 5.

The simplified rate is $\frac{3}{1}$. This is called a unit rate because we have found the cost "for just one." Now we substitute the simplified rate, or unit rate, in the proportion for $\frac{15}{5}$.

$$\frac{\text{Cost}}{\text{Candles}} \qquad \frac{\$3}{1} = \frac{z}{7}$$

- We ask, "$1 \cdot ? = 7$?" The answer is 7. Now we complete the proportion: $\$3 \cdot 7 = z$. We find that $z = \$21$.

$$\frac{\text{Cost}}{\text{Candles}} \qquad \frac{\$15}{5} = \frac{\$21}{7}$$

Seven candles will cost $21 if the unit rate, or cost for one, is $3.

POWER CONCEPT

Simplifying the rate makes it easier to solve rate problems.

How do we solve word problems involving complex rates?

When we solve word problems involving rates, we have to remember many steps. Let's summarize the steps.

- Start by setting up a proportion with a variable that represents the rate problem being solved.

- Ask, "Is there an easy multiplication problem?" If there is, complete the proportion, and the problem is done.

- If there is not an easy multiplication problem, ask, "Can the rate be simplified?" If so, find the GCF for the two numbers and find the simplified rate. If possible, use the unit rate.

- Then substitute the simplified rate in the proportion and finish solving the problem.

If we work carefully and slowly through these basic steps, the problems are not difficult to solve. These kinds of math problems cannot be rushed. We need to work carefully and keep our work organized.

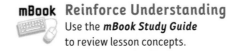

Problem-Solving Activity
Turn to *Interactive Text*,
page 114.

mBook **Reinforce Understanding**
Use the *mBook Study Guide*
to review lesson concepts.

Activity 1

Tell the Greatest Common Factor (GCF) for each pair of numbers.

1. 12 and 15
2. 16 and 18
3. 15 and 20
4. 24 and 36
5. 28 and 35

Activity 2

The rates tell how long it took different students to run laps. Tell which rates can be simplified. Then simplify them.

1. 4 laps in 10 minutes or $\frac{4}{10}$

2. 3 laps in 4 minutes or $\frac{3}{4}$

3. 5 laps in 15 minutes or $\frac{5}{15}$

4. 6 laps in 18 minutes or $\frac{6}{18}$

5. 12 laps in 28 minutes or $\frac{12}{28}$

6. 13 laps in 15 minutes or $\frac{13}{15}$

Activity 3

Complete the proportion for each of the rates. Simplify when necessary.

1. $\frac{4}{6} = \frac{6}{x}$
2. $\frac{6}{8} = \frac{x}{16}$
3. $\frac{6}{12} = \frac{5}{x}$
4. $\frac{8}{10} = \frac{x}{15}$
5. $\frac{4}{10} = \frac{8}{x}$

Activity 4 • Distributed Practice

Solve.

1. $438 - a = -399$
2. $\frac{2}{5} \cdot \frac{3}{4} = b$
3. $43.7 + 29.8 = c$
4. $d + 199 = 207$
5. $\frac{11}{12} \div \frac{1}{3} = e$
6. $13.05 - 4.8 = f$
7. $72 \div g = 8$
8. $h - 125 = 375$

▶**Double Inequalities**

Vocabulary
double inequality

How do we write double inequalities?

The inequalities we looked at in previous lessons go in one direction on the number line. Each inequality had either a lower boundary (it's greater than a certain number) or an upper boundary (it's less than a certain number). Let's look at some inequalities on the number lines.

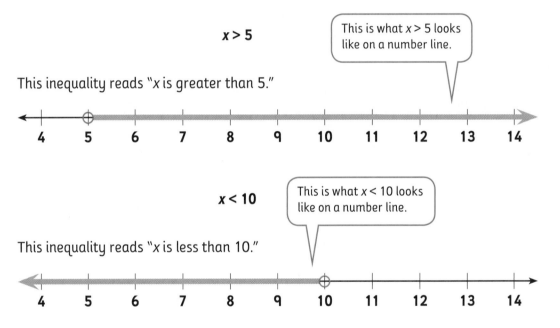

$x > 5$

> This is what $x > 5$ looks like on a number line.

This inequality reads "x is greater than 5."

$x < 10$

> This is what $x < 10$ looks like on a number line.

This inequality reads "x is less than 10."

Some problems give both upper and lower boundaries.

For instance, we might be told that something is greater than 5 but less than 10. In other words, the unknown value is between 5 and 10. We can write this statement using inequalities.

$$5 < x < 10$$

This inequality reads "5 is less than x, and x is less than 10."

This type of inequality is called a **double inequality** . A double inequality shows a range with an upper boundary and a lower boundary.

The double inequality $5 < x < 10$ means that x is between 5 and 10. Think about the two statements $5 < x$ and $x < 10$ coming together to form one statement.

$$5 < x \text{ and } x < 10$$

$$5 < x < 10$$

Now let's look at this inequality on a number line:

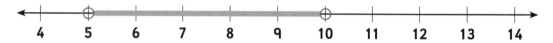

- Notice there are open circles on 5 and 10.
- Notice, too, that 5 and 10 are not included.

The value for x is somewhere between 5 and 10, but x does not equal 5 or 10.

We can also write double inequalities with the ≤ and ≥ symbols.

The following example shows there are at least 5 students in the class, but no more than 10. We can express this as a number sentence using the symbol ≤.

$$5 \leq x \leq 10$$

This statement reads "5 is less than or equal to x, and x is less than or equal to 10."

This is also called a double inequality. It shows a range with an upper boundary and a lower boundary.

This double inequality means that x is between 5 and 10, and both 5 and 10 are possible values for x. Think about the two statements coming together to form one statement.

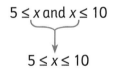

$$5 \leq x \text{ and } x \leq 10$$

$$5 \leq x \leq 10$$

POWER CONCEPT

A double inequality allows us to show a range of values between two numbers.

Here is how to show this inequality on a number line.

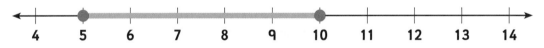

Apply Skills
Turn to *Interactive Text*, page 116.

mBook **Reinforce Understanding**
Use the *mBook Study Guide* to review lesson concepts.

▶**Problem Solving: Using Inequalities in the Real World**

What are some real-life ways that we use double inequalities?

We often use double inequalities when we describe temperature range. Meteorologists record the temperature throughout the day. Example 1 shows this situation.

Example 1

Write a double inequality and graph it on a number line.

Problem:

Let T = temperature throughout the day. We know that at one time during the day the temperature was 19 degrees, but it never went lower than 19 degrees. We also know that at another time during the day the temperature was 33 degrees, but it never went higher than 33 degrees. At other times, the temperature was in between these two extremes. How would we write the inequality using the symbol ≤?

$$19 \le T \le 33$$

Here's what this inequality looks like on a number line.

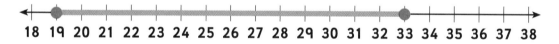

18 19 20 21 22 23 24 25 26 27 28 29 30 31 32 33 34 35 36 37 38

The number line shows us a range of temperatures. At one time during the day, the temperature equaled 19 degrees. At other times, it was greater than 19 degrees. At one time during the day, it equaled 33 degrees. At other times, it was less than 33 degrees. One statement using inequalities can say all of these things.

$$19 \le T \le 33$$

This is also a good way to think about negative numbers. In many places, temperatures reach below 0 degrees Fahrenheit in the winter.

Example 2 shows a double inequality that involves a negative number.

Example 2

Write a double inequality and graph it on a number line.

Problem:

On a very cold winter day in Green Bay, Wisconsin, the low temperature was −12 and the high temperature was 2. How would we write this inequality and show it on a number line?

Our low benchmark is −12 and our high benchmark is 2. We put the variable in between. We must also think about whether −12 and 2 are included in the range of values. They are. So our double inequality looks like this:

$$-12 \leq x \leq 2$$

Now we can graph the inequality on a number line:

−12	−11	−10	−9	−8	−7	−6	−5	−4	−3	−2	−1	0	1	2	3

> A benchmark is a significant point or point of reference.

It's important to recognize phrases that translate into double inequalities.

Look for statements such as *at least* x *but no more than* y, *between* x *and* y, *the high was* x *and the low was* y, and so on. These statements tend to be more complicated than statements such as, "It's less than 19 degrees outside."

Problem-Solving Activity
Turn to *Interactive Text*, page 117.

mBook Reinforce Understanding
Use the *mBook Study Guide* to review lesson concepts.

Tell whether each statement is true or false. On your paper, write T for true or F for false for each problem.

Model If $5 < x < 20$, a possible value of x is 20.   Answer: F

1. If $75 < y \le 99$, a possible value of y is 88.

2. If $75 < y \le 99$, a possible value of y is 75.

3. If $75 < y \le 99$, a possible value of y is 99.

4. If $75 < y \le 99$, a possible value of y is 79.

Tell if the number line shows the double inequality. Answer Yes or No. If no, tell how you would change it.

Model $43 < x \le 45$ Answer: No, the circle on 43 should be open.

1. $99 > m \ge 95$

2. $20 < n < 80$

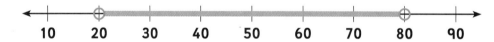

3. $18 > x \ge 15$

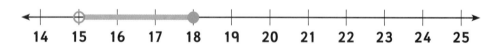

4. $34 \le z \le 43$

Activity 3

Write a statement that describes a situation using the given context (e.g., temperature, price, ounces).

Model $m < 5$ and $m > 2$, where m is Mickey's age in years.

Answer: Mickey is between 2 and 5 years old.

1. $10 \leq t \leq 50$, where t is the temperature in degrees.

2. $35 \leq p \leq 150$, where p represents the price in dollars of all the cameras at the department store.

3. $24 \geq w$ and $8 < w$, where w is the number of ounces of water a person drank in a day.

Activity 4 • Distributed Practice

Solve.

1. $11.05 \cdot 3 = a$

2. $537 + b = 601$

3. $\frac{1}{2} + \frac{1}{9} = c$

4. $70 \cdot d = 630$

5. $16.8 \div 2 = e$

6. $47.3 + 12.9 = f$

7. $g - 16 = 109$

8. $\frac{3}{8} - \frac{1}{3} = h$

9. $1.8 \cdot 4 = j$

► **Problem Solving: Comparing Different Rates**

How do we find the difference in the rates?

We do not always use rates to find equal ratios or proportions. Sometimes we want to solve a more complicated problem. These problems can require several steps, and finding the proportion is only one step in finding the answer. Example 1 shows how different rates can help us figure out how far apart cars would be in a race.

Example 1

Compare different rates.

Problem:

Jeff is near the front of the race. It takes him 5 minutes to drive 4 laps. Braxton is near the back of the race, and it takes him 5 minutes to drive 3 laps. How far apart will they be after 30 minutes?

We begin solving this problem by finding how many laps each driver will have gone after 30 minutes.

	Jeff	Braxton
Laps	$4 \cdot 6 = 24$	$3 \cdot 6 = 18$
Minutes	$5 \cdot 6 = 30$	$5 \cdot 6 = 30$

We multiply the minutes by 6 because we want to know the number of laps in 30 minutes. We multiply the laps by 6 so that our new ratios are equivalent to the ratios we started with.

This means that after 30 minutes, Jeff will have gone 24 laps and Braxton will have gone 18 laps. Now we can figure out how far apart they will be.

Jeff   Braxton

24   –   18   =   6 laps

After 30 minutes, Jeff will be 6 laps ahead of Braxton.

There are a number of times when we want to make a decision based on different rates. It may take one group longer to do something than another group, and we need to find the difference. Example 2 shows a case where we want to find out how much work two different crews are doing.

Example 2

Compare different rates.

Problem:

Ace Auto Rental has two different car lots in the city. Every time a car is returned, it has to be washed and cleaned for the next customer. At the south end car lot, the crew washes and cleans 10 cars an hour. The crew at the north end car lot can wash 25 cars in two hours. At first we might think, "That isn't much of a difference." But how much faster will the north end crew wash 100 cars?

	South End Crew	North End Crew
Cars	$10 \cdot 10 = 100$	$25 \cdot 4 = 100$
Hours	$1 \cdot 10 = 10$	$2 \cdot 4 = 8$

We multiply the number of cars by 10 because we want to see how long it takes to wash 100 cars. We multiply the number of hours by 10 so that our ratios are equivalent to the ratios we started with.

This means that for 100 cars, it takes the south end crew 10 hours and the north end crew 8 hours. What is the difference in the time?

South end crew		North end crew		
10	−	8	=	2 hours

The north end crew can get the job done 2 hours faster.

What is the problem asking for?

Solving a rate problem takes time. We need to start by asking, "What is the problem asking for?"

- In the first example, we wanted to know, "How far apart will the two cars be after 30 minutes?"

- In the second example, we wanted to know, "How much faster will the north end crew be able to wash 100 cars?"

When we have answered these questions, we are done with the problem. Solving the proportions is only part of the problem. We are not done until the question is answered.

POWER CONCEPT

Knowing what the problem is asking for helps us solve the whole problem.

✎ **Problem-Solving Activity**
Turn to *Interactive Text*, page 119.

mBook **Reinforce Understanding**
Use the *mBook Study Guide* to review lesson concepts.

Activity 1

Tell the faster crew in each situation by comparing rates.

1. Crew A makes 4 sandwiches in 5 minutes. Crew B makes 6 sandwiches in 10 minutes. Which crew works faster? Compare their work after 30 minutes.

2. Crew C washes 5 cars in 10 minutes. Crew D washes 8 cars in 15 minutes. Which crew works faster? Compare their work after 30 minutes.

3. Crew E makes 5 signs in 10 minutes. Crew F makes 12 signs in 20 minutes. Which crew works faster? Compare their work after 30 minutes.

Activity 2

Select the double inequality that best represents the word statement in each problem.

1. A child must be at least 2 years old and no more than 6 years old to attend the preschool. Use the variable a in a double inequality to represent the ages allowed at the school.
   (a) $a \leq 2 < 6$ 　　　(b) $2 < a \leq 6$ 　　　(c) $2 \leq a \leq 6$

2. The range of test scores on the last test was no less than 50 and no higher than 80. Use the variable t in a double inequality to represent the range of test scores.
   (a) $50 < t < 80$ 　　　(b) $50 \leq t \leq 80$ 　　　(c) $50 < t \leq 80$

3. John has more than 50 CDs in his collection but no more than 100. Use the variable c in a double inequality to represent the number of CDs he has.
   (a) $50 < c \leq 100$ 　　　(b) $50 \leq c \leq 100$ 　　　(c) $50 < c < 100$

Activity 3

Select the number line that represents the inequality.

1. $-5 < x \le 3$

(a) ⊕————●————→
      -5   3

(b) ●————⊕————→
      -5   3

(c) ●————●————→
      -5   3

2. $30 \le y \le 80$

(a) ⊕————⊕————→
      30   80

(b) ●————⊕————→
      30   80

(c) ●————●————→
      30   80

3. $50 > w > 10$

(a) ⊕————⊕————→
      10   50

(b) ●————⊕————→
      10   50

(c) ●————●————→
      10   50

4. $3 \ge t > -1$

(a) ⊕————●————→
      -1   3

(b) ●————⊕————→
      -1   3

(c) ●————●————→
      -1   3

Activity 4 • Distributed Practice

Solve.

1. $54 \div a = 6$

2. $\frac{3}{4} \cdot \frac{5}{6} = b$

3. $200.01 - 98.76 = c$

4. $d + 300 = 800$

5. $\frac{4}{9} \div \frac{1}{3} = e$

6. $22.8 + 47.6 = f$

7. $g \cdot 40 = 320$

8. $h = \frac{1}{3} + \frac{1}{9}$

▶**Showing the Range on a Number Line**

What does a number line with more than one range look like?

We have learned how to use number lines to show that a variable can stand for a range of values. In a previous lesson, we were given a problem like this one.

Example 1

Show a range of temperatures on a number line.

Problem:

Today was cloudy and cold. The low for the day was −8 degrees and the high was 4 degrees.

Let *z* equal today's temperature.

$$-8 \leq z \leq 4$$

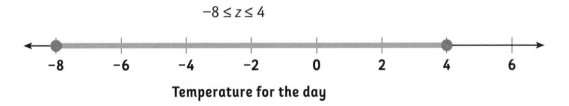

Temperature for the day

Notice that there is one range of values between −8 and 4.

Example 2 shows us that representing a range of numbers on a number line can be more complicated. We see that the number line now shows two ranges of numbers.

Example 2

Show two ranges of numbers on a number line.

Problem:

Carmen's softball team has 15 players. Seven of the players are taller than 66 inches and 8 of the players are from 60 to 63 inches. One of the players is 60 inches tall and one is 63 inches tall. Show the height of the players on Carmen's team on a number line.

Let k equal the height of the players.

$60 \leq k \leq 63$ or $k > 66$

We can also show ranges on a number line where the range of values for a variable applies to almost all of the number line.

Example 3

Show two ranges of numbers on a number line where the variable represents most of the numbers.

Problem:

There is a play structure in the mall on which kids can jump around on big cushions and not get hurt. However, the owners of the mall found that teenagers and young adults play too rough, so they are not allowed. The sign says, "Only ages 4 to 12 and 25 or older can play here."

> Notice that this part of the number line is not shaded.

Let m equal the age of people who can play on the play structure.

$4 \leq m \leq 12$ or $m \geq 25$

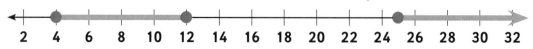

We have filled in most of the number line. The parts that are not shaded include only a few values since we do not include any ages below 0.

How should we think when we solve these problems?

When we use a variable to represent a range of values on the number line, we must read the problem carefully. Look for the way some sentences include a range of values.

For example, the problem in Example 3 said, "ages 4 to 12." That means 4 and 12 are included in the range along with all of the values in between.

Also think about those values that do not get included on the number line. Again, Example 3 does not allow people older than 12 or younger than 25 on the play structure. This part of the number line is not shaded.

%÷
<x **Apply Skills**
Turn to *Interactive Text*,
page 122.

mBook **Reinforce Understanding**
Use the *mBook Study Guide*
to review lesson concepts.

Activity 1

Tell if the number line matches the inequality statements. Answer Yes or No.

1. $10 < x < 30$ and $x > 80$
   Does this number line match?

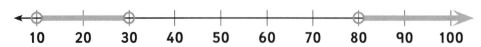

2. $-5 \leq y < 3$ and $y \geq 4$
   Does this number line match?

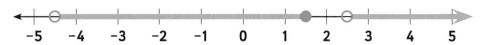

3. $10 \leq w \leq 60$ and $w \geq 90$
   Does this number line match?

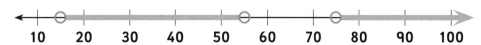

Activity 2

Tell if the value is within the range of values that satisfy the inequalities. Answer Yes or No.

1. $10 < w < 20$ and $w > 40$
   Is 10 in the range of values?

2. $10 \leq x \leq 15$ and $x > 50$
   Is 10 in the range of values?

3. $10 \leq a \leq 20$ and $a > 80$
   Is 80 in the range of values?

4. $-4 < b < 4$ and $b > 10$
   Is −3 in the range of values?

5. $-4 < c < 5$ and $c > 10$
   Is −5 in the range of values?

Activity 3

Select the number line that represents the inequality.

1. $-2 < x \le 4$

(a)
-2   4

(b)
-2   4

(c)
-2   4

2. $3 \le y \le 8$

(a)
3   8

(b)
3   8

(c)
3   8

3. $-1 > w > -5$

(a)
-5   -1

(b)
-5   -1

(c)
-5   -1

4. $0 \ge t > -4$

(a)
-4   0

(b)
-4   0

(c)
-4   0

Activity 4 • Distributed Practice

Solve.

1. $a - 297 = 468$

2. $\frac{11}{9} - \frac{2}{3} = b$

3. $12.6 \cdot 4 = c$

4. $90 \cdot d = 810$

5. $\frac{3}{5} + \frac{2}{10} = e$

6. $29.6 \div 4 = f$

7. $224 \div 7 = g$

8. $287.91 + 396.84 = h$

►Inequalities

How do we show inequalities?

We have been learning how to show inequalities in several different ways. In Review 1 we show an inequality on a number line.

> Remember to use an open circle when the symbol is > or <, and a closed circle when the symbol is ≥ or ≤.

Review 1

How do we show inequalities on a number line?

$x > 17$

$51 \leq q < 60$

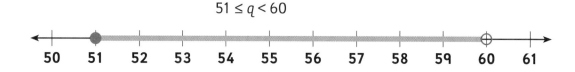

$j < 75$ and $j \geq 100$

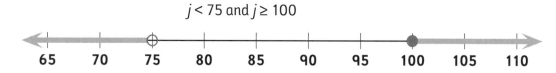

Notice that the range of values for j can be found on two parts of the number line.

We have also learned to recognize word statements that describe inequalities. We use these kinds of statements every day, but we may not realize that we are talking about inequalities. Statements such as *at least, at most, no more than,* and *no less than* often indicate inequalities.

Review 2 shows several ways in which everyday statements can be translated into inequalities.

Review 2

How do we use inequalities to represent everyday statements?

Since we got on the main highway, we were able to drive more than 50 miles per hour.

Let t equal how fast we were driving.

$$t > 50$$

This part of the ocean starts at 70 feet deep but then drops off to 120 feet deep.

Let k equal the depth of this part of the ocean.

$$70 \leq k \leq 120$$

The rainfall on this part of the coast is more than 100 inches but less than 130 inches.

Let y equal the amount of rainfall.

$$100 < y < 130$$

The people who live in this town are either under 35 years old or older than 60 years of age.

Let f equal the age of the people.

$$f < 35 \text{ and } f > 60$$

Finally, we learned we can create statements to help us think about a range of values for a variable. It is helpful to think about everyday events that happen around us. Review 3 shows how we can use common statements based on inequalities.

Review 3

How do we create statements based on inequalities?

Inequality:	$55 \leq k \leq 82$
Statement:	The temperature today went from a low of 55 degrees to a high of 82 degrees.
Inequality:	$r < 65$
Statement:	All of the shoes in the store are priced less than $65.
Inequality:	$z < 30$ and $z > 150$
Statement:	There are only two kinds of seats left for the concert. The cheap kind costs less than $30, and the other kind costs more than $150.

Remember to look for key phrases such as:

- at least x but no more than y.
- between x and y.
- the high was x and the low was y.

% ÷
= x
< x **Apply Skills**
Turn to *Interactive Text*, page 124.

mBook **Reinforce Understanding**
Use the *mBook Study Guide* to review lesson concepts.

How are rates a special kind of proportion?

Rates are comparisons between two different kinds of units. We may compare miles with hours or the cost of meat by the pound. Often rates involve proportions that help us find out how long it takes to do something.

> ### Review 1
>
> **How do we use proportions to solve rate problems?**
>
> **Problem:**
>
> A jet that travels at the speed of sound travels 1,320 miles in 2 hours. How far will it travel in 6 hours?
>
> $$\frac{\text{Miles}}{\text{Hours}} \qquad \frac{1{,}320}{2} = \frac{x}{6}$$
>
> - Looking at the denominators, we see the proportion asks us to think about 3 times the amount because $6 \div 2 = 3$.
>
> $$\frac{\text{Miles}}{\text{Hours}} \qquad \frac{1{,}320}{2} = \frac{3{,}960}{6}$$
>
> **The jet will travel 3,960 miles in 6 hours.**
>
> **Problem:**
>
> A 4-pound package of hamburger costs $8. How much will 2 pounds of hamburger cost?
>
> $$\frac{\text{Cost}}{\text{Pounds}} \qquad \frac{\$8}{4} = \frac{y}{2}$$
>
> - We can think of the proportion as taking half of 4 and half of 8, or we can ask, "2 times what is 8?"
>
> $$\frac{\text{Cost}}{\text{Pounds}} \qquad \frac{\$8}{4} = \frac{\$4}{2}$$
>
> **Two pounds of hamburger cost $4.**

One of the most common ways that we think about rate is through unit rates. We often use unit rates when we buy food or supplies. Unit rates tell us how much we get for 1 of something. Review 2 shows us two different cases of unit rate.

Review 2

How do we use proportions to find unit rates?

Problem:

Your family fills up the car at the gas station. You get 10 gallons of gas, and it costs $30. What is the price of a gallon of gas?

$$\frac{\text{Cost}}{\text{Gallons}} \qquad \frac{\$30}{10} = \frac{x}{1}$$

- An easy way to think about this is 10 times what is 30? We use the number 10 because we have 10 gallons of gas. Because $10 \cdot 3 = 30$, we know that the cost for one gallon of gas must be $3.

$$\frac{\text{Cost}}{\text{Gallons}} \qquad \frac{\$30}{10} = \frac{\$3}{1}$$

Gas costs $3 a gallon.

It is important to remember that a unit rate will always have a 1 in the denominator. This represents one unit.

Let's look at another problem.

Problem:

Coffee is sold in a 3-pound bag, and it costs $18. How much does coffee cost by the pound?

Since our unit rate is dollars per pound, we set up the proportion with cost in the numerator and pounds in the denominator.

$$\frac{\text{Cost}}{\text{Pound}} \qquad \frac{\$18}{3} = \frac{f}{1} \qquad\qquad \frac{\text{Cost}}{\text{Pound}} \qquad \frac{\$18}{3} = \frac{\$6}{1}$$

When we solve this problem, we think, "What number times 3 equals 18?" Because $3 \cdot 6 = 18$, we know that the cost per pound of coffee is $6.

Coffee costs $6 per pound.

We can also think about rates in more complex problems. We can use proportions to find unit rates for more than one situation. This allows us to compare the situations and see which is faster or better.

When we solve more complex problems, we need to be sure that we have answered the question that is asked. This usually means we have to do more than just solve the proportions.

Review 3 shows how we can use rates in a window-washing situation.

Review 3

How do we find the difference in rates?

Problem:

Bill's window-washing company has more workers than Janet's company. Bill's company can wash 40 windows in an hour. Janet's company can wash 25 windows in an hour. How many more windows will Bill's company wash after 4 hours?

Bill's Company

$$\frac{\text{Windows}}{\text{Hours}} \qquad \frac{40}{1} = \frac{z}{4} \qquad\qquad \frac{\text{Windows}}{\text{Hours}} \qquad \frac{40}{1} = \frac{160}{4}$$

- Bill's company washes 160 windows in 4 hours.

Janet's Company

$$\frac{\text{Windows}}{\text{Hours}} \qquad \frac{25}{1} = \frac{d}{4} \qquad\qquad \frac{\text{Windows}}{\text{Hours}} \qquad \frac{25}{1} = \frac{100}{4}$$

- Janet's company washes 100 windows in 4 hours.

We then find the difference between Bill's and Janet's companies after 4 hours.

$$160 - 100 = 60$$

Bill's company can wash 60 more windows after 4 hours.

We also use proportions to find larger quantities. For example, we can use proportions when we double a recipe for making cookies. We frequently use proportions to find unit rates when we want to know how much one of something costs. Finally, we use proportions to help us think about more complex problems.

 **Problem-Solving Activity**
Turn to *Interactive Text*, page 127.

 **mBook Reinforce Understanding**
Use the *mBook Study Guide* to review lesson concepts.

A WORKER ANT CAN LIFT
TWENTY TIMES
ITS OWN WEIGHT.

IF YOU WEIGHED 100 POUNDS AND YOU HAD THE PROPORTIONAL STRENGTH OF AN ANT, **YOU WOULD BE ABLE TO LIFT...**

An elephant seal

Seven football linemen

A small car

Building Number Concepts

- Use variables to represent numeric patterns
- Use variables to analyze patterns and make predictions
- Represent even and odd numbers and divisibility rules using algebraic equations

Problem Solving

- Represent part-to-whole and part-to-part relationships using ratios
- Solve real-world problems involving ratios
- Use percents to make comparisons

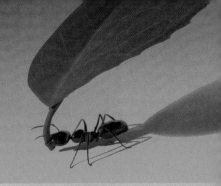

▶**Algebraic Patterns**

How do variables help us describe algebraic patterns?

Airlines make more money selling tickets to people who travel for business than they do selling tickets to vacation travelers.

Business travelers often have to change their plans and make reservations at the last minute. For this convenience, the airlines charge them a lot of money for a seat. Vacation travelers usually plan ahead and try to find the least expensive tickets. They tend to stick to their plans and do not change their trips at the last minute.

Let's say that an airline charges two times as much money for a ticket for a business traveler than a vacation traveler.

Example 1 shows this relationship or pattern using a variable. We can substitute any amount for the price of a vacation ticket and find the price of a business ticket.

Example 1

Use a variable to show the difference in ticket prices if a business traveler pays twice as much for a ticket as a vacation traveler.

Let q = the price of a vacation ticket.

The price of a business ticket is $2 \cdot q$.

Word problems are just one way we use variables to show a relationship or pattern. We can also use visual patterns with variables and numbers to help us understand and predict patterns.

Let's look at the pattern in Example 2. Notice how the number of circles in each box increases.

Example 2

Use a table to determine how many circles will be in the 10th box.

Box 1	Box 2	Box 3	Box 4	Box 5
OO	OO OO	OOO OOO	OOOO OOOO	OOOOO OOOOO

A quick look at the pattern shows that there are two more circles in each new box as we move to the right.

One way to solve this problem is to make a table that shows boxes 1 to 10 and how many circles there are in each box.

Box Number	1	2	3	4	5	6	7	8	9	10
Number of Circles	2	4	6	8	10	12	14	16	18	20

There are 20 circles in the tenth box.

Making a table is just one way to solve this problem. We can also figure out the number of circles in the 10th box by counting by two 10 times. That means counting 2, 4, 6, 8, 10, 12, 14, 16, 18, and 20. Again we find that there are 20 circles in the 10th box.

Using tables or counting can take a long time. Suppose we want to find the number of circles in the 60th box. It would take a long time to make the table or to count by two 60 times.

A simpler method is to look at the relationship between the number of the box and the number of the circles.

The number of circles is always two times more than the number of the box. We show this using a variable as **2 · n**, where *n* is the box number and 2 · *n* is the number of circles in the box.

Let's check that this works for the first three boxes.

- Box 1 has 2 · 1 or 2 circles.
- Box 2 has 2 · 2 or 4 circles.
- Box 3 has 2 · 3 or 6 circles.

Now let's check Box 10.

box number
↓
2 · *n*
⎫
number of circles in the box

We know that 2 · 10 = 20. We also know there are 20 circles in the 10th box. How about the 100th box?

Example 3 shows how easy it is to figure out the number of circles when we use a variable and substitution.

Example 3

Use a variable to find how many circles are in the 100th box.

First, we represent the pattern with 2 · n, where *n* is the box number. To find the number of circles in the 100th box, we substitute 100 for *n*.

2 · 100 = 200

There are 200 circles in the 100th box.

It takes a long time to write out a table from 1 to 100 or to count by two 100 times. It's much easier to use algebra to figure it out. This example shows just how powerful algebra can be.

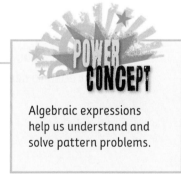

POWER CONCEPT

Algebraic expressions help us understand and solve pattern problems.

Apply Skills
Turn to *Interactive Text*, page 130.

Reinforce Understanding
Use the *mBook Study Guide* to review lesson concepts.

▶**Problem Solving: Another Way to Show Ratios**

What is a different way to think about ratios?

In the last two units, we learned different ways to think about ratios and proportions.

A common way to show either a ratio or a proportion is to write it vertically the way we write fractions. Example 1 shows how the ratio of boys, girls, and total students in a class are presented vertically.

Example 1

Solve the word problem by writing a ratio vertically.

Problem:

There are 16 girls and 14 boys in Mr. Hemley's sixth-grade classroom. What are the ratios in the classroom?

$$\frac{\text{Girls}}{\text{Boys}} \quad \frac{16}{14} \qquad \frac{\text{Girls}}{\text{Class}} \quad \frac{16}{30} \qquad \frac{\text{Boys}}{\text{Class}} \quad \frac{14}{30}$$

> It is important to notice the differences in each ratio.

These are all the ratios for looking at the comparisons between boys and girls in the classroom. We think about them like this:

- The ratio of girls to boys is a *part-to-part* relationship. A fraction is always a *part-to-whole* relationship. Although it looks like a fraction it is not.

- The ratios of girls to the class and boys to the class are part-to-whole relationships.

The difference between part-to-part and part-to-whole relationships is not that easy to see. That is why it's important to always use labels.

There is also another way to write ratios. We use a colon between the numbers and write the ratio as shown in Example 2.

Example 2

Write a ratio using a colon.

Problem:
There are 16 girls and 14 boys in Mr. Hemley's sixth-grade classroom.
What is another way to show the ratios in the class?

16 : 14 *There is a ratio of 16 girls to 14 boys.*

16 : 30 *The ratio of girls to total students is 16 to 30.*

14 : 30 *The ratio of boys to total students is 14 to 30.*

One advantage of showing ratios horizontally is that we can use the words "to" or "for" to talk about the different units in the ratio.

POWER CONCEPT

We can write ratios either vertically, like fractions, or horizontally with a colon.

Problem-Solving Activity
Turn to *Interactive Text*,
page 131.

mBook Reinforce Understanding
Use the *mBook Study Guide*
to review lesson concepts.

Activity 1

Write the missing numbers in the patterns on your paper. Use the letters to label your answers.

1. 16, 15, __(a)__, 13, 12, __(b)__, 10, __(c)__

2. 1, 3, 5, __(d)__, 9, 11, 13, __(e)__, 17, 19, __(f)__

3. __(g)__, 160, 150, 140, __(h)__, 120, __(i)__, 100, 90

4. 8, 13, 18, 23, __(j)__, __(k)__, 38, 43, 48, __(l)__

5. __(m)__, 70, __(n)__, 60, 55, 50, 45, __(o)__, 35, 30

Activity 2

Look at the algebraic pattern. Find the visual pattern that matches. The variable n represents the box number.

1. $2 \cdot n$

(a)
Box 1	Box 2	Box 3	Box 4	Box 5	Box 6
OO	OO OO	OOO OOO	OOOO OOOO	OOOOO OOOOO	OOOOOO OOOOOO

(b)
Box 1	Box 2	Box 3	Box 4	Box 5	Box 6
O	OO	OOO	OOOO	OOOOO	OOOOOO

(c)
Box 1	Box 2	Box 3	Box 4	Box 5	Box 6
OO	OO O	OO OO	OOO OO	OOO OOO	OOOO OOO

2. $n \cdot 4$

    (a)

Box 1	Box 2	Box 3	Box 4	Box 5	Box 6
OOOO OOOO	OOOO OO	OOOO O	OOOO	OOO	OO

    (b)

Box 1	Box 2	Box 3	Box 4	Box 5	Box 6
OOOO	OO	OOOO	OO	OOOO	OO

    (c)

Box 1	Box 2	Box 3	Box 4	Box 5	Box 6
OOOO	OOOO OOOO	OOOO OOOO OOOO	OOOO OOOO OOOO OOOO	OOOO OOOO OOOO OOOO OOOO	OOOO OOOO OOOO OOOO OOOO OOOO

3. $5 \cdot n$

    (a)

Box 1	Box 2	Box 3	Box 4	Box 5	Box 6
O	OO	OOO	OOOO	OOOOO	OOOOOO

    (b)

Box 1	Box 2	Box 3	Box 4	Box 5	Box 6
OOOOO	OOOOO OOOOO	OOOOO	OOOOO OOOOO	OOOOO	OOOOO OOOOO

    (c)

Box 1	Box 2	Box 3	Box 4	Box 5	Box 6
OOOOO	OOOOO OOOOO	OOOOO OOOOO OOOOO	OOOOO OOOOO OOOOO OOOOO	OOOOO OOOOO OOOOO OOOOO OOOOO	OOOOO OOOOO OOOOO OOOOO OOOOO OOOOO

Activity 3

Write the different ratios for each of the problems.

> **Model**   There are 15 girls in the class out of a total 27 students.
>
> Answer:
>
> Girls : Class 15 : 27
>
> Boys : Class 12 : 27
>
> Girls : Boys 15 : 12

1. There are 30 students on the varsity soccer team. They are all juniors or seniors. There are 22 seniors.

2. Of the 100 people at the rally, 55 of them are women.

3. The baseball team plays 40 games during its season. The team won 27 of its games.

Activity 4 • Distributed Practice

Solve.

1. $\frac{4}{5} + \frac{2}{9} = a$

2. $1.75 + 2.39 = b$

3. $4.2 \cdot 3 = c$

4. $\frac{3}{8} \div \frac{1}{4} = d$

5. Write the decimal number 0.20 as a percent.

6. Write the fraction $\frac{2}{4}$ as a decimal number.

7. Write 75% as a fraction.

8. Write the fraction $\frac{1}{4}$ as a percent.

Lesson 2 | Problem Solving: ▶Comparing Ratios

▶**Problem Solving: Comparing Ratios**

What's the best deal?

Ratios show relationships between different units.

Many stores give a better price if we buy a larger quantity of an item—but that's not always the case. So we have to look at the ratios carefully. We have to ask, "Which is the better deal?"

When we are looking for the best deal, we compare ratios. The units are cost (how much) and quantity (how many). In these kinds of cases, we are given all the numbers for both ratios. We make a comparison in order to answer the question.

When making comparisons, we do not use proportions or equivalent ratios. Instead, we find out which ratio gives us the most of something for the lowest price. Let's look at our choices for buying candy in the following example.

Problem:

Lorenzo's Candy Store has two prices for chocolate candy. We could buy:

- 5 pieces for $0.32
- 10 pieces for $0.52

Which one is the better deal? Are we getting a better deal per piece if we buy 10 pieces instead of 5 pieces?

Think of these two choices as ratios.

- 5 pieces for $0.32 is 5 : 0.32
- 10 pieces for $0.52 is 10 : 0.52

We answer the question by looking at the numbers in the ratios.

Example 1 shows how we set up ratios like these. To make the comparison, we make either the pieces or the costs the same. We use good number sense to figure out which numbers to make the same.

Example 1

Compare ratios to find the best deal.

$$\frac{\text{Pieces}}{\text{Cost}} \qquad \frac{5}{\$0.32} \qquad \frac{10}{\$0.52}$$

Good number sense tells us that it is easiest to make the *pieces* the same. That means that we have to change the first ratio.

$$\frac{\text{Pieces}}{\text{Cost}} \qquad \boxed{\frac{5}{\$0.32}} \quad \frac{\textcircled{10}}{\$0.52}$$

$$\frac{\text{Pieces}}{\text{Cost}} \qquad \frac{5}{\$0.32} \cdot \frac{2}{2} = \frac{\textcircled{10}}{\$0.64} \quad \text{Pieces are the same.}$$

Now we substitute the new ratio to make the comparison.

The ratio 5 : 0.32 is the same as 10 : 0.64.

$$\frac{\text{Pieces}}{\text{Cost}} \qquad \frac{10}{\$0.64} \qquad \frac{10}{\$0.52}$$

Buying 10 pieces for $0.52 is a better deal per piece.

These kinds of comparisons happen all the time in stores. To encourage us to buy more of something, a store will give us a better deal per unit if we buy more units of a product.

Let's look at another example. This time we will make the *costs* the same in the ratio.

Example 2

Compare ratios to find the best deal.

Problem:

  Lorenzo's Candy Shop sells 3 gumballs for $0.20. They also sell 16 gumballs for $0.80. Which is the better deal?

Once again we are given all the information we need for two ratios.

The first ratio is 3 : 0.20. The second ratio is 16 : 0.80.

When we use good number sense, we see it is easier to make the costs the same.

$$\frac{\text{Gumballs}}{\text{Cost}} \quad \boxed{\frac{3}{\$0.20}} \quad \frac{16}{\$0.80}$$

$$\frac{\text{Gumballs}}{\text{Cost}} \quad \frac{3}{\$0.20} \cdot \frac{4}{4} = \frac{12}{\$0.80} \longleftarrow \text{Costs are the same.}$$

Next we substitute the new ratio to make the comparison.

The ratio 3 : 0.20 is the same as 12 : 0.80.

$$\frac{\text{Gumballs}}{\text{Cost}} \quad \frac{12}{\$0.80} \quad \frac{16}{\$0.80}$$

Buying 16 gumballs for $0.80 is a better deal per piece.

Comparing ratios is easy once we find the equivalent ratios that make either the quantity the same or the cost the same. Then we ask ourselves, "What is the best deal?"

Making comparisons between ratios is a different kind of problem than we have worked before. We need to make sure that we look at all the numbers.

We keep asking ourselves these questions when we compare ratios:

- **What is the problem asking for?**
  In this lesson, the problems are asking us to make a comparison and find the best deal.

- **What do we know about the numbers?**
  We need to find equivalent ratios for either the quantity or the cost so we have something to compare. Look for the numbers that are easiest to multiply.

- **Does the answer make sense?**
  We always try to explain the answer to ourselves or someone else.

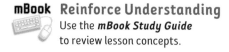

Problem-Solving Activity
Turn to *Interactive Text*, page 134.

mBook **Reinforce Understanding**
Use the *mBook Study Guide* to review lesson concepts.

Activity 1

For each comparison of ratios, tell what you are making the same—the quantity (Q) or the cost (C).

Model $\dfrac{\text{Lip Gloss}}{\text{Cost}}$ $\boxed{\dfrac{3}{\$4}}$ $\dfrac{5}{\$8}$

$\dfrac{6}{\$8}$ $\dfrac{5}{\$8}$

Answer: (C) We are making the cost the same.

1. $\dfrac{\text{Pears}}{\text{Cost}}$ $\boxed{\dfrac{2}{\$1}}$ $\dfrac{5}{\$3}$

$\dfrac{6}{\$3}$ $\dfrac{5}{\$3}$

2. $\dfrac{\text{Baseball Cards}}{\text{Cost}}$ $\dfrac{10}{\$25}$ $\boxed{\dfrac{5}{\$10}}$

$\dfrac{10}{\$25}$ $\dfrac{10}{\$20}$

3. $\dfrac{\text{Earrings (pairs)}}{\text{Cost}}$ $\boxed{\dfrac{3}{\$10}}$ $\dfrac{6}{\$24}$

$\dfrac{6}{\$20}$ $\dfrac{6}{\$24}$

4. $\dfrac{\text{DVDs}}{\text{Cost}}$ $\dfrac{5}{\$80}$ $\boxed{\dfrac{3}{\$40}}$

$\dfrac{5}{\$80}$ $\dfrac{6}{\$80}$

5. $\dfrac{\text{Candy Bars}}{\text{Cost}}$ $\boxed{\dfrac{3}{\$2}}$ $\dfrac{15}{\$9}$

$\dfrac{15}{\$10}$ $\dfrac{15}{\$9}$

Activity 2

Write the algebraic pattern that matches the visual patterns.

Model   What is the pattern?

Box 1	Box 2	Box 3	Box 4	Box 5	Box 6
OO	OO OO	OOO OOO	OOOO OOOO	OOOOO OOOOO	OOOOOO OOOOOO

Answer: 2 · n

1. What is the pattern?

Box 1	Box 2	Box 3	Box 4	Box 5	Box 6
OOO	OOO OOO	OOOOO OOOO	OOOOOO OOOOOO	OOOOO OOOOO OOOOO	OOOOOO OOOOOO OOOOOO

2. What is the pattern?

Box 1	Box 2	Box 3	Box 4	Box 5	Box 6
O	OO	OOO	OOOO	OOOOO	OOOOOO

3. What is the pattern?

Box 1	Box 2	Box 3	Box 4	Box 5	Box 6
OOOO	OOOO OOOO	OOOO OOOO OOOO	OOOO OOOO OOOO OOOO	OOOOO OOOOO OOOOO OOOOO	OOOOOO OOOOOO OOOOOO OOOOOO

Activity 3

Select the better deal per unit in each problem. Find the equivalent ratio to make either the quantity the same or the cost the same. Then tell which is the better deal by writing either (a) or (b) on your paper.

1. (a) 6 apples for $2 or
   (b) 12 apples for $3

2. (a) 2 CDs for $20 or
   (b) 3 CDs for $40

3. (a) 3 lip glosses for $10 or
   (b) 9 lip glosses for $35

4. (a) 4 video games for $100 or
   (b) 8 video games for $160

Activity 4 • Distributed Practice

Solve.

1. $17.1 - 8.6 = a$

2. $\frac{4}{5} \cdot \frac{2}{3} = b$

3. $1.6 \div 4 = c$

4. $\frac{8}{9} + \frac{4}{3} = d$

5. Write 25% as a decimal number.

6. Write the decimal number 0.08 as a fraction.

7. Write the fraction $\frac{4}{5}$ as a decimal number.

8. Write the fraction $\frac{3}{4}$ as a percent.

▶Complex Patterns

Problem Solving:
▶Rounding and Ratios

▶Complex Patterns

How do we analyze more complex patterns?

Algebra is filled with all kinds of patterns. The ones that we have looked at so far are fairly easy to understand. Now we will look at some complex patterns. Let's look at the pattern below.

Box 1	Box 2	Box 3	Box 4	Box 5
	O	OO	OO O	OO OO

This seems like an easy pattern, except the first box has no circles. We cannot just start at the second box because that would not tell us about the entire pattern.

We examine the numbers in the pattern by organizing them in a table. Example 1 shows how we use a table to analyze the pattern and come up with an algebraic pattern.

Example 1

Write an algebraic pattern and tell how many circles there would be in the 10th box.

Box 1	Box 2	Box 3	Box 4	Box 5
	O	OO	OO O	OO OO

We show what is happening with the pattern of circles by writing the pattern using numbers and organizing them in a table.

Box	1	2	3	4	5
Circles	0	1	2	3	4

Lesson 3

Reading the table from left to right helps us see the pattern. The number of circles is increasing by 1 each time. This pattern is consistent. We write this as +1.

Box	1	2	3	4	5
Circles	0	1	2	3	4

+1   +1   +1   +1

> The pattern in the table helps us write an algebraic pattern.

Reading the table from top to bottom also shows a pattern. There is one less circle than the box number each time. We can write this as −1.

Box	1	2	3	4	5
	↓	↓	↓	↓	↓
	−1	−1	−1	−1	−1
Circles	0	1	2	3	4

+1   +1   +1   +1

> This table also helps us see the pattern.

Based on the relationship between the box number and the number of circles, we write the pattern.

Let n be the box number.

- First let's use $n - 1$ to represent the number of circles in each box.
- Then we substitute the box number for n to figure out the number of circles.

$$n - 1$$
$$\downarrow$$
$$10 - 1$$

- Now we compute the number of circles.

The 10th box would contain 9 circles.

> Now that we know the algebraic pattern, we can find the number of circles in any box in this pattern.

The next problem shows another example of how we use a table to write an algebraic pattern.

Example 2

Write an algebraic pattern and tell how many circles there would be in the 10th box.

Box 1	Box 2	Box 3	Box 4	Box 5
ooo	oooo	ooooo	oooooo	ooooooo o

We show what is happening with the pattern of circles by writing the pattern using numbers and organizing them in a table.

Box	1	2	3	4	5
Circles	3	4	5	6	7

Box	1	2	3	4	5
Circles	3	4	5	6	7

+1   +1   +1   +1

> As we read from left to right, we are increasing by 1 circle each time. We can write this as +1.

When we read from top to bottom, we see that there are 2 more circles than the box number each time. This helps us write the pattern.

Box	1 $\downarrow$ +2	2 $\downarrow$ +2	3 $\downarrow$ +2	4 $\downarrow$ +2	5 $\downarrow$ +2
Circles	3	4	5	6	7

+1   +1   +1   +1

Again, let n be the box number.

- First, we use $n + 2$ to represent the number of circles in each box.
- Next we substitute 10 for the n in the pattern.

$$n + 2$$
$$\downarrow$$
$$10 + 2 = 12$$

There would be 12 circles in the 10th box.

Complicated patterns take a lot of thinking. Tables help us organize the numbers. When we use a table, we:

- get a sense of the pattern by reading the numbers left to right.
- can connect the box number with the pattern by reading the numbers top to bottom.

By analyzing the table, we find the algebraic pattern. We then use the algebraic pattern to find the number of circles in any box in the pattern.

Apply Skills
Turn to *Interactive Text*,
page 137.

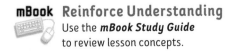

Reinforce Understanding
Use the *mBook Study Guide*
to review lesson concepts.

▶Problem Solving: **Rounding and Ratios**

How do we use rounding to compare costs?

Sometimes it is difficult to compare ratios because the numbers in the ratio don't convert easily.

We might have all the information we need for the ratios, but the units are not equivalent. We may find that there is no easy way to change either of the ratios to an equivalent ratio.

We see examples like this a lot when we shop. Store managers always want the prices to seem less than they really are, so they use numbers like $2.99 or $99.99 because they seem less than $3 or $100. Shoppers think $2.99 is a smaller number than $3, when it's really only a 1¢ difference. This is called a marketing strategy.

When we encounter situations like this, we must find a way to make an easier comparison. We need to find an equivalent ratio for the cost or the quantity. We use rounding to do this.

Rounding decimal numbers to whole numbers helps make the process easier. Example 1 shows how to use rounding to compare ratios. Using several steps helps us make these comparisons.

Example 1

Solve the word problem by rounding to compare the ratios.

Problem:

At the T-Hut, the price of 3 T-shirts is $19.99. We can also buy 7 of them for $39.99. Which is the better deal?

Steps for Using Rounding to Compare Ratios

STEP 1
Round each of the prices to the nearest whole number.

$19.99 rounds to $20
$39.99 rounds to $40

STEP 2

Find an equivalent ratio.

We want to make the quantities in both ratios equivalent.

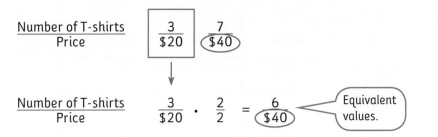

STEP 3

Substitute the new ratio and make the comparison.

$\frac{3}{\$20}$ is the same as $\frac{6}{\$40}$

Number of T-shirts		
Price		
	$\frac{6}{\$40}$	$\frac{7}{\$40}$

STEP 4

Make the comparison.

We can use a calculator to compare the ratios.

Buying 7 T-shirts for $40 is a better deal per unit.

 Problem-Solving Activity
Turn to *Interactive Text*,
page 139.

mBook **Reinforce Understanding**
Use the *mBook Study Guide*
to review lesson concepts.

Activity 1

Select the visual pattern that matches the algebraic pattern.

1. $n - 1$

(a)

Box 1	Box 2	Box 3	Box 4	Box 5
O	OO	OOO	OOOO	OOOOO

(b)

Box 1	Box 2	Box 3	Box 4	Box 5
	O	OO	OOO	OOOO

(c)

Box 1	Box 2	Box 3	Box 4	Box 5
OO	OOO	OOOO	OOOOO	OOOOOO

2. $n + 1$

(a)

Box 1	Box 2	Box 3	Box 4	Box 5
O	OO	OOO	OOOO	OOOOO

(b)

Box 1	Box 2	Box 3	Box 4	Box 5
	O	OO	OOO	OOOO

(c)

Box 1	Box 2	Box 3	Box 4	Box 5
OO	OOO	OOOO	OOOOO	OOOOOO

3. $n + 0$

(a)

Box 1	Box 2	Box 3	Box 4	Box 5
O	OO	OOO	OOOO	OOOOO

(b)

Box 1	Box 2	Box 3	Box 4	Box 5
	O	OO	OOO	OOOO

(c)

Box 1	Box 2	Box 3	Box 4	Box 5
OO	OOO	OOOO	OOOOO	OOOOOO

Activity 2

Round to the nearest whole number that would make comparing the ratios easier. Then write the new problem.

Model 4 for $9.99 and 5 for $18.99

Answer: You would round $9.99 to $10 and $18.99 to $20.

The new problem is: 4 for $10 and 5 for $20.

1. 4 for $24.99 and 5 for $49.99

2. 3 for $2.99 and 4 for $5.99

3. 2 for $19.99 and 3 for $39.99

4. 6 for $35.99 and 4 for $17.99

Activity 3

Name the better deal.

1. Would you rather buy 5 packs of gum for $1.19 or 10 packs of gum for $2.99?

2. Would you rather buy 4 CDs for $59.99 or 2 CDs for $24.99?

3. Would you rather buy 3 candy bars for $0.99 or 6 candy bars for $1.49?

4. Would you rather buy 8 pencils for $3.99 or 5 pencils for $1.99?

Activity 4 • Distributed Practice

Solve.

1. $\frac{11}{12} - \frac{1}{6} = a$

2. $6.2 \cdot 0.2 = b$

3. $\frac{4}{8} \div \frac{2}{8} = c$

4. $119.05 + 230.99 = d$

5. Write the decimal number 0.17 as a percent.

6. Write the fraction $\frac{2}{5}$ as a decimal number.

7. Write 35% as a decimal number.

8. Write the fraction $\frac{2}{4}$ as a percent.

▶ **Problem Solving: Ratio Problems**

What are the different kinds of ratio problems?

We learned about several different kinds of problems involving ratios.

Sometimes, we are given two ratios with a missing part. We must find the value of the missing part so the two ratios are equal. Example 1 shows this type of proportion problem.

Example 1

Solve the word problem to find the missing value.

Problem:

We are reading a map, and the scale shows 1 inch equals 500 miles. How many miles is a 3-inch distance on the map?

First, we set up the proportion like this:

$$\frac{\text{Inches}}{\text{Miles}} \qquad \frac{1}{500} = \frac{3}{x}$$

When we solve for x we are solving the proportion. The top number has been multiplied by 3, so we have to multiply the bottom number by 3 to find the missing value.

$$500 \cdot 3 = 1{,}500$$

Now we write the completed proportion.

$$\frac{\text{Inches}}{\text{Miles}} \qquad \frac{1}{500} = \frac{3}{1{,}500}$$

A 3-inch distance on the map represents 1,500 miles.

Other times, we are given problems where we need to find out how much "one of something" costs. These are called unit rate problems.

Example 2

Solve the word problem to find the unit rate.

Problem:

If 10 gallons of gas costs $30, how much does 1 gallon of gas cost?

We set up a proportion to solve this kind of problem as well. The difference is that one of the ratios has the number 1 as the unit.

$$\frac{\text{Gallons of Gas}}{\text{Cost}} \qquad \frac{10}{\$30} = \frac{1}{x}$$

We know how much 10 gallons costs. We use this information to figure out how much 1 gallon costs. We complete the proportion as a unit rate:

$$\frac{\text{Gallons of Gas}}{\text{Cost}} \qquad \frac{10}{\$30} = \frac{1}{\$3}$$

The unit rate is 1 gallon for $3.

Some other ratio problems do not involve making equal ratios at all.

When we shop for the best deal, we look at the different ratios. Our job is to compare them. We already have all the information for the two ratios, but they are not equivalent. We have to use good number sense and make either the quantity or the cost the same so that we can make a comparison. Example 3 shows a best-deal problem.

Example 3

Solve the word problem by comparing ratios.

Problem:

Marty's Quick Mart is selling bags of potato chips at the rate of 1 bag for $2.99. The grocery store down the street sells the same potato chips at the rate of 2 bags for $5. Which is the better deal per bag?

We start by rounding the first ratio. We round $2.99 to $3. Now let's write the two ratios:

$$\frac{\text{Bag of Chips}}{\text{Cost}} \qquad \frac{1}{\$3} \qquad \frac{2}{\$5}$$

We use number sense to make either the cost or the quantity even, then compare the ratios.

$$\frac{\text{Bag of Chips}}{\text{Cost}} \qquad \boxed{\frac{1}{\$3}} \qquad \frac{2}{\$5}$$

$$\downarrow$$

$$\frac{\text{Bag of Chips}}{\text{Cost}} \qquad \frac{2}{\$6} \qquad \frac{2}{\$5}$$

The rate of 2 for $5 is the better deal. We save a dollar when we buy 2 bags from the other store.

As we work these kinds of problems, we ask ourselves:

- What is the problem asking for?
- What ratios are we given?
- Are we given both ratios? If so, we compare them and determine the best deal.
- Are we given two ratios with one missing part? If so, we solve for the missing part so that the two ratios are equal. This is called a proportion.
- Are we given two ratios with one missing part and one part equal to 1? If so, we find the unit rate.
- Does our answer make sense?
- Could we explain the answer to someone else?

> It's important to keep all of these things in mind when solving ratio problems.

How do we use ratios to compare data in tables?

We often use ratios when we analyze the information given in a table of data.

Example 1 shows wholesale prices for food products. The data are given in a table. Below the table are proportion problems based on the data. We do not actually solve the problem. Instead, we explain what kind of ratio problem it is.

Example 1

Describe the proportion.

Problem:

Jahnella Keets owns a truck stop near a freeway. Besides selling gas, she also sells food and basic supplies. She buys goods for her store from a supplier. She makes comparisons and tries to find good deals so she can keep costs down at the truck stop.

DHM Suppliers faxes Jahnella the costs and weekly specials for items. She calls in her weekly order. Here is a part of the fax from DHM Suppliers.

Item	Quantity and Price	Weekly Special
Delmont Cookies	2 packages for $3	no
Frozen Pizza	1 box for $2.50	no
Fruit Juice	5 cases for $15.50	10 cases for $29
Potato Chips	6 bags for $3	no
Ice Cream	4 gallons for $10	15 gallons for $30
Bottled Water	5 cases for $20	no

Describe the kind of problem that each question represents:

1. **Jahnella wants 10 packages of Delmont cookies. How much will this cost?**

   What kind of problem is this? We know the price for 2 packages. This is a proportion problem. We create an equivalent ratio.

2. **People are drinking a lot of fruit juice. Is the weekly special a good deal?**

   We are comparing two ratios. We are also given all the information. The question is asking, "What is the best deal?" We use number sense and make the cases of juice the same. Then we compare the rates.

3. **How many bags of potato chips can Jahnella buy for $1?**

   We want to know how much we can get for just $1. This is a unit rate problem. We make an equivalent ratio.

Answering questions about data in a table can be challenging because sometimes we have to make adjustments to the data we find in the table. We need to set up different kinds of ratio problems. There are added steps that we need to do besides just reading the data from the table.

Problem-Solving Activity
Turn to *Interactive Text*, page 141.

mBook Reinforce Understanding
Use the *mBook Study Guide* to review lesson concepts.

Tell if the problem is (a) a proportion problem, (b) a best deal problem, or (c) a unit rate problem.

1. What is the cost for one box of pencils?

Boxes of Pencils	10	1
Cost	$5	x

2. If 3 bags of chips cost $5, how much will it cost for 6 bags of chips?

Bags of Chips	3	6
Cost	$5	x

3. What's the better deal: 2 pairs of jeans for $50 or 4 pairs of jeans for $80?

Pairs of Jeans	2 pairs	4 pairs
Cost	$50	$80

4. If 12 cans of fruit juice cost $3, how much will you pay for 24 cans?

Fruit Juice	12 cans	24 cans
Cost	$3	x

Match the visual pattern with the algebraic pattern given.

1. $2 \cdot n$

(a)

Box 1	Box 2	Box 3	Box 4	Box 5
OOOOO	OOOO	OOO	OO	O

(b)

Box 1	Box 2	Box 3	Box 4	Box 5
OOO	OOOOOO	OOOOOO OOO	OOOOOO OOOOOO	OOOOOO OOOOOO OOO

(c)

Box 1	Box 2	Box 3	Box 4	Box 5
OO	OO OO	OOO OOO	OOOO OOOO	OOOOO OOOOO

2. $n + 3$

(a)

Box 1	Box 2	Box 3	Box 4	Box 5
ooooo	oooo	ooo	oo	o

(b)

Box 1	Box 2	Box 3	Box 4	Box 5
oooo	ooooo	oooooo	ooooooo	ooooooo

(c)

Box 1	Box 2	Box 3	Box 4	Box 5
oo	oo oo	ooo ooo	oooo oooo	ooooo ooooo

3. $3 \cdot n$

(a)

Box 1	Box 2	Box 3	Box 4	Box 5
ooooo	oooo	ooo	oo	o

(b)

Box 1	Box 2	Box 3	Box 4	Box 5
ooo	oooooo	oooooo ooo	oooooo oooooo	oooooo oooooo ooo

(c)

Box 1	Box 2	Box 3	Box 4	Box 5
oo	oo oo	ooo ooo	oooo oooo	ooooo ooooo

Answer the questions about the table of data. Use ratios to set up your solutions. The data represent supplies that Tom needs to run his business— a hot dog stand at the park.

Tom's Hot Dog Stand Supplies	
Item	Quantity and Cost
Napkins	15 boxes for $45
Hot Dogs	20 packages for $200
Buns	10 packages for $50
Ketchup	6 bottles for $30
Mustard	6 bottles for $28

1. How much does it cost for 30 boxes of napkins?

2. What is the unit rate for the packages of hot dogs?

3. What's the better deal, the ketchup or the mustard?

4. How many packages of hot dog buns can Tim buy for $200?

Solve.

1. $100.01 - 98.79 = a$

2. $\frac{5}{6} \cdot \frac{6}{11} = b$

3. $32.8 \div 4 = c$

4. $\frac{1}{6} + \frac{1}{9} = d$

5. Write the decimal number 0.03 as a fraction.

6. Write the fraction $\frac{4}{8}$ as a percent.

7. Write 1% as a fraction.

8. Write 5% as a decimal number.

▸**Patterns in Tessellations**

How do tessellations follow algebraic patterns?

Tessellations allow us to use simple geometric shapes to make algebraic patterns. Remember that tessellations are shapes that are translated, reflected, or rotated in order to make a larger pattern.

In the tessellation pattern below, we combine more and more small triangles each time to create the next shape in the pattern.

Is there a way to predict how many small triangles will be needed to create the 10th shape in the tessellation pattern?

  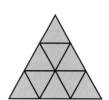 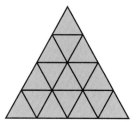

We represent the pattern with numbers by counting the number of little triangles in each shape and organizing these numbers in a table.

Example 1 shows how we use the table to understand the pattern and predict how many little triangles will make up each shape in the pattern.

Example 1

Use a table to determine how many triangles are needed to create the 10th shape in the tessellation pattern.

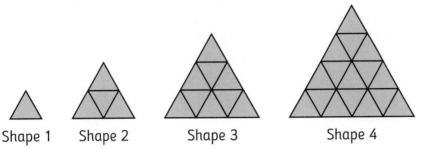

Shape 1   Shape 2   Shape 3   Shape 4

First we analyze how the number of small triangles changes from one shape to the next.

Shape	1	2	3	4
Small Triangles	1	4	9	16

We see a pattern when we read the numbers from left to right. Each difference is odd and it increases by 2: first 3, then 3 + 2 or 5, then 5 + 2 or 7, and so on.

Shape	1	2	3	4
Small Triangles	1	4	9	16

+ 3   + 5   + 7

We also find a pattern when we read the numbers from top to bottom. This shows a consistent relationship between the shape number and the amount of small triangles.

Shape	1	2	3	4
	$\downarrow$	$\downarrow$	$\downarrow$	$\downarrow$
	1^2	2^2	3^2	4^2
Small Triangles	1	4	9	16

The pattern is the number of the shape times itself. If we let x = the number of the shape, then the pattern is $x \cdot x$ or x^2.

The 10th shape in the pattern contains 10^2 or 100 small triangles.

Another way to find the number of small triangles in this tessellation is by drawing the next shape in the pattern. Then we count the triangles. Example 2 shows how we get the same answer with either strategy.

Example 2

Find how many small triangles are in the 5th shape in the pattern.

We create the 5th shape by adding a new row of 9 small triangles.

  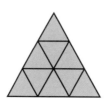 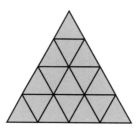 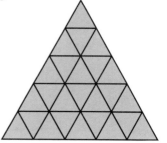

When we count the triangles, we see that the 5th shape has 25 small triangles.

Our algebraic pattern tells us that the 5th shape should have 5^2 or 25 small triangles.

The 5th shape in the pattern has 25 small triangles.

The powerful thing about algebra is that it gives us a way to think about shapes in the pattern that would be too difficult to draw.

Algebra helps us think about patterns that are too difficult to draw.

Apply Skills
Turn to *Interactive Text*, page 143.

Monitoring Progress
Quiz 1

mBook Reinforce Understanding
Use the *mBook Study Guide* to review lesson concepts.

Activity 1

Draw the next shape for each of these patterns on your paper.

Model

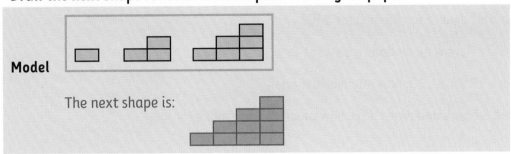

The next shape is:

1.

2.

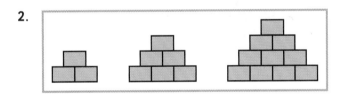

3.

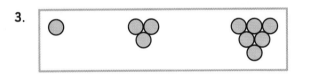

Activity 2

Tell what kind of ratio problem each is and then solve.

1. Which is the best deal: 2 for $5 or 3 for $10?

2. If it costs $8 for 4, how much does it cost for 2?

3. If balloons are 12 for $1.20, how much is just one?

4. If you worked 8 hours and made $16, how much did you make for just one hour?

5. Which is the best deal: 3 for $12 or 5 for $24?

Activity 3

Select the visual pattern that matches the algebraic pattern.

1. x^2

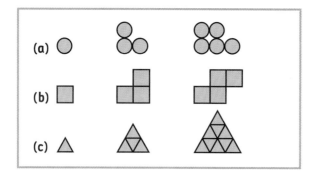

2. $x + 1$

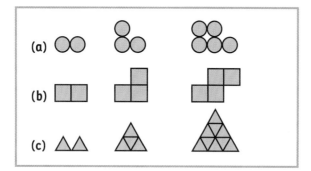

3. x

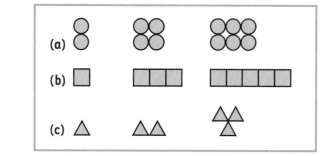

Activity 4 • Distributed Practice

Solve.

1. $\frac{7}{9} - \frac{2}{3} = a$

2. $27.8 \cdot 0.1 = b$

3. $\frac{2}{8} \div 4 = c$

4. $109.75 + 137.25 + 128.50 = d$

5. Write the decimal number 0.22 as a percent.

6. Write the fraction $\frac{1}{2}$ as a decimal number.

7. Write 150% as a decimal number.

8. Write 45% as a fraction.

▶**Number Machines**

What is the pattern in the number machine?

Number machines are another way to learn how to analyze patterns and write them using algebra.

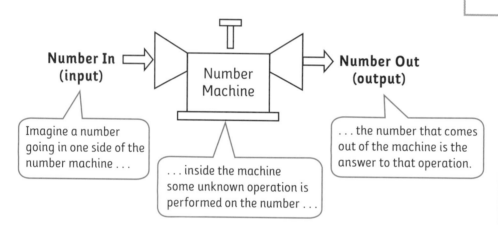

Number In (input) Imagine a number going in one side of the number machine . . .

Number Machine

. . . inside the machine some unknown operation is performed on the number . . .

Number Out (output) . . . the number that comes out of the machine is the answer to that operation.

The number going in is also called the **input**. The number coming out is also called the **output**.

In Example 1 we will make a table to show what happens when we input numbers. The numbers going in are not in any particular order.

To find the pattern of the output, we use the strategy of **guess and check**. We look for a pattern by guessing what is happening to the input that would produce the output.

When we find that our guess works for every pair of input and output numbers, we have found the pattern. Then we are ready to write an algebraic expression.

Example 1

Find the pattern that predicts the output of the number machine.

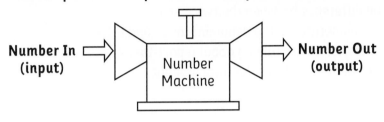

Number In (input) → **Number Machine** → **Number Out (output)**

STEP 1
Find out what is going on in the pattern.

- In the first ratio, the output is 5 times bigger than the input.
- In the second ratio it is 5 times bigger.
- We see a pattern in each row in the table. The output is always 5 times bigger than the input.

Input	Output
4	20
8	40
3	15
10	50

STEP 2
Create an algebraic expression.
Let g = the number going in. The number coming out is $5 \cdot g$.

The algebraic expression for the pattern is $5 \cdot g$.

Improve Your Skills

When we work with number machines, we need to think about the questions below and make sure we can answer them.

- *Can I use guess and check to find a pattern that works every time a number moves from the input to the output side of the table?*

- *Can I make up a number not in the table and then predict what the number will be when it goes through the number machine?*

Apply Skills
Turn to *Interactive Text*, page 147.

mBook Reinforce Understanding
Use the *mBook Study Guide* to review lesson concepts.

▶**Problem Solving: Mixtures**

How do we use ratios when we work with mixtures?

We have learned that ratios can be part-to-part and part-to-whole relationships. One way to tell the difference between the two is to ask ourselves, "Do we need to add the numerator to the denominator to find the total amount?" If the answer is yes, we are talking about a part-to-part relationship. In this case, we call the whole, or the total amount, the **mixture**.

Let's say we are making chocolate milk. We make it by combining chocolate syrup with milk. The bottle of syrup reads:

Directions: To make chocolate milk, use 2 ounces of syrup and 8 ounces of milk.

Ingredients: cocoa

We can also say that we are going to use *2 parts syrup* and *8 parts milk* to make a *total of 10 ounces of chocolate milk*. The total of 10 ounces is the mixture.

Let's look at three ratios we can make based on the mixture. We get the total amount by adding the two parts together.

Ratios for the Chocolate Milk Mixture			
Part-to-Part Ratio	$\frac{Syrup}{Milk}$	$\frac{2}{8}$	or 2 : 8
Part-to-Whole Ratio	$\frac{Syrup}{Mixture}$	$\frac{2}{10}$	or 2 : 10
Part-to-Whole Ratio	$\frac{Milk}{Mixture}$	$\frac{8}{10}$	or 8 : 10

How are ratio and percent related?

We might want to ask, "What percent of the mixture is syrup?"

To answer the question, we need to know what the whole amount is. Remember that percents are like fractions. They are part-to-whole relationships.

In this case, we are asking about the relationship between the 2 ounces of syrup and the total mixture of 10 ounces. Example 1 shows how to find the percent of syrup in the mixture.

Example 1

Find the percent of syrup in the chocolate milk.

Problem:

The chocolate milk is a mixture of 2 ounces of chocolate syrup and 8 ounces of milk. What percent of the mixture is syrup?

Part-to-Whole Ratio

$$\frac{\text{Syrup}}{\text{Mixture}} \qquad \frac{2}{10}$$

This ratio is just like a fraction because it is part-to-whole. We can change it into a decimal number and then into a percent.

$$\frac{2}{10} = 0.2 = 20\%$$

The mixture is 20% syrup.

📝 **Problem-Solving Activity**
Turn to *Interactive Text*,
page 149.

⌨ **mBook Reinforce Understanding**
Use the *mBook Study Guide*
to review lesson concepts.

Activity 1

Convert the fractions to percents. Remember to make them hundredths.

1. $\frac{1}{5}$ 2. $\frac{15}{20}$ 3. $\frac{1}{10}$

4. $\frac{3}{25}$ 5. $\frac{4}{50}$ 6. $\frac{1}{2}$

Activity 2

Tell all the different ratios involved in each of the mixtures.

Model   The pink paint is made up of 2 parts red and 1 part white.

$$\frac{\text{Red}}{\text{White}} \quad \frac{2}{1} \qquad\qquad \frac{\text{Red}}{\text{Total Mixture}} \quad \frac{2}{3} \qquad\qquad \frac{\text{White}}{\text{Total Mixture}} \quad \frac{1}{3}$$

1. The pancake batter is 3 parts water to 2 parts mix.

2. The sore throat remedy is 10 parts water to 1 part salt.

3. The caramel latte is 2 parts caramel to 12 parts milk.

Activity 3

In each problem, tell what percent the part is compared to the whole mixture.

1. The lemonade is made from 6 cups of water and 1 cup of powdered lemon concentrate. What percent of the mixture is water?

2. The orange paint is made with 3 parts red paint and 2 parts yellow paint. What percent of the mixture is red paint?

3. The pancake batter is made with 2 cups of mix and 3 cups of water. What percent of the pancake batter is the mix?

Activity 4 • Distributed Practice

Solve.

1. $30.27 - 25.38 = a$ 2. $\frac{11}{12} \cdot \frac{1}{2} = b$

3. $16.8 \div 0.2 = c$ 4. $\frac{1}{3} + \frac{1}{9} + \frac{1}{6} = d$

5. Write the decimal number 0.008 as a fraction.

6. Write the fraction $\frac{1}{3}$ as a percent.

7. Write 150% as a mixed number.

8. Write 20% as a decimal number.

▶**More Complicated Number Machines**

What do more complicated patterns look like?

The number machine can perform any operation and produce any kind of number. Earlier, the operations involved multiplication patterns. But the patterns can be more complex, too.

Example 1

Use the steps to find the pattern.

Number In (input) ⇨ **Number Machine** ⇨ **Number Out** (output)

Steps for Finding an Algebraic Pattern

STEP 1

Find out what is going on in the pattern.
Guess and check is a good strategy here. We could try division, as in 15 ÷ ? = 5. The operation would then be "divide by 3." But we know that 20 ÷ 3 does not equal 10.

Input	Output
15	5
20	10
12	2
28	18

STEP 2

Try another operation.
Let's look at the input numbers and output numbers. Each output number is 10 less than the input number. This pattern works for all the pairs of input and output numbers.

STEP 3

Create an algebraic expression.
Let y = the number going in.

The output is $y - 10$.

The algebraic expression is $y - 10$.

Sometimes the inputs and outputs are rational numbers. This makes the patterns even more complex. Example 2 shows what happens when some of the input and output numbers are fractions and decimal numbers.

Example 2

Find the pattern.

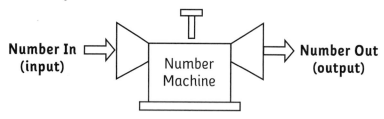

Number In (input) → Number Machine → Number Out (output)

STEP 1
Find out what is going on in the pattern.
A good way to begin analyzing the pattern is to compare the inputs and outputs. In this table, the output numbers are always smaller than the input numbers.

Input	Output
1	$\frac{1}{2}$
4	2
16	8
5	2.5

STEP 2
Create an algebraic expression.
We see that all of the output numbers are half of the input numbers. The operation must be "divide by 2."

Let n = the number going in.

The algebraic expression is $n \div 2$.

> Notice that one of our output numbers is a fraction $\left(\frac{1}{2}\right)$ and another output number is a decimal number (2.5). We can have both types of numbers in these kinds of patterns.

The important thing to remember with complex number machines is to use good number sense. We compare input and output numbers. Which are bigger? How much bigger? Good number sense and the guess-and-check strategy can help us figure out difficult patterns.

 **Apply Skills**
Turn to **Interactive Text**, page 151.

 **mBook Reinforce Understanding**
Use the **mBook Study Guide** to review lesson concepts.

▶**Problem Solving: Simple Experiments**

What kind of mixtures do we use in experiments?

Chemistry experiments can be fun. Sometimes they produce interesting results. Here is an easy way to make a slimy blob from simple ingredients.

Recipe for Slime

Ingredients

> 1 part borax soap
>
> 7 parts water
>
> 8 parts white glue

Directions

1. Mix the water and the soap in a bowl.

2. Slowly stir the glue into the water and soap. This will make a slime.

3. Squeeze it back and forth until it dries.

The more we play with the slime, the less sticky it becomes.

The recipe above makes a small amount of slime. But what if we want to make a lot of it?

Let's say that we want to make 3 times as much. We could use a ratio table to make sure that we are using the right parts, or amounts, for the bigger mixture. Example 1 shows how to set up a ratio table to find the ingredients for a larger batch of slime.

Example 1

Use a ratio table to find the ingredients for a larger batch of slime.

Problem:

We are making slime. We would like to make 3 times the amount on the recipe. How can we find the right amount of ingredients to use?

When we triple each ingredient, the proportions stay the same, no matter what type of comparison we are making.

Ingredient	Original Amount	Tripled Amount
Borax Soap	1	3
Water	7	21
Glue	8	24
Total Mixture	16	48

When we make a part-to-part comparison between one ingredient and another, the proportions stay the same. When we make a part-to-whole comparison about one of the ingredients to the whole mixture, the proportions stay the same.

Part-to-Part	Original Amount	Tripled Amount
Soap to Water	$\frac{1}{7}$	$\frac{3}{21}$
Soap to Glue	$\frac{1}{8}$	$\frac{3}{24}$
Water to Glue	$\frac{7}{8}$	$\frac{21}{24}$

Part-to-Whole	Original Amount	Tripled Amount
Soap to Mixture	$\frac{1}{16}$	$\frac{3}{48}$
Water to Mixture	$\frac{7}{16}$	$\frac{21}{48}$
Glue to Mixture	$\frac{8}{16}$	$\frac{24}{48}$

Tables are helpful if we have many parts in a mixture. We can take part-to-part or part-to-whole relationships and see that each one is the same proportion.

Problem-Solving Activity
Turn to *Interactive Text*, page 153.

mBook Reinforce Understanding
Use the *mBook Study Guide* to review lesson concepts.

Activity 1

Select the correct algebraic pattern that matches the number machine.
In each problem, *n* represents the input value.

1. Select the correct pattern.

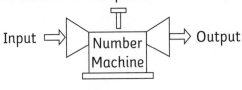

Input	Output
24	3
16	2
1	$\frac{1}{8}$
56	7

    (a) $n + 8$ **(b)** $n \cdot 8$ **(c)** $n \div 8$

2. Select the correct pattern.

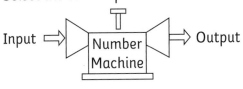

Input	Output
15	14
111	110
1	0
5	4

    (a) $n - 1$ **(b)** $n \cdot 1$ **(c)** $n \div 1$

3. Select the correct pattern.

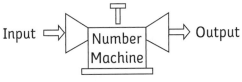

Input	Output
5	5
16	16
$\frac{1}{6}$	$\frac{1}{6}$
3.2	3.2

    (a) $n + 1$ **(b)** $n \cdot 0$ **(c)** $n - 0$

Activity 2

Write the operation (+, −, × , ÷) that makes the following statements true.

1. 5 _____ 7 = 12   2. 8 _____ 6 = 48   3. 42 _____ 7 = 6

4. 8 _____ 6 = 2   5. 42 _____ 7 = 35   6. 35 _____ 7 = 5

Activity 3

Answer the questions about the recipe proportions.

Here are the ingredients for making a bouncing ball:

6 parts water

3 parts white glue

2 parts corn starch

1 part borax soap

1. If you use 6 cups of water, how much white glue will you use?

2. If you use 1 cup of Borax soap, how much corn starch will you use?

3. If you use 3 cups of white glue, how much corn starch will you use?

4. If you use 12 cups of water, how many cups of Borax soap will you need?

Activity 4 • Distributed Practice

Solve.

1. $\frac{4}{5} - \frac{3}{10} = a$

2. $200.2 \cdot 2 = b$

3. $\frac{10}{12} \div \frac{1}{2} = c$

4. $149.78 + 228.39 = d$

5. Write the decimal number 0.048 as a percent.

6. Write the fraction $\frac{1}{100}$ as a decimal number.

7. Write 0.2% as a decimal number.

8. Write 0.5% as a fraction.

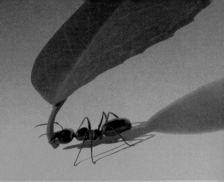

Lesson 8 ▸Patterns and Types of Numbers
Problem Solving:
▸Ratios and Percents

▸**Patterns and Types of Numbers**

Vocabulary
odd even prime number

How do we describe odd, even, and prime numbers using variables?

It's not hard to tell someone what an **odd** or **even** number is.

"Even numbers are numbers like 2, 4, 6, and 8. Odd numbers are numbers like 1, 3, 5, and 7."

We use another definition that better captures the pattern of even numbers. We say that:

"An even number is any number that can be divided by 2 with no remainder."

> This means an even number can be divided into two equal groups.

For example, 8 pennies can be divided into two equal groups of 4.

Nine pennies cannot be divided equally.

There is a simple way to use algebra to describe an even number.

- First, we remember the definition of even numbers: "An even number is any number that can be divided by 2 with no remainder."
- Next, we let k be any integer.

We can describe any even number as $2 \cdot k$, because we know that number will always be divided into two equal parts. Remember that $2 \cdot k = k + k$.

> **Even numbers:**
> We can describe any even number as $2 \cdot k$.

This rule is more powerful than we might think. For example, many people cannot tell us if zero is an even or an odd number. But if we use our rule and substitute zero for k, we know that zero is an even number.

The algebraic expression for an odd number builds on the rule for an even number. We define an odd number as any number that has a remainder when divided by 2.

Example 1 shows how we use algebra to describe an odd number.

Example 1

Use algebra to represent an odd number.

First, let's recall how even numbers differ from odd numbers.

> • An even number *does not* have a remainder when divided by 2.
> • An odd number *does* have a remainder when divided by 2.

We need to write an algebraic expression that will always have a remainder.

Next, we let k be any integer.

> **Odd numbers:**
>   We describe any odd number as $2 \cdot k + 1$.

If we substitute any integer for k, we will get an odd number. That's because of the "+1" part of the rule. It creates a remainder when we divide by 2.

We use the same kind of thinking to represent prime numbers. Let's describe the pattern of primes using variables.

Remember that **prime numbers** such as 3, 7, 11, and 37 are numbers that can only be divided by 1 and themselves.

When we divide a prime number by any other number, we get a remainder. For example, we know that 37 is a prime number because when we divide 37 by 1 and by 37 there is no remainder. If we divide 37 by another number, there will be a remainder.

Example 2

Use algebra to represent prime numbers.

First, let's recall the definition of prime numbers.

> **Prime numbers:**
> A prime number is a number that can be evenly divided *only* by 1 and by itself.

Next, let z = any prime number.

Some numbers have consistent, predictable patterns and we can use simple algebraic expressions to describe them. For instance, even numbers may be written as $2 \cdot k$ and odd numbers may be written as $2 \cdot k + 1$.

However, some numbers do not have consistent, predictable patterns. In this case, we can use algebra to describe their basic properties but we have to add conditions.

For instance, we write prime numbers using the algebraic expressions $z \div 1$ and $z \div z$, but then we have to add the condition where 1 and z are the only divisors of z.

Using variables to talk about different types of numbers helps us see their basic patterns.

Algebra helps us think about numbers like evens, odds, and primes. The algebra pattern is based on rules that differentiate these numbers from other numbers.

Apply Skills
Turn to *Interactive Text*, page 156.

Reinforce Understanding
Use the *mBook Study Guide* to review lesson concepts.

▶Problem Solving: **Ratios and Percents**

How do percents help us think about ratios?

We learned that a percent is a special kind of ratio. It is a part-to-whole relationship where the whole is 100.

We use percentages to compare changes. When we compare ratios (or percents), we are trying to find out which ratio (percent) is bigger.

Let's say your mother tells you that she just got off the phone with her sister. She says, "Your cousins both grew 2 inches last year."

You know your cousins both grew 2 inches, but was the percent increase the same for each cousin? In Example 1, we see a case where the cousins are identical twins. They were the same height last year.

Example 1

Find the percent change.

Problem:

Your cousins Tammy and Juanita both grew 2 inches last year. Was the percent increase the same if the heights were the same?

> We want to know if the two ratios are the same

Each cousin's height one year ago in inches

Tammy	40 inches
Juanita	40 inches

Let's write these as ratios. We are comparing heights a year ago to how much your cousins have grown since that time. We write this as:

Amount of Growth This Year : Height of Cousins One Year Ago

	Tammy	Juanita
Inches Grown in One Year	2	2
Height One Year Ago (in inches)	40	40

The height of 40 inches is the whole, or total amount, so we can change each ratio into a percent.

Tammy $\dfrac{2}{40}$ ⎫
    ⎬ $\dfrac{5}{100}$ → 0.05 → or 5%
Juanita $\dfrac{2}{40}$ ⎭

Both cousins grew by the same percent.

But what if the cousins are six years apart in age? Tammy is 7 and Juanita is 13. They are also different heights. This means that the percent change is going to be different. Let's look at Example 2.

Example 2

Find the percent change.

Problem:

Your cousins Tammy and Juanita both grew 2 inches last year. Was the percent increase the same if their heights one year ago were different?

Each cousin's height one year ago in inches

Tammy	40 inches
Juanita	50 inches

We can write these as ratios. Again, we are comparing their heights a year ago to how much they have grown since that time.

Amount of Growth This Year : Height of Cousins One Year Ago

	Tammy	Juanita
Inches Grown in One Year	2	2
Height One Year Ago (in inches)	40	50

The heights of 40 and 50 inches are the wholes, or total amounts, so we can change each ratio into a percentage.

Tammy $\quad\quad \dfrac{2}{40} \;=\; \dfrac{5}{100} \;=\;$ 0.05 or 5%

Juanita $\quad\quad \dfrac{2}{50} \;=\; \dfrac{4}{100} \;=\;$ 0.04 or 4%

Each cousin grew by a different percent. We can say that Tammy grew at a faster rate.

Another example of this kind of thinking involves the weather.

Suppose we hear on the radio that it has been dry throughout the United States for the month of April. Cities as far apart as Baltimore, Maryland, and Phoenix, Arizona, had three more days with clear skies than they did a year ago in the month of April.

Example 3 shows us that the percent increase is not the same.

Example 3

Find the percent change.

Problem:

Baltimore and Phoenix both had 3 more days with clear skies in the month of April than a year ago. Baltimore and Phoenix had the same increase in clear days, but was the percent increase the same?

We have to look at averages to answer that question. Baltimore typically does not have as many clear days in April as Phoenix. This makes the percent increase different.

Average number of clear days in April

| Baltimore | 8 days |
| Phoenix | 15 days |

We write these as ratios.

Extra Number of Clear Days : Average Number of Clear Days

	Baltimore	Phoenix
Extra Number of Clear Days	3	3
Average Number of Clear Days	8	15

Finally, we change each ratio into a percent.

Baltimore $\frac{3}{8}$ =   0.375 or 37.5%

Phoenix $\frac{3}{15}$ =   0.20 or 20%

The three extra days of clear skies was a much bigger change for Baltimore than for Phoenix.

If we are just interested in how much the change is, that is one thing. In the case of clear days, the increase was the same number of days for both cities.

But if we are interested in the percent of change, that is a different question. When we compare the two percent changes, we understand the effect of the change on each unit.

POWER CONCEPT

Reading a problem carefully will help us understand what kind of question we are being asked.

Problem-Solving Activity
Turn to *Interactive Text*, page 157.

mBook Reinforce Understanding
Use the *mBook Study Guide* to review lesson concepts.

Activity 1

Select the algebraic pattern that matches the type of number.

1. An even number (*n* is any integer)
   - **(a)** $2 + n$
   - **(b)** $2 \cdot n$
   - **(c)** $2 - n$

2. An odd number (*n* is any integer)
   - **(a)** $2 + n \cdot 1$
   - **(b)** $2 + n + 1$
   - **(c)** $2 \cdot n + 1$

3. A prime number (*n* is any integer)
   - **(a)** divisible only by *n* and 1
   - **(b)** divisible only by 2
   - **(c)** divisible only by 1, 2, and *n*

Activity 2

Tell which is the bigger percent increase.

1. **Plant A** was 4 inches tall and grew 1 inch.
   Plant B was 5 inches tall and grew 2 inches.
   Which plant had the bigger percent increase in growth?

2. **City A** normally has 5 clear days in April and had 1 extra clear day this year.
   City B normally has 3 clear days in April and had 3 extra clear days this year.
   Which city had the bigger percent increase in clear days?

3. **Rebecca** was 48 inches tall and grew 1 inch.
   Charlie was 52 inches tall and grew 1 inch.
   Which student had the bigger percent increase in height?

Activity 3

Tell if the problems are proportion problems, unit rate problems, or best deal problems.

1. You are doubling a recipe that calls for 2 cups of water and 1 cup of sugar.

2. You are comparing 3 packs of gum for $4 and 2 packs of gum for $3.

3. Batteries are sold in a 12-pack for $12.99. You want to know how much for just 1 battery.

4. You are mixing green paint using 2 parts blue and 1 part yellow. You need 4 times that amount to finish the room.

5. ABC Grocery sells a dozen donuts for $3.99. You want to know how much 1 donut costs.

Activity 4 • Distributed Practice

Solve.

1. $100.01 - 99.989 = a$

2. $\frac{5}{8} \cdot \frac{4}{10} = b$

3. $12.75 \div 3 = c$

4. $\frac{3}{9} + \frac{4}{6} = d$

5. Write the decimal number 0.001 as a fraction.

6. Write the fraction $\frac{1}{9}$ as a repeating decimal number.

7. Write 40% as a fraction.

8. Write 100% as a decimal number.

▶More Number Patterns

What are other ways to use variables to describe types of numbers?

We should always use number sense when we work with numbers. We learned that even numbers can be divided by 2 and not have a remainder.

There are other rules that help us figure out whether a number can be divided with no remainder. These are called divisibility rules.

For example, let's look at the following divisibility rule:

Divisibility Rule for 3:

If the sum of the digits in a number is divisible by 3, then the number is divisible by 3.

In a divisibility rule, there is no remainder after the division.

Example 1 shows how we use this divisibility rule.

Example 1

Use a divisibility rule to solve the problem.

Problem:

You and your two friends want to split the cost of tickets to a professional football game. The total cost for 3 tickets is $114. Can you divide this number by 3 and not get a remainder?

STEP 1
Add up all the digits in 114. 1 + 1 + 4 = 6

STEP 2
Divide 6 by 3. Is there a remainder? No.

The number 114 is divisible by 3.

Let's look at some divisibility rules.

Divisibility Rules	
2	The last digit in the number can be divided by 2.
3	The sum of the digits can be divided by 3.
4	The last two digits can be divided by 4.
5	The last digit in the number is 0 or 5.
6	If the sum of the digits can be divided by 3 and by 2, then the number can also be divided by 6.
9	The sum of the digits can be divided by 9.
10	The number ends in 0.

Let's figure out how to use variables to represent some of these rules. The variable is used as part of the expression.

Divisibility Rule for 3

- Let v = the sum of the digits in a number.
- We describe the divisibility rule as $v \div 3$.

Divisibility Rule for 5

- Let p = the last digit in a number.
- We describe the divisibility rule as "if p = 5 or 0."

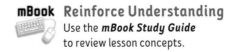

Apply Skills
Turn to *Interactive Text*,
page 159.

mBook Reinforce Understanding
Use the *mBook Study Guide*
to review lesson concepts.

▶Problem Solving: **Percent Decrease**

What happens when there is a decrease?

In the last lesson, we looked at ratios where there was a percent increase. We wanted to know if the percent change was the same for the two ratios. We want to know the same thing here, but now the question is about something that decreases instead of increases.

Example 1

Find the percent decrease.

Problem:

It has not rained very much all year. The reports on the radio talk about how everyone will have to save water this summer. In fact, Wilson Lake and Saturn Lake are 5 feet lower than they were a year ago. Both lakes are down the same amount. But have they both decreased by the same percent?

The depths of the two lakes last year

Wilson	125 feet
Saturn	50 feet

We can write these as ratios.

Amount of Decrease : Depth of Lake Last Year

Wilson $\dfrac{5}{125}$

Saturn $\dfrac{5}{50}$

Finally, we change each ratio into a percent.

Wilson $\dfrac{5}{125}$ = 0.04 or 4%

Saturn $\dfrac{5}{50}$ = 0.10 or 10%

The percent change is different for each lake.

Saturn Lake is down more than Wilson Lake.

Problem-Solving Activity
Turn to *Interactive Text*,
page 160.

mBook Reinforce Understanding
Use the *mBook Study Guide*
to review lesson concepts.

Homework

Activity 1

Tell what type of number or pattern is being described by each of the algebraic patterns.

1. $2 \cdot n$
   (a) prime
   (b) divisible by 3
   (c) even

2. $\frac{n}{5}$
   (a) even
   (b) divisible by 5
   (c) odd

3. $2 \cdot n + 1$
   (a) even
   (b) divisible by 2
   (c) odd

4. $\frac{n}{2}$ and $\frac{n}{3}$
   (a) even
   (b) divisible by 3
   (c) divisible by 6

Activity 2

Tell the numbers in each list that apply to the rule. Use the algebra rules to help you.

1. Which numbers are prime?
   1   2   4   5   7   9   11   12   13   15   21   23

2. Which numbers are divisible by 3?
   111   122   124   135   157   169   211   212   313   414   521   523

3. Which numbers are divisible by 6?
   51   62   64   65   77   99   111   312   413   515   621   723

4. Which numbers are divisible by 5?
   15   23   42   55   60   75   95   96   97   100   210   230

Activity 3

Tell the percent decrease.

1. Jones Lake was 100 feet deep and Taylor Lake was 88 feet deep last year. Both lakes dropped 4 feet this year. What was the percent decrease for each lake?

2. The Scatter Plots sold 3,427 CDs last year. They sold 1,500 fewer this year. What was the percent decrease in sales?

3. There were 500 students in the senior class last year. This year there were 150 fewer students. What was the percent decrease in the number of students?

Activity 4 • Distributed Practice

Solve.

1. $\frac{6}{9} - \frac{1}{8} = a$

2. $32.4 \cdot 5 = b$

3. $\frac{7}{11} \div \frac{4}{5} = c$

4. $1,698.25 + 4,876.19 + 2,500.47 = d$

5. Write the decimal number 0.99 as a percent.

6. Write the fraction $\frac{3}{8}$ as a decimal number.

7. Write 54% as a fraction.

8. Write 0.1% as a decimal number.

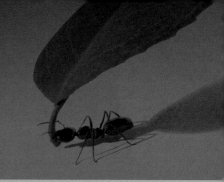

▶**Algebraic Patterns**

How do we use variables to describe algebraic patterns?

We use variables in algebra because we can substitute a range of values for the variable.

Sometimes there are an infinite number of values that we can substitute for the variable. Patterns help us think about how variables are used. We look at examples of a pattern and see how it can go on forever.

The power of an expression with variables is that it can represent the entire pattern. Review 1 shows two cases of patterns and how variables are used in the pattern.

Review 1

How does the variable help us represent the pattern?

Pattern 1:

Box 1	Box 2	Box 3	Box 4
o	88	○○○ ○○○ ○○○	○○○○ ○○○○ ○○○○ ○○○○

When we look at the relationship between the number of the box and the amount of circles in the box, we see this pattern.

Box	1	2	3	4
Number of Circles	1	4	9	16

When we think about the relationship, we see that if we multiply the box number times itself, we get the number of circles in the box.

The pattern is represented as the expression $x \cdot x$ or x^2.

Pattern 2:

Box 10	Box 11	Box 12	Box 13
OOOOO OO	OOOOO OOO	OOOOO OOOO	OOOOO OOOOO

When we look at the relationship between the number of the box and the amount of circles in the box, we see this pattern.

Box	10	11	12	13
Number of Circles	7	8	9	10

When we think about the relationship, we see that there are always 3 fewer circles than the number of the box. In box 11, there are 8 circles, and in box 12 there are 9 circles.

The pattern is represented by the expression $x - 3$.

Using expressions with variables to represent patterns helps us make predictions.

Let's look at the number machines in Review 2. We can predict the output numbers based on the expression that represents the pattern.

Review 2

How do we make predictions with variables?

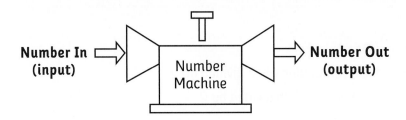

Number In (input) → Number Machine → Number Out (output)

The pattern for the first three sets of numbers is clear. The number in the output column is always 7 less than the number in the input column. That means the pattern is $x - 7$.

Input	Output
9	2
15	8
7	0
158	
10,007	

What are the numbers in the output column that are missing?

$$158 \rightarrow 151$$
$$10,007 \rightarrow 10,000$$

Variables help us see the general pattern for number concepts.

We learned simple divisibility rules for dividing numbers. With each of the rules, there is no remainder when we divide.

Variables help us represent the general pattern behind these rules. We see cases of this in Review 3 and Review 4.

Review 3

How do we use algebra to represent even and odd numbers?

Remember the rules for even and odd numbers:

Even and Odd Numbers

- An even number does not have a remainder when divided by 2.
- An odd number does have a remainder when divided by 2.

We know from our rule that an even number can be divided into two equal groups. We can multiply a number by 2 and get an even number.

Even number = $2 \cdot x$

An odd number cannot be divided into two equal groups. There is one more in one group than the other.

Odd number = $2 \cdot x + 1$

Review 4

How do we use algebra to represent divisibility rules?

Let's recall our divisibility rule for the number 3.

Divisibility Rule for the Number 3

If we add up all the digits in a number and get a sum that is divisible by 3, then the number is divisible by 3.

Let r = the sum of the digits in a number.

The divisibility rule for 3 is $r \div 3$.

Apply Skills
Turn to *Interactive Text*,
page 162.

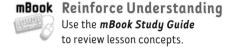

mBook Reinforce Understanding
Use the *mBook Study Guide*
to review lesson concepts.

▶Problem Solving: **Ratios**

How do we think flexibly about ratios?

Ratios look a lot like fractions. For this reason, it is easy to think that they are just fractions. However, that is not always true.

- Fractions are always part-to-whole relationships.
- Ratios can be part-to-whole relationships, but they can also be part-to-part relationships.

Ratios are special. One way they are special is they can always be shown horizontally. Review 1 shows how to find and write ratios.

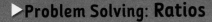

Review 1

How do we find the different ratios for a problem?

Problem:

An apartment building has 15 apartments for rent. They are empty right now. The other 35 apartments have families living in them, which means they are occupied. The total number of apartments in the building is 15 + 35 or 50. What are the different ratios in this problem?

	Part-to-Part Ratio	
Empty	15	
Occupied	35	
15 : 35	empty to occupied	

	Part-to-Whole Ratio	
Empty	15	
Total	50	
15 : 50	empty to total	
Occupied	35	
Total	50	
35 : 50	occupied to total	

Another special thing about ratios is we do not always have to make them equivalent.

Because they don't have to be equivalent, we don't always have to have proportions.

For example, when we are looking for the best deal, we don't want the ratios to be equal. We want to use number sense to make the quantities or costs the same so that we can make a comparison. Review 2 shows how we compare ratios to find the best deal.

Review 2

How do we compare ratios to find the better deal?

Problem:

You're going to buy shoes for your baby sister. The sign in the store says, "2 pairs of baby shoes for $12 or 4 pairs of shoes for $19." Which is the better deal?

$$\frac{\text{Pairs of Shoes}}{\text{Cost}} \qquad \frac{2}{\$12} \qquad \frac{4}{\$19}$$

We use number sense to see that we can change the first ratio so that the number of pairs of shoes is the same.

$$\frac{4}{24} \qquad \rightarrow \qquad \frac{4}{19}$$

Now we make the comparison by substituting the new ratio for the old one.

$$\frac{\text{Pairs of Shoes}}{\text{Cost}} \qquad \frac{4}{\$24} \qquad \frac{4}{\$19}$$

We find that 4 : 19 is a better ratio. If we need 4 pairs of shoes, this is a better deal.

We learned that when we have part-to-whole relationships, we can think about percent. For example, we can think of the percent of something in a mixture. We can also think about percent increase or decrease. Review 3 shows how to find a percent of a mixture.

Review 3

How do we use ratios in mixture problems?

Find the percent of ice cream in the mixture.

<table>
<tr><td align="center">Mixture</td></tr>
</table>

The ingredients for a large root beer milkshake are:

- 1 cup root beer
- 1 cup milk
- 3 cups ice cream

The total amount is 1 + 1 + 3 = 5 cups.

What is the ratio of ice cream to the total mixture?

3 : 5 ice cream to mixture

What is the percent of ice cream in the mixture?

$\frac{3}{5}$ = 0.6 or 60%

Finally, we learned that a percent is a special kind of ratio. It is a part-to-whole relationship where the whole is 100.

Percents allow us to compare changes. When we compare ratios (or percents), we are trying to find out which ratio (percent) is bigger. Review 4 shows us how to find out which ratio is bigger.

Review 4

How do we make comparisons using the percent of increase or decrease?

Problem:

It is the holiday season and everyone in the office has to work an extra 5 hours to make sure that all of the work gets done. That might seem like it is the same amount of extra work, but what is the percent increase for different workers?

- Manny is part-time and only works 25 hours per week.
- Luisa is full-time and works 40 hours per week.

Manny $\frac{5}{25}$ = 0.2 or 20% increase

Luisa $\frac{5}{40}$ = 0.125 or 12.5% increase

The number of extra hours has a greater effect on Manny than Luisa.

We can use ratios in many different ways. We have to be flexible in the way that we think about them. Some ratios are part-to-part relationships, and some are part-to-whole relationships.

When working with ratio problems, we need to think carefully and answer the question, "What is the problem asking for?"

Problem-Solving Activity
Turn to *Interactive Text*, page 165.

mBook **Reinforce Understanding**
Use the *mBook Study Guide* to review lesson concepts.

Two dimensions are fine in a book but

3-D

shapes have more dimensions.

Powerful
Pyramids

Pyramids of Giza, Egypt

Spectacular
Spheres

Montreal Biosphere

Modern houses in Rotterdam, the Netherlands

Colorful
Cubes

Los Angeles hotel towers

Cerebral
Cylinders

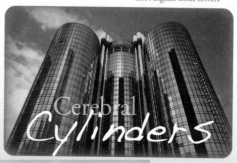

TOTALLY TUBULAR!

OBJECTIVES

Building Number Concepts

- Evaluate numeric expressions using order of operations rules

- Recognize like and unlike terms in an algebraic expression

- Simplify algebraic expressions using the properties of numbers

Problem Solving

- Identify the attributes of three-dimensional shapes

- Use formulas to find the surface area of cylinders and prisms

- Find the surface area of pyramids and polyhedrons by breaking the shapes into familiar parts

Lesson 1 ▶ Order of Operations

Problem Solving:
Three-Dimensional Shapes

▶**Order of Operations**

What is the order of operations?

We begin solving problems in algebra by evaluating and simplifying expressions. Here are some important terms:

- When a math statement does not have an equals sign or an inequality symbol, we call it an **expression** .

- If our expression has numbers only, it is called a **numeric expression** .

- When we use a variable, we call it an **algebraic expression** .

Here are some numeric and algebraic expressions.

Numeric Expressions

$2 + 3$ $3 \cdot 6$ $4 + 3 - 2$ 15

Algebraic Expressions

$x + 5$ $10 - y$ $z \cdot 2$ x

When we solve an expression, we call this **evaluating the expression** . Example 1 shows how we evaluate a numeric expression to get a single number for a solution.

Example 1

Evaluate the numeric expressions.

$2 + 3$ and $3 \cdot 6$

We evaluate $2 + 3$ by solving it. The solution is 5.
We evaluate $3 \cdot 6$ by solving it. The solution is 18.

Most of the numeric expressions we used in the past involved just one operation, such as $7 + 8$, $2 \cdot 9$, $13 - 7$, or $24 \div 3$. In higher level math we often see a mix of operations in one expression. This can cause a problem if we don't know the correct order for evaluating the expression.

Example 2 shows that we get two different answers if we evaluate a numeric expression using different orders of operation.

Example 2

Evaluate the numeric expression $4 - 1 + 2$.

Solution 1:

$4 - 1 + 2$ ←   Subtract 1 from 4.

$3 + 2$ ←   Add 3 and 2.

5 ←   This is the solution.

When we evaluate the problem this way, we get 5.

Solution 2:

$4 - 1 + 2$ ←   Add 1 and 2.

$4 - 3$ ←   Subtract 3 from 4.

1 ←   This is the solution.

When we evaluate the problem this way, we get 1.

The problem in Example 2 looks like an easy problem to evaluate. But depending on the order in which we solve it, we get two different answers. Which one is correct? The first one. Read on to see why.

In math, we can't have situations where there's more than one correct answer for the same problem. For this reason, mathematicians created rules so people can agree on one correct answer. The rules are called the **order of operations**.

In this unit, we will learn the complete set of rules for evaluating expressions that involve two or more operations.

For now, we will look at the order for the four basic operations—addition, subtraction, multiplication, and division. We think of the operations as being organized into two levels.

How to Think About Basic Operations
Level 1—Multiplication and Division Evaluate all multiplication and division problems first. If there are many in one expression, evaluate them in order from left to right. Do these operations before solving any addition or subtraction problems.
Level 2—Addition and Subtraction Evaluate all addition and subtraction problems next. If there are many in one expression, evaluate them in order from left to right.

Example 3 shows how to analyze problems and apply the rules for order of operations when expressions contain more than one operation.

Example 3

Evaluate the expressions using the order of operations.

Expression 1:

$$20 \div 2 \div 2 \cdot 9$$

This expression has all multiplication and division operations. So we evaluate it by working from left to right, following the order of operations.

$20 \div 2 \div 2 \cdot 9 \quad \leftarrow$ Divide 20 by 2.

$10 \div 2 \cdot 9 \quad \leftarrow$ Divide 10 by 2.

$5 \cdot 9 \quad \leftarrow$ Multiply 5 by 9.

$45 \quad \leftarrow$ **This is the solution.**

Expression 2:

$$10 - 2 \cdot 4 \div 2 + 1$$

This expression has a mix of operations. Follow the order of operations.

$10 - 2 \cdot 4 \div 2 + 1$ ←   Multiply 2 by 4.

$10 - 8 \div 2 + 1$ ←   Divide 8 by 2.

$10 - 4 + 1$ ←   Subtract 4 from 10.

$6 + 1$ ←   Add 6 and 1.

7 ←   **This is the solution.**

In Expression 2, when we followed the rules for order of operations and solved the multiplication and division first, we had to start in the middle of the problem. That's different from the way we solved problems in the past. Algebra helps us think differently about solving problems.

Apply Skills
Turn to *Interactive Text*, page 169.

mBook **Reinforce Understanding**
Use the *mBook Study Guide* to review lesson concepts.

▶**Problem Solving: Three-Dimensional Shapes**

Vocabulary

3-D
height
width
depth
face
edge
base
attributes

What are common attributes of three-dimensional shapes?

Let's think about how people design new cars. Before a car is built, engineers draw a design. They use computers to help design the car.

Engineers learn a lot about the actual design of the car by studying its image on the computer. They can turn it, rotate it, and look at it from many different angles. If the engineers like the design they have drawn, they will have artists or designers make clay models of the car. This helps the designers see the car before they actually make it.

Designing cars on computers or with clay models is just one example of how people work with three-dimensional shapes. A two-dimensional, or 2-D, object has just height and width. A three-dimensional, or **3-D**, object has **height**, **width**, and **depth**.

Example 1

Compare the dimensions of a 2-D object and a 3-D object.

Two-Dimensional Object

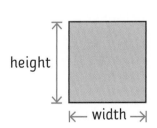

Three-Dimensional Object

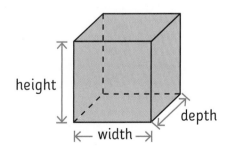

The 3-D object has an additional dimension. We call it *depth*.

Mathematicians have special terms to describe the parts of a 3-D shape. What we think of as a flat "side" of a shape, mathematicians call a **face** . Where the faces come together is called an **edge** . There is one special face of the shape that we call the **base** . It is usually the face that is at the bottom of the shape. The base is the part of the shape that makes it unique.

In a cube, all of the faces are squares, so the base is a square. Here is a cube with these parts labeled so that we can see how the terms are used.

3-D Cube

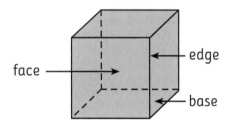

- The cube has faces that are squares.
- The place where two squares meet is called an edge.
- The face at the bottom is called the base.

In this shape, the faces and the base are all the same shape. They are all squares.

We call the bottom of the cube the base. But it is easy to get confused when we use this term, because the word "base" will be used two different ways when we start working with 3-D shapes.

How do we define "base" in 2-D and 3-D objects?

The word "base" has different meanings depending on if we are working with 2-D objects or 3-D objects.

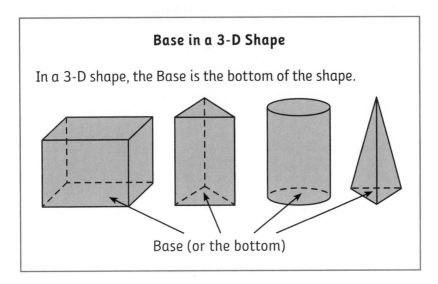

Base in a 3-D Shape

In a 3-D shape, the Base is the bottom of the shape.

Base (or the bottom)

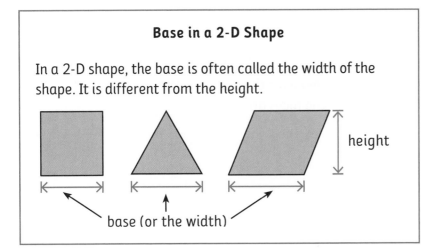

Base in a 2-D Shape

In a 2-D shape, the base is often called the width of the shape. It is different from the height.

height

base (or the width)

We need to make sure that we know what kind of shape we are working with when we see the word "base."

Working with three-dimensional shapes that are drawn on paper requires an ability to imagine faces of the object that are not clearly visible on the page. In the example above, it's difficult to picture all the faces of the cube. A cube actually has six faces.

How can we see all the faces in a 3-D object?

A good way to see all the faces of a three-dimensional object is to "unfold" the object into a two-dimensional shape. Let's look at what happens when we unfold a cube. The unfolded cube is shown on the right in the example.

Example 1

Unfold a cube to see all of its faces.

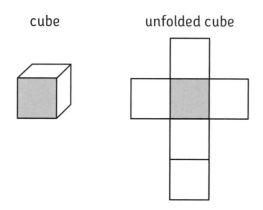

cube   unfolded cube

One of the faces of the cube is shaded to help us see what happens when the cube is unfolded. The shaded section remains in the middle of the drawing, and we can see what happens to the faces around it.

Let's look at some other three-dimensional shapes we see in our everyday lives: a cylinder and a cone.

We see cones when we look at party hats or ice cream cones. We see cylinders in objects such as soda cans. Imagine these shapes unfolded. These shapes have different kinds of faces, bases, and edges. We call the different features of the shape its **attributes** . We classify shapes based on their attributes.

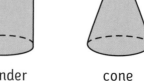

cylinder   cone

 Problem-Solving Activity
Turn to *Interactive Text*, page 170.

 mBook **Reinforce Understanding**
Use the *mBook Study Guide* to review lesson concepts.

Activity 1

Evaluate the numeric expressions. Be sure to follow the order of operations.

1. $18 - 8 \cdot 2$
   (a) 2
   (b) 3
   (c) 20

2. $4 + 8 \cdot 2 - 1$
   (a) 23
   (b) 18
   (c) 19

3. $15 \div 3 - 2 + 2$
   (a) 5
   (b) 17
   (c) 15

Activity 2

Evaluate the expressions. Be sure to follow the order of operations.

1. $15 + 6 - 4 \cdot 4$

2. $5 + 36 \div 9 \cdot 2$

3. $12 + 4 - 9 \cdot 0$

4. $1 + 3 \cdot 6 \div 9 - 3$

5. $44 \div 11 + 2 \cdot 3 - 9$

6. $12 \div 3 + 3$

Activity 3

Answer the questions about two- and three-dimensional shapes.

1. A three-dimensional shape is different from a two-dimensional shape because it has the added dimension of _____.
   (a) height   (b) depth   (c) width

2. A flat surface on a three-dimensional shape is called a(n) _____.
   (a) edge   (b) face   (c) side

3. An unfolded cube looks like which of the following?

    (a)   (b)   (c)

4. In a cube, the base is the same shape as the faces, and that shape is a _____.
   (a) circle   (b) triangle   (c) square

5. An edge on a 3-D shape is _____.
   (a) the place where two cylinders meet
   (b) the place were two faces meet
   (c) the same as a base

Activity 4 • Distributed Practice

Solve.

1. $12 + a = 24$

2. $\frac{1}{3} + \frac{1}{6} = b$

3. $c - 14 = 17$

4. $\frac{5}{8} - \frac{1}{4} = d$

Problem Solving:
▶**Sorting and Classifying Shapes**

▶**Order of Operations: Parentheses**

How do we evaluate expressions with parentheses?

In the last lesson, we learned the correct order to perform operations when we evaluate an expression. Parentheses add something else to think about when we do order of operations. Parentheses are grouping symbols that go around part of an expression. The rule is simple.

> **Rule:**
> If the expression has parentheses, we evaluate the problems inside the parentheses before we do anything else.

Example 1 shows how this works. After we evaluate the problems inside the parentheses, we use order of operations.

Remember that in order of operations, all multiplication and division is done before addition and subtraction.

Example 1

Evaluate the expression.

$12 - 4 \cdot (3 + 5) \div 4$

Following the rules, we solve what is in the parentheses first.

$12 - 4 \cdot (3 + 5) \div 4$ ←   Work inside the parentheses first: $3 + 5 = 8$.

$12 - 4 \cdot 8 \div 4$ ←   Multiply 4 by 8.

$12 - 32 \div 4$ ←   Divide 32 by 4.

$12 - 8$ ←   Subtract 8 from 12.

4 ←   **This is the solution.**

Do the parentheses make a difference? Let's see what happens when we take them away.

Example 2

Evaluate the same expression without parentheses.

12 − 4 · 3 + 5 ÷ 4

12 − 4 · 3 + 5 ÷ 4   ←   Multiply 4 by 3.

12 − 12 + 5 ÷ 4   ←   Divide 5 by 4.

12 − 12 + $\frac{5}{4}$ ←   Subtract 12 from 12.

0 + $\frac{5}{4}$ ←   Add 0 and $\frac{5}{4}$.

$\frac{5}{4}$ ←   **This is the solution.**

In Example 2 we get a different solution because the order was different without the parentheses.

When there is more than one set of parentheses in a problem, we evaluate them in order from left to right.

Example 3

Evaluate the expression with two sets of parentheses.

(4 · 3) + 12 ÷ (3 − 2)

(4 · 3) + 12 ÷ (3 − 2)   ←   Evaluate the first set of parentheses.

12 + 12 ÷ (3 − 2)   ←   Evaluate the second set of parentheses.

12 + 12 ÷ 1   ←   Divide 12 by 1.

12 + 12   ←   Add 12 and 12.

24   ←   **This is the solution.**

It's important to look at the entire expression before we begin evaluating the expression. Once we know where to start and what to do, we go to the toolbox and use the correct rule for order of operations.

% ÷ Apply Skills
< ×
Turn to *Interactive Text*, page 172.

mBook Reinforce Understanding
Use the *mBook Study Guide* to review lesson concepts.

▶**Problem Solving: Sorting and Classifying Shapes**

How do we classify shapes based on attributes?

In geometry, one of the things mathematicians like to do is classify shapes into groups. This grouping makes the shapes easier to describe. It also makes it easier to figure out the formulas for the volume of shapes.

Mathematicians classify shapes based on common characteristics or common attributes of the shapes. Attributes make a shape unique and make it look a certain way. Tops and bottoms of shapes that are the same size—shapes that are congruent—are a common attribute of some shapes.

Grouping is hard to do when we look at these shapes on a flat piece of paper. It is a lot easier when we have physical models of three-dimensional shapes. Example 1 shows one way to classify shapes. We will call this Group 1.

Example 1

Find the common attributes of these 3-D shapes.

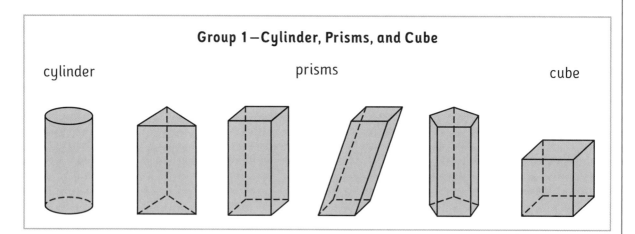

Group 1—Cylinder, Prisms, and Cube

cylinder   prisms   cube

All of these shapes have two common attributes.

- The tops and bottoms in each shape are parallel to each other.
- The tops and bottoms are the same size—they are congruent.

Let's classify other 3-D shapes based on different attributes. We will call this Group 2.

Example 2

Find the common attributes of these 3-D shapes.

Group 2 shows a different classification of shapes.

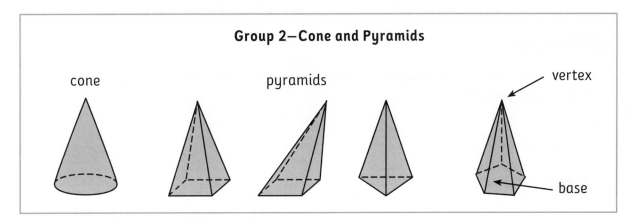

Group 2—Cone and Pyramids

cone

pyramids

vertex

base

All of these shapes have two common attributes.

- All of the shapes have a flat bottom or base.
- All of them meet at a point at the top called the vertex.

Making observations about common attributes of shapes is a good way to help us understand three-dimensional geometry.

Problem-Solving Activity
Turn to *Interactive Text*,
page 173.

mBook Reinforce Understanding
Use the *mBook Study Guide*
to review lesson concepts.

Activity 1

Choose the correct solution.

1. $20 - 12 + 2 - 4$
   (a) 10
   (b) 6
   (c) 2

2. $20 - (12 + 2) - 4$
   (a) 10
   (b) 6
   (c) 2

3. $(20 - 12) + 2 - 4$
   (a) 10
   (b) 6
   (c) 2

Activity 2

Evaluate the expressions using order of operations. Show your work and answers on your paper.

1. $27 \div (3 \cdot 3)$

2. $27 \div 3 \cdot 3$

3. $15 - 8 + 14$

4. $14 - (3 + 4)$

Activity 3

From the list provided, select the attribute that both shapes have in common.

1. Shape A   Shape B

   (a) They both have a vertex.
   (b) They both have parallel bases.
   (c) They are both cubes.

2. Shape A   Shape B

   (a) They both have a vertex.
   (b) They both have parallel bases.
   (c) They are both cones.

Activity 4 • Distributed Practice

Solve.

1. $21.3 + 42.7 = a$

2. $9 \cdot b = 72$

3. $c \div 8 = 7$

4. $\frac{4}{3} \div \frac{1}{3} = d$

5. $2.3 \cdot 0.1 = e$

6. $160 \div f = 80$

7. $\frac{3}{5} \cdot \frac{6}{8} = g$

8. $199.01 - 175.98 = h$

▶**Putting PEMDAS in the Toolbox**

What do we do with exponents?

We have learned almost all of the rules for order of operations. There is just one left. It involves exponents. We learned that we work parentheses first when we evaluate expressions. Before we solve any other operations, the next step is to evaluate any exponents in the expression. Example 1 shows this.

Example 1

Evaluate the expression that contains an exponent.

$4^2 - (15 \div 3) \cdot 2$

$4^2 - (15 \div 3) \cdot 2$	← Work inside the parentheses.
$4^2 - 5 \cdot 2$	← Solve the exponent 4^2.
$16 - 5 \cdot 2$	← Multiply 5 by 2.
$16 - 10$	← Subtract 10 from 16.
6	← **This is the solution.**

Example 2 shows how we combine all the rules to evaluate an expression. It includes exponents, parentheses, and all four operations.

Example 2

Evaluate the expression using the correct order of operations.

$(2 + 5^2) \div 9 + 7 - 2 \cdot 3$

$(2 + 5^2) \div 9 + 7 - 2 \cdot 3$	← Work inside the parentheses. Solve the exponent first: $5^2 = 25$.
$(2 + 25) \div 9 + 7 - 2 \cdot 3$	← Add within the parentheses.
$27 \div 9 + 7 - 2 \cdot 3$	← Divide 27 by 9.
$3 + 7 - 2 \cdot 3$	← Multiply 2 by 3.
$3 + 7 - 6$	← Add 3 and 7.
$10 - 6$	← Subtract 6 from 10.
4	← **This is the solution.**

POWER CONCEPT

Using the order of operations will help us evaluate expressions correctly.

We had to analyze the problem first before we could start to solve it. It is very important to remember this when we evaluate expressions.

What is PEMDAS?

When we put the order of operations rules together, it seems like a lot of rules to keep straight. There is a strategy for remembering them. It's called PEMDAS. Here is the entire set of rules for order of operations and an explanation of PEMDAS.

PEMDAS—The Rules for Order of Operations		
Step 1	**P** – Parentheses	Work what is inside the parentheses.
Step 2	**E** – Exponents	Work any numbers with exponents.
Step 3	**M** – Multiplication **D** – Division	Work multiplication or division problems from left to right.
Step 4	**A** – Addition **S** – Subtraction	Last of all, work addition or subtraction problems from left to right.

There is a simple phrase that will help us remember PEMDAS:

Please **E**xcuse **M**y **D**ear **A**unt **S**ally.

There are all kinds of expressions that have different combinations of parentheses, exponents, and operations. Most of the time, we will not use all of the rules of PEMDAS in a problem. Example 1 shows how to use PEMDAS correctly to evaluate two different numeric expressions.

Example 1

Evaluate the expressions using PEMDAS.

$3 + 2 \cdot (4 - 1)$

$3 + 2 \cdot (4 - 1)$ ← Work inside the parentheses: $4 - 1 = 3$.

$3 + 2 \cdot 3$ ← Multiply 2 by 3.

$3 + 6$ ← Add 3 and 6.

9 ← **This is the solution.**

$4 + 2 \cdot (17 - 9) \div 2^2$

$4 + 2 \cdot (17 - 9) \div 2^2$ ← Work inside the parentheses: $17 - 9 = 8$.

$4 + 2 \cdot 8 \div 2^2$ ← Solve the exponent: $2^2 = 4$.

$4 + 2 \cdot 8 \div 4$ ← Multiply 2 by 8.

$4 + 16 \div 4$ ← Divide 16 by 4.

$4 + 4 =$ ← Add 4 and 4.

8 ← **This is the solution.**

PEMDAS

Now we can build our Algebra Toolbox. We begin with the PEMDAS rules as our first set of rules. We will add other tools as we go.

%÷ **Apply Skills**
=<x Turn to *Interactive Text*,
page 175.

mBook **Reinforce Understanding**
Use the *mBook Study Guide*
to review lesson concepts.

▶**Problem Solving: Identifying Ways Shapes Are Different**

How are shapes different from one another?

Let's look again at the shapes we grouped together in the last lesson. We discussed common attributes in that lesson. This time we want to look for how the shapes differ from one another. Example 1 shows the shapes in Group 1 and describes the ways these shapes are different.

Example 1

Describe the ways cylinders, prisms, and cubes are different.

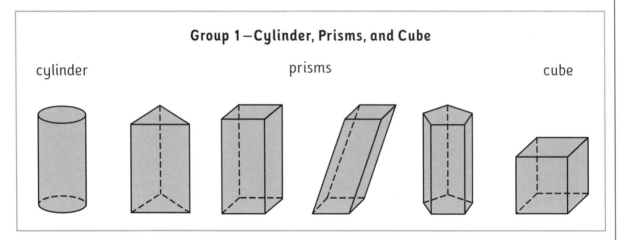

Group 1—Cylinder, Prisms, and Cube

cylinder   prisms   cube

- Cylinders have a circular base and no edges.
- Cubes and prisms have edges and they are parallel.
- Prisms have rectangles or parallelograms for faces.
- A cube has squares for each of its faces.
- Prisms can have many different shapes or polygons for bases.

Now let's examine how the shapes in Group 2 are different from one another.

Example 2

Describe the ways cones and pyramids are different.

Group 2—Cone and Pyramids

cone   pyramids

- Cones have a circular base and no edges.
- Pyramids have faces that are triangles.
- Pyramids can have many different shapes or polygons for bases.

Three-dimensional geometry involves a lot of new vocabulary. Here is a summary of the key words we have learned so far.

New Vocabulary for Three-Dimensional Shapes

Base—Usually the bottom of a three-dimensional object.

Face—What we see first when we look at an object. It is the outside flat surface of the object we have been studying so far.

Edge—The line we see when two faces come together.

Surface—We use this term to talk about the curved outside (or face) of a cone or cylinder.

Vertex—The point where all of the edges of a pyramid meet. In the case of the cone, it is the point.

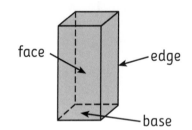

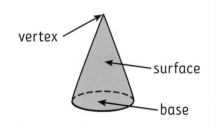

 Problem-Solving Activity
Turn to *Interactive Text*, page 176.

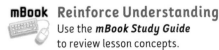 **Reinforce Understanding**
Use the *mBook Study Guide* to review lesson concepts.

Activity 1

Using the PEMDAS rules, tell which part of the problem you would solve first in each of the problems. You do not need to solve the whole problem.

Model $4 + 2 \cdot 7 - (8 + 2)$

Answer: $8 + 2$

1. $12 \div 4^2 + 7 - 8$
2. $27 - 8 \cdot 2 + 3$
3. $54 \div 3^2 + (2 - 2)$
4. $6 \cdot 4 + 8 \cdot 2$
5. $3 + 2 - 1 + 0 \cdot 2$
6. $15 - 8 + 5 - 10 + 2$

Activity 2

Evaluate the numeric expressions by using PEMDAS. Be sure to show each step as you go.

Model $4 \cdot 6 + (3 \cdot 4)$

Answer: $4 \cdot 6 + \mathbf{(3 \cdot 4)}$

$4 \cdot 6 + 12$

$24 + 12$

36

1. $2^2 \cdot (4 + 3) - 8$
2. $6 + 2 \cdot 5 - 8$
3. $25 \div (2 + 3) \cdot 8$
4. $3 + 12 \div 4 - 5$
5. $(3 + 5) \cdot 3^2 - 50$
6. $99 + (100 - 99) \cdot 10$

Activity 3

Select the attribute that makes the shapes different from one another.

1.

(a) a vertex
(b) a face
(c) a base

2.

(a) a base
(b) a curved face
(c) a vertex

3.

(a) a vertex
(b) a face
(c) the shape of the base

Activity 4 • Distributed Practice

Solve.

1. $47 + a = 257$
2. $1.25 \cdot 4 = b$
3. $18.8 \div 2 = c$
4. $d - 499 = 307$
5. $\frac{4}{5} + \frac{1}{10} = e$
6. $\frac{3}{11} - \frac{1}{11} = f$
7. $229 \cdot g = 458$
8. $407.29 + 319.91 = h$

Lesson 4 ▶Adding and Subtracting Integers

▶**Adding and Subtracting Integers**

<table>
<tr><td>Vocabulary</td></tr>
<tr><td>integer
absolute value</td></tr>
</table>

What is an integer?

Integers are positive and negative whole numbers that include the number 0. The number line shows a range of integers in order.

Integers on a Number Line

There are no fractions or decimal numbers. Positive and negative integers can be opposites based on their distance from zero.

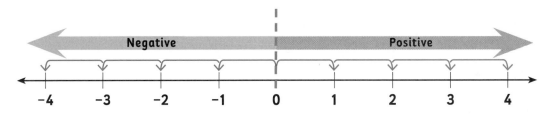

−4 and 4 are opposites

The integers −4 and 4 are opposites because they are the same distance from zero in opposite directions. We can think of a line at zero being the dividing line, or line of symmetry, with four units on either side.

What is absolute value?

Another helpful way to think about opposites is with a concept called absolute value. The **absolute value** of a number is its distance from zero on a number line. This means the absolute value of a number is never negative.

This makes sense when we think about distances. They are never measured using negative numbers. We don't travel −50 miles in a car or describe ourselves as being −3 yards away from the house.

Absolute value allows us to talk about distance from zero using only positive numbers. We write absolute value this way:

$$|-5| = 5 \qquad \text{or} \qquad |5| = 5$$

Since absolute value means the distance from zero, in both of the cases above, the value is 5.

One more important thing to notice about integers on a number line is that any integer on the left of any other integer is smaller. For instance, 3 < 4 and −4 < −3. The smaller number is always on the left.

POWER CONCEPT

The absolute value of a number is always positive.

How do we add and subtract integers?

There are specific rules for performing operations on integers. When we add integers, we move in a positive or negative direction on the number line, depending on the sign.

Example 1

Add 1 + −3.

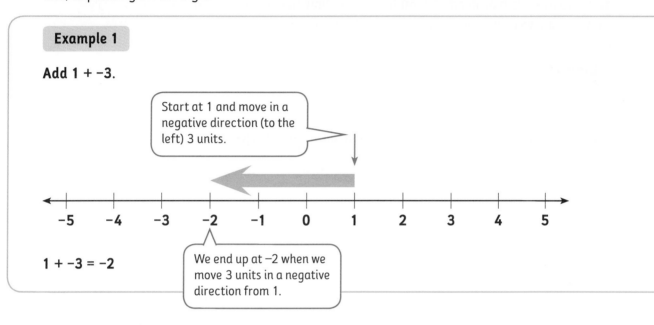

Start at 1 and move in a negative direction (to the left) 3 units.

We end up at −2 when we move 3 units in a negative direction from 1.

1 + −3 = −2

When we subtract integers, we change the problem to "add the opposite" and then perform the addition.

Example 2

Subtract −2 − −4.

We start by adding the opposite. The opposite of −4 is 4. We change the − to +. The problem becomes −2 + 4.

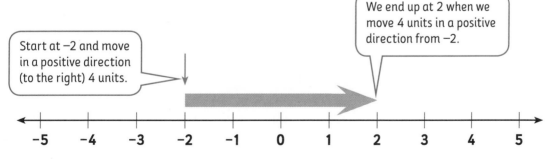

We end up at 2 when we move 4 units in a positive direction from −2.

Start at −2 and move in a positive direction (to the right) 4 units.

−2 − −4 = 2

We can't always draw a number line, because it would take too much time. For example, 200 + −300 would be a difficult problem to do with a number line because the integers are so large. But we can visualize a number line without numbers on it and decide which direction we need to move to solve a problem. Example 3 shows how to use a modified number line to think about addition with larger integers.

Example 3

Solve 200 + −300.

We start with a simple number line marked with a zero in the middle.

0

With this modified number line, we estimate the location of 200 and what it would look like to add −300 to it.

> If 200 is about here . . .

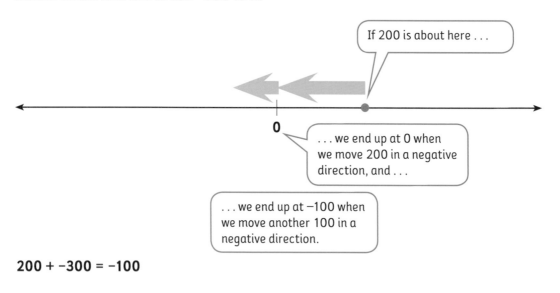

0

> . . . we end up at 0 when we move 200 in a negative direction, and . . .

> . . . we end up at −100 when we move another 100 in a negative direction.

200 + −300 = −100

One more important thing to remember about integer addition is that when we add a number to its opposite, the answer is always 0. The numbers "cancel each other out." We move a certain distance in one direction, then we move the exact same distance in the other direction. We always end up at 0.

Example 4

Show that a number plus its opposite equals 0.

$5 + -5 = 0$

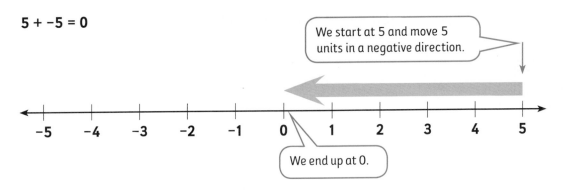

We start at 5 and move 5 units in a negative direction.

We end up at 0.

$-3 + 3 = 0$

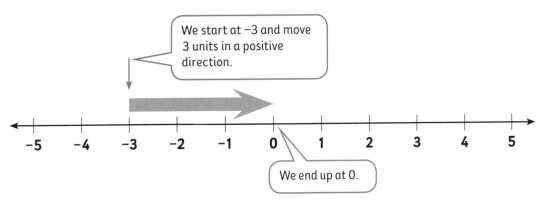

We start at −3 and move 3 units in a positive direction.

We end up at 0.

$100 + -100$

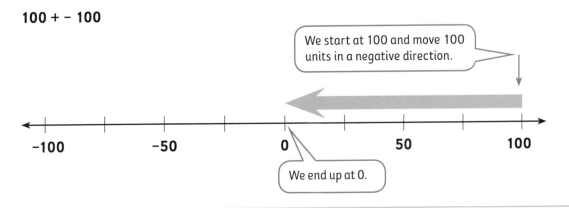

We start at 100 and move 100 units in a negative direction.

We end up at 0.

We now have two different tools in our Algebra Toolbox. We have PEMDAS and we have Operations Rules. We will continue to add more tools to the toolbox as we go.

Operations Rules

Rules for adding and subtracting integers are important when we solve algebra problems. We add these rules to our Algebra Toolbox.

Improve Your Skills

Your friend solves the problem −50 − −120. Here is her work:

−50 − −120
−50 + −120
−170

Your friend says that the answer is −170. **ERROR**

Remember that subtracting is the same as adding the opposite. The correct response looks like this:

−50 − −120
−50 + 120
70

The correct answer is 70. **CORRECT**

How do we build number sense about integer operations?

One way to build number sense is to solve problems in the opposite way than we usually solve them. In algebra, we call this "doing" and "undoing." With integer addition and subtraction, we are used to being given a problem to solve. For example, $-5 + -2$. We look for the answer, which is -7. But we can do the problem in the opposite way. We can "undo" it. Example 1 shows how this works.

Example 1

Fill in + or − to write the problem.

- Write the problem $-8 \;\square\; -9$ where the answer is -17.

    Answer: $-8 + -9 = -17$

    In this problem, we need the plus sign to make the problem equal -17.

- Write the problem $-2 \;\square\; -3 \;\square\; 2$ where the answer is 3.

    Answer: $-2 - -3 + 2 = 3$

    In this problem, we subtract -3 and then add 2 to get 3.

These kinds of activities require problem-solving strategies. We pay attention to the strategies when we work these kinds of problems, because they help us build good number sense.

Apply Skills
Turn to *Interactive Text*, page 178.

mBook Reinforce Understanding
Use the *mBook Study Guide* to review lesson concepts.

Homework

Activity 1

Evaluate the expressions. Select the correct answer for each by using the rules for integer addition and/or subtraction.

1. $4 - -9$
   (a) -13
   (b) 13
   (c) 5

2. $5 - 6$
   (a) 1
   (b) -1
   (c) 11

3. $-45 + -20$
   (a) 25
   (b) -65
   (c) -25

4. $-56 - -8$
   (a) -64
   (b) -48
   (c) 49

Activity 2

Tell the absolute value, or opposite, for each.

1. $|-3|$

2. What is the opposite of -3?

3. $|3|$

4. What is the opposite of 3?

5. $|-5|$

6. What is the opposite of -5?

Activity 3

Use integer rules and PEMDAS to evaluate the numeric expressions.

1. $-5 + 2 \cdot 3$

2. $5 - -8 - 3$

3. $(-5 + -2) \cdot -6$

4. $-50 \cdot (-1 \cdot 2) - 100$

Activity 4 • Distributed Practice

Solve.

1. $\frac{5}{8} \cdot \frac{4}{3} = a$

2. $229 + b = 337$

3. $\frac{11}{12} \div \frac{1}{6} = c$

4. $342 - d = -299$

5. $179.05 - 85.99 = e$

6. $\frac{1}{6} + \frac{2}{9} = f$

7. $g \cdot 50 = 350$

8. $14.2 + 17.9 = h$

▶**Problem Solving: Surface Area**

Vocabulary

surface area

What is surface area?

The work we do with three-dimensional shapes—folding, unfolding, finding common attributes, identifying important vocabulary—helps us understand how certain measurements are computed for different shapes. One type of measurement is surface area. **Surface area** is the sum of all the areas of the faces, bases, and surfaces of a three-dimensional shape.

In past lessons, we worked with shapes that were all grouped together because of common attributes:

- a parallel top and bottom.
- a point at the top called a vertex.

Let's think about the ways in which we measure these shapes. For this exercise, we are going to imagine that these shapes are solid.

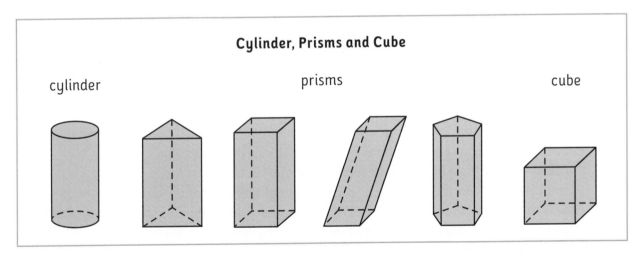

Cylinder, Prisms and Cube

cylinder   prisms   cube

How do we find the surface area of a cylinder?

To find the surface area of a cylinder, we divide the cylinder into sections and find the areas of those sections. Here are three areas we need to compute in order to find the surface area of a cylinder.

To find the surface area of the cylinder, we need to add:

- the area of the base (bottom)
- the area of the other base (top)
- the area of the surface

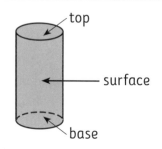

Steps for Finding the Surface Area of a Cylinder

STEP 1

Find the area of the base, or bottom.

Finding the area of the base is easy to do because it's the same as finding the area of a circle. We use the formula $A = \pi \cdot r^2$.

STEP 2

Find the area of the top.

The top is the same area as the base. In fact, it's also a base, because a cylinder is the same right-side-up as it is upside-down.

We can just double the bottom base to give us the area of both the bottom and the top. We make the formula $2 \cdot \pi \cdot r^2$.

STEP 3

Find the area of the curved face, or surface of the cylinder.

The distance around the cylinder is the circumference of the circular base or top. We have found the circumference of a circle before. It's computed by the formula $C = 2 \cdot \pi \cdot r$. The height of the cylinder is the distance from the base to the top. This is something else that can be measured. We find the area of the surface by computing the circumference times the height of the cylinder. The area formula is $2 \cdot \pi \cdot r \cdot$ height.

STEP 4

Add together all the parts.

Here is the formula for the surface area of a cylinder and an example where we apply the formula.

Formula for the Surface Area of a Cylinder

Area of two bases		Area of surface
$(2 \cdot \pi r^2)$	$+$	$(2\pi r \cdot h)$

We compute the surface area for this cylinder by substituting values for the variables.

$r = 2$

$h = 5$

$\pi = 3.14$

$r = 2$

$h = 5$

Surface Area of a cylinder $= (2 \cdot \pi \ r^2) + (2 \cdot \pi \ r \cdot h)$

$$= (2 \cdot 3.14 \cdot 2^2) + (2 \cdot 3.14 \cdot 2 \cdot 5)$$

$$= (2 \cdot 3.14 \cdot 4) + (6.28 \cdot 2 \cdot 5)$$

$$= 25.12 + 62.8$$

$$= 87.92$$

The surface area of the cylinder $= 87.92$ square units.

Because area is measured in square units, the sum of the areas or surface area is also measured in square units.

Next let's look at the surface area of a triangular prism.

How do we find the surface area of a triangular prism?

There are two bases on a triangular prism. They are both the same size and they are both triangles. Also, the faces of the shape's sides are all rectangles.

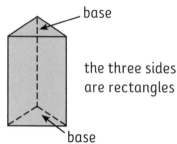

base

the three sides
are rectangles

base

Formula for the Surface Area of a Triangular Prism

2 · (Area of triangle) + 3 · (Area of rectangle)

We compute the surface area for this prism by substituting values for the variables. We start by finding the areas of each of the 2-D parts of the 3-D shape.

The Area of a triangle = $\frac{1}{2}$ · (base · height)

$= \frac{1}{2}$ · (6 · 2)

$= 6$ in^2

The Area of a rectangle = base · height

$= 6 · 10$

$= 60$ in^2

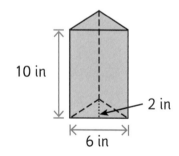

10 in

2 in

6 in

Remember that we can write square inches as in^2.

Surface Area of a triangular prism = 2 · (Area of Triangle) + 3 · (Area of Rectangle)

$= 2 · 6 + 3 · 60$

$= 12 + 180$

$= 192$ in^2

The surface area of the triangular prism is 192 in^2.

How do we find the surface area of a cube?

The surface area of a cube is the easiest of them all. Every face or base of the cube is a square. If we unfold a cube we will find six faces.

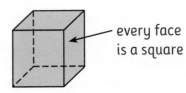

every face is a square

Formula for the Surface Area of a Cube

base · height · 6

$b \cdot h \cdot 6$

We compute the surface area for this cube by substituting values for the variables.

Surface Area of a cube = $b \cdot h \cdot 6$

$\qquad = 4 \cdot 4 \cdot 6$

$\qquad = 16 \cdot 6$

$\qquad = 96$

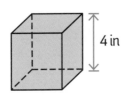

4 in

The surface area of the cube is 96 square inches.

When computing surface area of 3-D shapes, the most important step is to determine what 2-D shapes make up the bases and faces. The faces of prisms are always rectangles. The bases, however, can be different shapes. So far we have looked at shapes with circles, squares, and triangles for bases.

Problem-Solving Activity
Turn to *Interactive Text*, page 180.

Monitoring Progress
Quiz 1

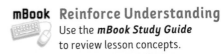

mBook Reinforce Understanding
Use the *mBook Study Guide* to review lesson concepts.

Activity 1

Select the correct answer to each question about surface area.

1. The surface area of a shape is the sum of _____.
   - **(a)** the areas of each base
   - **(b)** the areas of each face, base, and surface
   - **(c)** the perimeters of each face

2. The area formula for a circle is helpful for finding the surface area of which shape?
   - **(a)** cube
   - **(b)** cylinder
   - **(c)** pyramid

3. The area formula for a square is helpful for finding the surface area of which shape?
   - **(a)** cube
   - **(b)** triangular pyramid
   - **(c)** cone

Activity 2

Evaluate the expressions using the rules of PEMDAS and integers.

1. $3 + -2 + 6$

2. $4 \cdot (3 + -3)$

3. $7 - 8 - 3$

4. $24 \div (-4 + 12) + 2^2$

Activity 3

Find the surface area of each shape. Surface area is the sum of all of the areas of the shape.

1. What is the surface area of this triangular prism?

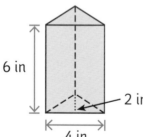

HINT: This shape is made up of three rectangles that have the same area and two triangles that have the same area. The area formula for a rectangle is Area = base • height. The area formula for a triangle is Area = $\frac{1}{2}$ • (base • height).

2. Compute the surface area of the cube.

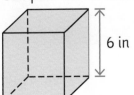

6 in

HINT: This shape is made up of six squares that have the same area. The area formula for a square is Area = base · height. Since the length of the base and height are the same on a square, we can also use $A = s^2$ where s is the length of a side.

Activity 4 • Distributed Practice

Solve.

1. $a \div 9 = 6$

2. $\frac{4}{5} \cdot \frac{3}{6} = b$

3. $5.10 \div 0.5 = c$

4. $d \cdot 4 = 32$

5. $2.6 \cdot 4 = e$

6. $f + 709 = 1{,}025$

7. $\frac{3}{7} - \frac{1}{3} = g$

8. $\frac{2}{3} + \frac{1}{9} = h$

▶**Algebraic Expressions and Special Symbols**

What are algebraic expressions?

In the last few lessons, we evaluated numeric expressions. These are expressions that contain only numbers. There is another kind of expression called an algebraic expression. It contains numbers and variables or only variables.

Numeric Expressions			
$2 + 3$	$12 \div 8$	$32 - (15 \div 3) \cdot 6^2$	15
Algebraic Expressions			
$a + 3$	$x \div y$	$32 - (b \div 3) \cdot 6^2$	x

Algebraic expressions are made up of parts called terms. There are two types of terms. There are **variable terms** and **number terms** . Variable terms and number terms are very different and cannot be combined.

A Typical Algebraic Expression
$w + 3$

When we see an expression like this, we cannot just add the w and the 3 together. The expression $w + 3$ cannot be rewritten as $w3$ or $3w$ because 3 is a number term and w is a variable term.

We have special symbols to show the difference between these terms.

- The V-shaped symbol represents a variable term.
- The N-shaped symbol represents a number term.
- Black symbols are positive.
- Red symbols are negative.

**Symbols That Help Us Understand
Terms in an Algebraic Expression**

 is a positive number term.

 is a negative number term.

 is a positive variable term.

 is a negative variable term.

Example 1 shows how we represent expressions using the special symbols.

Example 1

Represent the expressions $c + 2$ and $c + -3$ using symbols.

$c + 2$

c + 2

V + N N

$c + -3$

c + −3

V + N N N

What are coefficients?

This is a place where many students get confused. Our special symbols help us understand what is going on. Look at the box.

Another Typical Algebraic Expression

$3m + 1$

We just said that we can't combine variable terms and number terms. So how do we get $3m$ in the expression above? The 3 in 3m is called a **coefficient** and it means 3 times m. The coefficient represents the number of variables we have.

What does the coefficient mean in an expression?

Let's look at the same algebraic expression, $3m + 1$, using our special symbols.

$$3m \qquad + \quad 1$$

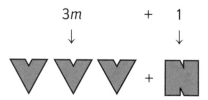

In this expression, the coefficient 3 means we have 3 of the variables, m, in our expression.

The coefficient and the variable make up the entire variable term.

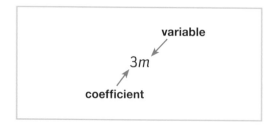

All variables have coefficients, even though there are two cases where they are hard to see. Sometimes the coefficients are "invisible." We call this type of coefficient an **implied coefficient**. Example 1 shows two expressions with implied coefficients.

Example 1

Find the implied coefficient in the expressions.

x + −2

$$x \quad + \quad -2$$

The implied coefficient is 1. The variable *x* is the same as 1 · *x*.

−*x* + 3

$$-x \quad + \quad 3$$

The implied coefficient is −1. The variable −*x* is the same as −1 · *x*.

An implied coefficient will always be 1 or −1.

How do we solve word problems involving expressions with coefficients?

Sometimes the answer to a problem is an expression. It's important to be able to identify situations in word problems where the answer is an algebraic expression with a coefficient. In word problems, we can think of the coefficient as the words in the problem that tell you "how many times." The table shows some of the key phrases we will see that represent coefficients.

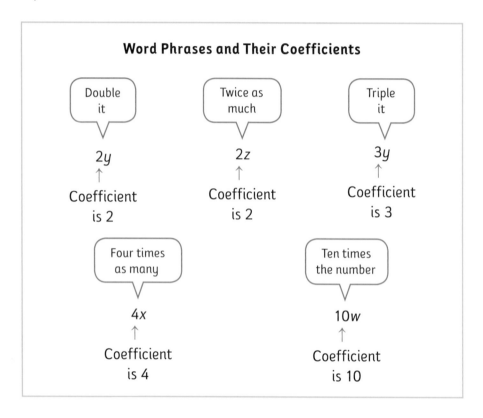

Word Phrases and Their Coefficients

Double it
$2y$
↑
Coefficient is 2

Twice as much
$2z$
↑
Coefficient is 2

Triple it
$3y$
↑
Coefficient is 3

Four times as many
$4x$
↑
Coefficient is 4

Ten times the number
$10w$
↑
Coefficient is 10

We should be sure to read all word problems carefully before we begin to solve them. If we have an algebraic equation with a coefficient in a word problem, we circle the coefficient. This will help us see the connection between the words in the word problem and the symbols in the algebraic expression.

 **Apply Skills**
Turn to *Interactive Text*, page 183.

 **mBook Reinforce Understanding**
Use the *mBook Study Guide* to review lesson concepts.

Activity 1

Rewrite the problems with special symbols as algebraic expressions.

Model   ▽ ▽ + ◪◪

Answer: $-2x + 2$

1. ▽ + ◪◪◪◪

2. ▽ + ◪◪

3. ▽ ▽ ▽ + ◪◪◪◪

4. ▽ ▽ + ◪

Activity 2

Number your paper from 1 to 4. Write the letter that matches the expression.

1. $x + -3$ (a) ▽▽▽ + ◪◪

2. $3x + -2$ (b) ▽ ▽ + ◪◪◪

3. $2x + 3$ (c) ▽ + ◪

4. $-x + 1$ (d) ▽ + ◪◪◪

Activity 3

Write an expression for each phrase. Circle the coefficient in the expression.

1. two times a number

2. triple a number

3. 10 times a number

4. a number doubled

5. a number tripled

6. four times as many

Activity 4 • Distributed Practice

Solve.

1. $\frac{5}{4} \div \frac{1}{4} = x$

2. $29 \cdot b = 58$

3. $c \div 20 = 90$

4. $1.25 + 2.75 = d$

5. $\frac{3}{5} \cdot \frac{7}{8} = e$

6. $13.2 \cdot 0.2 = f$

7. $320 - g = 690$

8. $\frac{8}{9} + \frac{1}{6} = h$

▸**Simplifying Expressions by Combining Like Terms**

How do we simplify expressions?

Simplifying algebraic expressions means combining as many parts as possible. There are rules about combining parts or terms in an expression.

- We only combine variable terms with other variable terms.
- We only combine number terms with other number terms.

This is what we mean when we say *combining like terms*.

Example 1 shows how to combine like terms using special symbols.

Example 1

Simplify the expression 2x + 3x + 2 + 1.

We demonstrate the problem with our special symbols.

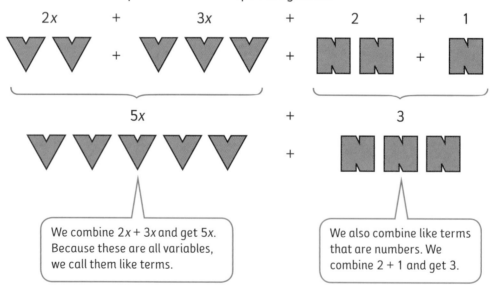

We combine 2x + 3x and get 5x. Because these are all variables, we call them like terms.

We also combine like terms that are numbers. We combine 2 + 1 and get 3.

The simplified expression is 5x + 3. That's as simple as it gets because we have combined all of the like terms.

It can be hard to realize that we are done simplifying when the answer is an expression. The expression $5x + 3$ doesn't look like the kind of answer we are used to getting. But it is the answer.

- The variable term is $5x$ and is represented by 5 ▼s.
- The number term is 3 and is represented by 3 ◼s.
- We can't combine ▼s and ◼s. They are not like terms.

Example 2 shows another situation where the answer is an expression.

Example 2

Simplify the expression $2x + 1 + 2$.

We can use special symbols to represent the problem.

$2x$ +   1   +   2

▼ ▼ + ◼ + ◼ ◼

$2x$ 3

▼ ▼   ◼ ◼ ◼

We can combine the ◼s. So the simplified expression is $2x + 3$.

That is as simplified as it gets. We have a variable term ($2x$) and we have a number term (3).

The simplified expression is $2x + 3$.

POWER CONCEPT

In an algebraic expression, variable terms and number terms cannot be combined.

When we write expressions, we always write the variable before the number. The expression is not completely simplified if it is not written this way.

Example 3 shows how we move the terms around to shift the variable to the front.

Example 3

Simplify the expression 2 + 3 + 1 + x.

First we combine like terms. We use the special symbols.

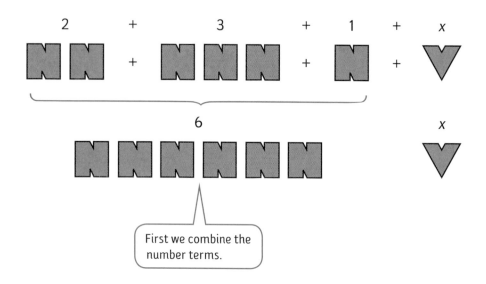

The expression is 6 + x. We can't combine any more terms. But we have one more step. We move the x term to the front to make x + 6.

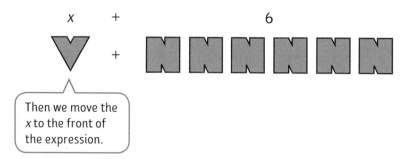

Now the expression is completely simplified. This is the way it should be written.

2 + 3 + 1 + x = x + 6.

When we simplify expressions, we only combine like terms. That means sometimes our answer is a single term such as $2x$ or 5 or it is an expression like $2x + 3$. Now we can add Like Terms to our toolbox.

Like Terms

- When two or more terms have the same variables, they are like terms.

- When two or more terms include only numbers, they are like terms.

Apply Skills
Turn to *Interactive Text*,
page 186.

Reinforce Understanding
Use the *mBook Study Guide*
to review lesson concepts.

▶**Problem Solving: Surface Area of Pyramids**

Vocabulary
slant height

How do we find the surface area of a pyramid?

Pyramids have attributes that are different from prisms. Pyramids have one base and opposite of the base is a point called the vertex. The faces of a Pyramid are triangles, and the base can form many different shapes. Let's look at the diagrams below.

vertex

all sides are triangles

base

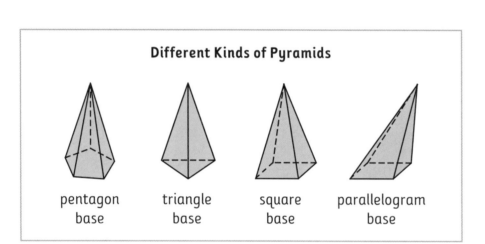

Different Kinds of Pyramids

| pentagon base | triangle base | square base | parallelogram base |

We compute the surface area of a pyramid by breaking it up into two-dimensional shapes. Then we use the area formulas for these shapes to find a formula for the surface area of the pyramid.

Surface Area Formula for a Pyramid

Area of the base   +   Area of the faces

Let's begin with a triangular pyramid.

Steps for Finding the Area of a Triangular Pyramid

STEP 1

Break apart the shape. We have a triangular base and three triangular faces.

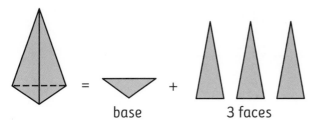

base   3 faces

STEP 2

Find the area for the base and the area for one of the faces.

Use the area formula for a triangle: $\frac{1}{2} \cdot b \cdot h$. We have two different heights for the triangular pyramid—the **slant height**, which is the height of the triangle face, and the base height, which is the height of the triangle base.

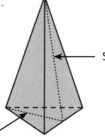

← slant height of the face

height of the base

STEP 3

Multiply the area of the face by 3 to get the total area of the faces.

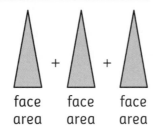

face area + face area + face area

STEP 4

Add the total area of the faces to the area of the base.

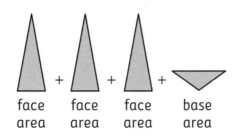

face area + face area + face area + base area

We compute the surface area for this triangular pyramid by substituting values for the variables. Let's look at an example.

Example 1

Find the surface area of the pyramid.

STEP 1
Break apart the shape.

STEP 2
Find the area for the base and one of the faces.

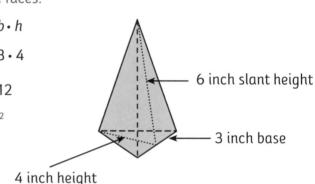

6 inch slant height

3 inch base

4 inch height

$$\text{Area of the base of the pyramid} = \frac{1}{2} \cdot b \cdot h$$
$$= \frac{1}{2} \cdot 3 \cdot 4$$
$$= \frac{1}{2} \cdot 12$$
$$= 6 \text{ in}^2$$

$$\text{Area of one of the faces} = \frac{1}{2} \cdot b \cdot h$$
$$= \frac{1}{2} \cdot 3 \cdot 6$$
$$= \frac{1}{2} \cdot 18$$
$$= 9 \text{ in}^2$$

STEP 3
Multiply the area of the face by 3 to get the total area of the faces.
We have 3 faces, so the total area for the faces is $3 \cdot 9 \text{ in}^2$ or 27 in^2.

STEP 4
Add the total area of the faces to the area of the base.
$6 + 27 = 33 \text{ in}^2$

Surface area of the pyramid = 33 in²

Finding the surface area of a pyramid takes several steps. We have to remember all of the faces because when pyramids are drawn on paper, we cannot see all of them.

 Problem-Solving Activity
Turn to **Interactive Text**, page 187.

 mBook **Reinforce Understanding**
Use the **mBook Study Guide** to review lesson concepts.

Activity 1

Select the simplified expression.

1. $2x + 4x + 3 + 5$
   (a) 14
   (b) $6x + 8$
   (c) $2x + 8 + 4x$

2. $3x + 2x + 8x$
   (a) $5x + 8x$
   (b) $13x$
   (c) $12x$

3. $2 + 5 + 7x$
   (a) $7x + 7$
   (b) $7 + 7x$
   (c) 14

4. $6x + 3x + 5x + 2 + 5 + 2$
   (a) $23x$
   (b) 23
   (c) $14x + 9$

Activity 2

Simplify the expressions. Be sure to write your answer with the variable first.

Model $7 + 2 + x + 2x + 3x$
Answer: $6x + 9$

1. $2x + 3x + 5$

2. $x + x + 2 + 7$

3. $3 + -5 + x$

4. $6x + 2x + 8$

5. $2x + 5x + 3x + 2$

6. $x + x + x + 3$

7. $1 + 2 + 3 + 2x$

8. $5 + 2 + 3 + 6x$

Activity 3

Tell which area formulas are needed to find the surface area of each shape. Select the correct answer.

1. What area formulas do we need to find the surface area of this shape?
   - **(a)** circle and rectangle
   - **(b)** rectangle and triangle
   - **(c)** triangle and circle

2. What area formulas do we need to find the surface area of this shape?
   - **(a)** triangle and rectangle
   - **(b)** rectangle and parallelogram
   - **(c)** parallelogram and triangle

3. What area formulas do we need to find the surface area of this shape?
   - **(a)** rectangle and triangle
   - **(b)** triangle and pentagon
   - **(c)** trapezoid and rectangle

4. What area formulas do we need to find the surface area of this shape?
   - **(a)** triangle
   - **(b)** triangle and rectangle
   - **(c)** rectangle and trapezoid

Activity 4 • Distributed Practice

Solve.

1. $240 \div a = 60$

2. $\frac{3}{5} \cdot \frac{1}{4} = b$

3. $12.3 \cdot 0.1 = c$

4. $d - 80 = 70$

5. $603.09 + 298.12 = e$

6. $\frac{8}{9} - \frac{1}{3} = f$

7. $500 + g = 1{,}100$

8. $\frac{5}{6} + \frac{4}{9} = h$

Lesson 8 | ▸Adding Properties to the Toolbox
Problem Solving: ▸Polyhedrons

▸Adding Properties to the Toolbox

How do we use properties to simplify expressions?

We can move terms around in expressions using the **commutative property** . We saw in the last lesson that it was okay to rewrite the expression $6 + x$ as $x + 6$. The commutative property tells us that if we are adding, we can add in any order.

Example 1 demonstrates the commutative property for addition.

<table>
<tr><td colspan="2" align="center">Vocabulary</td></tr>
</table>

Vocabulary

commutative
  property
associative property
property of opposites

Example 1

Use the commutative property for addition to rewrite the equations.

$3 + 2 = 5$	$\rightarrow$	$2 + 3 = 5$
$6 + 1 + 7 = 14$	$\rightarrow$	$7 + 1 + 6 = 14$
$1 + 2 + 3 + 4 = 10$	$\rightarrow$	$4 + 2 + 3 + 1 = 10$

It doesn't matter in what order we add the numbers. We get the same solution every time. This works for algebraic expressions with variables too. We can rewrite $4 + 3x$ as $3x + 4$ or $5 + x$ as $x + 5$. The commutative property is an important tool.

The **associative property** is also an important tool in working with expressions because it helps us group things together. With the associative property, we can regroup numbers in addition and multiplication problems without changing the answer. Sometimes we need to group things together because it makes the computation easier.

Example 2 demonstrates the associative property.

Example 2

Use the associative property for addition to rewrite the equations.

$(5 + 5) + 6 = 16$ → $5 + (5 + 6) = 16$
    $10 \ \ + 6$ $5 + \ \ 11$

$3 + (2 + 8) = 13$ → $(3 + 2) + 8 = 13$
$3 + \ \ 10$ $5 \ \ + 8$

$3 + (7 + 4) = 14$ → $(3 + 7) + 4 = 14$
$3 + \ \ 11$ $10 \ \ + 4$

In each case in Example 2, the grouping that adds up to 10 makes the problem slightly easier to solve. Most people are better at adding tens. The numbers 3 + 10 are easier to compute for most people than 5 + 8.

In algebra, it is also helpful to group numbers together that are opposites. The **property of opposites** tells us that any number plus its opposite equals zero.

Example 3 shows how we use properties to help simplify an expression.

In this lesson, we will use simple ▼s and ◼s to make it easier to write them on paper. We use red for negative terms and black for positive terms.

Example 3

Simplify the expression 2x + 2 + −2x.

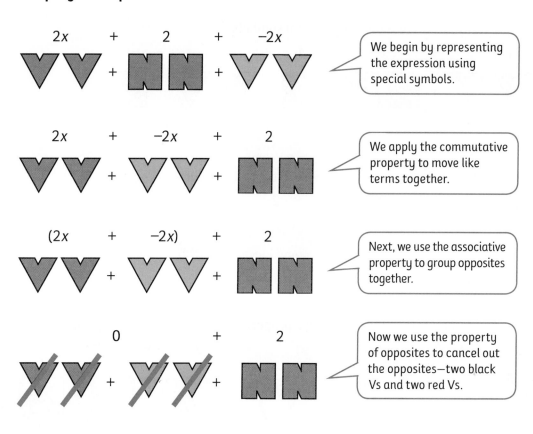

We begin by representing the expression using special symbols.

We apply the commutative property to move like terms together.

Next, we use the associative property to group opposites together.

Now we use the property of opposites to cancel out the opposites—two black Vs and two red Vs.

The simplified expression is 2.

Example 4

Simplify the expression $3x + 2 + 1 + -2x + -1$.

We begin by writing the expression using special symbols.

We apply the commutative property to move like terms together.

Next, we use the commutative and associative property to move and group opposites together.

Now we use the property of opposites to cancel out the opposites.

The simplified expression is $x + 2$.

After we used the commutative property to move like terms together, we used it again to move opposites together. Then we grouped them together using the associative property and cancelled out opposites using the property of opposites.

Rules	Properties
• PEMDAS	• Commutative property
• Operations rules	• Associative property
• Like terms	• Property of opposites

We now have all the tools we need in our Algebra Toolbox. It's very important to keep the toolbox in mind when we work algebra problems.

%÷ **Apply Skills**
=≤× Turn to *Interactive Text*,
page 189.

mBook **Reinforce Understanding**
Use the *mBook Study Guide*
to review lesson concepts.

▶**Problem Solving: Polyhedrons**

What is a polyhedron?

Polyhedrons are complex shapes that are made up of many faces that have identical shapes. Look at the polyhedrons below. We can see that the first one in the top row is made up of triangles and pentagons. The second is made up of triangles and squares. The last one in the bottom row uses hexagons and triangles. Some polyhedrons have a rounded shape like a ball, while others look like complex stars.

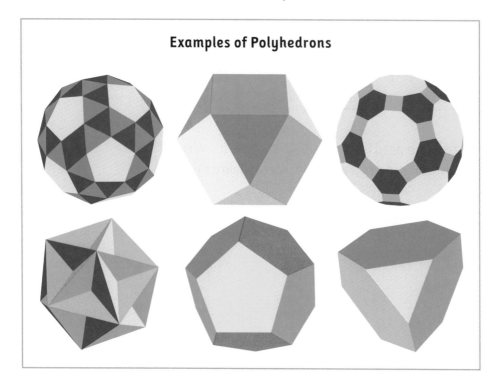

Examples of Polyhedrons

Polyhedrons are used in many different ways. Soccer balls and golf balls both use these patterns in their design. Some toys use polyhedrons to change from a ball to a star shape. Building models of polyhedrons help us see how they work.

Problem-Solving Activity
Turn to *Interactive Text*, page 190.

mBook **Reinforce Understanding**
Use the *mBook Study Guide* to review lesson concepts.

Activity 1

Select the expression that represents one of the properties we have learned: commutative property, associative property, or property of opposites.

1. $3 + 2$
   (a) $2 \cdot 3$
   (b) $2 + 3$
   (c) 0

2. $4 + -4$
   (a) 1
   (b) 0
   (c) -4

3. $5 + (8 + 2)$
   (a) $(5 + 8) + 2$
   (b) 0
   (c) 1

4. $6 \cdot 2 \cdot 8$
   (a) $2 + 8 + 6$
   (b) 0
   (c) $8 \cdot 2 \cdot 6$

Activity 2

Simplify the expressions using the properties and rules we have learned.

1. $2x + -3 + -x$

2. $-5 + x + 3$

3. $4 + -x + -3x$

4. $4x + -2x + -3x$

5. $-3 + -2 + 3x$

6. $4x + -2 + -3x + 3$

Activity 3

Select the 2-D shapes you see in the polyhedrons. You may select more than one.

1. (a) circle
   (b) square
   (c) hexagon

2. (a) triangle
   (b) pentagon
   (c) square

3. (a) triangle
   (b) circle
   (c) pentagon

4. (a) triangle
   (b) square
   (c) hexagon

Activity 4 • Distributed Practice

Solve.

1. $397 - x = -228$

2. $\frac{4}{5} - \frac{1}{10} = y$

3. $72.8 \div 0.8 = z$

4. $w + 90 = 170$

5. $30 \cdot a = 120$

6. $2.75 + 3.25 + 5.50 = b$

7. $\frac{7}{9} + \frac{2}{3} = c$

8. $d \div 60 = 8$

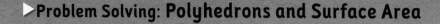

▶Problem Solving: **Polyhedrons and Surface Area**

How do we find the surface area of a polyhedron?

In the last lesson, we learned about polyhedrons. We saw one polyhedron that was made up of a cube in the center and six rectangular pyramids around the sides.

Remember, when we measure surface area, we are only interested in the surfaces that are on the outside. That means the cube in the center is not considered in the formula for surface area because we don't see any of its surfaces on the outside.

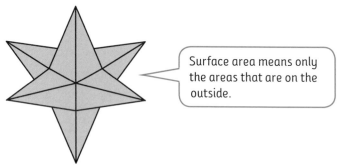

Surface area means only the areas that are on the outside.

The measurement of the outside of the polyhedron involves finding the sum of all the areas of the faces of the shapes that are showing on the surface of the polyhedron. Let's look at an example of how this is computed.

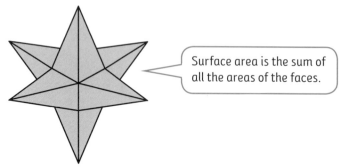

Surface area is the sum of all the areas of the faces.

We can see that the polyhedron has six pyramids. Each pyramid has four triangles, so we determine the surface area of the polyhedron based on these triangles.

Steps for Finding the Surface Area of a Polyhedron

STEP 1
Break the shape into smaller parts.

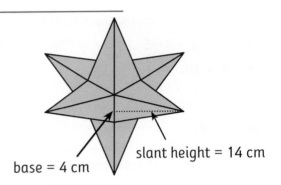

- There are four triangles in each pyramid.
- There are six pyramids. That means we have 24 triangles that make up the shape.
- All of these triangles have the same dimensions, a base of 4 and a height of 14.

base = 4 cm

slant height = 14 cm

STEP 2
Compute the area of one triangle.

Area of one triangle = $\frac{1}{2}$ · base · slant height

Area of one triangle = $\frac{1}{2}$ · 4 · 14

$= 28 \text{ cm}^2$

STEP 3
Find the sum of all the areas of the faces in order to find the surface area of the polyhedron.

We are adding 28, 24 times. This is the same as multiplying 28 · 24.

Surface area of the polyhedron = 28 · 24

$= 672 \text{ cm}^2$

The process of finding the surface area of a polyhedron shows that we can solve complex problems by working slowly and breaking the task into smaller, more manageable subtasks. It also shows how important simple shapes are in complex geometry.

Problem-Solving Activity
Turn to *Interactive Text*, page 193.

mBook **Reinforce Understanding**
Use the *mBook Study Guide* to review lesson concepts.

Activity 1

Evaluate the numeric expressions.

1. $-3 + 2 + 8 - 5$

2. $4 \cdot -5 + (3 + 2)$

3. $5^2 - 10 \cdot 2 + (-3 + -2)$

4. $(-3 - -2) - (-4 + -1) + 3^2$

5. $72 \div (12 - 4) + 4^2$

6. $6 + 24 \div (4 \cdot 3) - 2^2$

Activity 2

Simplify the algebraic expressions.

1. $x + 2x + -3$

2. $-3x + -2x + 5$

3. $-4 + x - -5$

4. $-x + -3 + 2x + 5$

5. $5 + -x + -2x - 4$

6. $5x + 15 + -12 + -3x$

Activity 3

Tell whether each statement is true or false. Then explain your answer.

1. When you are finding the surface area of a 3-D shape, you are finding the sum of the areas of all the faces.

2. Surface area is the measurement of the inside of the shape.

3. A polyhedron is a complex shape made up of cubes.

4. The surface area of a polyhedron may be found by finding the sum of all the areas of all the faces.

Activity 4 • Distributed Practice

Solve.

1. $2.30 \cdot 0.6 = a$

2. $\frac{3}{4} + \frac{1}{8} = b$

3. $\frac{4}{9} \cdot \frac{3}{5} = c$

4. $d - 70 = 80$

5. $90 + e = 150$

6. $120 \div f = 30$

7. $27.9 \div 9 = g$

8. $h \cdot 50 = 300$

▶**Algebraic Expressions**

Why is PEMDAS important?

Expressions are a key part of algebra. Numeric expressions are one kind. They have just numbers. Unless we have rules for working with numeric expressions, we will get different answers. That is why mathematicians created the rules for order of operations.

One easy way to remember the rules and their order is to think PEMDAS—Please Excuse My Dear Aunt Sally.

PEMDAS—The Rules for Order of Operations		
Step 1	**P** – Parentheses	Work what is inside the parentheses.
Step 2	**E** – Exponents	Work any numbers with exponents.
Step 3	**M**– Multiplication **D** – Division	Work multiplication or division problems from left to right.
Step 4	**A** – Addition **S** – Subtraction	Last of all, work addition or subtraction problems from left to right.

One other rule to remember is that if we have an expression with operations at the same level, we work left to right. Review 1 shows two different cases. The first case has multiplication and division operations. These are at the same level in PEMDAS, so we work left to right. The second case has a mix of operations.

Review 1

How do we evaluate numeric expressions?

Expression 1:
$50 \div 10 \cdot 4 \div 2$

The operations are at the same level. They are multiplication and division, so we work left to right.

$50 \div 10 \cdot 4 \div 2$ ← Divide 50 by 10.

$5 \cdot 4 \div 2$ ← Multiply 4 by 5.

$20 \div 2$ ← Divide 20 by 2.

10

The solution is 10.

Expression 2:
$6^2 - (8 - 2) \div 5$

There is a mix of operations, so we use PEMDAS.

$6^2 - (8 - 2) + 5$ ← P—Parentheses
Work inside the parentheses.

$6^2 - 6 + 5$ ← E—Exponents
Evaluate any numbers with exponents.

$36 - 6 + 5$ ← AS—Addition/Subtraction
The operations are at the same level. Work left to right.

$30 + 5$

35

The solution is 35.

How do we compute with integers?

Positive and negative integers are used a lot in algebra. If we don't remember what to do when we add or subtract these numbers, we'll get the wrong answer. The most important idea to remember is: Subtraction is the same as adding the opposite. Movement on the number line also helps us remember what is going on when we add or subtract integers.

Review 1

What is happening when we add using negative numbers?

$-4 + 6 = 2$

We start at -4 and move 6 in the positive direction.

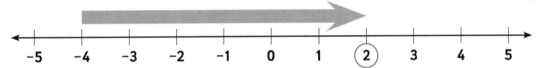

$-1 + -2 = -3$

We start at -1 and move 2 in the negative direction.

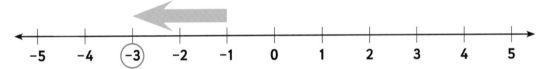

$-2 - -5$ Rule: Subtraction is adding the opposite.

$-2 + 5 = 3$

We start at -2 and move 5 in the positive direction.

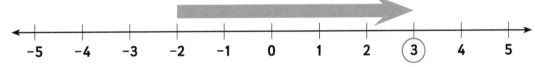

How do we work with algebraic terms?

Algebraic expressions contain variables. They can also have numbers. One of the hardest rules for working with expressions has to do with how we work with terms (variables and numbers) in an expression.

The rule is: We cannot combine numbers and variables in an expression. They are unlike terms. The three expressions in the box are all correct, yet the last two look like numbers and variables have been combined. Why are they correct?

Algebraic Expressions

$x + 2$

$-3x$

$3x + 2$

Our special symbols help us see why all three expressions are correct. The reason is simple. Terms such as $3x$ are just a way of showing the coefficient in the expression. The coefficient tells us how many variables we have. It also tells us whether the variables are positive or negative.

Review 1

What do expressions look like using special symbols?

$x + 2$ One positive variable and two numbers

$-3x$ Three negative variables

$3x + 2$ Three positive variables and two numbers

How do we simplify algebraic expressions?

There is more to algebra than rules. There are also properties. Two of the more common properties are the commutative and associative properties. Special symbols help us see why these properties are useful when we simplify expressions.

Review 1

How do we simplify algebraic expressions using the commutative property?

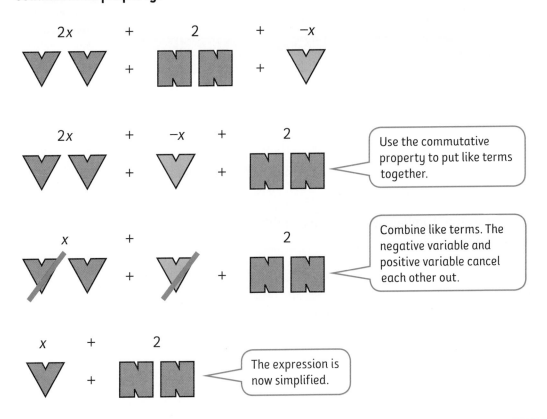

$2x$ + 2 + $-x$

$2x$ + $-x$ + 2

Use the commutative property to put like terms together.

x + 2

Combine like terms. The negative variable and positive variable cancel each other out.

x + 2

The expression is now simplified.

Review 2

How do we simplify algebraic expressions using the associative property?

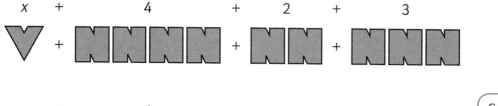

> Combine 2 + 3 using the associative property of addition to combine all like terms.

> Finish by using the associative property of addition to combine all like terms.

Here's another way to combine like terms using the associative property for the same expression.

$x + 4 + 2 + 3$

We combine 4 + 2 using the associative property of addition.

$x + 6 + 3$

$x + 9$

Apply Skills
Turn to *Interactive Text*,
page 196.

mBook **Reinforce Understanding**
Use the *mBook Study Guide*
to review lesson concepts.

▶Problem Solving: **Surface Area of Three-Dimensional Shapes**

What is the surface area of 3-D shapes?

Understanding the surface area of many 3-D shapes begins with sorting shapes into groups that have common attributes. In this unit, we sorted shapes into two groups.

Review 1

What are the attributes of 3-D shapes?

Group 1—Cylinder, Prisms, and Cube

cylinder   prisms   cube

- Cylinders have a circular base and no edges.
- Cubes and prisms have edges and their tops and bottoms are parallel.
- Prisms have rectangles or parallelograms for faces.
- A cube has squares for each of its faces.
- Prisms can have many different shapes or polygons for bases.

Group 2—Cone and Pyramids

cone   pyramids

- Cones have a circular base and no edges.
- Pyramids have faces that are triangles.
- Pyramids can have many different shapes or polygons for bases.

Once we separate these shapes into two groups, we start to think about ways to compute the surface area of each shape. Reviews 2 and 3 show how to think about the area of three different shapes.

Review 2

What are the formulas for the surface areas of a cylinder and triangular prism?

Formula for the Surface Area of a Cylinder

Area of two bases   Area of surface

$(2 \cdot \pi r^2)$ + $(2\pi r \cdot h)$

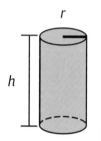

Formula for the Surface Area of a Triangular Prism

2 · (Area of triangle) + 3 · (Area of rectangle)

- The area of a triangular base is $\frac{1}{2}$ · base · height.

- We have two bases so the area is $2 \cdot \left(\frac{1}{2} \cdot \text{base} \cdot \text{height}\right)$.

- The area of a rectangular face is base · height.

- We have three rectangular faces so the area is 3 · (base · height).

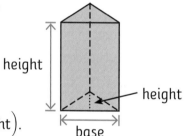

Review 3

How do we find the surface area of a pyramid?

To find the surface area of a pyramid, we need to find the area of the base and the area of each side. Then we add the areas to find the total surface area.

Let's look at a pyramid with a square base. It has four triangular faces.

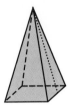

base

Pyramid = Area of the base + Area of 4 faces

Area of the base of the pyramid = $b \cdot h$

Area of one of the faces = $\frac{1}{2} \cdot b \cdot$ slant height

Surface Area of pyramid = $(b \cdot h) + 4 \cdot \left(\frac{1}{2} \cdot b \cdot h \right)$

Knowing how to find the surface area of basic three-dimensional objects helps us find the surface area of more complex objects. Polyhedrons are one type of complex three-dimensional shapes. Review 4 shows how we use what we know about basic shapes to find the surface area of a polyhedron.

Review 4

How do we find the surface area of a polyhedron?
Let's look at the steps for finding the surface area of a polyhedron.

STEP 1
Break the shape into smaller parts.

STEP 2
Compute the area of each of the smaller parts.

STEP 3
Find the sum of all the areas of the faces in order to find the surface area of the polyhedron.

Finding the surface area of a complex shape like a polyhedron is easier when we take our time and work carefully through each step.

Problem-Solving Activity
Turn to *Interactive Text*,
page 198.

mBook Reinforce Understanding
Use the *mBook Study Guide*
to review lesson concepts.

Got volume?

$$V = B \cdot h$$

A single cow can produce as much as 8 gallons of milk in one day.

- Two cups of milk make one pint.
- Sixteen cups of milk make one gallon.
- A large milkcan holds about 8 gallons.
- A transport truck carries about 7,000 to 8,000 gallons of milk.
- Large silos hold as much as 50,000 gallons of milk.

I DIDN'T KNOW I HAD IT IN ME!

OBJECTIVES

Building Number Concepts

- Use order of operations rules to evaluate algebraic and numeric expressions
- Use substitution to evaluate algebraic expressions
- Apply the distributive property to algebraic expressions

Problem Solving

- Use formulas to find the volume of cylinders and prisms
- Find the volume of pyramids and cones by comparing them to prisms and cylinders
- Use a formula to find the volume of a sphere

▶**Multiplication and Division of Integers**

Vocabulary
PASS rule

How do we multiply and divide integers?

In previous lessons we learned rules for adding and subtracting integers. We included these rules in our Algebra Toolbox.

Now we will look at the rules for *multiplying* and *dividing* integers. We will also add these to our toolbox. We can use a simple rule.

Rule

When the signs are the same in a problem, the answer is always positive.

The acronym **PASS** (**P**ositive **A**nswers **H**ave the **S**ame **S**igns) helps us remember this. If there is no sign in front of a number, the number is positive. Let's look at some multiplication examples.

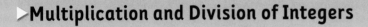

Positive　　**A**nswers　　**S**ame　　**S**ign

When we multiply two negative numbers:

Problem　　　　　Answer

$-5 \cdot -7 \ = \ 35$

The answer is positive because the signs in the problem are the same.

negative sign　　negative sign

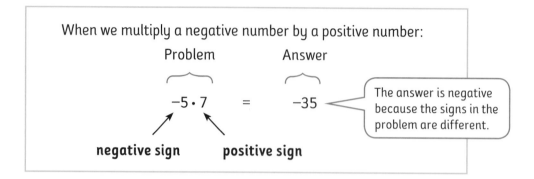

When we multiply a negative number by a positive number:

Problem   Answer

$-5 \cdot 7$ = -35

negative sign   positive sign

The answer is negative because the signs in the problem are different.

We use the same rule for dividing integers.

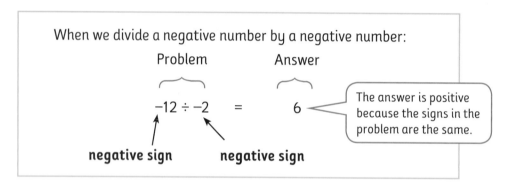

When we divide a negative number by a negative number:

Problem   Answer

$-12 \div -2$ = 6

negative sign   negative sign

The answer is positive because the signs in the problem are the same.

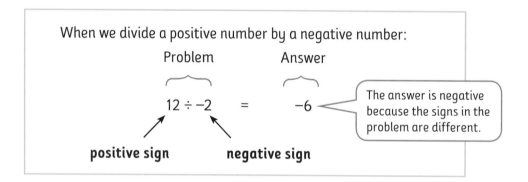

When we divide a positive number by a negative number:

Problem   Answer

$12 \div -2$ = -6

positive sign   negative sign

The answer is negative because the signs in the problem are different.

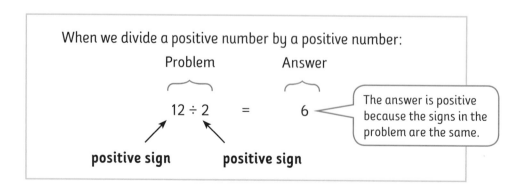

When we divide a positive number by a positive number:

Problem   Answer

$12 \div 2$ = 6

positive sign   positive sign

The answer is positive because the signs in the problem are the same.

We now have the complete list of rules for integer operations in our Algebra Toolbox.

When we evaluate complex expressions, we must use PEMDAS (*multiplication* and *division* before *addition* and *subtraction*) and our rules for integer operations.

Example 1 shows how we use our rules from the toolbox to find the answer.

Integer Operation Rules

Think about:

• Subtraction is the same as adding the opposite.

• Addition is about direction.

• When you multiply or divide integers, use the PASS rule.

Example 1

Evaluate a complex expression using PEMDAS and integer rules.

5 + 40 ÷ −10 · −3

STEP 1
PEMDAS

$5 + \boxed{40 \div -10} \cdot -3$

Remember the PASS rule for division: A positive divided by a negative is a negative. The answer is negative because the signs in the problem are different.

STEP 2
PEMDAS

$5 + \boxed{-4 \cdot -3}$

Remember the PASS rule for multiplication: A negative times a negative is a positive. The answer is positive because the signs in the problem are the same.

STEP 3

$\boxed{5 + 12}$

Remember the rule for adding integers: When we start with a positive number and move in a positive direction, we get a positive answer.

We see 17 is our answer.

Apply Skills
Turn to *Interactive Text*, page 201.

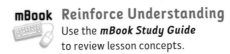

mBook **Reinforce Understanding**
Use the *mBook Study Guide* to review lesson concepts.

▶**Problem Solving: Concept of Volume**

Vocabulary
volume

How do we measure what's inside a three-dimensional object?

In the last unit, we learned to use a number of special vocabulary terms such as *face, edge,* and *base* when we talk about *three-dimensional,* or 3-D, objects. These terms are shown below.

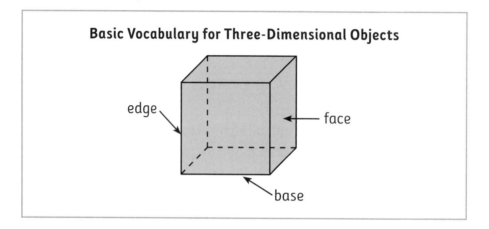

Basic Vocabulary for Three-Dimensional Objects

edge

face

base

We also learned that the *surface area* of a three-dimensional object is the measurement of the outside of the object. We can think of surface area as the "skin" or "wrapping paper" on the object.

Now we will learn to find out how much space is inside a three-dimensional object. When we measure the amount of space inside a three-dimensional object, we are measuring the object's **volume**.

The volume of a 12-ounce cup of coffee

Juice

The volume of a 2-liter bottle of juice

We talk about volume all the time, but we don't use the word. Instead, we use phrases such as "a 12-ounce cup of coffee," or "a 2-liter bottle of juice." Both statements refer to the volume of the containers.

We can accurately measure the volume of an object with tools and formulas. For example, cooks use measuring spoons and cups when they prepare meals. They use these measuring tools to make exact measurements.

However, it is also important to know how to estimate the volume of different objects. Estimation helps us understand how we get the different formulas that measure the volume of different three-dimensional objects.

Small three-dimensional cubes (such as dice or sugar cubes), and other items such as marbles, beans, packing peanuts, sand, rice, and water are different materials we can use to estimate the volume of larger three-dimensional objects.

Material for Filling Three-Dimensional Objects

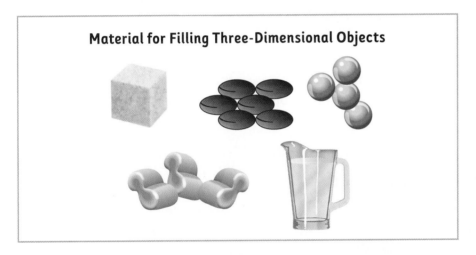

When we use these common three-dimensional objects to fill large three-dimensional objects such as the ones shown below, we are estimating volume.

Common Three-Dimensional Objects in Everyday Life

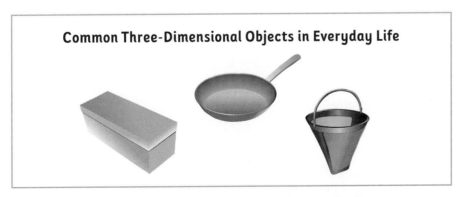

 Problem-Solving Activity
Turn to *Interactive Text*, page 202.

 mBook **Reinforce Understanding**
Use the *mBook Study Guide* to review lesson concepts.

Homework

Activity 1

Use the integer rules to solve the problems.

1. $-3 \cdot 5$
2. $15 \div -3$
3. $15 - 27$
4. $-6 + -8$
5. $-24 \div -8$
6. $-5 \cdot -3$
7. $5 + -7$
8. $-56 \div 7$

Activity 2

Use PEMDAS and integer rules to evaluate the numeric expressions.
Remember to do diagnostics first, and then go to the Algebra Toolbox.

1. $5 + 2 - -3 + (3 \cdot -6)$
2. $9 \cdot (-6 + -4) + 2^2$
3. $-15 \div -3 \cdot (8 - -2)$
4. $-24 + -38 - 3^2$

Activity 3

Choose the material that would most likely be used for estimating the volume
of the item.

1. The volume of a sauce pan is about 3
   (a) cups of water.   (b) marbles.   (c) grains of sand.

2. The volume of a shoe box is about 5
   (a) marbles.   (b) sugar cubes.   (c) cups of rice.

3. The volume of a waffle cone is about 15
   (a) cups of water.   (b) marbles.   (c) cups of beans.

Activity 4 • Distributed Practice

Solve.

1. $\frac{1}{5} \cdot \frac{5}{3} = a$
2. $-3 - 9 = b$
3. $\frac{1}{12} \div \frac{1}{6} = c$
4. $3^2 + (3 \cdot 4) - 2 = d$
5. $\frac{3}{4} - \frac{3}{8} = e$
6. $-9 + -9 = f$
7. $(5 - 10) + 2^2 = g$
8. $8 + 4 \div 2 = h$

▶ **Problem Solving: Measuring Volume and Cubic Units**

Vocabulary
cubic inch
cubic unit

How do we measure volume exactly?

Filling a rectangular prism with marbles is a good method of estimating its volume. However, it is not an exact method of measurement.

Estimating the Volume of a Rectangular Prism With Marbles

When we use marbles as a unit to measure the volume of a rectangular prism, *it will not be exact* because of the spaces between the marbles.

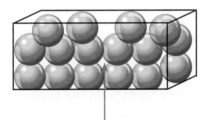

Space between the marbles

A more exact way to measure an object—and to understand the concept of volume—is to use something that fits exactly inside the object.

One of the best ways to find the volume of a three-dimensional object is to fill it with smaller objects that create a repeated pattern. This doesn't work for every three-dimensional object, but it works for objects like cubes, cylinders, and prisms.

 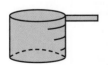 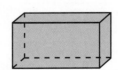

How do we find the volume of a rectangular prism?

Before we can find the volume of a rectangular prism, we must determine the height, width, and depth. Then, to get the volume, we multiply height times width times depth. But why does that work?

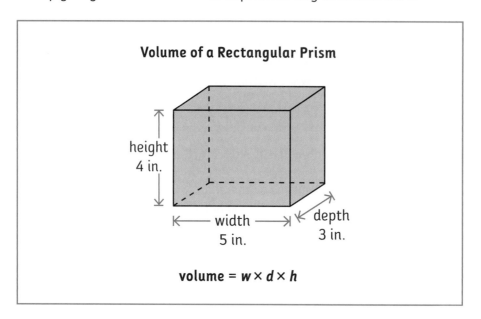

Volume of a Rectangular Prism

height
4 in.

width
5 in.

depth
3 in.

volume = $w \times d \times h$

Finding volume is like stacking cards. We stack cards from the bottom up until we reach the top. As we stack one card on top of the next card, we are creating a repeating pattern. We can think about the cards as a stack of bases.

This stack of bases helps us understand the volume formula for the rectangular prism. We find the volume by:

- Finding the area of the base.
- Multiplying the area of the base times the height.

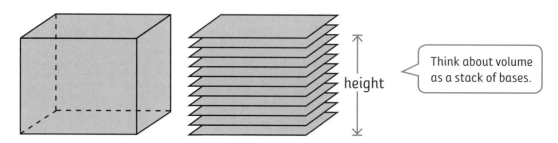

height

Think about volume as a stack of bases.

Example 1 shows how to find the volume by stacking bases.

Example 1

Find the volume of the rectangular prism.

The volume of the prism is the area of the base times the height.

Steps for Finding the Volume of a Rectangular Prism

STEP 1
Find the area of the base.

The area of the base is $5 \cdot 3 = 15$ square inches, or $15\ \text{in}^2$.

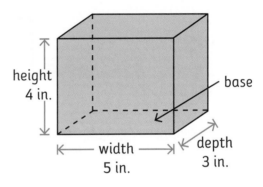

STEP 2
Multiply the area of the base times the height.
We can think of it as stacking these bases
to a height of 4 inches.

The volume of a rectangular prism equals
the area of the base times the height.

So we multiply 15 by 4.

$$15 \cdot 4 = 60$$

This is the same as multiplying width
times depth times height.

$w \times d \times h$

$$5 \cdot 3 \cdot 4 = 60$$

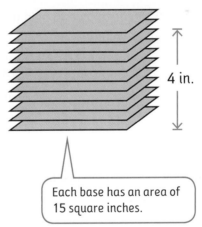

Each base has an area of
15 square inches.

What unit do we use to measure volume?

We just computed the volume of the prism in the previous example as 60, but 60 what? It is not 60 square inches.

Example 1 shows how to use square units to measure a two-dimensional, or 2-D, shape such as a rectangle.

Example 1

Find the area of the rectangle.

height = 3 units

base = 5 units

Area = 3 · 5, or 15 square units

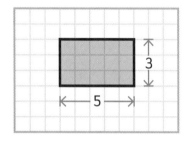

We use *square inches* to measure two-dimensional, or 2-D, objects.

We can check the answer by counting the squares in the rectangle.

Three-dimensional objects have depth, so one way we can measure them is in **cubic inches** .

Let's use small cubes similar to dice to help us understand why the word *cubic* is in the formula for volume.

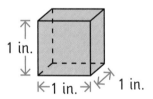

The cube is the basic unit of measurement for three-dimensional objects.

Example 2 shows how we can find out how many cubes will fill a prism.

Example 2

Find the volume of the prism.

How many 1 × 1 × 1 inch cubes will fill a prism with the dimensions 5 × 3 × 4?

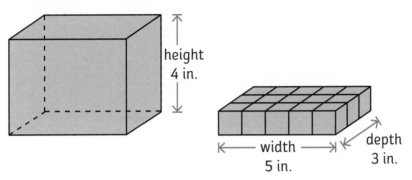

height
4 in.

width
5 in.

depth
3 in.

Notice that we use little cubes to measure the base of the prism.

The base of the prism = 5 · 3, or 15 cubes.

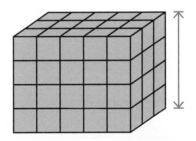

We can stack four bases that are each 1 inch in height to fill the prism.

The volume of the prism = 5 · 3 · 4 = 60 cubes, or 60 cubic inches.

We can now see why volume is measured in   **cubic units** . The cube is the basic unit of measurement in a three-dimensional object. We write cubic units as in^3 or cm^3.

Problem-Solving Activity
Turn to *Interactive Text*, page 204.

mBook Reinforce Understanding
Use the *mBook Study Guide* to review lesson concepts.

Activity 1

Use the integer rules for all four operations to solve the problems.

1. $-2 \cdot -3$
2. $-4 + -33$
3. $32 \div -8$
4. $15 - -3$
5. $8 \cdot -10$
6. $-49 \div -7$

Activity 2

Use PEMDAS and integer rules to evaluate the numeric expressions. Remember to do diagnostics first, and then go to the Algebra Toolbox.

1. $5 + (-4 + -1) - 3 \cdot -3$
2. $-3 \cdot (-2 \cdot 3) + -15$
3. $18 \div -3 \cdot 2 - 2^2$
4. $-5 + 3^2 \div -3 - -5$
5. $-12 - (-3 + -5) \cdot -2$

Activity 3

Select the correct measurement for each object.

1. The area of the rectangle is:
   (a) 12 units (b) 12 units^2 (c) 12 units^3

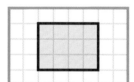

2. The length of the line is:
   (a) 10 cm (b) 10 cm^2 (c) 10 cm^3

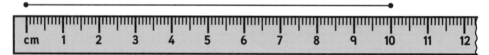

3. The volume of the cube is:
   (a) 8 in. (b) 8 in.^{2} (c) 8 in.^{3}

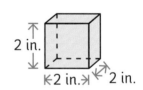

2 in.

2 in. 2 in.

Activity 4 • Distributed Practice

Solve.

1. $-4 - -5 = a$
2. $\frac{2}{3} \cdot \frac{3}{2} = b$
3. $(3 \cdot 5) - 3^2 = c$
4. $\frac{1}{4} \div \frac{1}{8} = d$
5. $\frac{1}{4} - \frac{1}{8} = e$
6. $(8 - 12) + -3 = f$
7. $-8 \div -1 = g$
8. $107 + 4 \div 4 = h$

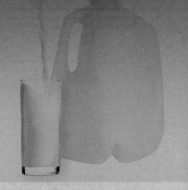

Lesson 3 | ▶Evaluating Algebraic Expressions

Problem Solving:
▶Bases and the Volume of Prisms

▶Evaluating Algebraic Expressions

How do we evaluate algebraic expressions?

We learned to simplify algebraic expressions by using properties such as the commutative property. When we work with these expressions, we must remember that we can only combine like terms.

Example 1 shows how we combine variable terms with variable terms, and number terms with number terms.

Example 1

Simplify the algebraic expression.

$3x + 2 + 4x + 7$

STEP 1
Use the commutative property to put like terms together.

$3x + 4x + 2 + 7$

STEP 2
Combine variable terms.

$7x + 2 + 7$

STEP 3
Combine number terms.

$7x + \quad 9$

Our solution is $7x + 9$.

We cannot combine variable terms and number terms in this expression.

We evaluate algebraic expressions by substituting a number for a variable.

With algebra, we can substitute any value for the variable to show the pattern represented by the expression.

Example 2 shows how to evaluate the algebraic expression $c + 7$ using different values for c.

Example 2

Evaluate the expression $c + 7$ using different values for c.

Let $c = 9$

$$c + 7$$
$$\downarrow$$
$$9 + 7 = 16$$

Let $c = -100$

$$c + 7$$
$$\downarrow$$
$$-100 + 7 = -93$$

Let $c = 5,000$

$$c + 7$$
$$\downarrow$$
$$5,000 + 7 = 5,007$$

POWER CONCEPT

When we evaluate an algebraic expression, we substitute a value for the variable.

We evaluated the expression in Example 2 using only one step. The expression was already simplified, so we just substituted different values.

More complicated expressions may require that we simplify the expression first and then evaluate it. Simplifying the expression first can make substitution easier when we evaluate the expression.

Example 3 shows two different ways to solve the same problem.

- In Method 1, we simplify the expression first and then substitute.
- In Method 2, we substitute and evaluate without simplifying.

We get the same answer using either method.

Example 3

Evaluate the expression using both methods.

$3m + 5 + 2m - 1$

Let $m = 2$

Method 1:

Simplify by using the commutative property, and then evaluate.

$3m + 5 + 2m - 1$ ←   Use the commutative property.

$3m + 2m + 5 - 1$ ←   Combine like terms.

$5m \quad + \quad 4$ ←   Substitute 2 for m.   ⟨ Remember, we let $m = 2$. ⟩

$5 \cdot 2 + 4$ ←   Use PEMDAS—multiplication and division before addition and subtraction.

$10 + 4$

Our solution is 14.

Method 2:

Substitute first and then evaluate.

$3m + 5 + 2m - 1$ ←   Substitute 2 for m.

$3 \cdot 2 + 5 + 2 \cdot 2 - 1$ ←   Use PEMDAS—multiplication and division before addition and subtraction.

$6 \quad + 5 + 4 \quad - 1$ ←   Use PEMDAS—All operations are addition and subtraction, so work left to right.

$11 \qquad + 4 - 1$ ←   Use PEMDAS—All operations are addition and subtraction, so work left to right.

$15 \quad - 1$

Our solution is 14.

The solution is the same using either method.

Working a math problem two different ways requires us to be flexible in our thinking. We must think about the problem and then use the right tools from the Algebra Toolbox.

% ÷
≡ × **Apply Skills**
< × Turn to *Interactive Text*,
       page 207.

mBook **Reinforce Understanding**
Use the *mBook Study Guide*
to review lesson concepts.

▶**Problem Solving: Bases and the Volume of Prisms**

How do we stack bases to find volume?

Stacking bases helps us understand the ways in which volume formulas are the same for many different three-dimensional objects.

We will use Volume = Base • height as a basic part of the formula. We capitalize the word *Base* because we are talking about the area of the base of the object, which has two dimensions—depth and width. Once we find this two-dimensional base, we multiply it by the height of the object. These drawings show bases for prisms.

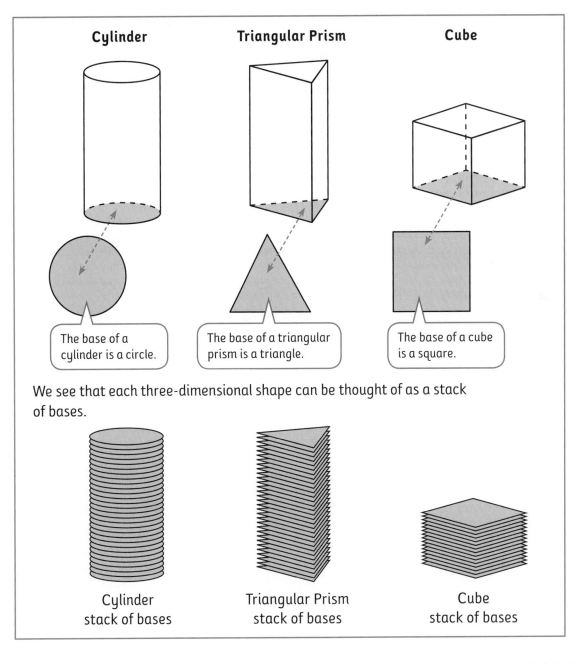

Cylinder

Triangular Prism

Cube

The base of a cylinder is a circle.

The base of a triangular prism is a triangle.

The base of a cube is a square.

We see that each three-dimensional shape can be thought of as a stack of bases.

Cylinder
stack of bases

Triangular Prism
stack of bases

Cube
stack of bases

We can use the same kind of thinking to find the volume of a triangular prism. We see in Example 1 that we can stack triangle-shaped bases to make the triangular prism.

Example 1

Find the volume of the triangular prism.

Volume of a prism = Base · height

STEP 1

First find the area of the triangular base.

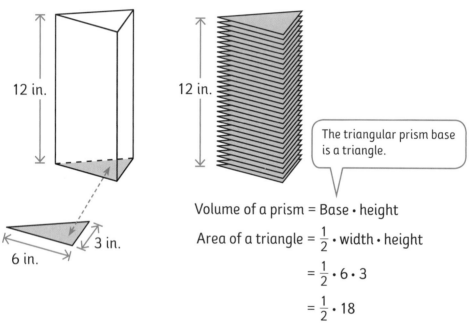

The triangular prism base is a triangle.

Volume of a prism = Base · height

Area of a triangle = $\frac{1}{2}$ · width · height

$= \frac{1}{2} \cdot 6 \cdot 3$

$= \frac{1}{2} \cdot 18$

Base of the triangular prism = 9 in²

STEP 2

Now find the volume of the triangular prism.

Base is the area of the triangular prism base.

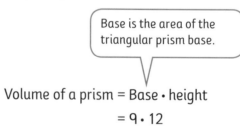

Volume of a prism = Base · height

$= 9 \cdot 12$

Volume of the triangular prism = 108 in³

Notice we use the height of the triangle to find the area of the base, but we use the height of the prism to find the volume of the triangular prism.

We can find the volume of a cylinder this way, too.

Example 2

Find the volume of the cylinder.

Volume of a cylinder = Base · height

STEP 1
First find the area of the cylinder base.

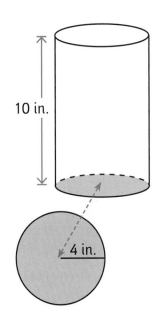

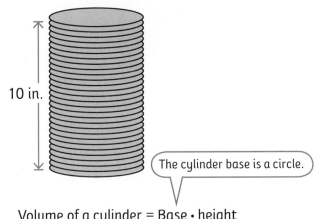

The cylinder base is a circle.

Volume of a cylinder = Base · height

Area of a circle = πr^2 = 3.14 · r^2

= 3.14 · 4^2

= 3.14 · 16

Base of the cylinder = 50.24 in²

Remember, we round π to 3.14 when we solve formulas.

STEP 2
Now find the volume of the cylinder.

Base is the area of the cylinder base.

Volume of a cylinder = Base · height

= 50.24 · 10

Volume of the cylinder = 502.4 in³

Example 3

Find the volume of the cube.

Volume of a cube = Base · height

STEP 1

First find the area of the cube base.

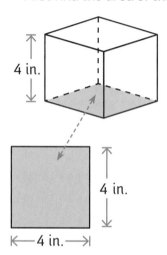

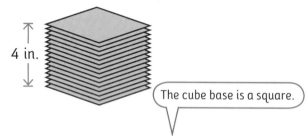

The cube base is a square.

Volume of a cube = Base · height

Area of a square = depth · width

= 4 · 4

Base of the cube = 16 in²

STEP 2

Now find the volume of the cube.

Base is the area of the cube base.

Volume of a cube = Base · height

= 16 · 4

Volume of the cube = 64 in³

Working with cylinders, prisms, and cubes shows us how important the base is to each volume formula. In each case, Volume = Base · height.

$$V = B \cdot h$$

Problem-Solving Activity
Turn to *Interactive Text*,
page 208.

mBook Reinforce Understanding
Use the *mBook Study Guide*
to review lesson concepts.

Activity 1

Evaluate the algebraic expressions by substituting the given value for the variable and then simplifying.

Model $x + 2x + 3x$ for $x = 2$

Answer: Substitute: $2 + \mathbf{2 \cdot 2} + 3 \cdot 2$

Simplify: $2 + 4 + \mathbf{3 \cdot 2}$

$\mathbf{2 + 4} + 6$

$\mathbf{6 + 6} = 12$

1. Evaluate $x + 10 + x + 5$ for $x = -5$. 2. Evaluate $4w + w - 3$ for $w = -2$.

3. Evaluate $14 + 2z + 21$ for $z = 10$.

Activity 2

Evaluate the expressions by simplifying them and then substituting the value for the variable.

Model $2x - x + 3 + 2x$ for $x = -1$

Answer: Simplify: $2x - x + 2x + 3$

$x + 2x + 3$

$3x + 3$

Substitute: $3 \cdot -1 + 3$

$-3 + 3 = 0$

1. Evaluate $2x + 3 + 4x + 5$ for $x = -5$.

2. Evaluate $w + w - 3$ for $w = -2$.

3. Evaluate $z + 3z + 8$ for $z = 10$.

Activity 3

Find the volume for each object given the Base and the height.

1. 3 cm   If the Base (the area of the circle) is 6 cm², what is the volume of the cylinder?

2. 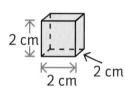 2 cm   2 cm   2 cm   If the Base (the area of the square) is 4 cm², what is the volume of the cube?

3. 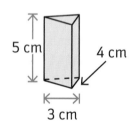 5 cm   4 cm   3 cm   If the Base (the area of the triangle) is 6 cm², what is the volume of the triangular prism?

4. 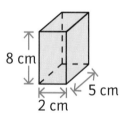 8 cm   5 cm   2 cm   If the Base (the area of the rectangle) is 10 cm², what is the volume of the rectangular prism?

Activity 4 • Distributed Practice

Solve.

1. $6 - {-2} = a$

2. $\frac{2}{5} \cdot \frac{1}{2} = b$

3. $\frac{1}{3} \div \frac{1}{6} = c$

4. $(3 \cdot 6) - 4^2 = d$

5. $(8 \cdot 2) \div 4 = e$

6. $\frac{1}{4} - {-\frac{2}{4}} = f$

7. $-7 + {-1} + 7 = g$

8. $16 \div 4 \div 4 = h$

▶**Writing and Evaluating Expressions**

Vocabulary
consecutive numbers number grid

How do we describe patterns of numbers using variables?

The power of variables is that they can be used to describe many kinds of number patterns.

We can write expressions that are general statements about a pattern and then substitute values for the variables to find specific instances of the pattern.

One kind of pattern involves **consecutive numbers** . Two or more integers listed in order are *consecutive numbers*.

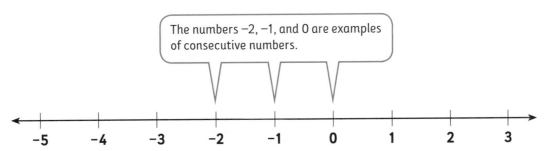

The numbers −2, −1, and 0 are examples of consecutive numbers.

There are many examples of consecutive numbers on this number line. For example, the numbers −2, −1, and 0 are consecutive. So are the numbers 0, 1, and 2.

Another place we can look at patterns of consecutive numbers is on a **number grid** . A number grid is a table of consecutive numbers.

Let's look at a simple example involving consecutive numbers shown on a number grid.

First, let's write expressions for the three consecutive numbers 6, 7, and 8, where $x = 6$.

1	2	3	4	5	6	7	8	9	10
11	12	13	14	15	16	17	18	19	20

If $x = 6$, we can write 7 as $x + 1$. That means we can write 8 as $x + 2$.

Our three consecutive numbers on a number grid can be written using the expressions:

$$x \qquad x + 1 \qquad x + 2$$

Expressions for three consecutive numbers

When variables describe patterns, we can use the same expressions to describe three other consecutive numbers on a number grid.

Example 1 shows us that the pattern works when we substitute the variable with the value for the first of three consecutive numbers.

Example 1

Look at the three consecutive numbers in the grids. Show the pattern:

$$x \qquad x + 1 \qquad x + 2$$

In this grid, the three consecutive numbers are 18, 19, and 20.

1	2	3	4	5	6	7	8	9	10
11	12	13	14	15	16	17	18	19	20

When we substitute 18 for x, we see that the pattern works.

$x = 18$
$x + 1 = 18 + 1$, or 19
$x + 2 = 18 + 2$, or 20

In this grid, the three consecutive numbers are 12, 13, and 14.

1	2	3	4	5	6	7	8	9	10
11	12	13	14	15	16	17	18	19	20

When we substitute 12 for x, we see the pattern works with these numbers too.

$x = 12$
$x + 1 = 12 + 1$, or 13
$x + 2 = 12 + 2$, or 14

What other expressions can be used to describe the general pattern?

Substituting variables to make a statement about a pattern is an important tool in algebra. When we use variables, we can describe the same pattern of numbers using different expressions.

Let's look at another series of three consecutive numbers. In the last example, we used a variable to represent the first of the three numbers.

In Example 1, we will show that we can use many different expressions to describe three consecutive numbers.

Example 1

Use models to represent three consecutive numbers.

Our three consecutive numbers are 46, 47, and 48.

Model 1:

Substitute x for the first number in the series of consecutive numbers.

$x = 46$

Our expression for our three consecutive numbers is:

$$x \qquad x + 1 \qquad x + 2$$

31	32	33	34	35	36	37	38	39	40
41	42	43	44	45	46	47	48	49	50

We see that our expression works. $\longrightarrow$

$x = 46$
$x + 1 = 46 + 1$, or 47
$x + 2 = 46 + 2$, or 48

Now let's represent these three consecutive numbers another way.

Model 2:

Substitute x for the second number in our consecutive numbers.

In this model, $x = 47$.

Our expression for our three consecutive numbers is now:

$$x - 1 \qquad x \qquad x + 1$$

31	32	33	34	35	36	37	38	39	40
41	42	43	44	45	46	47	48	49	50

$x - 1 = 47 - 1$, or 46
$x = 47$
$x + 1 = 47 + 1$, or 48

Now, let's have x stand for the last number in the consecutive numbers.

Model 3:

Substitute x for the last number in our consecutive numbers.

In this final model, $x = 48$.

Our expression for the three consecutive numbers is now:

$$x - 2 \qquad x - 1 \qquad x$$

31	32	33	34	35	36	37	38	39	40
41	42	43	44	45	46	47	48	49	50

$x - 2 = 48 - 2$, or 46
$x - 1 = 48 - 1$, or 47
$x = 48$

%÷
≡
<✕ **Apply Skills**
Turn to **Interactive Text**, page 212.

mBook Reinforce Understanding
Use the **mBook Study Guide** to review lesson concepts.

Activity 1

Tell the three numbers described in each problem by substituting values in the expressions given to represent the pattern.

Model If $y = 4$ and the pattern is described by the expressions $y - 1$, y, and $y + 1$, what are the three numbers?

Answer: 3, 4, and 5

1. If $y = 4$ and the pattern is described by the expressions y, $y + 2$, and $y + 4$, what are the three numbers?

2. If $z = 100$ and the pattern is described by the expressions $z - 10$, z, and $z + 10$, what are the three numbers?

3. If $a = -5$ and the pattern is described by the expressions $a - 1$, a, and $a + 1$, what are the three numbers?

4. If $b = 130$ and the pattern is described by the expressions $b - 2$, $b - 1$, and b, what are the three numbers?

Activity 2

Write three different expressions to show the same general pattern for each problem.

Model 34, 35, and 36

Answer:

Method 1: If $x = 34$, the series is x, $x + 1$, and $x + 2$.

Method 2: If $x = 35$, the series is $x - 1$, x, and $x + 1$.

Method 3: If $x = 36$, the series is $x - 2$, $x - 1$, and x.

1. 10, 20, 30   2. 55, 66, 77   3. −1, 0, 1

Activity 3

Tell two different sets of numbers that may be represented by the expressions.

Model $x - 5, x, x + 5$

Answer: Set 1: 5, 10, 15

Set 2: 45, 50, 55

1. $y - 20, y - 10, y$

2. $z - 10, z, z + 10$

3. $w, w + 2, w + 4$

4. $m - 100, m, m + 100$

Activity 4 • Distributed Practice

Solve.

1. $(5 \cdot 2) \div 5 = a$

2. $\frac{2}{4} \div \frac{3}{2} = b$

3. $\frac{1}{3} \div \frac{1}{3} = c$

4. $4^2 + 6 \div 2 = d$

5. $-4 \cdot -3 = e$

6. $\frac{1}{4} \cdot \frac{1}{4} = f$

7. $-6 + -1 \cdot -6 = g$

8. $5 \cdot -5 \cdot -2 = h$

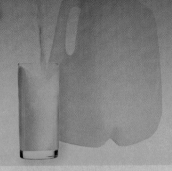

▶**Commonsense Algebraic Properties**

Vocabulary
multiplicative additive

What are some algebraic properties that "just make sense"?

There are many properties of numbers that we need to remember when we evaluate expressions.

We have talked about the commutative and associative properties. We use these two properties to move and group numbers.

Commutative Property

We can change the order of the numbers in an addition or multiplication problem without changing the answer.

$$x + 3 + 2x + -5 = x + 2x + 3 + -5$$

Associative Property

We can group the numbers in an addition or multiplication problem without changing the answer.

$$x + 3 + 7 + -2 = x + (3 + 7) + -2 = x + 3 + (7 + -2)$$

Now we can add some more properties to our Algebra Toolbox. These properties "just make sense." Since they are based on common sense, they are not hard to learn.

Let's begin by looking at three commonsense properties that involve zero. These properties involve two new terms. **Multiplicative** means that the property involves multiplication. **Additive** means that the property involves addition.

Identity Property of Addition

Any number plus zero equals the same number.

$$-3 + 0 = -3 \qquad 0 + 5 = 5$$
$$\frac{1}{2} + 0 = \frac{1}{2} \qquad n + 0 = n$$

Multiplicative Property of Zero

Any number times zero equals zero.

$$-3 \cdot 0 = 0 \qquad 0 \cdot 5 = 0$$
$$\frac{1}{2} \cdot 0 = 0 \qquad n \cdot 0 = 0$$

Additive Inverse Property

Any number plus its inverse equals zero.

$$3 + -3 = 0 \qquad -5 + 5 = 0$$
$$\frac{1}{2} + -\frac{1}{2} = 0 \qquad n + -n = 0$$

> Each of these properties contains a statement that uses a variable. The statement shows the general pattern of the property.

Now let's look at two commonsense properties that have to do with the number one.

Identity Property of Multiplication

Any number times one equals itself.

$$-3 \cdot 1 = -3 \qquad \frac{1}{2} \cdot 1 = \frac{1}{2}$$
$$1 \cdot 5 = 5 \qquad n \cdot 1 = n$$

Multiplicative Inverse Property or Reciprocal Property

Any number times its inverse equals one.

$$\frac{1}{2} \cdot \frac{2}{1} = 1 \qquad -3 \cdot -\frac{1}{3} = 1 \qquad \frac{1}{5} \cdot 5 = 1$$

$$n \cdot \frac{1}{n} = 1 \qquad \frac{a}{b} \cdot \frac{b}{a} = 1$$

Let's add these new properties to our Algebra Toolbox. We have grouped them in ways that are easier to remember than the properties shown in the examples.

Number Properties

Properties about moving and grouping numbers

- Commutative Property: $a + b = b + a$
$$a \cdot b = b \cdot a$$

- Associative Property: $a + (b + c) = (a + b) + c$
$$a \cdot (b \cdot c) = (a \cdot b) \cdot c$$

Properties about zero

- Multiplicative Property of Zero: $n \cdot 0 = 0$
- Additive Inverse Property of Zero: $n + -n = 0$
- Identity Property of Addition: $n + 0 = n$

Properties about one

- Identity Property of Multiplication: $x \cdot 1 = x$
- Reciprocal Property: $\dfrac{a}{b} \cdot \dfrac{b}{a} = 1$

$$n \cdot \dfrac{1}{n} = 1$$

Apply Skills
Turn to *Interactive Text*, page 216.

mBook **Reinforce Understanding**
Use the *mBook Study Guide* to review lesson concepts.

Activity 1

Use properties to help you decide what goes on the right side of the equal sign in each problem.

1. $3 + 4 = ?$
   (a) 0
   (b) $4 + 3$
   (c) $3 \cdot 4$

2. $2 \cdot 1 = ?$
   (a) 0
   (b) 1
   (c) 2

3. $4 \cdot 6 = ?$
   (a) $4 + 6$
   (b) $6 \cdot 4$
   (c) 0

4. $\frac{4}{3} \cdot \frac{3}{4} = ?$
   (a) 0
   (b) 1
   (c) 2

5. $5 + -5 = ?$
   (a) 0
   (b) 1
   (c) 2

Activity 2

Choose the example that matches the property.

1. Property of Zero
   (a) $\frac{1}{2} + 0 = \frac{1}{2}$
   (b) $\frac{1}{2} \cdot 0 = 0$
   (c) $\frac{1}{2} + -\frac{1}{2} = 0$

2. Property of Reciprocals
   (a) $\frac{2}{3} \cdot 1 = \frac{2}{3}$
   (b) $\frac{3}{5} + 0 = \frac{3}{5}$
   (c) $\frac{4}{6} \cdot \frac{6}{4} = 1$

3. Identity Property
   (a) $4 \cdot 1 = 4$
   (b) $4 \cdot 0 = 0$
   (c) $4 + -4 = 0$

4. Inverse Property
   (a) $3 + 0 = 3$
   (b) $3 + -3 = 0$
   (c) $3 \cdot 1 = 3$

Activity 3

Tell what shape the base is when you look at the volume for each of these shapes.

1.

2.

3.

4.

Activity 4 • Distributed Practice

Solve.

1. $\frac{2}{1} \cdot \frac{1}{2} = a$

2. $\frac{2}{1} \div \frac{1}{2} = b$

3. $\frac{4}{3} - \frac{1}{6} = c$

4. $4^2 + 3^2 + 2^2 = d$

5. $(6 \cdot 6) \div 6 = e$

6. $-3 \cdot \frac{1}{3} = f$

▶**Problem Solving: The Volume of Cones and Pyramids**

What happens when we can't stack bases to find the volume?

Our volume formula for cylinders, prisms, and cubes ($V = B \cdot h$) works because we can stack bases until we reach the top of each object.

However, we can't always stack bases to find volume. For example, the formula does not work when we try to find the volume of cones or pyramids.

In cones and pyramids, the shape at the top is not the same size as it is at the bottom because the faces of the shape come together at a single point, called the vertex.

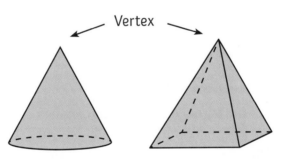

Vertex

What happens when we try to stack bases for a cone to find its volume?

Let's compare a cone and the stacked circular base of the cone.

We see that if we stack circular bases we create a cylinder.

If we draw lines on the picture of the cylinder, we can make an informal comparison of the volumes of the cone and the cylinder that is formed by the stacked bases.

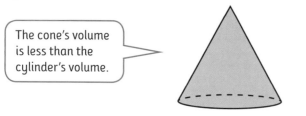

The cone's volume is less than the cylinder's volume.

We see the same type of situation with pyramids.

Pyramids have many different shapes for bases. Let's look at what happens when we stack bases of a pyramid.

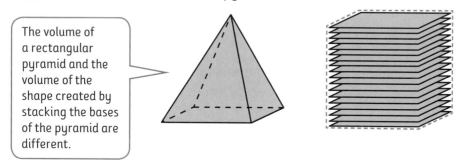

The volume of a rectangular pyramid and the volume of the shape created by stacking the bases of the pyramid are different.

The stacked rectangular base would make a rectangular prism.

If we draw the shape of the pyramid on the picture of the rectangular prism, we can make an informal comparison of the volumes of the pyramid and the prism.

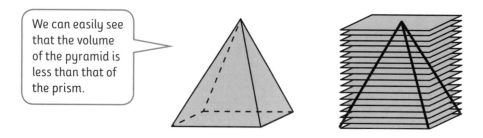

We can easily see that the volume of the pyramid is less than that of the prism.

How can we use cylinders and prisms to help us find the volume formula for cones and pyramids?

In earlier illustrations, we compared cones and pyramids with drawings of their stacked bases.

When comparing the shapes, the volumes of the cones or pyramids looked like they were about $\frac{1}{3}$ the size of the stacked bases.

In fact, if we were to fill a cone with sand and pour the sand into a cylinder with the same-sized base and height, it would take exactly three cones of sand to fill it up.

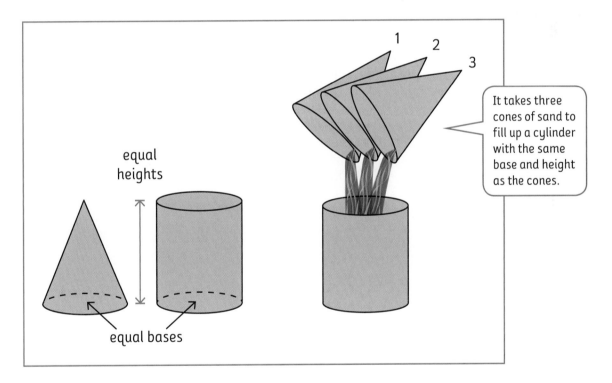

equal heights

equal bases

1
2
3

It takes three cones of sand to fill up a cylinder with the same base and height as the cones.

Now let's see how this affects the volume formula. The most important thing to notice is that we can pour the volume of three cones into a cylinder with the same base and height as each cone. This will help us remember the volume formula for a cone.

If we can pour three cones into the cylinder, this means the volume of the cylinder is three times the volume of the cone.

Volume of a cylinder = 3 • Volume of the cone

That means the volume of one cone is $\frac{1}{3}$ the volume of the cylinder. Now we can get our volume formula for cones. The $B \cdot h$ in the formula is the volume of the cylinder.

Volume of a cone = $\frac{1}{3} \cdot B \cdot h$

Example 1

Find the volume of the cone.

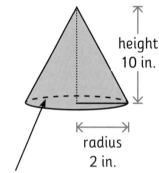

height
10 in.

radius
2 in.

Area of a circle = πr^2

$= 3.14 \cdot 2^2$

$= 3.14 \cdot 4$

Base of the cone = 12.56 in²

Volume of a cone = $\frac{1}{3} \cdot B \cdot h$

$= \frac{1}{3} \cdot 12.56 \cdot 10$

$= 4.187 \cdot 10$

Volume of the cone = 41.87 in³

This kind of thinking also works for pyramids and prisms. It doesn't matter what kind of pyramid it is, as long as we compare it to a prism with the same base and the same height.

Example 2

Find the volume of the pyramid.

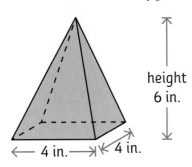

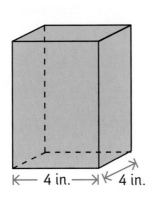

height
6 in.

← 4 in. →|← 4 in.

rectangular pyramid

rectangular prism

Area of Base = 4 · 4

Base of pyramid = 16 in²

Volume of a rectangular pyramid = $\frac{1}{3} \cdot B \cdot h$

$\downarrow \quad \downarrow \quad \downarrow$

$= \frac{1}{3} \cdot 16 \cdot 6$

$= \frac{1}{3} \cdot 96$

> Notice that we used the Associative Property to multiply 16 by 6 first. It's easier to multiply $\frac{1}{3} \cdot 96$, which equals 32, than to multiply $\frac{1}{3} \cdot 16$, which equals 5.3333.

Volume of the pyramid = 32 in³

📝 **Problem-Solving Activity**
Turn to *Interactive Text*, page 218.

⌨ **mBook Reinforce Understanding**
Use the *mBook Study Guide* to review lesson concepts.

Homework

Write a general statement for the properties shown.

Model   Multiplicative Property of Zero

Examples: $1 \cdot 0 = 0$ $2 \cdot 0 = 0$ $3 \cdot 0 = 0$ Answer: $n \cdot 0 = 0$

1. Additive Inverse Property
Examples:
$$5 + -5 \ \ = 0$$
$$10 + -10 = 0$$
$$2 + -2 \ \ = 0$$

2. Identity Property of Addition
Examples:
$$3 + 0 \ \ \ \ = 3$$
$$\tfrac{2}{3} + 0 \ \ \ \ = \tfrac{2}{3}$$
$$6{,}000 + 0 = 6{,}000$$

3. Multiplicative Inverse Property
Examples:
$$2 \cdot \tfrac{1}{2} = 1$$
$$3 \cdot \tfrac{1}{3} = 1$$
$$5 \cdot \tfrac{1}{5} = 1$$

Activity 2

**Use PEMDAS and integer rules to evaluate the numeric expressions.
Remember to do diagnostics first, then go to the Algebra Toolbox.**

1. $-6 \cdot -6 + -6 - 6$ **2.** $5 - 10 + -7$ **3.** $8 + -72 \div 9 - 1$

4. $-24 \div (-8 - -2) + -2$ **5.** $18 - 25 + 4 - -1$

Activity 3

Tell the volume of each shape.

1. height = 10 inches
Base = 15 square inches

2. height = 12 inches
Base = 21 square inches

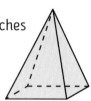

Activity 4 • Distributed Practice

Solve.

1. $2 - -2 + -2 = a$ **2.** $4^2 + 6 - 5 = b$ **3.** $(-3 + -1) \cdot (-5 + 4) = c$

4. $\tfrac{6}{1} \div \tfrac{1}{2} = d$ **5.** $\tfrac{2}{1} \cdot \tfrac{1}{2} = e$ **6.** $-\tfrac{1}{3} \cdot \tfrac{1}{3} = f$

7. $(-3 + -4) \cdot -2 = g$ **8.** $\tfrac{8}{1} \cdot \tfrac{1}{8} = h$

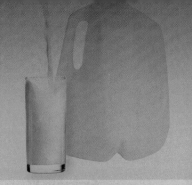

Lesson 7 ▶Distributive Property

▶**Distributive Property**

What is the distributive property?

We have looked at several properties now, and we have placed them in our Algebra Toolbox. The properties so far have involved either addition or multiplication.

Properties
Identity Property of Addition: $a + 0 = a$
Additive Inverse Property of Zero: $A + -A = 0$
Associative Property of Multiplication: $(a \cdot b) \cdot c = a \cdot (b \cdot c)$
Identity Property of Multiplication: $a \cdot 1 = a$
Reciprocal Property: $\frac{a}{b} \cdot \frac{b}{a} = 1$

Vocabulary
distributive property

Now we'll look at the **distributive property** , one of the most important properties in algebra.

When we use the distributive property, we work with a quantity that is inside a set of parentheses. The number (or variable) that is on the outside of the parentheses is the coefficient.

Let's look at an expression with a coefficient and a quantity:

coefficient   quantity

$2(x + 3)$

In Example 1 we see how to use the distributive property when evaluating an algebraic expression.

Example 1

Use the distributive property to evaluate this expression:

$$2(x + 3)$$

STEP 1
Distribute the coefficient across both terms inside the parentheses.

The terms inside the parentheses cannot be combined because we have a variable and a number.

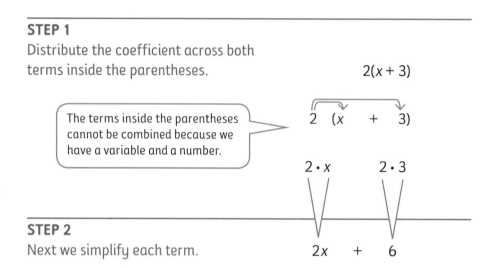

$$2(x + 3)$$

STEP 2
Next we simplify each term.

$$2x + 6$$

We have now simplified the expression using the distributive property.

Using our special symbols from the last unit, our expression looks like this:

The distributive property can be used to simplify many different kinds of expressions.

Remember to multiply, or "distribute," the coefficient across all the terms inside the parentheses.

Let's look at some other ways we can use this property.

Simplified Expressions Using the Distributive Property

$$2(x - 3)$$

$$2 \quad (x \quad - \quad 3)$$

$$2 \cdot x \quad - \quad 2 \cdot 3$$

$$\mathbf{2x - 6}$$

$$2(2x - 3)$$

$$2 \quad (2x \quad - \quad 3)$$

$$2 \cdot 2x \quad - \quad 2 \cdot 3$$

$$\mathbf{4x - 6}$$

$$x(x - 3)$$

$$x \quad (x \quad - \quad 3)$$

$$x \cdot x \quad - \quad x \cdot 3$$

$$\mathbf{x^2 - 3x}$$

Let's put the distributive property in our toolbox.

Properties

Associative Property

$(a + b) + c = a + (b + c)$

$(a \cdot b) \cdot c = a \cdot (b \cdot c)$

Commutative Property

$x + y = y + x \qquad x \cdot y = y \cdot x$

Identity Property of Zero

$x + 0 = x \qquad x \cdot 1 = x$

Additive Inverse Property of Zero

$a + -a = 0$

Multiplicative Property of Zero

$b \cdot 0 = 0$

Reciprocal Property

$\dfrac{a}{b} \cdot \dfrac{b}{a} = 1$

Distributive Property

$a(b + c) = ab + ac$

How do we translate statements into algebraic expressions?

Translating statements into algebraic expressions is a good way to understand any number of expressions, particularly those where we might use the distributive property.

Let's start with a simple phrase and then build up. We will use the letter n any time we need a variable.

"a number plus 2"

The phrase "a number plus 2" does not tell us which number. We don't have enough information, so we must use a variable. We can substitute a variable for "a number" and write the expression:

Phrase	Expression
"a number plus 2"	$n + 2$
"3 times a number"	$3 \cdot n$, or $3n$
"3 times a number plus 2"	$3n + 2$

Now let's see how we would translate a statement into an expression that has a coefficient. These are more complicated expressions. We can still use the distributive property to simplify them.

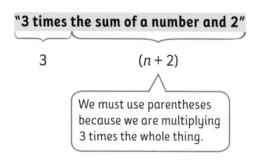

"3 times the sum of a number and 2"

3            $(n + 2)$

We must use parentheses because we are multiplying 3 times the whole thing.

Phrase	Expression
"3 times the sum of a number and 2"	$3(n + 2)$

%÷ Apply Skills
 =÷
 <× Turn to *Interactive Text*, page 222.

mBook Reinforce Understanding
Use the *mBook Study Guide* to review lesson concepts.

Homework

Activity 1

Prove the distributive property works by solving these problems two ways. First distribute, then find the sum in the parentheses before distributing the coefficient.

Model $2(8+2)$

Answer: $2 \cdot 8 + 2 \cdot 2 = 16 + 4 = 20$

$2 \cdot 10 = 20$

The answers are the same.

1. $4(3+4)$
2. $5(6+2)$
3. $2(5+6)$
4. $10(7+8)$

Activity 2

Practice using the distributive property by simplifying these algebraic expressions.

Model $3(x+5) \rightarrow 3 \cdot x + 3 \cdot 5 \quad 3x + 15$

1. $4(x+2)$
2. $5(1+d)$
3. $2(z+8)$
4. $a(a+7)$
5. $-6(b+20)$

Activity 3

Evaluate the expression using the properties you have learned.

1. $4+0=?$
    (a) 0
    (b) 1
    (c) 4

2. $2 \cdot 0 = ?$
    (a) 0
    (b) 1
    (c) 2

3. $3 \cdot 0 = ?$
    (a) 0
    (b) 1
    (c) $\frac{1}{3}$

4. $5 + -5 = ?$
    (a) 0
    (b) 1
    (c) $\frac{1}{5}$

5. $a \cdot \frac{1}{a} = ?$
    (a) 0
    (b) 1
    (c) $\frac{a}{1}$

Activity 4 • Distributed Practice

Solve.

1. $\frac{2}{3} \div \frac{2}{3} = a$
2. $\frac{3}{4} + \frac{1}{2} = b$
3. $(-4 \cdot -1) \cdot (-8 \div 4) = c$
4. $3^2 + 2^2 - 10 = d$
5. $\frac{18}{1} \cdot \frac{1}{18} = e$
6. $-\frac{1}{3} - \frac{1}{3} = f$
7. $\frac{2}{4} + -\frac{2}{8} = g$
8. $\frac{8}{1} \cdot \frac{1}{16} = h$

► **Problem Solving: The Volume of Spheres**

How do we find the volume of a sphere?

The volume of a sphere is difficult to think about because we cannot see any kind of base. The formula for the volume is even more complicated.

$$\text{Volume of a sphere} = \frac{4}{3}\pi r^3$$

One way to think about a sphere's volume is similar to the way we thought about the volume of a cone.

Example 1 will:

- Help us visualize the volume.
- Give us a step-by-step way to think about how we can find the volume for a sphere based on what we already know about shapes and volume.

Example 1

Find the volume of a sphere.

Steps for Finding the Volume of a Sphere

STEP 1
Begin by cutting a sphere in half.
Let's pretend the sphere is a basketball. When we cut it in half, we have a hemisphere.

sphere
(basketball)

hemisphere
(half of a basketball)

STEP 2

Fill the hemisphere with sand and pour it into a cylinder with the same height and base as the sphere.

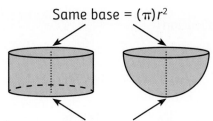

Same base = $(\pi)r^2$

height of the cylinder = the radius (r) of the hemisphere

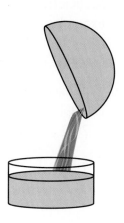

The volume of the hemisphere fills $\frac{2}{3}$ of the cylinder.

The volume of the hemisphere = $\frac{2}{3} \cdot$ Base $\cdot$ height.

Remember, the height of the cylinder is the same as the radius of the hemisphere. That means the volume of the hemisphere is:

$$\frac{2}{3} \cdot \pi \cdot r^2 \cdot r, \text{ or } \frac{2}{3}\pi r^3$$

STEP 3

Multiply the volume of the hemisphere times 2 to give us the volume of a sphere.

We multiply by 2 because we know that 2 hemispheres make a sphere, as two halves make a whole.

$$2 \cdot \frac{2}{3}\pi r^3 = \frac{4}{3}\pi r^3$$

The volume of a sphere = $\frac{4}{3}\pi r^3$.

 Problem-Solving Activity
Turn to *Interactive Text*, page 225.

mBook Reinforce Understanding
Use the *mBook Study Guide* to review lesson concepts.

Write a general statement about each property below. Use the examples provided to help you.

Model Commutative Property for Multiplication

Examples: $5 \cdot 6 = 6 \cdot 5$ $3 \cdot 4 = 4 \cdot 3$ Answer: $a \cdot b = b \cdot a$

1. Associative Property
Examples:
$$1 + (2 + 3) = (1 + 2) + 3$$
$$2 + (4 + 5) = (2 + 4) + 5$$

2. Distributive Property
Examples:
$$3(x + 2) \ = 3x + 6$$
$$-2(3 + w) = -6 + -2w$$

3. Multiplicative Inverse Property
Examples:
$$\frac{2}{3} \cdot \frac{3}{2} = 1$$
$$\frac{2}{1} \cdot \frac{1}{2} = 1$$

4. Commutative Property for Addition
Examples:
$$4 + 2 = 2 + 4$$
$$3 + w = w + 3$$

Use PEMDAS and integer rules to evaluate the numeric expressions. Remember to do diagnostics first, then go to the Algebra Toolbox.

1. $-8 + (-2 + -3) \cdot -7$

2. $15 + (-8 - -1) \cdot -2$

3. $10 - -2 \cdot -3 + -2^2$

4. $-16 \div -4 \cdot (-1 - -8)$

Find the volume of each sphere. Use the formula: $V = \frac{4}{3}\pi r^3$. Use 3.14 as the approximation for pi.

1. $r = 3$

2. $r = 0.5$

3. $r = 1$

Solve.

1. $\frac{2}{3} + \frac{2}{6} = a$

2. $\frac{3}{4} - \frac{1}{2} = b$

3. $(-2 \cdot -2) \cdot -4 \div 4 = c$

4. $4^2 - 2^2 = d$

5. $\frac{6}{1} \cdot \frac{1}{6} = e$

6. $-2 - -4 = f$

7. $\frac{2}{4} \div \frac{2}{8} = g$

8. $\frac{10}{1} \cdot \frac{1}{10} = h$

▶**Problem Solving: Finding the Volume of Complex Objects**

What are the key volume formulas?

In this unit we have learned to use the relationship of the height and the area of the base of an object as a way to find its volume.

Cylinders and cones are two basic types of three-dimensional objects where we use the two-dimensional base and the height to find the volume.

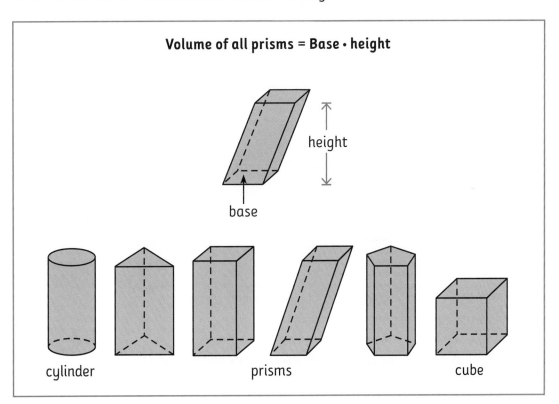

Volume of all prisms = Base · height

height

base

cylinder   prisms   cube

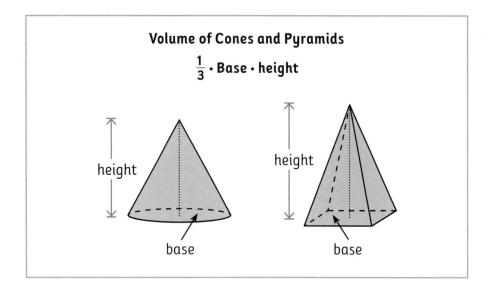

Volume of Cones and Pyramids

$$\frac{1}{3} \cdot \textbf{Base} \cdot \textbf{height}$$

height · base · height · base

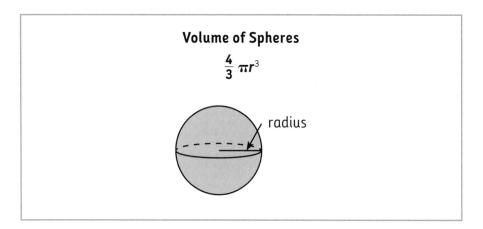

Volume of Spheres

$$\frac{4}{3}\pi r^3$$

radius

Knowing the volume of these basic objects helps us when we have to compute the total volume of a more complex object.

Example 1 shows us how to find the volume of a complex object made of three cans. If we look closely, we see three cylinders. We can combine the volume of each cylinder to get a total volume of the object.

Example 1

What is the volume of the three cans?

We have two small cans of tomato sauce and one large can of tomato sauce. We need to find the volume of all three cans.

To find the total volume, we:

- find the volume of each of the cylinders.
- add the volume of each of the cylinders together.

The radius for the taller can is 2 inches. Each of the shorter cans also has a radius of 2 inches. So we know each can has the same area for the base.

STEP 1

First, find the area of the base of the cans.

$$\text{Area of a circle} = \pi r^2$$
$$= 3.14 \cdot r^2$$
$$= 3.14 \cdot 2^2$$
$$= 3.14 \cdot 4$$

The area of each base = 12.56 in².

STEP 2

Find the volume of the taller can of tomato sauce.

$$\text{Volume of a cylinder} = \text{Base} \quad \cdot \quad \text{height}$$
$$\downarrow \qquad\qquad \downarrow$$
$$= 12.56 \quad \cdot \quad 8$$

The volume of the taller can = 100.48 in³.

STEP 3

Next we must find the volume of a shorter can of tomato sauce.

We know the area of the base of the shorter can is the same as the area of the base of the taller can. So the base of each of the cans is 12.56 in².

Volume of a cylinder =   Base   •   height
                           ↓   ↓
                    = 12.56   •   4

The volume of the shorter can = 50.24 in³.

STEP 4

Now we can add the volume of the cans to find the total volume of all three cans.

50.24 + 50.24 + 100.48 = 200.96

The total volume of the cans = 200.96 in³.

How do we find the volume of polyhedrons?

We studied polyhedrons in the last unit when we were working on surface area.

It is difficult to see all of the parts of the polyhedron shown because it is a three-dimensional object drawn on paper.

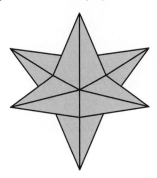

However, if we think about the pattern of pyramids that go around the center, we see that there are six pyramids in the drawing.

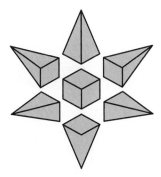

It is easier to see the parts of this polyhedron if we break it apart into familiar shapes. This will help us find the volume of the whole polyhedron.

Let's look at one of the pyramids so that we can see the height and dimensions of the base. We also need to look at the cube to see its dimensions.

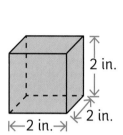

2 in.

2 in.

2 in.

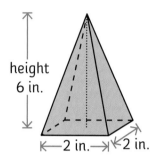

height
6 in.

2 in.

2 in.

The measurements for the pyramid and the cube are all that we need to figure out the volume of the polyhedron.

Steps for Finding the Volume of the Polyhedron

STEP 1
Find the volume of one pyramid.

Remember, Volume = $\frac{1}{3}$ · Base · height

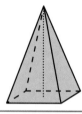

STEP 2
Find the volume of the cube in the center.

Volume of a cube = depth · width · height

STEP 3
Add the volumes of six pyramids and the cube to find the total volume.

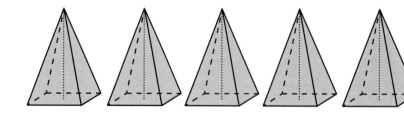

 Problem-Solving Activity
Turn to *Interactive Text*,
page 228.

 mBook Reinforce Understanding
Use the *mBook Study Guide*
to review lesson concepts.

Activity 1

Select the attribute that the two shapes have in common.

1.

   (a) vertex
   (b) circular base
   (c) square base

2.

   (a) vertex
   (b) circular base
   (c) square base

3.

   (a) vertex
   (b) a base
   (c) circular base

4.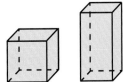

   (a) vertex
   (b) circular base
   (c) square base

Activity 2

Add together all of the volumes of the compound shapes to find the total volume of the shape.

1. The volume of the cube is 10 cm³.
   The volume of each rectangular prism is 12 cm³.
   What is the total volume?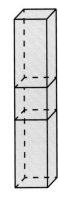

2. The volume of the cylinder is 30 cm³.
   The volume of each cone is 10 cm³.
   What is the total volume?

Activity 3

Give a general pattern for each of the properties named below. An example of the property is provided to help you.

1. Distributive Property, $4(n + 3) = 4n + 12$

2. Multiplicative Inverse Property, $5 \cdot \frac{1}{5} = 1$

3. Identity Property of Addition, $100 + 0 = 100$

4. Identity Property of Multiplication, $5 \cdot 1 = 5$

5. Multiplicative Property of Zero, $25 \cdot 0 = 0$

6. Commutative Property for Addition, $2.5 + 3.7 = 3.7 + 2.5$

Activity 4 • Distributed Practice

Solve.

1. $-5 \div 5 + 7 - 2 = a$

2. $\frac{3}{6} \div \frac{1}{2} = b$

3. $-6 + 6 = c$

4. $3^2 - (3 \cdot 3) = d$

5. $3^2 - (-3 \cdot 3) = e$

6. $9 - -8 = f$

7. $\frac{2}{3} \div \frac{2}{3} = g$

8. $\frac{3}{1} \cdot \frac{1}{3} = h$

▶**Algebraic Rules and Properties**

What rules help us evaluate algebraic expressions?

To get the same answer every time we evaluate an algebraic expression, we need rules that we can depend on.

Review 1

What are the rules we use when working with algebraic expressions?

Mathematicians have created two major rules that we can use with algebraic expressions.

The first major rule involves adding, subtracting, multiplying, and dividing integers. We use these rules all the time when we work with algebraic expressions and equations.

Addition/Subtraction	Multiplication/Division
Remember, subtraction is the same as adding the opposite. $9 - -2 = 9 + 2$ $9 - 2 = 9 + -2$	Remember PASS: **P**ositive **A**nswers **H**ave the **S**ame **S**igns $8 \cdot -5 = -40$ $-8 \cdot -5 = 40$

The second major rule involves the order of operations. The acronym PEMDAS helps us think about how we evaluate numeric expressions.

PEMDAS—The Rules for Order of Operations		
Step 1	**P**—Parentheses	Work what is inside the parentheses.
Step 2	**E**—Exponents	Work any numbers with exponents.
Step 3	**M**—Multiplication **D**—Division	Work multiplication or division problems from left to right.
Step 4	**A**—Addition **S**—Subtraction	Last of all, work addition or subtraction problems from left to right.

These two major rules give us all the information we need to evaluate expressions like the ones shown in Review 2.

Review 2

How do we use rules for integers and PEMDAS to evaluate expressions?

$10 \cdot 4 \div -2 - 3^2$

$10 \cdot 4 \div -2 - 3^2$ ←   Work with exponents.

$10 \cdot 4 \div -2 - 9$ ←   Multiplication/division: Work left to right and use PASS.

$40 \div -2 - 9$ ←   Multiplication/division: Work left to right and use PASS.

$-20 + -9$ ←   Add the opposite.

-29 ←   Solution.

We can also evaluate algebraic expressions that use variables if we know the value of the variable. We just have to substitute the value and then evaluate.

Review 3

How do we use substitution to evaluate expressions?

$$-3j + 8 - j$$
$$\text{Let } j = 10$$

$-3j + 8 - j$ ← Substitute 10 for j.

$-3 \cdot 10 + 8 - 10$ ← Multiplication/division: Work left to right and use PASS.

$-30 + 8 - 10$ ← Addition/subtraction: Work left to right and use subtraction (same as adding the opposite).

$-22 + -10$

-32 ← Solution.

Finally, we look at the distributive property, which is one of the most important properties we will use in beginning algebra.

When we use the distributive property, we distribute the coefficient across everything inside the parentheses. The coefficient means that we are multiplying, so we multiply the coefficient times each term inside the parentheses.

Review 4

How do we use the distributive property to simplify expressions?

$3(r + 3)$ $-10(m + 6)$ $9(w - 3)$

$3(r + 3)$ $-10(m + 6)$ $9(w - 3)$

In each case, we remove the parentheses by multiplying each value inside the parentheses by the coefficient

$3r + 3 \cdot 3$ $-10m + -10 \cdot 6$ $9w - 9 \cdot 3$

$3r + 9$ $-10m + -60$ $9w - 27$

Apply Skills
Turn to *Interactive Text*, page 232.

mBook Reinforce Understanding
Use the *mBook Study Guide* to review lesson concepts.

▶Problem Solving: **Volume of Three-Dimensional Shapes**

What is the volume of three-dimensional shapes?

When we studied surface area in the last unit, we sorted three-dimensional shapes based on attributes. This sorting helps us think about volume formulas. Here are the two groups of shapes that we used.

Group 1

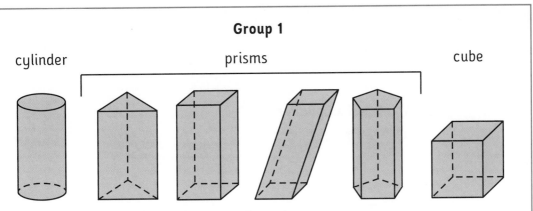

cylinder   prisms   cube

1. Cylinders have a circular base and no edges.

2. Prisms have rectangles or parallelograms for faces.

3. Cubes and prisms have edges and are parallel.

4. A cube has squares for each of its faces.

5. Prisms can have many different shapes, including polygons, for bases.

Group 2

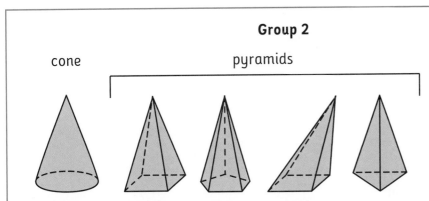

cone   pyramids

1. Cones have a circular base and no edges.

2. Pyramids have faces that are triangles.

3. Pyramids can have many different shapes, including polygons, for bases.

Now let's review different volume formulas. First let's look at finding the volume for cylinders.

We will use Volume = Base • height as a basic part of the formula to find the volume of three-dimensional shapes. We capitalize the word Base because we are talking about the area of the base of the object, which has two dimensions—depth and width. Once we find this two-dimensional base, we multiply it by the height of the object.

Review 1

How do we find the volume of a cylinder?

> **Volume of a Cylinder**
> Volume = Base • height

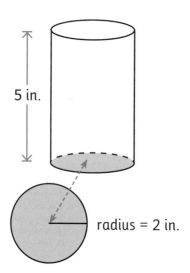

5 in.

radius = 2 in.

Base of a cylinder = Area of a circle

$$= \pi r^2$$
$$= 3.14 \cdot 2^2$$
$$= 3.14 \cdot 4$$

Base of the cylinder = 12.56 in².

Now we can find the volume of the cylinder.

Volume of a cylinder = Base • height   ⟵ Base is the area of the cylinder base.

$$= 12.56 \cdot 5$$

Volume of the cylinder = 62.8 in³.

Review 2

How do we find the volume of a prism?

Let's review our formula first.

Volume of a Prism
Volume = Base · height

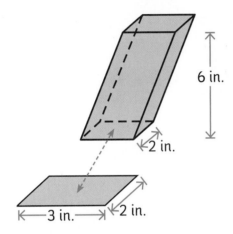

Base of a prism = Area of a parallelogram

= width · depth

= 3 · 2

Base of the prism = 6 in²

Now we can find the volume of the prism.

Volume of a prism = Base · height

= 6 · 6

> Base is the area of the prism base.

Volume of the prism = 36 in³

Review 3

How do we find the volume of a cube?

Let's review our formula first.

Volume of a Cube

Volume = Base · height

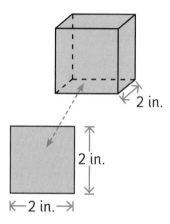

2 in.

2 in.

←2 in.→

Base of a cube = Area of a square

= width · depth

= 2 · 2

Base of the cube = 4 in²

Now we can find the volume of the cube.

Volume of a cube = Base · height

= 4 · 2

> Base is the area of the cube base.

Volume of the cube = 8 in³

Review 4

How do we find the volume of a cone?

Let's review our formula.

Volume of a Cone
Volume = $\frac{1}{3}$ · Base · height

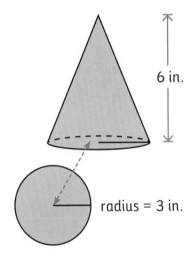

6 in.

radius = 3 in.

Base of a cone = Area of a circle

$\qquad$ = πr^2

$\qquad$ = $3.14 \cdot 3^2$

$\qquad$ = $3.14 \cdot 9$

Base of the cone = 28.26 in^2

Now we can find the volume of the cone.

Volume of a cone = $\frac{1}{3}$ · Base · height ← Base is the area of the circle.

$\qquad$ = $\frac{1}{3} \cdot 28.26 \cdot 6$

$\qquad$ = $9.33 \cdot 6$

Volume of the cone = 56.52 in^3

We can find the volume of a pyramid the same way.

Review 5

How do we find the volume of a pyramid?

Let's review our formula.

> **Volume of a Pyramid**
>
> Volume = $\frac{1}{3}$ • Base • height

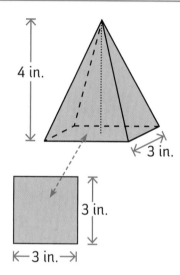

4 in.

3 in.

3 in.

3 in.

Base of a pyramid = Area of a square

= width • depth

= 3 • 3

Base of the pyramid = 9 in²

Now we can find the volume of the pyramid.

Volume of a pyramid = $\frac{1}{3}$ • Base • height   *(Base is the area of the square.)*

= $\frac{1}{3}$ • 9 • 4

= 3 • 4

Volume of the pyramid = 12 in³

 Problem-Solving Activity
Turn to *Interactive Text*,
page 234.

 mBook Reinforce Understanding
Use the *mBook Study Guide*
to review lesson concepts.

Unit 7 | Introduction to Algebraic Equations

Problem Solving: Geometric Construction and Angle Measurement

eee-YAAAAAH!!!!!

He said he's going too fast, and the jump is steeper than he thought.

I knew that.

OBJECTIVES

Building Number Concepts

- Understand the basic properties of algebraic equations

- Balance equations involving symbols or variables

- Solve problems involving algebraic equations

Problem Solving

- Use a compass and straightedge to construct basic figures

- Use algebraic reasoning to find missing angle measur

- Explore the properties of triangles that have congruent angles

▶Introduction to Algebraic Equations

Problem Solving:
▶**Geometric Construction and Angle Measurement**

▶**Introduction to Algebraic Equations**

What are algebraic equations?

In this unit, we will start working with equations. An **equation** is a math statement that shows that one expression is equal to another expression.

The following statements are equations. The expressions on each side of the equal sign do not look the same, but they are equal. The sides have to be equal to make it an equation. When the expression on one side of an equation equals the expression on the other side, we say the equation is **balanced** .

Vocabulary

equation
balanced

POWER CONCEPT

When the expression on one side of an equation equals the expression on the other side, the equation is balanced.

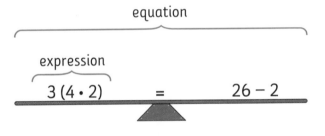

equation

expression

$3(4 \cdot 2)$ = $26 - 2$

$n + 25$ = 30

52 = $4c$

$3x + 1$ = $x + 16$

We learned that both sides of an equation are equal even though they do not look the same in the beginning. Let's explore this concept further. The examples use numeric equations to show that the two expressions are equal. We can solve the equation in Example 1 by starting on either side of the equal sign.

Example 1

Show that the expressions are equal by simplifying.

$$3(4 + 3) - 1 = 2 \cdot 2 \cdot 2 \cdot 2 + 2 + 2$$

Start on the right side of the equal sign and use PEMDAS.

$3(4 + 3) - 1 = 2 \cdot 2 \cdot 2 \cdot 2 + 2 + 2$

$3(4 + 3) - 1 = \quad 4 \cdot 2 \cdot 2 + 2 + 2$

$3(4 + 3) - 1 = \quad 8 \cdot 2 + 2 + 2$

$3(4 + 3) - 1 = \quad 16 + 2 + 2$

$3(4 + 3) - 1 = \quad 18 + 2$

$3(4 + 3) - 1 = \quad 20$

> **PEMDAS**
>
> **P**arentheses first
>
> **E**xponent next
>
> **M**ultiplication and
>
> **D**ivision (left to right)
>
> **A**ddition and
>
> **S**ubtraction (left to right)

Now go to the left side of the equal sign and use PEMDAS.

$3(4 + 3) - 1 = 20$

$3(7) - 1 \quad = 20$

$21 - 1 \quad = 20$

$\mathbf{20} \quad = \mathbf{20}$

Now it is clear that both sides are equal. They are balanced.

We could have solved the problem in Example 1 by starting on the left side of the equal sign. We would find the same answer, 20 = 20. The main idea with numeric equations is that the two sides are the same, or balanced. We prove they are the same by simplifying each expression.

Now let's explore how we can start on the left side first and show that the two expressions are equal. We follow the PEMDAS rules for each step.

Example 2

Solve the equation starting with the left side.

Use PEMDAS and start inside the parentheses.

$6 \div 2 + 3(4 - 3) = 5(2 + 1) - 3^2$

$6 \div 2 + 3(1) \quad = 5(2 + 1) - 3^2$

$6 \div 2 + 3 \quad = 5(2 + 1) - 3^2$

$3 + 3 \quad = 5(2 + 1) - 3^2$

$6 \quad = 5(2 + 1) - 3^2$

PEMDAS
Parentheses first
Exponent next
Multiplication and
Division (left to right)
Addition and
Subtraction (left to right)

Now go to the right side and use PEMDAS.

$6 = 5(2 + 1) - 3^2$

$6 = \quad 5(3) - 3^2$

$6 = \quad 5(3) - 9$

$6 = \quad 15 - 9$

$6 = \quad 6$

Now it is clear that both sides are equal. They are balanced.

We can see if both sides of a numeric equation are balanced by simplifying the expressions. This is helpful later on when we look at different kinds of equations.

%÷
=
<× **Apply Skills**
Turn to *Interactive Text*,
page 236.

mBook **Reinforce Understanding**
Use the *mBook Study Guide*
to review lesson concepts.

▶**Problem Solving: Geometric Construction and Angle Measurement**

What terms are important in geometric construction?

Vocabulary is an important part of geometry. It is one thing to memorize the terms, and it is another thing to use them. We are going to use our vocabulary terms as we make parallel and perpendicular lines using just a compass and a ruler or straightedge.

Vocabulary

line segment
arc
perpendicular
right angle
midpoint
parallel

Example 1

Steps for Making a Perpendicular Line Segment

Practice using the terms you learn in geometry as you are drawing and using your compass.

STEP 1
Draw a line segment with endpoints A and B.
A **line segment** is a part of a line that has a definite length.

A   B

STEP 2
Put the sharp end of the compass at one endpoint and stretch the compass to create an arc above the center of the segment.
An **arc** is a part of a circle.

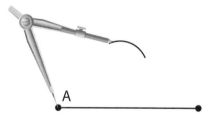

STEP 3
Do the same thing from the other endpoint so that the two arcs intersect.

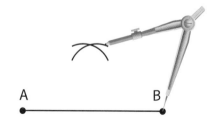

STEP 4

Draw another set of arcs on the opposite side of the line segment. Make sure not to change the width of the compass.

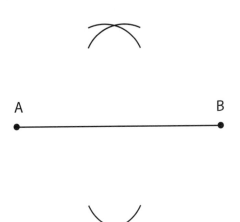

STEP 5

Finally, use a ruler or straightedge to draw a line segment that crosses through the two points where the arcs intersect.

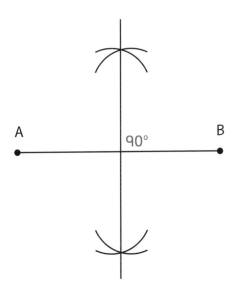

The two line segments are **perpendicular** to each other. This means the line segments form a **right angle** where the line segments intersect. A right angle is an angle whose measure is 90 degrees. The place where they intersect is the **midpoint** on the lines.

We make a parallel line segment by following the steps shown
in Example 2.

Example 2

Steps for Making a Parallel Line Segment

STEP 1
Draw a line segment.

_____

STEP 2
Make point A above the line segment and draw a diagonal line through
point A.

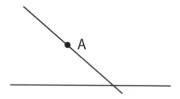

STEP 3
Draw an arc through both lines about halfway to point A. Do not change
the width of the compass.

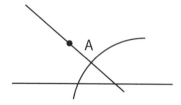

STEP 4

Put the sharp end of the compass on point A and make another arc above point A. Label the intersection of the arc and the line point B.

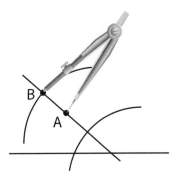

STEP 5

Put the sharp end of the compass on the point where the first arc and the horizontal line meet. Use your compass to measure the distance to the point where the first arc and the diagonal line intersect. Do not change the width of the compass after measuring.

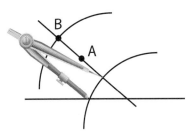

STEP 6

Put the sharp end of your compass on point B. Draw an arc as shown below.

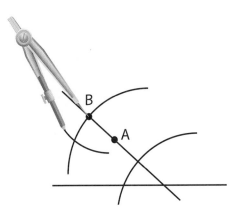

STEP 7

Use your straightedge or ruler to draw a line segment through the intersecting arcs and point A.

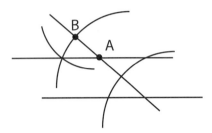

The new line segment is **parallel** to the original line segment. Parallel lines are lines that will never intersect.

Problem-Solving Activity
Turn to *Interactive Text*, page 238.

mBook Reinforce Understanding
Use the *mBook Study Guide* to review lesson concepts.

Activity 1

Simplify the sides of each equation and tell if the equation is balanced.

1. $5 + 2 \cdot 3 = 21 - 5 + 6$

2. $2 \cdot 2 \cdot 2 \cdot 2 + 3 + 4 = 5^2 - 1 \cdot 1 - 1$

3. $27 = (4 + 5) \cdot (2 + 1)$

4. $3 + 2 \cdot 6 = 10 + 10 + 10$

Activity 2

Select the geometric term that matches each of the following.

1. _____

   (a) line
   (b) line segment
   (c) arc

2.

   (a) line
   (b) line segment
   (c) arc

3. _____

   (a) perpendicular
   (b) parallel
   (c) arc

4.

   (a) perpendicular
   (b) parallel
   (c) arc

Activity 3 • Distributed Practice

Solve.

1. $\frac{1}{3} \cdot \frac{3}{1}$

2. $-4 - 2$

3. $-4 \cdot -2$

4. $-4 \div -2$

5. $\frac{3}{4} \div \frac{1}{8}$

6. $3^2 + (6 - -3)$

7. $(6 - -3) + 3^2$

8. Simplify using the distributive property: $3(x + 2)$

▷**Balancing an Equation**

How do we balance an equation with only half the information?

We proved that a numeric equation is balanced by simplifying each expression. We ended up with two numbers that were the same.

What happens when we want to balance an equation, but only have half the information? The illustration shows how we have an expression on only one side. Once we simplify it, we can create another expression that is different from the first one to balance the equation.

$$7(5 \cdot 2) - 20 \qquad =$$

Start by using PEMDAS.

$$7(5 \cdot 2) - 20 =$$
$$7(10) - 20 =$$
$$70 - 20 =$$
$$50 =$$

Now write an expression that is equal to 50.

$$50 = 5 \cdot 10$$

PEMDAS
Parentheses first
Exponent next
Multiplication and
Division (left to right)
Addition and
Subtraction (left to right)

Finally, put this expression on the right side of the equal sign to balance the equation.

$$7(5 \cdot 2) - 20 \qquad = \qquad 5 \cdot 10$$

These expressions do not look the same, but they are equal. When we simplify them, we know that 50 = 50.

We can use the same problem and create a different expression that is equal to 50. Another expression that is equal to 50 is:

$$50 = 5 \cdot 2 \cdot 5$$

Now we can balance the equation this way:

$$7(5 \cdot 2) - 20 \quad = \quad 5 \cdot 2 \cdot 5$$

Both sides are equal.

We need to remember two important ideas. First, the expressions on each side of an equation do not have to look the same. In fact, they almost always look different when we begin solving them. Second, equations must always balance. The two sides need to be equal.

Example 1

Write an expression that makes the equation balanced.

$$6(3 \cdot 7) - 10 =$$

Using PEMDAS, we work the expression as follows:

$$6(21) - 10 =$$
$$126 - 10 =$$
$$116 =$$

Now, we need to find an equal expression:

$$116 = 58 \cdot 2$$

$$6(3 \cdot 7) - 10 \quad = \quad 58 \cdot 2$$

POWER CONCEPT

The expressions on either side of an equation do not have to look the same.

%÷
<X **Apply Skills**
Turn to *Interactive Text*, page 240.

mBook **Reinforce Understanding**
Use the *mBook Study Guide* to review lesson concepts.

▶Problem Solving: **Bisecting Angles**

Vocabulary

constructions
bisect

How do we bisect angles?

Angles and their measurements will become increasingly important in your study of mathematics. In this unit, we use what we know about angles and shapes like triangles to figure out the measurement of an unknown angle. The diagram shows common measurements for angles.

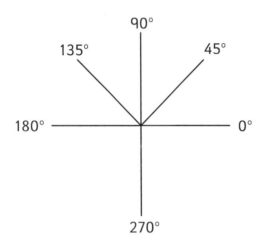

We can learn a lot about an angle by just using a ruler or a straightedge and a compass. **Constructions** are the drawing of geometric items, such as lines and circles, using only a compass and a straightedge. They allow us to **bisect**, or split in half, an angle without using a protractor.

Example 1

Steps for Bisecting an Angle With a Ruler and a Compass

STEP 1

Begin by drawing an angle using just a ruler.

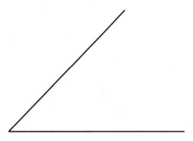

STEP 2

Put the sharp end of the compass at the vertex of the angle and draw an arc across both sides of the angle.

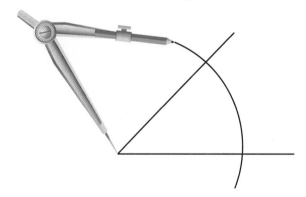

STEP 3

Now, put the sharp end of the compass at the point where the arc crosses one side of the angle. Make another arc in between the two lines near the middle.

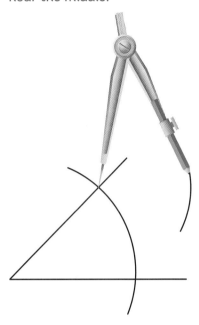

STEP 4

Next, put the sharp end of the compass on the other point where the arc crosses the side of the angle. Draw another arc. Now we can draw a line from the vertex through the point where the two arcs cross. Our line bisects the angle. We can check this by measuring the angles with our protractor.

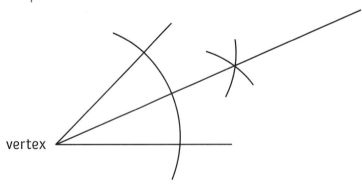

vertex

Problem-Solving Activity
Turn to *Interactive Text*,
page 242.

mBook Reinforce Understanding
Use the *mBook Study Guide*
to review lesson concepts.

Activity 1

Prove that the sides of the equations are equal by simplifying.

1. $8 + 5 \cdot 2 = 6 \cdot 3$

2. $2 \cdot 5 + 1 + 1 = 3 + 7 + 2$

3. $9^2 - 5 + 2 = 40 + 41 + -3$

4. $1 + 2 + 3 - 1 = 40 \div (9 - 1)$

Activity 2

Write an expression that will balance the right side of the equation with the left side. Use the operation given.

Model

$$3(4 \cdot 2) \qquad = \qquad \underline{\quad\quad} - 6$$

Answer: 30

Reasoning:

$3(4 \cdot 2) = 3 \cdot 8 = 24$

$\underline{\quad\quad} - 6 = 24$

$30 - 6 = 24$

1.
$$25 \div (2 + 3) \qquad = \qquad 17 - \underline{\quad\quad}$$

2.
$$8 + 9 - 7 \qquad = \qquad 100 \div \underline{\quad\quad}$$

3.
$$37 - 3 \cdot 3 \qquad = \qquad \underline{\quad\quad} \cdot 4$$

Activity 3

Tell the measurement of each bisected angle.

1. If the large angle is 90 degrees, what is the measure of $\angle a$?

2. If the large angle is 60 degrees, what is the measure of $\angle b$?

3. If the large angle is 120 degrees, what is the measure of $\angle c$?

4.  If the large angle is 20 degrees, what is the measure of $\angle d$?

Activity 4 • Distributed Practice

Solve.

1. $\frac{2}{3} - \frac{1}{9}$

2. $\frac{2}{3} \div \frac{1}{9}$

3. $-8 - -5$

4. $(6 \div 3) + 6 \cdot 2$

5. $4^2 - 3^2$

6. $2^2 \cdot 1^2$

7. $(-6 + -3) + (4 \cdot -2)$

8. Simplify using the distributive property: $4(x - 1)$

►**Another Way to Think About Balancing Equations**

How do the weights of different-shaped objects help us understand equations?

So far, we have worked with equations involving numeric expressions. We have learned that even though the expressions do not look the same, they need to be equal if they are going to be used in an equation.

$$3(2 + 1) + 1 \quad = \quad 11 - 1$$

To be balanced, expressions need to be equal to each other.

When we start including variables in equations, it is even harder to remember that both expressions are equal and that the equation is balanced.

We can use shapes to represent the numbers in an equation. This makes it easier to see the relationships between the numbers. Moving and substituting shapes to balance the scale is a lot like moving and substituting numbers when we work with algebraic equations.

Example 1 helps us think about balancing equations. It shows how substitution can prove that both sides are equal. We use three shapes of different weights to show that the scale is balanced, even though the two sides do not look the same.

Example 1

Balance the scale with the same shapes on each side using substitution.

The relative weight for each shape is shown here.

We begin with the shapes below on a balanced scale.

We can substitute on the right side. We trade three triangles for the circle that was there.

Next, we can substitute on the left side. We trade one triangle for two of the squares that were there. We now see that both sides are equal. They have exactly the same shapes on each side. The scale is balanced.

Speaking of Math

Here is how you can explain your thinking when balancing equations.

- *First, I look for things that are equivalent.*
- *Then, I substitute for equivalent values.*
- *Finally, I check both sides to see that they are the same, or balanced.*

How do we use substitution to balance the weight of different objects?

There is another way to think about shapes and balance scales. We can look at balancing as a problem-solving activity, where it is important to figure out the weight of one shape based on another shape. Example 1 shows how we use information from two different balance scales to figure out the weight of the triangle.

Find the weight of one triangle using substitution.

We can figure out the weight of the triangle by using information from the scale on the right. We see that we can take the square from the scale on the left and substitute it with two circles.

Now we see that there are two triangles for six circles. This is the same as one triangle for three circles.

We can say that one triangle weighs the same as three circles.

Sometimes we can solve these kinds of problems by using another strategy. We just cancel out the same shapes on each side of the same balance scale. In Example 2, we can figure out how much one circle weighs by canceling out squares and circles on each side of the scale.

Example 2

Figure out the weight of the circle by cancelling out the same shapes on each side.

First, we cross out those shapes on either side of the scale that are equal to each other.

We end up with one circle on the left side and two squares on the right. The scale is still balanced because we began with a balanced scale and crossed out equally on both sides.

We can say that one circle weighs the same as two squares.

%÷
=
<× **Apply Skills**
Turn to *Interactive Text*,
page 244.

mBook Reinforce Understanding
Use the *mBook Study Guide*
to review lesson concepts.

Homework

Activity 1

Tell if the scales are balanced by writing yes or no. Use these equivalences:

■ = ▲▲   ●●● = ▲

1.

2.

3.

4.

Activity 2

Find each value. Use cancellation.

1. Find the value of the diamond.

2. Find the value of the circle.

3. Find the value of the triangle.

Activity 3 • Distributed Practice

Solve.

1. $\frac{1}{2} \cdot \frac{1}{4}$

2. $\frac{1}{2} + \frac{1}{4}$

3. $\frac{1}{2} \div \frac{1}{4}$

4. $\frac{1}{2} - \frac{1}{4}$

5. $-6 \cdot -3$

6. $-6 \div -3$

Lesson 4 ▶ Equations With Variables

Problem Solving:
▶ Determining Measurements of Angles

▶ Equations With Variables

Vocabulary
property of equality

How do we solve simple equations?

We have learned about expressions with like and unlike terms. Now it is time to use these expressions in equations. The following illustration shows one of the simplest kinds of equations. It involves a single variable and a number as one expression and a number on the other side of the equal sign.

$$x + 2 = 3$$

When we solve these kinds of equations, we use special symbols for *variables* (▽) and *numbers* (▨). These symbols remind us which terms can be combined and which cannot. The goal in these equations is to solve for the variable. In Example 1, we are solving for *x*. That means we want to get *x* by itself on one side of the equal sign.

Example 1

Solve for *x*.

$$x \; + \; 2 \; = \; 3$$

▽ + ▨▨ = ▨▨▨

To get *x* by itself, we need to try to cancel the 2 next to it. Remember, we can only cancel numbers or symbols if we can cancel the same thing on both sides of the equation.

A number plus its opposite equals zero, so we add the opposites to both sides to keep the equation balanced. The numbers cancel each other out.

$$x \; + \; 2 \; + \; -2 \; = \; 3 \; + \; -2$$

▽ + ▨▨ + ▨▨ = ▨▨▨ + ▨▨

▽ + ▧▧ + ▧▧ = ▧▧▨ + ▧▧

▽ = ▨

$$x \; = \; 1 \qquad \textbf{We see that } x = 1.$$

How do we check to see if the answer is correct? We substitute 1 for x in the original equation.

$$x + 2 = 3$$
$$1 + 2 = 3 \qquad \leftarrow \text{ Substitute 1 for } x.$$
$$3 = 3$$

This problem used a new property from the toolbox. Notice that we got the variable by adding the opposite of the number to each side. We added −2 to 2 and −2 to 3. This property is the **property of equality**. It reminds us that when we do something to one side of the equation, we have to do the same thing to the other side. We use the same kind of thinking when we begin an equation with a negative number. This property is demonstrated in Example 2.

ALGEBRA TOOLBOX

Property of equality

When we do something to one side of the equation, we have to do the same thing to the other.

Example 2

Solve the equation involving negative numbers. Use the property of equality.

$$x \quad - \quad 2 \quad = \quad 1$$

$$\vee \; - \; \blacksquare\blacksquare \; = \; \blacksquare$$

$$x \quad + \quad -2 \quad = \quad 1$$

$$\vee \; + \; \blacksquare\blacksquare \; = \; \blacksquare$$

Subtraction is the same as adding the opposite.

$$x \quad + \quad -2 \quad + \quad 2 \quad = \quad 1 \quad + \quad 2$$

We add the opposites to both sides to keep the equation balanced. A number plus its opposite equals zero, so the numbers cancel each other out. On the right side, we add the like terms and we have our answer.

$$\vee \; = \; \blacksquare\blacksquare\blacksquare$$

$$x \quad = \quad 3$$

To check if the answer is correct, substitute 3 for x in the original equation.

$x - 2 = 1$

$3 - 2 = 1$ $\leftarrow$ Substitute 3 for x.

     $1 = 1$

The answer is correct because 1 = 1 is a true statement.

Improve Your Skills

Your friend solved the equation $x + 5 = 7$. His work looked like this:

$x + 5 = 7$	Check:
$x + 5 - 5 = 7 + 5$	$12 + 5 = 7$
$x = 12$	$17 = 7$ **ERROR**

What did your friend do wrong?

When he subtracted 5 from the left side of the equation, he should have subtracted 5 from the right side. Instead, he added 5. He should have subtracted instead of adding.

$x + 5 = 7$	Check:
$x + 5 - 5 = 7 - 5$	$2 + 5 = 7$
$x = 2$	$7 = 7$ **CORRECT**

The *property of equality* means you do the same thing to both sides of the equation.

% ÷
≤ × **Apply Skills**
Turn to *Interactive Text*, page 247.

mBook **Reinforce Understanding**
Use the *mBook Study Guide* to review lesson concepts.

▶**Problem Solving: Determining Measurements of Angles**

How do we find the measure of an unknown angle?

We know a lot about the properties of angles and lines based on what they look like. Even though the pictures below have no angle measures given, we can determine the measurements just by looking at them. They are based on common benchmarks we learned earlier.

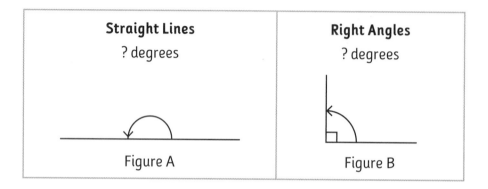

Straight Lines	**Right Angles**
? degrees	? degrees
Figure A	Figure B

In Figure A, we know that straight lines always measure 180 degrees.

In Figure B, we know that right angles always measure 90 degrees. The small box in Figure B is a symbol that tells us that it is a right angle.

What happens when we are given only some of the information about the measure of an angle? How do we figure out the measure of the angle that has a variable? We can use the same kind of algebraic equation that we learned earlier in the lesson.

Example 1

Figure the measure of ∠c.

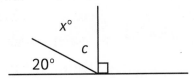

We know that the right angle is 90 degrees. We also know that all the angles add up to 180 degrees because we have a straight line. We can write the equation this way:

$$x + 90 + 20 = 180$$

$$x + 110 = 180 \qquad \leftarrow \text{We combine like terms.}$$

$$x + 110 + \boxed{-110} = 180 + \boxed{-110} \qquad \leftarrow \text{We add the opposite to both sides to keep the equation balanced.}$$

$$x + 0 = 70 \qquad \leftarrow \text{A number plus its opposite equals zero.}$$

$$x = 70$$

measure of ∠c = 70°

To check the answer, substitute 70 for *x* in the original equation.

$$x + 90 + 20 = 180$$

$$70 + 90 + 20 = 180$$

$$160 + 20 = 180$$

$$180 = 180$$

Speaking of Math

Here's how to explain your thinking about angles:

- *I know that a right angle is 90 degrees.*
- *I know that a straight line is 180 degrees.*
- *When using equations to find what degree an angle is, I add the opposite to both sides to keep the equation balanced.*

 Problem-Solving Activity
Turn to *Interactive Text*, page 248.

mBook **Reinforce Understanding**
Use the *mBook Study Guide* to review lesson concepts.

Activity 1

Solve the equations. Be sure to show all your work and check your answers at the end.

1. $3 + x = 12$

2. $y - 4 = 3$

3. $1 + w = -5$

4. $z - -5 = -2$

5. $-4 + a = -2$

6. $3 - 4 = n$

Activity 2

Tim got the following answers for each equation. Substitute Tim's answer in each equation to see if it is correct. If he was correct, write "correct." If Tim got the answer wrong, write "incorrect."

Model $z + 5 = 12$ $6 + 5 = 12$
          Answer: $z = 6$ $11 = 12$
                         6 is not correct

1. $x - -4 = 1$ Answer: $x = 5$

2. $-3 + z = 2$ Answer: $z = 5$

3. $w + 7 = -4$ Answer: $w = -11$

4. $12 - n = 2$ Answer: $n = -10$

Activity 3

Tell the measure of the missing angle in each problem.

1.

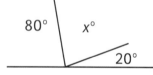

2.

3.

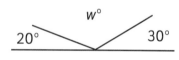

Activity 4 • Distributed Practice

Solve.

1. $4 - -3$

2. $4 - 3$

3. $4 \cdot -3$

4. $\frac{1}{2} \cdot \frac{1}{2}$

5. $\frac{1}{2} \cdot \frac{2}{1}$

6. $\frac{1}{2} \div \frac{1}{2}$

7. Simplify using the distributive property: $5(2x + 2)$

▶**Equations With Coefficients**

Vocabulary
coefficient

How do coefficients change the way we work equations?

We already learned that terms such as $3x$ or $5x$ involve a coefficient and a variable. A **coefficient** is a number that is being multiplied by an unknown quantity. Our special symbols remind us that we are not combining unlike terms. Instead, the 3 in $3x$ tells us how many x's we have.

$$x + x + x \quad = \overset{\text{coefficient}}{\underset{\text{variable}}{3x}}$$

We can use what we know about variables with coefficients to solve equations. The example below shows us what $3x = 15$ looks like when we use our special symbols.

Stacking the symbols helps us see what x equals. There are exactly five Ns for every variable. This tells us that one variable is worth five Ns.

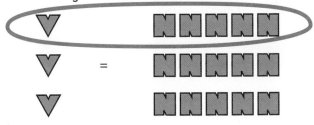

So, $x = 5$. We can tell this because we know that both sides of an equation must be equal.

Let's see how the coefficient helps us solve many different equations.

A variable is an unknown quantity, so its value can be different in different equations. In the equation $3x = 15$, x is equal to 5. But the variable x will not always be equal to 5, even if some of the numbers in the equation are the same. Let's look at some more equations. Our goal is to solve for x.

Example 1

Find the value of x in the equation.

$$3x \quad = \quad 30$$

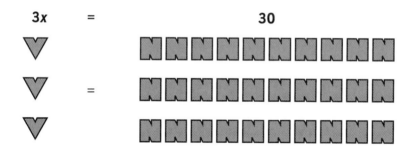

We divided the 30 from the right side of the equal sign into three groups. Since we want to know the value of x, we only need to look at the first row.

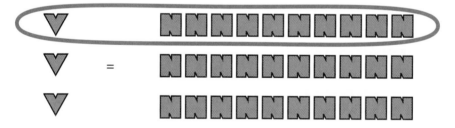

There are three groups of exactly ten Ns.

In this case, $x = 10$.

We have seen the number 3 used as a coefficient twice. Now let's look
at an equation that uses a different coefficient.

Example 2

Find the value of *x* in the equation.

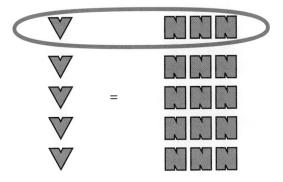

$$5x \quad = \quad 15$$

Remember that the coefficient tells us how many of the variable we
have. In this case, we have five *x*'s.

When we divide 15 Ns into five groups, there are exactly three Ns in
each group.

We know that $x = 3$.

%÷ = < x **Apply Skills**
Turn to **Interactive Text**,
page 251.

Monitoring Progress
Quiz 1

mBook **Reinforce Understanding**
Use the **mBook Study Guide**
to review lesson concepts.

Unit 7 • Lesson 5   **541**

Activity 1

Use the special symbols to find the value of x.

1. $2x = 10$

2. $4x = 12$

3. $3x = 9$

4. $5x = 10$

Activity 2

Find the measure of the missing angle in each problem.

1.
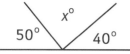

2.
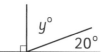

3.

Activity 3 • Distributed Practice

Solve.

1. $4 \div -2$

2. $-4 \div -2$

3. $-2 - -6$

4. $-2 + -6$

5. $5 + (6 \cdot 5) - 5$

6. $2 \cdot -6$

7. $(3^2 + 2) - 9$

8. Simplify using the distributive property: $2(-x + 1)$

▶More Equations With Coefficients

Problem Solving:
▶Finding the Measure of Two Angles

▶More Equations With Coefficients

Vocabulary
reciprocal

How do we solve equations with coefficients?

Using special symbols helps us solve equations with coefficients. For example, in the equation $4x = 12$, x is equal to 3.

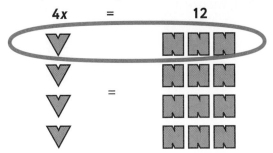

The original equation tells us that four x's equal 12, but to solve the problem without using special symbols, we need to find out what a single x equals. To do this, we multiply each side by the **reciprocal**, or inverse, of our coefficient, 4.

Since $4 = \frac{4}{1}$, the reciprocal of $\frac{4}{1}$ is $\frac{1}{4}$.

Example 1

Solve the problem $4x = 12$.

$$4x = 12$$

$$\frac{1}{4} \cdot 4x = 12 \cdot \frac{1}{4}$$ ← We multiply by the reciprocal of the coefficient. To keep the equation balanced, we need to multiply both sides.

$$\frac{4}{4}x = 3$$

$$1x = 3$$

$$x = 3$$ ← A number times 1 is the same number.

This is the same answer we got using the special symbols.

To check our answer, substitute 3 for x in the original equation.

$$4x = 12$$

$$4 \cdot 3 = 12 \quad \leftarrow \text{Substitute 3 for } x.$$

$$12 = 12$$

How do we solve equations when the coefficients are fractions?

Example 1 shows what happens when we have a fraction for a coefficient. The steps are almost the same. Once again, we use a coefficient to get x by itself.

Example 1

Find the value of x in the equation $\frac{1}{4}x = 10$.

$$\frac{1}{4}x = 10$$

$$\mathbf{4} \cdot \frac{1}{4}x = 10 \cdot \mathbf{4} \quad \leftarrow \text{Multiply each side by 4. Multiplying each side}$$
keeps the equation balanced. Four is the reciprocal of $\frac{1}{4}$. This will get x by itself.

$$\frac{4}{4}x = 40$$

$$1x = 40$$

$$x = 40 \quad \leftarrow \text{A number times 1 is the same number.}$$

We have solved for x.

To check the answer, substitute 40 for x in the original equation.

$$\frac{1}{4}x = 10$$

$$\frac{1}{4} \cdot 40 = 10 \quad \leftarrow \text{Substitute 40 for } x.$$

$$\frac{40}{4} = 10$$

$$10 = 10$$

How do proportions relate to algebra?

In earlier units, we worked proportion problems like the one shown below. We solved these problems by making equivalent fractions. Now we will learn a shortcut based on algebraic equations.

Example 1

Solve the word problem by setting up a proportion.

Problem:

Latisha is hiking in the mountains. Her map shows that she needs to go north to get to camp. Two inches on the map is equal to 500 yards. Based on the map, it is four inches to camp. How far will she have to walk?

We know:	We can say:	We write it like this:
2 inches = 500 yards 4 inches = x yards	2 is to 500 as 4 is to x	$\dfrac{2}{500} = \dfrac{4}{x}$

We write an equation for this problem by using cross multiplication.

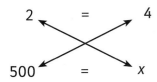

> When we cross multiply, we get an algebraic equation, and we solve it using the same steps that we learned.

$$2x = 500 \cdot 4$$

$$2x = 2{,}000$$

$$\tfrac{1}{2} \cdot 2x = 2{,}000 \cdot \tfrac{1}{2} \quad \leftarrow \text{Multiply each side by the same amount.}$$

$$\tfrac{2}{2}x = \tfrac{2{,}000}{2}$$

$$1x = 1{,}000$$

$$x = 1{,}000 \quad \leftarrow \text{A number times 1 is the same number.}$$

Latisha has 1,000 yards to walk before she gets to camp.

Improve Your Skills

Ms. Case asked three students to find the value of n when $3n = 21$. Rianna found the correct answer. What mistakes did her friends Lena and Forest make?

Lena: **ERROR**

> $3n = 21$
>
> $3 \cdot 3n = 21 \cdot 3$ ← Lena multiplied the coefficient by 3 instead of $\frac{1}{3}$. She
> $n = 63$ did not use the reciprocal to solve the equation.

Forest: **ERROR**

> $3n = 21$
>
> $\frac{1}{3} \cdot n = 21 \cdot \frac{1}{3}$ ← Forest did not write the entire expression on the left
> $\frac{1}{3}n = 7$ side of the equal sign. He wrote $\frac{1}{3} \cdot n$ instead of $\frac{1}{3} \cdot 3n$.
> $3 \cdot \frac{1}{3}n = 7 \cdot 3$ He left off the coefficient 3.
> $n = 21$

Rianna: **CORRECT**

> $3n = 21$
>
> $\frac{1}{3} \cdot 3n = 21 \cdot \frac{1}{3}$ ← Rianna multiplied both sides by the reciprocal
> $\frac{3}{3}n = 7$ of the coefficient.
> $n = 7$

It is important to multiply by the reciprocal on both sides of the equation.

%÷
=
<x **Apply Skills**
Turn to *Interactive Text*, page 253.

mBook **Reinforce Understanding**
Use the *mBook Study Guide* to review lesson concepts.

▶Problem Solving: Finding the Measure of Two Angles

supplementary angles

How do we use algebra to find the measure of angles?

We have worked on problems where we found the measure of the angle by using what we know about the measure of straight lines. We have also created a simple equation to solve the problem.

As we read through the next example, think about the rules for the properties used at each step.

Example 1

Find the measure of one unknown angle.

$$x + 20 + 75 = 180 \qquad \leftarrow \text{The sum of the angles in a}$$
$$\text{straight line is } 180°.$$

$$x + 95 = 180$$

$$x + 95 + \boxed{-95} = 180 + \boxed{-95} \qquad \leftarrow \text{Add } -95 \text{ to both sides of the}$$
$$\text{equation to get } x \text{ by itself.}$$

$$x + 0 = 85$$

$$x = 85$$

The measure of $\angle a = 85°$.

We are now able to solve more complicated problems with angles. In these cases, we have more than one angle that is unknown. At first, the problem does not look like it can be solved because we are not given the measurement for the two angles. However, we can use algebra and what we know about the measurement of straight lines to solve this problem.

- We know that a straight line is 180 degrees.
- So we know that angle *a* and angle *b* add up to 180 degrees.

Angles that add up to 180 degrees are called **supplementary angles** .

- So we know that angles *a* and *b* are *supplementary angles*.

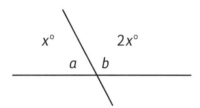

Since we know that the two angles added together equal 180 degrees, we write the equation like this:

$x + 2x = 180$

Then we solve for *x*.

$x + 2x = 180$

$3x = 180$ $\quad$ ← Combine like terms.

$\frac{1}{3} \cdot 3x = 180 \cdot \frac{1}{3}$ $\quad$ ← We want *x* by itself, so we need to multiply by $\frac{1}{3}$. Also, we multiply both sides by $\frac{1}{3}$ to keep the equation balanced.

$\frac{3}{3}x = \frac{180}{3}$

$1x = 60$

$x = 60$ $\quad$ ← A number times 1 is the same number.

Since $x = 60$, that means the measure of $\angle a = 60°$ and the measure of $\angle b = 2 \cdot 60$ or $120°$.

Example 2

Find the measure of the angles.

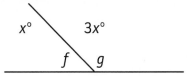

We know that f and g are supplementary angles.

We know we can set the equation up like this:

$x + 3x = 180$

Then we solve for x:

$x + 3x = 180$

$4x = 180$ ← Combine like terms.

$\frac{1}{4} \cdot 4x = 180 \cdot \frac{1}{4}$ ← Multiply both sides of the equation by $\frac{1}{4}$ to get x by itself.

$1x = 45$

$x = 45$ ← A number times 1 is the same number.

Now we can use the value of the variable to find all of the angle measurements.

$x° = 45°$ and $3x° = 3 \cdot 45$ or $135°$

The measure of $\angle f = 45°$.

The measure of $\angle g = 135°$.

We use algebra to help us solve many different problems involving angles.

Problem-Solving Activity
Turn to *Interactive Text*, page 254.

mBook Reinforce Understanding
Use the *mBook Study Guide* to review lesson concepts.

Activity 1

Solve each equation by using properties of equality and reciprocals.

1. $3x = 24$

2. $5y = 15$

3. $2w = 6$

4. $\frac{1}{3}z = 4$

5. $\frac{1}{2}a = 6$

6. $\frac{2}{3}b = 1$

Activity 2

Find the measures of the missing angles.

1. What is the measure of $\angle c$?

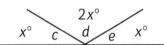

2. What is the measure of $\angle a$?

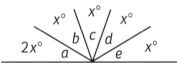

Activity 3

Solve the proportions by using cross multiplication.

1. $\frac{3}{4} = \frac{x}{6}$

2. $\frac{w}{5} = \frac{8}{10}$

3. $\frac{2}{5} = \frac{12}{z}$

4. $\frac{1}{a} = \frac{5}{15}$

Activity 4 • Distributed Practice

Solve.

1. $4 + -2$

2. $-4 + -2$

3. $-2 \cdot -6$

4. $-2 \cdot 6$

5. $5 \cdot (6 - 5) - 5$

6. $(3^2 - 2) + 9$

7. Simplify using the distributive property: $2(-x + 1)$

▶**Equations With Negative Numbers**

How do we work with negative numbers in an equation?

Sometimes equations with a lot of negative numbers can be confusing. When we work with these difficult equations, it is important to remember the rules for integers.

Rules for Working With Integers	
Rule	**Example**
Addition and Subtraction	
Subtraction is the same as adding the opposite.	$4 - 1$ is the same as $4 + -1$
When adding two numbers with the same sign, the sign on the answer is always the same.	• $4 + 3 = 7$ • $-6 + -2 = -8$
When the signs are different, the sign of the answer depends on the values in the problem.	• $-2 + 6 = 4$ • $2 + -6 = -4$
Multiplication and Division	
PASS: Positive answers have the same signs in multiplication and division.	• $-6 \cdot -3 = 18$ • $-6 \div -3 = 2$ • $6 \cdot 3 = 18$ • $6 \div 3 = 2$
When the amount of negative numbers being multiplied or divided is an odd number, the answer is negative.	• $2 \cdot -1 \cdot 3 \cdot 4 = -24$ • $6 \div -3 = -18$
When the amount of negative numbers being multiplied or divided is an even number, the answer is positive.	• $2 \cdot -1 \cdot -3 \cdot 4 = 24$

A good understanding of rules for operation on integers is important to being successful in algebra. We use these rules all the time.

Examples 1 and 2 show how important these rules are when we work the kinds of equations that we have seen in this unit. Whenever we see negative signs, it is important to slow down and remember the integer rules in the toolbox.

Example 1

Use the rules for integers to solve the equation $-3 + x - 2 = 8$.

$$-3 + x - 2 = 8$$

$$-3 + x + -2 = 8 \qquad \leftarrow \text{Subtraction is the same as adding the opposite. Instead of subtracting 2, we will be adding a } -2.$$

$$x + -3 + -2 = 8 \qquad \leftarrow \text{We commute so that we can combine the same terms.}$$

$$x + -5 = 8$$

$$x + -5 + \boxed{5} = 8 + \boxed{5} \qquad \leftarrow \text{We add 5 to both sides to get } x \text{ by itself. We have added 5 on both sides to keep the equation balanced.}$$

$$x + 0 = 13$$

$$x = 13$$

Check to make sure the answer is correct with substitution.

$$\overset{\displaystyle 13}{\underset{\downarrow}{}}$$

$$-3 + x - 2 = 8$$

$$-3 + 13 - 2 = 8$$

$$-3 + 13 + -2 = 8$$

$$10 + -2 = 8$$

$$8 = 8$$

In the next example, we see how the rules for integers apply to variables with coefficients.

This is where we need to use PASS as a way to think about multiplication and division.

Example 2

Use the rules for integers to find the value of x.

$$-5x = -30$$

$-\dfrac{1}{5} \cdot -5x = -30 \cdot -\dfrac{1}{5}$ ← We multiply each side by $-\dfrac{1}{5}$ to get a positive x by itself.

$$\dfrac{-5}{-5}x = \dfrac{-30}{-5}$$

$1x = 6$ ← The PASS rule works for both numbers. In both cases we are dividing a negative by a negative.

$x = 6$ ← A number times 1 is the same number.

> The reciprocal of a number will have the same sign.

%÷
=
<× **Apply Skills**
Turn to *Interactive Text*, page 257.

mBook **Reinforce Understanding**
Use the *mBook Study Guide* to review lesson concepts.

▶**Problem Solving: Missing Angles in Triangles**

What are important properties of triangles?

We have studied four common types of triangles. Each of these triangles share a common property. Their interior angles all add up to 180 degrees.

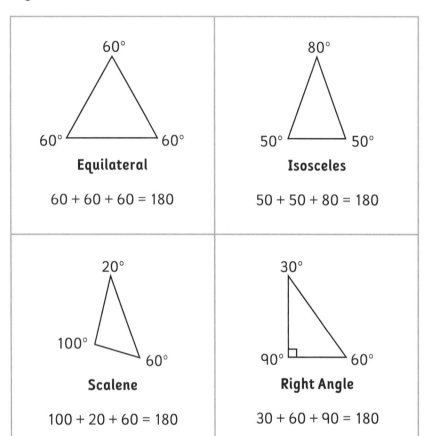

Equilateral

60 + 60 + 60 = 180

Isosceles

50 + 50 + 80 = 180

Scalene

100 + 20 + 60 = 180

Right Angle

30 + 60 + 90 = 180

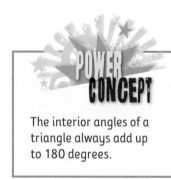

POWER CONCEPT

The interior angles of a triangle always add up to 180 degrees.

A simple way to prove that the interior angles of any of these triangles add up to 180 degrees is to tear off the corners and put them side by side. The picture below shows us that when the triangles are put together, the bottom forms a straight line, or 180 degrees.

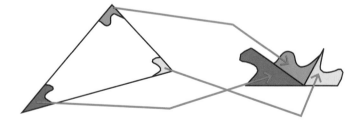

How do we use algebra when working with triangles?

We use the information about the interior angles of triangles to figure out the measure of unknown angles. Example 1 shows how we figure out the measure of the unknown angle *e*. We use an algebraic equation to find the measure of angle *e*.

Example 1

Find the measure of the missing angle.

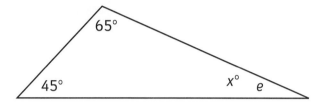

$x + 65 + 45 = 180$

$x + 110 = 180$ ← Combine like terms.

$x + 110 + \boxed{-110} = 180 + \boxed{-110}$ ← Add −110 to both sides of the equation to get *x* by itself.

$x + 0 = 70$

$x = 70$

The measure of ∠*e* is 70°.

Check to see if the answer is correct by substituting.

70
↓

$x + 65 + 45 = 180$

$70 + 65 + 45 = 180$

$135 + 45 = 180$

$180 = 180$

 Problem-Solving Activity
Turn to *Interactive Text*,
page 258.

 mBook **Reinforce Understanding**
Use the *mBook Study Guide*
to review lesson concepts.

Activity 1

Simplify each expression by combining like terms.

1. $-5x + x + -4x$
2. $x - 4 - 3$
3. $2x - -3 + 4 - x$
4. $7x + -2 + -7 + -6x$

Activity 2

Solve the equations using the rules for integers. Check your answer at the end using substitution.

1. $-4 + -3 + x = 14$

2. $2x - 5 + 5 - x = 12$

3. $x - -4 - 3 = 1$

4. $-2 + 2x - -2 + 3x = 20$

Activity 3

Find the missing angles in each of the triangles.

1. What are the measures of $\angle x$ and $\angle y$ in the equilateral triangle?

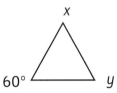

2. What is the measure of $\angle x$?

3. What is the measure of $\angle x$?

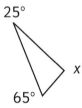

Activity 4 • Distributed Practice

Solve.

1. $\frac{1}{4} \div \frac{1}{2}$
2. $\frac{1}{4} \cdot \frac{1}{2}$
3. $-2 \cdot -6$
4. $4^2 \div 2 + 6$
5. $2 \cdot 4^2 + 3$
6. $(-5 \cdot -2) - 6$

7. Simplify using the distributive property: $2(3x + 2)$

Problem Solving:
▸**Triangles With Congruent Angles**

▸**Rate Problems and Algebra**

How do we convert proportion rate problems?

We have learned to use algebra to solve proportion problems. One kind of proportion involves rate. Let's see how we convert a rate problem from proportions into a simple algebraic equation.

Problem:

In the last play of the football game, Quentin threw a long pass that went more than half the distance of the field. It traveled 30 yards every 2 seconds. How long did it take for the ball to go 60 yards?

We know:	**We can say:**	**We write it like this:**
2 seconds = 30 yards g seconds = 60 yards	2 is to 30 as g is to 60.	$\dfrac{2}{30} = \dfrac{g}{60}$

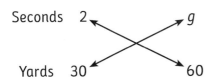

Seconds 2 g

Yards   30   60

We write an equation for this problem by using cross multiplication.

$30 \cdot g = 2 \cdot 60$ ← When we cross multiply, we get this equation.

$30g = 120$ ← We simplify the problem this way.

$\dfrac{1}{30} \cdot 30g = 120 \cdot \dfrac{1}{30}$ ← We multiply each side by $\dfrac{1}{30}$ to get x by itself.

$\dfrac{30}{30}g = \dfrac{120}{30}$

$1g = 4$

$g = 4$ ← A number times 1 is the same number.

It took the ball 4 seconds to go 60 yards.

Using proportions and cross multiplication is just one way to solve a rate problem. Another way is to substitute for variables using an algebraic formula.

We can use a formula called the *distance formula*, or $D = rt$. The **D** stands for *distance*, the **r** stands for *rate*, and the **t** stands for *time*.

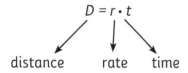

$$D = r \cdot t$$

distance   rate   time

Example 1

Find the distance using the distance formula.

Problem:
Josie is the fastest player on her basketball team. She can run 20 feet per second. If she runs 60 feet, how long does it take?

We know:

- The rate is 20 feet per second, so $r = 20$.
- The distance is 60 feet, so $D = 60$.

The question is asking "how long," or the amount of time, it will take. When we substitute what we know into the formula, we have an algebraic equation.

$$D = r \cdot t$$
$$60 = 20 \cdot t$$

We now treat this like any other algebra problem.

$$60 = 20t$$

$$\frac{1}{20} \cdot 60 = 20t \cdot \frac{1}{20}$$ ← We multiply both sides of the equation by $\frac{1}{20}$ to get *t* by itself.

$$3 = 1t$$

$$3 = t$$ ← A number times 1 is the same number.

It takes Josie 3 seconds to run 60 feet.

The distance formula allows us to use algebra to find rate, time, or distance. In the next example, let's find the rate.

Example 2

Find the rate using the distance formula.

Problem:

Roxy is a serious snowboarder. She won the final race with her best time. She completed a 1,000-yard course in 50 seconds. What was her rate of speed?

We know:

- She traveled 1,000 yards, so $D = 1,000$.
- It took her 50 seconds, so $t = 50$.

The question asks for the rate. In this case, we want to know yards per second. Now we can substitute the information we know into the formula.

$$r \cdot t = D \qquad \leftarrow \text{This time we reverse the equation so the}$$
$$\text{variable is on the left.}$$

$$r \cdot 50 = 1,000$$

$$50r = 1,000 \qquad \leftarrow \text{We use the commutative property to}$$
$$\text{change } r \cdot 50 \text{ into } 50r.$$

$$\frac{1}{50} \cdot 50r = 1,000 \cdot \frac{1}{50} \qquad \leftarrow \text{We multiply each side by } \frac{1}{50} \text{ to get } r \text{ by}$$
$$\text{itself.}$$

$$1r = 20$$

$$r = 20 \qquad \leftarrow \text{A number times 1 is the same number.}$$

Roxy traveled at a rate of 20 yards per second.

% ÷
= =
< × **Apply Skills**
Turn to *Interactive Text*, page 261.

mBook **Reinforce Understanding**
Use the *mBook Study Guide* to review lesson concepts.

▶**Problem Solving: Triangles With Congruent Angles**

What do we need to know about triangles to solve difficult problems?

When we are not given a lot of information in a problem, it can be difficult to solve. We know that isosceles triangles have two equal sides and two equal angles. We also know that all sides and all angles are equal in an equilateral triangle. The triangles below have marks that show the congruent sides and angles.

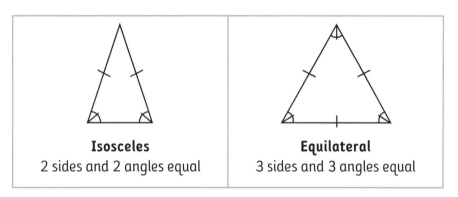

Isosceles
2 sides and 2 angles equal

Equilateral
3 sides and 3 angles equal

This information is useful in solving the problem on the next page. Notice that only the measure of one of the angles is given.

Example 1

Find the measure of ∠k in this isosceles triangle.

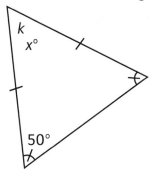

k
$x°$
$50°$

We know that the angles at the bottom measure 50 degrees because the marks on the angles show they are congruent.

Now we can write and solve an equation.

$$x + 50 + 50 = 180$$
$$x + 100 = 180 \qquad \leftarrow \text{ Combine like terms.}$$
$$x + 100 + \boxed{-100} = 180 + \boxed{-100} \leftarrow \text{ Add } -100 \text{ to both sides.}$$
$$x + 0 = 80$$
$$x = 80$$

The measure of ∠k = 80°

Speaking of Math

Here's how you can explain your thinking when you find the measurement of an angle in a triangle.

- *First, I look at the triangle to see what I know.*
- *Next, I look for congruent sides and angles.*
- *Then, I label the triangle with the information I learned based on the congruent sides and angles.*
- *Last, I write and solve my equation.*

Problem-Solving Activity
Turn to *Interactive Text*,
page 263.

mBook **Reinforce Understanding**
Use the *mBook Study Guide*
to review lesson concepts.

Activity 1

Solve the proportions using cross multiplication.

1. $\frac{1}{3} = \frac{12}{f}$

2. $\frac{10}{2} = \frac{15}{v}$

3. $\frac{t}{4} = \frac{6}{3}$

4. $\frac{10}{5} = \frac{m}{3}$

Activity 2

Find the missing angle.

1. What is the measure of $\angle b$?

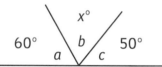

Activity 3

Use the distance formula $D = r \cdot t$ to solve these problems.

1. A baseball travels through the air at 100 feet per second. How far does it travel in 4 seconds?

2. It takes 30 seconds for a diver to rise from under water. She travels 5 feet per second. How far does she travel in 30 seconds?

3. Snow is sliding down the side of the mountain at the rate of 50 feet per second. It travels 300 feet before it stops. How long did it take the snow to travel the 300 feet?

Activity 4 • Distributed Practice

Solve.

1. $\frac{4}{5} - \frac{1}{2}$

2. $\frac{4}{5} \cdot \frac{5}{4}$

3. $4^2 \div (2 + 6)$

4. $(3 \cdot -6) \div 2$

5. $4^2 \div 2^2$

6. $6 \cdot 3 + 3$

7. $-5 \cdot -2 + 10$

8. Simplify using the distributive property: $3(-2x + 1)$

▶**Writing Equations From Words**

How do we write algebraic equations from word statements?

Much of this unit has involved solving algebraic equations. We have learned to solve for x by using properties and rules from our toolbox. Let's review the steps in solving a typical equation.

Example 1

Solve the equation $3x + x = 19 + 1$.

$3x + x = 19 + 1$

$4x = 20$ ← We add like terms on both sides of the equation.

$\frac{1}{4} \cdot 4x = 20 \cdot \frac{1}{4}$ ← We multiply each side by $\frac{1}{4}$ to get x by itself.

$\frac{4}{4}x = \frac{20}{4}$

$1x = 5$

$x = 5$ ← A number times 1 is the same number.

Sometimes we are given an equation using words instead of variables. Let's look at how we change words into equations.

We need to be able to translate words into numbers and variables. It is trickier than it seems, because we have to read the problem carefully and put the numbers and symbols in the right order. Example 2 demonstrates this.

Example 2

Translate this statement into an equation.

Statement: *Three times a number is equal to eight plus one.*

STEP 1

Begin with the first part of the statement: "Three times a number..." We do not know what the number is. That means we are working with an unknown, or a variable. We write this part of the statement using a variable. In this case, we will use n.

$3 \cdot n$ or $3n$

STEP 2

Translate the rest of the sentence. The rest of the sentence is easier to translate: "...is equal to eight plus one."

The phrase "is equal to" is the same as =. We translate this part of the statement this way:

$= 8 + 1$

STEP 3

Put the equation together.
Now we have the entire statement.

$3n = 8 + 1$

How do we write algebraic equations from word statements with negative numbers?

Translating negative numbers in statements can be difficult. Example 1 shows how we have to pay extra attention to the symbols that we use.

Example 1

Translate this statement with negative numbers into an equation.

Statement: *A number plus negative three is equal to nine minus five.*

STEP 1
Begin with the first part of the statement: "A number plus negative three…"
We do not know what the number is. That means we are working with an unknown, or a variable. We write this part of the statement using a variable. In this case, we will use *v*.

$v + -3$

STEP 2
Translate the rest of the statement. The rest of the statement is easier to translate: "…is equal to nine minus five."

The phrase "is equal to" is the same as =. We translate this part of the statement this way:

$= 9 - 5$

STEP 3
Put the equation together.
Now we have the entire statement.

$v + -3 = 9 - 5$

> Give extra care and attention when working with negative numbers.

%÷
=×
< × **Apply Skills**
Turn to *Interactive Text*, page 265.

mBook **Reinforce Understanding**
Use the *mBook Study Guide* to review lesson concepts.

▶**Problem Solving: Word Problems and Algebra**

How do we translate word problems?

Word problems require even more translation than simple statements for algebraic equations. It is important to check and double-check our work as we work through the problem. Example 1 shows how we have to think about the relationship first before we write the equation.

Example 1

Translate the word problem and solve.

Zach is three times older than his sister Rebecca. Zach is 15 years old. How old is Rebecca?

STEP 1
Think about what we know and what we don't know in the problem.
We know:

- Zach is three times older than Rebecca.
- Zack is 15 years old.

We don't know:

- Rebecca's age

STEP 2
Figure out what the variable is.
We do not know Rebecca's age, so that is the unknown. Let's use t to represent Rebecca's age.

t = Rebecca's age

We have a variable for Rebecca's age, and we know that Zach is three times older than Rebecca.

Zach's age = $3 \cdot t$, or $3t$

STEP 3
Write the equation.
Now we can use the two things we know about Zach to write the equation. We can write the equation because the two sides are balanced.

$3t = 15$

STEP 4

Solve the problem.

Now that we have written the problem, we know how to solve it.

$3t = 15$

$\frac{1}{3} \cdot 3t = 15 \cdot \frac{1}{3}$ ← Multiply both sides of the equation by $\frac{1}{3}$ to get t by itself.

$\frac{3}{3}t = \frac{15}{3}$

$1t = 5$

$t = 5$ ← A number times 1 is the same number.

Rebecca is five years old.

We can check our answer by substituting in the original equation.

5
$\downarrow$
$3t = 15$
$3 \cdot 5 = 15$
$15 = 15$

📝 **Problem-Solving Activity**
Turn to *Interactive Text*,
page 266.

⌨ **mBook** **Reinforce Understanding**
Use the *mBook Study Guide*
to review lesson concepts.

Activity 1

Write algebraic expressions for each of the phrases. Use any of the four operation symbols as well as > and < to write your expressions.

1. a number times five

2. three less than a number

3. four more than a number

4. a number greater than six

5. seven more than three times a number

6. eleven is more than a number

Activity 2

Write algebraic equations for each of the phrases. You do not need to solve the equation.

1. a number plus seven equals fourteen

2. twenty minus a number equals three times two

3. four hundred divided by a number equals negative four

Activity 3

Set the word problems up as algebraic equations and then solve.

1. Joanna earns $8 for every hour she works at her mom's store, plus $5 for cleaning the floors. Yesterday she made $37 at her mom's store. How many hours did she work?

2. Blake has a CD case that holds the same number of CDs on each page. He has enough CDs to fill 6 full pages, plus put 2 more CDs on the next page. He has 62 CDs in all. How many CDs fit on a full page?

3. You can make $2 for every program you sell at the game, plus $5 for helping at the food stand. How many programs did you sell at the game if you made $55?

Activity 4 • Distributed Practice

Solve.

1. $\frac{6}{5} - \frac{1}{5}$

2. $\frac{6}{5} \cdot \frac{5}{6}$

3. $4^2 \div (2^2 - 2)$

4. $3 \cdot -4 \div 2$

5. $4^2 \div 2 - 3$

6. Simplify using the distributive property: $-2(-2x + 4)$

▶Introduction to Algebraic Equations

How do we work with equations?

Throughout this unit we balanced equations. We defined an equation as a math statement that shows one expression is equal to another expression. These two expressions usually do not look the same, but that doesn't matter. If it is an equation, the two expressions must be equal. All of the equations below are balanced.

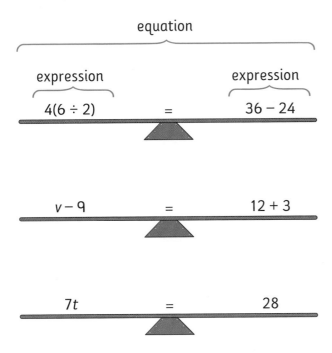

equation

expression   expression

$4(6 \div 2)$ = $36 - 24$

$v - 9$ = $12 + 3$

$7t$ = 28

The goal in working with equations is to solve for the variable. We use properties and rules from our toolbox to find the value of the variable.

Review 1

How do we keep equations balanced when solving?
When we solve an equation, we need to remember to do the same thing to each side of the equation. This keeps the equation balanced.

$5 + x - 4 = 27$

$5 + x + -4 = 27$ ← Subtraction is the same as adding the opposite.

$x + 5 + -4 = 27$ ← We commute so that we combine the same terms.

$x + 1 = 27$

$x + 1 + \boxed{-1} = 27 + \boxed{-1}$ ← We add -1 to both sides to get x by itself.

$x + 0 = 26$

$x = 26$

We check this answer to make sure it is correct by using substitution.

$$26$$
$$\downarrow$$
$$5 + x - 4 = 27$$
$$5 + 26 - 4 = 27$$
$$5 + 26 + -4 = 27$$
$$31 + -4 = 27$$
$$27 = 27$$

Our answer was correct.

Sometimes balancing equations with negative numbers is difficult. We need to remember the rules from our toolbox that involve operations on integers. Knowing the PASS rules and remembering that subtraction is adding the opposite helps us make sure we solve the equation correctly.

Review 2

How do we solve equations that contain negative numbers?
When we solve equations that have negative numbers in them, we need to use the rules for integers.

$$-2x = 16$$

$-\frac{1}{2} \cdot -2x = 16 \cdot -\frac{1}{2}$ ← We multiply each side by $-\frac{1}{2}$ to get x by itself.

$$\frac{-2}{-2}x = \frac{16}{-2}$$

$1x = -8$ ← The PASS rule works for both numbers.

On the left side of the equal sign, we are dividing a negative by a negative. Both numbers have the same signs, which means that the answer is positive.

On the right side of the equal sign, we are dividing a positive by a negative number. The signs are different, which means the answer is negative.

$x = -8$ ← A number times 1 is the same number.

We always check our work. We can substitute -8 for x.

$$-8$$
$$\downarrow$$
$$-2x = 16$$
$$-2 \cdot -8 = 16$$
$$16 = 16$$

How do we solve distance problems using algebra?

One of the big advantages of algebra is that it gives us a general way to represent and solve word problems.

Proportions are a good example of how we can solve a problem quickly using algebra. All we need to do is cross multiply.

Review 1

How do we solve proportion problems using algebra?

Problem:

A map shows 3 inches for every 500 miles. The distance on the map between Los Angeles and Denver is about 6 inches. How many miles is it from Los Angeles to Denver?

We begin by setting up the proportion. In this case, the proportion is $\frac{3}{500} = \frac{6}{x}$.

We then cross multiply to create an algebraic equation.

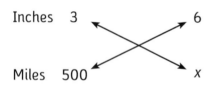

Inches   3   6

Miles   500 x

Now we can solve our equation to find the value of x.

$$3x = 500 \cdot 6$$

$$3x = 3,000$$

$$\frac{1}{3} \cdot 3x = 3,000 \cdot \frac{1}{3} \quad \leftarrow \text{We multiply both sides of the equation by } \frac{1}{3}$$
$$\text{to get } x \text{ by itself.}$$

$$\frac{3}{3}x = \frac{3,000}{3}$$

$$1x = 1,000$$

$$x = 1,000 \quad \leftarrow \text{A number times 1 is the same number.}$$

It is about 1,000 miles from Los Angeles to Denver.

We also use algebra to solve rate problems. We learned a formula for distance: $D = r \cdot t$. This formula is more efficient and flexible than setting up each problem as a ratio. Let's look at an example.

Review 2

How do we solve rate problems using algebra?

Problem:

When a person jumps out of a plane with a parachute, they can fall as fast as 175 feet per second. How long does it take to fall 875 feet?

We know:

- Rate = 175 ft./sec.
- Time is unknown.
- Distance = 875 ft.

Now we substitute our values into the equation.

$$875 \quad 175$$
$$\downarrow \qquad \downarrow$$
$$D \;=\; r \cdot t$$
$$875 = 175t$$
$$\frac{875}{175} = \frac{175}{175}t$$
$$5 = 1t$$
$$t = 5$$

It takes about 5 seconds for a person to fall 875 feet.

%÷
≡×
<× **Apply Skills**
Turn to *Interactive Text*, page 268.

mBook **Reinforce Understanding**
Use the *mBook Study Guide* to review lesson concepts.

▶**Problem Solving: Geometric Construction and Angle Measurement**

What are constructions?

Geometric constructions allow us to create lines and angles without protractors. They also give us a method for using some of the key vocabulary of geometry.

We made perpendicular and parallel lines using just rulers and protractors. We also bisected angles. Remember the following drawings.

Review 1

How do we construct a perpendicular line bisecting a segment?

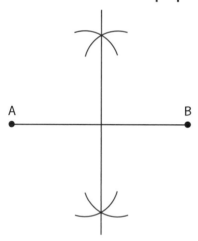

Review 2

How do we bisect an angle?

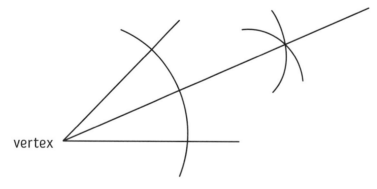

How do we measure angles using algebra?

Once we begin working with angles, we see the connection to algebraic equations. The equations help us figure out the measure of unknown angles. If we know certain properties of angles, we can set up simple algebraic equations to solve different kinds of problems.

Review 1

How do we solve for the measure of angles in a triangle?

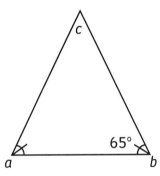

The marks tell us that $\angle a$ and $\angle b$ are equal. We also know that the measure of the interior angles on all triangles totals 180 degrees.

We can set up our equation using x for the measure of $\angle c$.

$$65 + 65 + x = 180$$
$$130 + x = 180 \qquad \leftarrow \text{Combine like terms.}$$
$$\boxed{-130} + 130 + x = 180 + \boxed{-130} \qquad \leftarrow \text{Add } -130 \text{ to both sides of the equation.}$$
$$0 + x = 50$$
$$x = 50$$

The measure of $\angle c = 50°$

Review 2

How do we find the measure of more than one angle in a triangle?

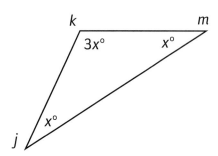

We know that the interior angles on all triangles total 180 degrees. That means all of the angles have to total 180 degrees. We set up the equation this way:

$x + 3x + x = 180$

Then we solve.

$x + 3x + x = 180$

$4x + x = 180$ ← Combine like terms.

$5x = 180$

$\frac{1}{5} \cdot 5x = 180 \cdot \frac{1}{5}$ ← Multiply both sides of the equation by $\frac{1}{5}$.

$\frac{5}{5}x = \frac{180}{5}$

$1x = 36$

$x = 36$ ← A number times 1 is the same number.

We can now substitute to find the measure of each angle.

- If $\angle j = x$, then the measure of $\angle j = 36°$
- If $\angle k = 3x$, then the measure of $\angle k = 3 \cdot 36$, or $108°$
- If $\angle m = x$, then the measure of $\angle m = 36°$

 Problem-Solving Activity
Turn to *Interactive Text*, page 269.

 mBook Reinforce Understanding
Use the *mBook Study Guide* to review lesson concepts.

WHAT DO YOU GET IF YOU CROSS TWO TRACKS WITH ONE TRACK?

A TRANSVERSAL?

YES, A TRANSVERSAL.

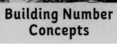

EVERYDAY TRANSVERSALS

OBJECTIVES

Building Number Concepts

- Use a variety of rules and properties to solve algebraic equations

- Use algebraic equations to describe a given situation

- Solve word problems involving algebraic equations using models and check answers for reasonableness

Problem Solving

- Use algebra to find the measures of interior angles in a polygon

- Use angle rules to solve problems involving related angles (vertical, corresponding, right, and supplementary)

- Complete simple proofs involving angle measures

▶Thinking About Algebraic Equations

What are the four steps for solving algebraic equations?

As algebraic equations become more complex, it's easier to make mistakes. Sometimes we don't know where to start to solve the problem.

Here is a way to think about how we approach equations:

Steps for Solving Equations

STEP 1
Look at the entire equation.

STEP 2
Look for the **parts** of the equation that seem different.

STEP 3
Remember the goal: Solve the equation so that we have a **positive variable on one side**.

STEP 4
Use the rules or properties we need to reach our goal.

Use the following exercise as a reminder to think about the first two steps.

Let's look at Figure 1 and Figure 2.

- Are they the same?
- If there is a change from one figure to the next, where is it?

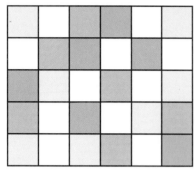

Figure 1

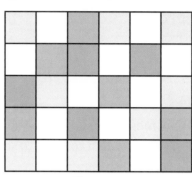

Figure 2

There is a difference, but it is a very small one. To find it, we look carefully at both figures and go back and forth. The change is in the top row.

Let's start on the top row of Figure 1 and count across four boxes. This box is blue. The color in the same box in Figure 2 is a little lighter. Unless we look carefully and think about what we are seeing, we'd think that Figure 1 was exactly like Figure 2.

So how does this apply to algebraic equations? Let's look at these equations. Are they the same, or is there a difference?

$3x = 25 + 3 + {-15} + {-1}$ $3x = 25 + 3 + 15 + {-1}$
Equation 1   **Equation 2**

There is one difference between the two equations. There is a **−15** in Equation 1 and **15** in Equation 2.

$3x = 25 + 3 + \mathbf{-15} + {-1}$ $3x = 25 + 3 + \mathbf{15} + {-1}$
Equation 1   **Equation 2**

Example 1 shows how much of a difference this little change can make.

Example 1

Solve each equation.

Equation 1	Equation 2
$3x = 25 + 3 + -15 + -1$	$3x = 25 + 3 + 15 + -1$
$3x = 28 + -16$	$3x = 28 + 14$
$3x = 12$	$3x = 42$
$x = 4$	$x = 14$

The answers to the equations are entirely different.

Improve Your Skills

A student looked for the difference between two equations.

$2x = 14 + 10$ $\qquad$ $-2x = 14 + 10$

Equation 1 $\qquad$ **Equation 2**

He says that there is no difference. **ERROR**

There is a difference between the two equations. In Equation 2, the coefficient 2 is negative instead of positive. **CORRECT**

Let's see how we use the four steps we learned earlier to solve an equation.

Example 2

Use the four steps for solving equations. $-2x = 14 + 10$

STEP 1
Look at the entire equation.
Look at both sides of the equation.

$$\underbrace{-2x} = \underbrace{14 + 10}$$

STEP 2
Look for the **parts** of the equation that seem different.
We have a negative number: $-2x$. We need to pay attention to this when solving the problem.

$$-2x = 14 + 10$$

STEP 3
Remember the goal: Solve the equation so that we have a **positive variable on one side**.
We need to solve for positive x.

$$-2x = 14 + 10$$

STEP 4
Use the rules or properties we need to reach our goal.
We add like terms. $\rightarrow$

$$-2x = 14 + 10$$
$$-2x = \ \ 24$$

We multiply each side by $-\frac{1}{2}$ so that we will $\rightarrow$
end up with x by itself. We multiply each
side by $-\frac{1}{2}$ to keep the equation balanced.

$$-\frac{1}{2} \cdot -2x = 24 \cdot -\frac{1}{2}$$

$$\frac{-2}{-2}x = \frac{24}{-2}$$

We use integer rules for division:

A negative number divided by a negative number
is a positive number.

$\rightarrow \dfrac{-2}{-2} = 1$

A positive number divided by a negative number
is a negative number.

$\rightarrow \dfrac{24}{-2} = -12$

One times a number is the same number.

$\rightarrow \quad x = -12$

We use the same properties and rules that we learned before to solve
for x.

We did not have to solve the equation in an entirely different way. We
just had to look at the whole equation first and find something that
might be different.

Apply Skills
Turn to *Interactive Text*,
page 273.

mBook **Reinforce Understanding**
Use the *mBook Study Guide*
to review lesson concepts.

▶Problem Solving: Interior Angle Measurement of Regular Polygons

How do we write equations for the measure of interior angles of regular polygons?

Regular polygons are shapes where the measure of each angle is the same. There is an interesting pattern that happens with regular polygons.

Look at the table. Notice what is happening to the total measure of the interior angles as we add one more side to a polygon. Remember that interior angles are the angles inside the shape. When we talk about the total measure of these angles, we mean their sum when we add them all up.

Table of Measures for Regular Polygons			
Shape	Number of Sides	Total Measure of the Interior Angles	Measure of Each Interior Angle
Triangle	3	180°	60°
Square	4	360°	90°
Pentagon	5	540°	108°
Hexagon	6	720°	120°

The total measure of the interior angles increases 180 degrees each time we add a side to a polygon. Why does this happen?

Let's look at the shapes below. We can make a new triangle each time we add a side to a polygon.

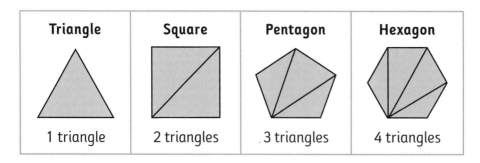

Triangle	Square	Pentagon	Hexagon
1 triangle	2 triangles	3 triangles	4 triangles

Each triangle has a sum of 180 degrees. That is how we get to the pattern.

We can write three different algebraic equations based on the angles of regular polygons. Example 1 shows the equations we write for a square.

Example 1

Write different algebraic equations for a square.

Equation based on the measure of one angle.

Let x = the number of angles in a square.

$90x = 360$

Equation based on the total measure of the interior angles.

Let x = the total measure of the interior angles.

$x = 4 \cdot 90$

Equation based on the number of triangles in the shape.

Let x = the total number of triangles in the square.

$180x = 360$

Problem-Solving Activity
Turn to *Interactive Text*,
page 274.

mBook Reinforce Understanding
Use the *mBook Study Guide*
to review lesson concepts.

Homework

Look at Figures 1 and 2. One is slightly different than the other. Tell the difference on your own sheet of paper.

1.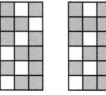

    Figure 1   Figure 2

2.

    Figure 1   Figure 2

3.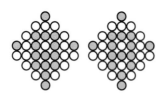

    Figure 1   Figure 2

Activity 2

Look at each pair of equations labeled (a) and (b). One is slightly different than the other. Tell the difference.

1. **(a)** $2x + 3 = 7$ **(b)** $2x + -3 = 7$ 2. **(a)** $-x + y = 10$ **(b)** $x + y = 10$

3. **(a)** $y = -5 + x$ **(b)** $y = -5 + -x$

Activity 3

Use the formula to answer the question about the shape.

1. $3m = 180$
    What is the measure
    of one angle in a
    triangle?

2. $4 \cdot 90 = y$
    What is the total
    measure of all the
    angles in a square?

Activity 4 • Distributed Practice

Solve.

1. $\frac{1}{x} = \frac{3}{6}$

2. $-3 + -7 = y$

3. $2x = x + 7$

4. $\frac{3}{5} \cdot \frac{z}{3} = 1$

5. $w = -2 - -8$

6. $3^2 \cdot 8 + 5 = w$

▶**Invisible Coefficients**

What is difficult to see in an algebraic equation?

Let's think about negative numbers. When we look at a number like −6, it is easy to think of it as any other number on the number line.

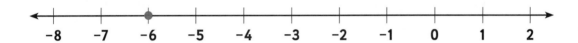

Now that we know about rules for operations on integers, there is another way to think about negative numbers: They are the product of −1 times a positive number.

Think of −1 as an invisible coefficient.

$-6 = -1 \cdot 6$

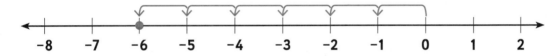

$-10 = -1 \cdot 10$

$-540 = -1 \cdot 540$

$-77 = -1 \cdot 77$

This kind of understanding is important when it comes to certain kinds of algebraic equations. Let's review the four steps for solving equations.

Steps for Solving an Equation

STEP 1
Look at the entire equation.

STEP 2
Look for the **parts** of the equation that seem different.

STEP 3
Remember the goal: Solve the equation so that we have a **positive variable on one side**.

STEP 4
Use the rules or properties we need to reach our goal.

Let's look at the following equations. There is one difference between them.

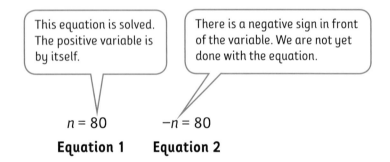

This equation is solved. The positive variable is by itself.

There is a negative sign in front of the variable. We are not yet done with the equation.

$n = 80$ $-n = 80$

Equation 1 **Equation 2**

Example 1 shows what rules we use to make the variable positive and solve the equation.

Example 1

Solve the equation using variable rules.

$-n = 80$

$-1 \cdot n = 80$ ← The number -1 is an invisible coefficient: $-n$ is the same as $-1 \cdot n$.

> We use integer rules for multiplication to solve the equation.

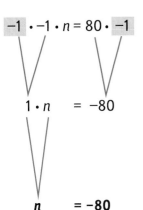

$-1 \cdot -1 \cdot n = 80 \cdot -1$ ← We multiply by -1 so that we will end up with a positive n. We multiply each side by -1 to keep the equation balanced.

$1 \cdot n = -80$ ← Integer rules for multiplication: A negative number times a negative number is a positive number. A positive number times a negative number is a negative number.

$n = -80$ ← One times a number is the same number.

The equation is solved because there is a positive variable by itself on one side of the equal sign.

%÷
=÷
<× **Apply Skills**
Turn to *Interactive Text*, page 277.

mBook **Reinforce Understanding**
Use the *mBook Study Guide* to review lesson concepts.

Unit 8 • Lesson 2   **589**

▶**Problem Solving: Exterior Angle Measurement of Regular Polygons**

How do we find the measures of exterior angles?

In the last lesson, we looked at the interior angles of regular polygons. These are the angles inside the shape. A polygon also has exterior angles, as we see in the following illustration. These angles are on the outside of the shape.

Each exterior angle in the illustration is labeled with a variable.

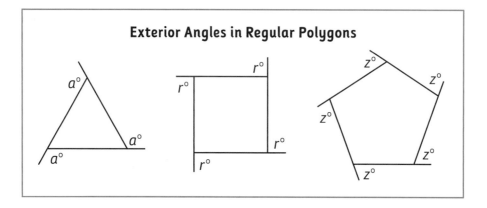

Exterior Angles in Regular Polygons

In each polygon, the variable for each angle is the same. That means each angle has the same measure.

How do we figure out the measure of the exterior angles for each polygon? We need to remember what we know about angles and straight lines to answer this question.

Let's look closely at just one part of the triangle. Example 1 takes a close-up look at the lower right-hand corner of the triangle. We have labeled the angles:

Angle *s* is the interior angle.
Angle *t* is the exterior angle.

We can tell a lot about these angles by remembering what we learned about the properties of angles and lines.

Example 1

Use what we know about the measure of angles in a regular triangle to find the measure of exterior ∠t.

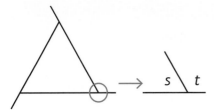

- We know that a straight line measures 180 degrees.

- We know from the last lesson that the interior angle of a regular triangle measures 60 degrees.

Let n = the measure of ∠t.

We write an algebraic equation this way:

interior measures of
a regular triangle

measure
of ∠t

measure of
a straight line

$$n + 60 = 180$$

$n + 60 + \boxed{-60} = 180 + \boxed{-60}$ ← We add −60 to both sides to keep the equation balanced.
A number plus its opposite equals 0.

$$n + 0 \quad = 180 + -60$$

$$n = \quad 120$$

The measure of ∠t = 120 degrees.

We can check our work by adding the measure of ∠s and ∠t to make sure they add up to 180 degrees.

$$60 + 120 = 180$$

That means the measure of all the exterior angles for a regular triangle is 120 degrees.

We need to think about straight lines when we think about exterior angles. We use this information to write an equation for the sum of the exterior angle measurements.

Example 2

Write an equation to find the sum of the measures of the exterior angles for a regular triangle.

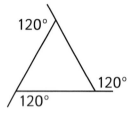

Let $z =$ the sum of the measures of the exterior angles for a regular triangle. We write the equation this way:

$$z = 3 \cdot 120$$
$$z = 360$$

The sum of the measures of the exterior angles is 360 degrees.

We will explore other shapes to show that the sum of the exterior angles is always 360°.

Problem-Solving Activity
Turn to *Interactive Text*, page 278.

mBook **Reinforce Understanding**
Use the *mBook Study Guide* to review lesson concepts.

Activity 1

Tell the coefficient in each question.

1. $-x = 7$
2. $y = 7$
3. $w = 12$
4. $-12 = z$
5. $3 + -m = 14$
6. $y = 17$

Activity 2

Solve the equations.

1. $2c + 12 = c$
2. $-a = -10$
3. $-b = 4$

Activity 3

Answer the questions about interior and exterior angles.

1. The measure of one interior angle of a triangle is 60 degrees. What is the total measure of all the interior angles?

2. The measure of one interior angle of a pentagon is 108 degrees. What is the measure of one exterior angle?

3. The total measure of the interior angles of a square is 360 degrees. What is the measure of one interior angle, and what is the measure of one exterior angle?

Activity 4 • Distributed Practice

Solve.

1. $4 - 2 \cdot 3 = w$
2. $2z + 7 = 21$
3. $4a = -12$
4. $5d = -30$
5. $\frac{2}{b} = \frac{6}{15}$
6. $-4 \cdot -\frac{1}{4} = c$

▶**Multistep Equations**

Where do we start with multistep equations?

Until now, we have worked with relatively simple equations. Solving the equations usually means that we used a reciprocal to change the coefficient so that it equals 1. Other times, we added an opposite so that a single variable was by itself.

Example 1 shows how we solve each of these types of equations.

Example 1

Solve a simple equation.

Use a Reciprocal	**Add the Opposite**

Use a Reciprocal

$$3x = 15$$

$$\frac{1}{3} \cdot 3x = 15 \cdot \frac{1}{3}$$

$$\frac{3}{3}x = \frac{15}{3}$$

$$1x = 5$$

$$x = 5$$

Add the Opposite

$$x + 3 = 20$$

$$x + 3 + \boxed{-3} = 20 + \boxed{-3}$$

$$x + 0 = 17$$

$$x = 17$$

Now let's look at equations where we have to change the coefficient and add the opposite. This is the first of many kinds of complex, multistep equations we will work on. Solving these kinds of equations takes a little more time.

We will use the four steps we learned for solving equations.

Steps for Solving Equations

STEP 1
Look at the entire equation.

STEP 2
Look for the **parts** of the equation that seem different.

STEP 3
Remember the goal: Solve the equation so that we have a **positive variable on one side**.

STEP 4
Use the rules or properties we need to reach our goal.

Example 2

Solve a multistep equation.

$$4x - 2 = 22$$

$4x + -2 = 22$ ←   Subtraction is the same as adding the opposite.

$4x + -2 \boxed{+2} = 22 \boxed{+2}$ ←   We add 2 so that we end up with $4x$ by itself. We add 2 to both sides to keep the equation balanced.

$4x + 0 = 22 + 2$ ←   A number plus its opposite equals 0.

$4x = 24$

$\boxed{\frac{1}{4}} \cdot 4x = 24 \cdot \boxed{\frac{1}{4}}$ ←   We multiply by $\frac{1}{4}$ so that we end up with x by itself. We multiply each side by $\frac{1}{4}$ to keep the equation balanced.

$\frac{4}{4}x = \frac{24}{4}$

$1x = 6$

$x = 6$ ←   A number times 1 is the same number. This is the solution.

> We add the opposite first. Then we work on the coefficient.

Let's look at the equation in Example 3. We will use the equation from the previous example, but we will change the −2 to 2.

We use our Algebra Toolbox to solve the equation.

Example 3

Solve a multistep equation.

$$4x + 2 = 22$$

$$4x + 2 + \boxed{-2} = 22 + \boxed{-2}$$ ← We add −2 so that we will end up with $4x$ by itself. We add −2 to both sides to keep the equation balanced.

$$4x + 0 \qquad = 22 + -2$$

$$4x \qquad = \quad 20$$ ← A number plus its opposite equals 0.

$$\boxed{\tfrac{1}{4}} \cdot 4x = 20 \cdot \boxed{\tfrac{1}{4}}$$ ← We multiply by $\frac{1}{4}$ so that we end up with x by itself. We multiply each side by $\frac{1}{4}$ to keep the equation balanced.

$$\frac{4}{4}x \;=\; \frac{20}{4}$$

$$1x = 5$$

$$x = 5$$ ← A number times 1 is the same number. This is the solution.

% ÷
= x **Apply Skills**
< X Turn to *Interactive Text*, page 281.

mBook **Reinforce Understanding**
Use the *mBook Study Guide* to review lesson concepts.

▶Problem Solving: **Angle Measurements of Irregular Polygons**

What do we know about the measurement of exterior angles?

We learned an important idea about exterior angles in the last lesson. It doesn't matter what kind of polygon it is, the sum of the exterior angles is always 360 degrees.

The illustrations below show why this is true. Even if we shrink each shape, the sum of the exterior angles always adds up to 360 degrees.

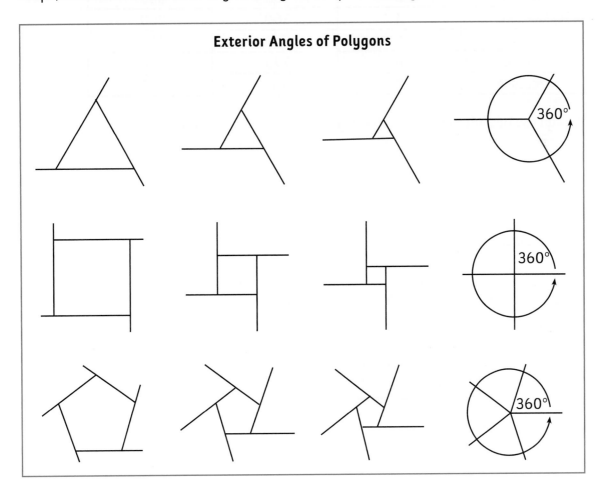

Exterior Angles of Polygons

How do we use multistep equations to find angle measurements?

The following table shows information about polygons.

Polygons and the Sums of the Measures of Interior and Exterior Angles			
Shape	Number of Sides	Sum of Interior Angles	Sum of Exterior Angles
Triangle	3	180°	360°
Quadrilateral	4	360°	360°
Pentagon	5	540°	360°
Hexagon	6	720°	360°
Octagon	8	1,080°	360°

We can use this information to solve angle problems using algebraic equations. In Example 1, we use the sum of the interior angles for a triangle to write an algebraic equation.

Example 1

Show the measure of each interior angle.

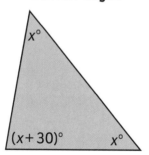

We know that the sum of the interior angles of a triangle is 180 degrees. That means we can set up the equation this way.

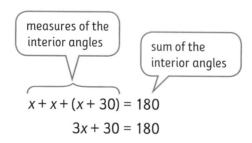

measures of the interior angles

sum of the interior angles

$$x + x + (x + 30) = 180$$
$$3x + 30 = 180$$

$$3x + 30 + \boxed{-30} = 180 + \boxed{-30}$$ ← We add −30 to get $3x$ by itself. We add −30 to both sides to balance the equation.

$$3x + 0 = 180 + -30$$ ← A number plus its opposite equals 0.

$$3x = 150$$

$$\frac{1}{3} \cdot 3x = 150 \cdot \frac{1}{3}$$ ← We multiply by $\frac{1}{3}$ to get x by itself. We multiply each side by $\frac{1}{3}$ to balance the equation.

$$\frac{3}{3}x = \frac{150}{3}$$

$$1x = 50$$

$$x = 50$$ ← A number times 1 is the same number. This is the solution.

We substitute for x in the triangle and get the measures of each interior angle.

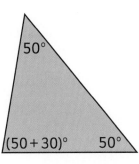

50°

(50 + 30)°   50°

Our Confirming answer is:

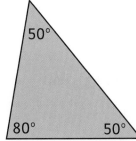

50°

80°   50°

We know this works because 50 + 50 + 80 = 180.

Problem-Solving Activity
Turn to *Interactive Text*,
page 282.

mBook **Reinforce Understanding**
Use the *mBook Study Guide*
to review lesson concepts.

Activity 1

In each problem, tell what step is first.

1. $3x + 12 = 24$
   - (a) Multiply each side by $\frac{1}{3}$.
   - (b) Add -12 to each side.
   - (c) Multiply each side by 12.

2. $4x = 16$
   - (a) Add -4 to each side.
   - (b) Add -16 to each side.
   - (c) Multiply each side by $\frac{1}{4}$.

Activity 2

Solve the equations.

1. $4z + 14 = 26$
2. $w + -7 = -12$
3. $-16 = -x + -4$
4. $27 = 8y + 3$
5. $8a + -3 = 5$
6. $-3 + -b = 1$

Activity 3

Find the measurements of the interior angles for each shape.

1. What is the measure of each angle?

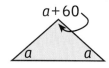

2. What is the measure of each angle?

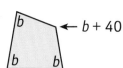

3. What is the measure of each angle?

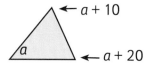

Activity 4 • Distributed Practice

Solve.

1. $\frac{x}{12} = \frac{2}{6}$
2. $-4 = \frac{12}{y}$
3. $9w = -81$
4. $-54 + z = -60$
5. $4^2 + 2 \cdot -3 = b$
6. $5 + x = 0$

▶**Translating Numbers Into Equations**

How do we translate simple numeric equations using variables?

We learned to translate numeric equations into algebraic equations. In these kinds of problems, we looked for a pattern in the numeric equations, then substituted a variable for the part of the equation that kept changing. Let's look at three different patterns.

$$0 + 7 = 7$$
$$0 + 82 = 82$$
$$0 + 9.99 = 9.99$$

What is the general pattern? $0 + y = y$

$$55 - 55 = 0$$
$$0.9 - 0.9 = 0$$
$$\frac{3}{4} - \frac{3}{4} = 0$$

What is the general pattern? $h - h = 0$

$$44 + 22 = 22 + 44$$
$$0.6 + 0.3 = 0.3 + 0.6$$
$$694 + 255 = 255 + 694$$

What is the general pattern? $m + r = r + m$

In the first two patterns, we ask the question, "What is the same and what is changing?" The variable is used to represent what is changing.

In the third pattern, both numbers on each side of the equal sign keep changing. That is why we use two variables to represent that pattern.

How do we use variables in word problems?

Another way to use variables to represent numbers is in word problems.

Example 1

Solve the word problem by using variables.

Problem:

Two numbers add up to 50. The larger number is 6 greater than the smaller number. What are the two numbers?

What happens if we use two variables to try to solve the problem?

- Let x = the smaller number.
- Let y = the larger number.
- $x + y = 50$

In this equation, the variables x and y stand for the two different numbers. But there is no way to solve this problem using what we know about algebraic equations. The only way to solve this problem is to use the guess-and-check method.

The key to solving a problem like this is to think about the relationship between the two numbers.

- Instead of using x and y, we use just one variable.
- If we let x = the smaller number, then $x + 6$ = the larger number.

Now we have a way of solving this kind of problem.

	smaller number		larger number		
	x	$+$	y	$=$	50
becomes $\rightarrow$	x	$+$	$x + 6$	$=$	50

$$x + x + 6 = 50$$
$$2x + 6 = 50$$

$2x + 6 + \boxed{-6} = 50 + \boxed{-6}$ ←   We add −6 so we can start to get x by itself. We add −6 to both sides to balance the equation.

$2x + 0 \quad = 50 + -6$ ←   A number plus its opposite equals 0.

$$2x \quad = \quad 44$$

$\frac{1}{2} \cdot 2x = 44 \cdot \frac{1}{2}$ ←   We multiply by $\frac{1}{2}$ so that we end up with x by itself. We multiply each side by $\frac{1}{2}$ to balance the equation.

$$\frac{2}{2}x \quad = \quad \frac{44}{2}$$
$$1x = 22$$
$$x = 22$$

←   A number times 1 is the same number. This is the solution.

That means:

- **The smaller number is 22.**
- **The larger number is 22 + 6 or 28.**

We check if this is correct by substituting the numbers 22 and 28 into the original equation.

22
↓ ↓

$$x + x + 6 = 50$$
$$22 + 22 + 6 = 50$$
$$50 = 50$$

> It is important to think about the problem and the relationship between the numbers. We do this by substituting our answer into the original equation.

This step proves that we answered the problem correctly.

These word problems look simple because they are just a couple of sentences, but they are more complicated than we might think.

Example 2

Solve the word problem by using variables.

Problem:

Two numbers add up to 80. One of the numbers is 3 times the other number. What are the two numbers?

The larger number is 3 times bigger than the smaller number. We use variables to show this relationship.

- Let y = the smaller number.
- Let $3y$ = the larger number.

$$y + 3y = 80 \qquad \leftarrow \text{ We combine like terms.}$$

$$4y = 80$$

$$\frac{1}{4} \cdot 4y = 80 \cdot \frac{1}{4} \leftarrow \text{ We multiply by } \frac{1}{4} \text{ to get } y \text{ by itself.}$$

We multiply each side by $\frac{1}{4}$ to balance the equation.

$$\frac{4}{4}y = \frac{80}{4}$$

$$1y = 20$$

$$y = 20 \qquad \leftarrow \text{ A number times 1 is the same number.}$$

That means:

- **The smaller number is 20.**
- **The larger number is 3 · 20 or 60.**

Check by substituting the numbers 20 and 60 into the original equation.

$$20 \quad 20$$
$$\downarrow \quad \downarrow$$
$$y + 3y = 80$$
$$20 + 60 = 80$$
$$80 = 80$$

We proved that we answered the problem correctly by substituting our answer into the original equation.

%÷ Apply Skills
<× X Turn to *Interactive Text*, page 284.

mBook Reinforce Understanding
Use the *mBook Study Guide* to review lesson concepts.

Activity 1

Tell the general pattern for each property shown.

1. $12 + 0 = 12$

   $\frac{1}{2} + 0 = \frac{1}{2}$

   $-7 + 0 = -7$

   (a) $12 + x = 12$
   (b) $x + 0 = x$
   (c) $x + y = z$

2. $-5 + 5 = 0$

   $-\frac{1}{3} + \frac{1}{3} = 0$

   $-7.2 + 7.2 = 0$

   (a) $-5 + \frac{1}{5} = 0$
   (b) $-\frac{1}{3} + \frac{1}{3} = x$
   (c) $-x + x = 0$

Activity 2

Translate the words into expressions.

1. 5 more than a number

2. a number minus 6

3. a number plus 7

4. 17 minus a number

5. 4.7 divided by a number

6. 3 less than a number

Activity 3

Write the word problems using algebra, then solve.

1. The sum of two numbers is 130. One of the numbers is 50 more than the other number. What are the two numbers?

2. The sum of three numbers is 60. The smallest number is 10 less than the middle number. The biggest number is 10 more than the middle number. What are the three numbers?

Activity 4 • Distributed Practice

Solve.

1. $25 = 4 + 3z$

2. $4h = -40$

3. $\frac{3}{5} = \frac{9}{a}$

4. $16 = 2(-2 + x)$

5. $b = -3 + 5$

6. $c + -\frac{1}{2} = 0$

▶**Problem Solving: Angles of Quadrilaterals**

How do we use algebra to find the measure of each angle?

We studied different types of quadrilaterals. One fact that we learned about quadrilaterals is that the sum of the interior angles is always 360 degrees.

Some quadrilaterals, such as squares, rectangles, and parallelograms, have consistent properties. For example, squares and rectangles always have angle measurements that are 90 degrees. The little square at each angle tells us this.

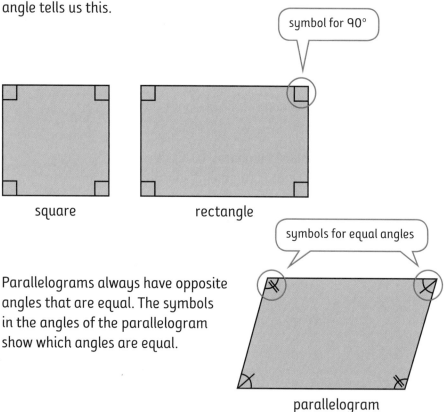

symbol for 90°

square   rectangle

symbols for equal angles

Parallelograms always have opposite angles that are equal. The symbols in the angles of the parallelogram show which angles are equal.

parallelogram

Other quadrilaterals might have a pair of angles that are the same and two others that are different.

Let's look at a kite. This shape has only two angles that are equal. ($\angle d = \angle f$).

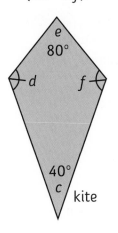

kite

Some quadrilaterals have different measures for each angle, like the shape in this illustration.

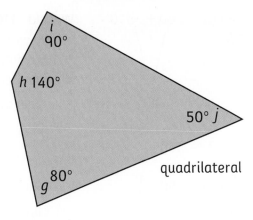

quadrilateral

Algebra helps us find the measure of each angle when we create equations. Example 1 shows how to find the measure of angles using an algebraic equation.

Example 1

Find the measure of each angle in the kite.

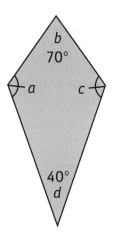

The symbols show that $\angle a$ and $\angle c$ are equal. Let x = the measure of each unknown angle.

We also know that the sum of the interior angles for all quadrilaterals is 360 degrees.

We set up the equation this way:

$x + x + 70 + 40 = 360$

$x + x + 70 + 40 = 360$ ←   We add like terms to simplify the equation.

$2x + 110 = 360$

$2x + 110 + \boxed{-110} = 360 + \boxed{-110}$ ←   We add −110 so that we will end up with 2x by itself. We add −110 to both sides to balance the equation.

$2x + 0 \qquad = \qquad 250$ ←   A number plus its opposite equals 0.

$2x = 250$

$\frac{1}{2} \cdot 2x = 250 \cdot \frac{1}{2}$ ←   We multiply by $\frac{1}{2}$ so that we get x by itself. We multiply each side by $\frac{1}{2}$ to balance the equation.

$\frac{2}{2}x \quad = \quad \frac{250}{2}$

$1x = 125$

$x = 125$ ←   A number times 1 is the same number. **That means the measure of $\angle a$ = 125 and $\angle c$ = 125.**

We substitute these values into the original equation to check our answer.

$\qquad 125$
$\qquad \downarrow \quad \downarrow$

$x + x + 70 + 40 = 360$
$125 + 125 + 70 + 40 = 360$
$250 + 70 + 40 = 360$
$320 + 40 = 360$
$360 = 360$

We cannot solve angle measurement problems if we are not given enough information.

When isn't it possible to find the measurement of an angle?

Look at the quadrilateral. The measures for ∠r and ∠u are not given.

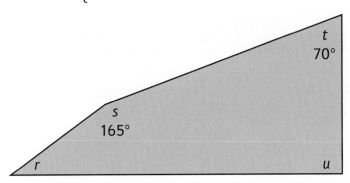

There are no symbols that show the angles are equal, so we cannot figure out their measurement.

Problem-Solving Activity
Turn to *Interactive Text*,
page 287.

Monitoring Progress
Quiz 1

mBook Reinforce Understanding
Use the *mBook Study Guide*
to review lesson concepts.

Activity 1

Solve.

1. $30 + 60 + x = 180$
2. $45 + 40 + 35 + w = 360$
3. $z = 3 \cdot 60$
4. $4 \cdot m = 360$

Activity 2

Write an equation for each of the word problems. You do not need to solve it.

1. If the sum of the interior angles of a square is 360, write an equation to show the measurement of one interior angle.

2. If a triangle has angles with measures of 90 and 30 degrees, write an equation to show the measurement of the third angle.

Activity 3

Tell the missing angle measures.

1. What are the measures of $\angle a$ and $\angle b$?

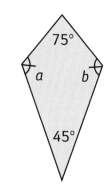

2. What is the measure of $\angle x$?

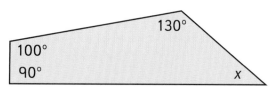

Activity 4 • Distributed Practice

Solve.

1. $\frac{12}{24} = \frac{x}{6}$
2. $2(a + 6) = -24$
3. $7b = -49$
4. $-22 + x + -9 = -50$
5. $\frac{1}{4} \cdot g = 1$
6. $d + -4 = 0$

▶Negative Coefficients

What difference does a negative coefficient make?

Look at the following equations. There is a difference between them. The equation on the right has a −3 as a coefficient.

$$3x + 5 = 14 \qquad -3x + 5 = 14$$

> We need to use what we know about integer rules when we solve for x.

Example 1 shows the steps for solving an equation with a negative integer.

Example 1

Solve the equation using integer rules.

$$-3x + 5 = 14$$

$-3x + 5 + \boxed{-5} = 14 + \boxed{-5}$ ← We add −5 so that we get −3x by itself. We add −5 to both sides to balance the equation.

$-3x + 0 \quad = \quad 9$ ← A number plus its opposite equals 0.

$$-3x = 9$$

$\boxed{-\dfrac{1}{3}} \cdot -3x = 9 \cdot \boxed{-\dfrac{1}{3}}$ ← We multiply by $-\dfrac{1}{3}$ so that we end up with a positive x by itself. We multiply each side by $-\dfrac{1}{3}$ to keep the equation balanced.

$\dfrac{3}{3}x \quad = \quad -\dfrac{9}{3}$ ← Integer rule for multiplication: A negative times a negative is a positive. A positive times a negative is a negative.

$$1x = -3$$

$$x = -3$$ ← A number times 1 is the same number. This is the solution.

What happens when we make one more small change? Look at the following equations. Do you see the difference between them?

$$-3x + 6 = 18 \qquad -3x - 6 = 18$$

The equation on the right uses subtraction in one of the expressions. Subtraction is the same as adding the opposite. Example 2 shows the steps in solving this type of equation.

Example 2

Solve the equation using what we know about rules.

$$-3x - 6 = 18$$

$-3x + -6 = 18$ ← Subtraction is the same as adding the opposite.

$-3x + -6 \boxed{+6} = 18 \boxed{+6}$ ← We add 6 to get $-3x$ by itself. We add 6 to both sides to keep the equation balanced.

$-3x + 0 = 24$ ← A number plus its opposite equals 0.

$-3x = 24$

$\boxed{-\frac{1}{3}} \cdot -3x = 24 \cdot \boxed{-\frac{1}{3}}$ ← We multiply by $-\frac{1}{3}$ to get a positive x by itself. We multiply each side by $-\frac{1}{3}$ to keep the equation balanced.

$\frac{3}{3}x = -\frac{24}{3}$ ← Integer rule for multiplication: A negative times a negative is a positive. A positive times a negative is a negative.

$1x = -8$

$\mathbf{x = -8}$ ← A number times 1 is the same number. This is the solution.

-8
↓

$-3x - 6 = 18$
$-3 \cdot -8 - 6 = 18$
$24 - 6 = 18$
$18 = 18$

> We check the answer by substituting -8 for x in the original equation.

% ÷
≡ ·
< × **Apply Skills**
Turn to *Interactive Text*, page 289.

mBook **Reinforce Understanding**
Use the *mBook Study Guide* to review lesson concepts.

▶**Problem Solving: Using Drawings to Solve Problems**

Why are drawings important for problem solving?

Algebra word problems can be difficult to solve. Sometimes a drawing helps us better understand the problem. In this lesson, we are going to work problems involving money. We will see how to:

- start with a drawing.
- figure out how to use a variable.

Example 1

Figure out how much money is in the first jar.

Problem:

Latisha puts extra money into three jars in the kitchen.

- The second jar has twice as much money as the first jar.
- The third jar has three times as much money as the first jar.
- Latisha counted all of her money yesterday, and she has $60.

How can we use a drawing to figure out how much money is in each jar?

STEP 1

Begin with a drawing.

Draw three jars and label each one.

What do we know?   We know how much money she has.

What don't we know?   How much money is in each jar.

Jar 1	+	Jar 2	+	Jar 3	=	60
Some money		2 times Jar 1		3 times Jar 1		

STEP 2

Figure out what the variable is.

We don't know how much money is in each jar. Let's use w to represent how much is in Jar 1.

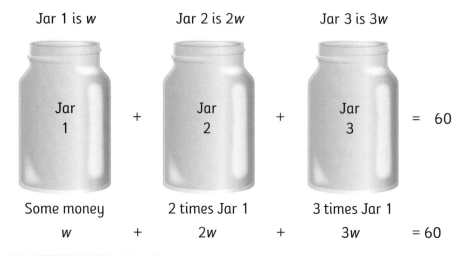

Jar 1 is w		Jar 2 is $2w$		Jar 3 is $3w$	
Jar 1	+	Jar 2	+	Jar 3	= 60
Some money		2 times Jar 1		3 times Jar 1	
w	+	$2w$	+	$3w$	= 60

STEP 3

Solve the equation.

$$w + 2w + 3w = 60$$

$$6w = 60$$

$$\frac{1}{6} \cdot 6w = 60 \cdot \frac{1}{6}$$

$$\frac{6}{6}w = \frac{60}{6}$$

$$1w = 10$$

$$w = 10$$

STEP 4

Answer the question.

Substitute 10 for w in the original equation to find out how much is in each jar.

$$\begin{array}{ccc} 10 & 10 & 10 \\ \downarrow & \downarrow & \downarrow \end{array}$$

$$w + 2w + 3w = 60$$

$$10 + 2 \cdot 10 + 3 \cdot 10 = 60$$

$$10 + 20 + 30 = 60$$

That means there is $10 in Jar 1, $20 in Jar 2, and $30 in Jar 3.

 Problem-Solving Activity
Turn to *Interactive Text*,
page 291.

 mBook Reinforce Understanding
Use the *mBook Study Guide*
to review lesson concepts.

Activity 1

Tell the next step to solve each problem.

1. $-3x + 11 = 20$
   $-3x + 11 + -11 = 20 + -11$
   $-3x = 9$

   What is the next step?

2. $-2x + 2 = 16$
   $-2x + 2 + -2 = 16 + -2$
   $-2x = 14$

   What is the next step?

Activity 2

Solve.

1. $-4x + 10 = 50$

2. $-6x + -2 = -20$

3. $-2x - 4 = 20$

Activity 3

Write the word problems using algebra, then solve. Draw a picture to help you understand the problem better.

1. Maria saves baseball cards. She has two boxes of cards. The first box has 4 times as many cards as the second box. Altogether, she has 75 cards. How many cards does she have in each box?

2. Penny and Sheldon are both working as servers in a restaurant. At the end of the evening, they count their tips. Penny has $10 less than 3 times as much money in tips as Sheldon. Altogether they have $74. How much money does each one have in tips?

Activity 4 • Distributed Practice

Solve.

1. $3(x + 4) = 12$

2. $\frac{4}{5} = \frac{w}{10}$

3. $5 + w = 0$

4. $-100 \div a = 25$

5. $\frac{1}{5} \cdot z = 1$

6. $4(x - 3) = 4$

Problem Solving:
▶**Rate Problems**

▶**Variables on Both Sides of the Equal Sign**

What do we do about variables in each expression?

Look at the following equations. There is a difference between them.

$$2x - 3 = 17 \qquad 2x - 3 = x + 17$$

The second equation has a variable to the right of the equal sign. Remember our goal. We want to have a positive x by itself on the left side of the equal sign.

Example 1

Solve the equation using what we know about opposites.

$2x - 3 = x + 17$

$2x + -3 = x + 17$ ← Subtraction is the same as adding the opposite.

$2x + -3 \; \boxed{+\, 3} = x + 17 \; \boxed{+\, 3}$ ← We add 3 to get $2x$ by itself. We add 3 to both sides to keep the equation balanced.

$2x + 0 \quad = \quad x + 17 + 3$ ← A number plus its opposite equals 0.

$2x \quad = \quad x + 20$

$\boxed{-x} + 2x = \boxed{-x} + x + 20$ ← We add $-x$ to cancel out the x on the right side of the equation. We add $-x$ to each side to keep the equation balanced.

$x \quad = \quad 0 + 20$ ← A variable plus its opposite equals 0.

$x = 20$

Sometimes, equations like the one in Example 1 can be solved in more than one way. In fact, it is important in algebra to be flexible.

Example 2 uses the same equation. This time we start by cancelling out the *x* on the right side. We end up with the same answer.

Example 2

Find another way to solve the same equation.

$$2x - 3 = x + 17$$

$$\boxed{-x} + 2x - 3 = \boxed{-x} + x + 17 \qquad \leftarrow$$

We add −*x* to cancel out the *x* on the right side of the equation. We add −*x* to each side to keep the equation balanced.

$$x - 3 \quad = \quad 0 + 17$$

$$x - 3 = 17$$

$$x \boxed{+} -3 = 17 \qquad \leftarrow$$

Subtraction is the same as adding the opposite.

$$x + -3 \boxed{+ 3} = 17 \boxed{+ 3} \qquad \leftarrow$$

We add 3 to get *x* by itself. We add 3 to both sides to keep the equation balanced.

$$x + 0 \quad = \quad 20 \qquad \leftarrow$$

A number plus its opposite equals 0.

$$x = 20$$

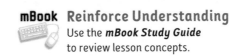

**%÷
<x** **Apply Skills**
Turn to *Interactive Text*, page 294.

mBook **Reinforce Understanding**
Use the *mBook Study Guide* to review lesson concepts.

▶Problem Solving: **Rate Problems**

How do we use drawings to solve rate problems?

In the previous unit we learned how to do simple rate problems. The formula used in a simple rate problem is this equation:

> **Rate Formula**
> $r \cdot t = d$

r = rate $\qquad$ t = time $\qquad$ d = distance

A rate problem can be more complicated than the one where we just substitute for one of the unknown variables.

To solve a complicated problem, it often helps to make a drawing to represent what is going on in the problem.

Let's use the four steps to solve a problem.

Example 1

Use a drawing to solve the problem.

Problem:

Two planes take off from an airport at the same time going opposite directions. One plane is flying 150 miles per hour. The second plane is flying 350 miles per hour. How long will it take them to be 1,000 miles apart?

STEP 1

Begin with a drawing.

Plane 1 $\qquad\qquad\qquad$ Plane 2

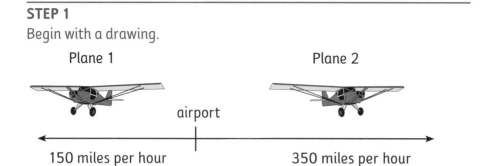

airport

150 miles per hour $\qquad\qquad$ 350 miles per hour

STEP 2

Figure out what the variable is.

We use a variable for something we don't know. The question asks how long it will take the planes to be 1,000 miles apart. That means we do not know the time.

Let's use the variable k to represent the time.

Both planes will be flying for the same amount of time, so we use the variable to show rate times time.

	$r \cdot t$
	$\downarrow \quad \downarrow$
Plane 1	$150k$
Plane 2	$350k$

We put this information into the basic rate equation:

$r \cdot t = d.$

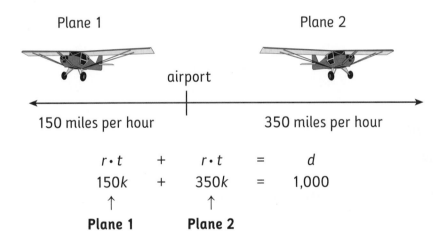

Plane 1   Plane 2

airport

150 miles per hour   350 miles per hour

$$r \cdot t \quad + \quad r \cdot t \quad = \quad d$$
$$150k \quad + \quad 350k \quad = \quad 1{,}000$$
$$\uparrow \qquad\qquad \uparrow$$

    Plane 1   **Plane 2**

STEP 3

Solve the equation.

$$150k + 350k = 1{,}000$$

$$500k = 1{,}000$$

$$\frac{1}{500} \cdot 500k = 1{,}000 \cdot \frac{1}{500}$$

$$\frac{500}{500}k = \frac{1{,}000}{500}$$

$$1k = 2$$

$$k = 2$$

STEP 4

Answer the question.

We substitute the value for k in the original equation to check the answer to our equation and to answer the question asked in the problem.

$$
\begin{array}{cc}
2 & 2 \\
\downarrow & \downarrow
\end{array}
$$

$$150k + 350k = 1{,}000$$

$$150 \cdot 2 + 350 \cdot 2 = 1{,}000$$

$$300 + 700 = 1{,}000$$

$$1{,}000 = 1{,}000$$

The planes will be 1,000 miles apart after 2 hours.

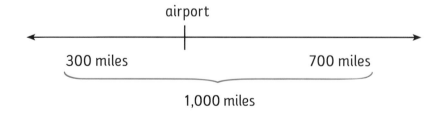

airport

300 miles   700 miles

1,000 miles

Problem-Solving Activity
Turn to *Interactive Text*,
page 296.

mBook Reinforce Understanding
Use the *mBook Study Guide*
to review lesson concepts.

Activity 1

For each problem, select the two different ways you could start solving them (choose two answers).

1. $2x + 7 = -x + 5$
   - (a) Add x to each side.
   - (b) Add -5 to each side.
   - (c) Divide each side by 7.
   - (d) Multiply each side by 2.

2. $y - 8 = 12 + 2y$
   - (a) Multiply each side by 2.
   - (b) Add 8 to each side.
   - (c) Add $-y$ to each side.
   - (d) Add 12 to each side.

Activity 2

Solve.

1. $a + 10 = 2a - 2$

2. $4 - 2b = b + 1$

3. $-3 - c = c + 2$

4. $x - 4 = 3x + 8$

Activity 3

Solve the rate problems using the formula $r \cdot t = d$.

1. Raj's family was traveling at about 60 mph to visit cousins living 100 miles away. About how long will it take them to get there?

2. If a satellite is 4,000 miles away from its target and it is traveling 200 miles per minute, how many minutes before it reaches its target?

Activity 4 • Distributed Practice

Solve.

1. $-5 - -2 = y$

2. $-18 + w = 2$

3. $\frac{1}{3} \cdot z = 1$

4. $\frac{5}{7} = \frac{h}{42}$

5. $4,000 = 200t$

6. $12 = 3(a + 2)$

▶**The Distributive Property in Equations**

How does the distributive property work in equations?

Look at the following equations. There is a difference between them.

$$2x + 4 = 18 \qquad 2(x + 4) = 18$$

The equation on the right contains parentheses.

We learned about expressions with parentheses when we worked with the distributive property. Let's stop and think about how to approach expressions like these.

What we know:

- We cannot combine terms that are different or unlike terms. In this case, we cannot combine the $2x$ and the 4.

$$2x + 4$$

The Distributive Property and Expressions

- We can "distribute" the 2 to each term when we simplify the expression. We multiply 2 times both terms inside of the parentheses.

$$2(x + 4)$$
$$2x + 8$$

Now let's use what we know about the distributive property to help solve equations.

Once we use the property, all we have to do is use the other rules and properties in our Algebra Toolbox.

Example 1

Use the distributive property to solve the equation.

$$2(x + 4) = 18$$
$$2x + 8 = 18 \qquad \leftarrow \quad \text{The distributive property: } 2 \cdot x = 2x \text{ and } 2 \cdot 4 = 8.$$

$$2x + 8 + \boxed{-8} = 18 + \boxed{-8} \qquad \leftarrow \quad \text{We add } -8 \text{ to cancel out the 8 on the left side of the equation. We add } -8 \text{ to each side to keep the equation balanced.}$$

$$2x + 0 \quad = \quad 10$$

$$2x = 10$$

$$\boxed{\tfrac{1}{2}} \cdot 2x = 10 \cdot \boxed{\tfrac{1}{2}} \qquad \leftarrow \quad \text{We multiply by } \tfrac{1}{2} \text{ to get } x \text{ by itself. We multiply each side by } \tfrac{1}{2} \text{ to keep the equation balanced.}$$

$$\tfrac{2}{2}x \quad = \quad \tfrac{10}{2}$$

$$1x = 5$$

$$x = 5 \qquad \leftarrow \quad \text{A number times 1 is the same number.}$$

Notice what happens when we substitute for x in the original equation. We can add inside of the parentheses because both terms are the same. They are like terms.

5
↓

$2(x + 4) = 18$ ←   We substitute 5 for x.

$2(5 + 4) = 18$ ←   We add $5 + 4$ because they are like terms.

$2(9) = 18$ ←   The equation $2(9)$ is the same as $2 \cdot 9$.

$2 \cdot 9 = 18$ ←   The numbers are the same.

$18 = 18$

We see two important ideas in Example 1:

- First, we begin by checking what is inside of the parentheses. If they are like terms, we combine them. If they are unlike terms, we cannot do anything.
- Second, we have to distribute the term on the outside across all terms that are inside of the parentheses.

Let's look at another example.

Example 2

Use the distributive property to solve the equation.

$5(2x - 1) = 25$

$10x - 5 = 25$ ←   The distributive property: $5 \cdot 2x = 10x$ and $5 \cdot 1 = 5$.

$10x + {-5} = 25$ ←   Subtraction is the same as adding the opposite.

$10x + {-5} \;{+5} = 25 \;{+5}$ ←   We add 5 to cancel out the 5 on the left side of the equation. We add 5 to each side to keep the equation balanced.

$10x + 0 \;\; = \;\; 30$

$10x = 30$

$\frac{1}{10} \cdot 10x = 30 \cdot \frac{1}{10}$ ←   We multiply by $\frac{1}{10}$ to get x by itself. We multiply each side by $\frac{1}{10}$ to keep the equation balanced.

$\frac{10}{10}x = \frac{30}{10}$

$1x = 3$

$x = 3$ ←   A number times 1 is the same number.

Remember what happens when we substitute for x in the original equation. We can add inside of the parentheses because both terms are now the same. They are like terms.

3

$\downarrow$

$5(2x - 1) = 25$

$5(6 - 1) = 25$ ←   We substitute 3 for x and $3 \cdot 2 = 6$.

$5(5) = 25$ ←   We subtract $6 - 1$ because they are like terms.

$5 \cdot 5 = 25$ ←   The equation $5(5)$ is the same as $5 \cdot 5$.

$25 = 25$ ←   The numbers are the same.

%÷
=
< x   **Apply Skills**
Turn to *Interactive Text*,
page 299.

mBook Reinforce Understanding
Use the *mBook Study Guide*
to review lesson concepts.

▶**Problem Solving: Angles and Intersecting Lines**

What is the relationship between angles and intersecting lines?

Let's look at the properties of a rectangle.

Properties of a Rectangle

- Not all of the sides are equal in length.
- The opposite sides of rectangle are parallel.
- Every interior angle measures 90 degrees. That is what the little square stands for in each angle.

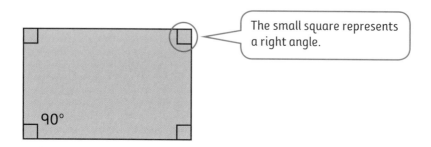

The small square represents a right angle.

90°

What happens when we extend the sides of a rectangle as shown in the next figure?

∠2, ∠3, and ∠4 are exterior angles to the rectangle.

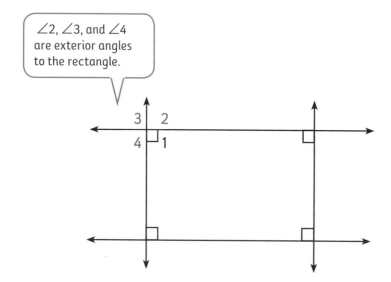

How do we find the measure of exterior angles?

By extending the sides of the rectangle, we created exterior angles. How do we find the measures of the exterior angles 2, 3, and 4?

We need to remember one important property of straight lines to answer this question:

- The measure of any straight line is 180 degrees.

Let's look closely at the corner of the rectangle and especially at the intersecting lines. We added labels to the line segments so that we can talk about them.

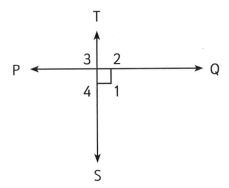

Example 1 shows how we find the measures of the exterior angles.

Example 1

Find the measures of ∠2, ∠3, and ∠4.

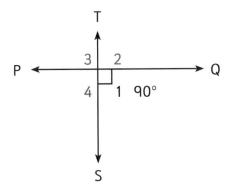

First, what is the measure of ∠2?

The vertical line ST has ∠1 and ∠2.

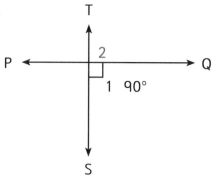

- We know that ∠1 = 90 degrees.
- We also know that line ST measures 180 degrees.
- Let x = the measure of ∠2.

$$x + 90 = 180$$
$$x + 90 + -90 = 180 + -90$$
$$x + 0 = 90$$
$$x = 90$$

The measure of ∠2 = 90°

What is the measure of ∠3?

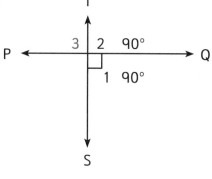

- We know that ∠2 = 90 degrees.
- We know the line PQ is straight so it measures 180 degrees.
- Let y = the measure of ∠3.

$$y + 90 = 180$$
$$y + 90 + -90 = 180 + -90$$
$$y + 0 = 90$$
$$y = 90$$

The measure of ∠3 = 90°

What is the measure of ∠4?

- We can use either line PQ or line ST to figure out the measure of ∠4.

- If we add angles 1, 2, and 3 we get 270 degrees.

- We know that the sum of the measurements of angles 1, 2, 3, and 4 is 360 degrees.

- Let's see why the measure of ∠4 is 90 degrees. We know that the measure of ∠4 must be 360° − 270° = 90°.

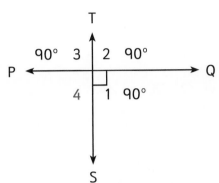

When we extend the sides of a trapezoid, the same thing happens. We create exterior angles. In the picture below, the exterior angles are labeled ∠2, ∠3, and ∠4.

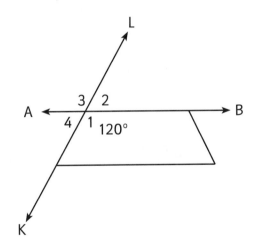

In Example 2 we find the measures of the exterior angles for the upper left corner of a trapezoid.

Example 2

Find the measures of ∠2, ∠3, and ∠4.

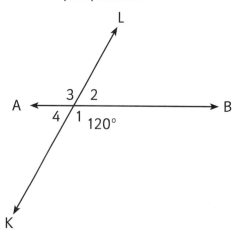

We know that lines AB and KL are straight lines. That means these lines measure 180 degrees.

What is the measure of ∠2?

Let x = the measure of ∠2.

$$x + 120 = 180$$
$$x + 120 + -120 = 180 + -120$$
$$x + 0 = 60$$
$$x = 60$$

The measure of ∠2 = 60°

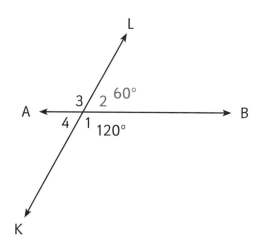

What is the measure of ∠3?

- Let y = the measure of ∠3.
- We know that ∠2 = 60°.

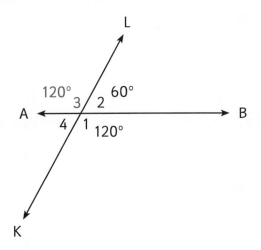

$$y + 60 = 180$$
$$y + 60 + -60 = 180 + -60$$
$$y + 0 = 120$$
$$y = 120$$

The measure of ∠3 = 120°

What is the measure of ∠4?

Repeating the process will help us figure out the measure of ∠4.

We know that ∠2 = 60° and that ∠3 = 120°.

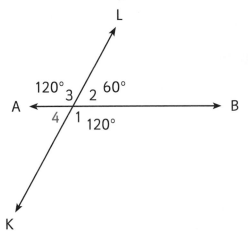

- We can use either line AB or line KL to figure out the measure of ∠4.
- We know that the measure of ∠4 = 60 degrees because ∠1 + ∠2 + ∠3 = 300.

$$300 + 60 = 360$$

Problem-Solving Activity
Turn to *Interactive Text*, page 300.

mBook **Reinforce Understanding**
Use the *mBook Study Guide* to review lesson concepts.

Activity 1

For each problem, answer "yes" if you can combine the terms inside the parentheses and "no" if you cannot.

1. $2(x + 4) = 6$
2. $4x = 3(4 + 5)$
3. $3(x + 2x) = 12$
4. $15 = 3(x + 3)$
5. $20 = 2(4 + w)$
6. $2(2 + 4) = 2x$

Activity 2

Solve.

1. $2(a + 1) = 6$
2. $24 = 3(b + 1)$
3. $25 = 5(1 + x)$
4. $-2(-z - 3) = 18$

Activity 3

Find the missing angles using the diagram.

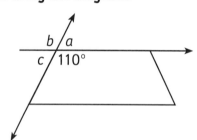

1. What is the measure of $\angle a$?

2. What is the measure of $\angle b$?

3. What is the measure of $\angle c$?

Activity 4 • Distributed Practice

Solve.

1. $\frac{a}{2} = \frac{10}{4}$
2. $2(2 - y) = -12$
3. $x + 5 = 0$
4. $y = -12 + -17$
5. $-12 = 2t$
6. $-5 + w = -12$

▶**Flexibility and the Distributive Property**

What is another way to solve an algebra equation?

In the last lesson, we learned how to solve equations using the distributive property. Two ideas were important:

- We cannot combine terms inside of the parentheses if they are not like terms.
- We must distribute what is outside of the parentheses over both terms inside the parentheses.

Example 1 is a reminder of how we use the distributive property.

Example 1

Solve the equation using the distributive property.

$8(x - 1) = 24$

$8x - 8 = 24$ ← The distributive property: $8 \cdot x = 8x$ and $8 \cdot 1 = 8$.

$8x + -8 = 24$ ← Subtraction is the same as adding the opposite.

$8x + -8 \boxed{+ 8} = 24 \boxed{+ 8}$ ← We add 8 to cancel out the 8 on the left side of the equation. We add 8 to each side to keep the equation balanced.

$8x + 0 = 32$

$8x = 32$

$$\frac{1}{8} \cdot 8x = 32 \cdot \frac{1}{8}$$

← We multiply by $\frac{1}{8}$ to get x by itself. We multiply each side by $\frac{1}{8}$ to keep the equation balanced.

$$\frac{8}{8}x = \frac{32}{8}$$

$$1x = 4$$

$$x = 4$$

Distributing the number outside of the parentheses is one way to solve this problem. But we can also solve it another way.

To get the same solution, we use the rules and properties in our Algebra Toolbox.

Example 2

Use rules and properties other than the distributive property to solve the equation.

$$8(x - 1) = 24$$

$$\frac{1}{8} \cdot 8(x - 1) = 24 \cdot \frac{1}{8}$$

← We multiply by $\frac{1}{8}$ to get x by itself. We multiply each side by $\frac{1}{8}$ to keep the equation balanced.

$$\frac{8}{8}(x - 1) = \frac{24}{8}$$

$$1(x - 1) = 3$$

$$(x - 1) = 3$$ ← A number times 1 is the same number.

$$x - 1 = 3$$ ← Remove the parentheses.

$$x + -1 = 3$$ ← Subtraction is the same as adding the opposite.

$$x + -1 \boxed{+1} = 3 \boxed{+1}$$ ← We add 1 to cancel out the −1 on the left side of the equation. We add 1 to each side to keep the equation balanced.

$$x + 0 = 4$$

$$x = 4$$

This is the same answer we got in Example 1.

Example 2 reminds us that the 8 outside of $(x - 1)$ is a coefficient. This means it is like the 5 in $5a$.

That means we can use its reciprocal to change it to 1.

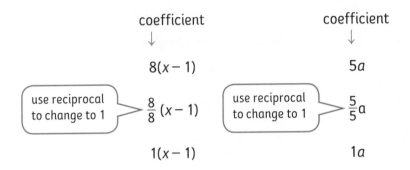

coefficient   coefficient
↓   ↓
$8(x - 1)$ $5a$

use reciprocal to change to 1 → $\frac{8}{8}(x - 1)$ use reciprocal to change to 1 → $\frac{5}{5}a$

$1(x - 1)$ $1a$

%÷
=
<× **Apply Skills**
Turn to *Interactive Text*,
page 303.

mBook **Reinforce Understanding**
Use the *mBook Study Guide*
to review lesson concepts.

▶**Problem Solving: Angles and Parallel Lines**

How do parallel lines help us understand angles?

In the previous lesson, we worked with different kinds of quadrilaterals. We extended lines from the sides of quadrilaterals so that we could find properties of intersecting lines. Let's review what we learned and look at some important definitions and rules.

Vertical Angles	Supplementary Angles
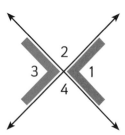	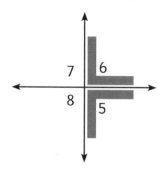
Two angles whose sides are opposite rays.	**The sum of two angles is 180 degrees.**
$\angle 1 = \angle 3$	$\angle 6 = \angle 8$
$\angle 2 = \angle 4$	$\angle 5 = \angle 7$
Angle 1 and angle 3 are vertical angles because the point of intersection makes rays for each angle. They are opposite each other.	Angle 5 and angle 6 are supplementary. When we combine the angles, they form a straight line. We know a straight line measures 180 degrees.

Vertical Angles Rule

The measures of vertical angles are equal.

We proved this in the previous lesson using algebra.

Let's look at parallelograms.

This quadrilateral has opposite sides that are parallel. Working with this shape helps us see how to make inferences about angles on parallel lines.

We begin by extending lines along each side of the parallelogram.

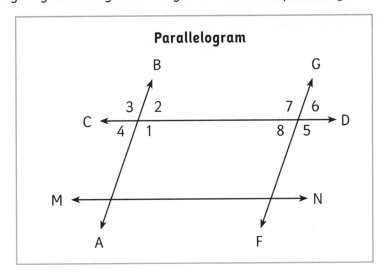

Parallelogram

Lines AB and FG are parallel. That means we could move AB over and put it on top of FG and it would be at the same line. If that is true, then ∠1, ∠2, ∠3, and ∠4 would fit on top of ∠5, ∠6, ∠7, and ∠8.

This means that when we have parallel lines and a straight line that intersects the two lines, the angles that are in the same position are equal.

In this case,

- measure of ∠1 = measure of ∠5
- measure of ∠2 = measure of ∠6
- measure of ∠3 = measure of ∠7
- measure of ∠4 = measure of ∠8

When two lines are crossed by another line, like CD on the previous page, they form angles that match or are in the same position.

Because ∠1 and ∠5 below are corresponding angles, we know that the measure of angle 1 = the measure of angle 5.

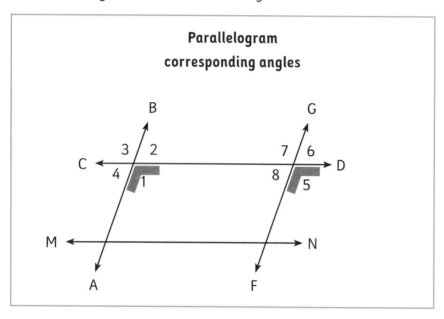

Parallelogram
corresponding angles

Corresponding Angle Rule

When two parallel lines (like AB and FG) are crossed by another line (like CD), the angles formed have equal measurement.

We use this understanding to make inferences. We figure out the measure of one angle based on another angle in a different position. Example 1 shows us how this is done.

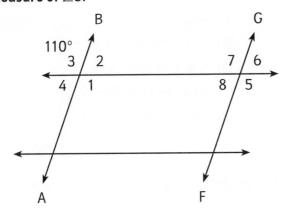

Example 1

Find the measure of ∠5.

Notice that ∠3 = 110 degrees.

We figure out the measure of ∠5 by making an inference. It is based on two rules:

- The vertical angles rule.
- The corresponding angles rule.

We know that:

- the measure of ∠3 = 110°

We infer that:

- the measure of ∠3 = the measure of ∠1 (vertical angles rule)
- the measure of ∠1 = the measure of ∠5 (corresponding angles rule)

This means that:

- the measure of ∠3 = the measure of ∠5
- the measure of ∠5 = 110°

Problem-Solving Activity
Turn to *Interactive Text*,
page 305.

mBook Reinforce Understanding
Use the *mBook Study Guide*
to review lesson concepts.

Activity 1

Select two different ways you could start solving the problems (choose two answers).

1. $-2(x + 4) = 6$
   (a) Add $\frac{1}{6}$ to each side.
   (b) Multiply each side by $-\frac{1}{2}$.
   (c) Distribute to get $-2x + -8$.
   (d) Multiply each side by $\frac{1}{4}$.

2. $8 = 4(y - 2)$
   (a) Distribute to get $4y - 8$.
   (b) Add $\frac{1}{8}$ to both sides.
   (c) Multiply each side by $\frac{1}{4}$.
   (d) Multiply each side by $-\frac{1}{4}$.

Activity 2

Solve the problems. Use the distributive property for problems 1 and 2. Use the reciprocal for problems 3 and 4.

1. $3(a + 1) = 9$

2. $35 = 5(b + 1)$

3. $30 = 5(1 + x)$

4. $-2(-z - 3) = -14$

Activity 3

Find the missing angles using the diagram.

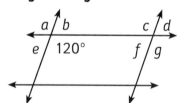

1. What is the measure of $\angle a$?

2. What is the measure of $\angle c$?

3. What is the measure of $\angle f$?

Activity 4 • Distributed Practice

Solve.

1. $2w = 6,000$

2. $\frac{a}{10} = \frac{2}{5}$

3. $\frac{1}{5} \cdot b = 1$

4. $0 = 4 + x$

5. $-15 \div z = 5$

6. $3(x + 1) = 27$

▶**Area Formulas and Algebraic Equations**

How do we use the distributive property in geometry?

Simple algebraic formulas are used to describe the area of two-dimensional shapes.

The three shapes below use base and height to calculate area.

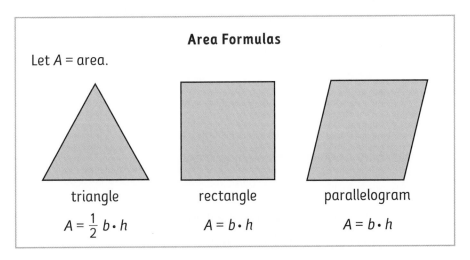

Area Formulas

Let A = area.

triangle
$A = \frac{1}{2} b \cdot h$

rectangle
$A = b \cdot h$

parallelogram
$A = b \cdot h$

Now that we know how to solve simple algebra equations, we can find more than just the area of two-dimensional shapes using base and height.

Example 1 and Example 2 show that for a two-dimensional object, we can find:

- the base if we know the height and area.
- the height if we know the base and area.
- the area if we know the base and height.

Example 1

Find the base of the triangle if the area of the triangle is 24 in².

We know:

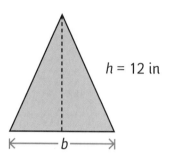

$h = 12$ in

- the height of the triangle is 12 inches.
- the area of the triangle is 24 square inches.
- $A = \frac{1}{2}b \cdot h$.

We begin by substituting the information we are given.

$$24 \quad\quad 12$$
$$\downarrow \quad\quad\quad \downarrow$$

$$A = \frac{1}{2}b \cdot h$$

$$24 = \frac{1}{2}b \cdot 12$$

$$24 = \frac{1}{2} \cdot 12 \cdot b \leftarrow$$ We use the commutative property to reorder the equation so we can combine $\frac{1}{2}$ and 12.

$$24 = 6b$$

$$\frac{1}{6} \cdot 24 = \frac{1}{6} \cdot 6b \leftarrow$$ We multiply by $\frac{1}{6}$ to get b by itself. We multiply each side by $\frac{1}{6}$ to keep the equation balanced.

$$\frac{24}{6} = \frac{6}{6}b$$

$$4 = 1b$$

$$4 = b$$

The base of the triangle = 4 inches.

Example 2

**Find the height of the parallelogram if the area of
the parellelogram is 80 in².**

We know:

- the base of the parallelogram is
  10 inches.
- the area of the parallelogram is
  80 square inches.
- $A = b \cdot h$.

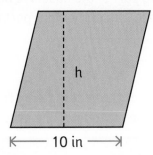

$\longleftarrow$ 10 in $\longrightarrow$

We begin by substituting the information we are given.

$$\underset{\downarrow}{80} \quad \underset{\downarrow}{10}$$

$$A = b \cdot h$$

$$80 = 10 \cdot h$$

$$80 = 10h \qquad \leftarrow \quad \text{The expression } 10h \text{ is the same as } 10 \cdot h.$$

$$\frac{1}{10} \cdot 80 = \frac{1}{10} \cdot 10h \quad \leftarrow \quad \text{We multiply by } \frac{1}{10} \text{ to get } h \text{ by itself. We}$$
$$\text{multiply each side by } \frac{1}{10} \text{ to keep the}$$
$$\text{equation balanced.}$$

$$\frac{80}{10} = \frac{10}{10}h$$

$$8 = 1h$$

$$8 = h$$

The height of the parallelogram is 8 inches.

Rectangles present another way to use what we have learned about algebra.

Example 3 shows a rectangle broken into two parts. We are given the measure for only part of the base. We must use the distributive property to find the length of the right part of the base.

Example 3

Find the base length of the rectangle by first finding the base length of the right side of the rectangle. The area of the rectangle is 40 in².

4 in

7 in   x

We know:

- the area of the rectangle is 40 square inches.
- the height is 4 inches.
- the base is $7 + x$ inches.
- $A = b \cdot h$.

So that we do not make a mistake in the order of operations, we put the base in parentheses.

We begin by substituting the information we are given.

$$
\begin{array}{ccc}
40 & (x+7)4 & \\
\downarrow & \downarrow & \downarrow \\
A & = b \cdot & h \\
40 & = (x+7) & 4
\end{array}
$$

There are two methods we can use to figure out the base of the rectangle.

- Method 1 uses the commutative property.
- Method 2 uses the distributive property.

Method 1: Using the Commutative Property

$$40 = (x + 7)4$$

$40 = 4(x + 7)$ ← We use the commutative property so that the coefficient is in front of the parentheses.

$\frac{1}{4} \cdot 40 = \frac{1}{4} \cdot 4(x + 7)$ ← We multiply by $\frac{1}{4}$ so that we get x by itself. We multiply each side by $\frac{1}{4}$ to keep the equation balanced.

$\frac{40}{4} = \frac{4}{4}(x + 7)$

$10 = 1(x + 7)$

$10 = (x + 7)$ ← A number times 1 is the same number.

$10 = x + 7$ ← Remove the parentheses.

$-7 + 10 = x + 7 + -7$ ← We add −7 to cancel out the 7 on the right side of the equation. We add −7 to each side to keep the equation balanced.

$3 = x + 0$

$3 = x$

The missing part of the base for the rectangle is 3 inches.

Remember what the question is asking for. We need to find the base.

The base of the rectangle is 3 + 7 or 10 inches.

Method 2: Using the Distributive Property

$$40 = (x + 7)4$$

$40 = 4(x + 7)$ ←   We use the commutative property so that the coefficient is in front of the parentheses.

$40 = 4x + 28$ ←   Distributive property: $4 \cdot x = 4x$ and $4 \cdot 7 = 28$.

$\boxed{-28} + 40 = 4x + 28 + \boxed{-28}$ ←   We add −28 to cancel out the 28 on the right side of the equation. We add −28 to each side to keep the equation balanced.

$$12 \quad = \quad 4x + 0$$

$$12 = 4x$$

$\dfrac{1}{4} \cdot 12 = \dfrac{1}{4} \cdot 4x$ ←   We multiply by $\dfrac{1}{4}$ to get x by itself. We multiply each side by $\dfrac{1}{4}$ to keep the equation balanced.

$$\dfrac{12}{4} = \dfrac{4}{4}x$$

$$3 = 1x$$

$$3 = x$$

This solution gives us the same answer for the part of the rectangle that is missing. The missing part of the rectangle is 3 inches.

The base of the rectangle is 3 + 7 or 10 inches.

% ÷
= ×
< X   **Apply Skills**
Turn to *Interactive Text*, page 308.

Monitoring Progress
Quiz 2

mBook   **Reinforce Understanding**
Use the *mBook Study Guide* to review lesson concepts.

Activity 1

Solve.

1. $A = 5 \cdot 7$
2. $P = 2 \cdot 4 + 2 \cdot 8$
3. $A = \frac{1}{2} \cdot 3 \cdot 2$
4. $5^2 = A$
5. $A = 2(x + 2)$
6. $A = 4 \cdot 6$

Activity 2

Use the area formula for a rectangle, $A = b \cdot h$, to solve the problems.

1. What is the length of the base of this rectangle if its area is 20 square inches?

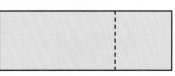

2 in   4 in b

2. What is the height of this rectangle if its area is 40 square inches?

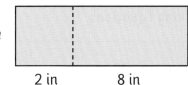

n 2 in   8 in

Activity 3

Use the area formula for a triangle, $A = \frac{1}{2} \cdot b \cdot h$, to solve the problems.

1. What is the length of the base of this triangle if its area is 10 square units?

5
b

2. What is the height of this triangle if its area is 12 square units?

h
3

Activity 4 • Distributed Practice

Solve.

1. $\frac{2}{a} = \frac{4}{6}$
2. $-54 \div y = -6$
3. $\frac{2}{3} \cdot c = 1$
4. $-\frac{1}{2} + w = 0$
5. $-4 + z = -8$
6. $14 = 2(x + 6)$

▶**Commutative and Associative Properties**

What do we do when equations look complicated?

It's important to have a flexible approach for solving algebraic equations. Often, we try to memorize just one way to solve an equation, then get stuck when we run into an equation that is slightly different.

Here are the four main steps we use.

Steps for Solving Equations

STEP 1
Look at the entire equation.

STEP 2
Look for the **parts** of the equation that seem different.

STEP 3
Remember the goal: Solve the equation so that we have a **positive variable on one side**.

STEP 4
Use the rules or properties we need to reach our goal.

The equation in Example 1 looks complicated because the expression on the left side is long. We use the commutative property to change the equation and make it easier to solve.

Example 1

Use the commutative property to make it easier to solve the equation.

$2x + 3 + 5x - 4 = 13$

$2x + 5x + 3 - 4 = 13$ ←   We use the commutative property to put like terms next to each other.

$2x + 5x + 3 + -4 = 13$ ←   Subtraction is the same as adding the opposite.

$7x + -1 = 13$ ←   We combine like terms.

$7x + -1 \boxed{+1} = 13 \boxed{+1}$ ←   We add 1 to cancel out the −1 on the left side of the equation. We add 1 to each side to balance the equation.

$7x + 0 = 14$

$7x = 14$

$\boxed{\frac{1}{7}} \cdot 7x = \boxed{\frac{1}{7}} \cdot 14$ ←   We multiply by $\frac{1}{7}$ to get x by itself. We multiply each side by $\frac{1}{7}$ to balance the equation.

$\frac{7}{7}x = \frac{14}{7}$

$1x = 2$

$x = 2$

% ÷ Apply Skills
< x   Turn to *Interactive Text*, page 310.

mBook Reinforce Understanding
Use the *mBook Study Guide* to review lesson concepts.

▶**Problem Solving: Proving Angles Are Equal**

What does it mean to prove something in geometry?

Throughout this unit we have been following a series of steps to solve algebraic equations.

The previous example showed how we solved an equation. For most of the steps, we described the rule or property from the Algebra Toolbox that explains the reason behind the step.

We can do something similar in geometry, and the process is called a **proof**. When we do a proof, we show the steps we use to make an inference about something.

Another property we need to learn to help us do this is the **transitive property**. This property is an easy way to show how different objects are related to each other.

Let's imagine three people: Cara, Gabriella, and Ramon. Let's say we know that Cara is the same height as Gabriella, and Gabriella is the same height as Ramon. We use this information to say that Cara and Ramon are the same height. The transitive property looks like this.

The Transitive Property

| Cara is the same height as Gabriella. | Ramon is the same height as Gabriella. | Therefore, Cara is the same height as Ramon. |

| Cara = Gabriella | Gabriella = Ramon | Cara = Ramon |

How do we use inferences in proofs?

Example 1 shows a line that cuts across two parallel lines. This line is called a **transversal** . The transversal can cut across the lines at any angle. We can prove that the angles created by the transversal line are equal by using the rules we have learned in previous lessons.

No measurements are given in Example 1. However, we can make inferences to prove that details about the angles are true. We don't need to use numbers. We will just use rules and properties.

Example 1

Use an inference to prove that ∠2 and ∠8 are equal.

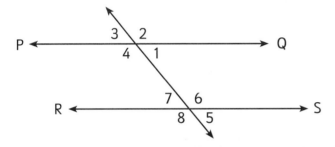

Proof	
Steps	**Reasons**
measure of ∠2 = measure of ∠4	Vertical Angles Rule
measure of ∠4 = measure of ∠8	Corresponding Angles Rule
measure of ∠2 = measure of ∠8	Transitive Property

> Remember the example of Cara, Gabriella, and Ramon when using the transitive property.

We can extend our thinking to more complicated problems. Example 2 shows how we make inferences to prove that different angles on a parallelogram are equal.

Example 2

Use an inference to prove that ∠1 and ∠11 are equal.

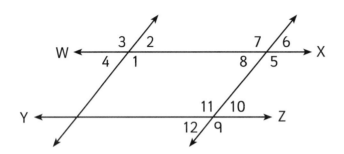

Proof	
Steps	**Reasons**
measure of ∠1 = measure of ∠3	Vertical Angles Rule
measure of ∠3 = measure of ∠7	Corresponding Angles Rule
measure of ∠7 = measure of ∠11	Corresponding Angles Rule
measure of ∠1 = measure of ∠11	Transitive Property

Problem-Solving Activity
Turn to *Interactive Text*, page 311.

mBook Reinforce Understanding
Use the *mBook Study Guide* to review lesson concepts.

Activity 1

Combine like terms using the commutative and associative properties in the expressions.

1. $x + 7 + x$
2. $-4 + y + -8$
3. $-w + 11 + 2w$
4. $6 + -a - 3$
5. $-2m + 4 + -3m + 6$
6. $8 + n + 2 + -3$

Activity 2

Solve.

1. $18 = 2x + -3 + -2x + 3x$
2. $3 + w + -7 = 21$
3. $a + 2a + -3 + a = 20$
4. $4 + b + -2 + 2b = 8 + b$

Activity 3

Tell the reasons for each of the steps proving that $\angle 1$ and $\angle 11$ are equal.

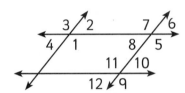

Proof	
Steps	Reasons
1. measure of $\angle 1$ = measure of $\angle 3$	
2. measure of $\angle 3$ = measure of $\angle 7$	
3. measure of $\angle 7$ = measure of $\angle 11$	
4. measure of $\angle 1$ = measure of $\angle 11$	

Activity 4 • Distributed Practice

Solve.

1. $x \cdot \frac{4}{3} = 1$
2. $-9 \cdot -8 = m$
3. $a + -1.2 = 0$
4. $\frac{z}{15} = \frac{3}{5}$
5. $-27 + b = 30$
6. $15 = 3(m + 1)$

▸**Fractions as Coefficients**

How do we solve an equation when the coefficient is a fraction?

Let's look at the following two equations. There is a difference between them.

$$2x + 4 = 20 \qquad \tfrac{1}{2}x + 4 = 20$$

The equation on the right has a fraction as a coefficient. This might look like a big change, but it doesn't make that much of a difference. We use the same rules and properties from our Algebra Toolbox to solve for x.

Example 1

Solve each equation.

$$\tfrac{1}{2}x + 4 = 20$$

$$\tfrac{1}{2}x + 4 + \boxed{-4} = 20 + \boxed{-4} \quad \leftarrow \quad$$ We add -4 to get x by itself. We add -4 to both sides to keep the equation balanced.

$$\tfrac{1}{2}x + 0 \quad = \quad 16$$

$$\tfrac{1}{2}x = 16$$

$$\boxed{2} \cdot \tfrac{1}{2}x = 16 \cdot \boxed{2} \quad \leftarrow \quad$$ We multiply by 2 to get a positive x by itself. We multiply each side by 2 to keep the equation balanced.

$$\tfrac{2}{2}x \quad = \quad 32$$

$$1x = 32$$

$$x = 32$$

We use the same kind of thinking when we work equations that involve the distributive property.

We get rid of the fraction coefficient by using a reciprocal. This method makes solving the equation much easier.

Example 2

Solve the equation using the distributive property.

$$\frac{4}{3}(x + 1) = 8$$

$$\frac{3}{4} \cdot \frac{4}{3}(x + 1) = 8 \cdot \frac{3}{4}$$ ← We multiply by $\frac{3}{4}$ to get a positive x by itself. We multiply each side by $\frac{3}{4}$ to keep the equation balanced.

$$\frac{12}{12}(x + 1) = \frac{24}{4}$$

$$1(x + 1) = 6$$

$$(x + 1) = 6$$ ← A number (or a quantity) times 1 is the same number.

$$x + 1 = 6$$

$$x + 1 + \boxed{-1} = 6 + \boxed{-1}$$ ← We add −1 to get x by itself. We add −1 to both sides to keep the equation balanced.

$$x + 0 = 5$$

$$x = 5$$

% ÷
= x
< x **Apply Skills**
Turn to *Interactive Text*, page 314.

 **mBook Reinforce Understanding**
Use the *mBook Study Guide* to review lesson concepts.

▶**Problem Solving: Making Inferences in Geometry**

How do we figure out the measure of unknown angles?

We learned about proof and inference in geometry. We learned about rules and properties that help us make inferences in geometry.

Let's review some other ideas about the measures of angles.

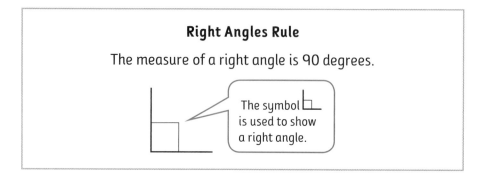

Right Angles Rule

The measure of a right angle is 90 degrees.

The symbol ⌐ is used to show a right angle.

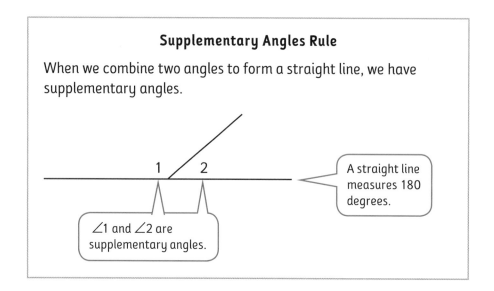

Supplementary Angles Rule

When we combine two angles to form a straight line, we have supplementary angles.

1   2

∠1 and ∠2 are supplementary angles.

A straight line measures 180 degrees.

Vertical Angles Rule

Vertical angles are two angles whose sides are opposite rays. Vertical angles have equal measurement.

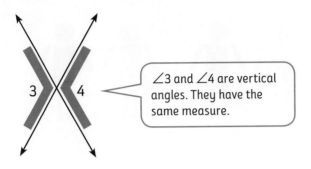

∠3 and ∠4 are vertical angles. They have the same measure.

Corresponding Angles Rule

When parallel lines are crossed by a transversal, corresponding angles have equal measurement.

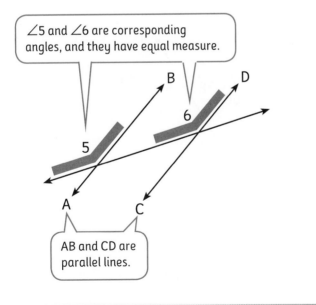

∠5 and ∠6 are corresponding angles, and they have equal measure.

AB and CD are parallel lines.

Transitive Property Rule

The transitive property shows relationships between quantities.

If $A = A$ and $B = C$, then $A = C$.

| $A = B$ | $B = C$ | $A = C$ |

We use these ideas to solve complex problems involving angles. Let's look at the problem in Example 1.

Example 1

Use interior angles to find the measure of ∠15.

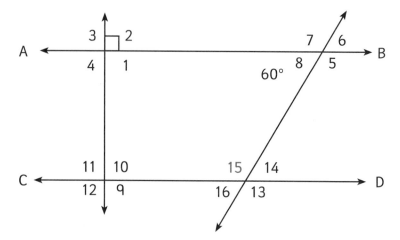

Lines AB and CD are parallel.

We start by looking for what we know. We know that:

- ∠2 = 90°
- ∠8 = 60°
- the sum of the interior angles of a quadrilateral = 360°

What inferences can we make?

$$\angle 2 = \angle 10 \qquad \leftarrow$$ These are corresponding angles. This means $\angle 10 = 90°$.

$$\angle 2 + \angle 1 = 180° \qquad \leftarrow$$ These are supplementary angles. We use algebra to find the measure of $\angle 1$.

Let x = the measure of $\angle 1$.

$$90 + x = 180$$
$$-90 + 90 + x = 180 + -90$$
$$0 + x = 90$$
$$x = 90$$

That means $\angle 1 = 90°$.

Now we have all the information we need to figure out the measure of $\angle 15$.

$$
\begin{array}{cccc}
90 & 60 & 90 & y \\
\downarrow & \downarrow & \downarrow & \downarrow \\
\angle 1 \;\; + & \angle 8 \;\; + & \angle 10 \;\; + & \angle 15 = 360°
\end{array}
$$

We substitute the values for the angles that we know.

Let y = the measure of $\angle 15$.

$$90 + 60 + 90 + y = 360$$
$$150 + 90 + y = 360$$
$$240 + y = 360$$
$$-240 + 240 + y = 360 + -240$$
$$0 + y = 120$$
$$y = 120$$

The measure of $\angle 15$ is 120°.

What we have learned about angles helps us make the inferences we need to solve this kind of problem.

 Problem-Solving Activity
Turn to *Interactive Text*,
page 315.

 **Reinforce Understanding**
Use the *mBook Study Guide*
to review lesson concepts.

Activity 1

For each expression, tell what you would multiply by to change the coefficient in front of the variable to 1.

1. $\frac{2}{3}x$

2. $2x$

3. $-x$

4. $\frac{1}{3}x$

5. $\frac{4}{5}x$

6. $-3x$

Activity 2

Solve.

1. $\frac{2}{3}z = 8$

2. $6 = \frac{1}{5}w$

3. $\frac{1}{2}x + 4 = 10$

4. $\frac{1}{4}y - 4 = 2$

Activity 3

Find the missing angle measures using the diagram. Lines AB and CD are parallel.

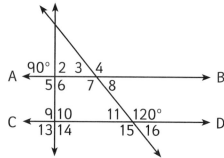

1. What is the measure of $\angle 10$?

2. What is the measure of $\angle 6$?

3. What is the measure of $\angle 3$?

4. What is the measure of $\angle 15$?

Activity 4 • Distributed Practice

Solve.

1. $\frac{3}{4} = \frac{b}{24}$

2. $2w = -8$

3. $1 = \frac{5}{4} \cdot d$

4. $a + -10 = 0$

5. $2(x + 5) = 3$

6. $-100 = -30 + x$

▶**More Fractions as Coefficients**

What do we do when an expression includes a fraction?

Let's look at the two equations below. There is a difference between them.

$$x = 20 \qquad \frac{x}{2} = 20$$

The equation on the right looks different from anything we have solved before because it includes a fraction.

But it is less challenging than we might think. We just have to remember rules about multiplication of fractions.

Let's look at the following patterns.

$$\frac{3}{4} = \frac{1}{4} \cdot 3 \text{ because } \frac{1}{4} \cdot \frac{3}{1} = \frac{3}{4}$$

$$\frac{7}{5} = \frac{1}{5} \cdot 7 \text{ because } \frac{1}{5} \cdot \frac{7}{1} = \frac{7}{5}$$

$$\frac{x}{2} = \frac{1}{2} \cdot x \text{ because } \frac{1}{2} \cdot \frac{x}{1} = \frac{x}{2}$$

A number or variable divided by 1 is the same number or variable.

One way to work problems like $\frac{x}{2} = 20$ is to convert the expression $\frac{x}{2}$ into $\frac{1}{2} \cdot x$ or $\frac{1}{2}x$.

Example 1 shows how to solve these kinds of equations.

Example 1

Solve an equation that includes a fraction.

$$\frac{x}{2} = 20$$

$\frac{1}{2} \cdot x = 20$ ←   The fraction $\frac{x}{2}$ is the same as $\frac{1}{2} \cdot x$.

$\boxed{2} \cdot \frac{1}{2}x = 20 \cdot \boxed{2}$ ←   We multiply by 2 to get x by itself. We multiply each side by 2 to keep the equation balanced.

$\frac{2}{2}x \quad = \quad 40$

$1x = 40$

$x = 40$

The process is a little more complicated with expressions like the following one. There are two unlike terms in the numerator.

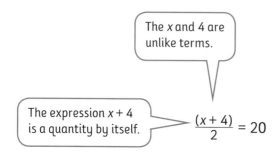

The x and 4 are unlike terms.

The expression $x + 4$ is a quantity by itself.

$$\frac{(x + 4)}{2} = 20$$

When we pull out the $\frac{1}{2}$, we need to remember that:

- we are multiplying the entire $x + 4$ by $\frac{1}{2}$.

- we must use order of operations to make sure that this happens.

- we do not want to multiply $\frac{1}{2}$ times either x or 4 by itself.

We use a similar process to solve the equation in Example 2. The key idea is to think about the numerator.

Example 2

Multiply fractions to solve the equation.

$$\frac{(x + 4)}{2} = 20$$

$\frac{1}{2} \cdot (x + 4) = 20$ ←   We put parentheses around $x + 4$ because we are multiplying the whole quantity.

$2 \cdot \frac{1}{2}(x + 4) = 20 \cdot 2$ ←   We multiply by 2 to get x by itself. We multiply each side by 2 to keep the equation balanced.

$\frac{2}{2}(x + 4) = 40$

$1(x + 4) = 40$

$(x + 4) = 40$ ←   A number times 1 is the same number.

$x + 4 = 40$

$x + 4 + -4 = 40 + -4$ ←   We add −4 to get x by itself. We add −4 to both sides to keep the equation balanced.

$x + 0 = 36$

$x = 36$

When we have an expression in fractional form like the ones shown in Examples 1 and 2, we need to think, "What is the coefficient in front of the variable?" Once we have identified the coefficient, we work the equation using the rules and properties from the Algebra Toolbox just like any other equation.

%÷
<x **Apply Skills**
Turn to *Interactive Text*, page 318.

mBook **Reinforce Understanding**
Use the *mBook Study Guide* to review lesson concepts.

▶Problem Solving: Word Problems

Why are drawings helpful for solving a word problem that involves a person's age?

Problems involving ages are like the money problems and rate problems we have solved before. We use drawings to help us understand what is going on in the problem.

Steps for Using Drawings to Help Solve Equations

STEP 1
Begin with a drawing.

STEP 2
Figure out what the variable is.

STEP 3
Solve the equation.

STEP 4
Make sure to answer what the question is asking for.

Here is an example of a problem involving different ages.

> We don't always need a drawing, but sometimes it helps.

Example 1

Find the ages of the three sisters.

Problem:

Amanda, Joanna, and Emily are sisters. Emily is the youngest, Joanna is in the middle, and Amanda is the oldest. Joanna is 2 years older than Emily. Amanda is 5 years older than Emily. When you add up their ages, it totals 67. How old is each sister?

STEP 1
Begin with a drawing.

| Emily | Joanna: 2 years older than Emily | Amanda: 5 years older than Emily |

STEP 2

Figure out what the variable is.

We use variables for what we don't know. We don't know how old each sister is.

Let's use *b* to represent Emily's age. If we do that, then we can represent the age difference of the other two sisters.

Emily	Joanna	Amanda
b	*b* + 2	*b* + 5

We set up the equation this way:

$b + (b + 2) + (b + 5) = 67$

STEP 3

Solve the equation.

$b + b + 2 + b + 5 = 67$

$b + b + b + 2 + 5 = 67$ ← We use the commutative property so that like terms are next to each other. Combine like terms.

$3b + 7 = 67$

$3b + 7 + \boxed{-7} = 67 + \boxed{-7}$ ← We add −7 to get *b* by itself. We add −7 to both sides to keep the equation balanced.

$3b + 0 = 60$

$3b = 60$

$\boxed{\frac{1}{3}} \cdot 3b = \boxed{\frac{1}{3}} \cdot 60$ ← We multiply by $\frac{1}{3}$ to get *b* by itself. We multiply each side by $\frac{1}{3}$ to keep the equation balanced.

$\frac{3}{3}b = \frac{60}{3}$

$1b = 20$

$b = 20$

STEP 4

Make sure to answer what the question is asking for.

We check our answer to make sure it is correct by using substitution.

Substitute the value for b in the original equation to find the age of each sister.

$$\text{Emily} = 20$$
$$\text{Joanna} = 20 + 2 \text{ or } 22$$
$$\text{Amanda} = 20 + 5 \text{ or } 25$$

$$
\begin{array}{ccccccc}
20 & & 20 & & 20 & & \\
\downarrow & & \downarrow & & \downarrow & & \\
b & + & b+2 & + & b+5 & = & 67 \\
20 & + & 22 & + & 25 & = & 67 \\
& & 42 & + & 25 & = & 67 \\
& & & & \mathbf{67} & = & \mathbf{67}
\end{array}
$$

Problem-Solving Activity
Turn to *Interactive Text*, page 321.

mBook Reinforce Understanding
Use the *mBook Study Guide* to review lesson concepts.

Activity 1

Solve.

1. $\frac{x}{2} = 10$

2. $\frac{10}{y} = -5$

3. $\frac{12}{z} = 6$

4. $\frac{a}{9} = 3$

5. $-\frac{27}{b} = -3$

6. $\frac{c}{3} = -9$

Activity 2

Solve.

1. $\frac{(m+4)}{2} = 4$

2. $\frac{(n+2)}{3} = 6$

3. $\frac{1}{(g+1)} = 2$

4. $\frac{1}{(2z)} = 3$

Activity 3

Use a drawing to help solve the problems.

1. Teri is 4 years younger than her brother Christopher. When you combine their ages, it totals 24. How old are Teri and Christopher?

2. Matt is Ava's father. Matt is 5 times older than Ava. When you add their ages together, it is 60. How old are Matt and Ava?

Activity 4 • Distributed Practice

Solve.

1. $-\frac{36}{h} = -9$

2. $4 + -12 = x$

3. $g \div -8 = -9$

4. $-\frac{4}{5} \cdot c = 1$

5. $0 = 500 + d$

6. $-112 - -399 = e$

▶**Negative Numbers**

What do we do when an expression contains a negative number?

Let's look at the following equations. There is a difference between them.

$$3x + 3 = 18 \qquad -3x - 3 = -18$$

The equation on the right is different because of the negative numbers. While this looks like a big change, it isn't. We just need to remember the rules about operations on integers.

Example 1

Solve an equation that contains negative numbers.

$$-3x - 3 = -18$$

$-3x + -3 = -18$ ← Subtraction is the same as adding the opposite.

$-3x + -3 \boxed{+3} = -18 \boxed{+3}$ ← We add 3 to get x by itself. We add 3 to both sides to keep the equation balanced.

$-3x + 0 = -15$ ← A number plus 0 is the same number.

$-3x = -15$

$\boxed{-\frac{1}{3}} \cdot -3x = -15 \cdot \boxed{-\frac{1}{3}}$ ← We multiply by $-\frac{1}{3}$ to get a positive x by itself. We multiply each side by $-\frac{1}{3}$ to keep the equation balanced.

$\frac{3}{3}x = \frac{15}{3}$ ← Integer rule for multiplication: A negative times a negative is a positive, so $-\frac{1}{3} \cdot -3 = \frac{3}{3}$ and $-15 \cdot -\frac{1}{3} = \frac{15}{3}$.

$1x = 5$

$x = 5$

Integer rules apply to expressions that contain fractions, too. When we "pull out" the fraction from the expression, we also pull out the negative value.

Example 2

Use integer rules for multiplication to solve this equation.

$$-\frac{x}{5} + 6 = 31$$

$$-\frac{x}{5} + 6 + \boxed{-6} = 31 + \boxed{-6}$$ ← We add −6 to get x by itself. We add −6 to both sides to keep the equation balanced.

$$-\frac{x}{5} + 0 = 25$$

$$-\frac{x}{5} = 25$$ ← The fraction $-\frac{x}{5}$ is the same as $-\frac{1}{5} \cdot x$.

$$-\frac{1}{5} \cdot x = 25$$

$$-\frac{1}{5}x = 25$$ ← The fraction $-\frac{1}{5} \cdot x$ is the same as $\frac{1}{5}x$.

$$\boxed{-5} \cdot -\frac{1}{5}x = 25 \cdot \boxed{-5}$$ ← We multiply by −5 to get a positive x by itself. We multiply each side by −5 to keep the equation balanced.

$$\frac{5}{5}x = -125$$ ← Integer rules for multiplication: a negative times a negative is a positive, so $-5 \cdot -\frac{1}{5} = \frac{5}{5}$. A negative times a positive is a negative number, so $25 \cdot -5 = -125$.

$$1x = -125$$

$$x = -125$$

% ÷
≧ ÷
< x **Apply Skills**
Turn to *Interactive Text*,
page 324.

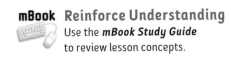

mBook Reinforce Understanding
Use the *mBook Study Guide*
to review lesson concepts.

▶**Problem Solving: Coin Problems**

How do we solve word problems with coins?

Algebra word problems that involve coins are a lot like rate, number, and age problems. We still follow the four steps for setting up and solving the equations.

Coin problems are different because we know the value of common coins. We know that a quarter equals 25 cents and a dime equals 10 cents.

The value of the coin is important because we use it as part of an equation.

How do we represent the value of different coins in an expression?

Steps for Using Drawings to Help Solve Equations
STEP 1 Begin with a drawing.
STEP 2 Figure out what the variable is.
STEP 3 Solve the equation.
STEP 4 Make sure to answer what the question is asking for.

Let's say we have some quarters, but we don't know how many quarters we have. Because the number of quarters is unknown, we use a variable.

Let y = the number of quarters.

The expression for the total value is:

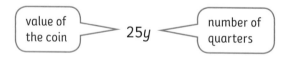

value of the coin ⟶ $25y$ ⟵ number of quarters

Let's use this kind of thinking to solve a coin problem. We need to remember the value of the coin when we represent the problem.

Example 1

Find the number of quarters in the coin problem.

Problem:

In my pocket are some quarters and four dimes. The amount of money in my pocket is 90 cents. How many quarters do I have?

STEP 1

Begin with a drawing.

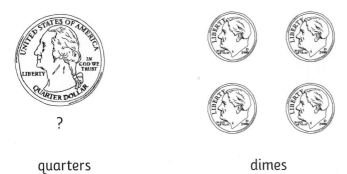

quarters   dimes

STEP 2

Figure out what the variable is.

- We don't know the number of quarters, so let h = the number of quarters.

- We do know the number of dimes. I have 4 dimes and each dime is worth 10 cents.

$$4 \cdot 10 = 40 \text{ cents}$$

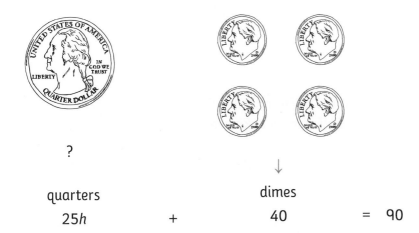

quarters   dimes
25h   +   40   =   90

STEP 3

Solve the equation.

$$25h + 40 = 90$$
$$25h + 40 + -40 = 90 + -40$$
$$25h + 0 = 50$$
$$25h = 50$$
$$\frac{1}{25} \cdot 25h = 50 \cdot \frac{1}{25}$$
$$\frac{25}{25}h = \frac{50}{25}$$
$$1h = 2$$
$$h = 2$$

I have two quarters.

STEP 4

Make sure to answer what the question is asking for.
We check to see if two quarters is correct by substituting for the variable in the original equation.

$$\overset{2}{\underset{\downarrow}{}}$$
$$25h + 40 = 90$$
$$25 \cdot 2 + 40 = 90$$
$$50 + 40 = 90$$
$$\mathbf{90 = 90}$$

Let's change this problem slightly. Suppose we don't know the number of dimes we have. Can we still solve the problem?

We need to think carefully about the different coins. But we can still solve problems where the number of coins is unknown.

Example 2

Find the number of quarters and dimes in the coin problem.

Problem:

I have some quarters and dimes in my pocket. I have twice as many dimes as I have quarters. The total amount of money in my pocket is 90 cents. How many quarters and dimes do I have?

STEP 1

Begin with a drawing.

   ?   ?

   quarters dimes

2 times as many dimes as quarters

STEP 2

Figure out what the variable is.

- We don't know the number of quarters or dimes.
- There are two times as many dimes as quarters.

Let v = the number of quarters.

That means the number of dimes is $2v$. We need to show the value for each coin.

quarter = v dime = $2v$

There are 2 times as many dimes as quarters.

  $25v$ + $10 \cdot 2v = 90$

 quarters dimes

STEP 3

Solve the equation.

$$25v + 10 \cdot 2v = 90$$

$$25v + 20v = 90 \qquad \leftarrow \quad \text{We use order of operations to make}$$
$$10 \cdot 2v = 20v$$

$$45v = 90$$

$$\frac{1}{45} \cdot 45v = 90 \cdot \frac{1}{45}$$

$$\frac{45}{45}v = \frac{90}{45}$$

$$1v = 2$$

$$v = 2$$

If I have two times as many dimes as quarters, that means I have $2 \cdot 2$ or 4 dimes.

I have 2 quarters and 4 dimes.

STEP 4

Make sure to answer what the question is asking for.

We check to see if two quarters is correct by substituting for the variable in the original equation.

$$\begin{array}{cc} 2 & 2 \\ \downarrow & \downarrow \end{array}$$

$$25v + 10 \cdot 2v = 90$$

$$25 \cdot 2 + 10 \cdot 2 \cdot 2 = 90$$

$$50 + 10 \cdot 4 = 90$$

$$50 + 40 = 90$$

$$\mathbf{90 = 90}$$

Problem-Solving Activity
Turn to *Interactive Text*,
page 325.

mBook Reinforce Understanding
Use the *mBook Study Guide*
to review lesson concepts.

Activity 1

Solve.

1. $-5x = 10$

2. $-24 = -4y$

3. $-\frac{1}{2}x = 4$

4. $-72 = -9z$

5. $-3m = 12$

6. $-\frac{2}{3}z = -1$

Activity 2

Solve.

1. $-5x + 6 = 16$

2. $-2(3 + x) = -22$

3. $-32 = -4x - 8$

4. $1 - x + 8 + -5x = -x + 7$

Activity 3

Solve the word problems involving coins.

1. Donny reached in his pocket and pulled out 75 cents, all in dimes and nickels. He had twice as many dimes as he had nickels. How many nickels did he have? How many dimes did he have?

2. Trinity needed to borrow some money for lunch. She asked Cassandra for money. Cassandra gave her all the change in her pocket. It was a total of 57 cents. There was one quarter, one dime, seven pennies, and the rest were nickels. How many nickels were there?

Activity 4 • Distributed Practice

Solve.

1. $\frac{2}{5} = \frac{h}{35}$

2. $3(x + 1) = 30$

3. $-15 + -27 = m$

4. $1 = \frac{1}{3} \cdot z$

5. $-5,000 = -5x$

6. $0 = 1,000 + x$

Lesson 15 | Unit Review
▸Solving Different Kinds of Algebraic Equations

Problem Solving:
▸**Lines and Angles**

What is important when we solve different algebraic equations?

Sometimes we get confused when we move from one equation to the next. The equations look different, and we might think, "I haven't seen this before. I don't know where to start."

Throughout this unit we learned the rules and properties we need to solve these equations. They are in our Algebra Toolbox. We keep in mind the four steps for working equations.

Steps for Solving Equations

STEP 1

Look at the entire equation.

STEP 2

Look for the **parts** of the equation that seem different.

STEP 3

Remember the goal: Solve the equation so that we have a **positive variable on one side**.

STEP 4

Use the rules or properties we need to reach our goal.

We use similar properties in the two equations in Review 1. The equations are slightly different from one another, but most of the properties and rules are the same.

Review 1

Review 1

How do we use rules and properties to solve equations?

Equation 1:

$$5x + 4 = 54$$

$$5x + 4 + \boxed{-4} = 54 + \boxed{-4}$$ ← We add −4 to get x by itself. We add −4 to both sides to keep the equation balanced.

$$5x + 0 \quad = \quad 50$$

$$5x = 50$$

$$\frac{1}{5} \cdot 5x = 50 \cdot \frac{1}{5}$$ ← We multiply by $\frac{1}{5}$ to get a positive x by itself. We multiply each side by $\frac{1}{5}$ to keep the equation balanced.

$$\frac{5}{5}x \quad = \quad \frac{50}{5}$$

$$1x = 10$$ ← A number times 1 is the same number.

$$x = 10$$

Equation 2:

$$\frac{x}{5} + 4 = 54$$

$$\frac{x}{5} + 4 + \boxed{-4} = 54 + \boxed{-4}$$ ← We add −4 so that we will end up with x by itself. We add −4 to both sides to keep the equation balanced.

$$\frac{x}{5} + 0 \quad = \quad 50$$ ← A number plus 0 is the same number.

$$\frac{x}{5} = 50$$ ← The fraction $\frac{x}{5}$ is the same as $\frac{1}{5} \cdot x$.

$$\frac{1}{5} \cdot x = 50$$ ← The fraction $\frac{1}{5} \cdot x$ is the same as $\frac{1}{5}x$.

$$\frac{1}{5}x = 50$$

$$\boxed{5} \cdot \frac{1}{5}x = 50 \cdot \boxed{5}$$ ← We multiply by 5 to get x by itself. We multiply each side by 5 to keep the equation balanced.

$$\frac{5}{5}x \quad = \quad 250$$

$$1x = 250$$

$$x = 250$$

How do we solve algebra word problems?

We have looked at different types of algebra word problems in this unit. These problems are important because they show us how variables are used to represent unknown quantities.

Algebra also shows us that we can use equations to describe different situations. By using variables and equations, we can represent a wide range of problems.

Review 1 presents two types of problems that we have studied. Let's see how we use the four steps as we solve each problem.

Review 1

How do we use a drawing to solve problems?

Problem:

Every day, planes fly between Chicago and Los Angeles. A jet plane takes off from Los Angeles at 8 AM, flying to Chicago at 550 miles per hour. Another jet takes off from Chicago, flying to Los Angeles. It is up against strong winds, so it can only go 350 miles per hour.

The distance is about 1,800 miles between Chicago and Los Angeles. When will the two planes pass each other?

STEP 1
Begin with a drawing.

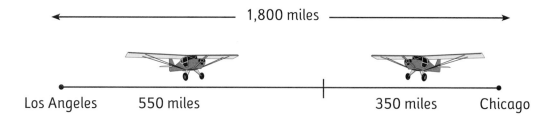

1,800 miles

Los Angeles   550 miles   350 miles   Chicago

STEP 2
Figure out what the variable is.
We know:

- the formula for rate is $r \cdot t =$ distance.
- the distance is 1,800 miles.
- the rate for each plane: 550 mph and 350 mph.

We don't know the time.

Let p = the time the planes are flying.

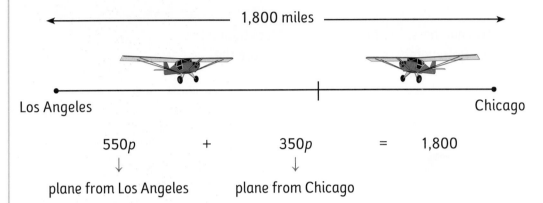

1,800 miles

Los Angeles   Chicago

$$550p \quad + \quad 350p \quad = \quad 1{,}800$$

plane from Los Angeles   plane from Chicago

STEP 3

Solve the equation.

$$550p + 350p = 1{,}800$$

$$900p = 1{,}800$$

$$\frac{1}{900} \cdot 900p = 1{,}800 \cdot \frac{1}{900}$$

$$\frac{900}{900}p = \frac{1{,}800}{900}$$

$$1p = 2$$

$$p = 2$$

The planes will be in the air for two hours before they pass each other.

STEP 4

Make sure to answer what the question is asking for.

We answered the question, but let's substitute for p in the original equation to make sure the answer works.

$$550p + 350p = 1{,}800$$

$$550 \cdot 2 + 350 \cdot 2 = 1{,}800$$

$$1{,}100 + 700 = 1{,}800$$

$$1{,}800 = 1{,}800$$

Review 2

How do we use a drawing to solve problems?

Problem:

I am thinking of two numbers. The first number is 4 less than 2 times the second number. Both numbers add up to 32. What are the two numbers?

STEP 1

Begin with a drawing.

first number   second number

We know that the first number is 4 less than 2 times the second number.

STEP 2

Figure out what the variable is.

We do not know either number, but we do know they add up to 32.

Figuring out the first number depends on the second number. Let w = the second number. That means we have to translate the first number.

Four less than 2 times w means $2w - 4$.

  $2w - 4$ w

Now we write an equation.

$2w - 4 + w = 32$

STEP 3

Solve the equation.

$$2w - 4 + w = 32$$
$$2w + -4 + w = 32$$
$$2w + w + -4 = 32$$
$$3w + -4 = 32$$
$$3w + -4 + 4 = 32 + 4$$
$$3w + 0 = 36$$
$$3w = 36$$
$$\frac{1}{3} \cdot 3w = 36 \cdot \frac{1}{3}$$
$$\frac{3}{3}w = \frac{36}{3}$$
$$1w = 12$$
$$\mathbf{w = 12}$$

STEP 4

Make sure to answer what the question is asking for.
The question asks what the two numbers are.

$$w = \text{the second number}$$
$$w = 12$$

$$2w - 4 = \text{the first number}$$
$$2 \cdot 12 - 4 = 24 - 4 \text{ or } 20$$

First number = 20
Second number = 12
$$\mathbf{20 + 12 = 32}$$

%÷
=
< x **Apply Skills**
Turn to *Interactive Text*,
page 328.

mBook **Reinforce Understanding**
Use the *mBook Study Guide*
to review lesson concepts.

▶**Problem Solving: Lines and Angles**

What do we know about lines and angles?

We learned that the total measure of the interior angles of different shapes is not the same.

- A triangle always has a total measure of 180 degrees for its interior angles.
- A rectangle has 360 degrees.
- A pentagon has 540 degrees.

But the total of the exterior angles is always 360 degrees.

We use information about interior and exterior angles to solve a range of algebra problems. The symbols we use to show that angles are equal give us a clue about what angles have the same measure.

Review 1

Find the measure of ∠w and ∠y.

Let a = the measure of each unknown angle.

We know that the sum of the interior angles for all quadrilaterals is 360 degrees.

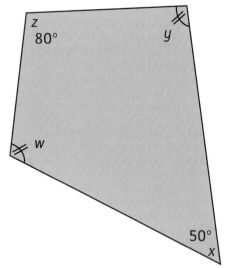

$$a + a + 80 + 50 = 360$$
$$2a + 130 = 360$$
$$2a + 130 + -130 = 360 + -130$$
$$2a + 0 = 230$$
$$2a = 230$$
$$\frac{1}{2} \cdot 2a = 230 \cdot \frac{1}{2}$$
$$\frac{2}{2}a = \frac{230}{2}$$
$$1a = 115$$
$$a = 115$$

The measure of ∠w is 115° and the measure of ∠y is 115°.

We also learned how to solve more complex problems using a set of rules and properties. This information helps us prove the measure of an angle or how angles are equal.

Key Ideas, Rules, and Properties

Right Angle Rule

The symbol ⌐ in the corner of an angle shows that the angle is a right angle. The measure of a right angle is 90 degrees.

Supplementary Angles Rule

When we combine two angles to form a straight line, we have supplementary angles. A straight line measures 180 degrees.

Vertical Angles Rule

These are two angles whose sides are opposite rays. Vertical angles have equal measurement.

Corresponding Angles Rule

When parallel lines are crossed by a transversal, corresponding angles have equal measurement.

Transitive Property

This is a property that shows relationships between quantities. If $A = B$ and $B = C$, then $A = C$.

We can use this information to solve a complex problem like the one in Review 2.

Review 2

How do we use angle rules to solve problems?
Lines HJ and PQ are parallel.

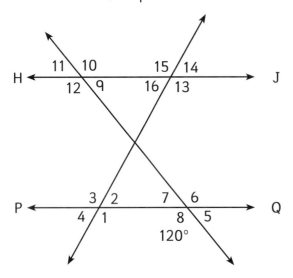

$$\angle 8 = \angle 12 \quad \leftarrow \quad \text{Corresponding angle rule.}$$
$$\angle 12 = 120°$$

$$\angle 11 + \angle 12 = 180° \quad \leftarrow \quad \text{These are supplementary angles.}$$

- Let x = the measure of $\angle 11$.
- Substitute $120°$ for $\angle 12$.

$$x + 120 = 180$$
$$x + 120 + -120 = 180 + -120$$
$$x + 0 = 60$$
$$x = 60$$

The measure of $\angle 11 = 60°$.

 Problem-Solving Activity
Turn to *Interactive Text*,
page 331.

mBook Reinforce Understanding
Use the *mBook Study Guide*
to review lesson concepts.

MATH-STRONAUT

Apollo 11 missed its landing coordinate by only 3.5 miles after a 250,000 mile trip.

On July 20, 1969, Apollo 11's lunar module carefully descended to the moon's surface. Out of the spacecraft stepped astronaut Neil Armstrong to put the first human footprint on the moon.

Did You Know?
Neil Armstrong carried with him to the moon a piece of the cloth and wood from the original 1903 Wright Flyer.

Algebra + Geometry = Unlimited Possibilities

OBJECTIVES

Building Number Concepts

- Use word problems and tables to think about functional relationships

- Interpret the slope and y-intercept of a function in a real-world situation

- Use a function to make predictions in a real-world situation

Problem Solving

- Graph linear functions on a coordinate graph

- Convert functions between representations (tables, graphs, and equations)

- Interpret the intersection of two functions in a real-world situation

▶Introduction to Functions

What is a function?

A **function** is a systematic relationship between two variables. There are many examples of functions in the world around us. An easy way to find one is to think about situations where one thing depends upon something else. Here are some examples of functions in everyday life.

Vocabulary
function

Statement:

I get paid for mowing lawns.

How much I get paid	⟷	How many lawns I mow

Relationship:

How much I get paid depends on how many lawns I mow.

Statement:

It costs money to put gas in my car.

The cost to fill up my car	⟷	The number of gallons I put in my tank

Relationship:

The cost to fill up my car depends on the number of gallons I put in the tank.

Statement:

The big rocks in the yard were hard to move.

| How easy it is to move a rock | | How much the rock weighs |

Relationship:

How easy it is to move a rock depends on how much it weighs.

One way to show a functional relationship is with a table. These number machines also represent functions because they show a systematic relationship between the input and the output.

In Example 1, the functional relationship between the input and the output is that the output is always five times the input. The value of the output depends on the value of the input.

Example 1

Define the functional relationship between the input and the output.

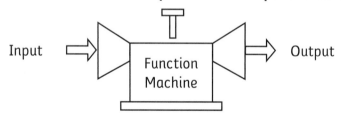

Input	Output
4	20
10	50
2	10
6	30

The functional relationship between the input and the output can be stated this way: We multiply the input by 5 to get the output.

 **Apply Skills**
Turn to *Interactive Text*,
page 334.

 **Reinforce Understanding**
Use the *mBook Study Guide*
to review lesson concepts.

▶**Problem Solving: Coordinate Graphs**

coordinate graph
coordinates
x-axis
y-axis
x-coordinate
y-coordinate
point of origin

What should we remember about coordinate graphs?

Coordinate graphs are used a great deal when we study algebra. Let's review some of the basic properties of coordinate graphs.

Properties of Coordinate Graphs

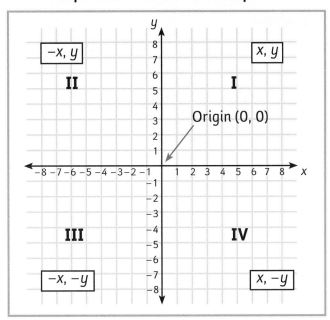

We use **coordinates** to describe the location of points on the coordinate graph. The first number in the coordinate tells us our location on the **x-axis**, or horizontal axis. The second number tells us our location on the **y-axis**, or vertical axis.

The pair of x and y coordinates in each quadrant tells us something about the value of the points that are plotted in that quadrant. The **x-coordinates** to the right of the y-axis are positive and those to the left are negative. The **y-coordinates** above the x-axis are positive and those below it are negative.

The point where the x-axis and y-axis intersect is called the **point of origin**. The coordinates of this point are (0, 0).

Example 1 shows a rectangle that cuts through all the quadrants. Each vertex of the rectangle has different *x*- and *y*-coordinates based on the quadrant. For example, the vertex in Quadrant III has the coordinates (−2, −3) because all coordinates in that quadrant are negative.

Example 1

Identify the coordinates in each quadrant.

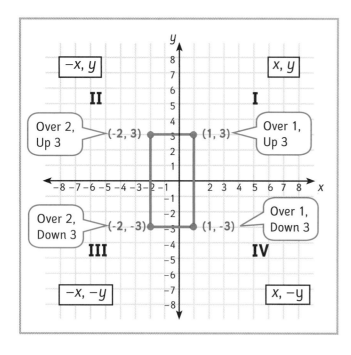

Problem-Solving Activity
Turn to *Interactive Text*,
page 337.

mBook Reinforce Understanding
Use the *mBook Study Guide*
to review lesson concepts.

Homework

Activity 1

In each of the statements, tell what part of the statement depends on another part.

1. Patricia makes $7 per hour for pulling weeds. _____ depends on _____

2. The cost of gas is $5 per gallon. _____ depends on _____

3. The heavier rocks are harder to move. _____ depends on _____

Activity 2

Look at the function machines and their inputs and outputs. Tell the relationship each one represents.

Model   The input ___minus 4___ equals the output.

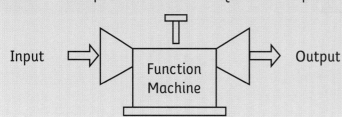

Input	Output
9	5
77	73
44	40
520	516
4	0

1. The input _____ equals the output.

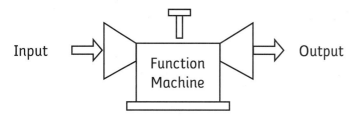

Input	Output
1	2
3	4
15	16
501	502
999	1,000

2. The input _____ equals the output.

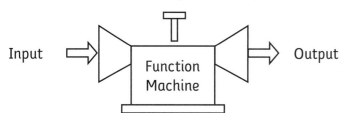

Input	Output
2	4
3	6
4	8
100	200
50	100

3. The input _____ equals the output.

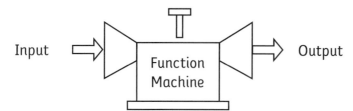

Input	Output
99	9
88	8
11	1
22	2
33	3

Activity 3

Identify the parts of the coordinate grid by selecting the word or phrase that describes it. Write a, b, or c on your paper.

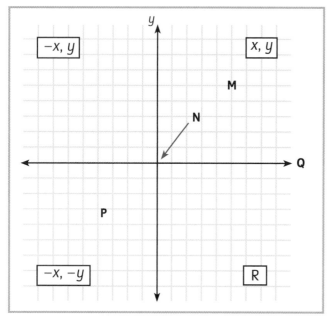

1. The section of the graph labeled **M** is called:
   (a) Quadrant III
   (b) Quadrant I
   (c) the origin

2. The section of the graph labeled **N** is called:
   (a) $(x, -y)$
   (b) Quadrant I
   (c) the origin

3. The part of the graph that is labeled **R** should say:
   (a) $(x, -y)$
   (b) Quadrant I
   (c) the x-axis

4. The section of the graph labeled **P** is called:
   (a) Quadrant III
   (b) Quadrant I
   (c) the origin

5. The section of the graph labeled **Q** is called:
   (a) $(x, -y)$
   (b) Quadrant I
   (c) the x-axis

Activity 4 • Distributed Practice

Solve.

1. $9 = 3x$

2. $2x + 3 = 7$

3. $3(x + 2) = 15$

4. $3x + 2x + 1 = 26$

5. $36 + 2x = 4 + 6x$

6. $-54 = -9x$

7. $-2x + 5 = -x + -2$

8. $x + 10 = 20$

▶**Functions From Everyday Life**

Vocabulary

systematic
relationship

How do we create a function from an everyday situation?

In the last lesson, we learned that functions show a **systematic relationship** between two variables. This means the change in one variable leads to a predictable change in another variable. This happens often in the world around us.

Example 1 shows two real-life examples of systematic relationships. In each case, we use a table to show the relationship between one variable and another variable.

Example 1

Show the function in a table and state the relationship.

Problem 1: Going Up in a Balloon

There are people who like to fly in hot air balloons. We often see the people in these balloons wearing jackets. Why? There is an interesting relationship between elevation and the temperature of the air. For every 500 meters up in the air, the temperature drops 6 degrees. Let's say it is 60 degrees on the ground when a balloon takes off. What is the change in temperature as the balloon goes up?

Height or Altitude (in meters)	Air Temperature (in degrees)
0	60
500	54
1,000	48
1,500	42
2,000	36

By the time the balloon gets to 2,000 meters, or about 6,500 feet, the air is 36 degrees.

How do we state the relationship?

The higher you rise in the balloon, the lower the temperature falls.

Problem 2: Changing the Oil

Vroom Oil Change changes oil for all kinds of cars. It charges different amounts depending on the size of the car's engine. Larger engines usually take more quarts of oil. The business charges $6 a quart to change oil. What would this look like on a table?

Number of Quarts	Total Cost
2	$12
3	$18
4	$24
5	$30

How do we state the relationship?

The total cost depends on the number of quarts.

In a function, a change in one variable results in a predictable change in the other variable.

Understanding functions means seeing the relationship between two variables in many different situations. Tables help us see this relationship between variables.

%÷ **Apply Skills**
≡ Turn to *Interactive Text*,
<x page 340.

mBook **Reinforce Understanding**
Use the *mBook Study Guide*
to review lesson concepts.

How do we make translations on a coordinate graph?

Translating shapes on a coordinate graph means sliding them either vertically or horizontally. It's important to keep track of the coordinates of a shape when we translate it. The patterns we see can help us learn more about geometry and movement on a coordinate graph.

Example 1 shows how we translate a trapezoid from Quadrant I to Quadrant II. The table shows how we move a distance of 9 on the graph.

Example 1

Translate the trapezoid by subtracting 9 from each x-coordinate.

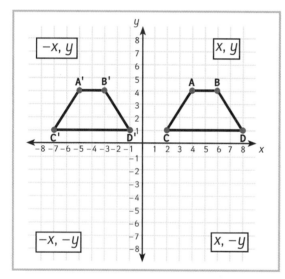

Notice that the coordinates of the translated shape are A', B', C', and D'. This is the way mathematicians write the coordinates of a translated shape.

Subtract 9 from each x-coordinate.

Start		End	
Vertices	**Coordinates**	**Vertices**	**Coordinates**
A	(4, 4)	A′	(−5, 4)
B	(6, 4)	B′	(−3, 4)
C	(2, 1)	C′	(−7, 1)
D	(8, 1)	D′	(−1, 1)

The change is only in the x-coordinates. Why is that? Since we are moving horizontally, we only see a change in the x-coordinate.

In each case, we end up with negative *x*-coordinates. The graph in Example 2 shows how the trapezoid is translated from Quadrant I to Quadrant IV.

Example 2

Translate the trapezoid by subtracting 6 from each *y*-coordinate.

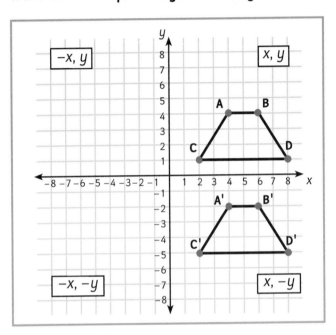

Subtract 6 from each *y*-coordinate.

Start		End	
Vertices	Coordinates	Vertices	Coordinates
A	(4, 4)	A′	(4, −2)
B	(6, 4)	B′	(6, −2)
C	(2, 1)	C′	(2, −5)
D	(8, 1)	D′	(8, −5)

Because we are moving vertically, we only see a change in the *y*-coordinate.

Problem-Solving Activity
Turn to *Interactive Text*,
page 342.

mBook Reinforce Understanding
Use the *mBook Study Guide*
to review lesson concepts.

Activity 1

Create the input/output table for each everyday function below. Then state the relationship between the input and output.

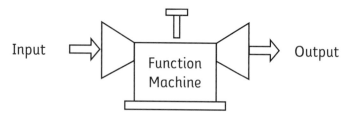

Input ⟹ | Function Machine | ⟹ Output

1. A gallon of gas costs $5.

2. There is a $5 processing fee for each ticket.

3. It takes Michael 10 minutes to read one page in his book.

Activity 2

Use the information from the tables in Activity 1 to answer the questions.

1. How many pages does Michael read in 30 minutes?

2. How many tickets did you buy if you paid $25 in processing fees?

3. If you paid $40 for gas, how many gallons did you buy?

4. How long did it take Michael to read 5 pages?

Tell the coordinates of the shape if you translate it one unit to the right.

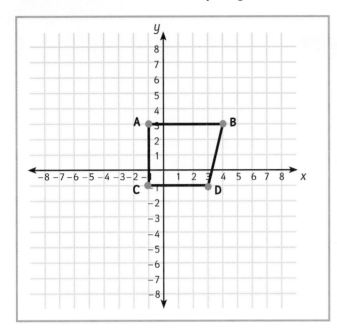

Evaluate the numeric expressions using the order of operations.

1. $-3 \cdot (4 + 3) + 10$

2. $5 - -2 + 7 - 11$

3. $5^2 - 4 \cdot 5 + -5$

4. $(3 + -4) \cdot (11 - -9)$

5. $9^2 \div 3^2 \cdot 7 - 5$

6. $-1 \cdot -1 \cdot -1 \cdot -1 \cdot -1$

7. $8 + -13 - 4 \cdot 8 + 10^2$

8. $1^2 + 2^2 + 3^2 + 4^2 \cdot 0$

▸**Graphing Functional Relationships**

What does the graph of a function look like?

Function machines and tables are great ways to see functions. When we look at the input and output of a function machine or the two columns in a table, we see the systematic relationship between two variables.

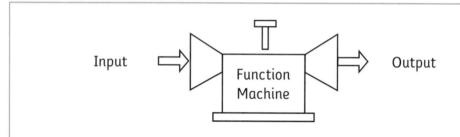

Input	Output
11	4
67	60
1	−6
9	2

Number of Quarts	Cost
2	$12
3	$18
4	$24
5	$30

How do we state the relationship?

We subtract 7 from x to get y.

How do we state the relationship?

We multiply 6 times the number of quarts to get the cost.

Another way to show a systematic relationship is to use a graph. We label each axis with the variables, then draw the relationship.

Example 1 shows the relationship between the number of hours worked and how much Tina made at the restaurant. The graph makes the relationship clearer than the table does. Each dot on the graph shows the relationship between input and output.

Example 1

Use a graph to solve the word problem.

Problem:

Tina works in the kitchen at Big Tom's Restaurant. She makes $10 an hour. The table shows how many hours she worked per week for six weeks and how much money she made. What is the relationship between how much she works and how much she gets paid?

Week	Hours Worked	Amount Paid
1	30	$300
2	25	$250
3	22	$220
4	35	$350
5	29	$290
6	38	$380

Let's draw a graph to show the relationship between hours worked and pay. In this graph, we find the first point on the graph by going over 30 (the input value) and going up 300 (the output value). Then we plot the remaining data from the table.

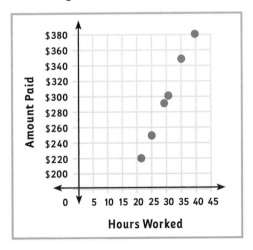

How do we state the relationship?

The more hours you work, the more you get paid.

The pattern on graphs can go the other direction too. In other words, one variable increases while the other decreases. We saw in the last lesson that as you go higher in elevation, the temperature gets lower.

Example 2

Use a graph to find the relationship between the temperature and the height of the balloon.

Height or Altitude (in meters)	Temperature
0	60°F
500	54°F
1,000	48°F
1,500	42°F
2,000	36°F

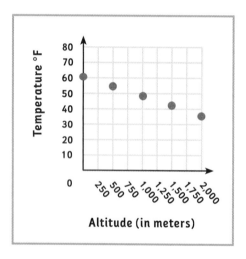

Altitude (in meters)

POWER CONCEPT

Graphing a function helps us see the relationship between the variables.

How do we state the relationship?

The higher you go in the balloon, the lower the temperature gets.

In each case, the graph helps us see the relationship between the variables. The graph also helps us make predictions about variables that are not in the table. This is one reason why functions are very important tools in mathematics.

 **Apply Skills**
Turn to *Interactive Text*, page 345.

 **Reinforce Understanding**
Use the *mBook Study Guide* to review lesson concepts.

How do we reflect a shape on a coordinate graph?

One way to think about a reflected line or shape is to think about a line of symmetry. When we reflect something, it flips across the line of symmetry an equal distance from the line.

Example 1 shows a reflected right triangle. We begin with a table of coordinates that shows the change from Quadrant II to Quadrant I. We are using the y-axis as a line of symmetry.

Example 1

Use the table to reflect the triangle from Quadrant II to Quadrant I.

Start		End	
Vertices	Coordinates	Vertices	Coordinates
A	(−1, 5)	A′	(1, 5)
B	(−4, 1)	B′	(4, 1)
C	(−1, 1)	C′	(1, 1)

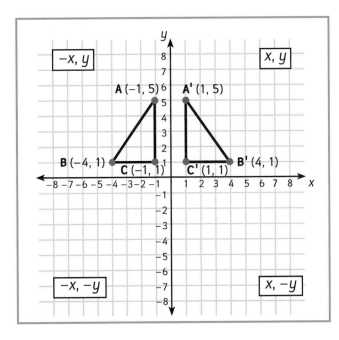

When we look at the coordinates in the reflected triangle, we see a pattern. We are reflecting the triangle across the y-axis. This means that the only changes are in the x-coordinates.

The x-coordinates are opposites. For example, the x-coordinate in Quadrant II is -4, but it changes to 4 in Quadrant I. This change is more than just going from a negative to a positive number. It shows how each coordinate is the same distance from the y-axis.

When we reflect shapes on a coordinate graph, we think about which signs we are changing. We also need to remember that these changes show that each coordinate is the same distance from the x- or y-axis.

Problem-Solving Activity
Turn to *Interactive Text*, page 346.

mBook Reinforce Understanding
Use the *mBook Study Guide* to review lesson concepts.

Activity 1

Create function tables for each problem.

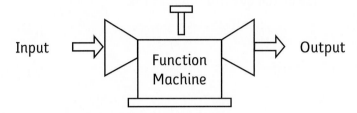

Input ⇨ Function Machine ⇨ Output

1. In basketball, each basket is worth 2 points.

2. At the Candy Shoppe in the mall, the price of a bag of candy is $5 per pound.

Activity 2

Draw a dot graph for each of the problems in Activity 1 on graph paper. Be sure to label the axes of your graph and use an appropriate scale. Use the graph to answer the following questions.

1. How many pounds of candy can you buy for $10?

2. How many points do you get for shooting 5 baskets?

3. What does it cost for 3 pounds of candy?

4. If you scored 6 points, how many baskets did you make?

Homework

Activity 3

Write the coordinates of all the vertices of the reflected triangles below. Use the letters to label your answers. Then answer the questions about the triangles.

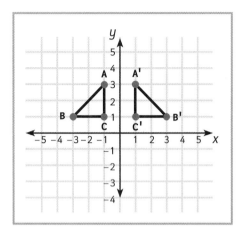

1. Look at the coordinates for A and A'. Do you see a pattern? Write a statement that tells the pattern.

2. Do you see the same pattern for B and B'? How about C and C'?

Activity 4 • Distributed Practice

Write a general statement that shows the property being used in each example.

1. Write a general statement using the variables a, b, and c to demonstrate the distributive property.
   Examples: $3(4+5) = 3 \cdot 4 + 3 \cdot 5$ $2(-1 + -2) = 2 \cdot -1 + 2 \cdot -2$

2. Write a general statement using the variables x and y to demonstrate the commutative property for multiplication.
   Examples: $4 \cdot 3 = 3 \cdot 4$ $-1 \cdot 2 = 2 \cdot -1$

3. Write a general statement using the variable w to demonstrate the multiplicative property of 0.
   Examples: $4 \cdot 0 = 0$ $-\frac{4}{5} \cdot 0 = 0$

4. Write a general statement using the variable z to demonstrate the additive inverse property.
   Examples: $0 = 6 + -6$ $0 = 15 + -15$

▶Analyzing Functional Relationships in a Set of Data

Vocabulary
data

How do we find functions in everyday data?

Every spring Mr. Raster's science class conducts an experiment outside the school cafeteria. Mr. Raster's students climb a ladder and measure the bounces of three different kinds of balls: a rubber ball, a tennis ball, and a golf ball. They drop each ball from different heights to see how the height of the bounce changes based on the type of ball. The students carefully measure each height where the ball is dropped. They also measure how high it returns after the bounce.

Example 1 shows the results of the experiment.

Example 1

Graph how high each ball bounces.

All heights are measured in inches.

Rubber Ball	
Drop Height	Bounce Height
24	19
30	24
36	29
40	32
50	40
60	48
70	56
80	64
90	72
100	80

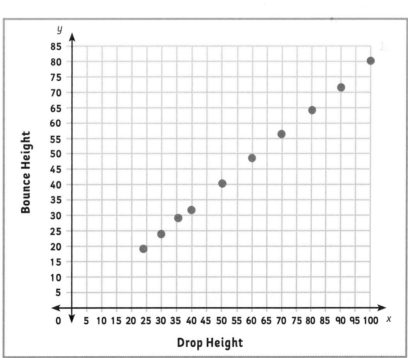

Tennis Ball	
Drop Height	Bounce Height
24	12
30	15
36	18
40	20
50	25
60	30
70	35
80	40
90	45
100	50

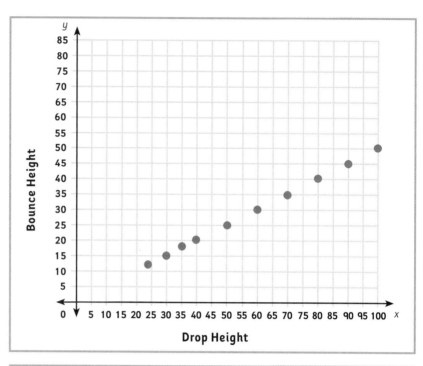

Golf Ball	
Drop Height	Bounce Height
24	18
30	23
36	27
40	30
50	38
60	45
70	52.5
80	60
90	67.5
100	75

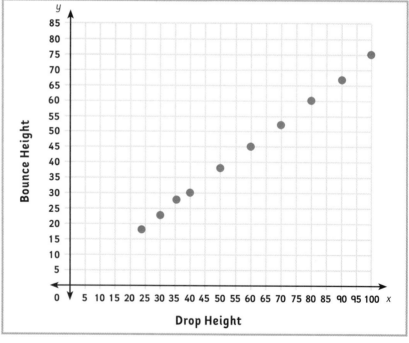

We see the relationship between the drop height and how high the ball bounces back up. We also see that each ball bounces back to different heights. The rubber ball bounces back the highest. That is why the trend in the graph is steeper than the other two. The tennis ball bounces back the least. Its trend is the flattest.

How do we collect our own data to analyze functions?

Classroom experiments involving functions work when we can see the relationship between a change in one variable and a change in the other variable.

In Mr. Raster's class, taking the ball to different heights was one variable. How far the ball bounced back was the other variable. At each step, his class collected **data** on how high the ball was before it was dropped and then measured, as carefully as they could, how high it bounced back up.

All of this information was added to a table before drawing a graph.

Rubber Ball	
Drop Height	**Bounce Height**
24	19
30	24
36	29
40	32
50	40
60	48
70	56
80	64
90	72
100	80

%÷
≡
<× **Apply Skills**
Turn to *Interactive Text*, page 349.

mBook **Reinforce Understanding**
Use the *mBook Study Guide* to review lesson concepts.

Activity 1

Select the statement that best describes the functional relationships shown in the tables. Write a, b, or c on your paper.

1.

Input	Output
2	4
5	10
10	20
25	50

(a) times 2
(b) plus 2
(c) plus 25

2.

Input	Output
12	4
9	3
24	8
3	1

(a) minus 8
(b) divided by 3
(c) times 3

3.

Input	Output
27	22
17	12
7	2
37	32

(a) minus 7
(b) divided by 3
(c) plus −5

Activity 2

Tell if there is a systematic relationship shown by the table of data in each problem. Answer yes or no.

1.

x	y
5	2
7	9
11	15
2	−5

Does this data represent a systematic relationship?

2.

x	y
1	4
2	8
3	12
4	16

Does this data represent a systematic relationship?

3.

x	y
1	5
2	10
3	15
4	20
5	25

Does this data represent a systematic relationship?

Tell the coordinates of the new shape.

1. Translate the rectangle one unit to the left.

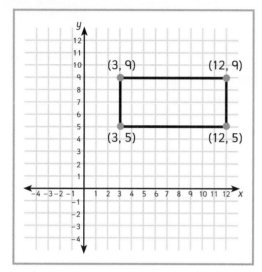

2. Reflect the triangle across the *y*-axis.

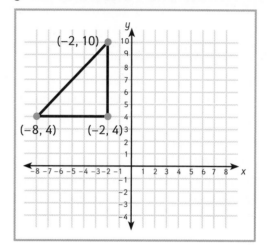

Solve.

1. $-25 - -15$

2. $270 \div -30$

3. $17 + -25$

4. $-80 \cdot -3$

5. $7 - 22$

6. $-100 \div -5$

7. $-125 + -125$

8. $-70 \cdot -7$

▶**The *X/Y* Table and Functions**

Vocabulary

independent variable
dependent variable

What is an *x/y* table?

We worked with tables and function machines to look at systematic relationships between variables. We described these variables as inputs and outputs.

We will now switch to a more algebraic form and write the variables as *x* and *y*. We will use Tina, who works at Big Tom's Restaurant, as the context. We learned in an earlier lesson that she earns $10 per hour, but the amount of time she works every week varies. The table shows how many hours she worked while she was going to school.

Week	Hours Worked	Amount Paid
1	5	$50
2	15	$150
3	8	$80
4	12	$120
5	10	$100

We can take the data from the table and put it in an *x/y* table. If that is all we did, it wouldn't be that much of a change. However, we describe all the data in the table using a simple equation. What is so important about functions is they let us summarize the systematic relationship between the two variables, usually represented by *x* and *y*, with an equation.

Example 1

Make an *x/y* table and a function from these data.

We will use the same data but just change the headings. Let *x* = the number of hours worked and *y* = the amount paid.

Hours Worked	Amount Paid
5	$50
15	$150
8	$80
12	$120
10	$100

x	*y*
5	50
15	150
8	80
12	120
10	100

The variable *x* represents the input data and *y* represents the output data. We said that Tina gets paid $10 per hour. We describe the relationship between the hours worked and the amount she gets paid this way:

$y = 10x$

What is the value of using an equation?

The value of using an equation is that it gives us a simple, general statement about a function that works for any data we are interested in.

There are three things to notice in the equation we created from the x/y table.

$$y = 10x$$

- First, we now have two different variables in the equation, x and y. This is different from the equations we studied in the last unit.

- Second, we write the equation starting with y on the left side of the equal sign. One way of talking about this function is to say, "What we get for y depends on what we substitute for x." We say that y depends on x. That is why x is called the **independent variable** and y is called the **dependent variable**.

> The importance of functions is that we can substitute any value for x and get a predictable value for y.

- Third, there is a connection between the relationship of x and y and proportions. The variables x and y have a proportional relationship. The proportion is $\frac{x}{y} = \frac{1}{10}$. Let's see how this is true.

The relationship between each set of x/y data is proportional.

$\frac{x}{y}$	$\frac{5}{50}$	$\frac{8}{80}$	$\frac{10}{100}$	$\frac{12}{120}$	$\frac{15}{150}$
	↓	↓	↓	↓	↓
$\frac{x}{y}$	$\frac{5}{50} = \frac{1}{10}$	$\frac{8}{80} = \frac{1}{10}$	$\frac{10}{100} = \frac{1}{10}$	$\frac{12}{120} = \frac{1}{10}$	$\frac{15}{150} = \frac{1}{10}$

This means that each pair of data is proportional to any other pair of x/y data. The x value is $\frac{1}{10}$ of the y value. We can also say it this way: The value of y is always 10 times the value of x.

That's where we get the function $y = 10x$.

Here is another function that shows a systematic relationship. We write an equation with two variables to show how x relates to y.

Example 1

Find the functional relationship between x and y.

x	y
3	−9
5	−15
−2	6
−4	12
10	−30

We get each y by multiplying x by −3. We write the function for the relationship this way:

$$y = -3x$$

A way to check the equation is to put a value in the x column and see if we get the correct value in the y column.

$$5$$
$$\downarrow$$
$$y = -3x$$
$$y = -3 \cdot 5$$
$$y = -15$$

The y value of −15 is associated with 5 in the x column. The equation is correct.

% ÷
≤ × **Apply Skills**
Turn to *Interactive Text*,
page 352.

Monitoring Progress
Quiz 1

mBook **Reinforce Understanding**
Use the *mBook Study Guide*
to review lesson concepts.

Activity 1

Solve the proportions by finding the value of the variable.

1. $\frac{y}{3} = \frac{6}{9}$

2. $\frac{2}{5} = \frac{z}{20}$

3. $\frac{3}{8} = \frac{27}{w}$

4. $\frac{4}{n} = \frac{24}{54}$

Activity 2

Use the x/y tables to write an equation.

1. What is this function?

x	y
2	4
5	10
10	20
25	50

2. What is this function?

x	y
1	5
2	10
3	15
10	50

3. What is this function?

x	y
4	36
7	63
3	27
8	72

Activity 3

The dot graph shows the functional relationship between how much Tina gets paid and how much she works. Answer the questions using the graph.

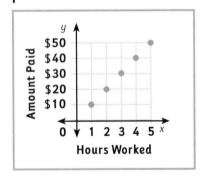

1. How much does Tina get paid for working 5 hours?

2. How many hours does Tina work if she gets paid $40?

3. How much does Tina get paid per hour?

4. If Tina worked 8 hours, how much would she get paid?

Activity 4 • Distributed Practice

Solve.

1. $3x + 2 = 14$

2. $-5z = 15$

3. $-27 = 3y$

4. $a + 16 = 17$

5. $15 = b - 2$

6. $3c = -24$

7. $5d + 10 = 25$

8. $-6e - 18 = -24$

▶**Writing Functions for Everyday Situations**

How do we write a function about an everyday situation?

Functions are everywhere around us. They describe a systematic relationship between two things, or variables. Let's see how to make a function from an everyday situation.

Situation:

Sunshine Bakery makes a lot of muffins every day. They send the muffins to stores and supermarkets around the city. They cook muffins on large trays. One tray makes 40 muffins at a time.

Steps for Writing Functions for Everyday Situations

STEP 1

Turn the situation into a function.

Based on the information, we know that 1 tray will make 40 muffins. That means 2 trays will make 80 muffins and 3 trays will make 120 muffins.

There is a relationship between the number of trays and the number of muffins.

We create an *x/y* table this way:

x = the number of trays
y = the total amount of muffins

x	y
1	40
2	80
3	120
4	160

STEP 2

Write the equation for the function.

We multiply 40 times the number of trays to get the total amount of muffins. If we have 3 trays, then we have 40 · 3 = 120 muffins. We use variables to make this equation:

$$y = 40x$$

Now we can check to see if the equation makes sense. Let's try a value for x and see if it works. Let's use 10 trays of muffins.

$$10$$
$$\downarrow$$
$$y = 40x$$
$$y = 40 \cdot 10$$
$$y = 400$$

Sunshine Bakery can make 400 muffins using 10 trays.

Speaking of Math

Here's how you can explain your thinking when you are writing an equation to represent a function.

- *First, I look for a relationship in the information.*
- *Next, I create a table so I can see the relationship.*
- *Then, I write an equation to represent the function. I start writing on the left side of the equal sign. The equation involves two variables that have a proportional relationship.*

It is important to know how to explain your thinking about functions.

% ÷
= ×
< × **Apply Skills**
Turn to *Interactive Text*,
page 355.

mBook **Reinforce Understanding**
Use the *mBook Study Guide*
to review lesson concepts.

▶**Problem Solving: Graphing Linear Functions**

What does the function look like on a graph?

When we show functions like $y = 40x$ on a graph, we use a line instead of a series of dots. This is why we call them **linear functions**—linear refers to the use of lines.

In Example 1, we draw a function on a coordinate graph and do not use labels for the axes. We just have the x- and y-axes.

Example 1

Show the linear function $y = 40x$ on a coordinate graph.

We get values for y by substituting different values for x. This lets us make a simple x/y table so that we can draw a line on the graph.

The graph of a linear function is a straight line.

x	y
0	0
1	40
2	80

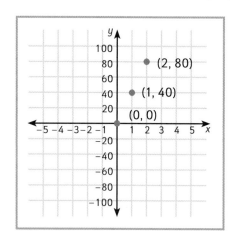

If we draw a line through these coordinates, we get a graph that shows a linear function.

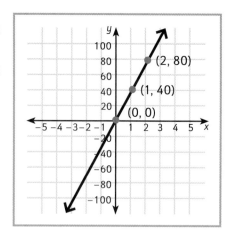

Example 2 shows what happens when Sunshine Bakery cuts back on the number of muffins for each tray. Rather than putting 40 muffins on each tray, they only put 25 muffins on a tray.

Example 2

Graph a linear function to show the number of muffins made per tray.

The number of muffins per tray is now 25.

Let x = the number of trays and y = the total amount of muffins.

x	y
1	25
2	50
3	75
4	100

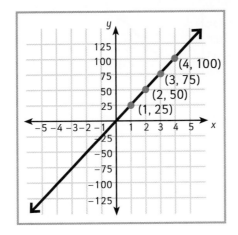

Function: $y = 25x$

The line in a linear function extends beyond what we can see in the graph on the page. Because of this, we can make predictions about other instances of this function.

How do we make predictions with functions?

In the last example, we used the line to predict how many muffins the bakery could make with 5 trays, 10 trays, or even 100 trays. All we need to do is look closely at the table and the graph and use number sense to extend the information we see there.

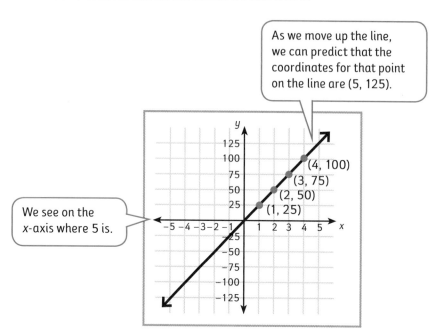

As we move up the line, we can predict that the coordinates for that point on the line are (5, 125).

We see on the x-axis where 5 is.

That means the number of muffins for 5 trays will be 125. We can't see 10 or 100 on the graph, but we can make predictions based on what we know about the relationships.

Problem-Solving Activity
Turn to **Interactive Text**, page 356.

mBook **Reinforce Understanding**
Use the **mBook Study Guide** to review lesson concepts.

Activity 1

Create an *x/y* table on your paper for each of the functions. Use −1, 0, 1, and 2 for the *x* values in the table. Then solve for *y* and fill in the *y* values.

Model $y = 2x$

Answer: The *x/y* table looks like this:

x	y
−1	−2
0	0
1	2
2	4

1. $y = 5x$

2. $y = 3x$

3. $y = 20x$

Activity 2

Write the functions for each of the following *x/y* tables with an equation. Use *x* and *y* and put *y* on the left of the equal sign.

1.

x	y
−1	−2
0	0
1	2
2	4

2.

x	y
2	8
10	40
−2	−8
20	80

3.

x	y
27	54
−2	−4
2	4
50	100

4.

x	y
40	400
3	30
200	2,000
6	60

5.

x	y
3	18
5	30
−7	−42
2	12

6.

x	y
16	80
−5	−25
4	20
25	125

Activity 3

Look at the functions shown by the equations and tables. Graph each on a sheet of graph paper. Label each point and connect them to show the line.

$y = 2x$

x	y
−1	−2
0	0
1	2
2	4

$y = 4x$

x	y
−1	−4
1	4
3	12
2	8

Activity 4 • Distributed Practice

Evaluate the numeric expressions using order of operations.

1. $-4 \cdot 8 \cdot -1 + 10$

2. $(3 + 17) \cdot (-4 + -5)$

3. $25 \div 5^2 + 10 - 15$

4. $17 - 25 + 45 - 3^2$

5. $3 \cdot (49 \div -7) + 40$

6. $-6 + -8 - -5 \cdot -8$

7. $(45 \div 3^2) - 5 + 15 - 10$

8. $-7 \cdot 6 \cdot -1 \cdot \frac{1}{6}$

Problem Solving:
▶Drawing Lines

▶**Slope and Linear Functions**

What is slope?

In the last lesson, we wrote functions based on x/y tables. Look at the function below. The relationship between x and y is the linear function y = 4x. That means we multiply the value of x times 4 to get the value of y.

x	y
1	4
2	8
3	12
4	16
5	20

What is the linear function?

y = 4x

Let's look at this function on a coordinate graph. It's important to notice the slant of the line. We use the word **slope** to describe the steepness or slant of a function. When we look at the equation for a linear function, the slope is the coefficient in front of the variable x. In this case, the slope is 4.

A Function With a Slope of 4

x	y
1	4
2	8
3	12
4	16
5	20

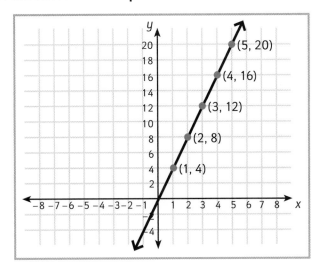

What is the slope for this line?

It is 4.

How do we determine the slope of a linear function?

We can also determine the slope of a linear function just by looking at the line on a graph.

Example 1 shows part of the graph we just made. This section shows how we describe horizontal movement on the graph as the **run** and vertical movement as the **rise** . We use the formula "rise over run" to calculate the slope.

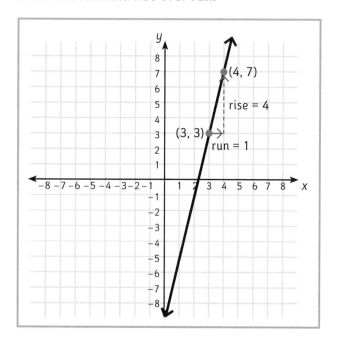
$$\text{Slope} = \frac{\text{rise}}{\text{run}} = \frac{4}{1} = 4$$

POWER CONCEPT

The slope tells us how steep or slanted the graph of a function is.

Slope doesn't always have to be a whole number. It can also be a fraction. Example 2 shows representations for a function that has a fraction as its slope. Notice in the *x/y* table that we multiply each *x* value by $\frac{2}{3}$ to get the *y* value. On the graph the rise is 2 and the run is 3.

Example 2

Find the slope of the line.

Here is the *x/y* table:

x	y
3	2
6	4
9	6
12	8
15	10

Here is the graph of the linear function $y = \frac{2}{3}x$:

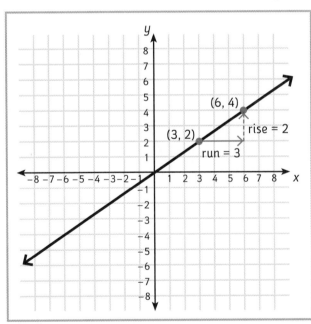

Slope $= \dfrac{\text{rise}}{\text{run}} = \dfrac{2}{3}$

The slope of this function is $\frac{2}{3}$.

 Apply Skills
Turn to *Interactive Text*, page 359.

mBook Reinforce Understanding
Use the *mBook Study Guide* to review lesson concepts.

How do we use slope to help us draw a line?

We saw how to figure out slope by looking at the rise over run of a line on a graph. We use the same idea to create a line with a slope from just one point on the graph. Example 1 shows how this works.

Example 1

Create a line with a slope of 2 that contains the point (1, 2).

We begin by plotting the point (1, 2) on the graph. We think about the rise and the run for a slope of 2.

$$\text{Slope} = \frac{\text{Rise}}{\text{Run}} = 2 \text{ or } \frac{2}{1}$$

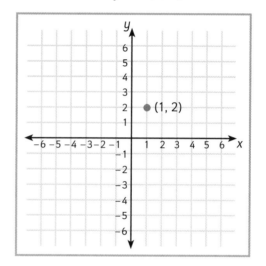

That means we move horizontally 1 for run and vertically 2 for rise.

We put a second point and then draw a line.

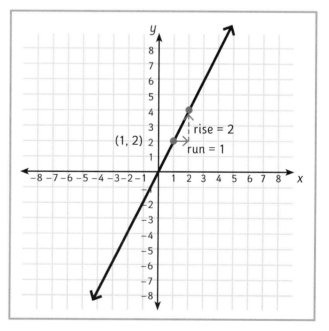

rise = 2
run = 1

 Problem-Solving Activity
Turn to *Interactive Text*,
page 361.

mBook **Reinforce Understanding**
Use the *mBook Study Guide*
to review lesson concepts.

Activity 1

Tell the slope by looking at the function written as an equation.

1. $y = 2x$

2. $y = \frac{1}{5}x$

3. $y = 6x$

4. $y = x$

5. $y = \frac{2}{3}x$

Activity 2

Tell the slope of the function by looking at rise over run on the graph of the function.

1.
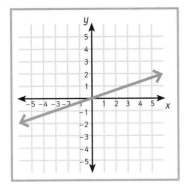

2.
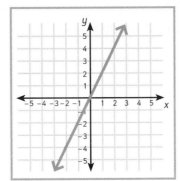

3.
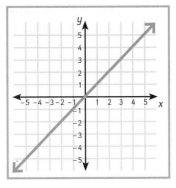

Activity 3

Draw the lines on graph paper. Be sure the line has the given slope and goes through the given point.

1. Draw a line with a slope of $\frac{1}{4}$ that goes through the point (4, 1).

2. Draw a line with a slope of −2 that goes through the point (1, −2).

3. Draw a line with a slope of $\frac{1}{3}$ that goes through the point (3, 1).

Activity 4 • Distributed Practice

Select the correct answer.

1. Select the name of the property represented by this general statement:
   $a + b = b + a$
   (a) Distributive Property
   (b) Identity Property of Addition
   (c) Commutative Property of Addition

2. Select the name of the property represented by this general statement:
   $a + 0 = a$
   (a) Distributive Property
   (b) Identity Property of Addition
   (c) Commutative Property of Addition

3. Select the name of the property represented by this general statement:
   $a + (b + c) = (a + b) + c$
   (a) Associative Property for Addition
   (b) Distributive Property
   (c) Identity Property of Addition

4. Select the name of the property represented by this general statement:
   $a(b + c) = ab + ac$
   (a) Distributive Property
   (b) Identity Property of Addition
   (c) Inverse Property of Addition

5. Select the name of the property represented by this general statement:
   $a + -a = 0$
   (a) Distributive Property
   (b) Identity Property of Addition
   (c) Inverse Property of Addition

6. Select the name of the property represented by this general statement:
   $\frac{a}{b} \cdot \frac{b}{a} = 1$
   (a) Inverse Property of Multiplication
   (b) Identity Property of Addition
   (c) Inverse Property of Addition

▶**Positive and Negative Slopes**

Vocabulary

positive slope
negative slope

What are some different kinds of slopes?

In the last lesson, we learned about the slope of a line. We know that the slope tells us how steep the line will be. Let's look at the functions graphed in Example 1 and see how the different slopes impact the graph of the line.

Example 1

Compare the slopes of the functions $y = \frac{2}{3}x$, $y = 2x$, and $y = 6x$.

How do the different slopes impact the graph of the line?

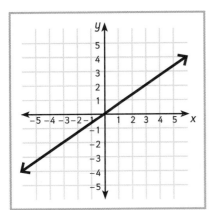

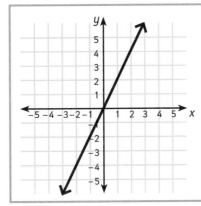

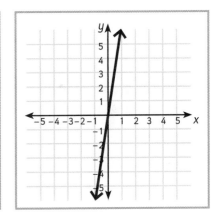

$y = \frac{2}{3}x$

Slope $= \frac{2}{3}$

$y = 2x$

Slope $= 2$

$y = 6x$

Slope $= 6$

The bigger the slope, the steeper the line.

The comparison in Example 1 involves slopes that are all **positive slopes** . These slopes are all greater than zero.

Another kind of slope is a **negative slope** . A negative slope is less than zero. Example 2 shows what a negative slope looks like as a line on a coordinate graph.

Example 2

Compare the graphs of the functions $y = x$, $y = -x$, and $y = -2x$.

What does the negative slope look like on the graph?

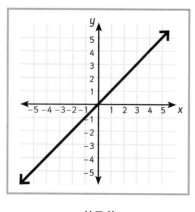

$y = x$

Slope = 1

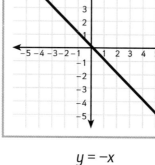

$y = -x$

Slope = −1

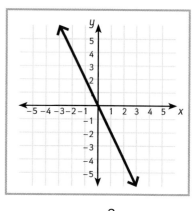

$y = -2x$

Slope = −2

The graphs of these functions show that positive slopes go up from left to right and negative slopes go down from left to right.

Negative slopes are the opposite of positive slopes when we think about steepness. With positive slopes, the bigger the number, the steeper the slope. In the case of negative slopes, the smaller the number, the steeper the slope. For example, a slope of −2 is steeper than a slope of −1 even though −1 > −2.

Example 3 shows the relative steepness of negative slopes.

Example 3

Compare the coordinate graphs of the following lines with negative slopes:

$y = -x$, $y = -\frac{1}{2}x$, and $y = -2x$.

How does the size of the negative slope impact the graph of the line?

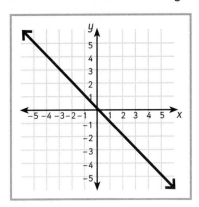

$y = -x$

Slope = -1

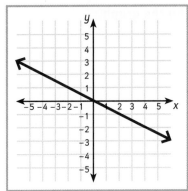

$y = -\frac{1}{2}x$

Slope = $-\frac{1}{2}$

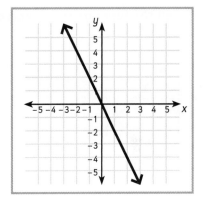

$y = -2x$

Slope = -2

When a slope is negative, the smaller the slope, the steeper the line.

It's important to become familiar with these different types of slopes and how slopes affect lines on the graph. This information helps us make even better analyses of functions.

POWER CONCEPT

- For positive slopes, bigger numbers mean steeper slopes.
- For negative slopes, smaller numbers mean steeper slopes.

%÷
<x **Apply Skills**
Turn to *Interactive Text*, page 363.

mBook **Reinforce Understanding**
Use the *mBook Study Guide* to review lesson concepts.

How do we use slopes to analyze functions?

Now that we understand different types of slopes, we can analyze functions. Sometimes we are given problems with incomplete information and we have to make assumptions about a function. Example 1 shows such a case.

Example 1

Tell the function represented by the graph.

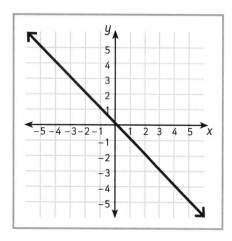

Which function is represented by this graph?

(a) $y = -x$

(b) $y = x$

(c) $y = 10x$

The answer is (a) $y = -x$.

This is the only answer that fits the graph since the line goes down from left to right. Only graphs with negative slopes have this characteristic. The other choices in the problem are positive slopes, which go up from left to right.

✎ **Problem-Solving Activity**
Turn to *Interactive Text*,
page 364.

mBook **Reinforce Understanding**
Use the *mBook Study Guide*
to review lesson concepts.

Tell the slope of each function.

1. $y = 3x$

2. $y = 4x$

3. $y = \frac{1}{4}x$

4. $y = -x$

5. $y = x$

6. $y = \frac{1}{3}x$

For each of the functions, look at the slope and tell whether the line on the graph will go up or down from left to right.

1. $y = -5x$

2. $y = \frac{2}{3}x$

3. $y = 10x$

4. $y = -x$

5. $y = -\frac{1}{2}x$

For each pair of functions, tell which line is steeper.

1. Line A: $y = -\frac{1}{2}x$
   Line B: $y = -x$

2. Line A: $y = 3x$
   Line B: $y = \frac{1}{3}x$

3. Line A: $y = -2x$
   Line B: $y = -x$

4. Line A: $y = \frac{5}{6}x$
   Line B: $y = 4x$

Solve.

1. $-27 + -35$

2. $-8 - 15$

3. $-5 \cdot -20$

4. $-540 \div 60$

5. $12 - -35$

6. $17 + -100$

7. $-20 \cdot 4$

8. $-54 \div -6$

Problem Solving:
▶The Advantages of Lines

▶Rate of Change

Vocabulary	
rate of change	

How do we use slope to compare everyday functions?

We have learned two ways to figure out the slope of a function.

The first is with an x/y table. We analyze the relationship between the x and y values in the table, then state it using words. Then we use the words to write an equation using x and y. The coefficient in front of x is the slope.

The second way to figure out the slope of a function is using the formula for rise over run of a line on a coordinate graph.

Both strategies give us the same function.

x	y
1	3
2	6
3	9
4	12

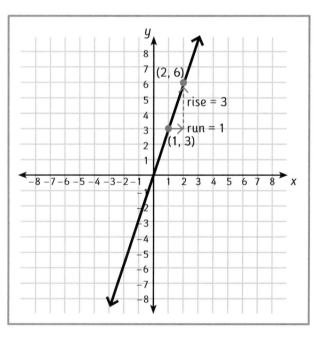

Look at the x/y table for a pattern. If we multiply each x by 3, we get y. We use this pattern to write the function $y = 3x$. The slope is 3.

We also find the equation for the function by measuring rise and run on the coordinate graph.

$$\text{Slope} = \frac{\text{rise}}{\text{run}} = \frac{3}{1} = 3$$

The slope is 3. We write the function $y = 3x$.

In the last lesson, we looked at how to tell the steepness or direction of a line just by looking at the slope. We were able to discuss these general rules about slope:

Lines With Positive Slopes:
- The bigger the slope, the steeper the line.
- Lines with positive slopes go up from left to right.

Lines With Negative Slopes:
- The smaller the slope, the steeper the line.
- Lines with negative slopes go down from left to right.

Looking at the steepness, or slope, of the line tells us something else that is very important. It tells us about the **rate of change**. The rate of change tells us how quickly a function is increasing or decreasing.

Example 1 shows why rate of change is important. We use it in everyday life when we think about how long it takes to reach a goal. In this example, Tina, who works at Big Tom's Restaurant, wants to make $60 to pay for college textbooks. Tina used to earn $10 per hour, then she got a raise to $15 per hour.

The tables and graph show two different functions for how Tina can earn $60.

Example 1

Show how Tina's old wage compares to her new wage using slopes.

Let x = the number of hours worked and y = dollars paid.

$10 per hour	
x	**y**
1	10
2	20
3	30
4	40
5	50
6	60

Function: $y = 10x$

$15 per hour	
x	**y**
1	15
2	30
3	45
4	60
5	75
6	90

Function: $y = 15x$

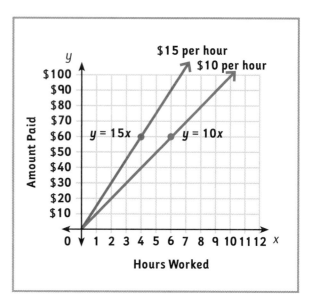

We compare the two lines. One line is steeper than the other. The $y = 15x$ line is steeper. Both lines get to $60, but the $y = 15x$ line gets there faster.

This means that Tina gets to the goal of $60 faster when she is paid $15 per hour. That is because the rate of change is larger. The rate of change helps us see how Tina gets to her goal faster when she earns $15 per hour.

One of the best ways to compare two functions is to compare their slopes. Slope tells us about the rate of change. This is important data for making comparisons.

%÷ **Apply Skills**
<X Turn to *Interactive Text*,
       page 367.

mBook Reinforce Understanding
Use the *mBook Study Guide*
to review lesson concepts.

▶**Problem Solving: The Advantages of Lines**

What are the advantages of using lines to make comparisons?

In the previous example, we compared how long it would take Tina to earn $60 based on two different rates of pay. In one case, the linear function showed her original rate of $10 per hour. In the other case, the linear function showed what she was earning after her raise to $15 per hour.

When we solve an equation, we can only find one value at a time. The advantage of a coordinate graph is that it lets us make comparisons at many different points in time.

Let's look at Example 1. The problem describes two different companies that wash windows on tall buildings. It shows different rates for washing windows. We can compare how many windows have been washed at different points in time.

Example 1

Use a graph to solve the word problem.

Problem:

Ajax Window Workers is trying to get contracts to wash windows for the buildings downtown. It is trying to beat Wonder Washers by advertising that it can do the job faster. Based on the data in the tables, which company washes windows faster?

Here are x/y tables for the two companies. The number of windows cleaned depends on the time they have to clean them.

Let x = hours and y = the number of windows cleaned.

Ajax	
x	**y**
1	3
2	6
3	9
4	12
5	15

Function: $y = 3x$

Wonder Washers	
x	**y**
1	2
2	4
3	6
4	8
5	10

Function: $y = 2x$

We make comparisons on the graph where the lines intersect points on the grid. We see three different comparisons.

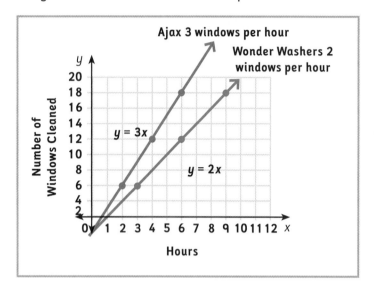

Ajax
6 windows in 2 hours
12 windows in 4 hours
18 windows in 6 hours

Wonder Washers
6 windows in 3 hours
12 windows in 6 hours
18 windows in 9 hours

We make our decision about these two companies by looking at which washes more windows in less time. Ajax washes the same number of windows in less time than Wonder Washers. That makes it the faster window-washing company.

Problem-Solving Activity
Turn to *Interactive Text*, page 368.

mBook Reinforce Understanding
Use the *mBook Study Guide* to review lesson concepts.

Activity 1

Look at the three lines on the graph and select the equation that matches each line. Use your knowledge of slope and steepness to help you.

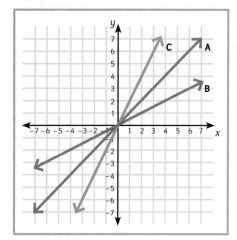

1. Which equation matches Line A?
    - (a) $y = 2x$
    - (b) $y = x$
    - (c) $y = \frac{1}{2}x$

2. Which equation matches Line B?
    - (a) $y = 2x$
    - (b) $y = x$
    - (c) $y = \frac{1}{2}x$

3. Which equation matches Line C?
    - (a) $y = 2x$
    - (b) $y = x$
    - (c) $y = \frac{1}{2}x$

Activity 2

Tell which line is steeper by comparing slopes. Write a or b on your paper.

1. Which line is steeper?
    - (a) $y = 3x$
    - (b) $y = \frac{1}{3}x$

2. Which line is steeper?
    - (a) $y = \frac{1}{2}x$
    - (b) $y = 2x$

3. Which line is steeper?
    - (a) $y = 2x$
    - (b) $y = 3x$

4. Which line is steeper?
    - (a) $y = \frac{2}{3}x$
    - (b) $y = x$

Activity 3

Look at the two lines on the graph. They show that Marcus earns $10 per hour at the restaurant and Elizabeth earns $12 per hour. Answer the questions using the graph.

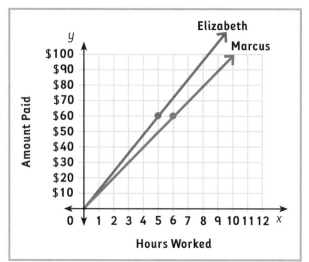

1. How many hours does Marcus have to work to earn $60?

2. How many hours does Elizabeth have to work to earn $60?

3. If the goal was to see who was first to earn $120, who would reach the goal faster, Elizabeth or Marcus?

Activity 4 • Distributed Practice

Solve.

1. $3x = -24$

2. $-4x + 5 = -27$

3. $72 = 9x$

4. $-6 + -6y = 36$

5. $x - 13 = 13$

6. $-6x + 1 = -5$

7. $170 = x + 80$

8. $210 = -30y$

▶The Y-Intercept

Vocabulary
y-intercept

What about lines that don't go through the origin?

Every linear function we have looked at so far has gone through the point of origin, or where the *x*- and *y*-axes intersect. The graph shows two different kinds of linear functions. Each one goes through the point of origin.

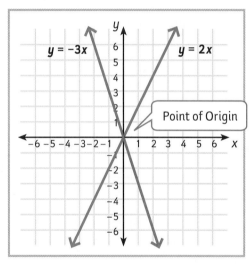

Some linear functions pass through the *y*-axis at some point other than (0, 0). The point where the line crosses the *y*-axis is called the **y-intercept** . We can see how a line crosses the *y*-axis at a point other than (0, 0) when we create a graph for a function such as the price Vroom Oil Change charges for an oil change.

Example 1 shows a table for the cost of oil based on the number of quarts a customer needs. Notice that Vroom Oil Change charges $3 to recycle the old oil from a car. We see that the line passes through (0, 3) on the y-axis of the graph.

The point (0, 3) on the graph means 0 quarts of oil and $3 to recycle the oil. This could happen if somebody changed their own oil and brought the used oil to Vroom Oil Change for recycling.

Example 1

Use a table, equation, and graph to solve the word problem.

Problem:

Vroom Oil Change charges $6 per quart to change oil. It charges $3 to recycle the old oil from your car. It doesn't matter how much oil you have, the recycling charge is always the same.

Here is a table showing all the charges. How much does it cost to recycle oil if Vroom doesn't change the oil?

Number of Quarts	Cost for Oil	Recycling Charge	Total Cost
1	$6	$3	$9
2	$12	$3	$15
3	$18	$3	$21
4	$24	$3	$27
5	$30	$3	$33

When we put this into an x/y table, we need to figure out the equation that will give us the total cost. Here is the x/y table showing quarts and total cost.

Let x = the number of quarts and y = the total cost.

x	y
1	9
2	15
3	21
4	27
5	33

We find the cost by multiplying 6 times the number of quarts and adding $3. That means our function is:

$$y = 6x + 3$$

We can check this by substituting one of the x values in the function to see if it gives us the correct y value.

$$
\begin{array}{c}
4 \\
\downarrow
\end{array}
$$

$$y = 6x + 3$$
$$y = 6 \cdot 4 + 3$$
$$y = 24 + 3$$
$$y = 27$$

Here is what the graph looks like for this linear function.

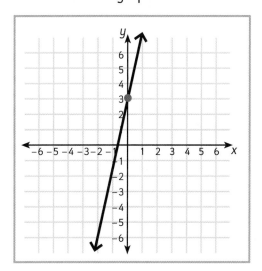

The function crosses the y-axis at (0, 3). The y-intercept for this function is 3.

What happens if Vroom Oil Change decides to change the price it charges for recycling the oil? Let's say that it now charges $4 to recycle the oil.

Example 2 shows the change from the old charge of $3 to the new charge of $4. The slope of the line does not change. The line has just moved up one unit on the y-axis. The lines are parallel because they have the same slope.

Example 2

Use a table, function, and graph to solve the word problem.

Problem:

Vroom Oil Change still charges $6 per quart to change oil. But it now charges $4 to recycle the old oil from your car. How does the function change?

Number of Quarts	Cost for Oil	Recycling Charge	Total Cost
1	$6	$4	$10
2	$12	$4	$16
3	$18	$4	$22
4	$24	$4	$28
5	$30	$4	$34

When we put this into an *x/y* table, we need to figure out the equation that will give us the total cost. Here is the *x/y* table showing quarts and total cost.

Let x = the number of quarts and y = the total cost.

x	y
1	10
2	16
3	22
4	28
5	34

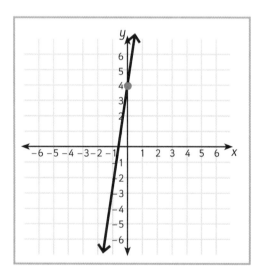

What is our function?

$y = 6x + 4$

Here is what the graph looks like for this function. The y-intercept is now 4. The line has shifted up one unit.

By adding a constant to linear functions, we move the y-intercept up the y-axis. A similar thing happens when we subtract a constant.

Let's imagine that Al's Auto Repair wants to get into the oil changing business. Al decides to change oil for $6 a quart, but he will not charge for recycling the oil.

Al has a big opening day celebration. On opening day, he will give everyone a discount of $5 off an oil change for coming to his shop. In this case, we are subtracting 5 in the function. This means the line intersects the y-axis at $(0, -5)$.

Example 3

Use a table, equation, and graph to show the $5 discount.

Number of Quarts	Cost for Oil	Discount	Total Cost
1	$6	$5	$1
2	$12	$5	$7
3	$18	$5	$13
4	$24	$5	$19
5	$30	$5	$25

When we put this into an x/y table, we need to figure out the equation that will give us the total cost.

Let x = the number of quarts and y = the total cost.

x	y
1	1
2	7
3	13
4	19
5	25

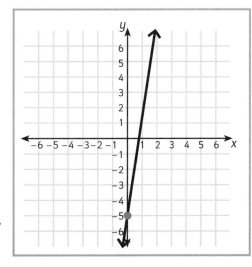

What is our function?

$y = 6x - 5$

The graph for this function tells us that the y-intercept is -5. However, in real life we could not walk into Al's shop and get $5 without an oil change.

 **Apply Skills**
Turn to *Interactive Text*, page 371.

Monitoring Progress
Quiz 2

 **Reinforce Understanding**
Use the *mBook Study Guide* to review lesson concepts.

Activity 1

Identify the *y*-intercept for each graph.

1.
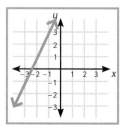

(a) (0, 0)
(b) (0, 2)
(c) (0, 5)
(d) (0, 10)

2.
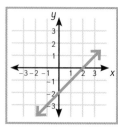

(a) (0, 2)
(b) (0, −2)
(c) (−2, 2)
(d) (−2, 0)

3.
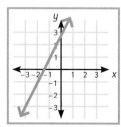

(a) (0, 3)
(b) (3, 0)
(c) (2, 3)
(d) (3, 2)

4.
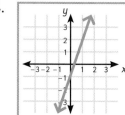

(a) (0, 1)
(b) (0, −1)
(c) (1, 0)
(d) (−1, 0)

Activity 2

Look at the graphs. Select the equation that matches each function. Use your knowledge of slope and steepness to help you.

1.
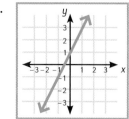

(a) $y = x + 1$
(b) $y = 2x + 1$
(c) $y = 3x + 1$
(d) $y = 4x + 1$

2.
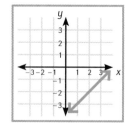

(a) $y = x$
(b) $y = x - 1$
(c) $y = x - 2$
(d) $y = x - 4$

3.
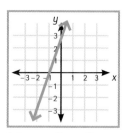

(a) $y = 3x + 3$
(b) $y = 2x + 3$
(c) $y = x + 3$
(d) $y = -x + 3$

Activity 3

Tell which line is steeper by comparing slopes. Write a or b on your paper.

1. Which line is steeper?
   (a) $y = x$
   (b) $y = \frac{1}{2}x$

2. Which line is steeper?
   (a) $y = 3x$
   (b) $y = x$

3. Which line is steeper?
   (a) $y = 5x$
   (b) $y = 2x$

4. Which line is steeper?
   (a) $y = \frac{2}{3}x$
   (b) $y = 2x$

Activity 4 • Distributed Practice

Solve.

1. $-3 + 2 \cdot -8 + 100$

2. $5^2 - (8 + 2) \cdot 2$

3. $100 \div 50 + 7 - 4$

4. $100 \div 5^2 + 7 - 4$

5. $20 \cdot 8 \cdot 0 - 100$

6. $-15 + -30 - -8 \cdot 10$

7. $24 \div (8 - 4) + -12$

8. $-8 \cdot -8 \div 32 + (2 - 9)$

Problem Solving:
▶**Graphing Linear Equations**

▶**Slope-Intercept Form: $y = mx + b$**

What is the equation for a linear function?

We are now ready to start working with the traditional equation for a linear function, which is $y = mx + b$. Each part of the equation shows what we have already learned in previous lessons. Let's look at each part of the equation for a linear function.

The value of y depends on $mx + b$.

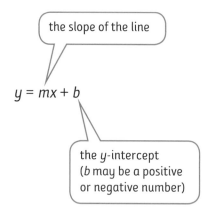

the slope of the line

$y = mx + b$

the y-intercept
(b may be a positive
or negative number)

We use this equation to create a table of data and then draw a line on a coordinate graph. All that we have to do is substitute a value for x and then solve the equation just like any other equation. Example 1 shows what this process looks like.

Example 1

Graph the function $y = 2x - 3$.

STEP 1

Substitute values for x and put the values for x and y into a table.

$y = 2x - 3$

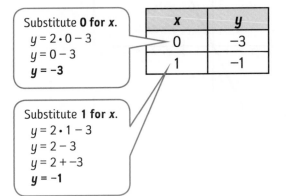

Substitute **0** for x.
$y = 2 \cdot 0 - 3$
$y = 0 - 3$
$y = -3$

x	y
0	−3
1	−1

Substitute **1** for x.
$y = 2 \cdot 1 - 3$
$y = 2 - 3$
$y = 2 + -3$
$y = -1$

Substitute **2** for x.
$y = 2 \cdot 2 - 3$
$y = 4 - 3$
$y = 1$

x	y
2	1
3	3

Substitute **3** for x.
$y = 2 \cdot 3 - 3$
$y = 6 - 3$
$y = 3$

STEP 2

Use the table to plot a line on a coordinate graph.

We check to see if we drew the line correctly by looking at the function.

Is the slope of the line 2? We use rise over run to find out.

$$\text{Slope} = \frac{\text{Rise}}{\text{Run}} = \frac{2}{1} = 2$$

In this case, b is a negative number. The line crosses the y-axis at $(0, -3)$. This is the y-intercept for the function.

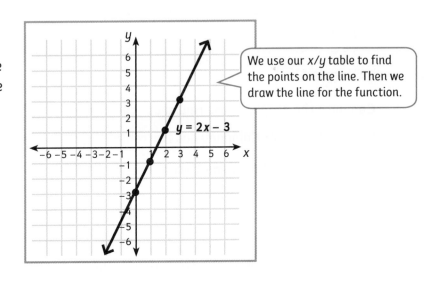

We use our x/y table to find the points on the line. Then we draw the line for the function.

$y = 2x - 3$

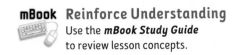

Apply Skills
Turn to *Interactive Text*, page 374.

mBook **Reinforce Understanding**
Use the *mBook Study Guide* to review lesson concepts.

▶**Problem Solving: Graphing Linear Equations**

What does $y = mx + b$ look like with no slope?

zero slope

We looked at two different kinds of slopes in this unit: positive and negative slopes. They go in opposite directions.

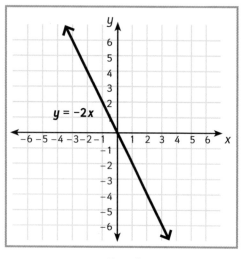

negative slope

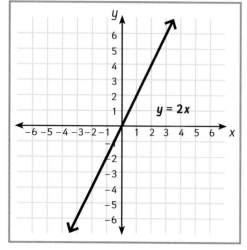

positive slope

There is one other kind of slope we need to know about— **zero slope** .

Example 1 shows how two different choices can lead to different kinds of graphs.

Example 1

Compare the graphs of the rental car choices.

Dented Rental Car Company has two rental choices.

Choice 1: Pay $20 a day for the car, and then 10 cents (or $0.10) for every mile driven.

Choice 2: Pay $25 a day for the car, and drive an unlimited number of miles for no extra charge.

We put each choice into a function, then graph it on a line.

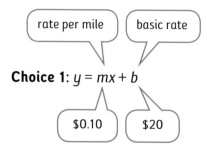

The function is $y = 0.10x + 20$.

We make a table based on the function.

Number of Miles Driven	Cost for Miles Driven	Basic Charge	Total Charge
0	$0	$20	$20
10	$1	$20	$21
20	$2	$20	$22
30	$3	$20	$23
40	$4	$20	$24
50	$5	$20	$25

Then we place the information in an *x/y* table.

Let x = number of miles driven and y = total cost.

x	y
0	$20
10	$21
20	$22
30	$23
40	$24
50	$25

Finally, our graph is a positive function that looks like this.

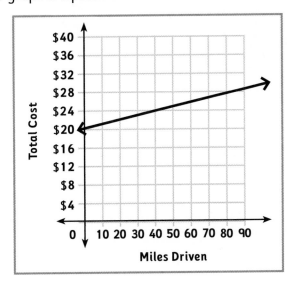

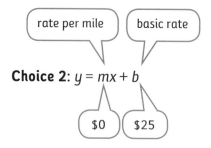

Choice 2: $y = mx + b$

The function is $y = 0x + 25$ or $y = 25$.

We make a table based on the function.

Number of Miles Driven	Cost for Miles Driven	Basic Charge	Total Charge
0	$0	$25	$25
10	$0	$25	$25
20	$0	$25	$25
30	$0	$25	$25
40	$0	$25	$25
50	$0	$25	$25

Then we place the information in an x/y table.

Let x = number of miles driven and y = total cost.

x	y
0	$25
10	$25
20	$25
30	$25
40	$25
50	$25

Our graph is a positive linear function that looks like this.

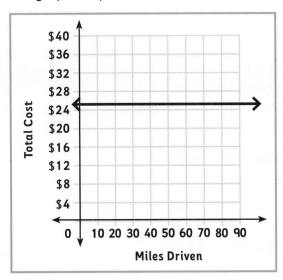

The slope of the second line is zero. It is a horizontal line that keeps going on and on. It doesn't matter how many miles we drive that day, the charge for the rental car will still be $25. This is a linear function with zero slope.

If we compare the two graphs, we see that Choice 1 is a better deal if we are going to drive less than 50 miles a day. If we are going to drive more than 50 miles a day, then Choice 2 is the better deal.

Problem-Solving Activity
Turn to *Interactive Text*,
page 376.

mBook **Reinforce Understanding**
Use the *mBook Study Guide*
to review lesson concepts.

Activity 1

Each of the functions is written in $y = mx + b$ form. Tell the slope and the y-intercept in each function.

1. $y = 2x + 3$
   (a) What is the slope?
   (b) What is the y-intercept?

2. $y = \frac{1}{2}x + 4$
   (a) What is the slope?
   (b) What is the y-intercept?

3. $y = 3x$
   (a) What is the slope?
   (b) What is the y-intercept?

4. $y = 4$
   (a) What is the slope?
   (b) What is the y-intercept?

Activity 2

Write the equation for each of the functions using $y = mx + b$ form.

1. Write the function whose slope is -1 and y-intercept is 5.

2. Write the function whose slope is 0 and y-intercept is 2.

3. Write the function whose slope is 1 and y-intercept is 0.

Activity 3

Create an x/y table and a graph for each of the functions you wrote in Activity 2.

Activity 4 • Distributed Practice

Write the general pattern for each of the properties. You are given examples to help you.

1. Additive Identity Property

   $3 + 0 = 3$

   $-\frac{1}{2} + 0 = -\frac{1}{2}$

   $2.3 + 0 = 2.3$

   Write the general pattern using the variable m.

2. Multiplicative Inverse (reciprocal) Property

   $\frac{2}{3} \cdot \frac{3}{2} = 1$

   $\frac{4}{3} \cdot \frac{3}{4} = 1$

   $\frac{2}{1} \cdot \frac{1}{2} = 1$

   Write the general pattern using the variables a and b.

3. Distributive Property

   $2(x + 5) = 2x + 10$

   $3(x + 7) = 3x + 21$

   $4(x + 9) = 4x + 36$

   Write the general pattern using the variables x, y, and z.

▸**Algebraic Equations and Functions**

How do we use what we learned about solving equations when working with functions?

We have learned a lot about how to solve algebraic equations. We have created an Algebra Toolbox. It is filled with properties and rules that help us solve equations step-by-step.

Algebra Tools

The tools in our Algebra Toolbox help us solve equations:

- Properties
- PEMDAS
- Operations Rules
- Like Terms

Knowing how to solve equations is very important when we work with functions. While functions help us see a predictable, systematic relationship between two variables, solving equations helps us find an exact point in that relationship. It is easiest to see that point when we graph a function.

Let's go back to the rental car example in the last lesson. We can rent the car for one day and pay $20 plus 10 cents (or $0.10) for every mile that we drive.

Example 1 shows the graph of the function. But let's say that we turn in the car, and the rental charge is $28. How many miles did we drive? We can look closely at the graph or use algebra to answer this question. Example 1 shows how we can do this.

Example 1

Use an algebraic equation to solve the word problem.

Problem:

I rented a car from Dented Rental Car Company, and I decided to use Choice 1. That means I pay $20 a day plus $0.10 per mile. That day, I drive from Baltimore to Washington, D.C., and back again. My total bill from Dented Rental is $28. How far did I drive?

Let x = number of miles driven and y = total cost.

The function is $y = 0.10x + 20$.

The graph shows a line. To find out exactly how many miles were driven, we start by finding $28 on the y-axis. Then we go across the graph until we reach the line to determine where this intersects with the x-axis. If we look closely, we see it is 80 miles.

Another way to solve this problem is to use an algebraic expression.

We know that the total cost is $28 and y = the total cost. All we have to do is substitute for y.

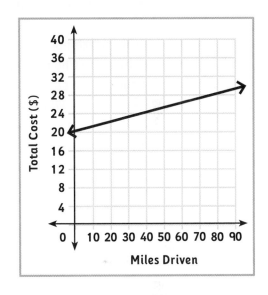

$$\overset{28}{\underset{\downarrow}{}}$$

What is the function?

$$y = 0.10x + 20$$
$$28 = 0.10x + 20$$
$$28 + \boxed{-20} = 0.10x + 20 + \boxed{-20}$$
$$8 = 0.10x + 0$$
$$8 = 0.10x$$
$$\frac{8}{0.10} = \frac{0.10}{0.10}x$$
$$80 = 1x$$
$$80 = x$$

I drove 80 miles. We get the same answer using algebra.

The advantage of using algebra is we often do not have the function on a graph. This means that we need to use algebra to solve the problem.

 **Apply Skills**
Turn to *Interactive Text*, page 379.

 **mBook** **Reinforce Understanding**
Use the *mBook Study Guide* to review lesson concepts.

▶**Problem Solving: More Graphs of Linear Functions**

How do we know what changes and what stays the same in a function?

Functions help us think about the systematic relationship between two variables. We have used equations involving x and y to represent each variable. We have also learned that the traditional way of showing a function is to use the equation $y = mx + b$.

When we solve an equation of a function algebraically, we need to think carefully about what each variable in the equation stands for. A good way to begin is to think about what is changing and what is staying the same.

In the rental car example, the amount that was changing was the number of miles. In Choice 2, we could have driven 10 miles or 50 miles. That part could have changed. What stayed the same was the basic cost of the rental car, which was always going to be $25 no matter how many miles were driven. When we look at the equation for the function, we see which parts are changing and which parts stay the same. The y-intercept, which we call b, is a constant. It stays the same.

Equation for a function: $y = mx + b$

Let's look at how to take a simple function and turn it into an algebraic equation we can solve. Example 1 shows how we translate it into an equation.

Example 1

Use algebra to solve the word problem.

Problem:

Tina is working at Big Tom's Restaurant and is paid $15 an hour. She has $50 in the bank, and she needs $350 to pay her rent this month. How many hours will she have to work until she has $350 to pay her rent?

STEP 1

Decide what is changing and what is staying the same.

The $50 Tina has in the bank is not changing. It stays there. What changes is the number of hours she is going to work.

Equation for a function: $y = mx + b$

STEP 2

Find what the variables represent in the function.

Let x = the number of hours she works and y = the total amount she has saved. The variable b does not change. That is the $50 Tina has in the bank. We use this to understand what y, x, and b stand for in the function equation.

STEP 3

Substitute for the variables in the function. This will give us a simple algebraic equation.

$$350 \quad 15 \quad 50$$
$$\downarrow \quad \downarrow \quad \downarrow$$

Equation for a function: $y = mx + b$

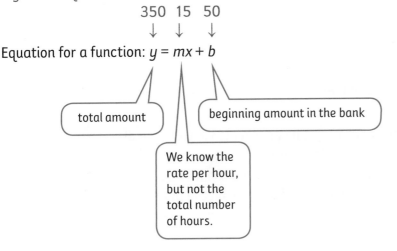

STEP 4

Solve the equation.

The equation is: 350 = 15x + 50

Solution:

$$350 = 15x + 50$$
$$350 + \boxed{-50} = 15x + 50 + \boxed{-50}$$
$$300 = 15x + 0$$
$$300 = 15x$$
$$\frac{300}{15} = \frac{15}{15}x$$
$$20 = 1x$$
$$20 = x$$

Tina will have to work 20 hours to save a total of $350.

We substitute to check if we are correct.

$$\overset{20}{\downarrow}$$

$$350 = 15x + 50$$
$$350 = 15 \cdot 20 + 50$$
$$350 = 300 + 50$$
$$350 = 350$$

Let's look at another problem using the equation $y = mx + b$. Tina also has a cell phone. She pays $30 a month and an additional $8 for every hour she talks on the phone each month. Example 2 shows how our function changes and how we solve it.

Example 2

Use algebra to solve the word problem.

Problem:

Tina has an inexpensive cell phone plan. She pays a monthly charge of $30, but has to pay an additional $8 for every hour she talks on the phone. The company just charges by the hour, not by the minute. Last month her bill was $54. How many hours did she talk on the phone?

STEP 1

Decide what is changing and what is staying the same.

Tina pays $30 each month for her cell phone. It doesn't matter how many hours she talks. This amount does not change. What changes is the number of hours she talks on the phone.

changes   stays the same

Equation for a function: $y = mx + b$

STEP 2

Find what the variables represent in the function.

Let x = the number of hours she talks on the phone and y = the total amount of her bill. The variable b does not change. That is the $30 she pays each month for her phone.

STEP 3

Substitute for the variables in the function. This will give us a simple algebraic equation.

$$54 \quad 8 \quad 30$$
$$\downarrow \quad \downarrow \quad \downarrow$$

Equation for a function: $y = mx + b$

total amount   monthly charge for her phone

We know the rate for every hour, but not the number of hours she talked on the phone.

STEP 4

Solve the equation.

The equation is: $54 = 8x + 30$

Tina talked for 3 hours on her cell phone last month.

Solution:

$$54 = 8x + 30$$
$$54 + -30 = 8x + 30 + -30$$
$$24 = 8x + 0$$
$$24 = 8x$$
$$\frac{24}{8} = \frac{8}{8}x$$
$$3 = 1x$$
$$3 = x$$

Problem-Solving Activity
Turn to *Interactive Text*, page 380.

mBook **Reinforce Understanding**
Use the *mBook Study Guide* to review lesson concepts.

Activity 1

Use algebra to solve the functions.

1. $y = 0.10x + 20$ for $y = 360$
2. $y = 0.20x + 10$ for $y = 210$
3. $y = 0.50x + 40$ for $y = 140$
4. $y = 0.30x + 30$ for $y = 930$

Activity 2

Write an equation for each function using the car rental contracts.

> **Model** A rental car costs $50 plus 20 cents per mile. Write the equation that describes this function.
>
> Answer: $y = 0.20x + 50$

1. A rental car costs $25 plus 10 cents per mile. Write the equation.

2. A rental car costs $100 plus 5 cents per mile. Write the equation.

3. A rental car costs $20 plus 30 cents per mile. Write the equation.

4. A rental car company only charges per mile. The rate is $1 per mile. Write the equation.

Activity 3

For each of the everyday functions, write the equation that describes the function. Use $y = mx + b$ form.

1. Todd is a busboy at a popular restaurant. He gets paid $8 per hour and $50 per night he works. Write an equation that describes this function.

2. Loretta has a babysitting business and she charges $10 per hour and a flat fee of $5 per job. Write an equation that shows this function.

3. The tickets for the baseball game cost $30 per ticket plus a $10 processing fee for each group purchasing tickets. Write an equation that shows this function.

Activity 4 • Distributed Practice

Solve.

1. $-24 + -18 + -14$
2. $27 - 4 - 8$
3. $-18 \div 9$
4. $-9 \cdot -8$
5. $-170 - -90$
6. $417 - 503$

Lesson 13 ▶Creating an X/Y Table From a Graph

Problem Solving:
▶ **The Point Where Functions Intersect on a Graph**

▶**Creating an X/Y Table From a Graph**

How do we create a table from a graph?

Up until now, we have been given functions and then plotted them on a coordinate graph. What happens when we reverse this process?

Example 1 shows how we can create a table by looking at points on a graph.

Example 1

Make an x/y table from the graph of a function.

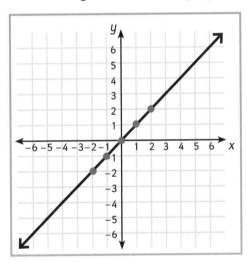

If we identify the coordinates of the points on this graph, we see x and y values for the function. The coordinates of the points are: (0, 0), (1, 1), (2, 2), (−1, −1), and (−2, −2). We just take the x and y values from these coordinates and put them in a table.

x	y
−2	−2
−1	−1
0	0
1	1
2	2

An x/y table shows the x values and y values for a function. These are very easily translated from (x, y) coordinates to x and y values in a table. This is also a way to find the equation of a function shown on a graph because once we show it in a table, it is easy to analyze the relationship between x and y. For the function shown in Example 1, the equation is y = x. Every input value is the same as every output value.

% ÷
≡ =
< x **Apply Skills**
Turn to *Interactive Text*,
page 382.

mBook Reinforce Understanding
Use the *mBook Study Guide*
to review lesson concepts.

▶**Problem Solving: The Point Where Functions Intersect on a Graph**

Where do two functions meet?

There are times when linear functions help us make important decisions. This often happens when we are given a choice and we can't decide what to do. Example 1 shows what different payment plans mean when we buy a used car. We use algebra to figure out the point where the plans cross.

Example 1

Use equations and a graph to solve the problem.

Problem:

Garrison Motors offers two payment plan choices when you buy a used car.

Plan 1: Pay $500 down and make payments of $100 per month.

Plan 2: Just pay $150 per month.

At what point will you have paid the same amount of money?

We begin by writing the two functions.

Plan 1: What is changing and what is the same?

When we pay $500 up front, that stays the same. What is changing is the number of months that we pay $100. The function for Plan 1 is $y = 100x + 500$.

Plan 2: What is changing and what is the same?

The only thing that is happening in Plan 2 is change. Nothing is staying the same. We pay $150 per month. The number of months that we pay changes. The function for Plan 2 is $y = 150x$.

We use algebra to figure out where the functions cross.
If $y = 100x + 500$ and $y = 150x$, that means $150x = 100x + 500$ because both of these expressions equal y.

Now we solve the problem using the rules and properties in our Algebra Toolbox.

$$150x = 100x + 500$$

$$150x + \boxed{-100x} = 100x + \boxed{-100x} + 500$$

$$50x = 0 + 500$$

$$50x = 500$$

$$\frac{50}{50}x = \frac{500}{50}$$

$$1x = 10$$

$$x = 10 \text{ or } 10 \text{ months}$$

Here is the graph with the two functions. The two functions cross at 10 months on the x-axis.

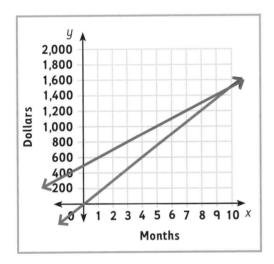

Problem-Solving Activity
Turn to **Interactive Text**,
page 383.

mBook **Reinforce Understanding**
Use the *mBook Study Guide*
to review lesson concepts.

Activity 1

For each of the graphs, create an *x/y* table.

1.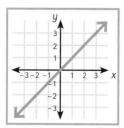

2.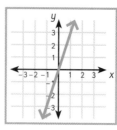

3.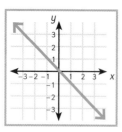

4.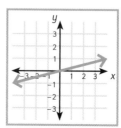

Activity 2

For each of the *x/y* tables, write an equation that represents the function.

1.

x	y
2	4
3	6
10	20
100	200

2.

x	y
4	2
6	3
20	10
200	100

3.

x	y
5	−5
10	−10
100	−100
0	0

4.

x	y
16	4
100	25
32	8
4	1

Activity 3

Look at each of the graphs. They show the relationship between two functions. Tell the point where the two functions intersect.

1.

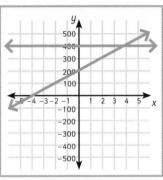

What are the coordinates of the point where the two functions intersect?

2.

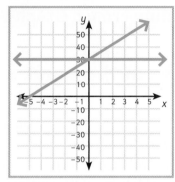

What are the coordinates of the point where the two functions intersect?

3.

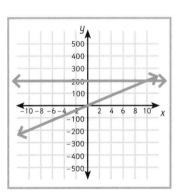

What are the coordinates of the point where the two functions intersect?

Activity 4 • Distributed Practice

Solve.

1. $3x + 4 = 12$

2. $-56 = -8x$

3. $4x + 7 = 15$

4. $-27 = 9 + -4x$

5. $90x = 180$

6. $-15 = 12 + 3x$

7. $-48x = -46 - 2x$

8. $x + 17 = 34$

▶**Creating an Equation From a Graph**

How do we figure out the equation of a function from a graph?

In the last lesson, we created an x/y table using the coordinates on a graph. We could then write the equation. But we can write the equation from the graph without creating a table first. How do we look at a line on a coordinate graph and figure out its equation? Just think about the two parts to a linear equation—the slope and the y-intercept.

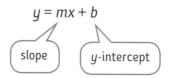

$$y = mx + b$$

slope y-intercept

Example 1 shows a line on a coordinate graph. The line goes through the origin. That means the value for b is 0, so all we look at is $y = mx$. We figure out m (or slope) by using rise over run. We begin by looking at two points on the line, (1, 2) and (2, 4). From these two points, we find the rise and run for computing the slope.

Example 1

Use the graph to write an equation for the function.

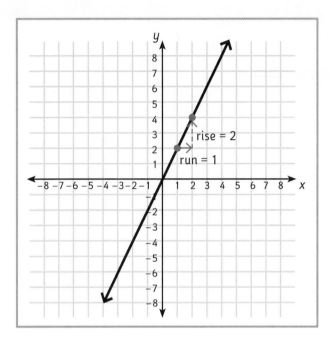

$\dfrac{\text{Rise}}{\text{Run}} = \dfrac{2}{1}$ or 2

The slope = 2

The graph goes through the origin (0, 0), so we know the y-intercept is zero.

The equation for the function is $y = 2x + 0$ or just $y = 2x$.

We can also figure out how to write functions with negative slopes just by looking at the graph. In this case, we have to pay attention to the direction we are moving. In Example 2, we look at the two points (−2, 1) and (−5, 2), which are in Quadrant II on the graph.

Example 2

Use the graph to write an equation for the function.

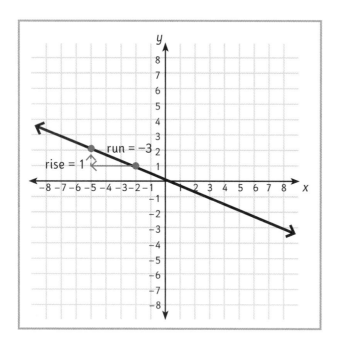

The run is going in the negative direction. We see this on the *x*-axis.

$$\frac{\text{Rise}}{\text{Run}} = \frac{1}{-3} \text{ or } -\frac{1}{3}$$

The slope $= -\frac{1}{3}$

The graph also goes through the origin (0, 0), so the *y*-intercept is zero.

The equation for this function is $y = -\frac{1}{3}x + 0$ or just $y = -\frac{1}{3}x$.

It's also important to be able to write an equation for a function that has a y-intercept other than 0. Example 3 shows a line that intersects the y-axis at the point (0, 2). That means the value for b is 2. Now we use rise over run to figure out the slope. Once again, we look at two points on the graph, (1, 3) and (2, 4). These two points are in Quadrant I.

Example 3

Use the graph to write an equation for the function.

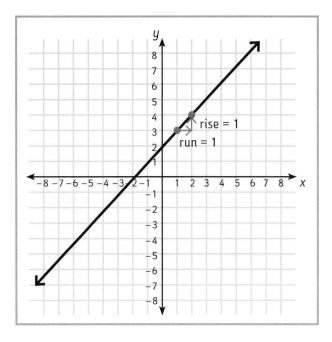

$\dfrac{\text{Rise}}{\text{Run}} = \dfrac{1}{1}$ or 1

The slope = 1

The line crosses the y-axis at the point (0, 2). This means that the y-intercept for this function is 2, or that $b = 2$.

The equation for the function is $y = x + 2$.

In Example 4, we have a function with a negative slope and a
y-intercept other than 0. In this function, the line goes through the
y-axis at the point (0, −6). This means *b* = −6.

Next, we find the slope, or *m*. We again look at two points to find the
slope, (−1, −4) and (−3, −1). The two points are found in Quadrant III this
time. These points are interesting because even though they each have
two negative coordinates, the rise is going up, so it is positive. To go from
−4 to −1 we add 3: −4 + 3 = −1. That is why the rise is a positive number.

Example 4

Use the graph to write an equation for the function.

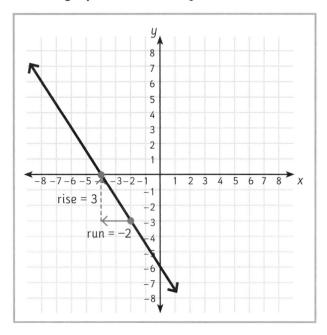

We are going the negative direction with run. We see on the *x*-axis that
we are moving to the left, or in a negative direction, two units.

$\frac{\text{rise}}{\text{run}} = \frac{3}{-2}$ or $-\frac{3}{2}$ The slope $= -\frac{3}{2}$

The graph crosses the *y*-axis at the point (0, −6), so the *y*-intercept,
or *b*, is −6.

The equation for this function is $y = -\frac{3}{2}x + -6$ **or** $-\frac{3}{2}x - 6$.

Apply Skills
Turn to *Interactive Text*,
page 385.

Reinforce Understanding
Use the *mBook Study Guide*
to review lesson concepts.

▶**Problem Solving: Using a Function to Find the Best Deal**

How do functions help us figure out the best deal?

Raul works in pizza delivery. He had to choose between two different companies to work for. Let's see which company would pay him more in a day.

Example 1

Solve the problem by finding the intersection of the functions.

Problem:

Raul has to choose between two companies to work for.

Bonzo Pizza will pay him $10 a day and $3 for every pizza he delivers. Too Hot to Eat Pizza will pay him $5 for every pizza he delivers. Which company will pay more in a day?

We solve the problem using algebra.

- Let x = pizzas delivered and y = total pay
- The function for Bonzo Pizza is $y = 3x + 10$
- The function for Too Hot to Eat Pizza is $y = 5x$

$$5x = 3x + 10$$
$$5x + -3x = 3x + -3x + 10$$
$$2x = 0 + 10$$
$$2x = 10$$
$$\frac{2}{2}x = \frac{10}{2}$$
$$1x = 5$$
$$x = 5 \text{ or } 5 \text{ pizzas}$$

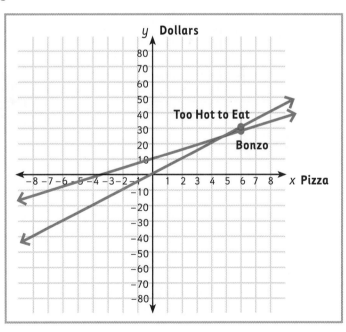

Look at the graph for the two linear functions. After six pizzas Raul is earning more working at Too Hot to Eat. By following the lines, we see that working at Too Hot to Eat pays more if Raul delivers more than five pizzas per day.

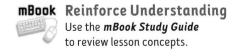

Problem-Solving Activity
Turn to *Interactive Text*, page 386.

mBook Reinforce Understanding
Use the *mBook Study Guide* to review lesson concepts.

Answer the questions for each of the graphs.

1.

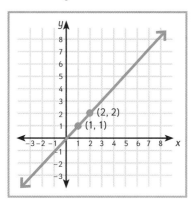

(a) What is the rise?

(b) What is the run?

(c) What is the slope?

2.

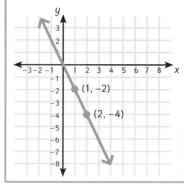

(a) What is the rise?

(b) What is the run?

(c) What is the slope?

Answer the questions for each of the graphs.

1.

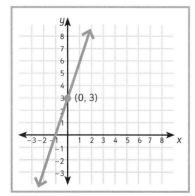

(a) At what point does the line cross the y-axis?

(b) What is the y-intercept?

2.

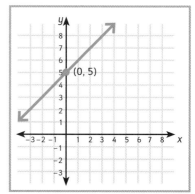

(a) At what point does the line cross the y-axis?

(b) What is the y-intercept?

Activity 3

Write the equation for the function shown in each graph by finding the slope and intercept.

1. What is the equation for this graph?

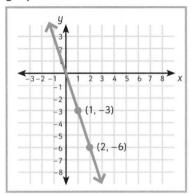

2. What is the equation for this graph?

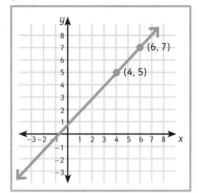

3. What is the equation for this graph?

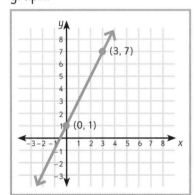

Activity 4 • Distributed Practice

Solve.

1. $3x = 4x + 2$

2. $5x + 3 = 2x + 2$

3. $x + 7 = -2x + 5$

4. $5 - x = 3x + -5$

5. $2x + 10 = -10 + -4x$

6. $-4x = -3x + 4$

7. $-2x - 2 = 2 + -x$

8. $4 - x = 5 + x$

▶Introduction to Functions

What is so different about functions?

We study functions when we learn about algebra. It is easy to mix functions and algebra together, but functions have important properties that need to be understood by themselves.

Functions show systematic relationships between two variables, *x* and *y*.

In the function $y = mx + b$, we say that the value of *y* depends upon what is in $mx + b$.

Word problems and tables of numbers are one way to understand how functions are all around us. Both word problems and tables show systematic relationships and help us make predictions.

Review 1

How do word problems and tables help us understand functions?

Problem:

Two clubs at Freemont High School are having a water balloon fight. They are doing this to raise money for charity. Both sides have catapults that launch water balloons. When we pull back on the catapult, the balloon flies out of the bucket. Based on the data the teams collected, what is the relationship between how far the catapult is pulled back and the distance the balloon travels?

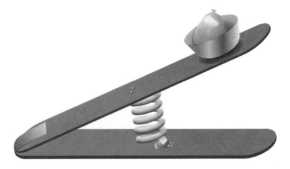

Amount We Pulled Back on Catapult (in inches)	Distance Traveled (in feet)
5	10
10	20
15	30
20	40

What is the relationship?

The more we pull back on the catapult, the farther the water balloon flies.

What is the function?

We multiply the number in the first column by 2 to get the number in the second column.

Let y = the distance traveled and x = the amount we pull back on the catapult.

$$y = 2 \cdot x \text{ or } y = 2x$$

In the catapult example, the distance the balloon travels depends on how far we pull back the catapult. We use the function to make predictions. If we pull back the catapult 30 inches, the balloon should go 60 feet.

Word problems that involve functions also require us to think about what parts of the problem are changing and what parts are staying the same. In the catapult problem, the amount we pull back on the catapult is always changing, and the distance the balloon travels always changes. Nothing is the same. There are a lot of cases where we have to determine what is changing and what stays the same so that we can write the function correctly.

Review 2

How do we decide what is changing and what stays the same?

Problem:

Most cell phone plans have a basic monthly fee and then there are additional charges for extra minutes that you use. Celia has a plan where she pays $58 per month for 500 minutes and then $0.10 per additional minute used.

What stays the same? The monthly charge of $58 per month.

What changes? How many minutes more than 500 she talks in a month.

What is the relationship?

Celia's monthly bill depends upon her monthly charge plus the amount for overtime minutes.

Let's say that last month Celia talked 560 minutes. That is 60 minutes more than the 500 she gets.

What is the function?

Let y = the total bill and x = the number of minutes more than 500.

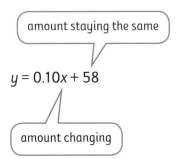

amount staying the same

$$y = 0.10x + 58$$

amount changing

What is the solution to the problem?

We substitute the extra 60 minutes into our function to find Celia's total bill.

$$60$$
$$\downarrow$$
$$y = 0.10x + 58$$
$$y = 0.10 \cdot 60 + 58$$
$$y = 6 + 58$$
$$y = 64$$

Celia's bill for the month is $64.

We can also use this function to make predictions about how much Celia's bill would be if she talked even longer on the phone that month.

The rate of change in a function is called the slope.

%÷
=
< × **Apply Skills**
Turn to *Interactive Text*,
page 388.

mBook **Reinforce Understanding**
Use the *mBook Study Guide*
to review lesson concepts.

▶**Problem Solving: Working With Coordinate Graphs**

What do functions look like on a coordinate graph?

We learned about functions on coordinate graphs that involve straight lines. These are linear functions. There is a specific formula for plotting the lines for these functions on a coordinate graph.

Formula for linear function:

$$y = mx + b$$

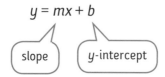
slope   y-intercept

We use this formula to plot a line on a graph. The simplest function is one where the y-intercept is the origin. This means the value for b is zero and we don't need to write it as part of our function.

The slope of a function tells us how quickly the function is increasing or decreasing. On a graph, we can find the slope by taking the rise over the run.

Review 1 shows different functions that go through the origin. They all show the different rates a car travels.

Review 1

How do we use slope to compare functions?

The bigger the number in front of x, the steeper the slope. The graph with the steepest slope has the greatest rate of change. That means the car going 60 miles in one hour is changing more (or going more miles) than the cars going 40 or 50 miles in one hour.

The steeper the slope, the greater the rate of change.

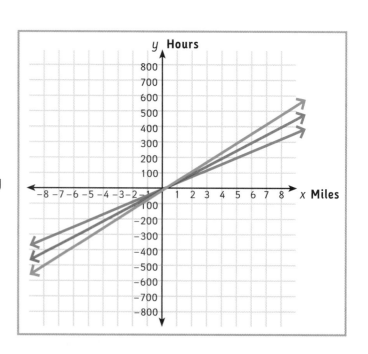

We use a formula to graph a line.

Review 2

How do we graph a function?

$y = 3x - 2$

We create an x/y table based on this function. We substitute values for x to get values for y.

x	y
0	−2
1	1
2	4

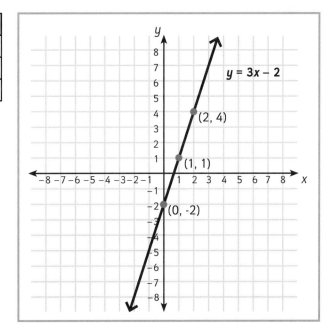

We can use the graph to write an equation. We need to remember "rise over run." Review 3 shows how to figure out the slope of the line using rise over run. Then we look for the place where the line crosses (or intercepts) the y-axis.

Review 3

How do we use a graph to write the equation for a function?

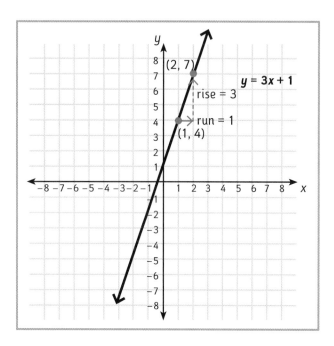

First we find rise over run. The rise is 3 and the run is 1, so our slope is $\frac{3}{1}$ or 3.

Find where the line crosses the y-axis. It crosses at 1.

Substitute the values for slope and y intercept into the formula.

$$\begin{matrix} 3 & 1 \\ \downarrow & \downarrow \end{matrix}$$
$$y = mx + b$$

The equation for the function is $y = 3x + 1$.

How do we make decisions based on functions?

One of the ways that we can use functions is to make comparisons. When we graph two linear functions, it is often possible to find where the two functions intersect. This is especially useful if we are comparing two plans that involve money.

Review 1

What happens at the intersection of two functions?

Problem:

Chantrelle needs to buy new furniture for her apartment. When she goes to the furniture store, they offer her two payment plans. When will she have paid the same amount?

Plan 1: Pay $400 down and $100 per month.

Plan 2: Pay $300 per month.

We use what we know about functions and algebra to answer this question.

What are the functions?

Plan 1: $y = 100x + 400$

Plan 2: $y = 300x$

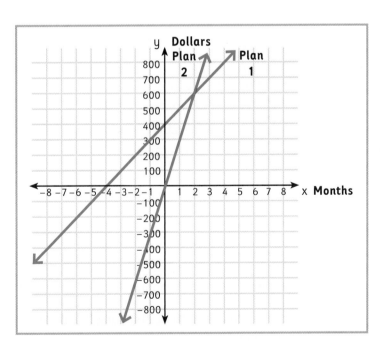

They both equal y, so:

$$300x = 100x + 400$$
$$300x + -100x = 100x + -100x + 400$$
$$200x = 0 + 400$$
$$200x = 400$$
$$\frac{200}{200}x = \frac{400}{200}$$
$$1x = 2$$
$$x = 2$$

At 2 months, Chantrelle would have paid the same amount of money regardless of the plan she selects. After that, she is paying more money per month if she chose Plan 2 (paying $300 per month).

Functions help us make decisions. We use functions to figure out what happens in the long run. Which choice is the better deal? Which job pays more money? These are just a few of the questions we can answer when we compare functions.

Review 2

How do we use functions to make comparisons?

Problem:

You are going to hire a company to paint your house. You get bids from two companies. Which one should you choose based on price alone?

Bid 1: TriFlex Painting will charge you $200 for paint and $30 per hour.

Bid 2: Randall's Painting will charge you $40 per hour, with no charge for the paint.

You can make a decision on which company you want if you have a good idea of how long it will take to paint your house. We can use algebra and graphs to answer the question.

What are the functions?

Bid 1: $y = 30x + 200$

Bid 2: $y = 40x$

We find out when they will cost the same using algebra.

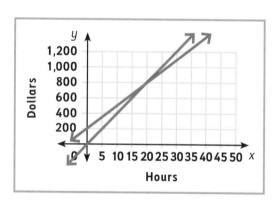

$$40x = 30x + 200$$
$$40x + -30x = 30x + -30x + 200$$
$$10x = 0 + 200$$
$$10x = 200$$
$$\frac{10}{10}x = \frac{200}{10}$$
$$x = 20$$

You will pay the same amount if the job takes 20 hours.

If the job takes more than 20 hours, it will cost you more to choose Bid 2 ($40 per hour).

Problem-Solving Activity
Turn to *Interactive Text*, page 389.

mBook Reinforce Understanding
Use the *mBook Study Guide* to review lesson concepts.

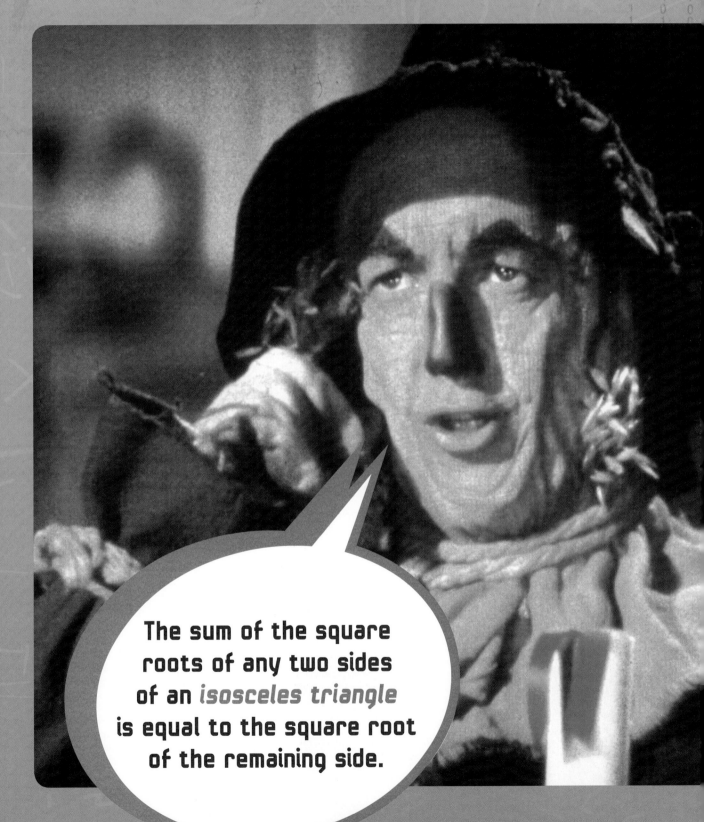

The sum of the square roots of any two sides of an *isosceles triangle* is equal to the square root of the remaining side.

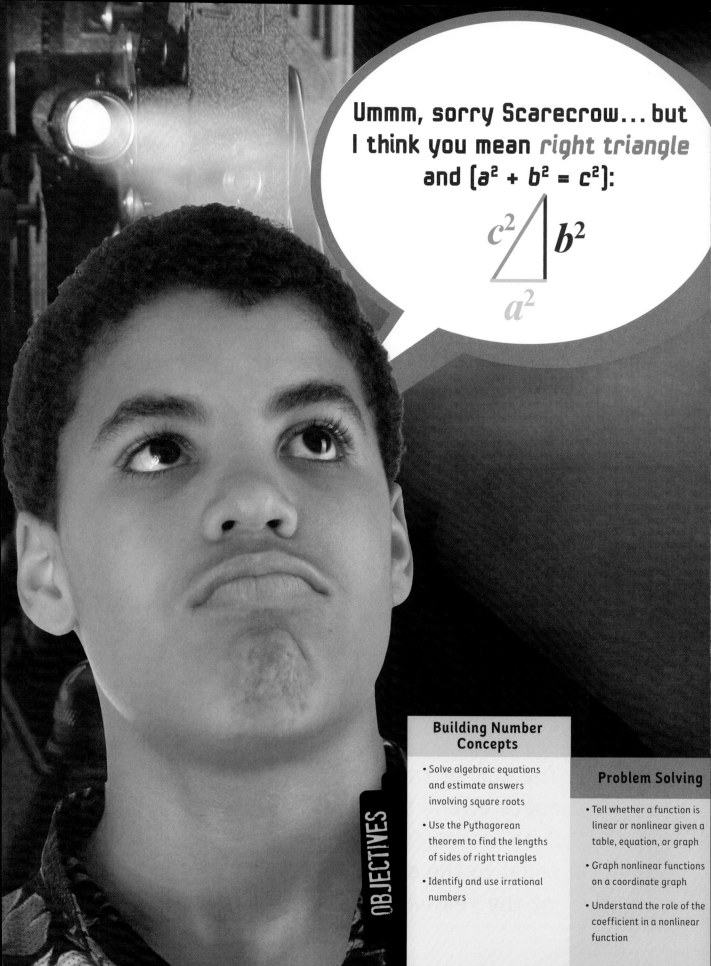

Building Number Concepts

- Solve algebraic equations and estimate answers involving square roots
- Use the Pythagorean theorem to find the lengths of sides of right triangles
- Identify and use irrational numbers

Problem Solving

- Tell whether a function is linear or nonlinear given a table, equation, or graph
- Graph nonlinear functions on a coordinate graph
- Understand the role of the coefficient in a nonlinear function

▶The Pythagorean Theorem

Vocabulary
Pythagorean theorem hypotenuse

What is the relationship between squares, rectangles, and triangles?

Squares and rectangles help us understand the area formula for triangles. We measure the area of two-dimensional shapes in square units, and a square is a good example of this kind of area measurement. Example 1 shows how square units are based on the measurement of each side of a square.

Example 1

Where do we get square units?

Each side of the square measures 4 units.

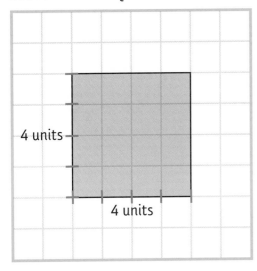

4 units

4 units

Our algebraic formula for the area of a square is:

Area = base · height, or $A = b \cdot h$

When we substitute 4 for b and 4 for h, we get:

$$\begin{array}{cc} 4 & 4 \\ \downarrow & \downarrow \end{array}$$

$A = b \cdot h$

$A = 4 \cdot 4$

$A = 16$ square units

We see the 16 units when we count the squares.

Our area formula for triangles makes sense based on what we know about the area of a square. We simply make two triangles out of the square by drawing a diagonal from one vertex of the square to the opposite vertex. Example 2 shows how we find the area formula of a triangle.

Example 2

How do we find the area of a triangle?

The square is divided into two congruent triangles.

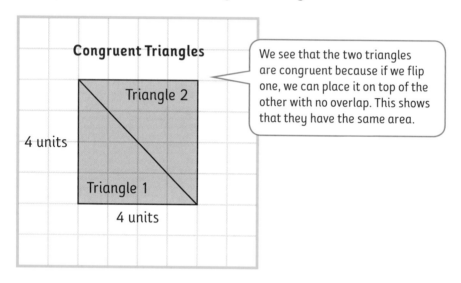

Congruent Triangles

Triangle 2

Triangle 1

4 units

4 units

We see that the two triangles are congruent because if we flip one, we can place it on top of the other with no overlap. This shows that they have the same area.

This means the area formula for a triangle is:

Area = $\frac{1}{2}$ · **base · height, or** $A = \frac{1}{2} \cdot b \cdot h$

$$4 \quad 4$$
$$\downarrow \quad \downarrow$$

$A = \frac{1}{2} \cdot b \cdot h$

$A = \frac{1}{2} \cdot 4 \cdot 4$

$A = \frac{1}{2} \cdot 16$

$A = 8$ square units

Counting the square units in each triangle also confirms that the area of Triangle 1 = $\frac{1}{2} \cdot b \cdot h$, or 8 square units.

Congruent Triangles in a Square

Area = 8 square units

The same kind of thinking applies to triangles and rectangles. It is easy to see how we get the area formula for a triangle from the area of a rectangle.

Example 3

How are the areas of rectangles and triangles related?

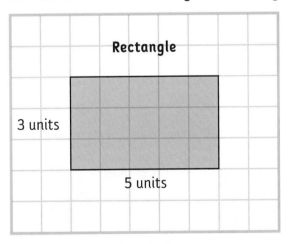

Rectangle

3 units

5 units

Area of a rectangle = $b \cdot h$

$$\begin{array}{cc} 5 & 3 \\ \downarrow & \downarrow \end{array}$$

$A = b \cdot h$

$A = 5 \cdot 3$

$A = 15$ square units

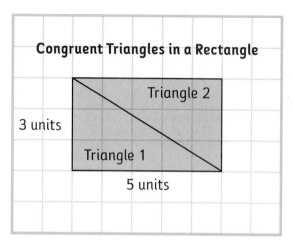

The area of Triangle 1 is $\frac{1}{2}$ the area of the rectangle. We see that the formula for the area of the triangle remains the same.

Area of a triangle = $\frac{1}{2} \cdot b \cdot h$

$$
\begin{array}{cc}
5 & 3 \\
\downarrow & \downarrow
\end{array}
$$

$A = \frac{1}{2} \cdot b \cdot h$

$A = \frac{1}{2} \cdot 5 \cdot 3$

$A = \frac{1}{2} \cdot 15$

$A = 7\frac{1}{2}$ square units

The triangle in Examples 2 and 3 are right triangles because one angle measures 90 degrees. However, the area formula applies to any triangle.

The formula $A = \frac{1}{2} \cdot b \cdot h$ works for all triangles.

| equilateral | isosceles | right | scalene |

What is the relationship between sides of squares and rectangles?

We can see a clear relationship between the different sides of a square or a rectangle if we think about the properties of these two shapes. All sides of a square are equal in length. The opposite sides of a rectangle are equal in length.

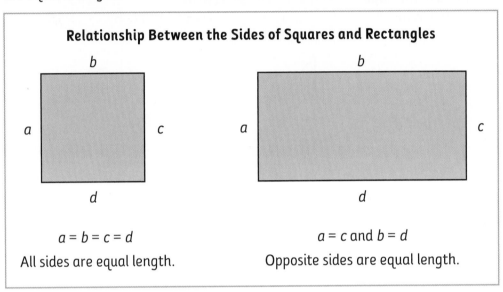

Relationship Between the Sides of Squares and Rectangles

$a = b = c = d$
All sides are equal length.

$a = c$ and $b = d$
Opposite sides are equal length.

What is the Pythagorean theorem?

There is a special relationship between the sides of a right triangle that is a bit more complicated. We can use the **Pythagorean theorem** to see this relationship. This formula only works for right triangles. We generally use it to figure out the length of the hypotenuse. The **hypotenuse** is the side opposite the right angle.

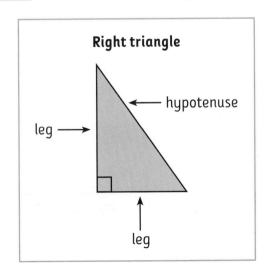

Right triangle

leg →

← hypotenuse

leg ↑

> In a right triangle, the sides that form the right angle are called legs.

The Pythagorean Theorem

The Pythagorean theorem tells us that the sum of the squares of the legs of a right triangle is equal to the square of the hypotenuse. In the Pythagorean theorem, we label the legs of the triangle a and b. The hypotenuse is c. This helps us write the formula for the theorem.

$$a^2 + b^2 = c^2$$

We can show that the Pythagorean theorem works by substituting numbers into the formula.

Example 1

Show that the Pythagorean theorem is true for this triangle.

Let $a = 12$
$\quad b = 5$
$\quad c = 13$

$a^2 + b^2 = c^2$
$12^2 + 5^2 = 13^2$
$144 + 25 = 169$
$\quad\quad 169 = 169$

We see that the formula, $a^2 + b^2 = c^2$, is true for this triangle.

We can prove that the Pythagorean theorem works using a simple drawing. Remember that the theorem tells us that we square each side of the triangle. We draw a square on each side to show this.

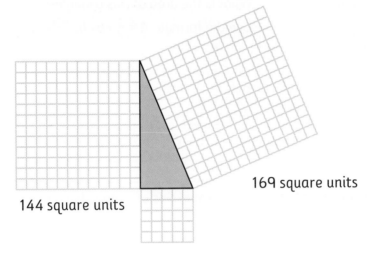

144 square units

169 square units

25 square units

Remember the theorem: the sum of the squares of the legs of a right triangle is equal to the square of the hypotenuse. This means that if we add the areas of the small and medium squares, they should equal the area of the large square.

25 + 144 = 169

169 = 169

The numbers are the same. We see that the formula $a^2 + b^2 = c^2$ is true for this triangle.

% ÷
≡
< X **Apply Skills**
Turn to *Interactive Text*,
page 392.

mBook **Reinforce Understanding**
Use the *mBook Study Guide*
to review lesson concepts.

Homework

Find the area of the shapes.

1. What is the area of this square?
Use the formula $A = s^2$.

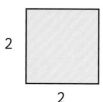

2. What is the area of this triangle?
Use the formula $A = \frac{1}{2} \cdot b \cdot h$.

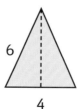

Activity 2

Write whether each of the statements about the properties of shapes is true or false. If the statement is false, rewrite it to make it true.

1. All the sides of a rectangle are always the same length.

2. All the sides of a square are always the same length.

3. All the sides of a triangle are always the same length.

4. The area of a triangle is half of the area of a rectangle if it has the same base and height.

5. The area of a square is half the area of a rectangle if it has the same base and height.

Activity 3

Prove the Pythagorean theorem works for these triangles.

1.

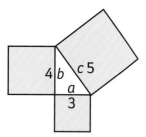

2.

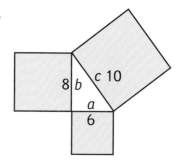

Activity 4 • Distributed Practice

Create x/y tables for each of the following functions.

1. $y = 3x$
2. $y = -x$
3. $y = \frac{1}{2}x$

▶Square Numbers and Square Roots

Vocabulary
square root radical sign

How do we find the length of the side of a right triangle?

In the last lesson, we proved the Pythagorean theorem by counting the number of square units in the squares for each side. We proved that for a right triangle, the formula $a^2 + b^2 = c^2$ was correct.

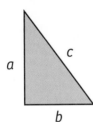

$$a^2 + b^2 = c^2$$

We see that this is true when $a = 4$, $b = 3$, and $c = 5$.

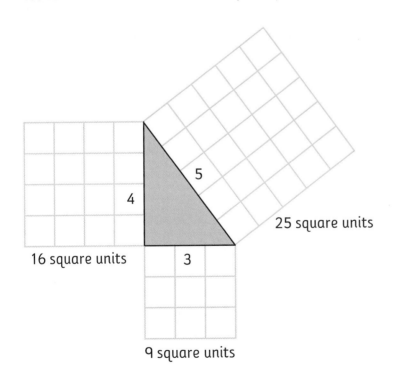

16 square units

9 square units

25 square units

$$4^2 + 3^2 = 5^2$$
$$16 + 9 = 25$$
$$25 = 25$$

We use this formula to find the missing length of any one side of a right triangle. Let's suppose that we do not know the length of the hypotenuse of this triangle.

Example 1

Use the Pythagorean theorem to find the length of the hypotenuse.

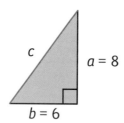

c $a = 8$

$b = 6$

We substitute the numbers for the variables in the formula for the Pythagorean theorem.

$$8 \qquad 6$$
$$\downarrow \qquad \downarrow$$
$$a^2 + b^2 = c^2$$
$$8^2 + 6^2 = c^2$$
$$64 + 36 = c^2$$
$$100 = c^2$$

At this point, we can use our number sense to find c. We know $c^2 = c \cdot c$ and $100 = 10^2$, or $10 \cdot 10$. So $c = 10$.

Number sense tells us this is correct.

The length of the hypotenuse is 10.

What is the relationship between square numbers and square roots?

It is not always easy to find the length of the hypotenuse using number sense as we did in the previous example. What we need to do is find the **square root** of a number. A square root is a number that, when multiplied by itself, becomes a square number.

$$100$$

We start with the square number 100. To find the square root of the number, we ask, "What number squared will give me this number?" In this case, the square root is 10.

$$10^2 = 100$$

When we want to show square roots, we write problems this way:

$$\sqrt{100} = 10$$

The $\sqrt{}$ sign over the 100 is called the **radical sign**.

The next example shows a surprising fact about square numbers and square roots.

As we can see, all numbers have a positive and negative square root. This makes sense when we think about the rule for negative numbers— a negative number times a negative number is a positive number.

Example 1

Use what we know about square numbers to find the square roots.

Square Number	Square Roots
$5 \cdot 5 = 25$ $-5 \cdot -5 = 25$	$\sqrt{25} = 5$ and -5
$7 \cdot 7 = 49$ $-7 \cdot -7 = 49$	$\sqrt{49} = 7$ and -7
$3 \cdot 3 = 9$ $-3 \cdot -3 = 9$	$\sqrt{9} = 3$ and -3
$20 \cdot 20 = 400$ $-20 \cdot -20 = 400$	$\sqrt{400} = 20$ and -20

How do we solve square roots that are not perfect squares?

Not all numbers have integers as square roots. When we try to find the square root of most numbers, our answer is often a decimal number. Usually we just enter a number and press the $\sqrt{}$ button on a calculator to find a square root. Here are some examples of square roots that are not integers. We have rounded the decimal number to the hundred-thousandths place.

Square Roots That are Decimal Numbers
$\sqrt{3}$ = 1.73205 and −1.73205
$\sqrt{10}$ = 3.16228 and −3.16228
$\sqrt{6}$ = 2.44949 and −2.44949
$\sqrt{150}$ = 12.24745 and −12.24745

Although we have been talking about both positive and negative square roots, when we use a calculator to compute the square root of a number, it is only shown as a positive number. For most applications of square roots, including the formula for the Pythagorean theorem, this is all we need. When we measure the length of something, it is always a positive number.

%÷
=×
< **Apply Skills**
Turn to *Interactive Text*, page 396.

mBook **Reinforce Understanding**
Use the *mBook Study Guide* to review lesson concepts.

Activity 1

Find the square root of the perfect square numbers. Remember the negatives.

1. $\sqrt{25}$

2. $\sqrt{49}$

3. $\sqrt{64}$

4. $\sqrt{100}$

5. $\sqrt{1}$

Activity 2

Find the square root of these nonperfect square numbers. Use a calculator. Round the answer to the nearest tenth.

1. $\sqrt{82}$

2. $\sqrt{5}$

3. $\sqrt{50}$

4. $\sqrt{17}$

5. $\sqrt{26}$

Activity 3

Find the length of the hypotenuse in each triangle. Use the Pythagorean theorem and a calculator. Round your answers to the nearest tenth.

1. What is the measure of side c?

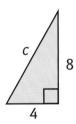

2. What is the measure of side c?

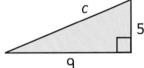

3. What is the measure of side c?

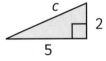

4. What is the measure of side c?

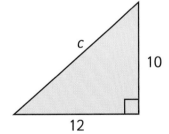

Activity 4 • Distributed Practice

Write an equation for each of the functions using the data found in the x/y tables.

1. What is the equation for this function?

x	y
1	2
2	4
3	6
4	8

2. What is the equation for this function?

x	y
9	3
12	4
15	5
18	6

3. What is the equation for this function?

x	y
1	6
2	12
3	18
4	24

4. What is the equation for this function?

x	y
50	25
40	20
30	15
20	10

▶**Applying the Pythagorean Theorem**

How do we find the lengths of other sides of a right triangle?

We have learned how to find the length of the hypotenuse of a right triangle by using the Pythagorean theorem. We use algebra to find the length of any one of the sides of a right triangle if we know the length of the other two sides.

In Example 1, we will use the length of the hypotenuse and one leg to find the length of the other leg. We will use algebra to find the length of the unknown side in each triangle.

Example 1

Use the Pythagorean theorem to find the missing lengths.

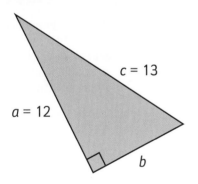

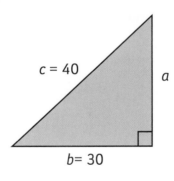

Pythagorean theorem: $a^2 + b^2 = c^2$

12   13

↓   ↓

$a^2 + b^2 = c^2$

$12^2 + b^2 = 13^2$

$144 + b^2 = 169$

$-144 + 144 + b^2 = 169 + -144$

$0 + b^2 \quad = 169 + -144$

> What we do to one side we do to the other side to keep the equation balanced.

$b^2 = \quad 25$

$\sqrt{b^2} = \sqrt{25}$

$b = 5$

30   40

↓   ↓

$a^2 + b^2 = c^2$

$a^2 + 30^2 = 40^2$

$a^2 + 900 = 1{,}600$

$a^2 + 900 + -900 = 1{,}600 + -900$

$a^2 + 0 \quad = 1{,}600 + -900$

$a^2 = \quad 700$

$\sqrt{a^2} = \sqrt{700}$

$a = 26.46$

Remember that the square root of a number can be either positive or negative. Notice that we only used the positive square root in these answers. This is because we only use positive numbers when we talk about the length of a side of a triangle.

POWER CONCEPT

The Pythagorean theorem helps us find the length of one side of a right triangle when we know the lengths of the other two sides.

How do we use the Pythagorean theorem in sports?

The Pythagorean theorem is surprisingly useful in many everyday applications, especially in sports. A very simple example is baseball. Suppose there is a runner on first base and one on second base. Both runners try to steal when the next pitch is thrown. Let's say that one runner is just as fast as the other runner. Where would it be faster to throw the ball to get one of the runners out? Should the catcher throw it to second base or third base?

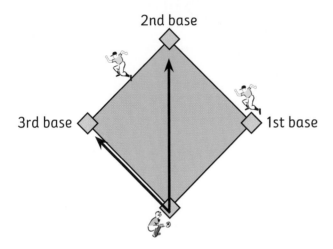

2nd base

3rd base

1st base

We need to think about baseball diamonds in order to answer the question.

- First, diamonds in baseball are actually squares. Each base is on a vertex, and the angles measure 90 degrees. If we cut the square in half, we have two right triangles.

- Second, if we look at the triangle on the left in Example 1, there is a right angle at third base. We also know that the distance between each base is 90 feet.

We can solve the problem using the Pythagorean theorem.

Example 1

Use the Pythagorean theorem to find the distance from home plate to second base.

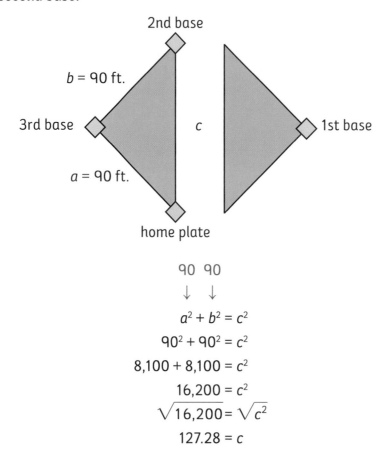

2nd base

b = 90 ft.

3rd base

c

1st base

a = 90 ft.

home plate

90   90

↓   ↓

$$a^2 + b^2 = c^2$$
$$90^2 + 90^2 = c^2$$
$$8{,}100 + 8{,}100 = c^2$$
$$16{,}200 = c^2$$
$$\sqrt{16{,}200} = \sqrt{c^2}$$
$$127.28 = c$$

The distance from home plate to second base is 127.28 feet or about 127 feet.

The catcher should throw the ball to third base because it is a shorter distance. It is only 90 feet instead of 127 feet.

We can use the same kind of thinking to understand why tennis players hit a ball from one corner of a tennis court to the other. They do this because the ball has a better chance of staying in the court if hit diagonally. We see this in Example 2.

Example 2

Use the Pythagorean theorem to find the distance diagonally across a tennis court. Then compare that distance to the length of the court.

When players play from the middle, they only have 78 feet. When they hit the ball across court, they have more room to hit the ball.

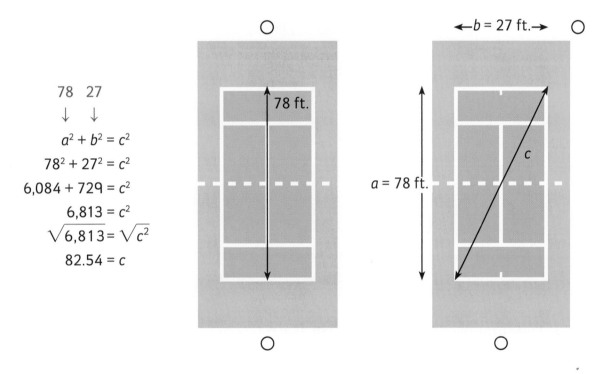

$$78 \quad 27$$
$$\downarrow \quad \downarrow$$
$$a^2 + b^2 = c^2$$
$$78^2 + 27^2 = c^2$$
$$6{,}084 + 729 = c^2$$
$$6{,}813 = c^2$$
$$\sqrt{6{,}813} = \sqrt{c^2}$$
$$82.54 = c$$

There is about 82 feet to hit the ball inside the court when we hit across a diagonal. That is 4 feet more than when players are hitting from the middle of the court.

Finally, soccer players often take penalty kicks during a game. The greater the distance that the ball travels, the better chance there is to block the ball. It is a shorter distance in front of the goal than it is off to the side.

Example 3

Use the Pythagorean theorem to find the distance the soccer ball travels in each situation.

The player kicks 20 yards centered in front of the goal.
Another player kicks from 30 yards to the left.

20   30
↓   ↓
$a^2 + b^2 = c^2$
$20^2 + 30^2 = c^2$
$400 + 900 = c^2$
$1{,}300 = c^2$
$\sqrt{1{,}300} = \sqrt{c^2}$
$36.06 = c$

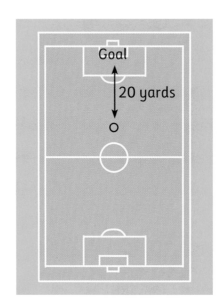

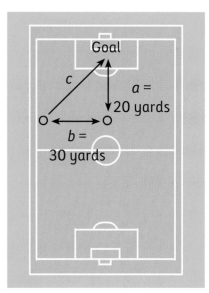

The player near the sideline kicks the ball 36 yards instead of 20 yards. That is an extra 16 yards.

Distance makes a difference when playing sports. Most of the time coming from an angle means that we will have to hit, kick, throw, or shoot the ball farther. With tennis, more distance means the ball has a better chance of staying in the court. With soccer and baseball, it means that we will have to kick or throw the ball farther.

Apply Skills
Turn to *Interactive Text*, page 400.

mBook Reinforce Understanding
Use the *mBook Study Guide* to review lesson concepts.

Activity 1

Solve the square roots. Use a calculator and round the answer to the nearest tenth. Remember the negatives.

1. $\sqrt{47}$

2. $\sqrt{55}$

3. $\sqrt{65}$

4. $\sqrt{82}$

5. $\sqrt{101}$

6. $\sqrt{75}$

Activity 2

Using the Pythagorean theorem, find the missing parts of the right triangle.

1. What is the measure of side c?

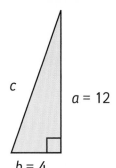

c
$a = 12$
$b = 4$

2. What is the measure of side a?

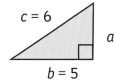

$c = 6$
a
$b = 5$

3. What is the measure of side b?

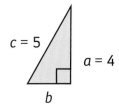

$c = 5$
$a = 4$
b

Activity 3

Solve the application problems using the Pythagorean theorem.

1. What is the length of the diagonal across the doubles match tennis court?

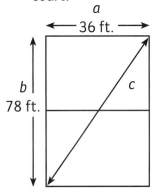

a

36 ft.

b

78 ft.

c

2. How far does the catcher throw from home plate to second base?

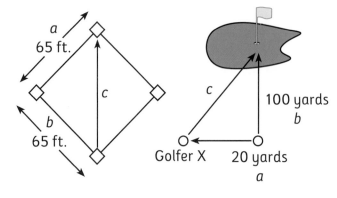

a

65 ft.

b

65 ft.

c

3. How far is it from Golfer X to the flag?

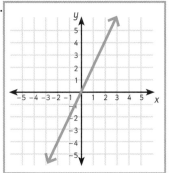

c

100 yards

b

Golfer X   20 yards

a

Activity 4 • Distributed Practice

Look at the graph for each function and write its equation.

1.

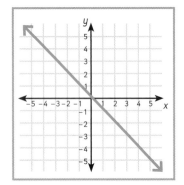

2.

3.

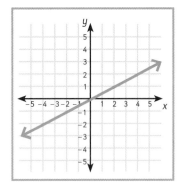

▶**Problem Solving: Nonlinear Functions**

What is the difference between linear and nonlinear functions?

Unit 9 presented key ideas about linear functions. These functions are systematic relationships between x and y whose graph is a line. We also learned that in a function such as $y = x + 1$, the value of y depends upon the value of x. That makes y the **dependent variable** and x the **independent variable**.

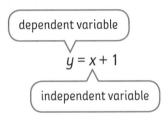

dependent variable

$$y = x + 1$$

independent variable

An x/y table helps us create graphs for functions. Example 1 shows the function $y = x$. The values in the x/y table are coordinates on the graph. We can draw a straight line through these coordinates.

Example 1

Use the table to graph the function $y = x$.

x	y
−2	−2
−1	−1
0	0
1	1
2	2

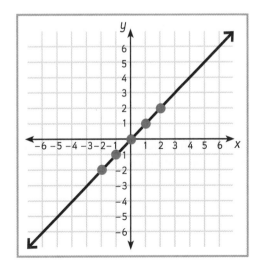

One difference between linear and nonlinear functions is that the value of the dependent variable does not change by the same amount each time in a nonlinear function. This happens when the x-variable has an exponent. Example 2 shows a function where y is the x-value squared. Look carefully at how this affects the y-values in the table.

Example 2

Create a table for the function $y = x^2$.

Let's see how the exponent changes the y-values in the table.

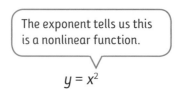

The exponent tells us this is a nonlinear function.

$$y = x^2$$

x	y
−2	4
−1	1
0	0
1	1
2	4

Notice that two different x-values have the same y-value in this function.

We substitute the value of x into $y = x^2$. When we substitute −2 for x, we get $y = (-2)^2$ or $y = 4$. We use the same process to complete the rest of the table.

Notice that the y-values do not increase by the same amount each time. This is one of the differences between linear and nonlinear functions. This makes it more difficult to predict what number will come next.

Nonlinear functions may have different exponents, not just squares. We may have x^3, x^4, x^5, etc., as our variable term.

POWER CONCEPT

In a nonlinear function, the values for the dependent variable do not increase by the same amount each time.

When we are working with exponents, we should use a calculator to compute these values. Many calculators have a y^x key. This is the key we use to find a power of something. For instance, if we are solving 2^5, we would enter 2, y^x, and then 5. The result is 32. If we multiply $2 \cdot 2 \cdot 2 \cdot 2 \cdot 2$, we would get the same result.

Example 3 shows an x/y table for a nonlinear function with an exponent other than 2.

Example 3

Create a table for the function $y = x^3$. Use a calculator to find the y-values.

$$y = x^3$$

x	y
0	0
1	1
2	8
3	27
4	64

We substitute each value for x into the function to find the y-values.

To find the value of y when x is 2, we would press these keys on the calculator:

What do nonlinear functions look like on a graph?

We learned that the y-values do not increase by the same amount each time in a nonlinear function. This tells us that the graph of the function will not be a straight line.

The shape of the line changes just by squaring the x. Let's look at an example.

Example 1

Use the table to graph the function $y = x^2$.

$y = x^2$

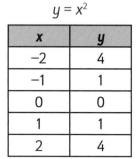

x	y
−2	4
−1	1
0	0
1	1
2	4

The line for a nonlinear function is a curve—not a straight line.

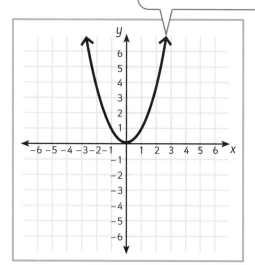

The graph of a nonliner function will always have at least one curve. It is never a straight line.

Problem-Solving Activity
Turn to *Interactive Text*, page 405.

mBook Reinforce Understanding
Use the *mBook Study Guide* to review lesson concepts.

Create *x/y* tables for the functions. Include these *x* values: −2, −1, 0, 1, and 2.

1. $y = x + 3$ **2.** $y = x^2$ **3.** $y = -x - 1$ **4.** $y = x^3$

Use your knowledge of nonlinear functions and symmetry to complete the graphs.

1. Complete this graph for the function $y = x^2$.

x	y
0	0
1	1
2	4

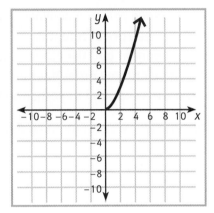

2. Complete this graph for the function $y = 2x^2$.

x	y
0	0
1	4
2	16

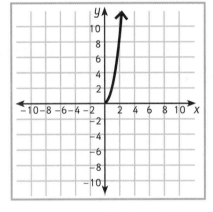

3. Complete this graph for the function $y = x^3$.

x	y
0	0
1	1
2	8

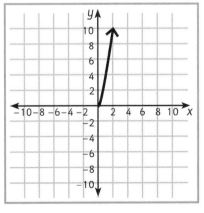

Activity 3

Choose the correct multiple choice answer.

1. One of the key differences between nonlinear and linear functions is how they are graphed. The way they are different is:
   (a) They are lines that go in different directions.
   (b) One is a line and one is a curve.
   (c) They are curves that curve in different directions.

2. Another key difference between nonlinear and linear functions is in the equation. The way they are different is:
   (a) One has an exponent and the other does not.
   (b) One has a slope and the other does not.
   (c) One has a y-intercept and the other does not.

3. In the function $y = x^2$, we see something different in the x/y table. What is it?
   (a) Two of the x/y values are the same.
   (b) Two y-values have the same x-value.
   (c) Two x-values have the same y-value.

Activity 4 • Distributed Practice

Write an equation for each of the functions using $y = mx + b$.

1. The cost of blueberries is $3 per pound.

2. The daily cost of the rental car is $0.10 per mile plus a base fee of $25.

3. The price of gas is $4 per gallon.

▶Properties of Irrational Numbers

Vocabulary
perfect square numbers
irrational numbers

What are rational numbers?

One way to change a simple fraction into an integer or a decimal number is to divide the denominator into the numerator. When we do this, we either get an integer, a decimal number that ends (or terminates), or a pattern in the decimal number place that repeats itself. They are all rational numbers.

Rational Numbers	
When we divide the numerator by the denominator . . .	**the resulting number is a rational number**
$\frac{24}{8} = 3$	an integer
$\frac{3}{8} = 0.375$	a decimal number that terminates
$\frac{7}{11} = 0.63636363\ldots$	a repeating pattern of decimal numbers

Something different happens when we compute the square root of a number. When we use a calculator or a spreadsheet to find the square root of a number, we usually get a long decimal number. Example 1 shows what kind of numbers we get when we find the square root of the numbers 1 through 10.

Example 1

What are the square roots of these numbers?

Number	Square Roots
1	1 and −1
2	1.4142 and −1.4142
3	1.7321 and −1.7321
4	2 and −2
5	2.2361 and −2.2361
6	2.4495 and −2.4495
7	2.6458 and −2.6458
8	2.8284 and −2.8284
9	3 and −3
10	3.1623 and −3.1623

The numbers 1, 4, and 9 are perfect square numbers.

Numbers like 1, 4, and 9 are called **perfect square numbers** because their square roots are integers. As we can see, most of the square roots are decimal numbers. The decimal numbers have been rounded to the ten-thousandths place. They are not rational numbers.

What are irrational numbers?

If we use a calculator or a spreadsheet to calculate square roots, we will also find something else—the decimal numbers for square roots do not end and they do not repeat themselves in a pattern. When a decimal number does not end and does not have a pattern, we call that number an irrational number .

We see this with the square root of 2.

$$\sqrt{2} = 1.4142135623731...$$

The decimal number does not end, and there is no pattern to the decimal numbers.

All of this means that we have to round square roots when we use them. We usually round the decimal number to the tenths or hundredths place. Remember to use rounding rules. Example 1 shows some positive square roots.

Example 1

Round these irrational numbers to the nearest tenths and hundredths place.

		Rounded to the Tenths Place	Rounded to the Hundredths Place
$\sqrt{2} =$	1.4142	1.4	1.41
$\sqrt{3} =$	1.7321	1.7	1.73
$\sqrt{5} =$	2.2361	2.2	2.24

 **Apply Skills**
Turn to *Interactive Text*, page 408.

Monitoring Progress
Quiz 1

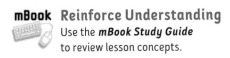 **Reinforce Understanding**
Use the *mBook Study Guide* to review lesson concepts.

Activity 1

Solve the square roots. Remember the negatives. Use your calculator and round to the nearest tenths place.

1. $\sqrt{9}$

2. $\sqrt{10}$

3. $\sqrt{4}$

4. $\sqrt{11}$

5. $\sqrt{2}$

6. $\sqrt{17}$

Activity 2

For each of the numbers, tell if it's an integer (IN), a rational number (R), or an irrational number (IR). Use the letter abbreviations.

1. 3.4

2. −4

3. $\sqrt{5}$

4. 0.1111111111111111111111111...

5. 2.23606797749978969640917366887313...

6. $\frac{2}{3}$

7. 0.375

8. 0.4285714285714285714285714285714857142...

Activity 3

Find the square roots of the numbers between 20 and 30 and answer the questions.

1. How many of the square roots between 20 and 30 are integers? What are they?

2. How many of the square roots between 20 and 30 are rational numbers? What are they?

3. How many of the square roots between 20 and 30 are irrational numbers? What are they?

Create an *x/y* table for the functions shown in the graphs.

1.

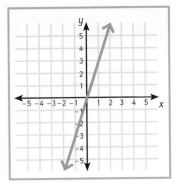

2.

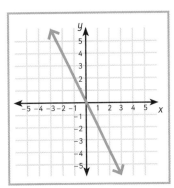

3.

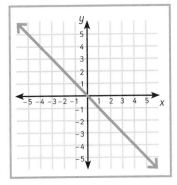

▶**Problem Solving: The Direction of Nonlinear Functions**

What happens when x is negative?

In Lesson 4, we saw the graph of the function $y = x^2$. The graph was a curve. This curve is called a **parabola** . Let's look at our parabola and the table again to see how x^2 makes the parabola.

Vocabulary
parabola

$y = x^2$

x	y
−3	9
−2	4
−1	1
0	0
1	1
2	4
3	9

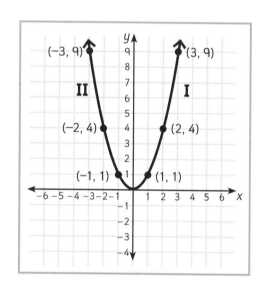

The parabola is in Quadrants I and II. This is because when we substitute any value for x in x^2, we get a positive output. Our Integer Rules help us understand why this happens.

> **Integer Rules**
> - When we substitute a positive value for x, we are multiplying a positive times a positive. The answer is positive.
> - When we substitute a negative value for x, we are multiplying a negative times a negative. The answer is positive.

That means the y-values for this function will always be positive.

Functions can get complicated, and it is important to think about what is happening when we work with negative numbers. Example 1 shows what happens when we substitute a negative number into functions with different exponents. Notice that if the exponent is odd, the result is a negative number.

Example 1

Substitute a negative integer for x in each function.

Let $x = -2$.

Remember to use the Integer Rules from the Algebra Toolbox.

Function	Multiplication	Result
$y = x^2$	$-2 \cdot -2 =$ same signs	4
$y = x^3$	$-2 \cdot -2 \cdot -2 =$ $4 \cdot -2 =$ different signs	-8
$y = x^4$	$-2 \cdot -2 \cdot -2 \cdot -2 =$ $4 \cdot -2 \cdot -2 =$ $-8 \cdot -2 =$ same signs	16
$y = x^5$	$-2 \cdot -2 \cdot -2 \cdot -2 \cdot -2 =$ $4 \cdot -2 \cdot -2 \cdot -2 =$ $-8 \cdot -2 \cdot -2 =$ $16 \cdot -2 =$ different signs	-32

POWER CONCEPT

In an equation such as $y = x^n$:

- When n is odd, a negative value for x will give a negative value for y.

- When n is even, a negative value for x will give a positive value for y.

Another important thing to consider when working with functions is whether the exponent has a negative coefficient. Remember that the negative sign in front of the x^2 in the function $y = -x^2$ is actually an invisible coefficient. It is −1.

Example 2

Determine how a negative coefficient changes the output of a function.

Function

$y = -x^2$

The equation $y = -x^2$ is the same as $y = -1 \cdot x^2$.

Let $x = 3$.

$$3$$
$$\downarrow$$

$y = -x^2$

$y = -1 \cdot 3^2$

$y = -1 \cdot 9$

$y = -9$

PEMDAS
Remember to use the PEMDAS rules from the Algebra Toolbox to work these kinds of problems. Always work the exponent before you do multiplication.

Function

$y = -2x^3$

The equation $y = -2x^3$ is the same as $y = -2 \cdot x^3$.

Let $x = -3$.

$$-3$$
$$\downarrow$$

$y = -2x^3$

$y = -2 \cdot (-3)^3$

$y = -2 \cdot -27$

$y = 54$

The negative coefficient changes the output for the function. A positive input into $y = -x^2$ gave a negative output instead of a positive output. A negative input into $y = -2x^3$ gave a positive output instead of negative output.

How does a negative coefficient affect the graph of a nonlinear function?

Now that we know how to find y-values for nonlinear functions, let's see what the functions look like on a coordinate graph. Example 1 shows two parabolas. The first is the graph of $y = 3x^2$, and the second is the graph of $y = -3x^2$.

Example 1

Compare the graphs of $y = 3x^2$ and $y = -3x^2$.

$y = 3x^2$

x	y
−2	12
−1	3
0	0
1	3
2	12

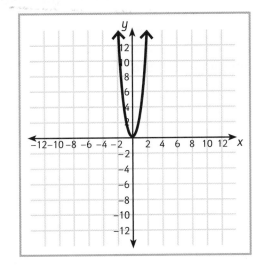

$y = -3x^2$

x	y
−2	−12
−1	−3
0	0
1	−3
2	−12

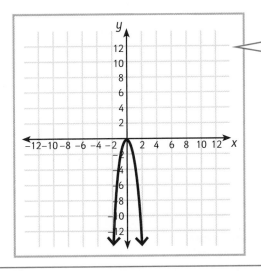

We see that the second graph points in the opposite direction of the first graph. This is because of the negative coefficient.

POWER CONCEPT

When a function has a negative coefficient, the graph is reflected over the x-axis.

 Problem-Solving Activity
Turn to *Interactive Text*, page 410.

 mBook Reinforce Understanding
Use the *mBook Study Guide* to review lesson concepts.

Activity 1

Solve the equations using substitution.

1. $y = x^2$ for $x = -1$
2. $y = -x^2$ for $x = -1$
3. $y = 2x^2$ for $x = -3$
4. $y = -2x^2$ for $x = -3$
5. $y = 3x^2$ for $x = -2$
6. $y = -3x^2$ for $x = -2$

Activity 2

Create x/y tables for the functions. Use the x-values −2, −1, 0, 1, and 2.

1. $y = x^2$
2. $y = -x^2$
3. $y = -2x^2$
4. $y = 2x^2$
5. $y = -\frac{1}{2}x^2$
6. $y = \frac{1}{2}x^2$

Activity 3

Look at the graphs of functions and tell if the function has a negative coefficient or a positive coefficient.

1.
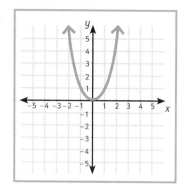

2.
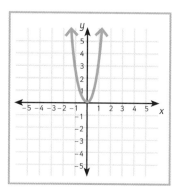

3.
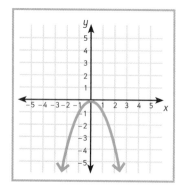

4.
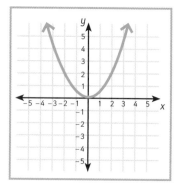

Activity 4 • Distributed Practice

Create an x/y table for each of the functions using the equations.

1. $y = 3x + 2$
2. $y = -x - 1$
3. $y = -2x + 5$

▸**The Radical Sign and Evaluating Numeric Expressions**

How do we use algebra to solve problems with square roots?

We have found the square roots of numbers using either number sense or a calculator. We use number sense when the number is a perfect square number, such as 25 or 36.

$\sqrt{36}$ — Number sense reminds us that 6 · 6 = 36, so 36 is a square number.

$\sqrt{36} = 6$ or -6

$\sqrt{25}$ — Number sense reminds us that 5 · 5 = 25, so 25 is a square number.

$\sqrt{25} = 5$ or -5

Sometimes we are given problems that have numeric expressions under the radical sign. The radical is the name of the square root symbol. When we solve this, we need to think about our rules for order of operation, PEMDAS.

The radical sign is a type of grouping symbol. First we evaluate the numeric expression under the radical and then we take its square root.

$\sqrt{}$

Remember that parentheses are always solved first. We extend this rule to any type of grouping symbol.

PEMDAS
Remember to use the PEMDAS rules from the Algebra Toolbox to work these kinds of problems. Always work the exponent before you do multiplication.

Example 1 shows this situation. We use the symbol ± when there is a positive and negative answer.

Example 1

Use PEMDAS to solve problems that have a radical sign.

Problem 1

$\sqrt{2 \cdot 8}$	←	The problem.
$\sqrt{2 \cdot 8}$	←	Evaluate the expression under the radical first.
$\sqrt{16}$	←	Find the square root using mental math.
$\sqrt{16} = \pm 4$	←	The answer is +4 and −4.

Problem 2

$\sqrt{30 \div 5}$	←	The problem.
$\sqrt{30 \div 5}$	←	Evaluate the expression under the radical first.
$\sqrt{6}$	←	Find the square root using a calculator.
$\sqrt{6} = \pm 2.45$	←	The answer is +2.45 and −2.45.

We might also have a case where the radical is just part of a larger expression. In this case, it's especially important to remember PEMDAS.

We also need to realize that we have two expressions to evaluate. Given the fact that the square root can be positive or negative, we have to solve for both. Example 2 demonstrates this situation.

Example 2

Find all the solutions to expressions with a radical sign.

Problem 1

$\sqrt{2 \cdot 8} + 2$ ←   The problem.

$\sqrt{16} + 2$ ←   Evaluate the expression under the radical.

$\pm 4 + 2$ ←   Find the square root, ±4.

$4 + 2$ $-4 + 2$ ←   Write the two expressions.

$4 + 2 = 6$ $-4 + 2 = -2$ ←   Solve the two expressions.

6 and −2   ←   The answers.

Problem 2

$3 \cdot \sqrt{30 \div 5} + 2$ ←   The problem.

$3 \cdot \sqrt{6} + 2$ ←   Evaluate the expression under the radical.

$3 \cdot \pm 2.45 + 2$ ←   Find the square root and round it.

$3 \cdot 2.45 + 2$ $3 \cdot -2.45 + 2$ ←   Write the two expressions.

$7.35 + 2$ $-7.35 + 2$ ←   Solve the two expressions.

9.35 and −5.35   ←   The answers.

POWER CONCEPT

Expressions with a radical sign will usually have two solutions.

When we work with radicals, we need to work carefully and be sure to find all the possible answers.

%÷ Apply Skills
=×
Turn to *Interactive Text*, page 414.

mBook Reinforce Understanding
Use the *mBook Study Guide* to review lesson concepts.

▶Problem Solving: **Changing the Shape of a Nonlinear Function**

How does changing the coefficient change the shape of a nonlinear function?

In the last lesson, we looked at how a negative coefficient changes the direction of a nonlinear function. We can also change the shape of a nonlinear function by changing the coefficient in front of the *x*-variable. Look at the three functions in Example 1.

Example 1

Compare the graphs of the functions.

$$y = \frac{1}{3}x^2$$

x	y
−3	3
−2	$\frac{4}{3}$
−1	$\frac{1}{3}$
0	0
1	$\frac{1}{3}$
2	$\frac{4}{3}$
3	3

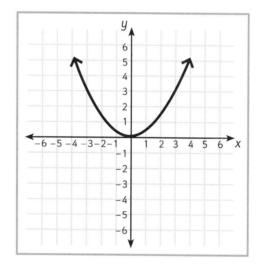

$$y = x^2$$

x	y
−3	9
−2	4
−1	1
0	0
1	1
2	4
3	9

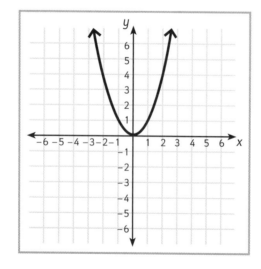

$y = 3x^2$

x	y
−3	27
−2	12
−1	3
0	0
1	3
2	12
3	27

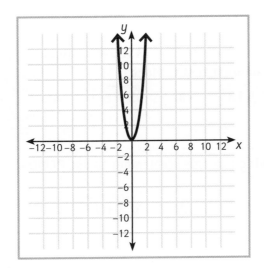

As we move from a coefficient of $\frac{1}{3}$ to a coefficient of 3, the parabola gets narrower.

We see that the coefficient changes the shape of the graph.

When the coefficient of x is between 0 and 1, the graph is wider than the graph of $y = x^2$.

When the coefficient of x is greater than 1, the graph is narrower than the graph of $y = x^2$.

$y = \frac{1}{3}x^2$

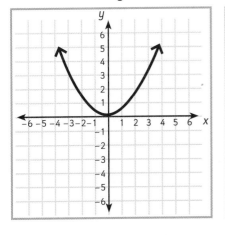

$y = x^2$

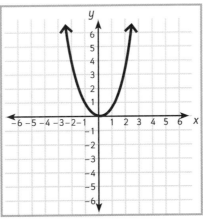

$y = 3x^2$

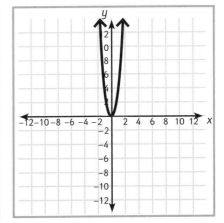

Problem-Solving Activity
Turn to *Interactive Text*, page 415.

mBook Reinforce Understanding
Use the *mBook Study Guide* to review lesson concepts.

Activity 1

Solve the expressions. Remember to use PEMDAS. Use a calculator if necessary and round to the nearest tenths place.

1. $\sqrt{2+4}$
2. $\sqrt{3+13}$
3. $\sqrt{55-6}$
4. $\sqrt{7+3}$

Activity 2

Solve the expressions involving radicals. Remember to use PEMDAS. Be sure to find all of the solutions.

1. $\sqrt{2+4}+9$
2. $2 \cdot \sqrt{3+13}$
3. $3 \cdot \sqrt{55-6}+2$
4. $-3 \cdot \sqrt{7+3}-8$

Activity 3

Match the functions with their graphs. Use the letters next to the parabolas to identify them.

1. $y = -\frac{1}{2}x^2$
2. $y = 3x^2$
3. $y = -3x^2$
4. $y = \frac{1}{2}x^2$

A

B

C
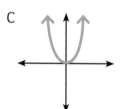

D
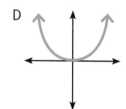

Activity 4 • Distributed Practice

Draw the graph for each of the functions.

1. $y = 3x$
2. $y = -x$
3. $y = 2x + -1$

Problem Solving:
▸**Other Nonlinear Functions**

▸**The Radical Sign and Algebraic Equations**

How do we use algebra to solve problems with square roots?

We have used simple algebra to find the square roots of numbers. When we solve the problem $x^2 = 36$, we are doing algebra.

Example 1

Find the value of x by finding the square root.

$$x^2 = 36$$

$$\sqrt{x^2} = \sqrt{36} \quad \leftarrow \quad \text{Take the square root of } x^2 \text{ and the square root of } 36 \text{ to keep the sides balanced.}$$

$$x = 6$$

We can work backward from our answers, such as $x = 6$, by squaring each side. Once again, what we do to one side, we have to do to the other side.

$$x = 6$$

$$x^2 = 6^2 \quad \leftarrow \quad \text{We square both sides in order to keep the equation balanced.}$$

$$x^2 = 36$$

Now that we know how to work with square numbers and radical signs, we can put both of these ideas together and solve equations like the one in Example 2.

Example 2

Solve the equation by squaring both sides.

$$\sqrt{x + 2} = 5$$

$$\left(\sqrt{x + 2}\right)^2 = 5^2 \quad \leftarrow \quad$$ We square both sides to keep the equation balanced.

$$x + 2 = 25 \quad \leftarrow \quad$$ When we square a square root, we remove the radical.

$$x + 2 + \boxed{-2} = 25 + \boxed{-2}$$

$$x + 0 \quad = 25 + -2$$

$$x + 0 = \quad 23$$

$$x = 23$$

Check to see if this is correct by substituting 23 for x in the original equation.

$$23$$
$$\downarrow$$
$$\sqrt{x + 2} = 5$$
$$\sqrt{23 + 2} = 5$$
$$\sqrt{25} = 5$$
$$5 = 5$$

The answer 23 is correct.

%÷
≡
<× **Apply Skills**
Turn to *Interactive Text*,
page 418.

mBook **Reinforce Understanding**
Use the *mBook Study Guide*
to review lesson concepts.

▶Problem Solving: **Other Nonlinear Functions**

What happens to the graph when our function is $y = x^3$?

The only kind of graph with a curve we have seen in this unit has been one with a parabola. This is because the x in our functions has been squared. The function $y = x^2$ is a common example.

The Graph for the Function $y = x^2$

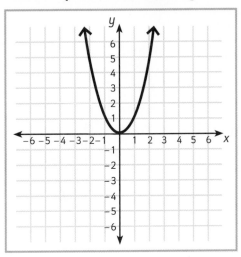

When we change the function to $y = x^3$, it seems like a small change. However, it makes a big difference when we look at the graph. Suddenly the shape of the line is entirely different. If we look at the x/y table, the change makes sense. The exponent is an odd number, so when we multiply three negative numbers together we get a negative answer or product.

Example 1

Graph the function $y = x^3$.

$y = x^3$

x	y
−3	−27
−2	−8
−1	−1
0	0
1	1
2	8
3	27

The Graph for the Function $y = x^3$

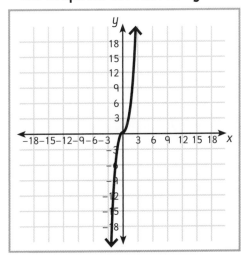

As we explore mathematics, we will learn about more nonlinear graphs. This is a summary of the different ways we have looked at nonlinear graphs in this unit. Each one is based on a function where the *x*-value has an exponent.

Squaring the *x* changes what was a straight line into a curve called a parabola.

$$y = x^2$$

x	y
−3	9
−2	4
−1	1
0	0
1	1
2	4
3	9

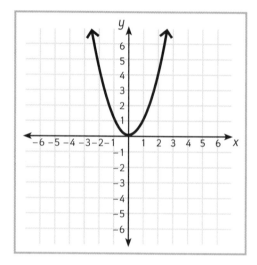

The negative coefficient in front of *x* turns the parabola upside down. It changes the direction of the function.

$$y = -x^2$$

x	y
−3	−9
−2	−4
−1	−1
0	0
1	−1
2	−4
3	−9

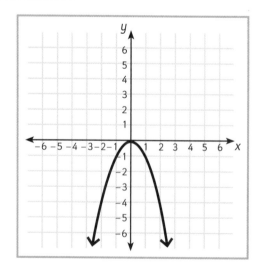

> Changing the constant or coefficient in front of the x changes the shape of the function. Smaller constants make the shape of the parabola wider. Bigger constants make the shape steeper.

$y = \frac{1}{2}x^2$

x	y
−3	$4\frac{1}{2}$
−2	2
−1	$\frac{1}{2}$
0	0
1	$\frac{1}{2}$
2	2
3	$4\frac{1}{2}$

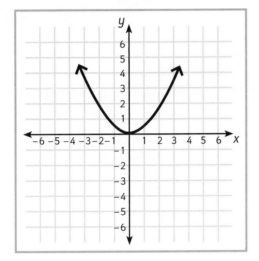

> By changing x^2 to x^3, the graph changes significantly.

$y = x^3$

x	y
−3	−27
−2	−8
−1	−1
0	0
1	1
2	8
3	27

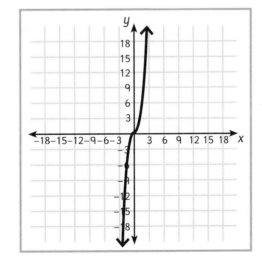

 Problem-Solving Activity
Turn to *Interactive Text*, page 419.

mBook Reinforce Understanding
Use the *mBook Study Guide* to review lesson concepts.

Square the numbers.

1. 5^2

2. $\left(\frac{1}{3}\right)^2$

3. x^2 when $x = -2$

4. $(5 + 2)^2$

5. 3.3^2

Solve the equations involving radicals. Remember, you can square each side to make the solution easier.

1. $\sqrt{x + 1} = 2$

2. $\sqrt{2 + x} = 4$

3. $\sqrt{x - 4} = \sqrt{9}$

4. $\sqrt{2x + 1} = 3$

5. $\sqrt{4x + 2} = 5$

Select the graph that matches each of the equations for functions. Use the letter next to the graph to identify it.

1. $y = x^2$

2. $y = \frac{1}{2}x$

3. $y = x^3$

4. $y = 2x$

5. $y = -2x^2$

(a)
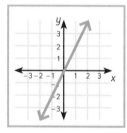

(b)
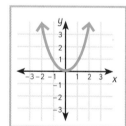

(c)
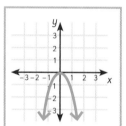

(d)
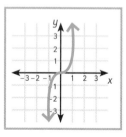

(e)
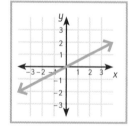

Activity 4 • Distributed Practice

Represent the functions given as equations using words. There are many different applications you can use. Some examples are car rentals, price per pound, cost per gallon, or dollars per hour.

1. Write a word statement for the function $y = 4x$.

2. Write a word statement for the function $y = x$.

3. Write a word statement for the function $y = 0.10x + 100$.

▶**Using Number Sense With Square Roots**

What are good estimates of square roots?

It's difficult to have good number sense about square roots if we just use a calculator to compute our answer. In some ways, the square root button makes things too easy. Part of the problem is since most square roots are irrational numbers, we see a long string of decimal numbers. We don't think about where the square number is on the number line. We also lose our ability to find a good estimate of a square root if we are only using a calculator.

We can begin building our number sense by thinking about square roots and perfect square numbers. Let's say that we need to find the square root of 10. We begin by thinking about the perfect squares that are near 10.

Example 1

Find $\sqrt{10}$ without using a calculator.

The number line helps us think about the answer to this problem.

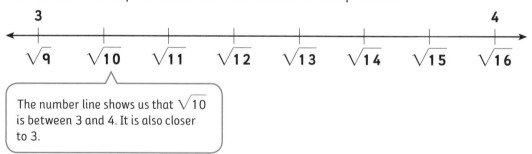

The number line shows us that $\sqrt{10}$ is between 3 and 4. It is also closer to 3.

A good estimate for $\sqrt{10}$ on the number line is that it is between 3 and 4, but it is much closer to 3. We can use decimal numbers to make an even closer estimate of $\sqrt{10}$.

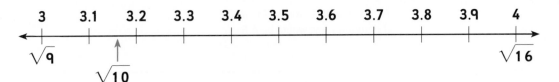

A more exact estimate of $\sqrt{10}$ would be 3.1 or 3.2.

Here is the calculator answer:
$\sqrt{10} = 3.162$

Our estimate was fairly close.

How do we find more exact square roots?

We just used a number line and perfect squares to find a good estimate of a square root. We can take this one step further. We can use a calculator to get an even more precise estimate of the square root of numbers. All we do is use the calculator for our multiplication.

Example 1

Use a calculator to estimate $\sqrt{21}$.

Find the value of $\sqrt{21}$.

STEP 1

Think about perfect squares we know above and below $\sqrt{21}$.

The perfect square below $\sqrt{21}$ is $\sqrt{16}$. We know $\sqrt{16} = 4$.

The perfect square above $\sqrt{21}$ is $\sqrt{25}$. We know $\sqrt{25} = 5$.

STEP 2

Place these numbers on a number line.

We know that $\sqrt{21}$ is between 4 and 5. It is about halfway between the two numbers.

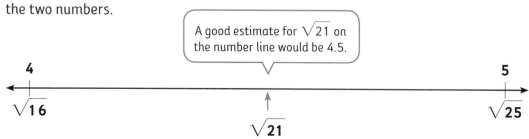

A good estimate for $\sqrt{21}$ on the number line would be 4.5.

4      $\sqrt{16}$ $\sqrt{21}$ 5 $\sqrt{25}$

STEP 3

Let's start there and use our calculator to multiply this decimal number times itself.

20.25

That's too low, so let's try 4.6

21.16

That's just a little too high, so let's go back and try 4.58.
This decimal number is just less than 4.6

20.98

That is very close. We can keep adding decimal number places to get even more exact. However $\sqrt{21}$ is an irrational number. That means it never ends, and we can never find the answers exactly.

%÷
≤× **Apply Skills**
Turn to *Interactive Text*, page 421.

mBook **Reinforce Understanding**
Use the *mBook Study Guide* to review lesson concepts.

Activity 1

Tell the perfect squares you would use above and below each of the numbers if you were estimating the square root.

1. $\sqrt{20}$ is between $\sqrt{?}$ and $\sqrt{?}$

2. $\sqrt{90}$ is between $\sqrt{?}$ and $\sqrt{?}$

3. $\sqrt{40}$ is between $\sqrt{?}$ and $\sqrt{?}$

4. $\sqrt{30}$ is between $\sqrt{?}$ and $\sqrt{?}$

5. $\sqrt{5}$ is between $\sqrt{?}$ and $\sqrt{?}$

Activity 2

Estimate the square roots.

1. $\sqrt{105}$
2. $\sqrt{88}$
3. $\sqrt{39}$
4. $\sqrt{2}$
5. $\sqrt{55}$

Activity 3

Use estimation and answer true or false.

1. A good estimate for $\sqrt{28}$ is 14.

2. A good estimate for $\sqrt{57}$ is 7.5.

3. A good estimate for $\sqrt{68}$ is 9.

4. A good estimate for $\sqrt{14}$ is 2.4.

5. A good estimate for $\sqrt{7}$ is 2.6.

Activity 4 • Distributed Practice

Represent the functions given in words using *x/y* tables.

1. The cost of gas is $3.50 per gallon.

2. The rental car cost $25 per day.

3. Britt makes $10 per hour.

▶Square Roots and Irrational Numbers

Why is a square root important?

In secondary mathematics, we spend a lot of time working with numbers that have exponents. Many times, these are square numbers like the one shown in the algebraic equation. Solving for x means that we need to find a square root.

Review 1

How do we use square roots to solve equations?

$$2x^2 + 1 = 29$$

$$2x^2 + 1 + -1 = 29 + -1$$

$$2x^2 = 28$$

$$\frac{1}{2} \cdot 2x^2 = 28 \cdot \frac{1}{2}$$

$$\frac{2}{2} x^2 = \frac{28}{2}$$

$$x^2 = 14$$

$$\sqrt{x^2} = \sqrt{14}$$

$$x = 3.74$$

One formula that helps us find the square root of a number is the Pythagorean theorem. Most of the time, the hypotenuse of a right triangle does not have an exact integer length. Square roots allow us to find the length of the hypotenuse.

Review 2

How do we use the Pythagorean theorem to find the lengths of the sides of a right triangle?

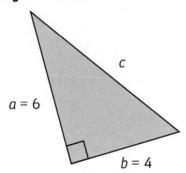

Pythagorean Theorem: $a^2 + b^2 = c^2$

$$6 \quad 4$$
$$\downarrow \quad \downarrow$$

$$a^2 + b^2 = c^2$$

$$6^2 + 4^2 = c^2$$

$$36 + 16 = c^2$$

$$52 = c^2$$

$$\sqrt{52} = \sqrt{c^2}$$

$$7.21 = c$$

The length of side $c = 7.21$.

We need to do more than use a calculator in order to work with square roots. We still need good number sense. We can find some square roots just by noticing that the number is a perfect square number. If we think of our multiplication facts and what we know about multiplying two negative numbers, we can find the square roots for that number.

Review 3

What are some perfect square numbers and their square roots?

Perfect Square Number	Square Roots
4	2 and −2
16	4 and −4
81	9 and −9
100	10 and −10

Most of the time it isn't this easy. When we use a calculator to find the square root of a number such as 15, we notice it's a decimal number with a long string of decimal places.

Review 4

What are irrational numbers?

Numbers like $\sqrt{15}$ do not end and they do not follow a pattern.

$$\sqrt{15} = 3.872983\ldots$$

These square roots are irrational numbers, or decimal numbers that do not terminate or repeat.

We can still use good number sense to find square roots by remembering that perfect square numbers are around a number like 15.

Review 5

How do we find a good estimate of a square root?

Find the value of $\sqrt{15}$.

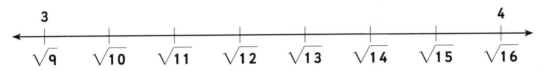

We know $\sqrt{15}$ is between the perfect square numbers $\sqrt{9}$ and $\sqrt{16}$. That means the square root is between 3 and 4. We also know $\sqrt{15}$ is much closer to $\sqrt{16}$ than $\sqrt{9}$, so its square root must be close to 4.

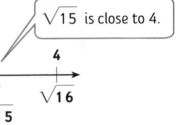

$\sqrt{15}$ is close to 4.

We can use decimal numbers to make an even closer estimate of $\sqrt{15}$.

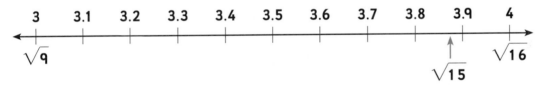

A more exact estimate of $\sqrt{15}$ would be 3.8 or 3.9.

Here is the calculator answer.

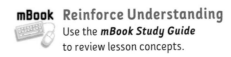

1 5 √   3.87

Apply Skills
Turn to *Interactive Text*,
page 423.

mBook Reinforce Understanding
Use the *mBook Study Guide*
to review lesson concepts.

What is the difference between linear and nonlinear functions?

The linear functions that we studied in Unit 9 are based on a special equation. The key parts of the equation are slope and *y*-intercept.

Equation for a Linear Function

$$y = mx + b$$

slope   *y*-intercept

When we substitute values into the equation, we can create a line on a coordinate graph. It is important to notice that the *y*-intercept is constant. It does not change. It is the *mx* part of the equation that changes. That is because we are substituting different values for *x*.

Review 1

What does a linear function look like on a graph?

Let *b* = 3

Let *m* = 2

We can substitute these values from our *x/y* table to create a graph.

$$y = 2x + 3$$

x	y
−2	−1
−1	1
0	3
1	5
2	7

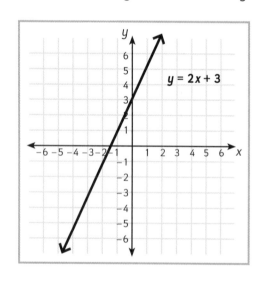

$y = 2x + 3$

The nonlinear functions that we studied in this unit have exponents as part of the equation. When x is squared or when it has a higher exponent, the shape of the line changes from a straight line to a curve. This makes sense when we look at a simple x/y table for the function $y = x^2$. In this case, the value of y is never negative because x is always squared. A negative number times a negative number is always positive.

Review 2

What does a nonlinear function look like on a graph?

$y = x^2$

x	y
-3	9
-2	4
-1	1
0	0
1	1
2	4
3	9

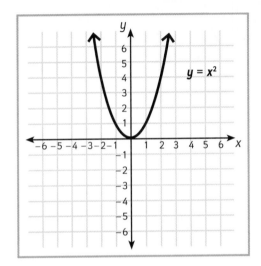

We can change the shape and direction of a nonlinear function by changing the coefficient in front of the x-variable. We can make the parabola wider or thinner depending upon how large the coefficient is. Negative coefficients make the parabola point down.

How can we change the direction and shape of a nonlinear function?

Begin with a simple nonlinear function.

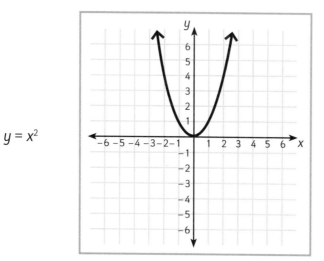

$y = x^2$

Change the shape by making the coefficient $\frac{1}{2}$. This makes the parabola wider.

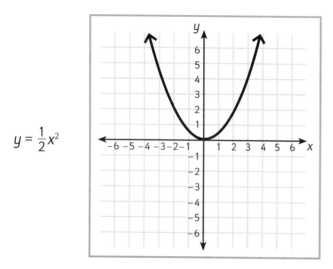

$y = \frac{1}{2}x^2$

We can make the parabola steeper by changing the coefficient from $\frac{1}{2}$ to 3.

$y = 3x^2$

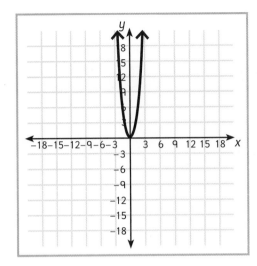

Finally, we can flip over the parabola by making the coefficient negative.

$y = -3x^2$

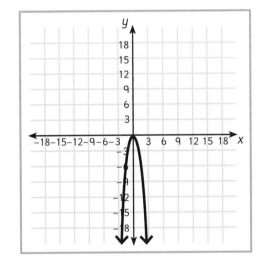

What are other nonlinear functions?

We learned about another nonlinear function, $y = x^3$. This function is different from $y = x^2$.

Review 1

What does the function $y = x^3$ look like?

Look at the graph of $y = x^3$.

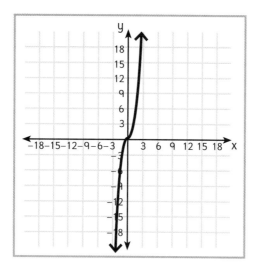

This graph is very different from the graph of $y = x^2$. We see that the graph is in Quadrants I and III, and that it is narrower than the graph of $y = x^2$.

We will learn about other nonlinear graphs as we continue to study mathematics.

Problem-Solving Activity
Turn to *Interactive Text*,
page 426.

mBook Reinforce Understanding
Use the *mBook Study Guide*
to review lesson concepts.

Glossary

3-D An object having length, width, and height (p. 450)

A

absolute value The distance of a number from zero on a number line (p. 394)

additive Involving addition (p. 475)

algebraic expression An expression that contains a variable (p. 373)

arc Part of the circumference of a circle (p. 514)

associative property Property that allows us to regroup numbers in addition and multiplication without changing the answer (p. 423)

attributes The different features of a shape (p. 380)

B

balanced When the expression on one side of an equation equals the expression on the other side (p. 511)

base The face at the top and bottom of a 3-D shape (p. 378)

benchmark A standard by which something can be measured or judged (p. 59)

bisect Split in half (p. 522)

box-and-whisker plots A kind of graph that helps us understand how all the data are distributed from high to low (p. 42)

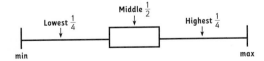

C

coefficient A number that is being multiplied by an unknown quantity; represents the number of variables, for example, $3m + 1$, 3 variables (p. 410)

common denominator Denominators that are the same (p. 12)

commutative property for addition Property that allows us to move numbers around when we add them (p. 127)

consecutive numbers Numbers that are next to each other on the number line (p. 469)

constructions The drawing of geometric items (p. 522)

coordinate graph A graph where points are plotted using x- and y-coordinates (p. 681)

coordinates Dots showing location on a graph (p. 689)

cubic inches Unit for measuring volume (p. 456)

cubic units How volume is measured; the basic unit of measurement for a 3-D object (p. 457)

D

data A collection of facts from which conclusions are drawn (p. 709)

dependent variable A variable in a logical or mathematical expression whose value depends on the independent variable (p. 811)

depth An additional dimension for a 3-D object (p. 377)

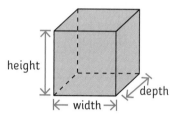

direct relationship A relationship that when one variable increases or decreases, the other variable does the same (p. 81)

distributive property Property that allows us to distribute a term over a quantity; $a(b+c) = ab + ac$ (p. 485)

double inequality An inequality that shows a range with an upper boundary and a lower boundary (p. 276)

E

edge Where the faces of a 3-D shape come together (p. 378)

equation A math statement that shows that one expression is equal to another expression (p. 511)

evaluating the expression When the expression is solved (p. 373)

even number Any number that can be divided by 2 with no remainder (p. 349)

exponent a mathematical notation indicating the number of times a quantity is multiplied by itself (p. 844)

expression A math statement that does not have an equals sign or an inequality symbol (p. 373)

F

face The flat side of a shape (p. 378)

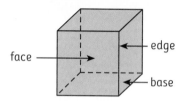

function A systematic relationship between two variables (p. 687)

G

guess and check A strategy used to find the pattern of the output (p. 338)

H

height One of the dimensions of a 3-D object (p. 377)

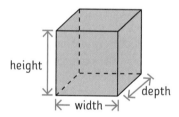

hypotenuse The side opposite the right angle (p. 793)

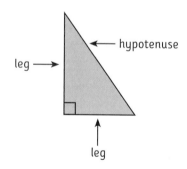

I

implied coefficient An invisible coefficient, always 1 or -1 (p. 411)

independent variable A variable whose values are independent of changes in other variables (p. 811)

indirect relationship A relationship that when the value of one variable goes up, the value of other variable in the relationship goes down (p. 88)

inequality A statement involving two expressions where one expression is greater than or less than the other (p. 233)

input The number going into a function (p. 338)

integers Numbers that include only positive and negative whole numbers and zero (p. 393)

irrational numbers Decimal numbers that never end but do not repeat (p. 60)

L

least common denominator The smallest number that two different denominators can divide into evenly (p. 14)

linear function A function that has a constant rate of change and can be modeled by a straight line (p. 720)

line of best fit A line placed through a scatter plot to clearly view the direction of the points (p. 94)

line segment Part of a line that has end points and a definite length (p. 514)

M

maximum The greatest number in the data set (p. 8)

mean The average of a set of data (p. 9)

median The middle number in a set of data (p. 22)

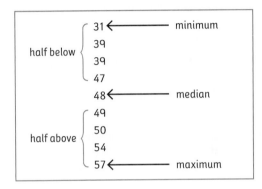

midpoint The middle point of a line segment (p. 515)

minimum The smallest number in a set of data (p. 8)

mixture The whole, or the total, amount (p. 340)

mode The number that appears the most in a data set (p. 8)

multiplicative Involving multiplication (p. 475)

N

negative slope The slope of a graph that decreases from left to right (p. 732)

number grid A table of consecutive numbers (p. 469)

number term Part of an algebraic expression that includes only numbers (p. 408)

numeric expression When an expression has only numbers (p. 373)

O

odd number Any number that does have a remainder when divided by 2 (p. 349)

order of operations Rules that were created so that people can agree on one correct answer (p. 374)

outlier Extreme numbers in a data set (p. 30)

output The number going out of a function (p. 338)

P

parabola The graph, or curve, of the function $y = ax^2$ (p. 822)

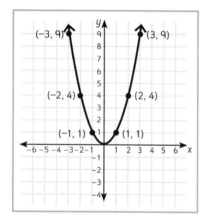

parallel Lines that do not intersect or meet (p. 518)

PASS Rule **P**ositive **A**nswers **S**ame **S**ign
1. When we multiply two negative numbers, the answer is positive
2. When we multiply a negative by a positive, the answer is negative
3. When we divide a negative by a negative, the answer is positive
4. When we divide a positive number by a negative number, the answer is negative
5. When we divide a positive by a positive, the answer is positive (p. 447)

perfect square number An integer that can be written as the square of some other integer; in other words, it is the product of some integer with itself (p. 818)

perpendicular A straight line at a right angle to another straight line (p. 515)

point of origin Where the x- and y-axes cross (0, 0) (p. 689)

positive slope The slope of a graph that increases from right to left (p. 731)

prime number A number that is only divisible by 1 and itself (p. 350)

proof The steps followed when making an inference to justify the solution to a problem (p. 650)

proper fraction A fraction where the numerator is less than the denominator (p. 69)

property of equality When we do something to one side of the equation, we do the same thing to the other side (p. 534)

property of opposites Tells us that any number plus its opposite equals zero (p. 424)

proportion Two or more ratios that are equal (p. 156)

Pythagorean theorem Formula for the length of the hypotenuse, telling us that the sum of the squares of the legs of a right triangle is equal to the square of the hypotenuse (p. 793)

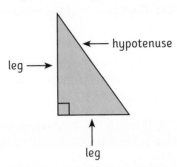

R

radical sign The $\sqrt{}$ sign over the number squared (p. 799)

range The difference between the biggest number and the smallest number in a data set (p. 8)

rate A comparison of numbers that are measured in different units (p. 238)

rate of change The speed at which a function is increasing or decreasing (p. 737)

ratio The comparison of two numbers (p. 142)

rational number Any number that can be expressed as a fraction (p. 48)

ray A line that extends in only one direction (p. 233)

reciprocal The multiplicative inverse of a number (p. 41)

repeating decimals Fractions that when turned into a decimal produce a repeating pattern (p. 60)

right angle An angle of 90 degrees (p. 515)

rise The vertical movement on the graph (p. 726)

run The horizontal movement on the graph (p. 726)

S

scatter plot A data analysis tool that shows the relationship between two variables (p. 69)

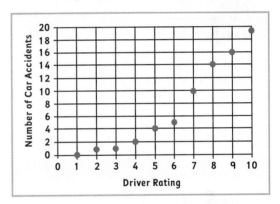

slope The steepness, or slant, of a function (p. 725)

square root A number that when multiplied by itself equals a given number (p. 799)

$$\sqrt{100} = 10$$

substitution Replacing a variable with a number value (p. 136)

supplementary angles Angles that add up to 180 degrees (p. 548)

surface area The sum of all the areas of the surfaces of a 3-D shape (p. 401)

systematic relationship The change in one variable leads to a predictable change in another variable (p. 694)

T

transitive property Property that says if $a = b$ and $b = c$, then $a = c$ (p. 650)

transversal A line that cuts across two parallel lines (p. 651)

U

unit rate How much of something is in one unit (p. 240)

V

variable term Part of an algebraic expression that contains a variable (p. 408)

volume The amount of 3-dimensional space inside an object (p. 450)

W

word statement Uses words to describe a relationship (p. 244)

width One of the dimensions of a 3-D object (p. 377)

X

x-axis The horizontal axis of the graph (p. 689)

x-coordinate The x portion of the coordinate (p. 689)

Y

y-axis The vertical axis of the graph (p. 689)

y-coordinate The y portion of the coordinate (p. 689)

y-intercept The point where the graph of a function or relation intersects the y-axis of the coordinate graph (p. 743)

Z

zero slope The slope of a horizontal line (p. 752)

Index

distances and, 239, 557–559, 572–573

drawings for solving problems, 618–620

finding differences in, 282–283, 298

problem examples, 239–241, 246–247, 268–272, 618–620

simplifying, 268–272

unit rate and. *See* unit rate

using proportion to solve problems, 246–247, 295

rational numbers, defined, 48, 817. *See also* decimal numbers; fractions

ratios. *See also* proportional relationships; proportions

colons in, 305

common mistakes with proportions and, 217–219

comparing, 309–312, 326, 368

comparing data in tables with, 327–328

defined, 142

everyday uses of, 143

flexible thinking about, 367–370

fractions compared to, 144–145, 367

mixtures and, 340, 341, 345–346, 369

percents and, 341, 352–355, 360, 369–370

questions to ask when comparing, 312

reviews, 228, 367–370

rounding, to compare, 320–321

simplifying, 208–211

solving word problems with, 146

types of problems with, 324–326, 367–370

ways to write, 142, 228, 304–305

rays

defined, 234

graphing inequalities on number lines, 234

reciprocals

defined, 41, 543

signs of, 553

solving equations with, 543–544, 546, 553

rectangles. *See* squares and rectangles

rectangular prisms. *See* prisms

repeating decimal numbers, 60

right angles

defined, 515

rule, 656, 683

symbol for, 606, 656

right triangles. *See also* Pythagorean theorem

area formula for, 792

determining length of sides, 797–798, 803–804, 845

hypotenuse of. *See* hypotenuse

Pythagorean theorem and. *See* Pythagorean theorem

reflecting, on graph, 703–704

right angle in, 554

rise, defined, 726. *See also* slopes

rounding

comparing costs with, 320–321

ratios, 320–321

rounding decimal numbers

benchmarks for, 59

helping in understanding meaning of number, 59

procedure for, 57–58

run, defined, 726. *See also* slopes

S

scalene triangles, 554

scaling factor, 182, 184, 185, 186

scatter plots

defined, 69

direct relationships on, 81–82, 94, 115

indirect relationships on, 88, 116

line of best fit on, 94–96

making and using, 69–71

without relationships, 116

shapes. *See also specific shapes*

classifying based on attributes, 384–385

fair shares of. *See* fair shares

reflecting, on graph, 703–704

similar. *See* similar shapes (similarity)

three-dimensional. *See* 3-D shapes

translating on coordinate graphs, 696–697. *See also* coordinate graphs

weight of, balancing equations and, 527–531

similar shapes (similarity)

described, 180–182

drawing, 183–186

proportions illustrating, 184, 186, 210–211, 230

rectangles, 183–184, 210–211

triangles, 180–182, 185–186

of negative numbers, 551, 668

supplementary angles, 548–549, 636, 656, 683

surface area
  of cubes, 405
  of cylinders, 402–403, 440
  defined, 401
  of polyhedrons, 430–431, 442
  of prisms, 404, 440
  of pyramids, 418–420, 441
  review, 440–442

surfaces, of 3-D shapes, 391

systematic relationship, defined, 694. *See also* functions

T

tables
  helping see parts of mixtures, 346
  ratios for comparing data in, 327–328

tessellations
  determining subsequent shapes, 332–334
  following algebraic patterns, 332–334

3-D shapes
  attributes of, defined, 380
  bases of, 378, 379, 390, 391
  classifying based on attributes, 384–385
  common attributes of, 377–378, 384–385
  depth of, 377
  differences among, 390–391
  edges of, 378, 390, 391
  in everyday life, 380
  faces of, 378, 390, 391
  height of, 377
  space inside. *See* volume
  surface area of. *See* surface area
  surfaces of, 391
  two-dimensional objects compared to, 377
  vertex of, 385, 391
  width of, 377

thumb units, 198–199

transitive property, 650, 651, 652, 658, 683

transversals, 651, 657, 683

trapezoids, translating on coordinate graph, 696–697

triangles. *See also* Pythagorean theorem; right triangles
  algebra to measure angles of, 555, 560–561
  algebraic expressions and area formulas, 641, 642
  area of, 149, 641, 790, 792
  with congruent angles, 560–561
  equilateral, 554, 560
  explaining thinking when find measurement of, 561
  important properties of, 554
  isosceles, 554, 560, 561
  measuring angles of, 555, 560–561, 575–576, 598–599
  measuring exterior angles of, 590–592
  measuring more than one angle of, 548, 576
  multistep equations to find angles of, 598–599
  polyhedrons and, 430–431
  proportional, 180–182
  reflecting, on graph, 703–704
  regular, specifications of, 584
  within regular polygons, 584
  relationship between squares, rectangles and, 789–792
  scalene, 554
  similar, 180–182, 185–186
  solving difficult problems about, 560–561
  in tessellations. *See* tessellations
  types of, 554

triangular prisms. *See* prisms

U

unit rate
  defined, 240, 255
  finding with proportions, 255–259, 272, 296
  solving word problems with, 258–259
  word problem, 325

units, different, number lines showing, 264–265

V

variable terms
  combining, 457
  defined, 408

Photo and Illustration Credits

PHOTO CREDITS

Unit 1 1 Batter © Rick Friedman/Corbis. Hitter ©istockphoto.com/Robert Kelsey. Softball and glove ©Jupiter Images.

Unit 2 Thumbprint (large) ©istockphoto.com/Nathan Fabro. Handprint ©istockphoto.com/omergenc. Eyeball ©istockphoto.com/Paul Kline. DNA ©istockphoto.com/Luis M. Molina. Chemist ©istockphoto.com/Laurence Gough. Thumbprint (small) ©istockphoto.com/appleuzr.

Unit 3 Geese ©istockphoto.com/Kevin Miller. Geese silhouette ©istockphoto.com/Gord Horne. Sky ©istockphoto.com/konradlew. Snow geese ©istockphoto.com/Ken Canning. Wetlands ©istockphoto.com/John Anderson. Birds ©istockphoto.com/Rob Pavey.

Unit 4 Ant with leaf ©istockphoto.com/Mark Evans. Elephant seal ©istockphoto.com/Nancy Nehring. Boy ©Jupiter Images. Car ©istockphoto.com/Crisian Lupu. Girl (two hands) ©Jupiter Images. Linemen ©istockphoto.com/George Peters. Girl (one finger) ©Jupiter Images.

Unit 5 Teens with 3D glasses ©istockphoto.com/Bob Ingelhart. Popcorn ©istockphoto.com/Amanda Rohde. Giza pyramids ©istockphoto.com/Volker Kreinacke. Montreal Biosphere ©istockphoto.com/Dan Moore. Modern houses ©istockphoto.com/LyaC. Los Angeles hotel towers istockphoto.com/Daniel Stein. 3D glasses ©istockphoto.com/Florian Röbig.

Unit 6 Woman ©istockphoto.com/Michael Krinke. Milk glass (first) ©istockphoto.com/Ina Peters. Milk glass (second) ©istockphoto.com/Sergey Mironov. Cow ©istockphoto.com/Michael Krakowiak. Milk churn ©istockphoto.com/Rtimages. Dairy silos ©istockphoto.com/steverts. Milk truck ©istockphoto.com/Nancy Brammer. Farm ©istockphoto.com/Aimin Tang. Rural road ©istockphoto.com/Maksym Dyachenko. Milk gallon ©istockphoto.com/DNY59.

Unit 7 Snowboarder ©istockphoto.com/Bob Ingelhart. Chairlift and mountains ©istockphoto.com/Superseker. Snowboarders standing ©istockphoto.com/Eric Belisle. Snowboarders sitting ©istockphoto.com/Denis Pepin. Snowboard jump ©istockphoto.com/Eugeny Shevchenko.

Unit 8 Tire tracks ©istockphoto.com/Jeff Chevrier. Stairs ©istockphoto.com/Mike Panic. Bridge ©istockphoto.com/javarman3. Construction ©istockphoto.com/Michael Braun. Freeway ©istockphoto.com/Maciej Noskowki. Roller coaster ©istockphoto.com/Paul Erickson. Barn door ©istockphoto.com/Jim Jurica. Field ©istockphoto.com/Rene Mansi. Rails ©istockphoto.com/fontmonster. Girl ©istockphoto.com/Justin Horrocks. Boy ©istockphoto.com/Eric Simard. Hatch marks ©istockphoto.com/Dietmar Klement.

Unit 9 Earth from moon, Apollo command and service modules, footprint courtesy of NASA. Lunar module ©istockphoto.com/P. Wei. Rocket man ©Fabrice Coffrini/AFP/Getty Images. Hand and pencil ©istockphoto.com/Yenwen Lu. Buzz Aldrin and flag on moon courtesy of NASA.

Unit 10 Scarecrow THE WIZARD OF OZ ©Turner Entertainment Co. A Warner Bros. Entertainment Company. All Rights Reserved. Movie projector ©istockphoto.com/Michael Kurtz. Boy ©istockphoto.com/Frances Wicks. T-square and triangle ©istockphoto.com/Joan Loitz.

ILLUSTRATION CREDITS

Unit 2 Cybermap ©istockphoto.com/Emrah Türüdü.

Unit 3 Globe ©istockphoto.com/zbruh.

Unit 4 Cartoon CALVIN AND HOBBES © 1986 Watterson. Dist. by UNIVERSAL PRESS SYNDICATE. Reprinted with permission. All rights reserved.

Unit 8 Airplane ©Jupiter Images.

Unit 9 Apollo 11, astronaut, moonscape illustrations based on photos courtesy of NASA.